L.F.

D0858554

In this important student text, Professor Freedman provides an exhaustive account of Soviet policy in the Middle East from the invasion of Afghanistan in December 1979 to withdrawal from the country ten years later.

Following an introductory chapter which views the period from World War II to the invasion, Robert Freedman examines policy motives and outcomes in a broadly chronological approach. Specific and detailed attention is paid to Soviet policy towards the Iran–Iraq war, the Arab–Israeli conflict, and intra-Arab policies. Throughout, Professor Freedman compares the policies of Gorbachev with those of his predecessors – Brezhnev, Chernenko, and Andropov. He concludes that continuity, not change, has characterized recent Soviet policy toward the Middle East. This can be seen, for example, in Soviet plans for a settlement of the Arab–Israeli conflict, in Soviet unwillingness to use military force to challenge either Israeli or American activities, and in the Soviet position on the Iran–Iraq war. However, as Robert Freedman observes, the Soviet withdrawal from Afghanistan, its sharp improvement of relations with Egypt, and the moderation of its relations with Israel, may represent a policy change which could be built upon in the future.

Moscow and the Middle East is based on a wealth of documentation. This includes interviews with Middle East politicians and government officials, Middle East and Soviet newspapers, speeches and statements of Soviet government ministers and official Moscow radio broadcasts in the Arab world. This book will provide students of Soviet foreign policy, the Middle East and international relations with an invaluable textbook. It will also prove an essential reference source for government officials and policy analysts.

Moscow and the Middle East

MOSCOW AND THE MIDDLE EAST
Soviet policy since the invasion of Afghanistan

Robert O. Freedman
Peggy Meyerhoff Pearlstone Professor of Political
Science and Dean of Graduate Studies
Baltimore Hebrew University

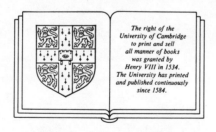

The right of the
University of Cambridge
to print and sell
all manner of books
was granted by
Henry VIII in 1534.
The University has printed
and published continuously
since 1584.

CAMBRIDGE UNIVERSITY PRESS
Cambridge
New York   Port Chester
Melbourne   Sydney

ALBRIGHT COLLEGE LIBRARY

Published by the Press Syndicate of the University of Cambridge
The Pitt Building, Trumpington Street, Cambridge CB2 1RP
40 West 20th Street, New York, NY 10011, USA
10 Stamford Road, Oakleigh, Melbourne 3166, Australia

© Cambridge University Press 1991

First published 1991

Printed in Great Britain at the University Press, Cambridge

British Library cataloguing in publication data

Freedman, Robert O. (Robert Owen)
  Moscow and the Middle East: Soviet policy since the
  invasion of Afganistan.
  1. Soviet Union. Foreign relations with Middle East
  I. Title
  327.47056

Library of Congress cataloguing in publication data

Freedman, Robert Owen.
    Moscow and the Middle East: Soviet policy since the invasion of
  Afghanistan / Robert O. Freedman.
      p.   cm.
    Includes bibliographical references.
    ISBN 0–521–35184–7. ISBN 0–521–35976–7 (pbk)
    1. Middle East – Foreign relations – Soviet Union.   2. Soviet Union –
  Foreign relations – Middle East.   3. Soviet Union – Foreign
  relations – 1975–1985.   4. Soviet Union – Foreign relations – 1985–
  I. Title.
  DS63.2.S65F72   1991
  327.47056 dc20 90 31056 CIP

ISBN 0 521 35184 7 hardback
ISBN 0 521 35976 7 paperback

327.47056
F 853 m
1991

235186

17.95

For Sharon, with love

Contents

Preface

I have been following the course of Soviet policy in the Middle East for two decades, and this is my second book on the topic. The first, *Soviet Policy Toward the Middle East Since 1970* (New York: Praeger, 1975, 1978, 1982) went through three editions and covered Soviet policy from the death of Nasser in September 1970 until the late Brezhnev era. This book, taking as its starting point the Soviet invasion of Afghanistan in December 1979, analyzes Soviet policy in the Middle East until the final withdrawal of Soviet troops in February 1989. Given the fact that no fewer than four different Soviet leaders presided over Soviet policy toward the Middle East from 1979 to 1989 (Leonid Brezhnev, Yuri Andropov, Konstantin Chernenko, and Mikhail Gorbachev), the book also offers the opportunity for a comparative analysis of the policies of the four leaders, so that some meaningful generalizations might be suggested about continuity and change in Soviet policy toward the Middle East.

In the course of my study of Soviet policy toward the Middle East, I have benefited from the counsel and advice of numerous individuals whom I would like to thank. These include Amos Jordan of the Center for Strategic and International Studies of Washington, DC; Martha Mautner of the Intelligence and Research Bureau of the State Department; Wayne Lemberg, Brian McCauley, and Melvin Goodman of the Central Intelligence Agency; David Albright of the Air War College; Galia Golan and Theodore Friedgut of The Hebrew University of Jerusalem; Yaacov Ro'i of Tel Aviv University; Rashid Khalidi of the University of Chicago; Karen Dawisha of the University of Maryland; Harold Saunders of the Brookings Institution; Carol Saivetz of the Russian Research Center of Harvard University; Pedro Ramet of the University of Washington, and Judge Russell Eisenberg of Milwaukee.

I am also indebted to a number of government officials who were kind enough to give of their time for interviews. These include Robert Pelletreau of the US State Department; Aryeh Levin and Yaacov Rosen of the Israeli Foreign Ministry; Nimrod Novick, Advisor to Israeli Foreign Minister Yitzhak Peres; Yasser Arafat and Yasser Abd Raboo of the Palestine Liberation Organization; Abdul Mohsin al-Duaij, Kuwaiti Ambassador to the Soviet Union; and Oleg Derkovsky of the Soviet Embassy in Washington, DC. I would also like to thank the Soviet colleagues with whom I spent a week discussing Middle East political problems during an IREX exchange visit to the Oriental Institute of the Soviet Academy of Sciences in January 1988. Needless to say, while I am indebted to all of the individuals listed above (and many more not listed) for sharing their views with me, I alone am responsible for all interpretations and errors in the book.

I also have many people to thank at Baltimore Hebrew University for their support in enabling me to write this book. First and foremost is my secretary, Mrs. Elise Baron, who typed the manuscript while also handling the affairs of the Graduate School in an expert manner; Mrs. Elaine Eckstein who helped maintain my research files; Mrs. Jeanette Katcoff and Dr. Arthur Lesley of Baltimore Hebrew University's Library who helped me obtain the necessary books and periodicals; and my colleagues Dr. Leivy Smolar, President of the University, and Dean Judy Meltzer who were highly supportive of my research efforts.

Finally, a word of thanks to my children, Deborah Colette and David Noam, who continue to be interested in their father's scholarly activities, and to my wife Sharon, a true companion for life, to whom this book is dedicated.

Introduction

Writing a historical analysis of Soviet policy toward the Middle East in the period between the Soviet invasion of Afghanistan in December 1979 and the final withdrawal of Soviet troops from that country in February 1989 presents a number of interesting challenges. In the first place there were no fewer than four different Soviet leaders during this period: Leonid Brezhnev, who presided over the invasion and who died in November 1982; Yuri Andropov, who died in February 1984; Konstantin Chernenko, who died in March 1985; and Mikhail Gorbachev who presided over the withdrawal from Afghanistan. While each of these Soviet leaders faced different Middle East problems, a comparative analysis of their policies toward the Middle East should provide a useful case study of continuity and change in Soviet policy toward the region.[1]

A second analytical problem is the fact that Soviet domestic politics and, to a lesser degree Soviet foreign policy, have been in a state of increasing flux under Gorbachev. Indeed, as these lines are being written, the newly elected Supreme Soviet is asserting its right to be a major factor in shaping Soviet domestic and foreign policy. Under the circumstances, any judgment made about the Gorbachev era will, of necessity, be only a tentative one. Nonetheless, the cut-off date of this analysis, the final withdrawal of Soviet troops from Afghanistan in February 1989, has been selected because it offers almost four full years of Gorbachev's period in office with which to compare the new Soviet leader with his three predecessors. Despite the flux in Soviet politics, it is hoped that this will be a sufficiently long period to make the necessary comparative analysis, however tentative it might be.

Third, there is the question as to which approach to take toward Soviet policy goals in the region. On this question, Western analysts are divided into three different schools of thought. These divergent views are of more than academic interest since very different policy prescriptions follow from them, including different views as to whether the United States should seek the cooperation of the Soviet Union in efforts to settle the Arab–Israeli and Iran–Iraq conflicts. The first Western school of thought as to Moscow's Middle Eastern goals may be characterized as the "offensive-successful" school.[2] This school of thought, looking primarily at Soviet military power in the region, argues not only that Moscow is offensively inclined and seeks to oust the West from the oil resources and strategic communication routes of the Middle East, replacing Western influence with Soviet influence, but also that it has been quite successful in exercising influence (i.e. getting a nation to do what Moscow wants it to do, or refrain from doing that which Moscow opposes),[3] primarily by intimidating the states of the region. According to this school of thought, not only should the USSR not be invited to participate in peace-making efforts in the region, but it must be confronted wherever possible to prevent the Middle East from falling into Soviet hands. On the opposite end of the spectrum of Western analysts of Soviet Middle Eastern goals, is what might be termed the "defensive-unsuccessful" school.[4] This school of thought argues that Moscow is basically defensively oriented in the Middle East, given higher priorities elsewhere in the world, and regional problems which the USSR finds unmanageable and which severely curtail Soviet influence. Given this situation, it is argued, Moscow can be invited to participate in peace-making efforts because it wants a stable situation along its Southern periphery. The final school of thought, to which the author of this book belongs, may be termed the "offensive–unsuccessful school."[5] This school of thought argues that while Moscow is essentially offensively oriented in the Middle East and has seized upon virtually any opportunity to weaken Western, and particularly American influence there, the USSR has been basically unsuccessful in extending its influence in the region because of the independence of the local actors and their resistance to Soviet control. This school of thought, looking at the offensive orientation of the USSR in the region, is wary of inviting Moscow to participate in any peace-making efforts, arguing that while there might well be tactical compromises by the USSR in varying situations, the USSR cannot be trusted to fulfil its part of any agreement in the long term. Indeed, in the Arab world in particular, the USSR seems to be involved in a zero-sum game competition with the United States for influence, where a gain by the United States becomes an equivalent loss for Moscow and vice versa. While one of the policy innovations of the Gorbachev period has been an explicit rhetorical denunciation of zero-sum game thinking and its replacement by a "balance of interests" approach to world politics, in practice, the Soviet Union, at least until its withdrawal from Afghanistan, has acted as if it were still engaged in the zero-sum game influence competition despite Gorbachev's rhetoric. It remains to be seen if there will be any genuine change in the post-Afghanistan period.

In looking to the roots of the offensive thrust of Soviet policy toward the Middle East, one can point to two main sources: the Tsarist legacy and the Marxist–Leninist ideological approach to the world. The Tsarist legacy dates back at least to Peter the Great and his offensive thrust against Turkey and Iran, that was continued by his successors with a good deal of success, particularly in the cases of Catherine the Great and Alexander I.[6] Indeed a prime cause of World War I was Tsarist efforts at expansion in the Balkans toward the Turkish Straits, control over which became one of the major aims of Russian policy during the war. A second major factor underlying the offensive nature of Soviet foreign policy has been Marxist–Leninist ideology. In addition to legitimizing the rule of the Communist Party of the Soviet Union, Marxist–Leninist ideology posits a conflictual model of the world, one which does not recognize the concept of a status quo. Thus, unless Moscow is advancing, it will, of necessity, be retreating.[7] While Gorbachev, in another policy innovation, has begun to talk about the "deideologization" of foreign policy, and its replacement by "universal human values," it is a very open question as to whether it is possible for a Soviet leader to have a domestic role for a legitimizing ideology, but maintain that the ideology has little or no significance in world affairs. In any case, so long as the Marxist–Leninist ideology provides the *Weltanschauung* (world view) for the Soviet leadership, it is difficult to see how its conflictual model can be removed from the practice of Soviet foreign policy.

While the Soviet Union is engaged in an influence competition with the United States in the Middle East, it should be noted that Moscow has other goals in the region as well. The Middle East provides waterways that are of major importance to the Soviet Union and its Warsaw Pact allies, so maintenance of the right of free passage is a central Soviet interest. In addition, Middle Eastern states, many of which are oil rich, are customers for Soviet arms and other Soviet products. Some, like Syria and South Yemen, also provide the Soviet Union with military "facilities" or bases and are sources of military and political intelligence for Moscow. Indeed, of all the Third World regions in which Moscow is active, the Middle East, being closest to the Soviet Union, is of the highest strategic and political importance, and Moscow clearly has had no desire to allow the region to be used as a base for military attack or political subversion against the USSR. Soviet leaders rarely omit references to the propinquity of the Middle East to the Soviet Union when they wish to underline the justification for a Soviet policy there. Thus Moscow can claim a legitimate defensive need to play a role in Middle East affairs, while at the same time utilizing its propinquity to play an offensive role in the region.

As it seeks to increase its influence in the Middle East, and especially in the Arab world, Moscow has used a number of tactics. First and foremost comes the supply of military assistance, whether in the form of Soviet arms, advisors, or training in Soviet military institutes. There is an extensive bibliography on Soviet military assistance to Third World states in general and to Middle Eastern states, which receive the bulk of Soviet military aid, in particular.[8] According to a US Government estimate, in the 1981 to 1988 period the USSR led all other outside suppliers in the delivery to the Middle East of tanks, self-propelled guns, artillery, armored personnel carriers and armored cars, major surface ships like destroyers and frigates, submarines, supersonic and subsonic aircraft, other aircraft and surface-to-air missiles (see Table 1).[9] Suffice it to say that Moscow hopes to receive influence in and hard currency from the state which receives Soviet arms (occasionally a third state, like Saudi Arabia, will pay for arms shipments to a Soviet client, like Syria). Indeed, according to the same government estimate, Moscow made $78.1 billion in the 1981–88 period from its arms deliveries to the Middle East out of a total value of $129.2 billion in arms sales to the Third World.[10] Yet, in offering military aid to Middle Eastern clients like Syria and Libya, Moscow runs the risk of the client states becoming involved in military actions not wanted by Moscow (i.e. Syria in Lebanon against the PLO or against Israel; and Libya in Chad). In addition, it is a very open question as to how much influence Soviet weapons supplies actually bring to Moscow. Indeed, one of the theses of this book is the very limited influence Moscow has in the region, despite all the military aid it has given to regional clients. Interestingly enough, with the greater freedom the Gorbachev policy of *glasnost* has brought to the Soviet press, even senior Soviet commentators have begun to question the dividends of Soviet arms sales to the region. Thus, in the aftermath of a Soviet arms sale agreement with Iran in June 1989,

Table 1. *Numbers of weapons delivered by major suppliers to Near East and South Asia*[a]

Weapons category	United States	USSR	Major Western European[b]
1981–1984			
Tanks and self-propelled guns	1,819	2,910	485
Artillery	684	5,965	1,235
APCs and armored cars	3,334	5,150	1,275
Major surface combatants	4	16	14
Minor surface combatants	16	20	47
Submarines	0	5	0
Supersonic combat aircraft	209	1,090	225
Subsonic combat aircraft	6	70	60
Other aircraft	18	170	150
Helicopters	4	545	150
Guided missile boats	0	10	31
Surface-to-air missiles (SAMs)	1,668	11,125	1,875
1985–1988			
Tanks and self-propelled guns	879	2,155	10
Artillery	469	3,500	550
APCs and armored cars	248	4,595	200
Major surface combatants	0	16	12
Minor surface combatants	0	13	35
Submarines	0	10	6
Supersonic combat aircraft	44	370	120
Subsonic combat aircraft	0	70	25
Other aircraft	36	200	95
Helicopters	29	490	100
Guided missile boats	0	0	1
Surface-to-air missiles (SAMs)	175	8,780	665
1981–1988			
Tanks and self-propelled guns	2,698	5,065	495
Artillery	1,153	9,465	1,785
APCs and armored cars	3,582	9,745	1,475
Major surface combatants	4	32	26
Minor surface combatants	16	33	82
Submarines	0	15	6
Supersonic combat aircraft	253	1,460	345
Subsonic combat aircraft	6	140	85
Other aircraft	54	370	245
Helicopters	33	1,035	250
Guided missile boats	0	10	32
Surface-to-air missiles (SAMs)	1,843	19,905	2,540

[a] All data are for calendar years given.
[b] Major Western European includes France, United Kingdom, West Germany, and Italy totals as an aggregate figure.
Source: Richard F. Grimmett, *Trends in Conventional Arms Transfers to the Third World by Major Suppliers 1981–1988* (Washington: Congressional Research Service 1989), p. 59.

Aleksander Bovin, speaking on the International Panorama program on Moscow TV, questioned:

> We have agreed to cooperate with Iran and in part, to strengthen its defense capacity. As always, this is a great secret. Naturally it is a question of weapons sales. Well the advantages here are obvious. First, it means hard currency or hard currency goods. Second, it means influence in Tehran, or at least a belief that there is such influence. Well, that's if we take a short-term look. But what if we look at it long-term? Here things are more complicated. *What we get is that we are continuing to pump weapons into the most restless region of our planet; and that means we are going to promote the preservation of that restlessness and instability.*
>
> According to the data regularly published throughout the world, we, together with the United States, are the leaders in the world's arms trade. *This, it seems to me, is difficult to reconcile with the postulates of new political thinking. If for example, the Kalashnikov assault rifle is found in possession of the warring sides throughout the world, this can hardly substantiate its universal human significance, so to speak, its universal human value. I would like to hope that weapons sales will be placed under control of the Supreme Soviet, and that glasnost – and that means also democracy – will reign supreme also in this important direction of our policy.*[11] (emphasis mine)

While the supply of arms is the primary Soviet tactic for increasing its influence in the Middle East, Moscow uses other tactics as well. Economic aid, in the 1950s, 1960s, and 1970s, usually took the form of large hydroelectric or industrial projects, like the Aswan Dam in Egypt, the Euphrates Dam in Syria, and steel mills in Iran. Primarily aimed at strengthening the government sector of the recipient state's economy, the USSR usually accompanied this aid with on-the-spot advisors and/or training programs in the Soviet Union. In addition, the USSR offered numerous scholarships for the students of Middle Eastern states to study in Moscow. In the 1980s, however, as Soviet resources began to shrink and the political dividends from the supply of major economic aid projects also shrank (Egypt, the biggest recipient of Soviet aid had repudiated its Treaty of Friendship and Cooperation with the USSR and gone over to the American camp), voices began to be raised in Moscow calling for a reappraisal of economic aid policies.[12] In addition, under Gorbachev, private initiative in the economy is being encouraged and Moscow, hitherto a provider of economic assistance to the Middle East, has now begun to seek investment from wealthy Middle East states like Kuwait in Soviet joint ventures.

If economic aid is rapidly diminishing as a tactic of increasing Soviet influence in the region, Moscow has also sought to solidify its influence through the conclusion of long-term friendship and cooperation treaties. The first was concluded with Egypt in 1971; Iraq followed in 1972, Somalia in 1974, Ethiopia in 1978, the Peoples Democratic Republic of Yemen (South Yemen) in 1979, Syria in 1980, and the Yemen Arab Republic (North Yemen) in 1984. Moscow began to use this tactic as its position began to be eroded in Egypt following the death of Nasser in 1970 as the Soviet leadership evidently sought to put state-to-state relations above the political whims of any individual Middle Eastern leader. Nonetheless, the repudiation of the treaties by Egypt in 1976 and Somalia in 1977 indicate that the Soviet tactic has not always met with success.[13] Another major tactic has been the establishment of party-to-party relations between the CPSU (Communist Party of the Soviet Union) and a number of the one-party regimes in the Arab world, such as the FLN in Algeria, and the Ba'ath parties of Syria and Iraq. In promoting party-to-party ties Moscow has sought to instill in the Arab party a Marxist–Leninist, anti-imperialist, *Weltanschauung*, and to urge it to maintain a large governmental sector in its economy. During the Brezhnev era, Moscow sought, in the Middle East as elsewhere in the Third World, to go one step further and transform one-party regimes into so-called Marxist–Leninist "Vanguard Parties" that, at least in theory, should be closely allied with the USSR. Ethiopia and South Yemen were the Middle Eastern countries which established these Vanguard parties, but both countries had serious economic problems as well as conflicts with their neighbors (Ethiopia also faced serious internal unrest), and Soviet specialists, in the latter part of the Brezhnev era, began to consider such regimes more liabilities than assets to the USSR.[14] There is also some question as to the future success of the Soviet tactic of using party-to-party relations to enhance Soviet influence. First, as Gorbachev, reacting to major Soviet economic failures, promotes the private sector, the Soviet model of a state-controlled economy loses significance. Second, with the "deideologization" of foreign policy, Moscow may see less need to promote Marxism–Leninism abroad. In any case, its attempts to promote a Marxist–Leninist *Weltanschauung* would appear to weaken, if the Soviet leaders are themselves confused about the relevance of ideology in the contemporary world. Finally, Moscow's use of the CPSU as a model for other parties in controlling state institutions and society may lose its luster if domestic unrest continues to escalate and the Communist leadership of the USSR seems unable to control it.

A related Soviet tactic aimed at gaining influence has been the provision of security infrastructure assistance to countries like South Yemen and Ethiopia, often with the help of East Germany. The value of this tactic may have been called into question, however, by Moscow's failure to either anticipate or prevent the events of January 1986 in the PDRY when an internecine struggle for power erupted between the top Communist leaders of the country,[15] or to help Ethiopia succeed in putting down ethnic insurgencies.

Another tactic used by Moscow to increase its influence has been its constant attempts to exploit the lingering memories of both Western colonialism that dominated the Middle East in the inter-war and immediate post World War II periods, and also Western threats against Middle East oil producers, made during the oil embargo of 1973–74. Yet another tactic used by Moscow has been disinformation, the deliberate telling of lies to undermine the US position in the Middle East. Soviet disinformation has ranged from Soviet media reports of an impending US attack on Iran in January 1981 on the eve of an agreement for the release of the US hostages (a clear attempt to sabotage the release and thereby prevent a possible US–Iran *rapprochement*) to claims that the Israeli planes that bombed PLO headquarters in Tunis in 1985 had taken off from US aircraft carriers (an attempt to undermine US attempts to act as an "honest broker" in an Arab–Israeli peace settlement).[16] Last but certainly not least, in its efforts to increase its influence in the Middle East Moscow has offered the Arabs aid of both a military and diplomatic character against Israel, although that aid has been necessarily limited in scope since Moscow continues to support Israel's right to exist – both for fear of unduly alienating the United States (with whom Moscow desires additional strategic arms agreements and improved trade relations), and because Israel serves as a convenient rallying point for potentially anti-Western forces in the Arab world.

While the USSR has used all these tactics, to a greater or lesser degree of success, over the last two decades, it has also run into serious problems in its quest for influence in the Middle East. First, are the numerous inter-Arab and regional conflicts that pervade the Middle East and make it the most strife-torn region in the world. While aiding one side to a conflict gives Moscow entrée to a regional state, the Soviet action has often meant alienating the other party and sometimes driving it into the arms of the West, as well as enabling the state receiving Soviet aid to exploit Soviet assistance by undertaking actions not necessarily to the liking of the Soviet leadership. Indeed, there have been a number of cases where a client's regional goals have differed sharply from Moscow's regional and global aims, and Soviet leaders have had a difficult time trying to follow an even-handed policy in such conflicts as the Ethiopian–Somali, Iranian–Iraqi, North Yemeni–South Yemeni, Moroccan–Algerian, Syrian–Iraqi, and Syrian–Palestinian, however much the Soviet leadership may have wished to spread the mantle of a "Pax Sovietica" over the region. Second, the existence of communist parties in the Middle East has, on balance, proven to be a handicap for Moscow. While in the few cases where local communist parties are legal and independent (Tunisia, Israel, Lebanon) they have played a modest role in reinforcing Soviet propaganda efforts in the region, in most countries of the Middle East they are feared by the one-party regimes as potential or actual competitors for power and Moscow is inevitably blamed when the local communist party is perceived as participating in an attempt to overthrow the regime. Examples of this problem have been the communist-supported *coup d'état* in the Sudan in 1971, communist efforts to organize cells in the Iraqi army in the mid and late 1970s, and the activities of the Tudeh (communist) party in Khomeini's Iran in the 1980s.[17] A third problem facing Moscow has been the wealth which flowed to the Arab world – or at least to its major oil producers – due to the quadrupling of oil prices in 1973. This enabled the Arabs to buy quality technology from the West and Japan, and this development helped weaken the economic bond between the USSR and such Arab states as Iraq and also enabled Saudi Arabia to try to pry away Moscow's Arab allies, like the PDRY, with promises of financial aid.[18] A fourth problem for Moscow since 1967, and particularly since the 1973 Arab–Israeli war, has been the resurgence of Islam. Western scholars have long been divided on the question as to whether fundamentalist Islam is a net asset or liability to Moscow.[19] Some argue that since fundamentalist Islam is basically anti-Western and attacks not only US policies in the Middle East but Western culture as well, and since the USSR is itself basically anti-Western, regimes like those of the Ayatollah Khomeini are *de facto* assets to Soviet policy in the Middle East. A very different argument is made by those Western scholars who emphasize the religious incompatibility of Islam and communism. Given the fact that one of the central components of Marxism–Leninism is atheism, it is argued that this factor precludes any genuinely close relationship between the Soviet Union and such countries as Khomeini's Iran or Saudi Arabia – particularly in the aftermath of the Soviet invasion of Afghanistan where Soviet troops were seen as fighting against essentially Islamic resistance forces. In this regard, Ayatollah Khomeini himself noted:

> We are fighting against international communism to the same degree that we are fighting against the Western world devourers led by America, Israel and Zionism. My dear friends, you should know that the danger from the communist powers is not less than America ... Once again I strongly condemn the dastardly occupation of Afghanistan by the plunderers and occupiers of the aggressive East. I hope that the Muslim and noble people of Afghanistan will as soon as possible achieve true victory and independence and be released from the grip of these so-called supporters of the working class.[20]

Some Western observers have further argued that the Soviet Union may itself be vulnerable to Islamic fundamentalism.[21] In this regard it should be pointed out that the vast majority of the Soviet Union's estimated 50 million Muslims are Sunni, not Shia like Iran (the only large Soviet Shia population, however, is in Azerbaizhan, bordering Iran), and the failure of Khomeini's brand of Islamic fundamentalism to penetrate to the Arab world, even to the Shia of Iraq and Eastern Saudi Arabia, would appear to make it unlikely to have a major impact on Soviet Muslims as a whole. Nonetheless, as ethnic unrest grows in Azerbaizhan and Soviet Central Asia for a number of reasons including overpopulation, underemployment, and rising ecological problems, some Soviet Muslims may turn to Islam as a protest movement, although the Gorbachev regime (or its successor) would have to make extraordinary mistakes in its nationality policies for Islamic fundamentalism to be a genuine threat to the USSR.[22]

A fifth problem facing Moscow has been the danger of a war erupting at a time or place not wanted by the Soviet leadership. The outbreak of the Iran–Iraq war in 1980 was in many ways "the wrong war at the wrong time at the wrong place" for Moscow. Not only did it cause a major split in the Arab world and divert Arab attention from the Arab–Israeli conflict, it led to an improvement in US ties to Saudi Arabia and the other Gulf states as well, thus strengthening the US political/military position in the region.[23] Similarly, the prevention of an outbreak of a war between Syria and Israel has been a major goal of the Gorbachev regime, for fear that it might lead to a US–Soviet confrontation that would jeopardize the Soviet leader's ambitious program of domestic *perestroika*.

To overcome these difficulties, Moscow has evolved one overall strategy: the development of a bloc of "anti-imperialist" states within the Arab world. In Moscow's view, these states should bury their internecine rivalries and join together, along with such political organizations as the Arab communist parties and the PLO (and, if at all possible, with Iran) in a united front against what the USSR has called the "linchpin" of Western imperialism in the Middle East – Israel. Under such circumstances it is the Soviet hope that the Arab states would then use their collective pressure against the United States to weaken the US position in the region. While with the exception of a brief period during the 1973 Arab–Israeli war Arab unity on an "anti-imperialist" basis has been a chimera, and, as mentioned above, it is doubtful that Moscow would want a repetition of such a war, nonetheless, so long as Soviet leaders continue to think in terms of such Leninist categories of thought as "united fronts" ("anti-imperialist" Arab unity, in Soviet parlance, is merely another way of describing a united front of Arab governmental and nongovernmental forces) and, so long as there is a deep underlying psychological drive for unity in the Arab world, Moscow can be expected to continue to pursue this overall strategy as a long-term goal.

Sources for the study of Soviet policy toward the Middle East

One of the central assumptions on which this study is based is that one cannot understand the true impact of Soviet policy in the Middle East unless one first understands the main currents of politics in the Middle East as whole as well as the domestic politics and foreign policies of such key Middle East actors as Syria, Israel, Egypt, Iraq, Iran, Jordan, and the PLO. To do this a regular reading of the Middle East press is essential,[24] and interviews with Middle Eastern politicians and government officials often helpful in understanding the nuances of a country's policy.[25] Second, given the fact that the United States is the main competitor to the Soviet Union in the Middle East, a knowledge of US policies and problems in the region is also required. In addition, since England, France, Germany, and Italy, sometimes acting in concert as the EEC and sometimes acting individually, also play roles in the Middle East, the interested student should be acquainted with their policies[26] as well as those of China which, in recent years through arms sales to such countries as Iran and Saudi Arabia, has also become a factor of importance in the region.

In turning to an examination of the sources of Soviet conduct in the

Middle East, beyond such general ones mentioned above as the Tsarist legacy, Marxist–Leninist ideology, and concern for Soviet security, difficulties emerge. Some scholars see Soviet policy in the Middle East (and elsewhere) as the outcome of battles between rival Soviet bureaucracies. While a number of useful insights have emerged from analyses of this type,[27] I do not feel sufficiently comfortable with the amount of data on which such studies are based to draw far-reaching conclusions about Soviet policy from them. Until *glasnost* reaches the point that Soviet officials are willing to write candid memoirs of their bureaucratic struggles – and the recent two volume memoirs of Andrei Gromyko were lacking in such information on the Middle East[28] – it will be necessary to view Soviet decisions on Middle East policy as either consensus agreements or as the outcome of a Politburo debate, and evaluate them as such, rather than try to determine the various sides to a possible controversy and then analyze who emerged victorious in the Politburo debate. This is not to say that a "rational actor," black-box, model of international relations will be the only one employed in this study. It is clear that both the Soviet Union and the US have, from time to time, acted irrationally in the Middle East, often on the basis of incorrect perceptions of the situation, and such apparent misperceptions will be pointed out. The second US intervention in Lebanon from September 1982 to February 1984 is a prime example of this as is the Soviet invasion of Afghanistan in 1979 which, Soviet scholars are beginning to say, was based on a misperception of the domestic situation in Afghanistan.

While the main focus of this book will be on policy outcomes, rather than the policy debate, it is nonetheless necessary to discuss the Soviet sources on which the analysis will be based. In terms of authoritativeness, speeches by the General Secretary of the Communist Party, government statements, and the speeches of the Soviet Foreign Minister and Prime Minister should be seen as the most authoritative. Next in importance would come editorials in *Pravda* and *Izvestia* and doctrinal articles in *Kommunist*. Third would come regular journalistic articles in *Pravda* and *Izvestia* and articles in the Soviet foreign policy monthly *Mezhdunarodnaia Zhizn* (International Affairs) which as of June 1989, had two deputy foreign ministers, Viktor Karpov and Vladimir Petrovsky and an assistant to Soviet Foreign Minister Shevardnadze, Termuroz Stepanov, on its editorial board. Interestingly enough, however, as *glasnost* became increasingly acceptable in Soviet foreign policy analyses and old stereotypes were gradually dropped, even *Mezhdunarodnaia Zhizn*, beginning with its May 1988 edition, added the notation on its table of contents that "material published in this journal does not necessarily reflect the views of the Editorial Board."

Sources of almost equal authoritativeness are official Moscow radio broadcasts to the Arab world in Arabic or to Iran in Farsi (Persian). These broadcasts often summarize Soviet policy toward the region or toward a particular country, and are useful sources of information as to the message Moscow is trying to get across at any particular time. The official Soviet radio voice, Radio Moscow, should be distinguished from the less authoritative and more blatantly ideological Radio Peace and Progress, which, nonetheless, in the 1980–86 period, often signalled the beginning of a new Soviet policy. By 1987, however, in its broadcasts to Iran, it appeared to be following a policy line highly critical of Iran while the Soviet government was attempting a *rapprochement* with that country. By contrast, its broadcasts to Israel emphasized Soviet attempts to improve relations with the Jewish state. On balance, therefore, Radio Moscow Peace and Progress should be seen as less authoritative, albeit perhaps more interesting, from 1987 on. *Novaia Vremiia* (*New Times*), the Soviet foreign policy weekly also went through a metamorphosis beginning in late 1987. While editorials and most articles in the journal clearly reflected Soviet government positions before that date, with articles by Dmitry Volsky of particular importance since in the pre-*glasnost* days he was by far the most candid Soviet commentator, in 1987 the journal as a whole began to increasingly emphasize internal developments in the Soviet Union while also becoming somewhat more daring in some of the foreign policy issues which it discussed.

One of the most hotly debated questions among analysts of Soviet foreign policy is the degree of authoritativeness of the articles appearing in the journals of the Soviet Union's three main research institutes that deal with the Middle East: *Mirovaia Ekonomika i Mezhdunarodnye Otnosheniia* (*World Economy and International Relations*) of the World Economy Institute; *Ssha* (*USA*) of the USA–Canada Institute, and *Aziia i Afrika Sevodnia* (*Asia and Africa Today*) of the Institute of Oriental Studies (co-published with the Soviet Afro-Asian Solidarity Committee). Related to this question is the issue as to how much influence Soviet academics have over Soviet foreign policy. While in his study of the debates within the Soviet academic institutes, Jerry Hough cites the words of an unnamed deputy director of an institute to his subordinates: "those who write don't decide; those who decide don't read,"[29] the issue is obviously far more complicated than this. At the

minimum, Soviet scholars in their articles outline the parameters of
Soviet policy options; sometimes, as Elizabeth Valkenier notes in her
book *The Soviet Union and the Third World: An Economic Bind*,[30]
Soviet scholars through their debates, have a major impact in changing
Soviet policy. In this context it is interesting to note that during interviews at the Oriental Institute in Moscow in January 1988, I was told
that 50 percent of the work of the scholars dealing with contemporary
Middle East issues was commissioned either by the Soviet Foreign
Ministry or by the International Department of the Central Committee
of the Communist Party. Clearly, therefore, the writings and opinions of
Soviet scholars are of importance in the formation of Soviet policy
toward the Middle East, although it is not possible to determine with
any degree of accuracy just how important. Nonetheless, articles in the
scholarly journals are a source of information on Soviet policy toward
the region, and some of the more significant ones will be cited in this
analysis although the primary source of information on which this study
is based are the statements of Soviet leaders, editorials and articles in
Pravda, *Izvestia*, and *New Times*, and Soviet radio broadcasts to the
Middle East.

1 On the eve: Soviet policy toward the Middle East from World War II until the invasion of Afghanistan

In the period from World War II until the fall of the Shah of Iran in 1979, the Soviet Union tended to pursue one line of policy toward the two northernmost nations of the Middle East – Iran and Turkey (hereafter called the Northern Tier) – and another toward the other Middle Eastern states. The reason for this may be traced to both geography and history. Iran and Turkey differ sharply from the other nations of the region in three important respects. Both nations have long borders with the Soviet Union, and both have fought numerous wars against invading Russian troops in the last 400 years. As a result, both Iran and Turkey have had a great deal of experience with Russian imperialism, and for this reason the Soviet leadership has had far greater difficulty in extending Soviet influence in these nations than in the other countries of the Middle East, which neither border on the USSR nor possess a long experience in dealing with Russian imperialism. Indeed, almost all the nations of what we shall call the Southern Tier have had bitter experience with *Western* imperialism – particularly that of Britain and France – which dominated the region from Morocco to the Persian Gulf in the interwar period. It is in this part of the Middle East that the Soviet Union has seen the greatest increase in its influence since the end of World War II, although the Russians have proven unable to expand their influence to the point of actual control in any nation of the area.[1]

The Stalinist heritage, 1945–1953

Stalin's foreign policy toward the Middle East was a relatively uncomplicated one. Immediately after World War II, he demanded that the Turkish government cede to Russia parts of eastern Turkey and grant the Soviet Union a military base in the Turkish straits. In addition, Stalin claimed the right to a trusteeship over Libya and postponed the withdrawal of Soviet occupation forces from Iran until well into 1946.

These relatively crude attempts at territorial aggrandizement were counterproductive. Instead of increasing Russia's security through the acquisition of territory (a similar motive governed Soviet policy in Eastern Europe during this period), Stalin's actions served only to drive the nations of the Northern Tier into the arms of the West.[2]

Stalin's policies toward the Southern Tier were scarcely more productive. Viewing the world in terms of two camps, communist and anticommunist, Stalin was either unable or unwilling to see that the leaders of the new nations of what we now call the Third World wished to belong to neither camp, but desired to remain neutral. The Soviet press called such leaders as Nasser, Shishakli, and Nehru "lackeys of the imperialists," and described the newly formed Arab League as an "instrument of British imperialism." The Soviet recognition of the state of Israel in 1948 and its diplomatic and military support for it during the first Arab–Israeli conflict (1947–49) seem to have been aimed at weakening Britain's position in the Middle East and depriving it of key military bases.[3] In any case it did not improve the Russian position among the Arab states, while the period of good relations between the USSR and Israel was of a very short duration.[4]

Thus, Soviet policy toward the Middle East under Stalin was unproductive, if not counterproductive, and Russian influence was at a low ebb in both the Northern and Southern Tiers of the region at the time of Stalin's death in March 1953.

The Khrushchev Era, 1953–1964

The death of Stalin brought a fundamental change in Soviet policy toward the Middle East. Although Moscow had begun to take the side of the Arabs in the Arab–Israeli conflict as early as 1954, when Malenkov was still premier, the real change in Soviet policy did not emerge until after Khrushchev ousted Malenkov from the premiership in February 1955. Unlike Stalin, Khrushchev was not afflicted with a two-camp view of the world. Instead, he saw the world as being divided into three main zones or blocs – the socialist bloc, the capitalist bloc, and the Third World, which he hoped to win over to communism through political support and large doses of economic and military aid.[5] An irony of this development was that the new American Secretary of State, John Foster Dulles, had a two-camp view of the world much like Stalin's and tended, therefore, to have little patience with the neutralist aspirations of Third World leaders. Hence, when Dulles tried to integrate a number of Arab states into a military alliance aimed against the Soviet Union, he greatly offended their sensibilities, particularly since England, the former colonial overlord of much of the Middle East, was to be a founding member of the alliance. Egypt's Nasser was particularly irritated by this development, since his principal Arab rival, Nuri Said of Iraq, embraced the alliance (the Baghdad Pact) – and the military and economic assistance that went with it. Nasser then turned to Moscow for arms, and the end result of the process was that Nasser, through the now famous arms deal of 1955, actually invited the Russians to participate in the politics of the Middle East.[6] By obtaining large amounts of sophisticated weaponry from the USSR, Nasser clearly demonstrated the Arabs' independence from their former colonial masters; for Moscow, on the other hand, it was a means of gaining influence in the Middle East.

Nonetheless, even in the process of gaining influence in the Middle East through the sale of weapons, the Soviet leaders got themselves involved in a dilemma that has persisted until today. Mere provision of weapons to a country, regardless of its need for the weapons, does not give the donor nation control over the policies of the recipient nation. To the contrary, the supply of advanced weaponry may enable the recipient nation to embark on a military adventure that the donor nation considers undesirable. Even worse, such a military adventure might threaten to drag the donor nation itself into a war it does not want. Although the supply of weapons to military regimes may be relatively inexpensive in terms of cost to the Soviet economy, in terms of the risk that Moscow might be involved in a war not of its choosing as a result of such military assistance, the cost of such aid can be very high indeed. The Russians became aware of this danger in 1956 with the outbreak of the Sinai campaign, and found themselves in an even more dangerous predicament with the outbreak of the Six-Day War in 1967 and the Yom Kippur War in 1973. Heavy arms shipments to Egypt preceded each conflict, and Moscow was in danger of involvement in each war.[7]

Besides running the risk of direct involvement in an Arab–Israeli war, Khrushchev faced yet another dilemma in his dealings with Nasser. While happily accepting large quantities of Soviet economic and military aid, as well as support against the West following the nationalization of the Suez Canal in 1956 and during the subsequent Suez crisis, Nasser declared the Egyptian communist party to be illegal and kept its leaders in prison. Indeed, he made it very clear that he differentiated between the Soviet Union as a "great friend" and the Egyptian communist party, which he considered a threat to his dictatorship. As early as August 16, 1955, Nasser had stated in an interview in the Lebanese paper *Al-Jarida* that "nothing prevents us from strengthening our economic ties with Russia even if we arrest the Communists at home and put them on trial."[8]

Such a situation posed a painful dilemma to Khrushchev, a dilemma that he never really resolved. Nasser was a useful ally in the cold war, regardless of his treatment of the Egyptian communist party. Nonetheless, since Khrushchev considered himself the head of the international communist movement, he felt constrained to try to protect the communist parties of the Middle East. On several occasions he complained to Nasser about the treatment of the Egyptian communists, but Nasser denounced such "interference" in Egypt's "internal affairs," and relations between the Soviet Union and Egypt deteriorated as a result.[9]

The role of the communist party was to prove a stumbling block in Khrushchev's policies toward Syria and Iraq as well. In 1957, Syria, of all the nations of the Southern Tier, seemed most ripe for a communist seizure of power. The Syrian communist party had grown rapidly since the overthrow of the Shishakli dictatorship in 1954, and the Syrian government was very pro-Russian. The USSR sent a great deal of economic and military aid to Syria in 1957,[10] and Syrian leaders were frequent visitors to the Soviet Union in that year. Yet even as Syria appeared on the brink of "going communist" (as some US newspapers speculated), an event occurred that could only have shocked and disappointed the Soviet leadership – the union of Syria and Egypt into the United Arab Republic.[11] And just as the Egyptian communist party had been banned by Nasser, so too was the Syrian communist party, hitherto the strongest in the Arab world. While the official Soviet response to the announcement of the formation of the United Arab Republic was restrained in tone,[12] the event marked a victory for Arab nationalism, as espoused by Nasser, and a defeat for Arab communism and, to a lesser degree, the USSR.

The conflict between Arab nationalism and communism (and indirectly the USSR) became even more acute following the overthrow of the pro-Western regime of Nuri Said in Iraq in July 1958. While Nasser, who later flew to Moscow to discuss this event, had high hopes that Arab nationalists who backed him would take power and bring Iraq into the Egyptian-dominated United Arab Republic, it soon transpired that Kassem, who emerged as the leader of the new regime, was an independent Arab nationalist, one who was willing to utilize the Iraqi communist party to combat Nasser's followers in Iraq. Indeed, the Iraqi communist party was prominently represented in the new Iraqi regime, and the Soviet leaders soon began to give Iraq large amounts of economic and military aid, much as they had done with Egypt and Syria earlier.[13] In addition, however, the Soviet Union came out in support of Kassem in his efforts to keep Iraq independent of Nasser's unity movement.[14] *Pravda* pointedly stated on March 30, 1959:

> It has lately become apparent that some public figures in the Near East mean by Arab nationalism the immediate and mechanical unification of all Arab states by one of them, regardless of whether they want it or not. All who do not agree with this are denounced as Zionists, communists and enemies of the Arab people.[15]

Despite a brief *rapprochement* with Nasser in 1960, Khrushchev once again clashed with Egyptian leaders in May 1961 during a visit by an Egyptian parliamentary delegation headed by Anwar Sadat, who was then chairman of the United Arab Republic's National Assembly. Khrushchev attacked the Egyptian leaders for opposing communism and told them, "If you want socialism, you should not oppose communism," since the one automatically followed the other. He also told the Egyptians, "Arab nationalism is not the zenith of happiness," and "Life itself will impose communism." The Egyptians retorted angrily and Soviet–Egyptian relations suffered another setback.[16]

Meanwhile, despite Soviet military, economic, and diplomatic support, Kassem had proven to be a difficult person for the Soviet leaders to work with. Although he pulled Iraq out of the Baghdad Pact (securing, in the process, a large Soviet loan), he also skillfully played the communists off against the Nasserites, weakening both, and emerged himself as the dominant force in Iraq.[17] By 1961 the communists had lost their last positions of power in his regime and Kassem ruled alone – although he tolerated the presence of communists in Iraq to a limited extent. The Iraqi communists lost even this tenuous degree of freedom, however, when an avowedly anti-communist group of army officers overthrew Kassem in 1963 and proceeded to execute hundreds of Iraqi communists and drive the remainder either underground or into exile. Although this regime was itself overthrown before its anti-communist policies led to too severe a breach with the USSR, its successor was not much more hospitable toward the Iraqi communist party.

By this time, however, Khrushchev had switched his primary interest in the Arab world to yet another country, Algeria. Following the end of the Algerian war of independence with France in 1962, the USSR established close relations with the regime of Ahmed Ben-Bella. Soviet economic and military aid was provided to Ben-Bella, who allowed a number of Algerian communists to participate, as individuals, in his regime (the party itself remained illegal) while also nationalizing a sizable portion of Algeria's agricultural land and industry. Relations between the two countries grew so warm that Ben-Bella was awarded the Lenin Peace Prize and decorated as a "hero of the Soviet Union" during his visit to Moscow in April 1964, and at the end of the visit the Algerian leader secured a major loan.[18]

These developments in Algeria, coupled with Nasser's nationalization of a large portion of Egyptian industry following the breakup of the union with Syria in the fall of 1961, encouraged Khrushchev to believe that the Arab nationalist leaders were turning toward socialism even without the help of the communist parties. Indeed, it probably appeared to Khrushchev that his prediction made to Sadat in 1961 was now coming true. By 1963 Soviet ideologists were casting around for an explanation for this behaviour, one that would justify increased Soviet support for such regimes. (The support most likely would have come anyway, but a new ideological concept would help justify it, both to suspicious communists who were suppressed under the Arab nationalist regimes, and to those in Moscow who questioned the wisdom of aiding leaders such as Ben-Bella and Nasser.)[19] Consequently, the terms "noncapitalist path" and "Revolutionary Democracy" were born. By "noncapitalist path" Soviet ideologists meant an intermediate stage between capitalism (or the primitive capitalist economies the nationalist leaders had inherited from the colonial period) and socialism, and the highly optimistic Khrushchev often used the terms "noncapitalist path" and "socialism" synonymously in describing the progress of such regimes as those of Nasser and Ben-Bella. The term "Revolutionary Democracy" was used to describe those states moving along the noncapitalist path toward socialism without the help of a communist party, which according to previous Marxist–Leninist theory was supposed to be the *sine qua non* of a transition to socialism.[20]

These semantics enabled Khrushchev to attempt to solve his dilemma of dealing with both nationalist leaders like Nasser and the communist parties of their states, a dilemma that had caused problems for Soviet policy makers in the past. Arguing that the Egyptian Communist Party would be more effective working from within Nasser's regime to win the Egyptian leader to "scientific socialism," Khrushchev – and his successors – urged the Egyptian Communist Party (a weak and faction-ridden organization) to dissolve and join the Arab Socialist Union (ASU), which was Nasser's mass political organization and the only one permitted in Egypt. In another policy innovation, the Soviet leadership moved to establish direct party-to-party relations between the CPSU and the ASU, such as had already been done with Ben-Bella's Front de Liberation Nationale (FLN), in which communists occupied key positions. In establishing direct party-to-party relations, the Soviet leaders claimed that this would enable the CPSU to directly transmit its revolutionary experience to the one-party regimes of the Arab states and thereby hasten the trip of Egypt and Algeria down the noncapitalist path toward communism.

As might be expected, a number of Arab communists took a rather dim view of these developments in Soviet strategy, which many of them saw as the effective end of their political existence. Writing in the *World Marxist Review*, a journal that served as a sounding board for the world's nonruling communist parties as well as for the CPSU, several Arab communists voiced their unhappiness with these Soviet ideological innovations. Thus, Fuad Nasser, Secretary General of the Jordanian communist party and generally a strong supporter of Soviet foreign policy (particularly in the Sino-Soviet conflict), stated in the course of a 1964 symposium on Arab socialism and Arab unity: "Latterly, there has been a great deal of talk about these ex-colonial countries taking the non-capitalist way, although *frankly speaking* we still are not sufficiently clear as to what this means" (emphasis added).[21]

Similarly, Khalid Bakdash, Secretary General of the Syrian communist party and perhaps the most prestigious communist leader in the entire Middle East (and also a staunch supporter of Soviet policy), pointedly stated:

> *Some people say*, and this can be heard in Syria as well, that the communist parties no longer play the role they used to. This is a shortsighted view, to say the least, and to say it would be tantamount to denying the need for the continued existence of the party.
> ... This is a shortsighted view because the role of the working class in our countries is bound to grow with the development of the national-liberation movement. The stronger the communist parties and the more ground the ideas of scientific socialism gain, the more certain our progress in the future.[22] (emphasis added)

A second area of disagreement that arose during the symposium dealt with the degree of criticism to which the Revolutionary Democratic leaders should be subjected by Arab communists. Bakdash took the lead in urging that the shortcomings of these regimes should be clearly pointed out, while other Arab communists argued that only the positive (that is, genuine socialist) aspects of Nasser's and Ben-Bella's programs should be commented upon because the main role of the Arab communists was to disseminate "scientific socialism" among the masses. Bakdash disagreed with their emphasis, arguing that while it was important for Arab communists to teach "scientific socialism" and to promote friendship between their countries and the Soviet Union, it was also important to point out the differences between the communists and the Revolutionary Democrats.[23]

While the Arab communists debated the advantages and disadvantages of assisting the Revolutionary Democratic leaders, Khrushchev paid a visit to Egypt in May 1964 to examine the situation for himself. Although the visit was supposed to demonstrate the *rapprochement* between the USSR and Egypt, as symbolized by the Aswan Dam, it also illustrated Khrushchev's fundamental inability to understand the major currents in Arab politics. According to an Egyptian account of his visit, the Soviet leader seemed amazed at the popular responses Iraqi President Aref got from the Egyptian crowds when he cited Koranic verses in his speech. In addition, Khrushchev clashed with Ben-Bella, who reportedly told the Soviet leader that he knew nothing about Arab unity or the Arabs. To this Khrushchev is supposed to have replied, "I must admit I don't understand you, for there is only one unity, the unity of the working class."[24] Nonetheless, the visit ended on a positive note, at least for the Egyptians, who were the recipients of a $277 million loan, and Nasser became the second Arab leader to be made a "hero of the Soviet Union."[25]

In addition to their activities in Egypt, Syria, Iraq, and Algeria during the Khrushchev period, the Russians also became active in other parts of the Arab world, although to a much smaller degree. The USSR gave military and economic aid to Yemen and Morocco (and was caught in the middle of the Algerian–Moroccan war of 1963) and granted economic assistance to Tunisia and the Sudan.[26] In addition, diplomatic relations were begun with Libya and Jordan, although repeated Soviet efforts to establish diplomatic relations with Saudi Arabia proved unsuccessful.

Khrushchev's policy toward the Northern Tier nations, Turkey and Iran, was far more limited in scope. Since these two nations were military allies of the United States, Khrushchev was not above rattling

Soviet rockets at them, much as he periodically did to Britain, France, and West Germany. This, as can be imagined, was not conducive to an improvement of relations. Nonetheless, toward the end of Khrushchev's reign, relations with both countries were moderated. In the case of Iran, this was primarily due to the Shah's announcement in 1962 that no foreign missiles would be permitted on Iranian soil. This led to a major improvement in Soviet–Iranian relations. Leonid Brezhnev made a state visit to Iran in 1963, and the USSR gave Iran a $38.9 million loan in the same year.[27] It should be pointed out, however, that Iran was sorely beset by internal difficulties at the time of the Shah's announcement. The major land reform campaign under way at the time had aroused a great deal of opposition to the Shah's government, and the improvement of relations with the USSR enabled the Shah to concentrate his attention on his internal opposition.[28]

Soviet–Turkish relations during the Khrushchev era were considerably cooler. While Moscow had renounced its territorial demands against Turkey soon after the death of Stalin, Khrushchev had threatened to go to war against Turkey in 1957 over an alleged Turkish plot to invade Syria. Although in the atmosphere of East–West detente following the Cuban missile crisis of October 1962 some Turks called for closer relations with the Soviet Union, Khrushchev's policy toward the Cyprus crisis, which involved support for the Greek position and military aid for the Cypriot regime of Archbishop Makarios, was a major stumbling block in the way of *rapprochement* between the two countries.[29]

All in all, the Soviet Union's position in the Middle East at the time of Khrushchev's fall in October 1964 was considerably better than when Khrushchev came to power. Of perhaps greatest significance, the Baghdad Pact had been all but destroyed by the withdrawal of its one Arab member, Iraq. In addition, Moscow had succeeded in establishing diplomatic relations with almost all the states in the Middle East and had given many of them military and economic aid. The Middle East was clearly no longer the Western sphere of influence it had been at the time of Stalin's death, and the Russians could justifiably consider themselves to be an important factor in Middle Eastern affairs.

The Soviet position, however, was far from a dominant one in 1964. In the countries in which the USSR could be said to have had the most influence – and in which it had spent the most money (Egypt, Syria, Iraq, and Algeria) – the communist parties remained illegal and many communists languished in jail. Voices were already being raised in

ALBRIGHT COLLEGE LIBRARY 235186

Moscow that too much had been spent with too little return. Although Arab leaders often joined the Russians in denouncing "imperialism," all had fairly good relations with the Western powers, and the USSR was unable to control any of them. It was beginning to appear that, far from being exploited by the Russians, as many in the West had feared when the USSR had made its dramatic entrance into the Middle East in 1955, the Arab nations were actually exploiting the Russians. They had gained large amounts of military and economic aid, while sacrificing none of their sovereignty. As a Soviet scholar, Nodari Simoniya, stated several years later:

> The existence of the world socialist system may be used to the advantage not only of Revolutionary Democrats or other representatives of the workers; certain judicious bourgeois circles in a number of countries are very successfully using this circumstance to strengthen the political sovereignty and economic development of their countries.[30]

Soviet gains were also limited in the realm of ideology. To be sure, the state sector had been enlarged and the private, or capitalist, sector reduced in many of the states of the region, particularly Egypt and Algeria. In addition, some foreign investments had been nationalized, and there had been a considerable amount of land reform. Nonetheless, these social reforms had been undertaken by nationalist regimes, operating independently of the communist parties of their countries. Khrushchev hailed these reforms as demonstrating that a number of Middle Eastern nations had taken the noncapitalist way, and in his usual optimistic way went on to equate the noncapitalist way with the road to socialism on which the communist nations of the world themselves had embarked. Khrushchev's successors, however, clearly differentiated between these two concepts. Simoniya, in assessing the overthrow of such pro-Russian regimes as Nkrumah's in Ghana and Sukarno's in Indonesia, noted ruefully that the noncapitalist road was by no means irreversible.[31]

In sum, when Khrushchev fell in October 1964, the Soviet position in the Middle East was far better than it had been at the time of Stalin's death (it could hardly have been worse), yet it was far from a position of dominance or even preponderance of power. The nations of the Northern Tier, Iran and Turkey, remained firm allies of the United States, although both had improved relations – to a point – with the Soviet Union. Soviet influence had risen fastest among the Arab states, particularly Egypt, Algeria, Syria, and Iraq, but even in these states it was clearly limited. Each of these countries had maintained its independence of action both domestically and in foreign policy and, as argued above, tended to extract far more from the Soviet Union in the form of economic and military support than it paid in political obedience. To be fair to Khrushchev, it should be pointed out that the Middle East was not the primary area of Soviet concern during the period in which he ruled. Khrushchev's main concerns were the problems of Eastern and Western Europe and the rapidly escalating Sino-Soviet conflict. With the rise of the Brezhnev–Kosygin leadership to power, however, Soviet interest began to focus more closely on the Middle East.

The Brezhnev era, 1964–1970

When the impulsive and energetic Khrushchev was replaced by the conservative and rather phlegmatic duo of Brezhnev and Kosygin, Western observers called the changeover in leadership "the triumph of the bureaucrats."[32] Like bureaucrats everywhere, they were tired of the constant administrative reorganizations of the Khrushchev era, along with his impulsive actions in foreign policy.[33] Unlike Khrushchev, who tried to spread Soviet influence everywhere in the world at a rapid pace, the new leaders seem to have decided to concentrate Soviet energies and resources on becoming the dominant power in the Middle East, while adopting a much more gradualist policy toward the growth of Soviet power in other parts of the noncommunist world. The Soviet drive for power and influence in the Middle East became increasingly evident in 1965 and 1966, both in the Northern Tier nations, which became the recipients of large amounts of Soviet economic aid, and in the Arab states of Egypt, Syria, Iraq, and Algeria. By early 1967 the new Soviet policy was in high gear, and at least part of the responsibility for the June 1967 Arab–Israeli war can be attributed to the USSR, which was exploiting the Arab–Israeli conflict to increase its influence among the Arab states.

While the Israeli victory in the Six-Day War was a temporary setback for Moscow, one consequence of the Arab defeat was a marked decline of American influence in the radical Arab states of the region.[34] As a result Moscow redoubled its efforts to oust Western influence from the Arab states, while cementing their newly improved relations with Iran and Turkey. Yet, by becoming more involved in the Middle East, the

Soviet leaders encountered a number of serious problems, and although by the death of Nasser, in September 1970, Soviet influence in the Middle East had reached its highest point since World War II, the Russians were still far from controlling the region. They instead found themselves paying a far higher price than ever before in terms of economic and military aid for their "influence," while running an increasingly serious risk of war with the United States – just at a time when the Sino-Soviet struggle was heating up.

In assessing the Brezhnev–Kosygin approach to the Middle East, it is first necessary to analyze the international situation that the new Soviet leadership faced when it took power in October 1964. Next, an examination will be made of the innovations and changes the new leadership made in Soviet policy toward the region. Finally, an assessment will be made of the Soviet position in the Middle East at the time of Nasser's death.

The new international situation

In surveying the Soviet position in the world after they took power in 1964, Brezhnev and Kosygin seem to have reached the conclusion that the further expansion of Soviet influence in Western Europe and Latin America was out of the question, at least for the time being, since these areas were of vital importance to the United States, which had demonstrated its clear military superiority over the Soviet Union during the Cuban missile crisis. Similarly, the active hostility of the Chinese communists had confronted the Russians with a clear danger as well as an obstacle to the spread of their influence in South and Southeast Asia. While the USSR still had several important footholds in Africa, the Soviet leaders evidently decided that, given the expanding opportunities in the Middle East, they should begin to concentrate their military and economic assistance there, an area contiguous to the USSR and one holding greater possibilities for Soviet gains.[35]

The growing influence of the Russian military, with its call for an expanded navy, probably was a contributing factor to this decision. The key naval communication routes that run through the Middle East, and the Russian need to cope with American missile-carrying Polaris submarines already cruising in the Mediterranean at the time of Khrushchev's fall, made the region a particularly important one for the Soviet military. In 1964 a special Mediterranean unit was formed as part of the Soviet Black Sea fleet.[36]

A second contributing factor to the Soviet decision was the increasing instability in the region itself. Nasser's prestige had begun to wane, as his regime was beset with increasing economic and political difficulties, not the least of which was the failure of Egyptian intervention in the Yemeni civil war. Egypt's relations with the United States also began to deteriorate badly in the 1965–66 period.[37] In addition, the endemic Arab–Israeli conflict had begun to worsen, the frequently changing Syrian and Iraqi regimes were unable to cope with internal difficulties, and the British were hard-pressed to maintain their position in riot-torn Aden. All these developments must have tempted the Russians into greater involvement.

The Soviet leaders' attempt to gain increased influence in the Middle East was also aided by a number of events occurring elsewhere in the world in the 1965–66 period. Perhaps the most important was the large American troop commitment to Vietnam in 1965. This was a major bonus to the Russians for a number of reasons. Not only did the Vietnam War cause increasing internal turmoil in the United States itself, but it also served another major Soviet goal – the containment of communist China. For with a half-million American troops to its south, a hostile India (supported by both the United States and the Soviet Union) to its Southwest, and fifty Russian divisions along its northern border, China was indeed "contained" – from the Russian point of view, that is. Another important consequence of US policy in Vietnam was that it tended to divert American energy and attention from other parts of the world, including the Middle East, thus enabling the Russians to operate more freely there.[38]

A second major bonus for the Soviet Union was China's so-called cultural revolution, which occurred in 1966. This effectively removed China from competition with Russia in the Third World and greatly reduced Chinese influence in the international communist movement. Not having to compete economically with China for influence throughout the Third World allowed the Soviet leaders to concentrate their resources in the Middle East.[39] It should be added that the cultural revolution, much like the US involvement in Vietnam, tended to divert Chinese attention from the Middle East.[40]

Yet another bonus for Moscow came with the British decision to pull out of Aden (now the People's Democratic Republic of Yemen) in February 1966. This, together with increasing discussion in England about the necessity for pulling out of the Persian Gulf as well, must have given the Russians the impression that a major power vacuum was opening up along the southern and eastern periphery of the Arabian Peninsula – a power vacuum that the Russians could fill. The fact that Western unity also seemed to be breaking down, as evidenced by deGaulle's 1966 decision to take French military forces out of NATO, also must have been encouraging to Moscow. This French move, coupled with the British decision to pull out of Aden, made it appear very unlikely that the western powers would develop a joint policy to confront the USSR in the Middle East.

Soviet failures elsewhere in the Third World also may have sharpened the Russian drive into the Middle East. The fall of Sukarno's regime in Indonesia in October 1965, a regime in which the Russians had invested nearly $2 billion in military and economic aid, was a blow to the Russians. Four months later, in February 1966, came the fall of Nkrumah's regime in Ghana, and the Russians lost their investment of nearly $500 million in military and economic aid. Both pro-Soviet regimes were replaced by pro-Western ones.[41]

These events must have made the Russians prize even more highly the good relations they still had with a number of Middle Eastern nations, particularly the regimes of the "radical" Arab states, in which they had similarly invested extensive economic and military assistance. This was particularly true of the Syrian regime, which took power after a *coup d'état* in February 1966 and announced its intention to undertake a major "socialist transformation" in Syria as well as work for improved relations with the Soviet Union. The fact that this regime took power so soon after the overthrow of Nkrumah must have been heartening for the Russians; even more heartening was the new regime's decision to permit the Syrian communist leader, Khalid Bakdash, to return from his eight-year exile in Europe.[42] Yet the Soviet leaders were to find that their initial enthusiasm for the new Syrian regime was to become a very costly one, for it was this regime, with its encouragement of the Palestinian guerrillas, that was to help precipitate the June 1967 Arab–Israeli War.

New policy initiatives

The decision of Brezhnev and Kosygin to make the Middle East a primary area of Soviet interest meant that the new Soviet leaders would have to come to grips with some of the dilemmas left unsolved from the Khrushchev era. Most important of these was the role the communist parties of the Middle East were to play in the political and economic life of the countries in which they operated. While Khrushchev had been generally ambivalent about this, the Brezhnev–Kosygin leadership adopted a clearer position. They no longer entertained much hope that any of the communist parties of the region would seize power; indeed, confronted by a hostile communist China, the Soviet leaders must have wondered if it was to their benefit if any more countries were taken over by independent communist parties. In any case the new Soviet leaders began to emphasize the importance of good state relations with the nationalist leaders of the Middle East, and generally let the communist parties of the region fend for themselves. In the case of the Northern Tier states, Moscow virtually disregarded the communist parties; in the case of the Revolutionary Democratic Arab states, the parties were urged to disband and their members urged to join the large state parties of their countries, such as Egypt's Arab Socialist Union, with which the Soviet leaders, in a policy change begun in Khrushchev's last months in power, were trying to develop party-to-party relations.

Thus, in April 1965 the Egyptian Communist Party was officially dissolved; a communiqué later published in *Al-Nahar* (Beirut) announced the termination

> of the existence of the Egyptian communist party as an independent body and the instruction of its members to submit – as individuals – their applications for membership in the Arab Socialist Union, and to struggle for the formation of a single socialist party which would comprise all the revolutionary forces in the country.[43]

Unfortunately for the Soviet leaders, the new strategy met with serious difficulties only two months later as Ben-Bella was ousted from office by Hoauri Boumedienne, the Algerian military chief, who had earlier complained about the growth of communist influence in the Ben-Bella government. Boumedienne purged the Algerian government and the FLN of its communist members and publicly stated that communists would have no part in his new government.[44] For reasons of international politics, the Soviet leadership did not break relations with the new regime, even when Algerian communists were imprisoned by it. The CPSU even continued party-to-party relations with the now communist-free FLN, perhaps hoping thereby to maintain socialist influence on the Boumedienne regime from above. Nonetheless, party relations with the FLN proved to be an embarrassment for the Soviet Union because the Algerian communist party, although now illegal, continued to operate. At the 23rd CPSU Congress in March 1966, the Algerian FLN, which was invited as a friendly (albeit non-communist) party, walked out rather than see the Algerian communist party seated as an official delegation.[45]

Thus, the new Soviet leaders had run into a dilemma. In seeking to develop close party ties with the non-communist state parties of the radical Arab states, they invited the Algerian FLN to the conference; yet, because of the Sino-Soviet conflict and for reasons of domestic legitimacy, they had to invite the Algerian communist party as well. The Soviet goal to remain the leaders of the international communist movement had once again come into conflict with its Middle Eastern policies. Unfortunately for Moscow, this particular conflict was to occur again.[46]

Meanwhile, in Egypt the decision to dissolve the communist party had not led to the hoped-for increase in communist influence in the Nasser regime, although it did remove a major irritant in Soviet–Egyptian relations. While the former members of the party were given posts in the Egyptian mass media, the Youth Bureau, the Ministry of Education, and even the Central Committee of the Arab Socialist Union, power remained in the hands of Nasser and his entourage, and there was no noticeable increase in socialist legislation as a result of the communist presence. While the Marxists may have hoped to form "vanguard cadres" in the Arab Socialist Union, they were unable to do so; indeed, the only vanguard organization within the ASU was a quasi-secret police cadre system controlled by Ali Sabry and Shaari Gomaa, which arrested and periodically imprisoned the former communists.[47]

Perhaps because of the apparent failure of the Egyptian experiments in communist party dissolution, or because of the prestige of Khalid Bakdash, who had strongly opposed it, the Soviet leadership did not actively pressure the Syrian communist party to dissolve following the coming to power of the pro-Soviet left-wing Ba'ath regime in Syria in February 1966. Instead, the CPSU established party-to-party relations with it, thus extending Soviet party relations to the third Arab state in the Middle East. The Soviet action was preceded by the decision by the new regime to permit Khalid Bakdash to return from exile, and the subsequent Soviet loan of $132 million to Syria for the construction of the Euphrates Dam. The timing of the loan, coming so soon after Bakdash's return, is clearly reminiscent of the $277 million loan to Egypt in 1964 following Nasser's decision to free imprisoned Egyptian communists. It appeared in the mid-1960s that a demonstrative act by a nationalist Arab leadership toward its communist party, one of little or no political cost to the leadership, might well bring a reward out of proportion to the cost involved.[48]

In addition to de-emphasizing the importance of the Middle Eastern communist parties and attempting to develop close party ties with the nationalist parties of the radical Arab states, there was another policy change under Brezhnev and Kosygin. This involved a revised estimate of the desirability of Arab unity. While Khrushchev was ambivalent on the issue of Arab unity and occasionally opposed it because he feared that it would be a barrier to the spread of Russian and communist influence, the new Soviet leadership gave it a strong endorsement. The reason for this change in policy lay in the fact that beginning in 1965 the USSR tried to forge a quasi-alliance of the "anti-imperialist" forces of the Middle East under Soviet leadership. The fact that perhaps the only issue on which all Arabs can agree is opposition to Israel had led the Russians to brand Israel as the "imperialist wedge" in the Middle East and to link closely the Arab struggle against Israel with the "struggle against imperialism." One of the Soviet goals in this process was to limit the internecine conflict among the Arab nations, particularly Egypt, Syria, and Iraq, which was as endemic to the Middle East as the Arab–Israeli conflict.[49] In addition, Moscow evidently hoped that, by becoming the champion of the Arab states against Israel, it could line up the Arab states against the West as well. Yet this policy, while it paid some dividends to the USSR, also proved to be a very dangerous one, since it almost got Moscow involved in the June 1967 Arab–Israeli War and into an open conflict with Israel and the United States in July 1970.

Soviet policy toward the Northern Tier under Brezhnev

When the new Russian leadership began to step up the Soviet drive in the Middle East, attention was first turned to the nations of the Northern Tier. A deliberate effort was made to improve relations with Turkey, and the Soviet leaders shifted their position on the Cyprus issue to gain Turkish support. Kosygin visited Ankara in September 1966, and a $200 million Soviet loan was worked out in which Moscow agreed to construct a steel mill and several other industrial projects. Interestingly enough, the agreement stipulated that the Soviet loan could be repaid by the shipment of certain types of Turkish products – products that had a difficult time finding markets in the West.[50]

Soviet relations improved even more rapidly with Iran. In July 1965 the Shah paid an official visit to the Soviet Union, and in January 1966 the Russians gave Iran a $288.9 million loan for a series of industrial projects.[51] Of greatest diplomatic importance was the Soviet–Iranian agreement reached at the same time, whereby the Russians would provide Iran with $110 million in military equipment, primarily small arms and transport equipment, in return for Iranian gas. While some Western commentators stated that the USSR was now making dangerous inroads in Iran, it appeared that the Shah was utilizing the Soviet arms for several purposes of his own. The first was to persuade the United States to sell Iran more sophisticated weapons, including anti-aircraft equipment, under the implicit threat that Iran would otherwise turn to the USSR.[52] Perhaps more important, however, was that the USSR, in supplying arms to Iran, had implicitly strengthened the Shah in his dealings with Iraq, a nation with good relations with the Soviet Union and one with which Iran was continuously in conflict; the new Soviet–Iranian detente enabled the Shah to focus his attention on the power struggle in the Persian Gulf. In any case, the Soviet leaders evidently found their *rapprochment* with Iran to be a most satisfactory one, because in April 1968, in another visit to Iran, Kosygin offered still another loan, this time for up to $300 million.[53]

By the summer of 1970 the Brezhnev–Kosygin leadership had agreed to provide no less than $788.9 million in economic aid to the nations of the Northern Tier, along with $110 million in military aid. Yet what had Moscow obtained in return? Relations had improved considerably with both Turkey and Iran, but both remained within the Western alliance system, and any thoughts of a drift toward neutralism seemed to have been aborted by the Soviet invasion of Czechoslovakia in August 1968. Soviet ships now visited Iran's Persian Gulf ports (along with Iraq's), but this merely made the Russian choice more difficult in case of a clash between the Persian Gulf powers. Indeed, as the politics of the Persian Gulf grew hotter with the British withdrawal from the region in 1971, the Soviet leaders were to find that Iran had exploited her newly improved relations with the USSR to achieve her own objectives in the region.[54] Similarly, although Moscow enjoyed a larger degree of freedom of maneuver through the straits as a result of its improved relations with Turkey, the Turks remained quite independent, as evidenced by their refusal, despite a great deal of Soviet pressure, to return the Lithuanians who had hijacked a Russian plane to Turkey in September 1970.

Soviet policy toward the Southern Tier under Brezhnev

The Soviet leadership's policy toward the Arab nations and Israel from 1964 until the death of Nasser was considerably more complex than their policy toward Iran and Turkey. Mention has already been made of the changed Soviet position on the desirability of Arab unity and the Soviet effort to promote close party relations between the CPSU and the radical Arab socialist parties of the region. Economic and military aid continued to play an important role in the Soviet–Arab relations, as it had done under Khrushchev, but Soviet political support for the radical Arab regimes, primarily Syria's, was perhaps even more important. The Syrian regime that had taken power in February 1966 espoused not only the need for a socialist transformation in Syria and close cooperation with the Soviet Union, but also military and financial assistance for the Palestine Fatah guerrilla organization led by Yasser Arafat, which began a series of guerrilla attacks against Israel. These attacks placed the narrowly based Ba'ath regime in danger of retaliatory attacks by Israel, which might cause its fall; in order to avoid such a possibility the Soviet leadership urged the other Arab states, especially Egypt, to join together with Syria against the "imperialists" and Israel. This was the theme of a visit by Soviet Premier Kosygin to Cairo in May 1966, in which the Soviet leader called for a united front of progressive Arab states "such as the United Arab Republic, Algeria, Iraq and Syria to confront imperialism and reaction."[55] Kosygin's visit to Cairo was followed by a trip by Iraqi Premier Bazzaz to Moscow in late July, in which the Soviet leadership publicly ended its rift with the Iraqi government over its persecution of the Kurds and the Iraqi communist party, and urged the Iraqis to join in the anti-imperialist front of the Arab states.[56] In November 1966 the Arab united front sought by the USSR began to take shape as Egypt and Syria signed a defensive alliance, and the Soviet leaders may have hoped that this would deter any major Israeli attack on Syria.[57] Nonetheless, the Syrian government seized on the alliance to step up its support for Palestinian guerrilla attacks on Israel, and by April 1967 the Syrian–Israeli and Jordanian–Israeli borders had become tinderboxes.

The Israelis had initially restricted themselves to retaliatory raids against the Jordanians, through whose territory the guerrillas had come from Syria. In early April they decided to retaliate directly against the Syrians. Following Syrian shelling of Israeli farmers from the Golan Heights, the Israeli air force took to the skies to silence the Syrian artillery and in the process shot down seven Syrian jets that had come to intercept them. This defeat was a major blow to the prestige of the Syrian government, and when coupled with anti-Ba'ath rioting led by Muslim religious leaders in early May it appeared that the shaky Syrian Ba'athist government was about to fall. These developments led the Soviet leaders, who were concerned about the collapse of their main Arab ally in the Middle East and the center of anti-Western activity, to give false information to the Egyptians that Israel was planning a major attack on Syria. Nasser, then at the low point of his prestige in the Arab world, apparently seized this opportunity to regain his lost prestige and again appear as the champion of the Arabs by ordering the UN forces to leave their positions between Israel and Egypt, and by moving Egyptian troops to the borders of Israel. In addition, he blockaded the Straits of Tiran to Israeli shipping and at the end of May signed a military alliance with his erstwhile enemy, King Hussein of Jordan. Following the military encirclement of Israel, it appeared that war was but a few days away, and on the morning of June 5, 1967, the Israelis decided to strike before they were attacked. In the course of six days the Israelis succeeded in defeating the armies of Egypt, Syria, and Jordan and capturing the Sinai Peninsula, the Jordanian section of the West Bank of the Jordan River, and the Golan Heights in Syria.[58]

While Arab leaders may have hoped that the Soviet position of support for the Syrian regime, Soviet efforts to tie it to Egypt through an alliance and Soviet efforts to rally an "anti-imperialist" anti-Israeli alliance among the Arab states would mean Soviet military support to the Arabs during the war with Israel, Soviet military aid was not forthcoming. The only substantive action the USSR took was to break diplomatic relations with Israel, an action also taken by the other Soviet bloc states in Eastern Europe (with the exception of Romania) and Yugoslavia.

As might be imagined, the lack of Soviet support during the war and the Soviet efforts to achieve a cease-fire with Israeli troops still occupying Arab territory were bitter pills for the Arabs to swallow, and Soviet prestige dipped in the Arab world as a result. In an effort to compensate for their limited support of the Arabs during the war, the Soviet leaders moved immediately to rebuild the armies of Syria and Egypt and offered Soviet weapons to Jordan in an effort to attract King Hussein to the Soviet side. In addition, the Soviet leaders attempted to capitalize on the heightened military weakness of the Arab states and their diplomatic isolation (much of it self-imposed) to increase Soviet influence throughout the Arab world. Having broken diplomatic relations with the United States and Britain during the war, Egypt, Syria, Iraq, and the Sudan had nowhere else to turn for sophisticated military equipment, although French President Charles deGaulle, in condemning Israel for attacking the Arabs, sought to spread French influence in the Arab states and at the same time to obtain new markets for France's battle-proven Mirage jet fighter-bombers. China also was not idle during this period. Immediately after the war, the Chinese diverted to Egypt four shiploads of Australian wheat destined for China and gave Egypt a $10 million loan.[59] The Chinese proved unwilling, however, to give the Egyptians what they really wanted – an atom bomb. As Mohammed Heikal relates in *The Cairo Documents*, the Chinese leaders refused the Egyptian request and told the Egyptian delegation that if they wanted atomic weaponry, they would have to develop it themselves, just as China had done.[60]

One consequence of the June war that the Soviet leaders welcomed was the oil embargo that the Arab states imposed on the United States, Britain, and West Germany. An article in the August 1967 issue of *International Affairs* stated:

> The oil weapon is a powerful weapon in the hands of the Arab countries. This is the first time in the history of the Middle East that the Western world has been made to feel who is the real owner of Arab oil. Let us add that the Western powers depend heavily on Arab oil.[61]

Despite Soviet urging, however, Arab solidarity on the oil embargo could not be maintained, particularly since the conservative Arab states – Saudi Arabia, Kuwait, and Libya – were demanding its termination.[62] In addition, both the United States (then possessing an oil surplus available for export) and Iran stepped up production to compensate for the Arab oil cutoff, and Western Europe was in no danger of running out of oil. Consequently, at the Arab summit conference in Khartoum in August 1967, the Arab states agreed to terminate the oil embargo. The rich oil states – Saudi Arabia, Kuwait, and Libya – agreed to provide Egypt and Jordan with an annual subsidy to compensate them for war losses. (Syria, which boycotted the conference, was not included in the subsidy arrangement.) In return, Nasser agreed to pull Egyptian troops out of Yemen, thus ending the threat to Saudi Arabia's southern border.

While not too pleased with the end of the Arab oil embargo and the end of "anti-imperialist" Arab unity created by the war, the Soviet leaders may have been relieved that the rich oil states were sharing with the USSR the expensive burden of supporting the chronically poor Egyptian economy. Writing in *New Times* after the conclusion of the Khartoum conference, Igor Belyayev and Yevgeny Primakov, two of the senior Soviet commentators on Middle Eastern affairs, seemed to agree with the Khartoum decision: "It was a matter of sober calculation. Refusal to pump oil for the United States, Britain and the Federal Republic of Germany caused no actual shortage of oil and oil products in Western Europe."[63]

Nasser's agreement at the Khartoum conference to withdraw Egyptian troops from Yemen appeared to most observers at the time to mean that the Saudi-backed Royalist forces would emerge victorious from the long and bloody Yemeni civil war. To prevent this from happening, the USSR engaged in a massive airlift of military equipment to the Republican forces in late 1967, and this helped prevent a Royalist victory. Unfortunately for Moscow, however, squabbling among the Republican forces was eventually to result in a coalition government of Royalists and Republicans and a Westward turn in Yemeni foreign policy.

To the south, in Aden, the Soviet leaders quickly recognized the nationalist regime, which came to power after the British withdrawal at the end of 1967, and which proclaimed Aden to be the People's Democratic Republic of South Yemen. Within two months the USSR had begun to send military equipment to the strategically located state at the entrance to the Red Sea, and it was not long before the South Yemeni Defense Minister journeyed to Moscow to ask for more aid. South Yemen, however, was plagued by a festering civil war between two radical nationalist groups who had fought each other as well as the British during the independence struggle. It was also beset by continuing tribal strife and an ill-defined border with North Yemen, which soon was the scene of military conflict. In this situation the Soviet Union tried to maintain as neutral a position as possible toward all groups while at the same time acquiring storage facilities and naval landing rights in the port city of Aden.[64]

While the Soviet Union became active in southern Arabian affairs following the June war because of the exigencies of the political situation (North Yemen) and perceived opportunities (South Yemen), the main focus of Soviet activity in the 1967–70 period lay in its relations with the war-weakened regime of Egyptian President Gamal Nasser. Soviet–Egyptian cooperation manifested itself primarily in the diplomatic and military spheres, but the USSR also continued to lend money to Egypt for industrialization. In November 1967 the United States and the Soviet Union, together with Britain, worked out a vague formula, UN Resolution No. 242, which called for Israeli withdrawal "from occupied territories" (without stating how far the withdrawal should go) in return for Israel's right to live in peace within "secure and recognized boundaries" (without stating where these boundaries should be or defining the word "secure"). Resolution No. 242 also created a UN mediator, Gunnar Jarring, who soon began a long, tedious, and ultimately unsuccessful series of meetings with Israel, Egypt, and Jordan, each of whom had accepted the resolution while interpreting it quite differently.[65]

The failure of Jarring's diplomatic efforts, as well as various Soviet-sponsored four-power and two-power conferences to obtain an Israeli withdrawal from the Sinai Peninsula, prompted Nasser to begin a war of attrition with his newly rebuilt army against Israel in April 1969. Hoping to use Egypt's superiority in artillery to cause unacceptable casualties to Israeli forces dug in along the canal, Egyptian guns began a steady pounding of the Israeli positions. The Israelis, with only a twelfth the population of Egypt, and inferior in artillery, decided to use the one weapon in which they had almost absolute superiority, their air force, to silence the Egyptian artillery. Having accomplished this with minimum losses in aircraft, the Israelis then embarked on a series of deep penetration raids into the heartland of Egypt in an effort to persuade Nasser to give up his war of attrition, and by January 1970 Israeli planes were flying at will through eastern Egypt.

This situation was humiliating to Nasser. Having lost the 1967 war and the Sinai Peninsula, he now seemed unable even to defend Egypt's heartland. Consequently, in an effort to remedy this politically intolerable situation, Nasser flew to Moscow and asked the Soviet leaders to establish an air-defense system manned by Soviet pilots and anti-aircraft forces, and protected by Soviet troops. The cost to Egypt, however, was a high one. To obtain Soviet aid, Nasser had to grant to the Soviet Union exclusive control over a number of Egyptian airfields as well as operational control over a large portion of the Egyptian army.[66]

In deciding to help the Egyptians, the Soviet leadership was faced with a difficult decision. On the one hand, failure to help Nasser might mean the Egyptian President's ouster by elements in the Egyptian leadership less friendly toward the USSR at a time when the United States was trying to rebuild its position in the Arab world. In addition, the airbases that the USSR would control could be used by Russian pilots not only to intercept the Israelis but also to fly covering missions for the Soviet Mediterranean fleet. This would be of great tactical benefit to Soviet commanders because the USSR possessed no genuine aircraft carriers of its own at the time. A final argument in favor of the Soviet commitment to Egypt was that it would be a demonstration to the Arab world that the USSR was an ally to be counted on.

Despite these clear advantages, there was one major disadvantage – the negative effect on the United States of the Soviet intervention. Up to this time, other than supplying limited numbers of military advisers, both superpowers had refrained from a major commitment of combat troops to any nation in the Middle East. Now, with between 10,000 and 15,000 Soviet troops to be stationed in Egypt and with Soviet pilots flying combat missions, there was the serious possibility of a superpower confrontation. Given American troop commitments in Vietnam and the harsh clamor in the United States not to commit any more Americans to combat duty, the Soviet leaders were probably safe in assuming that no American ground troops or pilots would be stationed in Israel. (In any case, the Israelis stated that they wanted only American material, not American troops). Nonetheless, there was still the possibility that in the event of a confrontation between the Soviet Union and Israel, the United States would be drawn in on the side of the Israelis.

Finally, perhaps reasoning that their investment in Egypt, still the most powerful and most influential of all the Arab states, was too great to give up, or perhaps believing that a Vietnam-burdened Nixon administration would not act decisively in the Middle East despite its public statements to the contrary, the Soviet leaders decided to take the risk and commit pilots and combat troops to Egypt. Fortunately for the Soviet leaders, Israeli Defense Minister Moshe Dayan stated that the Israeli air force would cease its deep penetration raids of Egypt so as to avoid a confrontation with the Soviet pilots; this, initially at least, took some of the heat out of the situation. By the end of June, however, with Soviet forces engaged in establishing the air-defense system near the Suez Canal, Soviet–Israeli clashes did occur, and on one occasion the Israelis shot down five Soviet-piloted MIGs. In addition, President Nixon publicly warned the Russians that the Middle East could drag the superpowers into a direct war, just as happened in 1914. Perhaps fearing such an eventuality, or perhaps wishing to consolidate their new military position in Egypt, the Soviet Union agreed to an American-sponsored ninety-day cease-fire arrangement after lengthy and "frank" consultations with Nasser in Moscow.[67] The cease-fire was eventually to last for more than three years; but soon after it came into effect (August 8, 1970), and in large part because of it, Jordan was to erupt into civil war, a development to be discussed below.

While the USSR had enhanced its military position in the eastern Mediterranean through its acquisition of bases in Egypt, both Soviet and communist influence in Nasser's regime still remained limited. Although Soviet commentator Georgi Mirsky had optimistically stated shortly after the June war in a *New Times* article, "It is not to be excluded that left socialist tendencies in the Arab world will gain as a result of the recent events,"[68] events were to prove otherwise. Perhaps emboldened by the results of the war, the Egyptian Marxists demanded the liquidation of the Nasser regime's right wing and the transfer of power to "revolutionary cadres."[69] These demands went unheeded. Nasser did purge some rightists, primarily to secure his own political base, although his action was widely interpreted at the time as a concession to the Russians. In an interview in *Jeune Afrique* on October 1, 1967, an Egyptian communist testified to the weakness of his movement in Egypt:

> We have committed major errors, we have been "drooling" so much during the years because Nasser had permitted us to participate in national life and had given us posts in editorial offices and the university, that we have let ourselves become embourgeoises. We have lost all contact with the masses and these, abandoned to themselves, are completely disorganized. The truth is that we are tired and not at all prepared to return to prison.[70]

Despite the aid he was receiving from the USSR, Nasser also tried to maintain some ties with the West. He continued to rely on American oil companies to search for oil in Egypt. He also reportedly advised the new Libyan leader Muammar Kaddafi, who came to power in September 1969 after overthrowing King Idris, to turn to France and not to the USSR for arms.[71]

While Soviet influence had increased quite sharply in Egypt, it remained quite limited in Syria and Iraq, the other two major recipients of Soviet attention in the region. For example, the Soviet leaders were unable to persuade either the Syrians or the Iraqis to accept the Soviet-backed UN Resolution No. 242 or to cooperate with Egypt in seeking a political settlement to the Middle East crisis. Syria and Iraq also rejected the cease-fire agreement of August 1970, much to the chagrin of the

Soviet Union. In Syria, Soviet efforts were hampered by the Syrian communist party, which actively campaigned against Defense Minister Hafiz Assad in his struggle for power with Salah Jedid, the ex-army officer who was head of the Ba'ath party. The Syrian communists not only harmed their own fortunes in Syria (limited as they were) but Soviet–Syrian relations as well, as the Soviet Ambassador, Nuradin Mukhdinov, was drawn into the power struggle pitting the communists and Jedid on one side against the ultimately victorious Assad on the other.[72]

In May 1969, Assad, who was angered both by Soviet meddling in Syrian politics and by the failure of the USSR to provide what he thought were sufficient weapons, dispatched his close friend, Syrian Chief of Staff Lt.-Gen. Mustafa Talas, on an arms procurement trip to China. There, perhaps acting on Assad's instructions, Talas allowed himself to be photographed waving the famous little Red Book of Chairman Mao's sayings. Coming only two months after the bloody Sino-Soviet clashes along the Ussuri River, Talas's action must have been particularly galling to the Russians after all the Soviet economic, military, and diplomatic support for Syria. According to the *Jerusalem Post*, Assad reportedly had said prior to Talas's journey: "Why should we not boycott the Soviet Union and its supporters inside the country? If we do so, we can force them to review their stand. Either they give us what we want and what is necesary or they will lose our friendship."[73]

The Soviet leaders may have taken Assad's warning seriously, or they may have concluded that it was counterproductive to get too closely involved in internal Syrian politics. In any case, by the end of 1969 they had disassociated themselves from the power struggle in Syria, which Assad seemed certain to win. The Soviet leaders may have taken some consolation from the fact that Assad was more willing to cooperate with the other Arab states than Jedid was, although the communist party of Syria, which had opposed him, continued to be persecuted. The persecution was severe enough for the Soviet press to take public notice; on July 18, 1970, the Soviet newspaper *Trud*, in an article signed "Observer," protested against the arrest and murder of a number of Syrian communists.[74]

The Soviet Union's relations with Iraq during the 1967–70 period were a bit warmer than with Syria, although the two states continued to disagree on such Middle Eastern political issues as UN Resolution 242, the Iraqi government's treatment of its Kurdish minority, and its persecution of the Iraqi communists. Iraq had long been isolated both in the Middle East as a whole and in the Arab world, and successive Iraqi governments looked to their tie to the USSR as a means of balancing off Iraq's strained relations with its pro-Western neighbors, Iran, Saudi Arabia, Jordan, Turkey, and Kuwait. From the Soviet point of view, the weak Aref regime in Iraq was not only yet another base for Soviet influence in the region; it was also a potential source of oil. By 1967 Soviet planners had begun to change their earlier optimistic predictions that the USSR would have sufficient oil and natural gas to meet all its internal needs as well as increasing amounts available for export to the Soviet bloc states of Eastern Europe and to hard-currency customers in Western Europe and Japan. While the USSR had large reserves of oil and natural gas, most of these were located in the frozen wastes of eastern and western Siberia and would have required large infrastructure investments before they could be developed. Consequently, in December 1967 the USSR signed an agreement with Iraq to provide credits and equipment for the northern Rumelia oil field, with the USSR to be partially repaid in crude oil. In the same year the Soviet Union had also signed long-term agreements with Afghanistan to import natural gas and with Iran to import both oil and natural gas. Soviet thinking at the time seemed to revolve around the idea that the USSR could import oil and natural gas from the Middle East to serve industries in the southern part of the Soviet Union while selling Soviet oil and natural gas to Eastern and Western Europe. Such a plan would also enable the Soviet leaders to postpone, at least for a while, the huge infrastructure investments needed to develop Siberian oil and natural gas.[75]

The coming to power of the Ba'athist Al-Bakr regime in July 1968 had little effect on Soviet–Iraqi relations at the state level, which continued to be very good, despite the fact that Iraqi communists continued to be persecuted. According to a reliable source, Al-Bakr even negotiated with the communists to obtain their participation in his government; but by demanding too much (that is, the Defense Ministry) the Iraqi communist party wound up with nothing.[76] Nonetheless, the Soviet leadership evidently found its relations with the Al-Bakr regime to be more than satisfactory, since in July 1969 another long-term oil agreement was signed between the two countries for the development of the oil fields of northern Rumelia. In this one the USSR was to be repaid for its credits and equipment exclusively in Iraqi crude oil.[77] A *Pravda* article by Yevgeny Primakov on September 21 had warm praise for the Al-Bakr regime, although it chided the regime for failing to agree with UN Resolution 242 and for failing to reach an agreement with the Kurds.[78]

While the USSR and Iraq were able to agree on oil development, and the Soviet government warmly hailed the agreement reached on March 11, 1970, between the Iraqi government and the Kurds, the two nations remained divided on policy toward the Arab–Israeli conflict. Iraq opposed the cease-fire agreement of August 1970, and a *Pravda* article of August 1, 1970 called the Iraqi opposition to the cease-fire "incomprehensible" and went on to note:

> the stand taken by the leadership of Iraq's Ba'ath party is surprising... *Without warning*, Baghdad began saying that "attempts are being made to dispose of the Palestine question" and so forth ... the negative attitude of Iraq's Ba'ath party leadership toward President Nasser's initiative and toward the position of the UAR government does not contribute to the actual struggle against the aggressor and the forces of Imperialism and Zionism that support aggression.[79] (emphasis added)

The fact that the Soviet leadership used the phrase "without warning" probably indicates that they were not even consulted by the Iraqi regime on this important policy statement. It is interesting to note that even after the Iraqi delegation went to Moscow for talks in early August, there was no change in Baghdad's position. Despite Iraqi opposition to this relatively important initiative backed by the USSR, Moscow not only did not exert any pressure on the Iraqi leadership (such as curtailing or even cutting off military or economic aid), they went ahead and signed a protocol on trade and economic cooperation with the Iraqis on August 13, 1970, which called for an increase in trade and Soviet assistance. Moscow then granted the Iraqis a $34 million loan on August 30.[80] These events indicate not only a limited degree of Soviet influence in Iraq but also a clear desire by the USSR to maintain good relations with the oil-rich and strategically located nation that had become Egypt's chief rival in the Arab world.

As the Soviet leaders stepped up their efforts to oust Western influence from the Middle East following the June war, developments in the Arab states of North Africa appeared to fall nicely into place for them. In Libya, as noted above, the pro-Western regime of King Idris was overthrown in September 1969 by a military junta headed by Muammar Kaddafi, whose first major foreign policy demand was for the United States and Britain to leave their military bases in Libya – a demand both Western nations speedily complied with. In Algeria, Boumedienne's decision to nationalize the French-owned oil industry led to a withdrawal of French technicians, and the Soviet Union immediately sent its own technicians to replace them. It should be mentioned, however, that in the cases of both Libya and Algeria, the steps taken by the nationalist regimes to lessen Western influence in their countries did not mean they had opened the door to Soviet control. Both Boumedienne and Kaddafi pursued indepedent foreign and domestic policies, as their frequent clashes with both the USSR and the United States clearly indicated.

One country where the Soviet Union appeared to make deep inroads was the Sudan. Following a military *coup d'état* in May 1969, Jaafar Nimeri came to power. He proclaimed the Sudan to be a democratic republic and defined the main foreign policy aims of his regime as the support of national liberation movements against imperialism, active support of the Palestinian struggle, and extension of the Sudan's ties to the Arab world and the socialist countries. Domestically, Nimeri proclaimed the formation of a single party of "workers, peasants, soldiers, national bourgeoisie and the progressive intelligentsia." Communists were prominently represented in Nimeri's first cabinet, although the communist party, like all other existing parties, was officially dissolved.[81]

The Soviet leadership wasted little time in consolidating its relations with Nimeri's regime. The Sudanese leader was invited to Moscow in November 1969, and agreements were signed for the expansion of trade and cultural and scientific cooperation.[82] State relations continued to improve in early January 1970, as Soviet navy warships paid a visit to Port Sudan and the USSR began to supply the Sudan with military equipment.[83] As Soviet–Sudanese relations improved, the Soviet leaders apparently decided that in order to solidify ties with the strategically located nation and to avoid possible future complications, the powerful Sudanese communist party should dissolve (as Nimeri had demanded), its members to join Nimeri's one-party regime as individuals, much as the Egyptian communist party had done earlier.[84] However, the Sudanese communist party was split, and the faction led by Secretary General Abdel Mahgoub apparently refused to comply with the Soviet requests. Nonetheless, Mahgoub was willing to support the Nimeri regime, and in an interview with the Soviet journal *Za rubezhom*, which was broadcast over Radio Moscow in Arabic on August 11, 1969, the Sudanese communist leader stated:

> The communists believe that the present government is a progressive one and that the May 25th movement had created the best circum-

> stances for continuing our people's struggle for realizing the tasks of
> the national democratic revolution. Therefore, the Communist Party
> sincerely supports the new government's policy.[85]

Yet, as the situation in the Sudan developed, it became clear that
Nimeri was using the Sudanese communists to weaken his right-wing
enemies, the Mahdiists. Once the Mahdiists were eliminated as a political force, Nimeri arrested and then exiled Mahgoub, who had become
increasingly critical of Nimeri's policies, including the entry of the
Sudan into a projected confederation with Egypt and Libya. While the
anti-Mahgoub faction remained allied to Nimeri and in the government,
it appeared that the Sudanese leader had learned the lesson, taught by
Kassem a decade earlier, of playing off the communists against other
political forces, and that the communist party's future in the Sudan was
limited indeed. Indeed, in July 1971 it was involved in a failed coup
attempt against Nimeri and its leadership slaughtered by the Sudanese
leader.

If the postwar atmosphere in the Arab world was conducive to
weakening Western influence, it also provided fertile ground for the
growth of the Palestinian resistance movement, a multitude of guerrilla
organizations, which launched attacks against Israel (most of them
unsuccessful), capturing the imagination of an Arab public still shocked
by Israel's defeat of the regular Arab armies. As the Palestinian guerrilla organizations increased in power, they began actively competing
with each other for recruits, funds, and prestige, while at the same time
increasingly becoming a challenge to the established governments in the
Arab world, particularly those in Jordan and Lebanon, where large
numbers of Palestinian refugees were located.[86] While the Soviet leadership initially played down the significance of the guerrilla organizations
because it preferred to work through the established Arab states,
Moscow could not long overlook either the growing power of the
Palestinian guerrilla movement as a factor in Middle Eastern politics or
the growing involvement of the Chinese communists in the movement.
By providing military equipment and ideological training to a number of
the guerrilla organizations, the Chinese were seeking to increase their
influence in the Middle East via the Palestinians.[87] By mid-1969 the
Soviet leadership evidently decided that it was time to get involved with
the guerrillas. It did so in a cautious manner, however, and it was not
until after the death of Nasser and the severe beating taken by the
Palestinians in the Jordanian civil war that the Soviet Union began to
court the guerrillas in a serious manner.

At the 7th World Trade Union Congress in Budapest in October 1969, Politburo member Aleksandr Shelepin came out with the first public sign of Soviet support for the guerrillas: "We consider the struggle of the Palestine patriots for the liquidation of the consequences of Israeli aggression a just anti-imperialist struggle of national liberation and we support it."[88]

By stressing the term "liquidation of the consequences of Israeli aggression," however, Shelepin was manipulating the meaning of the guerrilla organizations' fight to coincide with the Soviet-backed UN Resolution 242. Indeed, in 1969 the guerrilla organizations were virtually unanimous in proclaiming their intention to liquidate Israel itself, rather than to aid the Arab states in recovering the land lost to Israel in 1967. By the end of 1969, however, after observing how clashes with the guerrillas had shaken both the Lebanese and Jordanian governments, the Soviet leaders may have begun to envision the Palestinian movement as a useful tool for weakening or even overthrowing the two pro-Western regimes and replacing them with governments more friendly to the USSR.[89]

In February 1970, Yasser Arafat, who had replaced Ahmed Shukeiry as head of the Palestine Liberation Organization (PLO), the loose federation of the guerrilla organizations, after the 1967 war, was invited to Moscow (he had gone to Moscow in July 1968 as part of an Egyptian delegation), but the visit was kept in low key, as the invitation came from the Soviet Afro-Asian Solidarity Organization rather than from a higher-ranking organ of the Soviet government. The very next month, however, Arafat was given a high-level reception in Peking, and the Palestinian guerrilla leader warmly praised the Chinese for their assistance. As Sino-Soviet competition for the allegiance of the guerrillas grew, the Soviet leadership decided that its position would be improved if the communist parties of the Middle East formed their own guerrilla organization, which would be able to participate in, and hopefully influence, the PLO from the inside. Consequently, the communist parties of Lebanon, Syria, Jordan, and Iraq formed the Ansar guerrilla organization in March 1970, but as a Jordanian communist party member was to complain two years later, Ansar had very little influence in the PLO.[90]

One of the main problems plaguing the PLO was the very sharp competition among its constituent organizations for power. Some guerrilla groups were avowedly Marxist, such as the Popular Front for the Liberation of Palestine (PFLP) and the Popular Democratic Front for the Liberation of Palestine (PDFLP). Others were the instruments of Arab governments, such as Saiqa (Syria) and the Arab Liberation Front (Iraq). Still others, such as Fatah, the largest, proclaimed themselves ideologically neutral and were willing to accept aid from all sides. By June 1970 the intra-Palestinian struggle for power had reached a peak, with the PFLP openly challenging Fatah's leadership and seeking to bring down the regime of King Hussein in Jordan as well. By this time the guerrillas had established a virtual state-within-a-state in Jordan, and the compromise agreement worked out in June between Hussein and the guerrillas testified to their growing power. The acceptance by King Hussein of the American-sponsored cease-fire agreement (Egypt and Israel also agreed) in August set the stage for the final showdown. Fearing that the Palestinian cause would be overlooked in a direct settlement between Israel and Jordan and Egypt, and feeling that the time had come to topple the Hussein regime, the PFLP embarked on a skyjacking spree that resulted in the flying of three skyjacked passenger planes to a guerrilla-controlled airstrip in northern Jordan where they were destroyed, while the troops of King Hussein, which had surrounded the guerrilla airstrip, looked helplessly on.[91]

Hussein seized this opportunity to end the guerrilla threat to his regime and began military attacks on the guerrillas. While his army was attacking the guerrilla positions, the Syrian government, then headed by Salah Jedid, dispatched an armored brigade to help the guerrillas. At this juncture the United States moved the Sixth Fleet toward the battle area and, acting jointly with Israel, threatened to intervene if the Syrian forces were not withdrawn, as both Kissinger and Nixon clearly indicated that they would not permit the pro-Western regime of Hussein to be ousted by the invasion of a client state of the Soviet Union.[92] The Soviet leadership, during this period, after initially appearing to support the Syrian move, became conspicuous by its inaction.[93] For this reason, or because of the strong American–Israeli stand, or, most probably, because he saw a chance to embarrass Jedid, General Assad, who controlled the Syrian air force, refused to dispatch Syrian jets to fly covering missions for the Syrian tanks. The result of Assad's decision was that the Jordanian air force and tank units badly mauled the invading Syrian force, which was compelled to retreat in disarray to Syria. The emboldened Hussein then turned to finish off the guerrillas and had almost completed the job when an Arab League cease-fire arranged by Nasser came into effect.[94] It was to be the Egyptian President's last act as an Arab leader, however because on the very next day he died of a heart attack, an event that was to lead to a transformation of the Soviet position in the Middle East. Before this transformation is discussed, however, it is necessary to evaluate the Soviet Middle Eastern position at the time of Nasser's death.

The Soviet position in the Middle East at the time of Nasser's death: a balance sheet

In assessing the Soviet position in the Middle East at the time of Nasser's death, it is clear that the primary Soviet gain since Khrushchev's ouster had been an improvement in the Soviet military position in the region, although this was not an unmixed blessing for the Soviet leaders. The USSR had acquired air and naval bases in Egypt, and port rights in Syria, the Sudan, North Yemen, South Yemen, and Iraq. These bases in Egypt gave air cover to the Soviet fleet sailing in the eastern Mediterranean and thus were substitutes for aircraft carriers, which the Soviet navy did not then possess. Yet the large military presence of the Soviet Union in the Middle East also contained a major risk for the Soviet leadership. There were a number of Arabs who wanted to involve the USSR in a war against Israel, regardless of the international consequences of such an action. One of the reasons that the Soviet Union accepted the American cease-fire initiative in the summer of 1970 appears to have been a desire to cool down its rapidly escalating conflict with Israel, which might soon have involved the United States as well. Thus, while the Soviet military position in the Middle East had improved by the time of Nasser's death, so too had the chances of a military confrontation between the United States and the Soviet Union – a development the Soviet leaders probably wished to avoid at almost any cost, given the increasingly hostile relations between the USSR and China.

Other than improving their military position in the Middle East, there were few concrete gains the Russians could point to from their expensive involvement in the region at the time of Nasser's death. The Soviets seemed to have assumed the role of military supplier and financier of the economically weak radical Arab regimes of the area, and they appeared to be attempting to buy influence in the Northern Tier nations as well. Nonetheless, as Aaron Klieman pointed out in his 1970 study of the Soviet involvement in the Middle East, "In return for enabling the Soviets to claim influence, the Arabs expect Moscow to supply loans, weapons, technical advice, diplomatic support, and favorable terms of trade."[95] The obvious question is, who was exploiting whom in this relationship? In addition, Soviet "influence" was far from reaching a position of control over the policies of any of the regimes in the region. The continued opposition of Syria and Iraq to such Soviet-supported peace initiatives as UN Resolution No. 242 and the 1970 cease-fire agreement presented serious difficulties to Soviet policy makers, who sought to create a unified Arab stand on a Middle Eastern settlement that would be favorable to both the USSR and its Arab allies.

An even more serious problem for the Soviet Union at the time of Nasser's death was the re-emergence of the United States as an active factor in Middle Eastern politics. While the US position in the Arab world reached a low point following the Six-Day War, it appeared to have made a substantial recovery by September 1970. The Rogers Plan, formally announced on December 9, 1969, called for an almost total Israeli withdrawal from territories occupied in the 1967 war, and seemed to be a demonstration of the Nixon administration's "evenhandedness" in the Arab–Israeli conflict.[96] The cease-fire between Israel, Egypt, and Jordan that began in August 1970 was an American initiative, and although it was violated by Egypt (Israel received compensation for this by increased delivery of American weapons), it nonetheless seemed to set the climate for substantive peace negotiations. The strong American support for King Hussein's regime when Syrian tanks invaded Jordan in September 1970, during Hussein's crackdown on the guerrillas, helped restore a great deal of American influence in Jordan and in the region as a whole. The Soviet Union's disinclination to get involved in support of one of its erstwhile clients, Syria, against a client of the United States, Jordan, was also not lost on the Arab world.

Perhaps even more important, however, was the impression, spread in the Arab world by American declarations of an evenhanded policy in the Middle East, that the United States might be willing to assist the Arab states in regaining at least part, if not all, of the land lost to Israel in 1967 – something the Soviet Union had been unable to do by diplomacy and was still unwilling to do by force.

Thus, the specter of rising American influence in the Arab world and the disunity among the Soviet Union's Arab clients were the major problems confronting the Soviet leadership when Gamal Nasser, the man who had been the linchpin of Soviet strategy in the Middle East, departed from the scene.[97]

Brezhnev's Middle East policy, 1970–1979: an overview*

The death of Nasser led to the emergence of a new leader in Egypt, Anwar Sadat, a man who was to take a very different position toward the Soviet Union than his predecessor. While Nasser had mortgaged a good deal of Egypt's sovereignty to the Soviet Union in the form of bases in return for rebuilding his army after 1967, Anwar Sadat, who came to power in October 1970 after Nasser's death, was to adopt a different policy. When diplomatic efforts to bring about a Middle East peace plan stagnated, Sadat became increasingly disenchanted with the Soviets, whom he saw as unable to get the Israelis to withdraw by diplomatic means, unwilling to use military force for this purpose, and hesitant to supply the Arab states with the weaponry they needed to fight effectively.

The Soviet reluctance, which became increasingly evident during the 1971–72 period, may have resulted from three factors. In the first place, the strong US reaction to what was at least a tacitly Soviet-supported Syrian invasion of Jordan in September 1970 seems to have indicated to the Soviets that the United States was more willing to take action in the Middle East than it had been in January 1970, when the Soviet Union sent its pilots and missile crews to Egypt. Second, the long-feared Sino-US entente against the Soviet Union seemed suddenly on the horizon following Kissinger's surprise trip to Peking in July 1971 and the subsequent announcement of Nixon's visit to the Chinese capital. Finally, the long-delayed strategic arms talks, the centerpiece of Soviet–US detente, were nearing conclusion. In sum, the Soviet leaders clearly did not want – at that time – to jeopardize the benefits of detente to aid a rather fickle Arab ally such as Sadat, who had not only openly flirted with the Americans (US Secretary of State Rogers was invited to Cairo in May 1971), but who had also opposed Soviet policy in the Sudan by strongly backing Nimeri's suppression of the communist-supported coup attempt as well, particularly at a time when the United States, after the events in Jordan, was significantly strengthening its relationship with Israel.[98]

For his part, Sadat saw the emerging Soviet–US detente as taking place at Arab expense, and soon after the Soviet–US summit of May 1972 in Moscow, the Egyptian leader expelled the Soviet military troops

---

* For a detailed treatment of Soviet policy toward the Middle East during this period, see Robert O. Freedman, *Soviet Policy Toward the Middle East Since 1970*, 3rd edn (New York: Praeger, 1982).

from his country while also ending Soviet control over Egyptian air, naval, and army bases. While the Egyptian action was a serious blow to the Soviet Union's strategic position in the eastern Mediterranean, the subsequent Soviet pullout, not only of pilots and missile crews, but also of advisors, lessened the chances of any direct Soviet involvement in a future Egyptian–Israeli war, and this factor must have softened the impact of the exodus, which was clearly a major blow to the Soviet Union's Middle East position.[99]

Sadat's limited war against Israel

While Sadat may have hoped that his ouster of the Soviets would lead to action from the United States in the form of pressure on Israel to withdraw from the Sinai, such pressure was not to be forthcoming – at least, not for more than a year and a half. Therefore, having sought to mobilize both US and Soviet support for his policies, and having failed in both quests, Sadat moved to rally the Arabs, and particularly oil-rich Saudi Arabia, to his cause. By the spring of 1973 he had also secured a resumption in the flow of Soviet weapons, enough to enable him to launch a limited war against Israel, and by September he had achieved a general coordination of military planning with Syria. While the Soviet Union almost certainly knew about Sadat's plans for war, they did little to prevent it, and once both Egypt and Syria had demonstrated their military ability in the first days of the war, the Soviet leadership reinforced the Arab war effort with a major airlift and sealift of weaponry, as well as diplomatic support in the United Nations.[100] In taking such action, the Soviet Union was stepping back from its policy of supporting detente, which had reached its highest point at the time of the Moscow summit of 1972, and which seemed to be reconfirmed by the Washington summit of June 1973. The change in Soviet behavior may be explained by several factors. First, the Sino–US entente, which the Soviet Union had initially feared, had not come to fruition. Second, the Nixon administration, badly beset by Watergate, was in a weakened position *vis-à-vis* the Soviet Union. Indeed, by this time, one of the few positive achievements the Nixon administration could show was detente with the Soviet Union – a policy to which the administration was now wedded. These factors combined to give the Soviet Union more leverage *vis-à-vis* the United States and the Soviet leadership was not slow in taking advantage of the situation.[101]

The Arab coalition that Sadat had formed on the eve of the 1973 war fitted neatly into the overall Soviet plan of forming an "anti-imperial-ist" alliance of Arab states. The fact that this Arab coalition included not only such "progressive" Arab states as Syria and Iraq but also such conservative ones as Kuwait and Saudi Arabia may have been perceived as an added bonus, because the oil embargo imposed by these countries against the United States and its NATO allies seemed to be a major step on the road to ousting Western influence from the Arab world – the Soviet goal since the mid-1960s – as well as weakening the overall Western position in the world balance of power. For this reason, Moscow gave extensive military aid to Syria and Egypt during the war, and pressured the United States to halt a major Israeli advance as the war came to an end.[102]

Unfortunately for the Soviets, however, the aftermath was to see not only the collapse of the "anti-imperialist" Arab coalition they had so warmly endorsed but also a serious deterioration of the Soviet position in the Arab world, despite all the military and diplomatic support the Soviet Union had given the Arab cause during the war. While the Arab–Israeli conflict remained the most salient issue in Middle East politics, it was the United States that was to take an active role in working toward a diplomatic settlement, earning for itself in the process a greatly enhanced status in the Arab world. Under the mediating efforts of US Secretary of State Henry Kissinger, Egypt and Israel reached a disen-gagement agreement in January 1974 that led to the withdrawal of Israeli forces from both banks of the Suez Canal. Then, at the end of May 1974, Kissinger secured a disengagement agreement between Syria and Israel that led to a withdrawal of Israeli forces not only from territories captured in 1973 but also from the city of Kuneitra, captured in 1967. Yet another disengagement agreement was reached in late August 1975 between Israel and Egypt whereby the Israelis withdrew to the Mitla and Giddi passes in the Sinai Desert.[103]

While the United States was taking these initiatives, the Soviet Union was, essentially, sitting on the sidelines, although in the aftermath of the 1973 war a Geneva peace conference was convened under the co-chair-manship of the United States and the Soviet Union. It was quickly adjourned, however, and Kissinger, not the Geneva Conference, became the main instrument in working toward a settlement of the Arab–Israeli conflict. For its part, the Soviet leadership was clearly unhappy with the disengagement agreements – particularly the Sinai II agreement of 1975, which Moscow denounced – but they proved incap-able of influencing the course of events.

In an effort to directly affect the diplomacy surrounding the Arab–Israeli conflict in the aftermath of the 1973 war, the Soviet leadership tried a variety of tactics. Thus, at the Geneva Conference, Gromyko made a point of underlining Soviet support of Israel's right to exist and met privately with Foreign Minister Abba Eban to suggest Moscow's willingness to reestablish diplomatic relations with Israel once an Arab–Israeli settlement was reached.[104] (At the same time Moscow allowed a then record number of Soviet Jews to leave for Israel). Several months later, however, in the face of the first Egyptian–Israeli disengagement agreement and Kissinger's efforts to work out a similar agreement between Syria and Israel, Moscow took the opposite course by sending arms to Syria and supporting the war of attrition Syria was waging on the Golan Heights.[105] In taking this action, the Soviet leadership may have hoped to torpedo the negotiations or, at least, prevent the lifting of the oil embargo then being considered by the oil-rich Arab states. At the very minimum, the Soviets may have felt that their aid would strengthen Syria's hand in the bargaining process and thereby preserve the Soviet position and prevent Syria's slipping into the pro-US camp.

Another tactic used by the Soviet leadership during the Kissinger disengagement process was to urge the rapid reconvening of the Geneva Conference, although the Soviet calls did not meet with success. Even during the period from March to May 1975, when the Kissinger shuttle had been temporarily derailed and US Middle East policy was going through one of its periodic "reappraisals," the Soviet Union's efforts to seize the diplomatic initiative proved ineffectual. Despite dispatching Kosygin to Libya and Tunisia, and sending a number of signals to Israel of continued Soviet support of the Jewish state's existence (these included sending several Soviet officials to Israel), the Soviet leadership proved unable even to coordinate Arab positions on a settlement let alone work out the details of an Arab–Israeli agreement.[106] A fourth tactic used by the Soviet Union, as developments began to move in a way unfavorable to Soviet interests in the aftermath of the 1973 war, was a fundamental policy change toward the Palestinians. With Egypt moving toward the US camp, with the Saudi Arabian–Egyptian axis, tacitly supported by the Shah's Iran, now the dominant one in Arab politics, and with Syria still wavering despite large amounts of Soviet military aid, the Soviet leaders began openly to back the concept of an independent Palestinian state in the West Bank and Gaza regions.[107]

Following the Sinai II agreement and a UN meeting between Gromyko and Israel's new Foreign Minister Yigal Allon on September

24, 1975, Soviet plans for an overall settlement of the Arab–Israeli conflict, one facet of which would include an independent Palestinian state, became increasingly explicit, and the Soviet proposals were published, amid great fanfare, in April and October 1976. In their statements, the Soviets also came out for the immediate reconvening of the Geneva Conference with the full participation of the PLO, but this ploy proved ineffectual since neither Israel nor the United States would accept the PLO as a negotiating partner so long as it continued to call openly for Israel's destruction. In addition to US and Israeli opposition, the Soviet peace proposals, which included offers of Soviet guarantees, were not greeted with much enthusiasm by the Arabs, and the growing civil war in Lebanon further reduced the efficacy of the Soviet plan.[108]

Indeed, the civil war in Lebanon, which pitted the Christians against the Muslims and Palestinians over who would control Lebanon, became more complicated when Syria intervened militarily in June to aid the Christians against their enemies. The Syrian intervention posed a very serious problem for Soviet diplomacy as battles took place between Syrian and PLO forces in July 1976. Since the PLO, despite its disparate elements, was now a close ally of the Soviet Union in the Middle East, while Syria remained the key swing country the Soviet Union wanted to prevent from joining the Egyptian–Saudi Arabian axis, it was inevitable that the Soviet Union's relations with one or both would suffer no matter which position the Soviets took toward the Lebanese fighting. The end result was that the PLO complained about insufficient Soviet aid, while Syria was clearly unhappy with both the negative Soviet comments about Syrian policy in Lebanon and a slowdown in Soviet arms deliveries. Nonetheless, the Soviets were saved further diplomatic embarrassment when a settlement of the civil war was reached in October 1976 that preserved the PLO as an independent force in Lebanon, although the fact that the settlement had been worked out under Saudi Arabian mediation and that it also included a reconciliation between Syria and Egypt could not have been happily received in the Kremlin, which continued to fear the adhesion of Syria to the Egyptian–Saudi axis.[109]

President Carter's efforts

In the aftermath of the Lebanese civil war came the US presidential elections. With a new president in office, albeit one relatively inexperienced in foreign affairs, all sides expected new US initiatives to bring about a Middle East settlement. The Soviets, whose relations with the United States had hit a new low as a result of their involvement in Angola, but who hoped for a new SALT agreement and new trade agreements nevertheless, sent a number of signals to the incoming Carter administration that it would be willing to cooperate with the United States in bringing about a Middle East settlement.[110] The Soviet reasoning appeared to be that given the sharp diminution of Soviet influence in the Arab world due to US diplomatic successes and the establishment of a large pro-US camp in the Arab world (the only strongly pro-Soviet elements at this time were Libya and South Yemen – countries with relatively little influence in the area), Moscow would do well to have an overall settlement to consolidate the Soviet position in the region, even if the Soviets were not yet at the point where they could resume their offensive efforts to weaken and ultimately eliminate Western influence.

Fortunately for Moscow, Carter initially decided to jettison Kissinger's step-by-step approach and embarked on an effort to achieve a comprehensive Middle East peace settlement. In doing so he decided that Moscow could be a suitable partner in this endeavor. The end result of this process was the joint Soviet–American statement on the Middle East of October 1, 1977 which called, among other things, for the reconvening of the Geneva Conference by December 1977, thereby guaranteeing the USSR a principal role in the Middle East peacemaking process.

Yet in bringing Moscow back into the center of Middle East peace making – a major gain for Moscow – Carter made three serious misjudgments. Despite the clash between Moscow and both Syria and the PLO during the Lebanese civil war, Carter assumed Moscow could deliver both to the peace table. Secondly, Carter seemed to believe that unless Moscow was brought into the peace process, it would successfully sabotage it.[111] Finally, Carter erred seriously in failing to recognize that the Soviet conception of a Middle East peace settlement was very different from that of the United States. As it has evolved since 1973, the Soviet peace plan has been composed of three major components: (1) Israeli withdrawal from all territory captured in the 1967 war; (2) establishment of a Palestinian state on the West Bank and Gaza; and (3) acknowledgment of the right to exist of all states in the region, including Israel.

In assessing the Soviet peace plan, it is clear why Moscow found it to its advantage. In the first place such a plan would preserve the state of Israel, whose existence has become an important part of Soviet strategy.

As discussed earlier, the Soviet Union has sought to consolidate "anti-imperialist" Arab unity around Arab enmity toward Israel. The mere fact of an Israeli withdrawal to the pre-war 1967 lines would not remove the potential threat of a future Israeli attack on the Arabs (or vice versa) or the memories of the generations-long Arab–Israeli conflict. Indeed, by supporting the concept of a limited peace (and opposing the concept of a more extensive peace, in which Israel would have trade, cultural, and diplomatic relations with its neighbors)[112] the Soviet Union hoped to keep at least a certain amount of latent hostility alive in the Arab–Israeli relationship, thereby forcing the Arabs to retain at least a modicum of unity to confront the putative Israeli threat. The Soviet leaders evidently hoped they could then exploit that unity to enhance their own position in the Middle East and weaken the position of the United States. In any case, by ensuring that tension would remain in the Arab–Israeli relationship, Moscow's importance as an arms supplier to the Arabs would be reinforced; it should not be forgotten that the provision of arms has been the Soviet Union's most important means of influence in the Arab world for many years, as well as an important source of hard currency for the USSR.

A second benefit of such a plan for the Soviet Union would have been the termination of the American role as mediator in the Arab–Israeli peace process. This role has been a key to American influence in the Arab world since the 1973 war, for it demonstrated to the Arabs that it was the United States, and not the Soviet Union, that was able to secure Israeli territorial withdrawals. Once a final, as opposed to another partial, agreement was reached, the necessity for American mediation would be ended; and the Soviet leaders may have reasoned that this would lead to a drop in US prestige and influence in the Arab world, as well as an end to the quarrels between the Arab states over the making of peace with Israel, quarrels that have impeded the Soviet drive to help create the "anti-imperialist" Arab unity.

Yet another benefit of such a plan would be that, by preserving Israel, the United States would not be alienated. Given the strong emotional and political ties between the United States and Israel, which have been reiterated by successive American presidents, the Soviet Union, if it sought to destroy Israel, would clearly jeopardize the chances for a Senate ratification of another strategic arms agreement. For this reason, the Soviet leadership in speeches to Arab leaders as well as in its peace plans has endorsed Israel's right to exist as an independent state. Concomitantly, the establishment of a limited Arab–Israeli peace would also

lessen the possibility of a superpower conflict erupting from an Arab–
Israeli war.

The establishment of an independent Palestinian state, if it were
accepted, might well benefit the Soviet Union. The Soviet leadership
obviously hoped in 1977 that such a state, whose creation Moscow
began to advocate in late 1973, would be an ally of Soviet policy in the
Arab world and would help combat US influence in the region. Indeed,
the Soviet Union would clearly gain from having another ally in the very
center of the Middle East. In addition, the Soviet leadership may have
believed that a Palestinian state on the West Bank and Gaza would be
dependent on Soviet support because it would be sandwiched between a
hostile Israel, a suspicious Jordan, and probably hostile Syria, if Assad
were still in power when the state was formed.

While Moscow may have hoped for a number of benefits for its
Middle East position to emerge from the acceptance of its peace plan,
and may have believed that the momentum for such an acceptance
would be created by the convening of the Geneva Conference in
December 1977, such was not to be the case. Indeed, the joint Soviet–
American peace statement became moot, as the surprise visit of Anwar
Sadat to Jerusalem in November 1977 and the subsequent Camp David
agreements changed the face of Middle East diplomacy. Moscow was
again thrown on the defensive by Camp David, and quickly expressed
its concern that other Arab states would follow Egypt's example and
sign what the Soviet media decried as a "separate deal" with Israel.
Indeed, since September 1978 Moscow has been preoccupied with the
dangers of an expanded Camp David process and one of the central
thrusts of Soviet Middle Eastern policy until Gorbachev was to try to
isolate Egypt and prevent any expansion of Camp David.

Fortunately for Moscow in the period immediately after Camp David,
there was almost universal Arab antipathy toward the Camp David
agreements and the subsequent Egyptian–Israeli peace treaty of March
1979. Indeed, Moscow had hopes that the large Arab coalition which
had come together at Baghdad in November 1978 to denounce Camp
David – a coalition highlighted by the *rapprochement* between Syria and
Iraq – might form the "anti-imperialist" Arab bloc the USSR had
sought for so long.

Iraq's lead in forming the anti-Camp David bloc of Arab states was
particularly welcome to Moscow, because Soviet–Iraqi relations, once
very close (the 1972 Soviet–Iraqi Treaty of Friendship and Cooperation
and Soviet aid to Iraq in suppressing its Kurds in 1974 were high points

of the relationship), had begun to decline. The decline, interestingly enough, can be dated from the Iraq–Iran treaty of 1975 which, albeit only temporarily, ended the border war between the two countries. According to what became known as the Algiers Agreement, which was warmly welcomed by Moscow, the two nations delineated their long-disputed border and agreed to cease assistance to dissident groups within each other's territory. This meant a termination of Iranian aid to the Kurds, who were then in the midst of a life-and-death struggle with the advancing Iraqi army. With the end of the Iran–Iraq conflict (although it was to resume in September 1980), and an inevitable end in view for the Kurdish struggle for autonomy, the Soviet position in the Persian Gulf seemed to be greatly enhanced. The long-feared possibility that the USSR would be drawn into a war between Iran and Iraq was now eliminated, and the USSR could move to improve its relations with Iran as well as Iraq while also assuring itself of a continued flow of oil from Iraq and an uninterrupted flow of natural gas from Iran.

The Iraq–Iran agreement was to have another effect on Soviet policy, however. By removing the two main threats to the Iraqi government, the Ba'athists were now far less dependent for military aid on the USSR. In addition, since the quadrupling of oil prices in December 1973, the Iraqi government was no longer economically dependent on the USSR and, as it embarked on a major economic development plan, it began to increasingly place its orders for factories and other goods with Western European, Japanese, and even American firms rather than with the USSR and East Europe. Although Soviet–Iraqi trade was to sharply increase during this period, Iraqi exports were already out-stripping Soviet exports,[113] as the Iraqis began to repay previous Soviet loans. To be sure, the USSR remained actively involved in the Iraqi economy, training Iraqi workers, building factories, canals, and power stations and Iraq did sign a cooperation agreement with the Council for Mutual Economic Assistance in July 1975.[114] Nonetheless, the thrust of Iraqi economic relations was clearly in a Western direction, a development which was to become even more evident in the post-1975 period.

Following the signing of its treaty with Iran, Iraq embarked on a policy of improving relations with its other neighbors in the Gulf, particularly Saudi Arabia and the United Arab Emirates. Increased conflict with Syria and the PLO, however, clouded Iraq's efforts to assume a position of leadership of the Arab world and contributed to its continuing isolation there. Of even more serious concern to Moscow during this period was Iraq's continued opposition to Soviet peace initiatives in the

Middle East, and its persecution of the Iraqi communist party which had come out in open opposition to a number of Iraqi government policies.

The Iraqi government seems to have made a definite effort to improve relations with its once hostile Persian Gulf neighbors in the aftermath of the Iran–Iraq treaty. Thus, in July 1975, an agreement between Iraq and Saudi Arabia was signed, dividing the neutral zone which lay along their common border.[115] In addition, several Iraqi officials made tours of Gulf states in an effort to develop cooperation and enhance the Iraqi role in the Gulf. Iraq also began to extend economic assistance to Jordan during this period and a road between the Jordanian port of Aqaba and Iraq was planned. From the Soviet viewpoint, the new Iraqi initiatives held both advantages and disadvantages. Should Iraq draw closer to Saudi Arabia, it could conceivably influence the Saudi government to adopt a less pro-Western policy. On the other hand, however, by drawing closer to Saudi Arabia, Iraq might itself become influenced by the Saudis and draw further away from the USSR.

The primary Iraqi foreign problem, once its conflict with Iran was settled, was Syria, and this was one conflict in which the Iraqis could not call upon Moscow for assistance. Indeed, in his speech to the 25th Party Congress, in February 1976, Brezhnev publicly ranked Syria over Iraq in its list of Arab allies, something the Iraqi leadership may not have appreciated.[116] In any case, there were a number of issues dividing the rival Ba'athist regimes including Syria's cutting off of Euphrates River water to Iraq, Iraq's cutting off of oil supplies to Syria, and attempts by each government to assassinate the leaders of the other. The USSR, still seeking to forge an "anti-imperialist" alignment in the Arab world, was clearly concerned about the Syrian–Iraqi conflict and sought to overcome it through public admonishments and a mediation effort by Soviet Prime Minister Aleksey Kosygin who journeyed to both Baghdad and Damascus at the height of the Lebanese civil war (the two Ba'athist regimes backed opposing sides in the conflict), but to no avail.[117] Even when Syria and Iraq joined a number of other Arab states, including Libya, Algeria, and South Yemen, as well as the PLO, in forming an organization to protest Sadat's visit to Jerusalem in November 1977 (the Front of Steadfastness and Confrontation), this unity did not last as Iraq pulled out of the meeting, claiming that Syria wanted a deal with Israel.[118] Indeed, not only was Iraq in conflict with Syria over this point, it also became involved in an assassination campaign in the summer of 1978 against PLO leaders whom it claimed were seeking an agreement with Israel.[119]

By this time, Iraqi opposition even to Soviet-endorsed peace plans, such as the October 1977 joint statement with the United States, was becoming a problem for the USSR which was trying to rebuild its Middle East position by co-sponsoring the renewal of the Geneva Conference with the United States. Even more aggravating to the USSR during this period, however, was the continued westward turn of the Iraqi economy. Indeed, by 1977, as Soviet–Iraqi trade began to drop, Iraqi–American trade had sharply increased,[120] and the Soviet leadership, which had long emphasized the connection between economics and politics, could have drawn small comfort from the frequent Iraqi protestations that its economic ties in no way influenced its political relationships.[121]

Several additional problems clouded Soviet–Iraqi relations in 1978. Soviet aid to the Mengistu regime in Ethiopia in its war against the independence-seeking Eritreans, one faction of whom were backed by Iraq, clearly antagonized Baghdad just as Soviet aid to Ethiopia against Somalia caused major problems in Soviet–American relations.[122] On the other hand, however, in the spring of 1978 the Iraqi government announced the execution of a number of Iraqi communists, which could only anger Moscow.

Conflict between the Iraqi communist party (ICP) and the Iraqi Ba'athists had long been brewing. By 1976, the ICP had become increasingly unhappy with its virtually powerless position in the Iraqi government and began to openly advocate an increased role for itself in Iraq's National Front. In addition, the ICP began to advocate genuine autonomy for the Kurds (the Iraqi government had imposed an autonomy plan that left the central government in control of all key aspects of Kurdish life) and openly opposed the Ba'athist policy of resettling Kurds outside of Kurdistan. Clearly unhappy with the westward drift of the Iraqi economy, the ICP also condemned the growing power of "private capital" and Iraq's "continuing dependence on the capitalist world market."[123]

In addition to making these open criticisms of Ba'athist policy, the communists reportedly sought to form secret cells in the Iraqi armed forces and carried on anti-government propaganda among Iraq's Kurds and Shiites – the groups most disaffected with the Sunni Ba'athist rule in Iraq.[124] Indeed, the Ba'athists may well have suspected communist involvement in the February 1977 Shiite religious protest demonstrations. Given the nature of the Iraqi regime, which has not hesitated to liquidate any outspoken opponents of the regime whether or not they resided in Iraq, it appeared only a matter of time until the crackdowns occurred.[125] While persecution of the ICP became increasingly open in 1977, the Iraqi government decided to execute a number of communists in the spring of 1978. Possibly reacting to the army-based, pro-Soviet coup in nearby Afghanistan, the Ba'athist regime evidently decided that the crackdown took precedence over its relations with the USSR. Indeed, as Naim Haddad, one of the leaders of Iraq's ruling Revolutionary Command Council bluntly stated: "All communist parties all over the world are always trying to get power. We chop off any weed that pops up."[126]

The executions cast a pall over Soviet–Iraqi relations, despite the protestations of Iraqi leaders that they wanted good relations with the USSR. Significantly, however, Haddad stated: "the Soviet Union is a friend with whom we can cooperate as long as there is no interference in our internal affairs."[127] Nonetheless, the USSR must have been concerned about trends in Iraqi foreign and domestic policy, even as the Camp David agreements gave the USSR another opportunity to rebuild its position in the Middle East.

The aftermath of Camp David

While the Soviet leadership was undoubtedly unhappy with the results of Camp David, which seemed to indicate that Egypt and Israel were now well on their way to signing a peace agreement, Moscow could only have been pleased with a number of developments in the Arab world that were precipitated by the Egyptian-Israeli-American summit, including the reconciliations between Iraq and Syria, Jordan and the PLO, and Iraq and the PLO, and the Baghdad Conference of November 1978 which appeared to align almost the entire Arab world against Sadat. In addition, several months later Moscow received an unexpected bonus when the Shah of Iran was ousted and the Islamic government, which replaced his regime, left CENTO, proclaimed that Iran would pursue a neutralist policy, and offered full support to the Palestinian cause. Unfortunately for the USSR, however, just as its long-sought anti-imperialist bloc in the Arab world appeared to be forming (and had the possibility of expanding to include Iran), actions by Moscow's erstwhile ally, Iraq, served not only to divide the nascent bloc but also to run counter to Soviet policies in a number of areas.

While the Camp David summit was in progress, the USSR seemed particularly concerned that the United States would secure a military base in either Egypt or Israel.[128] Although the outcome of Camp David did not provide for such a military base, it was clear that the United States, by virtue of its mediating efforts between Egypt and Israel and its promises to them of economic and military aid, was becoming even more involved in both countries, and the USSR may well have feared that a more formal military arrangement was not far off and that the Camp David system might expand to include such states as Jordan and possibly even the PLO.

Not unexpectedly, therefore, the USSR greeted the agreements with hostility. In a major speech at Baku on September 22, Brezhnev denounced what he termed the US attempt to "split the Arab ranks" and force the Arabs to accept Israeli peace terms. In addition, he returned to the old three-part Soviet peace plan, emphasizing that Israel had to withdraw totally from all territory captured in the 1967 war and agree to the establishment of a Palestinian state in the West Bank and Gaza. Brezhnev also repeated the Soviet call for a return to the Geneva Conference, with full participation of the PLO. Interestingly enough, perhaps to balance the American success at Camp David, Brezhnev hailed events in Afghanistan in his Baku speech, emphasizing that the new left-wing government which had seized power in that country in April had embarked on the road to socialism.[129]

If the Soviet reaction to Camp David was hostile, the reaction of most of the Arab states was not much warmer. While President Carter dispatched a series of administration representatives to try to sell the agreement to such key Arab states as Saudi Arabia (a major financial supporter of Egypt); Jordan (which according to the Camp David agreements was to play a major role in working out the West Bank–Gaza autonomy plan); and Syria, they met with little success. Indeed, only three days after the announcement of the Camp David agreements, the Front of Steadfastness and Confrontation met in Damascus. Not only did it condemn Camp David which it terms "illegal," and reaffirm the role of the PLO as the sole representative of the Palestinian people, it also decided on the need to "develop and strengthen friendly relations with the socialist community led by the USSR."[130] Reinforcing Soviet satisfaction with this development, the PLO Moscow representative Mohammed Shaer stated that the Front for Steadfastness and Confrontation was "the core of a future broad pan-Arab anti-imperialist front."[131]

The Soviet Union, for its part, moved once again to reinforce its ties with key members of the Steadfastness Front as first Assad, then Henri

Boumadienne of Algeria and then Arafat of the PLO visited Moscow in October. The Soviet media hailed the visit of Assad who, it was noted, came as a representative of the Steadfastness Front; and one result of the meeting, besides the joint denunciation of Camp David and of attempts "to undermine Soviet–Arab friendship," was a Soviet decision to "further strengthen Syria's defense potential."[132]

While the visit of Assad to Moscow could be considered a success for the USSR in its efforts to prevent the Camp David agreement from acquiring further Arab support, the Arab leader's subsequent move toward a reconciliation with Iraq was even more warmly endorsed by the USSR. As discussed above, the Syrian–Iraqi conflict had long bedeviled Soviet attempts to create a unified "anti-imperialist" bloc of Arab states, and, therefore, when Assad announced that he had accepted an invitation to visit Iraq, the Soviet leadership must have seen this as a major step toward creating the long-sought "anti-imperialist" Arab bloc. While many observers saw Assad's visit as a tactical ploy to strengthen Syria's position in the face of the projected Israeli–Egyptian treaty, the USSR was effusive in its praise, with Moscow Radio calling it "an event of truly enormous importance which had considerably strengthened the position of those forces that decisively reject the capitulatory plans for a settlement drawn up at Camp David."[133]

While the Syrian–Iraqi reconciliation can be considered the most positive Arab development from the Soviet point of view to flow from Camp David, the limited *rapprochement* between the PLO and Jordan which occurred was also deemed a favorable development by the USSR, since it further reduced the chances of Jordanian participation in the Camp David accords and brought Jordan closer to an alignment with the anti-Sadat forces in the Arab world. The two *rapprochements* helped set the stage for the Baghdad Conference which appeared to further consolidate the bloc of Arab states opposing Sadat – a development warmly greeted by Moscow. At Baghdad, not only were the Camp David agreements condemned, with even Saudi Arabia participating in the condemnation (the Saudis may have been influenced, if not intimidated by the Syrian–Iraqi *rapprochement*), but a joint PLO–Jordanian commission was established, an event which appeared to foreshadow further cooperation between these two erstwhile enemies. In addition, another reconciliation took place as the PLO and Iraq, which had been involved in an assassination campaign against each other in the summer, also appeared to end their conflict. Besides these reconciliations, specific anti-Egyptian measures were decided upon at Baghdad. Thus, the Arab

League headquarters was to be removed from Cairo, and economic sanctions were planned against Egypt should Sadat go ahead with the signing of the treaty. Finally, the USSR must have been pleased by the Baghdad Conference's formula for a "just peace" in the Middle East: Israeli withdrawal from the territories captured in 1967 and the "right of the Palestinian people to establish an independent state on their national soil."[134] While the latter phrase was open to differing interpretations, the juxtaposition of the two statements seemed to indicate that even such radical states as Iraq and Libya might, for the first time, be willing to grudgingly accept Israel's existence. Although the Baghdad statement on peace was far from the trade, tourism, and normal diplomatic relations wanted by the Israelis, it was very close to the peace formula which had been advocated by the USSR since 1974. In sum, the Soviet leadership was undoubtedly pleased with the results of the Baghdad summit, with one Soviet commentator deeming it "a final blow to imperialist intentions aimed at dissolving Arab unity and pressuring other Arabs to join Camp David."[135]

Given the key role of Iraq in orchestrating the anti-Sadat forces at Baghdad, and helping to form what the USSR hoped might become the nucleus of the "anti-imperialist" Arab bloc Moscow had long wanted, it is not surprising that Soviet–Iraqi relations improved in the aftermath of the conference. Indeed, one month later, Saddam Hussein himself was invited to Moscow. While the main purpose of Hussein's visit was probably to coordinate the Soviet and Iraqi positions opposing Camp David, it appears that other issues occupied the discussions as well. These included Soviet–Iraqi trade relations, problems pertaining to Iraq's communist party, and the Soviet supply of arms to Iraq following Camp David. In this regard there were a number of reports in the Western press that both Syria and Iraq were asking for sharp increases in Soviet weapons supplies to compensate the Arabs for Egypt's departure from the Arab camp.[136] The USSR, however, reportedly told Syria and Iraq that since they were now cooperating they could pool their weapons.[137] In resisting the Syrian and Iraqi demands (if this, indeed, is what happened), the USSR may have been concerned that if the Syrians and Iraqis were too well armed they might provoke a war against Israel at a time inconvenient for the USSR,[138] or it may have simply been one more case where an arms supplier was unwilling to meet all the demands of its clients.

At any rate, while there appeared to have been progress on the question of economic relations during the talks, the outcome of the military aid question was not clear with the final communiqué stipulating only that "the sides reiterated their readiness to keep cooperating in strengthening the defense capacity of the Iraqi Republic."[139] Even less was said on the subject of the Iraqi communist party and the only public reference (and a veiled one at that) to this area of conflict in Soviet–Iraqi relations was made in a dinner speech by Kosygin who stated: "Friendly relations with the Republic of Iraq are highly valued in the Soviet Union and we are doing everything to make them more durable. This is our firm course and it is not affected by circumstantial considerations."[140]

If the Soviet leadership sought to use the Brezhnev–Hussein meeting to secure improved treatment for the Iraqi communists, they were not successful. Less than a month later, on January 10, *Pravda* published an editorial from the Iraqi communist paper *Tariq Ash-Shab* deploring "the widespread persecution of communists in Iraq and repression against the communist party's organization and press," and *Pravda* followed the editorial up three days later by publishing the statement of the December 1978 Conference of Arab communist parties which similarly condemned Iraq for its treatment of the ICP.[141]

The anti-Iraqi campaign in the Soviet press is of particular interest. In the past, the USSR had grudgingly tolerated attacks on local communist parties, so long as the regime responsible adopted a proper "anti-imperialist" stance. Indeed, the USSR had even gone so far as to urge the dissolution of Arab communist parties or their restriction to the role of teachers of "scientific socialism" in Third World countries to avoid such conflicts.[142] It may well be, therefore, that Moscow saw more than just a domestic problem in Iraq's persecution of the ICP which continued through the first half of 1979. Iraq, in leading the opposition to the Egyptian–Israeli treaty, was seeking to project itself as the leader of the Arab world. In order to successfully accomplish this task, however, Iraq had not only to arrange a *rapprochement* with Syria and the PLO, it had to establish a working relationship with Saudi Arabia as well, the Arab world's leading financier, and a growing Persian Gulf military power. The Soviet leadership may have suspected, therefore, that the overt anti-communist campaign in Iraq was designed to signal to the Saudis that Iraq was no longer a close ally of the USSR, and when Iraqi strongman Saddam Hussein went so far as to state that: "We reject the wide expansion by the Soviet Union in the Arab homeland" and that "the Arabs should fight anyone – even friends like the Soviets who try to occupy Saudi land," this may have confirmed Soviet suspicions.[143]

Yet another factor which may have tarnished somewhat Iraq's useful-ness to the USSR as a leader of the anti-Sadat and anti-American forces in the Arab world was the eruption of a serious quarrel between Iraq and the PDRY, the most Marxist of the Soviet Union's Arab allies. There appear to have been two major causes for the quarrel. In the first place, when the PDRY invaded North Yemen, then an American ally, in late February 1979, Iraq led an Arab mediation mission which, against the background of an American military build-up of North Yemen, succeeded in getting the South Yemenis to withdraw before any of their major objectives were achieved. Given the apparent Soviet support for the invasion, this would appear to have been a case where Soviet and Iraqi objectives were in conflict.[144] Secondly, several months later, an Iraqi communist party member, Taufiq Rushdi, who had been lecturing in the PDRY, was murdered – apparently by a "hit team" of Iraqi security men attached to Iraq's Aden embassy. In reprisal, a PDRY force stormed the Iraqi embassy and seized the gunmen, an action which provoked a storm of protest from Baghdad.[145]

If the unity of the anti-Sadat forces in the Arab world was threatened by the Iran–PDRY conflict, it was also endangered by the growing strife between Iraq and the Muslim fundamentalist government led by the Ayatollah Khomeini in Iran. The problem originated in Iranian Kurdis-tan where the Kurds, seizing the opportunity provided by the disintegra-tion of the Shah's regime – and of the Iranian army – demanded autonomy.[146] This, in turn, led to bloody clashes between the central authorities and Iran's Kurds, and, as the Iranian Kurds agitated for independence, this inevitably affected the Kurds living in Iraq who, after receiving arms from their brethren in Iran, rekindled their war against the Ba'athist regime in Iraq. This, in turn, led to Iraqi bombing of Kurdish border villages in Iran and a sharp deterioration in Iranian–Iraqi relations.[147] Further disturbing relations between the two states were charges by the Iranian Governor General of Khuzistan that Iraq had smuggled weapons into the region in which most of Iran's ethnic Arabs live, and an Iraqi crackdown on Shiite religious leaders in Iraq who had maintained close relations with Khomeini.[148] Iran's clash with Iraq also affected its relations with other Arab states when, in response to Iraqi demands that Iran return the three Arab islands in the Straits of Hormuz seized by the Shah in 1971, a religious leader close to Khomeini reasserted the Iranian claim to Bahrein which the Shah had renounced in 1970.[149]

The rise in Iranian–Arab tensions served to further split the camp of the anti-Sadat Arabs, with Kuwait and Bahrein lining up behind Iraq while Libya and the PLO, who had been early supporters of Khomeini, backed the Iranians who were also strongly opposed to Camp David.[150] It also negatively affected Iranian–Soviet relations which were already strained by growing anti-communist sentiment in Iran and Soviet support for what was perceived in Iran as the anti-Islamic Taraki regime of Afghanistan. Thus, a front page editorial in a government-supported newspaper, the *Islamic Republic*, claimed that "the ruling clique in Iraq" was plotting against Iran both to "prevent the spread of Iran's Islamic revolution into Iraq" and to "open the road to the warm waters of the Persian Gulf to their big master" – a clear reference to the Soviet Union.[151]

Then, in July 1979, the anti-Sadat unity world suffered another blow as the *rapprochement* between Iraq and Syria came to a sudden end as Iraq's new President, Saddam Hussein, accused Syria of being involved in a plot to overthrow him (Syria's unwillingness to subordinate itself to Iraq in the proposed union of the two countries, however, may have been the real cause of the split).[152] Fortunately for Moscow, however, the sharp deterioration in US–Iranian relations served to compensate the USSR for the weakening of the anti-Sadat coalition in the Middle East as Moscow saw itself emerging as the major zero-sum game winner in the influence competition for Iran as US–Iranian relations plummeted with the onset of the hostage crisis.

By mid-October 1979, the outlook for the Khomeini regime did not appear very bright. The economy was in a shambles, unemployment was rising, and the Kurds were scoring victories against Khomeini's forces. Meanwhile, Prime Minister Bazargan and his liberal allies, were losing out in the power struggle with the Islamic Revolutionary Council as clerical leaders such as Ayatollah Beheshti and non-clerical Islamic radicals such as Hassan Bani Sadr expressed growing displeasure with the Bazargan government. As one after another of Bazargan's allies were forced out of office, it seems to have appeared to Khomeini and the Islamic Revolutionary Council that a scapegoat was needed to help explain Iran's problems and regenerate revolutionary enthusiasm. Given the past record of the United States in Iran, the US was the obvious selection, and beginning in mid-October a virulent anti-American campaign was begun in the Iranian media. At the same time, the Tudeh party was allowed to reopen its newspaper as the Iranian leaders evidently felt they had to mend their fences somewhat with their northern neighbor if they were to mount a major confrontation with the

United States. It should be noted in this context that the anti-American campaign began more than ten days *before* the Shah came to the United States for medical treatment. His arrival, therefore, came at a time when the anti-American campaign was well underway and the atmosphere already prepared for action against the embassy. Whether or not Ayatollah Khomeini actually ordered the embassy seizure himself is not yet known; what is clear is that he prepared the atmosphere for the seizure and that he and his entourage were to exploit the hostage seizure to inject a new spirit into the Islamic revolution at a time when Iran was facing a very difficult time.[153]

The initial Soviet reaction to the embassy seizure was somewhat guarded as *Pravda* printed essentially factual accounts of the action of the students.[154] Several days later, however, as the situation became clearer, the USSR tilted toward a pro-Iranian position, with a Moscow Radio Persian language commentary on November 6 terming the student action "totally understandable and logical."[155] Soviet broadcasts continued in this vein – despite protests by Washington (a situation reminiscent of Soviet behavior the previous fall when the Shah was slipping from power) – until December 5 when *Pravda* itself took a strongly pro-Iranian position, in an article by A. Petrov which, after deploring the US naval build-up near Iran as "flagrant military and political pressure against Iran," stated:

> Instead of setting an example of restraint, responsibility and composure in the present circumstances, redoubling efforts to seek a reasonable way out of this situation and not letting emotions take the upper hand, certain circles in the US are leaning more and more toward the use of force. They claim that this is a response to the holding as hostages of US embassy personnel in Tehran, which is contrary to the norms of international law. To be sure, the seizure of the American embassy in and of itself does not conform to the international convention concerning respect for diplomatic privileges and immunity. However, one cannot pull this act out of the overall context of American–Iranian relations and forget about the actions of the US toward Iran, which are in no way consonant with the norms of law and morality ... The indisputability of the principle of immunity of diplomatic representatives cannot serve as justification, and even less as a pretext, for violating the sovereignty of an independent state – another principle that is at the heart of all international law.[156]

Petrov's rather convoluted analysis of international law ended with a warning: "Our country, as Comrade L. Brezhnev has stressed, opposes outside interference in Iran's internal affairs by anyone, in any form and under any pretext. This position of the Soviet Union remains unchanged."

In analyzing the reasoning behind Moscow's pro-Iranian position in the hostage crisis, at a time it was seeking the passage of the SALT II agreement in the US Senate, one can perhaps point to the uncertain handling of the crisis by the Carter administration. The administration's reluctance to impose economic, let alone military, sanctions at a time when the United States was being humiliated on a daily basis by street mobs parading with the sign "America can't do anything" may well have struck the Soviet leadership as a sign of weakness, particularly since President Carter emphasized so strongly that the lives of the hostages were the primary American concern. Indeed, the hostage situation weakened still further the position of the United States in the Middle East as many nations in the region began to openly wonder how likely it was that the United States would come to their aid if it could not even defend its own interests, a perception perhaps reinforced by Washington's passivity after its embassy in Pakistan was stormed and burned later in November. To be sure, when the hostage issue was initially raised in the United Nations, Moscow voted for two Security Council resolutions calling on Iran to free the hostages (after all, its own diplomats could one day find themselves in a similar situation); the latter one on December 4. Yet the *Pravda* article mentioned above which appeared one day after the December 4 vote (and which was broadcast by Tass International Service) seemed to convey the USSR's true feelings. As the hostage crisis went on, it appeared as if the Soviet leaders saw an excellent opportunity to drive a wedge between the US and Iran. At the same time, Moscow could exploit Carter's decision to send a naval task force toward Iran as a threat not only against that country, thereby reinforcing Iranian–American animosity, but against the Arab oil producers as well, in an effort to further weaken the American position in the Middle East. Indeed, this was to be the central theme of Soviet propaganda for the next few months. Apparently Moscow thought that given Carter's strong commitment to the SALT II agreement, and his tendency to overlook Soviet exploitation of Third World crises, the USSR could have its way in Iran and have SALT II also.[157]

The onset of the hostage crisis brought a change in the Iranian government as Prime Minister Bazargan resigned and Khomeini gave full governmental power to the Islamic Revolutionary Council. The change in government was welcomed by Moscow who saw in the liberal Bazargan an individual who was likely to seek good ties with the US.[158] Indeed, *Pravda* hailed the anti-US statements of Bani Sadr, one of the most influential members of the Islamic Revolutionary Council in the evident expectation that the anti-US thrust of the hostage seizure would become a basic policy of the new government.[159] Indeed, one of the first acts of the new government was to denounce the 1959 mutual security treaty between the US and Iran, an action clearly welcomed by Moscow, although the Soviet leadership was far less happy over the government's abrogation of the clauses of the 1921 Soviet–Iranian treaty which allowed Soviet troops to enter Iran if a foreign military force entered that country.[160]

As might be expected, the Tudeh party pledged its full support for the new regime and hailed the transfer of power from the "bourgeois liberal" Bazargan government to the revolutionary government,[161] and in an interview in *L'Humanité* which was cited in *Pravda*, Tudeh leader Kianouri claimed that a "new stage" of the Iranian revolution had begun whose two aims were to "eliminate all manifestations of American domination in Iran and deepen the revolution's class content by enlisting the popular masses in a more active struggle against the upper bourgeoisie." He also called for the establishment of a "broad national front" to rally all available forces, including national minorities, for "the struggle against American domination."[162] Kianouri's concern about the national minorities probably reflected the fact that by November, the Iranian government was fighting not only the Kurds but the Azerbaizhanis as well, and the Tudeh – and Moscow – may have worried that these conflicts would sap the power of the now strongly anti-American regime in Tehran. For its part, Moscow changed its reporting of the struggles of the national minorities to a far more sympathetic evaluation of the central regime and blamed US agents for "organizing separatist actions and provoking unrest in Iran."[163]

In sum, the hostage seizure and the subsequent rift between the United States and Iran was seen by the Soviet Union as a golden opportunity to reinforce its own ties with Iran while weakening the overall position of the United States in the region. Whether or not the Carter administration's lack of firmness in handling the Iranian crisis was a factor in the Soviet decision to proceed with a massive invasion of Afghanistan, in late December, is only a matter of conjecture. Nonetheless, it must have struck the Kremlin leaders that if the US was unwilling to intervene in Iran where it had major interests, it was very unlikely to take action in Afghanistan where American interests were almost non-existent. In any case, the Soviet invasion of Afghanistan was to cause Moscow serious problems throughout the Muslim world, and it is to Brezhnev's efforts to deal with that situation that we now turn.

2 Soviet policy from the invasion of Afghanistan until the death of Brezhnev

The impact of the Soviet invasion

The invasion of Afghanistan, which was to create major problems for Moscow in its drive to extend Soviet influence in the Middle East, came after more than a year and a half of Moscow's rising frustration with the communist leadership of Afghanistan which had ruled ineffectually since seizing power in April 1978.[1] The very narrowly based government of Noor Mohammed Taraki was in deep trouble almost from the time it seized power, and the signing of a Treaty of Friendship and Cooperation with the USSR in December 1978 did little to help the communist regime. Although Soviet military aid and advisers had poured into the country after the coup, and Taraki and his strong man Prime Minister, Hafizullah Amin, had begun to institute major land reform and social reform programs in the rural areas of Afghanistan, the new government had incurred the wrath of the Islamic religious leaders as well as tribal leaders who resisted Kabul's efforts to extend its control to their areas. While the rebels were divided among themselves, the heavy-handed actions of the central government which included the physical mistreatment of Muslim Mullahs and the indiscriminate bombing of rebel areas helped expand the opposition to the communist regime, and the rebels were also aided by the defection of a number of Afghani soldiers (many of whom belonged to non-Pathan ethnic minorities) and army officers as well. The government's efforts were further hampered by the fierce rivalry between the Khalq faction of the party led by Taraki and Amin and the rival Parcham faction led by Babrak Karmal. By June 1979 fighting was raging in more than three-quarters of Afghanistan's provinces, and an attack had been made in Kabul itself against the government.

The conflict in Afghanistan posed a major threat to Soviet prestige. Having signed a Treaty of Friendship and Cooperation with the Taraki regime, and having hailed the Afghani leader as a fellow revolutionary,[2] Brezhnev felt obligated to aid the new Afghani government – particularly since it shared a long border with the USSR. Consequently, as the Taraki regime began to lose control, the USSR expanded its military aid, sending helicopters and helicopter gun-ships to assist the Afghani government in fighting the rebels in Afghanistan's mountain regions,[3] and there were a number of reports of Soviet involvement in military actions.[4]

In addition to stepping up its military aid to Kabul, Moscow also moved on the diplomatic front to try to curb the Afghani rebels' use of sanctuaries in neighboring countries. Pakistan, the main rebel base, was singled out for Soviet censure, and Moscow exploited the fact that Pakistan was in a difficult position because of its conflict with the United States over the independent Pakistani nuclear development program, which had caused a sharp deterioration in Pakistani–American relations. Iran also came in for Soviet censure, and the USSR accused China, Egypt and the United States of aiding the rebels. Indeed, *Pravda* openly accused the CIA of involvement in the rebellion,[5] a charge that was termed "slanderous and baseless" by the United States.[6]

Neither Soviet charges of outside intervention nor the military aid which the USSR had thus far extended, however, managed to stem the tide which appeared to be flowing against the Taraki regime by June 1, 1979. The Soviet leadership then stepped up its diplomatic efforts to protect Taraki by issuing a formal warning in *Pravda* which stated:

> The USSR cannot remain indifferent to the violations of the sovereignty of the Democratic Republic of Afghanistan, the incursions into its territory from Pakistan, and the attempt to create a crisis situation in that area ... What is in question is virtual aggression against a state with which the USSR has a common frontier.[7]

This warning, however, did not serve to end the insurgency which, in any case, was locally based. Consequently, the Soviet leadership increasingly faced the choice of whether or not to commit its own troops (or possibly those of a client state such as Cuba) to help salvage the situation. A major troop commitment held both advantages and disadvantages for Moscow. On the one hand, Soviet military aid to Iraq in 1974, Angola in 1976, and Ethiopia in 1978, the latter two cases involving a sizeable Soviet military commitment, had succeeded in aiding its allies against insurgencies, and Moscow by now had experience in counterinsurgency operations. In addition, the propinquity of

Afghanistan's border to the USSR, and its treaty with Moscow, to say nothing of Soviet prestige and a desire to prevent the emergence of a solid band of increasingly militant Islamic states along its southern borders (Iran, Pakistan, and if the Muslim-dominated rebels were successful, Afghanistan) all militated for increased Soviet military activity. On the other hand, however, the Taraki regime was in a far weaker position than either the Iraqi Ba'ath in 1974 or even Mengistu's Ethiopian regime in 1978, and an increase in Soviet military activity in Afghanistan might also serve to drive both Iran and Pakistan back toward the United States while at the same time providing ammunition for the anti-SALT elements in the United States at a time when the SALT II treaty, which had to be ratified by the United States Senate, was already under heavy attack there.

The change in government in Afghanistan in September 1979 could only have further disturbed Moscow as Taraki was overthrown by Amin who took full control and soon clashed directly with the Russians, demanding the ouster of the Soviet Ambassador. It may have appeared to the Soviet leaders that Amin, who had studied for three years in the United States (at Columbia University), and who had met frequently with US Ambassador Adolph Dubs (who was assassinated in February 1979) might become an Asian Tito,[8] if he were not overthrown first by the Afghan rebels. Under these circumstances, and benefiting from the hostage crisis in Iran which diverted American attention (and noting the very weak reaction of the Carter administration to the hostage seizure) Moscow sent its troops into Afghanistan, deposed (and murdered) Amin, and replaced him with Babrak Karmal.

While the Soviet relationship with Afghanistan dated back to the nineteenth century, and while Soviet–Afghan relations both in the military and economic spheres had become increasingly close after World War II,[9] the dispatch of more than 80,000 Soviet combat troops to Afghanistan, the first Soviet military move of such magnitude outside of the Soviet bloc in Eastern Europe, stirred a great many fears in the Middle East and particularly among the oil producers in the Arab world, since Soviet forces, operating from airbases in Afghanistan, were now in fighter-bomber range of the Strait of Hormuz. In addition it created serious problems for Moscow in its relations with the United States (President Carter imposed a partial grain embargo, limited the sale of high-technology equipment, withdrew the SALT II treaty from Senate consideration, and cancelled American participation in the Moscow Olympics). The United States also seized upon the invasion to try to rally the Muslim states of the Middle East, many of whom were suspicious of the United States because of its role in Camp David, against the USSR while at the same time stepping up its search for Middle Eastern bases and hastening the deployment of its military forces near the Persian Gulf which Carter pledged to protect.[10] When the issue of Soviet intervention in Afghanistan came up for a vote in the United Nations in early January, only Ethiopia and South Yemen, among Moscow's Middle Eastern allies, voted against the resolution which condemned the USSR, while Algeria, Syria, and North Yemen abstained, with Libya taking a similar position by being absent from the vote.[11] Among the 104 countries voting against Moscow (only 18 states voted with the USSR while 30 abstained or were not present) was Iraq whose President, Saddam Hussein, publicly condemned the invasion, thus further demonstrating Iraq's independence of Moscow.[12] Also voting against Moscow were Saudi Arabia, Jordan, and Kuwait, all of whom Moscow had hoped to wean away from the West. As far as Iran was concerned, its Foreign Ministry issued a statement condemning the invasion, while its UN representative joined with the majority in voting for the anti-Soviet resolution.[13]

In an effort to overcome this Muslim backlash, which it feared the US would be able to exploit, Moscow made several moves. In the first place, its most trusted Arab allies, Syria, the PLO, Algeria, Libya, and the PDRY, who formed the Steadfastness and Confrontation Front, organized a meeting in Damascus in mid-January – two weeks before the Islamic Conference was scheduled to meet to discuss the invasion. The Steadfastness and Confrontation Front used its meeting as a platform to condemn the United States, while pledging friendship for the Soviet Union and solidarity with Iran. It also tried to divert the attention of the Arab world away from the Soviet invasion of Afghanistan by emphasizing American support for Camp David and calling for a postponement of the beginning of the Islamic Conference on January 26 because that was the date scheduled for the normalization of relations between Egypt and the "Zionist Entity" (Israel).[14]

Indeed, the Steadfastness Front, or at least key components of it such as Syria, the PLO (primarily the PFLP and DFLP) and the PDRY became almost adjuncts of Soviet policy during this period. Thus at the end of January, Gromyko visited Syria, and the joint communiqué issued at the end of his visit articulated the themes which Moscow and its Middle East allies were to use over the next few months to try to divert Muslim attention from the invasion of Afghanistan to the activities of "American-supported" Israel in the West Bank and Gaza. Fortunately for Moscow, the expansion of Israeli settlements on the West Bank and the US turnabout in the March 1, 1980 UN Security Council vote condemning Israeli policies were to prove most fortuitous for Soviet propaganda efforts.

Moscow's invective against Israel reached a new high during Gromyko's visit as the Soviet–Syrian communiqué attacked Israel not only for racial discrimination but also for the "desecration of objects of historical, religious and cultural value to the Arabs." The United States, however, received the brunt of the Soviet and Syrian criticism:

> Under the cover of an artificially fomented uproar over the events in Iran and Afghanistan, imperialist circles and their accomplices are striving to divert the Arab people's attention away from the struggle to liquidate the consequences of Israeli aggression, and are attempting to create a split in the ranks of the Arab and Moslem countries, drive a wedge between them and their friends – the USSR – and subvert the unity and principles of the non-aligned movement. [The USSR and Syria] condemn the continuing campaign by imperialist forces, led by the United States, which are displaying a false concern for Islam while simultaneously supporting Israel's seizure of the Holy places in Jerusalem [and] taking an openly hostile position toward the revolution in Iran.
>
> The facts indicate that imperialism has been and continues to be an enemy of all the Moslem countries as a whole and an enemy of Islam.[15]

The communiqué also mentioned further Soviet provision of military aid to Syria, and indeed, not only Syria but also Iraq, Algeria, South Yemen, and Libya reportedly received sharply increased amounts of Soviet weaponry in the post-invasion period as Moscow sought to bolster its position in these countries.[16] An arms deal was also signed with Kuwait in early February as Moscow sought to improve that country's relationship with the USSR.[17]

Nonetheless, while Moscow was seeking – and obtaining – the support of the Steadfastness Front in the post-Afghan invasion period, the Front itself was encountering serious problems. In addition to criticism from other Arab and Muslim states for their position on the Soviet invasion of Afghanistan, many of the Front leaders were encountering internal problems. In addition to the Muslim Brotherhood's attacks against the Syrian government, Libyan leader Kaddafi faced internal unrest, as well as condemnation from other Arab states for supporting an abortive attack against Tunisia. At the same time, Libya and the PLO became embroiled in a conflict because of Kaddafi's displeasure over a lack of PLO aggressiveness against Israel. Meanwhile, the new Algerian President, Chadli Ben-Jedid, faced the continuing problem of the Polisario rebellion which was draining Algerian, as well as Moroccan, resources and Algeria began to moderate its position toward the United States. Finally, a major power struggle was underway in the PDRY, which culminated five days after the end of the Steadfastness Conference in the ouster of PDRY President Abd al-Fattah Ismail, and his replacement by the more pragmatic Prime Minister Ali Nasser Moham-med – the second major government upheaval in South Yemen in less than two years. Moscow, whether or not it had a role in the ouster of Ismail may well have been pleased by the development since, in the post-Afghanistan invasion atmosphere in the Middle East, the USSR was trying to reduce the perception of the "Soviet threat." Ali Nasser Muhammed, who wanted to cooperate with his neighbors instead of trying to overthrow them as Ismail had advocated, was clearly the man to support the Soviet policy.[18]

Consequently, it was a weakened Steadfastness Front which met in April 1980, and although it managed to work out a temporary *rapprochement* between the PLO and Libya and denounced the normalization of relations between Israel and Egypt, the meeting was not particularly successful in working out any concrete measures to combat either Sadat or the United States.[19] While diplomatic relations were broken between the Steadfastness Front members and the Sudan, Somalia, and Oman which still maintained diplomatic relations with Egypt, and while the US (and its efforts to obtain bases in the Arab world) was severely denounced while Moscow was warmly praised, the Steadfastness meeting was not marked by any solid achievement. Moscow, however, took an optimistic view of the meeting pointing to its decision to establish a joint military command, and other coordinating bodies, and asserted that "the tendency towards the anti-imperialist united action of the Arab people is gaining momentum."[20] The previous failure of the Steadfastness Front members to coordinate their actions, however, must have raised serious questions, even in Moscow, as to the likelihood of success of these organizational moves.

In addition to obtaining the support of the Steadfastness Front, Moscow also appeared to draw somewhat closer to North Yemen with whom it signed a major arms deal. While the North Yemenis may well have turned to Moscow for arms to demonstrate their displeasure with the military supply arrangement made with Washington the previous year, an arrangement which Saudi Arabia, for its own reasons, was delaying, the overall impact of the North Yemeni turn to Moscow seemed to undercut US policy in the Arabian Peninsula and was to raise, once again, questions about the capability of US diplomacy.[21]

A similar development in South Asia was also to weaken the US position while strengthening that of the USSR. An election was held in India which brought Indira Ghandi back to power – the woman who, as Prime Minister, had been far more friendly to Moscow than her successor, Moraji Desai. While Mrs Ghandi criticized the Soviet invasion of Afghanistan, she was far more critical of the US aid offers to Pakistan to help counter the Soviet action. Then, when Pakistan's President Zia contemptuously rejected America's $400 million aid offer as "peanuts," American prestige dropped again, while Moscow sought to carefully cultivate India, a process which was to result in Indian recognition of the Vietnamese puppet government in Cambodia, and a major Soviet–Indian arms deal.[22]

In addition to bolstering its ties with India and utilizing the Arab Rejectionist Front to deflect Muslim criticism, Moscow stepped up its support for Iran in its confrontation with the United States in the period after the invasion of Afghanistan. Not only did the USSR veto a US-sponsored UN Security Council resolution calling for economic sanctions against Iran, it also strongly reiterated its warning against US military intervention in Iran with *Pravda*, on January 10, 1980 stating that Moscow would not tolerate any outside interference in Iranian internal affairs. While the USSR sought to project itself as the protector of Iran, it also sought to temper Iranian criticism of the Afghan invasion by having Babrak Karmal, the Soviet-installed leader of Afghanistan, write to Khomeini with an appeal for a common front against US imperialism.[23] To further placate the Ayatollah, his picture was published in two Kabul newspapers.[24] All these efforts, however, came to naught. The two leading candidates for the Iranian presidency, Hassan Bani Sadr and Foreign Minister Ghotbzadeh both attacked the USSR in campaign speeches in late January 1980, with Bani Sadr accusing Moscow of wanting to divide Iran and push to the Indian Ocean.[25] At the Islamic Conference, the Iranian representative joined in the general denunciation of Soviet policy and urged the conference to demand the withdrawal of Soviet forces from Afghanistan, although he also demanded that the conference condemn the US economic blockade of Iran and act to eliminate "US imperialist influence in Islamic countries."[26]

The Islamic Conference which not only condemned the USSR in very strong terms (despite the efforts of the Steadfastness Front) but also suspended the membership of Afghanistan, called on Islamic nations to break diplomatic relations with that country, and urged a boycott of the Moscow Olympics, was a major defeat for Soviet Middle Eastern policy.[27] The Soviet defeat was compounded in early February when Ayatollah Khomeini himself castigated the Soviet invasion for the first time, and pledged unconditional support for the Muslim insurgents fighting the Soviet-backed regime.[28] Iran's newly elected President, Bani Sadr, also denounced the USSR and promised that Iran would send supplies and equipment to the Afghan rebels.[29] By this time, the United States had softened its stance toward Iran, and, as part of its overall effort to rally the Muslim Middle East against the USSR, decided to postpone sanctions against Iran until after Bani Sadr had a chance to deal with the hostage issue.

As the Iranian leadership issued anti-Soviet statements, Moscow could not help but be concerned that the Iranians might come to agree with the US assertion that the USSR was the greater threat, and, with Soviet troops now bordering Iran in two directions, might release the US hostages and turn Iran back toward the United States. Consequently, the Soviet leadership took an increasingly unfavorable view of Bani Sadr who appeared to favor a speedy solution of the hostage conflict, and Moscow became far more supportive of both the militant students who wanted to hold onto the hostages to keep the revolution going and such clerical leaders as Ayatollah Beheshti, who supported them.[30] Khomeini, who sided with the students, was praised not only by the Tudeh which was now one of his most fervent supporters, but also by Moscow as *Pravda* on February 24 cited Khomeini's statement that the students holding the hostages had given a "crippling blow to the American imperialists."

As Moscow began to side increasingly with the clerical leaders of Iran, articles began to appear in Soviet journals and newspapers emphasizing the "progressive" nature of Islam, with Leonid Medvenko going so far as to assert in a *New Times* article that while Islam could be either progressive or reactionary depending upon the circumstances:

> What distinguishes the present stage of the national liberation movement, which often raises the banner of Islam, is that this movement is not spearheaded only against imperialism, but gradually turns against the very foundations of capitalism. The conflict between the capitalist West and Moslem East, which has latterly become sharper still, is a

vivid reflection of the ideological crisis of neo-colonialism, for it is in effect evidence of loss of faith in capitalism, which not so long ago regarded Islam as its ally. This evidently explains the West's fear of the process sometimes called the "regeneration of Islam."[31]

Interestingly enough, however, while Soviet observers tended to wax eloquent about the positive trends in Islam, Middle Eastern communists remained considerably more skeptical about the clergy and a symposium appearing in the *World Marxist Review* spoke openly of the "limits of the clergy's progressive impulses."[32] The Middle Eastern communists' caution was well taken because on March 20 Khomeini issued his strongest denunciation of the USSR to date, although he coupled it with strong criticism of the United States:

> We are fighting against international communism to the same degree that we are fighting against the Western world devourers led by America, Israel, and Zionism. My dear friends, you should know that the danger from the communist powers is not less than America...

> Once again I strongly condemn the dastardly occupation of Afghanistan by the plunderers and occupiers of the aggressive East. I hope that the Moslem and noble people of Afghanistan will as soon as possible achieve true victory and independence and be released from the grip of these so-called supporters of the working class.[33]

Then, in an attack on the Islamic Marxists and the Tudeh, Khomeini appeared to repudiate those Soviet writers who saw an anti-imperialist blending of Islam and Marxism:

> Most regretably, at times it can be seen that due to the lack of the proper and precise understanding of Islamic issues *some people have mixed Islamic ideas with Marxist ideas and have created a concoction which is in no way in accordance with the progressive teachings of Islam* ...[34] (emphasis mine)

Khomeini's attack, coupled with Iran's termination of natural gas deliveries to the USSR because of a dispute over price, seemed to signal a deterioration in relations with the Soviet Union.[35] Fortunately for Moscow, however, by this time the Carter administration had lost patience on the hostage issue and in early April the US expelled the Iranian diplomats from the US, announced the imposition of economic sanctions while urging its NATO allies to do likewise, and warned it had "other means" available to free the hostages if the sanctions did not work. Seizing the opportunity presented by the American actions, Moscow offered Iran land transit facilities to circumvent a potential

American naval blockade, and many of Moscow's East European allies, possibly concerned about the USSR's future inability to supply them with sufficient fuel, journeyed to Tehran to try to arrange barter deals where they would obtain Iranian oil for the food and manufactured goods that might be embargoed by the West. As US–Iranian tension again rose, Afghan leader Babrak Karmal, almost certainly acting on Soviet instructions, made another *démarche* to Tehran, this time to normalize relations with Iran (a similar note was sent to Pakistan).[36]

In sum, therefore, at the time of the abortive American hostage rescue on April 25, 1980, Moscow may have seen the Iranian government once again swinging back toward the USSR as the American threats took precedence over the Soviet invasion of Afghanistan.

Soviet policy from the abortive hostage rescue mission to the Iran–Iraq war

The ill-fated American rescue mission of April 25, 1980 appeared to provide a golden opportunity for Moscow to reinforce its ties with Iran while at the same time enabling it to demonstrate to the nations of the Middle East the dangers posed to them by the American military buildup in the Indian Ocean. It also aided Moscow in its efforts to divert Muslim attention from the Soviet invasion of Afghanistan, and Moscow lost little time in attacking the US for the rescue attempt, comparing it to the raid by the Tel-Aviv "cut-throats" at Entebbe,[37] and claiming that the raid was part of a larger plot to overthrow the government of Ayatollah Khomeini.[38] The USSR also thrust itself forth again as the protector of Iran – and other Muslim countries – with *Izvestia* on May 1 asserting:

> It is not for nothing that influential commentators in the US are admitting that the existence of the Soviet Union is the main factor that US hawks are forced to take into account in their plans concerning Iran – and that's not all. It is also indicative that these same commentators admit that bellicose circles in the US would long since have decided on extreme measures in their anti-Iranian schemes had they not taken into account certain indisputable facts of present day reality. Thus practical experience graphically shows whom the Islamic countries that are striving to consolidate their sovereignty and that want to be full masters in their own houses can rely upon.[39]

Writing in a similar vein, *New Times* Middle Eastern specialist Dmitry Volsky asserted that the rescue mission "showed how little respect

imperialist policymakers have for the sovereignty of Muslim countries."
Volsky, after then discussing NATO efforts to exploit the Afghan situation to build an anti-Soviet Muslim bloc, also asserted, rather optimistically, "it may already be said that the Muslim world as a whole refuses
to join in Washington's anti-Soviet strategy."[40] Unfortunately for
Volsky, the Islamic Conference which met several weeks after his article
appeared was to prove his assertion premature, and despite the Soviet
attempt to act as Iran's champion, it was to be Iran which led the
conference in its denunciation of the USSR's invasion and occupation of
Afghanistan.

The Islamic Conference meeting in mid-May was its second in 1980.
After the diplomatic battering the Muslim nations administered to the
USSR in January, Moscow may have expected better treatment at the
May meeting because of both the abortive US rescue mission and the
Begin government's decision, announced just before the start of the
session, to consider the formal annexation of East Jerusalem. Indeed,
Israel was strongly denounced by the Muslim nations, while the United
States also came in for a large share of criticism both for its support of
Israel and for its "recent military aggression" against Iran.[41]

Nonetheless, while there was widespread condemnation of the US,
the Soviet Union also had its share of difficulties at the conference. In
the first place, despite efforts of the PLO and other Steadfastness Front
members, Afghanistan, which had been suspended from the conference
in January, was not readmitted. Secondly, despite a gesture by the
Karmal government just before the meeting where the Soviet-installed
Afghan President invited Iran and Pakistan to participate in talks aimed
at arranging the withdrawal of Soviet troops from Afghanistan, Iran
severely denounced the USSR at the conference and went so far as to
include, as official members of its own delegation, eight Afghan rebel
leaders.[42] Foreign Minister Ghotbzadeh led the Iranian delegation and
denounced the USSR and the US in equally harsh terms, condemning
the Soviet Union's invasion of Afghanistan as "a flagrant violation of
international law carried out in total disrespect for the sovereignty and
territorial integrity of Afghanistan."[43] He also stated, in an obvious
effort to prevent the conference from being diverted to the Palestine–
Israel conflict, "For us, the liberation of Afghanistan is not less important than the liberation of Palestine." Ghotbzadeh was successful in his
quest, as the Islamic Conference, despite the efforts of the Steadfastness
Front, again called for the "immediate, total and unconditional withdrawal of all Soviet troops stationed on the territory of Afghanistan." It

also set up a three-man committee, composed of Ghotbzadeh, the Foreign Minister of Pakistan, and the Islamic Conference Secretary General to seek a solution of the Afghan problem.[44]

Despite the Islamic Conference's numerous criticisms of the United States, the May meeting must be considered another diplomatic defeat for the USSR which rejected the conference's Afghan Committee plan, and denounced the "representatives of reactionary Muslim quarters" who "succeeded in pushing through a resolution on the Afghan question couched in terms hostile to the people and government of Afghanistan."[45]

Once again, as was the case following the Islamic Conference in January, Moscow and its Arab allies sought to deflect Muslim criticism by concentrating their attention on Israeli actions in the West Bank and Gaza and purported American support for them. Fortunately for Moscow, Israel was again to give the USSR ammunition for its propaganda efforts. Thus, following a terrorist attack against Jews in the West Bank city of Hebron who were returning from Sabbath services, Israel expelled the Mayor and religious leader of that city and the Mayor of a nearby city who were accused of creating the atmosphere for the attack. A month later two West Bank Arab Mayors were maimed by bombs and, at the same time, the Begin government began to push the bill for the formal annexation of East Jerusalem through the Israeli Parliament. Moscow seized on these events to claim that Egypt had capitulated to Israel and to demonstrate that by backing these actions, the United States was, in fact, an enemy of Islam. The USSR also proclaimed its willingness to vote sanctions in the Security Council against Israel "by virtue of its solidarity with the Arab and other Islamic countries that considered it necessary for the Security Council to take some steps in connection with the Israeli occupier's defiant action."[46] Indeed, Moscow was to use the numerous condemnations of Israel by the UN in the spring and summer of 1980 – condemnations that were spearheaded by its Arab allies – to try to divert attention from Afghanistan where, despite a massive troop commitment, the USSR was facing serious difficulties in suppressing the rebels.[47]

Arab condemnation of Israeli actions in the West Bank, the passage of the May 26 deadline for the establishment of Palestinian autonomy, and the deterioration of Saudi–American relations led Moscow to float another trial balloon in July for the improvement of relations between Moscow and Riyadh. Writing in *Literaturnaia Gazeta*, Igor Belyayev, citing the statement of Saudi Defense Minister Prince Sultan that "in the end, it turns out that the US is only a colossus with feet of clay," noted that "certain members of the ruling family think it is time to resume diplomatic relations with the Soviet Union as well as with other Socialist countries." Belyayev also noted that the Soviet position on Camp David "coincides completely, for all practical purposes, with the position of the Wahabi Kingdom," and he also stated, a bit prematurely, that Saudi Arabia was making a "fundamental change" in its security doctrine. Belyayev asserted that because of US-spread rumors about the Saudi ruling family, American support for Camp David, and Saudi unhappiness about the abortive Iran rescue mission, the "special relationship" between the US and Saudi Arabia was coming to an end.[48]

While Saudi Arabia was to respond negatively to the Soviet trial balloon,[49] Saudi–American relations remained troubled and, in August, Saudi Arabia moved closer to Iraq as Saddam Hussein and King Khalid, in the first visit of an Iraqi leader to Saudi Arabia since 1958, jointly threatened to cut off aid to any nation which recognized Jerusalem as Israel's capital. Moscow could only welcome this development, as it further focused attention on Israeli actions while also appearing to pull Saudi Arabia farther away from the United States.

If the United States was encountering difficulty in rallying many Arab states in support of Camp David, it was having more success in improving its military position in the region. Thus, the United States and Turkey signed a major defense agreement in January 1980, and the military coup which took place in Turkey in September seemed to arrest that country's slide into anarchy. The US position was also bolstered by Greece's decision to return to NATO.[50] In the cases of both Greece and Turkey, the decisions of the national leadership to establish a closer military relationship with the United States seem to have been, at least in part, a consequence of the Soviet invasion of Afghanistan.

In addition to strengthening military relations with Turkey and Greece, the US was also successful in arranging military cooperation with Somalia, Oman, and Kenya. In addition, while not formally having a base in Egypt, the US began to develop a major military relationship with that country as by the spring and early summer of 1980 Egyptian and American forces began to carry out joint maneuvers. Needless to say, Moscow was very unhappy with these developments and used the joint US–Egyptian maneuvers to castigate Sadat as a traitor to the Arab cause.

An *Izvestia* article on July 15 summarized Moscow's concerns with

the growth of American military power in the Middle East and its efforts
to portray this development as a threat to Middle Eastern states:

> The US is speeding the implementation of its plans to create Middle
> Eastern "base states" where it could station large contingents of
> American military personnel, and the question is not one of deploying
> individual units, but, as observers point out – entire divisions together
> with the American fleet and the "rapid deployment force." Their
> purpose is to be the American militarists' "strike force" in the Middle
> East.
>
> Whom will the American bayonets be aimed against? First and fore-
> most against the national liberation processes that are taking place in
> the region and against those countries that oppose the dictat of the
> American oil companies. It is also no secret that the American forces
> could be used at any moment to seize the petroleum resources of that
> very rich area of the world.[51]

As Soviet concern grew over the rise in US military power in the
Middle East, increasing Soviet concern over internal developments in
Iran was also evident. While Moscow remained supportive of the
Islamic fundamentalists who insisted on holding onto the hostages, the
Soviet leadership was less happy with other actions of this group which
included the purging and closing of Iran's universities, and the growing
emphasis on the Islamization of Iranian society which seemed to give
little chance for left-wing groups to operate openly. Meanwhile, the
second stage of the Iranian parliamentary elections had brought about a
victory for the representatives of the Islamic Republican Party, a
development which, when combined with the revision of the new con-
stitution giving Khomeini almost total power, seemed to ensure the
further Islamization of Iranian life.[52]

While Moscow has always been willing to tolerate suppression of local
communists and left-wing forces so long as a country had good relations
with the USSR and was following an "anti-imperialist" foreign policy
line, its patience appeared to wear thin with Iran at the end of June
when Foreign Minister Ghotbzadeh expelled the First Secretary of the
Soviet Embassy in Iran, Vladimir Golvanov, on charges of espionage,
and followed this up two days later by again sharply criticizing the USSR
and ordering Moscow to reduce the size of its diplomatic personnel in
Iran to nine – the number of Iranian diplomats in the USSR.[53] Ghotbzadeh also stated that the Tudeh party was taking advantage of Iran's
preoccupation with the US hostages to conduct activities benefiting the

USSR. Two days later an estimated 500,000 Iranians marched in Tehran demanding the dissolution of the Fedayeen, Mujahadeen, and other left-wing groups.[54] Perhaps reacting to the rise in anti-leftist spirit as well as the denunciations by Ghotbzadeh, Moscow demanded more security at its embassy in Tehran, claiming that it had information that "elements hostile to the USSR" planned to seize the embassy.[55] While the Soviet embassy was not attacked at that time, the Tudeh party, which had been denounced by Ghotbzadeh, had its offices stormed on July 22 by a mob of Islamic militants.[56]

As the government of Iran took an increasingly hostile position toward the USSR, despite its continuing confrontation with the United States, Moscow continued to seek to convince the Iranians that they needed a good relationship with the USSR for protection against the United States. Thus *Pravda* on July 26 noted that the base agreement which the US had just signed with Oman, "unquestionably threatens the independence and national sovereignty of the Persian Gulf states, above all Iran." In addition, Moscow claimed that the United States was behind the major coup attempt against the Khomeini regime in July.[57] A *New Times* commentary on the abortive coup also noted that Iran suffered from the attempts of "some influential forces within the country to isolate it from its friends, the Soviet Union included." The commentary went on to say that these forces were "systematically conducting propaganda hostile to the USSR, slandering Soviet foreign policy, and distorting its character and aims so as to dull the vigilance of the Iranian people and distract their attention from the insidious acts of US imperialism." The *New Times* article also implicitly criticized Iran's Muslim fundamentalists by attacking "counter-revolutionaries who were inciting groups of religious fanatics to action against the democratic and other leftist forces, in particular against the Tudeh party, which backs Ayatollah Khomeini's anti-imperialist line."[58] While seeking to demonstrate the USSR's "true friendship" with Iran, Moscow also undertook a series of very sharp criticisms of Foreign Minister Ghotbzadeh,[59] culminating with a major attack in *Pravda* on August 27 which called him a man of "pro-American orientation" who "hopes to undermine relations" between Iran and the USSR and "weaken Iran's efforts to achieve independence." The *Pravda* article also warned Iran, "it is common knowledge that when Soviet–Iranian ties weakened, the aggressors stepped up their intrigues and subversive activity against Iran."

Neither Ghotbzadeh, nor Bani Sadr, who also was subjected to Soviet criticism, seemed cowed by the Soviet threats. Thus, on August 14, Ghotbzadeh strongly attacked the USSR in a letter to Soviet Foreign Minister Gromyko that was also broadcast on Tehran radio. In it Ghotbzadeh asserted that the USSR was no less "Satanic" than the US, and accused Moscow of giving arms and satellite intelligence photos to Kurdish rebels fighting for autonomy, and having its embassy and consulates spy on Iran. Ghotbzadeh also told Gromyko that Iran "shall not forget how the Soviet government treated our people during the past half century," in particular "the occupation of part of our sacred land and the emergence of a party which, since its founding, has served as a fifth column for your country in our beloved land."[60]

While Moscow's relations with Bani Sadr and Ghotbzadeh deteriorated, the Soviet leadership evidently held out hope for the new Prime Minister, Islamic fundamentalist Ali Rajai,[61] who took office in August, as well as the Ayatollah Beheshti, head of the Islamic Republican party, whom *New Times* Middle East specialist Dmitry Volsky cited as saying that Soviet–Iranian relations "are of a constructive nature and have a good chance of developing."[62] Apparently, Moscow reasoned that while Bani Sadr wanted the hostages released so that Iran could get on with its economic development, the hard-line Islamic Republicans, for whom Islamic purity took priority over economic development, would continue to drag out the hostage confinement, thereby preventing any Iranian–American reconciliation. While the Soviet leaders were far from happy with the suppression of Iran's leftist groups and ethnic minorities, particularly the Kurds who again began to receive favorable Soviet press coverage, at the very least Moscow seemed hopeful that the continued holding of the hostages would keep Iran out of the American camp and on the "anti-imperialist" path. Unfortunately for the USSR, however, the outbreak of war between Iran and Iraq appeared to change the hostage equation in Iranian politics and once again held out the possibility of a *rapprochement* between Iran and the United States, and also led to a major realignment in Arab politics.

The Iran–Iraq War

Tension had been building between Iran and Iraq almost from the time that Ayatollah Khomeini took power. Khomeini, who had been expelled from his place of exile in Iraq at the request of the Shah, was seen by the Iraqi leadership as a threat to the loyalty of its Shiite population, among whom Khomeini had lived for fifteen years. At the same time, Iran saw Iraq as a cause of the unrest in the Arab-populated province of Khuzistan. Behind these concerns were two very dfferent conceptions of the future. Iraq, which was seeking to become the leader of the Arab world, emphasized Arabism aş its main propaganda theme and in February 1980 issued a Pan-Arab charter in an effort to rally the Arab states behind its leadership. By contrast, the central theme for Iran was Islam, and Ayatollah Khomeini and his entourage, who made no secret of their desire to export Iran's Islamic revolution, sought to rally the Muslim world, both Arab and non-Arab, behind the banner of Islam. Superimposed on this conflict was the historic Gulf rivalry between Arab and Persian, and by April 1980 when a serious border conflict broke out between Iran and Iraq it seemed clear that each was trying to undermine the other's government. Indeed, Iraqi President Saddam Hussein blamed Iran for the grenade attack against Deputy Premier Tariq Aziz, and, in retaliation, expelled thousands of Iraqi Shiites of Iranian parentage, and demanded the renegotiation of the 1975 Iran–Iraq Treaty.[63] For their part, Ghotbzadeh and Khomeini pledged to overthrow the Iraqi regime which they depicted as the agent of the United States, and Bani Sadr delivered the ultimate insult to Iraq by claiming that Arab nationalism – Ba'athist or otherwise – was anti-Islamic and equivalent to Zionism.[64] Iran also claimed that Iraq was behind the assassination attempt against Ghotbzadeh when the Iranian Foreign Minister was visiting Kuwait.

For its part, Moscow was very uncomfortable as the Iran–Iraq conflict heated up in April, as it appeared that the USSR might have to choose sides. While Soviet reporting of the conflict reflected a relatively neutral position, Radio Moscow seemed a bit more sympathetic to Iran[65] although the overall theme of Soviet propaganda was that it was a most unfortunate conflict from which only "imperialism" could benefit. From the Soviet point of view a war would only serve to divide the anti-American forces in the Middle East,[66] and Moscow naturally encouraged mediation attempts such as the one undertaken by PLO leader Yasser Arafat in early May. Unfortunately for Moscow, the mediation effort was a failure with Radio Tehran in an Arabic broadcast on May 7 repudiating Arafat's mission:

> The PLO, headed by Arafat, should lead an Arab campaign of confrontation against the terrorist puppet regime in Baghdad, such as the one waged against the As Sadat regime in Egypt. As a matter of fact, the confrontation against the Baghdad regime must be even more severe, because the terrorist puppet regime in Baghdad is just as

dangerous to the Moslem Iraqi people and the Palestine question as the As Sadat regime is to the Arab cause. Moreover, the Baghdad regime's alliance with Israel and the United States is as strong as that of Anwar Sadat.[67]

The Iran–Iraq conflict continued to simmer during the summer and began to directly affect Soviet–Iranian relations in August when the Iranian Ambassador to the Soviet Union, Mohammed Mokri, told an embassy press conference that if Soviet military assistance to Iraq did not end, he doubted that Iran would keep its ambassador in Moscow.[68] The USSR then apparently sought to assuage the Iranians by offering to sell them arms (along with Iraq), albeit unsuccessfully, because two weeks later, Mokri announced at an embassy press conference, that Iran had turned down the offer because it did not want to be a "regional gendarme or waste money on weapons."[69]

When the border skirmishing erupted into a full-scale war in mid-September, the Soviet Union was in a very awkward position as a good argument could have been made in the Kremlin to aid either side. On the one hand, Moscow was linked to Baghdad by a Treaty of Friendship and Cooperation and had long been Iraq's main supplier of military weaponry. In addition, Iraq had been a leading foe of the US-sponsored Camp David agreements and, as a nation with pretensions to leadership in the Arab world, could one day become the focus of the "anti-imperialist" Arab unity which Moscow had sought for so long. Indeed, by its leadership at the two anti-Camp David Baghdad Conferences, Iraq demonstrated a potential for just such a role, and the growing relationship between Iraq and Saudi Arabia that was in evidence before the Iran–Iraq war erupted may have been seen by Moscow as a development that would further move the Saudis out of the American camp. Yet another argument that could have been made in the Kremlin for aiding Iraq was the fact that such aid would be a demonstration to the Arab world that Moscow was indeed a reliable ally (some Arab states had questioned this, despite Soviet aid to the Arab cause in the 1973 war). From the point of view of the Soviet economy, aid to Iraq would help assure the continued flow of Iraqi oil to the USSR and its East European allies.

Soviet opponents of aid to Iraq could point to the continued persecution of Iraqi communists,[70] and Iraq's clear move away from the USSR since the treaty was signed in 1972, as typified by its condemnation of Moscow because of the invasion of Afghanistan,[71] its February 1980 Pan-Arab Charter which called for the elimination of both superpowers from the Arab world,[72] and the growth of its economic and even military ties with France and other West European nations. On balance, however, since the Russians saw Iraq as "objectively" a major anti-Western force, a very good argument could have been made to aid the Iraqis in the war.

On the other hand, however, a very good case could also have been made for aiding Iran. First and foremost, the Khomeini revolution detached Iran from its close alignment with the United States, thereby striking a major blow to the US position in both the Persian Gulf and the Middle East as a whole. In addition, by holding onto the American hostages, the Khomeini regime carried on a daily humiliation of the United States, a factor which further lowered American prestige in the region. Consequently, any major Soviet aid effort to Iraq contained the possibility of ending the hostage impasse (indeed, as the war heated up, the Islamic fundamentalists in Iran suddenly seemed more responsive on the hostage issue and on November 2 the fundamentalist-dominated Parliament voted to release the hostages, albeit conditionally) and even moving Iran back toward the American camp because of Iran's dependence on US military equipment. Given Iran's large population (three times that of Iraq) and its strategic position along the Persian Gulf and at the Strait of Hormuz, such a development would clearly not be in Moscow's interest. Another strategic factor that the Soviet leadership had to take into consideration was that Iran, unlike Iraq, had a common border with the USSR, as well as with Soviet-occupied Afghanistan. While Iranian efforts on behalf of the Afghan rebels had so far been limited, one could not rule out a major increase in Iranian aid to the Afghan rebels should Moscow side with Iraq, as well as a more pronounced effort on the part of Khomeini to infect the USSR's own Muslims with his brand of Islamic fundamentalism.[73] Finally, as in the case of Iraq, there was an important economic argument. While Iran had cut off gas exports to the USSR, the signing of a major transit agreement between the two countries just before the war erupted[74] may well have seemed to Moscow as the first step toward the resumption of natural gas exports, and, given Iran's large available reserves of this fuel, Moscow may have wished to encourage the supply relationship, particularly if – as some experts predicted – the USSR might run short of oil in the mid-1990s.

Soviet opponents of aid to Iran could have pointed to the Islamic fundamentalists' treatment of the Tudeh, although it was not yet as brutal as Iraq's treatment of its communists, as well as its treatment of

Iranian minorities with whom the USSR hoped to cultivate a good relationship. Here again, however, Iran's treatment of its Kurds seemed no worse than Iraq's. Finally, opponents of aid to Iran could have pointed to Iran's leading anti-Soviet role in Islamic conferences, although again there may not have been too much to choose between Iran's and Iraq's anti-Sovietism. The main factor in the Soviet evaluation of both countries was that they seemed far more anti-American than anti-Soviet, and both contributed to the weakening of the American position in the Middle East. For this reason, Moscow needed a good relationship with both and could not afford to alienate either.

Given this situation, it is not surprising that Moscow remained neutral while urging a speedy settlement of the war lest the "imperialists" benefit. Indeed, the outbreak and prolongation of the war brought with it a number of rather serious problems for Moscow. In the first place, there was a major split in the anti-Sadat forces in the Arab world as Libya and Syria came out for Iran, while Jordan openly backed Iraq. In addition to Iraq breaking diplomatic relations with Syria and Libya, Saudi Arabia broke diplomatic relations with Libya,[75] and the Saudis began to increasingly support Iraq. The end result of this was a major disruption of the "anti-imperialist" Arab unity that Moscow had wanted for so long. As *New Times* commentator Alexander Usvatov lamented:

> Fought between two non-aligned countries pursuing anti-imperialist policies, the war is bound to weaken them in the face of intensified imperialist scheming, and sows division and disarray in the world's anti-imperialist front, creating a serious threat to peace and international security.[76]

In addition to the split in the anti-Sadat front, Moscow feared a major American gain in the conflict. The emplacement of American AWACS aircraft and ground radar personnel in Saudi Arabia (following Iranian threats against Saudi Arabia) seemed to demonstrate American willingness to help defend Saudi Arabia and other Arab states in time of need and helped refute Moscow's charge that the US military buildup in the Indian Ocean was a threat to the Arab world. Indeed, the AWACS move appeared to reverse the decline in Saudi–American relations and held out the possibility of a further improvement in relations.[77]

A related problem for the USSR was the formation of the Gulf Cooperation Council, an organization composed of Saudi Arabia, the United Arab Emirates, Oman, Bahrein, Qatar, and Kuwait. Precipitated by both the Soviet invasion of Afghanistan and the Iran–Iraq war, the organization was composed of conservative and basically pro-Western monarchies, three of whose members (Oman, Saudi Arabia, and Bahrein) had military ties to the United States while only one, Kuwait, then had diplomatic relations with the Soviet Union. As the organization took shape,[78] Moscow feared that it would provide both a military and political backdrop for increased American activity in the Persian Gulf, especially since Oman had already agreed to provide a base for the American Rapid Deployment Force.

Finally, as Iraq and Iran continued to bomb each other's oil installations, Moscow became concerned that, once the war was over, both countries might turn to the United States and Western Europe for aid in reconstruction. A *Tass* commentary on October 10 made clear this Soviet concern:

> It is easy to see in these conditions the imperialist powers are quite willing to turn the conflict to their advantage, to capitalize on the economic weakening of Iran and Iraq, so as to grant them imperialist economic aid on their own terms, whose aim will undoubtedly be to restore in those countries the positions of Western oil monopolies, to entangle them in the web of predatory financial agreements, in short, to restore their economic domination.[79]

As the war continued, Moscow appeared to be able to do little but urge its immediate end, proclaim Soviet neutrality, and warn both Iran and Iraq, along with the other countries of the Middle East, that the United States was exploiting the war for its own benefit. The Soviet media also highlighted American efforts to create an international armada to patrol the Persian gulf and emphasized the threat to the region posed by the visit of General David Jones, Chairman of the US Joint Chiefs of Staff, to Oman, Egypt, Saudi Arabia, and Israel.[80] In addition to denouncing American efforts to exploit the war, Moscow seemed to try to maintain some ties with both belligerents by allowing a limited amount of Soviet weaponry to be transshipped to both Iran and Iraq although the USSR publicly denied any such shipments.[81] As its frustration mounted over being unable to affect an end to the conflict which seemed to be greatly strengthening the Middle East position of the United States (and thereby weakening that of the USSR in the zero-sum game view of the Arab world held by Moscow),[82] the Soviet leadership made two moves. The first was to utilize the signing of a Friendship and Cooperation Treaty with Syria as a demonstration of the continued importance of Moscow to the Arab world. A second major Soviet effort was an open appeal for the neutralization of the Persian Gulf – a rather transparent device to reverse the gains made by the US as a result of the war – in a speech made by Brezhnev during the Soviet leader's visit to India in December.

Assad's visit to Moscow in October 1980, three weeks after the outbreak of the Iran–Iraq war, was highlighted by the signing of a Friendship and Cooperation Treaty between Syria and the Soviet Union. This document seemed to give the USSR a stronger foothold in Syria at a time when that country, as well as the entire Middle East, was wracked by the Iran–Iraq war. Given the fact that the USSR had long been pressing Assad to sign such a document, the treaty must be considered a victory for Soviet policy although Assad's growing domestic and foreign isolation appear to be the prime cause for his willingness to sign it. The Israeli–Egyptian peace treaty and the growing normalization between the two countries left Syria in a weakened position *vis-à-vis* Israel, while at the same time Syria's growing conflict with Iraq had left it even more exposed. In addition, besides being bogged down in Lebanon, Assad faced a growing internal threat from the Muslim Brotherhood which had been assassinating a number of prominent Alawi figures.[83] Adding to Syria's sense of isolation was a further cooling of its relationship with Jordan, which had become increasingly friendly with Iraq which was granting it a large amount of economic aid.[84] These developments had increased Assad's dependence on the USSR and lay at the root not only of his endorsement of the Soviet invasion of Afghanistan, but also of his decision to finally agree to a Friendship and Cooperation Treaty with Moscow, an action he had been resisting for almost a decade.[85]

Interestingly enough, however, despite the treaty, Assad continued to seek to keep a certain amount of flexibility in his relationship with the USSR. Thus, before signing the treaty with Moscow, he signed a unity agreement with Libya thereby demonstrating that Syria was not as isolated as either its friends or foes may have thought. In addition, despite the outward harmony of the visit, there were clearly continuing disagreements as the final communiqué noted "a thorough and fruitful exchange of opinions" had taken place in an "atmosphere of mutual understanding"[86] – code words for disagreement. Part of the problem may have lain in open Syrian support for Iran in the war while, as mentioned above, the USSR wanted to remain neutral, although Moscow may have leaned a bit in the direction of Syria on this point by warmly praising the Iranian revolution in the joint communiqué. For its part Syria endorsed the Soviet position on Afghanistan, stressed the need for Soviet participation in all stages of a Middle Eastern settlement and proclaimed Syria's willingness to "continue to repulse any attempts to undermine Soviet–Arab friendship." As far as Soviet military assistance was concerned, the joint communiqué merely stated that "questions of the USSR providing further assistance to Syria in strengthening her defense capability were discussed during the talks and relevant decisions adopted."

The treaty itself was a fairly standard Soviet Friendship and Cooperation Treaty, unique only in its denunciation of "Zionism as a form of racism" both in the preamble and in article 3.[87] Moscow, perhaps to maintain Syria's independent image, stated that it would "respect the policy of non-alignment pursued by Syria" (however, similar language had been used in the Soviet–Afghan Treaty of Friendship and Cooperation of December 1978).[88] As in other treaties, both sides promised to consult regularly, and to consult immediately in the case of situations jeopardizing the peace and security of one of the parties. In the area of military cooperation, article 10 of the treaty stated that "the parties shall continue to develop cooperation in the military field on the basis of appropriate agreements concluded between them in the interest of strengthening their defense capability." Essentially, the treaty codified the existing relationship between the USSR and Syria, and in the absence of any secret military clauses,[89] served to provide a formal foundation for the improved Syrian–Soviet relationship. Thus Moscow was assured of a formal presence in the very heart of the Arab world (the other Soviet Friendship and Cooperation Treaties still in effect with Arab states were with peripheral Iraq and South Yemen), while also formally demonstrating Soviet support for Syria in the face of its conflicts with surrounding Arab states and Israel.

Yet, for Moscow, the signing of the Treaty with Assad and the provision of additional military aid posed a number of problems. In the first place, beset by internal and external difficulties Assad might provoke an international crisis, either with Israel, or with one of his Arab enemies, and then drag in the USSR. Secondly, Assad, who had demonstrated his independence of Moscow on a number of occasions in the past, might do so again, thus complicating Soviet Middle Eastern policy at a time when, because of the Iran–Iraq war, Soviet policy was already in a state of disarray. Indeed, in the crisis with Jordan in late November 1980, and in the Lebanese "missile crisis" with Israel which began in April 1981,[90] Assad was to demonstrate just such an independent turn.

The war between Iran and Iraq continued through November and directly affected the Arab summit conference scheduled for the end of the month in Amman, Jordan. Fearing that the Arab states would condemn it for aiding non-Arab Iran in the war, Syria boycotted the conference and pressured Lebanon and the PLO to do so as well, while Libya (which was also aiding Iran), Algeria, and South Yemen, the other members of the Steadfastness Front also boycotted the meeting. The Syrian-led boycott of the Arab summit was a blow to Moscow's efforts to help rebuild "anti-imperialist" unity in the Arab world. An even more serious problem for Moscow took place in the aftermath of the summit when Syrian forces mobilized on Jordan's border in an effort to pressure King Hussein. Syria claimed that it was mobilizing because King Hussein was providing a base for the Muslim Brotherhood for its attacks on his regime, but it seems more likely that Assad was trying to punish Hussein for hosting the Arab summit which came out in support of Iraq in the Iran–Iraq war. In any case Moscow was pulled into the situation because Assad chose the time of the visit by Soviet Politburo member Vasili Kuznetzov, who had come to Damascus to transmit the Soviet–Syrian treaty ratification papers, to stage the crisis. In doing this, Assad clearly tried to demonstrate that Moscow backed him in the crisis. For his part, perhaps to dispell this impression, Kuznetzov in his Damascus speech at the height of the crisis, stressed the Soviet–Syrian treaty's importance in "eliminating hotbeds of dangerous tension in the Near East," and called for the peaceful solution of problems between Arab countries.[91] In any case, while Saudi Arabia was to ultimately mediate the crisis, the confrontation between Syria and Jordan helped to halt the slow *rapprochement* between Moscow and Amman (Hussein postponed a planned visit to Moscow) while once again reinforcing American–Jordanian ties which had been strained since Camp David. Indeed, Hussein turned to Washington with a request for arms to counter what he called a Soviet-backed threat to the security of his country.[92] Furthermore, as a result of the Syrian move, Moscow may well have felt that Jordan was more susceptible to American pressure to join the Camp David peace process.[93]

If the signing of the treaty with Syria was to cause Moscow more trouble than it expected, the Brezhnev visit to India and the proclamation of the Brezhnev plan for the neutralization of the Persian Gulf was not to prove much more efficacious. In many ways, India was an almost ideal place for Brezhnev to launch his Persian Gulf plan, which, like the Soviet Middle East peace plan launched at the height of the Lebanese civil war of 1976, seemed aimed at regaining the initiative for the Soviet Union at a time when Middle Eastern developments seemed out of Moscow's control.[94] The Indian government of Indira Ghandi was concerned about the growing military ties between the United States and Pakistan and by Chinese military aid to Pakistan. Indeed, these developments, coupled with the US military deployment in the Indian Ocean and the victory of Republican presidential candidate Ronald Reagan may have brought back memories of an earlier Republican administration's "tilt" to Pakistan in 1971. As a consequence, Indira Ghandi clearly felt the need for a close tie with Moscow, and the Russians, who had signed a major arms deal with India only a few months earlier, moved to reinforce the relationship further by agreeing to significantly increase Soviet shipments of oil and oil products to India to help compensate it for the petroleum imports lost because of the outbreak of the Iran–Iraq war.[95] In return for Soviet military, political, and economic support, India provided an important service to Moscow. As the largest non-aligned state, and as both one of the founders of the movement and the host of the February 1981 Non-aligned Conference, Indian political support for Moscow could be expected to assuage some of the non-aligned nations' unhappiness with Moscow because of its invasion of Afghanistan. Indeed, the final communiqué issued after the Brezhnev visit did not even mention Afghanistan and stated only that a "negotiated political solution alone can guarantee a durable settlement of the existing problems of the region," thereby echoing Moscow's call for Iran and Pakistan to begin negotiations with the pro-Soviet Afghan government. In addition, the communiqué also called for the dismantling of all foreign military and naval bases in the area "such as Diego Garcia" and the prevention of the creation of new bases, along with the return of Diego Garcia to Mauritius – a clear anti-American position.[96]

In addition to reaching agreement with India on these issues, Brezhnev also utilized his visit to call for the neutralization of the Persian Gulf. Given the importance of the Brezhnev plan, which received extensive publicity in the Soviet press, the five-point proposal, which was included in Brezhnev's speech to the Indian Parliament, is here printed in its entirety:

> We propose to the United States, other Western powers, China, Japan, all of the states which will show interest in this, to agree on the following mutual obligations:

Not to establish foreign military bases in the area of the Persian
   Gulf and adjacent islands; not to deploy nuclear or any other
   weapons of mass destruction there.

Not to use and not to threaten with the use of force against the
   countries of the Persian Gulf area, not to interfere in their
   internal affairs.

To respect the status of non-alignment, chosen by Persian Gulf
   states; not to draw them into military groupings with the
   participation of nuclear powers.

To respect the sovereign right of the states of the region to their
   natural resources.

Not to raise any obstacles or threats to normal trade exchange
   and the use of sea lanes that link the states of that region with
   other countries of the world.[97]

   It seems clear that the Brezhnev plan had three main goals: (1) revers-
ing the diplomatic and military gains which had accrued to the United
States as a result of the war, and the US naval buildup in the region, by
the call for the elimination of all "foreign" military bases; (2) preventing the formation of a Western-linked Persian Gulf security pact based
on a US-armed and supported Saudi Arabia, by the prohibition of
military groupings of Persian Gulf states linked to nuclear powers; and
(3) championing Iranian interests against the United States through the
call for free use of the sea lanes and normal trade exchange (the United
States had been considering a naval blockade against Iran as a step
toward freeing the hostages).[98]
   While the Brezhnev plan was warmly received in India, it was rejected by the United States and received only a mixed welcome in the
Middle East. If one of the goals of the Brezhnev plan was to win support
in Iran for Soviet policies, the Soviet plan did not meet with success.
Indeed, as the Iranian–American negotiations toward release of the
hostages moved into high gear, Soviet–Iranian relations appeared to
deteriorate as Afghan refugees stormed the Soviet embassy in Tehran
on the anniversary of the Soviet invasion of Afghanistan and burned the
Soviet flag. While Moscow strongly protested the action of "the unruly
mob" and called for the punishment of the attackers and their
organizers,[99] the official Iranian reply, while somewhat apologetic, said
the attackers were justified in their actions.[100] It is doubtful whether the
Soviet leaders noted the irony inherent in the Iranian statement since

only a year before the Soviet press had used similar terms in justifying the Iranian seizure of the American embassy in Tehran.

Nonetheless, the USSR apparently swallowed its anger, and Soviet broadcasts to Iran continued to emphasize that the USSR wanted friendly relations with Iran.[101] One cause of the Soviet effort to continue to seek close ties to Iran despite the embassy incident was the speed-up of the Iranian–American talks on freeing the hostages. Indeed as the date for the Carter administration's departure from office neared, the pace of the talks intensified and it appeared that an agreement might well be reached before Ronald Reagan took office. In an effort to prevent such a development, the Soviet media began to print and broadcast to Iran reports of an imminent American attack on that country,[102] and brushed aside American complaints that the Soviet broadcasts were harming the negotiations.[103] The Soviet ploy was ultimately to fail, however, and on January 20, 1981, the day Ronald Reagan was inaugurated, the hostages were finally released, thanks, in part, to the aid of Steadfastness Front member Algeria which played an important mediating role.

Moscow's response to the Reagan administration's Middle East policy

In surveying their Middle Eastern position at the time that the Reagan Administration took office, the Soviet leaders may well have felt that their position was a mixed one. In the first place, despite the divisions in the Arab world, Sadat remained isolated because of Camp David which no other Arab state had endorsed. In addition, Moscow had close relations with the Front of Steadfastness and Confrontation (Syria, Libya, Algeria, South Yemen, and the PLO) who were the most vocal of the anti-Sadat nations in the Arab world and who dutifully echoed the Soviet policy on such issues as Afghanistan in return for Soviet military aid and diplomatic support (Algeria was a partial exception to this pattern). In addition, Moscow had good relations with non-Arab and non-Muslim Ethiopia, a key African, as well as Middle Eastern, state, although at the cost of alienating Somalia which had gone over to the United States and which had granted the US port facilities as well as a base for the American Rapid Deployment Force. While benefiting from its increasingly close ties to Ethiopia and the Steadfastness Front, Moscow also faced a number of problems. In the first place, while the Steadfastness Front Arab states and Ethiopia were willing to overlook

the Soviet invasion of Afghanistan, both Iran and the Centrist,* or so-
called moderate, Arab states denounced the Soviet action, and
Moscow's efforts to demonstrate its fidelity to the Muslim cause by
championing Iran in its conflict with the United States over the hostages
and by diverting Muslim attention from the situation in Afghanistan to
the Arab–Israeli conflict had met with only limited success. The other
negative developments Moscow had to be concerned about as Reagan
took office included a possible reconciliation between Iran and the US,
the increasing diplomatic acceptability of the US military forces in the
Persian Gulf, a very severe split in the anti-Sadat grouping of Arab
states, and the possibility that Centrist Arab states like Jordan and
Saudi Arabia might yet be drawn into the American-sponsored Camp
David peace process. Moscow was soon to try to reverse these negative
trends.

By the time the CPSU convened its 26th Congress on February 23,
1981, the outline of the Reagan Administration's Middle East policy
was already clear. The US was seeking to build an anti-Soviet alliance of
Middle East states, regardless of their mutual conflicts, thereby pursuing a policy that was the mirror image of Soviet efforts to build an "anti-
imperialist" bloc in the region. In his speech to the CPSU Congress,
Brezhnev outlined the thrust of the Soviet response to the Reagan
policy and to the negative trends in the Middle East which had
hampered Moscow in its quest for influence in the region.[104] In the first
place, to counterbalance the growing military power of the United
States in the Persian Gulf and Indian Ocean region, and the growing
diplomatic acceptability of that presence because of both the Soviet
invasion of Afghanistan and the Iran–Iraq war, the Soviet leader
reiterated his call, first made in India in mid-December 1980, for an
international agreement to neutralize the Persian Gulf. The Soviet
leader also offered – for the first time – to combine discussions of the
Afghanistan situation with that of the Persian Gulf although he made it
clear that Afghanistan's internal situation (i.e. its communist government) was not a matter for discussion, and that the USSR would not
withdraw its forces from Afghanistan until the "infiltration of counter-

---

* Saudi Arabia, Kuwait, Jordan, the United Arab Emirates, North Yemen,
   Somalia, Bahrein, Qatar, the Sudan, Morocco, and Tunisia. Iraq, which at the
   time shared the Steadfastness stated goal of destroying Israel, but which was not
   a member of the Steadfastness Front because of its enmity toward Syria, also
   denounced the invasion while opposing Camp David. The Centrist Arab states
   seemed willing to entertain the idea of peace with Israel; the Steadfastness
   Front members did not.

revolutionary bands" was completely stopped, and treaties were signed between Afghanistan and its neighbors to ensure that no further infiltration would take place.

As far as the Iran–Iraq war was concerned, the Soviet leader once again called for its immediate termination, and stated that the Soviet Union was taking "practical steps" to achieve that goal. In discussing the Arab–Israeli conflict Brezhnev denounced the Camp David peace process, and again enumerated the tripartite Soviet solution for the conflict: (1) Israeli withdrawal from all territories captured in 1967; (2) the right of the Palestinians to create their own state; and (3) the ensuring of the security of all states in the region, including Israel. Brezhnev also repeated the Soviet call for an international conference on the Arab–Israeli conflict, with the participation of the Arabs, including the PLO, and Israel, along with the United States and some European states. All in all, the Soviet proposals on Afghanistan, the Persian Gulf, and the Arab–Israeli conflict, together with the announced efforts to end the Iran–Iraq war, seemed aimed at placing Moscow at the center stage of Middle Eastern diplomacy, a diplomatic position not enjoyed by the Soviet Union since the 1973 Arab–Israeli war.

Interestingly enough, the Soviet leader also made note in his speech of two related Middle Eastern phenomena to which the USSR was having difficulty in adjusting its policies: the Khomeini revolution in Iran and the rise of fundamentalist Islam. As far as Iran was concerned, Brezhnev noted that "despite its complex and contradictory nature, it is basically an anti-imperialist revolution, although domestic and foreign reaction is seeking to alter this character." Brezhnev also offered Soviet cooperation with Iran (no mention was made of Soviet–Iraqi relations in his speech), but only on the grounds of "reciprocity," perhaps a reference to continuing anti-Soviet speeches and activities in Iran. In discussing Islam, Brezhnev acknowledged that "the liberation struggle could develop under the banner of Islam," but also noted that "experience also indicates that reaction uses Islamic slogans to start counter-revolutionary insurrections."

In the aftermath of the 26th Party Congress, Moscow pursued two diplomatic policies. First, it sought to strengthen its ties with two of its Steadfastness Front allies – Libya and Algeria – with whom there had been some recent difficulties and it also sought to cultivate two Centrist Arab states – Kuwait and Jordan – to prevent them from moving toward the United States.

Libyan leader Muammar Kaddafi arrived in Moscow on April 27 at a time when he was isolated in the Arab world (the alliance with Syria, signed in September 1980 was inoperative)[105] and was also in difficulty with many of his African neighbors because of the Libyan intervention in Chad. Moscow appeared rather ambivalent about Libya's efforts at unity with Chad, in part because of its negative effects on other African states (especially the Sudan and Nigeria), while Kaddafi's ideological pretensions also continued to bother the Soviet leadership. Nonetheless, Kaddafi's vehement anti-Americanism was on balance an asset for Soviet diplomacy while his political isolation and increasing conflict with the United States (the US was to close Libya's diplomatic mission in Washington a week after Kaddafi's visit to Moscow, in part because of Libya's role in supporting international terrorism) made Libya increasingly dependent on the USSR.[106] For his part, Kaddafi, who made no secret of his desire to destroy Israel, continually requested more Soviet aid than Moscow was willing to offer and his request on behalf of the Steadfastness Front for more aid against Israel was made again during his visit to Moscow, his first since 1976.[107] Nonetheless, the final communiqué, which referred to the talks as having taken place in "an atmosphere of broad mutual understanding" (code words for disagreement over several issues), merely praised the Steadfastness Front (no specific promises of aid were announced), and in his welcoming speech, Brezhnev pointedly noted the differences – including ideological differences – between the USSR and Libya. Still, the USSR did go a long way toward legitimizing the Libyan role in Chad, (something Moscow was later to regret) as the final communiqué noted the "positive role that has been played by Libya's aid to Chad."[108] Moscow also denounced US efforts to brand Libya as a terrorist state and supported the Libyan–Algerian position in the dispute over the former Spanish Sahara by endorsing the call for the right of self-determination for the Western Saharan people. While Moscow got Libya's support for the Soviet call to make the Persian Gulf and Indian Ocean areas "zones of peace," Moscow evidently was unable to get Kaddafi's agreement for an international conference on the Arab–Israeli conflict as there was no mention of the conference – long a major Soviet goal – in the final communiqué.[109]

The second Steadfastness state leader to come to Moscow for talks with the Soviet leadership in 1981 was Algerian President Chadli Ben-Jedid who came to the Kremlin on June 8. While the USSR and Algeria had maintained close ties since Algerian independence in 1962, the death of Houari Boumadienne in 1979 had raised questions about the future course of Algerian foreign policy. In addition, despite US military aid to Morocco, the US and Algeria had developed close economic ties. (Interestingly enough, despite Soviet military aid to Algeria, Morocco and the USSR had also developed close economic ties.) Finally, Algeria's role in the freeing of the US hostages in Iran could not have been to Moscow's liking, although the Algerians were to deem it a "debt of honor" in repayment of John F. Kennedy's support of their drive for independence.[110] Nonetheless, the onset of the Reagan administration was to cause a chilling of US–Algerian ties. In the first place the US began to step up its military aid to Morocco, and stated that it would no longer link arms sales to Morocco with Moroccan progress in achieving a negotiated settlement of the Spanish Sahara conflict.[111] Secondly, the long negotiations between Algeria and El Paso Natural Gas on a major US–Algerian natural gas agreement fell through leaving Algeria with an infrastructure expense of $2.5 billion for natural gas wells, pipelines, and liquification plants.[112] Finally, Reagan's general "tough-line" toward the Third World on such issues as the Law of the Sea served to alienate the Algerians. Thus when Ben-Jedid came to Moscow, US–Algerian relations had cooled considerably and Moscow may have looked forward to a further consolidation of Soviet–Algerian relations.

Nonetheless, all was not complete harmony during Ben-Jedid's visit as evidenced by the joint communiqué's assertion that the talks had taken place in an atmosphere of "frankness," and, as in the case of Libya, there was no mention of Algerian support for Brezhnev's call for an international conference on the Middle East.[113] For its part, however, Moscow endorsed Algeria's position on the Sahara conflict, as the communiqué noted that both sides agreed that the people of the Western Sahara had the right of self-determination, and both Algeria and the USSR condemned foreign bases in the Persian Gulf.[114] Moscow also used the Algerian leader's visit to call for the transformation of the Mediterranean into a zone of peace, a maneuver which, if successful, would have meant the ejection of the US Sixth Fleet from the Mediterranean.[115]

In sum, it would appear that in the case of the visits of both Algerian President Chadli Ben-Jedid and Libyan leader Muammar Kaddafi, Moscow gave somewhat more in diplomatic support than it got in return. Nonetheless, at a time when the Middle East was in a great state of flux, with many trends moving in a negative direction as far as the

USSR was concerned, the Soviet leadership seemed willing to pay the diplomatic price to reinforce ties with both states. Interestingly enough, however, Moscow was to meet with greater diplomatic success during the visits of representatives of the Centrist wing in Arab politics, Kuwait and Jordan.

Even before Sheikh Sabah al Ahmad as Sabah of Kuwait and King Hussein of Jordan visited Moscow, a number of the Centrist Arabs seemed to be pulling back from the close tie with the United States which had been precipitated by the Iran–Iraq war.[116] Thus when the new American Secretary of State Alexander Haig toured the Middle East in early April in an effort to rally support for the US plan to create an anti-Soviet alignment while putting the Arab–Israeli dispute on the diplomatic "back burner," he met with little success as two of the Arab states he visited, Jordan and Saudi Arabia, indicated that they were more concerned with what they perceived as the threat from Israel (Saudi Arabia said this explicitly) than the threat from the Soviet Union.[117] In addition, fighting had once again escalated in Lebanon and Haig took the opportunity to condemn Syria strongly for its "brutal" actions in that country, a move not calculated to drive a wedge between Damascus and Moscow. The lack of success of the Haig visit arrested the momentum of American policy in the region, and set the stage for some diplomatic successes by the Soviet Union during the visits of Sheik Sabah and King Hussein.

Kuwait, whose Deputy Premier Sheik Sabah visited Moscow on April 23, was a key target of Soviet diplomacy. As the only state in the Gulf Cooperation Council (GCC) with diplomatic relations with Moscow, it was also the most "non-aligned" and the Soviet leaders evidently hoped to use Kuwait's influence within the GCC (it is the second most important country after Saudi Arabia) to prevent that organization from committing itself too closely to the American side. For its part Kuwait had been carefully cultivating a relationship with the USSR since 1975, the last time Sheik Sabah had journeyed to Moscow. Then, as in April 1981, Kuwait's regional problems made it seek protection.[118] In 1975 Kuwait was confronted with territorial demands by Iraq; in 1981, while relations had improved with Iraq, a far more serious problem lay on its border with Iran whose warplanes were occasionally bombing and strafing Kuwaiti territory because of Kuwaiti aid to the Iraqi war effort. Under these circumstances, the Kuwaitis evidently felt they needed support not only from the United States whose ability to aid Kuwait was increasingly in doubt since the fall of the Shah, but from the Soviet Union as well, and the Kuwaiti deputy Premier, who was also his country's foreign minister, went a long way toward meeting his hosts' diplomatic needs during his visit to Moscow.[119] Thus not only did he denounce Camp David, he also came out in favor of an international conference on the Middle East, thereby supporting a cardinal Soviet goal, something neither Libya nor Algeria was willing to do. In addition he also announced Kuwait's opposition to the creation of foreign military bases in the Persian Gulf, thus supporting yet another central Soviet foreign policy goal. Finally, he joined Moscow in calling for an international conference on the Indian Ocean aimed at turning it into a "zone of peace" thereby supporting another Soviet diplomatic ploy to eliminate the US military presence from the region.[120]

To be sure, there were areas of disagreement during the talks in which *Pravda* reported a "detailed exchange of views."[121] Probably the most important issue of disagreement was Afghanistan (Kuwait continued to oppose the Soviet presence in Afghanistan) of which no mention was made in the formal communiqué. Nonetheless, on balance it was a most successful visit as far as Moscow was concerned since it was able to obtain Kuwaiti support for a number of major Soviet Middle East policies.

The visit of Jordan's King Hussein in late May could also be considered a diplomatic success for Moscow. The USSR had been seriously concerned that because of Syrian military pressure, Hussein might be pushed back into the American camp and into support of Camp David (Jordan had distanced itself from the United States in 1978 because of Camp David). Perhaps heightening Soviet concern was the so-called "Jordanian option" which was being promoted by Israeli Labor Party leader Shimon Peres. Until May 1981, Peres's Labor Party was leading all the Israeli public opinion polls for the election scheduled for June 30 and Moscow may have seen a Peres victory as yet another enticement for Jordan to become involved in Camp David. For its part, however, since the 1978 Baghdad Conference, Jordan was very much a Centrist Arab state and saw far more benefit in maintaining close ties with Iraq and Saudi Arabia (which subsidized a considerable portion of the Jordanian economy) than in joining Israel and Egypt in the highly ambiguous autonomy negotiations.[122] By 1981, the once-isolated Jordanian monarch was now part of the general Arab consensus against Camp David, although Jordan's bitter dispute with Syria continued to simmer. The Syrian–Jordanian conflict (along with the Syrian–Israeli crisis over the emplacement of Syrian missiles in Lebanon)[123] was undoubtedly one of the topics of discussion between Brezhnev and Hussein, and *Pravda*'s reference to the talks having taken place in a "business-like atmosphere" may very well have referred to disagreements over Syria.[124] It is, in fact, possible that Hussein may have asked the USSR to use its influence with Syria to ease its pressure against Jordan, in return for Jordanian willingness to endorse Moscow's views on a number of key Middle Eastern issues. First and foremost was the convening of an international conference on the Middle East. Both in his speech at the welcoming banquet[125] and in the final communiqué Hussein supported this Soviet goal, thereby also demonstrating his opposition to the Camp David process. In addition Hussein also joined Moscow in opposing foreign bases in the Persian Gulf, thus supporting another key Soviet goal. Given the fact that the Jordanian Defense Minister accompanied Hussein, the groundwork may have also been laid during this visit for the subsequent Soviet–Jordanian SAM arms deal, as the joint communiqué noted that the two sides had agreed to work on further increasing trade, economic, cultural, and other (i.e. military related) matters. All in all, Moscow was quite pleased by Hussein's visit and *New Times* correspondent Alexander Usvatov summarized Moscow's satisfaction:

> It is no secret that Tel Aviv and Washington have always regarded Jordan as a "weak link" in the Arab world, counting on drawing it by hook or by crook into the separate Camp David process and into their anti-Arab and anti-Soviet plans.
>
> The results of King Hussein's talks with Leonid Brezhnev and other Soviet leaders were a disappointment for those who entertained such hopes.[126]

While Moscow had gained considerable diplomatic mileage from the visits of Jordan's King Hussein and Kuwait's Sheik Sabah, the diplomatic shift by Sudanese President Jaafar Nimeri ran counter to the Soviet goal of keeping Egypt isolated in the Arab world. Under pressure from Libyan forces in Chad (again, Moscow must have wondered if the Libyan move into Chad was of benefit to the USSR), Nimeri decided to come out in support of Sadat's Camp David policy by restoring full diplomatic relations with Egypt at the end of March and urging the other Arabs to do so as well. Further angering Moscow was the Sudanese offer of military bases to the US – if the United States would upgrade them first.[127] Moscow's unhappiness was reflected in an *Izvestia* commentary on April 14, two days after the Sudanese Ambassador returned to Cairo:

> Egypt is doing everything in its power to try to break out of its political isolation without renouncing Camp David and its commitment to the U.S. and Israel. It sees its rapprochement with the Sudan as a way out. But does Sudan need to come to Sadat's aid, especially on an anti-Libyan basis? Wouldn't it be better to remain with Libya in a single Arab family that resolutely condemns Egypt's capitulatory policy and shameful deal with Israel?

> Cairo is suffocating in its isolation. It is playing up to Khartoum and trying to take on the role of intermediary in relations between Sudan and the U.S., promising Sudan bags of dollars and piles of American weapons.[128]

Despite the Sudanese shift back toward Egypt, on balance Moscow's Middle Eastern diplomatic position had clearly improved by the spring of 1981, and the USSR was to try and exploit a series of Middle Eastern crises in the spring and summer to improve its position still further.

Moscow and the Middle East crises of 1981

The Syrian missile crisis

The first major crisis which the USSR sought to exploit, albeit very carefully, was the crisis over the emplacement of Syrian anti-aircraft missiles in Lebanon, a crisis which was also of considerable benefit to Syria.

At the outbreak of the April fighting in Lebanon, in which Syria attacked Phalangist positions in Beirut and near Zahle, a Christian Lebanese city which lay astride a major Syrian communication route into Lebanon (the Phalange was seeking to consolidate a communication link between Zahle and the Christian positions in Northern Lebanon), Syria remained in a state of isolation in the Arab world, primarily because of its support for Iran in the Iran–Iraq war. In addition, because Saudi Arabia and Kuwait had cut off funds for the Syrian force in Lebanon, Syria's economic position had weakened, a development exacerbated by the continuing domestic unrest in Syria. When Syrian attacks against the Christians near Zahle escalated, Israel responded by shooting down two Syrian helicopters involved in the operation. Syria responded by moving surface-to-air missiles across the border into Lebanon opposite Zahle, thus breaking the tacit agreement with Israel made in 1976 whereby Israel did not interfere with the Syrian invasion of Lebanon, so long as no SAM missiles were moved into Lebanon and no Syrian forces were sent to South Lebanon. Israeli Prime Minister Begin who appeared to be motivated during the crisis at least in part by electoral considerations, responded by saying that if the missiles were not moved back into Syria, Israel would destroy them. The crisis was on.

While the exact nature of the Soviet role in the missile crisis is not yet known, several things do appear clear. In the first place, Assad's decision to move the missiles seems to have caught the USSR by surprise (as in the November 1980 crisis with Jordan, Assad apparently took action without consulting Moscow – despite the Soviet–Syrian treaty)[129] and it was not until more than a week after the crisis began that Moscow made any public comment about it. Indeed, Moscow did not make any public comments about the crisis until after it became clear that other Arab countries, particularly such Centrist states as Saudi Arabia and Kuwait, were rallying to Syria's side.[130] Such a development benefited the USSR by moving its client out of isolation in the Arab world, and held out the possibility of rebuilding the anti-imperialist Arab unity that Moscow continued to hope for. An additional benefit flowing to the Soviet Union from the missile crisis was that it served to further weaken the American effort to build an anti-Soviet bloc of Arab states and further complicated relations between Saudi Arabia, which promised to aid Syria, and the United States, Israel's main supporter, at a time when relations had already become strained over Congressional opposition to the AWACs sale to Saudi Arabia.[131] Yet another benefit of the crisis for Soviet diplomacy, albeit a fleeting one, lay in the fact that in the initial stages of the conflict the United States sought Soviet assistance in defusing it,[132] thereby once again demonstrating the importance of the Soviet Union to Middle East peace-making. Although the US was not pleased by the subsequent lack of Soviet assistance during the crisis, Brezhnev was also to exploit it to repeat Moscow's call for an international conference to solve the crisis.

While Moscow sought to exploit the missile crisis for its own benefit; once that crisis was underway, the USSR faced a number of dangers as well. First and foremost was the possibility that a full-scale war between Syria and Israel might erupt, into which Moscow could be drawn. For Moscow, this was not an opportune time for such a war. With Reagan now willing to allow grain sales to the USSR and considering the resumption of the stalled SALT talks (a key Soviet priority), any major

Middle Eastern war in which Moscow got involved might well reinforce the basically anti-Soviet tendency of the Reagan administration, doom the SALT talks, and possibly reverse Reagan's decision on grain sales. While Moscow, as well as Damascus, would profit from the extension of the radar-SAM network to Lebanon,[133] it would be far better for Moscow if this could be done without war. So long as war threatened, but did not break out, the Arabs would rally around Syria, and attention would be focused on the Arab–Israeli conflict – and away from the continuing Soviet occupation of Afghanistan. In addition, Moscow may have feared that a Syrian–Israeli war would bring the collapse of the Syrian regime, one of Moscow's closest allies in the Arab world.[134]

A second problem facing Moscow lay in the fact that President Reagan had sent an experienced trouble shooter, Philip Habib, to the Middle East in early May to try to prevent war. While Moscow and Damascus utilized the respite granted by the Habib mission to strengthen the missile position in Lebanon (Israel was unlikely to strike a blow at the missiles with Habib in the Middle East lest US–Israeli relations be severely damaged), the Soviet leadership had to be concerned that Habib, in his shuttle diplomacy, might succeed in drawing Damascus away from Moscow, much as Kissinger had done in 1974.[135] For this reason Moscow bitterly attacked the Habib mission, claiming it was a device to impose Israel's will on Syria and the other Arabs.[136]

In the face of these dangers Moscow adopted the dual policy of discrediting US mediation efforts while also playing down the possibility of war. This strategy became evident in mid-May as the Soviet Ambassador to Lebanon, Aleksander Soldatov, on May 16, stated that the developments in Lebanon "are unrelated to the Soviet–Syrian treaty."[137] Soldatov's comments may well have been a response to the article which appeared several days earlier in the Syrian journal *al-Ba'ath* which stated that if Israel attacked the SAM batteries it would risk confronting not only Syria and its Arab supporters, but also "the strategic world of Syrian–Soviet friendship and cooperation."[138] Then *Pravda*, in a commentary by Soviet Middle East specialist Pavel Demchenko, on May 17, praised Syria as the main bastion of Arab forces opposed to Camp David and denounced Israel's demand for the removal of the Syrian missiles, which were there for "defensive" purposes, as a maneuver worked out by the US and Israel.[139] Brezhnev himself entered the Middle East commentary with a speech in Tibilisi on May 22 in which he warned of the dangerous situation in the region and blamed Israel and the United States, and also called for international talks to solve the crisis in a peaceful manner.[140] This was also the theme of his speech at the dinner honoring the visit of King Hussein on May 27 in which he also noted that the USSR wanted good relations with Israel.[141] Significantly, in neither speech did he mention the Soviet–Syrian treaty.

As the crisis continued, Syria obtained increasing support for its position from the other Arabs, as an Arab Foreign Minister conference, called on the initiative of Algeria and the PLO in late May, pledged financial support to Syria (Saudi Arabia and Kuwait, which had cut off funds for the Syrian forces in Lebanon, resumed their contributions), and the Arab states pledged "total" military assistance to Syria in case of an Israeli attack on Syrian forces in Lebanon or Syria.[142] Much to Moscow's satisfaction the Arab states also warned the US that continuation of its "unconditional" support to Israel "would lead to a serious confrontation between the Arab nation and the US."[143] Soon after this meeting, however, both Jordan and Iraq qualified their support to Syria, while for its part Syria did not even send a delegation to the Baghdad meeting of Islamic Foreign Ministers called to deal with the Lebanese crisis at the start of June.

The destruction of the Iraqi nuclear reactor

On June 9, however, the missile crisis seemed to pale in importance as another Middle Eastern crisis replaced it in the headlines.[144] On that date Israeli aircraft destroyed an Iraqi nuclear reactor which the vast majority of Israelis feared was being constructed to develop a nuclear weapon for use against Israel. The Israeli action inflamed the Arab world far more than did the Syrian–Israeli confrontation over the Syrian missiles in Lebanon, as many Arabs felt humiliated by the fact that Israeli aircraft, which flew over Jordanian and Saudi airspace on the way to and from Iraq, were able to come and go unscathed while eliminating the most advanced nuclear installation of any Arab country. As might be expected Moscow moved quickly to try to exploit this situation, not only condemning the Israeli raid but also pointing to the fact that the Israeli action was carried out with American-supplied aircraft and that it took place despite – or indeed because of – the US AWACs radar planes operating in Saudi Arabia.[145] Reagan's decision to postpone shipment of additional F-16 fighter-bombers to Israel because of the attack was deprecated by Moscow which sought to exploit the Israeli action by utilizing it to focus Arab attention on the "Israeli threat" to the Arab world (rather than the "Soviet threat") and to undermine the American position in the region as Israel's chief supporter, while at the same time improving Soviet–Iraqi relations. In addition, Moscow evidently hoped that the Israeli attack would help to rebuild the "anti-imperialist" Arab unity which had been so badly dissipated by the Iran–Iraq war. As a commentary by *Pravda* commentator Yuri Glukhov noted on June 16:

> (The Israeli raid) had again demonstrated the extent of the imperialist and Zionist threat hanging over the Arab countries, forcing them to set aside their differences, *which have become more pronounced of late* ...

> In order to carry out their schemes, the Israeli leaders and their patrons have also taken advantage of the situation that has come about in the Persian Gulf zone and the protracted and bloody conflict between Iraq and Iran. In recent months, Baghdad has virtually withdrawn from the Arabs' common front for the struggle to eliminate the consequences of Israeli aggression ...

> The criminal actions of Tel Aviv and its sponsors have demonstrated once again that the only enemy of the Arab peoples is imperialism and its henchmen, and that no task is more important than closing ranks in the face of the danger threatening their vital interests.[146] (emphasis added)

Moscow may have also seen the Israeli raid as undercutting Egyptian efforts to reenter the Arab mainstream, since it took place only a few days after a Begin–Sadat summit. In addition to reestablishing full diplomatic relations with the Sudan, Egypt had sold Iraq thousands of tons of Soviet ammunition and spare parts to aid it in its war with Iran[147] – something noted with displeasure in Moscow which was concerned about Sadat's lessening isolation.[148] Fortunately for Moscow, the Israeli raid did serve to abort, albeit only temporarily, any Iraqi–Egyptian *rapprochement*, despite Sadat's denunciation of the Israeli action.

Moscow, however, was to be less successful in its goal of exploiting the Israeli raid to undermine the US position in the Arab world, and in particular to improve Soviet ties with Iraq. While there had been calls in the Arab world to embargo oil to the US because of the raid, the Reagan administration's decision to join with Iraq in a UN Security Council vote condemning Israel seemed to deflate any such Arab pressures.[149] Indeed, the Iraqi–American cooperation at the UN seemed to set the stage for improved Iraqi–American relations, as Iraqi President Saddam Hussein, on the ABC television program "Issues and Answers" stated his interest in expanding diplomatic contacts with the

United States and announced that he would treat the head of the American interests section in the Belgian Embassy in Baghdad as the head of a diplomatic mission.[150]

In taking this posture, the Iraqi leader appeared to be trying to drive a wedge between the United States and Israel which was very unhappy with the US vote in the UN. On the other hand, Moscow may have seen that the US was seeking to drive a diplomatic wedge between the USSR and Iraq. In any case, Soviet–Iraqi relations had been declining for a number of years and they were not helped by Moscow's position of neutrality in the Iran–Iraq war. A further deterioration in Soviet–Iraqi relations had come in February 1981 at the 26th CPSU Congress (which the Iraqi Ba'athists had not attended) when the head of the Iraqi communist party Aziz Mohammed denounced the Iraqi government for its acts of repression against the ICP and the Iraqi Kurds, and also condemned the Iran–Iraq war and demanded the immediate withdrawal of Iraqi troops from Iran.[151] As Soviet–Iraqi relations were deteriorating, the US moved to improve relations with the regime in Baghdad. Secretary of State Haig noted the possibility of improved Iraqi–American relations in testimony to the Senate Foreign Relations Committee in mid-March (Iraq was seen as concerned by "the behavior of Soviet imperialism in the Middle Eastern area")[152] and followed this up by sending Deputy Assistant Secretary of State Morris Draper to Iraq in early April.[153] To improve the climate for the visit, the US approved the sale to Iraq of five Boeing jetliners.[154] While nothing specific came out of Draper's talks, Washington continued to hope that because of Iraq's close ties with Jordan and Saudi Arabia, the regime in Baghdad might abandon its quasi Steadfastness Front position and move toward a more Centrist position in the Arab world on the issue of making peace with Israel. Indeed, Saddam Hussein himself, in his ABC interview, gave some hints about just such a move. Nonetheless, the future direction of Iraqi policy remained to be determined, especially since, as the Iran–Iraq war dragged on, the possibility existed that Iraq might have to turn back to Moscow to get sufficient arms to score a major victory. Indeed, the report of a large shipment of Soviet tanks to Iraq in the late fall seemed to signal a Soviet desire to improve relations.[155]

The bombing of Beirut

While the furor of the Israeli attack on the Iraqi reactor slowly died, Middle East tensions were kept alive by a number of other events during the summer which Moscow sought to exploit. In the first place, following the reelection of Menahem Begin's Likud party, Israel launched a series of attacks against Palestinian positions in Lebanon in an effort to keep the PLO off balance and keep it from launching terrorist attacks against Israel. The fighting quickly escalated with the PLO shelling towns in Northern Israel and the Israelis bombing PLO headquarters in Beirut, causing a number of civilian casualties in the process. While the US condemned the bombing of Beirut and again delayed the shipment of F-16s to Israel – while at the same time sending Habib back to the Middle East to work out a cease-fire (something that he accomplished in late July) – Moscow seized the opportunity to once again link the Israeli actions to the US, and called for sanctions against Israel.[156] The bombing of Beirut also served to further inflame Arab tempers both against Israel and against the United States (there were once again calls for an oil boycott of the United States and heavy criticism of American support of Israel not only from the Steadfastness Front but also from such Centrist states as Jordan and Kuwait). All this activity, of course, served to further divert Arab attention from the continued Soviet occupation of Afghanistan while underlining the Soviet claim that it was US-supported Israel, not the Soviet Union, that was the main threat to the Arab world.

The Libyan–American clash over the Gulf of Sidra

The fourth in the series of Middle East crises occurring in 1981 took place in mid-August, and for the first time it was the United States, not Israel, which was directly involved. A number of questions remain about this incident which involved the shooting down of two Libyan interceptor aircraft (SU-22) which had initially fired upon two American aircraft protecting US maneuvers in the Gulf of Sidra, a region Kaddafi claimed as Libyan territorial waters but which the United States (and most of the international community, including the USSR) claimed were international waters.[157] In the first place, was the matter merely an accident in which an overeager Libyan pilot decided to fire his missiles (Libya had been challenging US maneuvers in the Gulf of Sidra for several years and there had already been a number of incidents) or was it deliberately staged by Kaddafi? Secondly, was Moscow involved in the planning of the event, or was it caught by surprise? As far as Libya's planning of the incident is concerned, there are two factors to consider. On the one hand, Kaddafi was out of the country negotiating a treaty in

South Yemen at the time of the incident. On the other hand, however, there were a number of coincidences which, when taken together, lead one to believe that there is a good possibility that Libya may indeed have planned the incident. In the first place, Libya was striving to emerge from its position of isolation in the Arab world, and had restored diplomatic relations with Morocco while also seeking to mend fences with Iraq and Saudi Arabia. Kaddafi may well have noted how Syria moved out of its position of isolation *vis-à-vis* the mainstream Arabs by means of its confrontation with Israel over the missiles in Lebanon, and since Israel did not border Libya, Kaddafi may have wished to utilize a military confrontation with the US – whose reputation among Centrist Arabs had suffered as a result of the Israeli bombings of Beirut and the Iraqi reactor – for a similar purpose. Secondly, since he was in the process of negotiating a tripartite alliance with Ethiopia and the PDRY, he may have wished to use the incident to demonstrate that the alliance was needed against "US imperialism" and was not directed at such Arab states as Saudi Arabia or North Yemen which otherwise might have been concerned about it. Third, an OPEC meeting was beginning in Geneva, and Kaddafi may have wished to use the incident as a backdrop for his demand for higher oil prices.[158] Finally, with a Soviet foreign office delegation led by Aleksey Shvedov visiting the country, and under increasing pressure from the United States, Kaddafi may have wished to utilize the incident as a justification for turning to Moscow for a Treaty of Friendship and Cooperation while ensuring that the US would not escalate its retaliation against Libya.

Whether or not Libya actually planned the incident, it did not take long for Moscow to try to exploit the battle over the Gulf of Sidra for its own benefit. Based on the initial Soviet reaction to the Gulf battle, it appears as if Moscow was caught by surprise. Nonetheless, after a day of reporting the events without commentary, once Moscow appeared certain that there would be no escalation, it began to try to show the Arabs that the incident demonstrated how dangerous it was for them to have an American fleet operating off their shores. Thus in a political commentary broadcast by Tass International Service, Sergei Kulik set a tone for later Soviet treatment of the event:

> In commenting on the reports of the attacks by US fighter planes on Libyan aircraft, many foreign observers agree that this dangerous incident has once again demonstrated the great threat which is created by the constant presence of American naval and air forces on the territories and waters belonging to other states thousands of kilometers

away from the US ... off Africa's eastern coastline, in the Indian Ocean and the Persian Gulf a whole armada of American vessels continues to parade while keeping the oil producing countries of the Near East in their sights.[159]

A French language Soviet broadcast to North Africa on August 26 made this point even more explicit:

> Until now, when Washington concentrated an armada of warships in the Mediterranean and the Persian Gulf, when it created a network of military bases in the vicinity of Arab countries, everybody understood it was a dangerous thing, but not everybody, *far from it*, realized to what extent this was dangerous.

> The US provocation in the Gulf of Sidra has made a great many people look at the American military presence in quite a different light.[160] (emphasis added)

In addition to using the Gulf of Sidra incident to try to lessen the diplomatic acceptability of the US military presence in the Persian Gulf, and also noting the highly negative Arab response to the American role in the incident, Moscow also cited it as justification for the signing of the Tripartite Treaty by Ethiopia, Libya, and South Yemen. The USSR also praised the treaty as "an important stage in strengthening the national liberation movement's solidarity and in stepping up their struggle against imperialism and reaction and for peace and progress."[161]

Moscow also maintained, however (in an apparent effort to reassure Saudi Arabia and North Yemen), that the treaty was "not directed against any other country or people."[162] Nonetheless, the text of the Tripartite Treaty which noted that one of its goals was the struggle against "reaction" – a commonly used term for the conservative Arab states of the Persian Gulf along with Egypt and the Sudan – could only prove counterproductive to Soviet efforts to improve relations with the conservative Gulf states, given the close tie between the Tripartite Treaty nations and Moscow.[163]

The upheaval in Iran

While Moscow was seeking to exploit the Libyan–American clash in the gulf of Sidra to weaken the US position in the Middle East, it was trying to follow the same policy during the upheavals in Iran which witnessed the ouster and escape to Europe of Iranian President Bani Sadr, the assassination of his successor Mohammed Ali Rajai along with a

number of key Iranian Islamic Republican party leaders such as Ayatollah Beheshti, and a series of additional bombings and other attacks
directed against the fundamentalist Khomeini government by the
opposition Mujahadeen.

The central Soviet concern in its policy toward Iran was a fear that
after the hostage release, the United States and Iran might move toward
a *rapprochement*, particularly because of Iranian military requirements
due to the Iran–Iraq war. Fortunately for Moscow, anti-Americanism
remained the central foreign policy theme of the Khomeini regime
during 1981 as it had been the previous year, and the regime's enemies
were usually branded American or Zionist agents. Given Moscow's
previous displeasure with Bani Sadr, his departure was no loss but the
Soviet leadership was quite unhappy with the assassination of Beheshti
whom *Pravda* characterized on July 3 as being "one of the most consistent proponents of an anti-imperialist, anti-American policy."[164] The
bombings at the end of June and at the end of August, while eliminating
a number of top Iranian leaders, gave Moscow the opportunity to
reinforce Tehran's suspicions that the CIA was behind the incidents.
Thus, in a Persian language broadcast immediately after the August
bombings, Moscow radio commentator Igor Sheftunov stated:

> It is impossible to deny Washington's role in the terrorist activities
> against the Islamic Republic of Iran and its leaders. Since the fall of the
> monarchy and the installation of the Islamic Republic, US imperialists
> have been doing their utmost to topple the republican regime and
> replace it with the old one ...
>
> Washington has shown its sympathy toward Bakhtiar, the last Prime
> Minister of the Shah, and Bani Sadr, the former President of Iran who
> is now a refugee. Both of these men are engaged in extensive terrorist
> activities against the Islamic Republic of Iran and its leaders.[165]

Moscow also sought to link US aid to the Afghan rebels (early in 1981
Reagan had announced publicly that the US was aiding the Afghani
resistance) with US aid to the opposition in Iran in an effort both to
discredit the Afghan resistance in Iran and to drive a further wedge
between Tehran and Washington.

Yet while Iranian–American relations remained highly strained, it did
not appear as if Moscow was making a great deal of headway in improving its own position in Iran. Iranian leaders continued to be suspicious of
Moscow both for its centuries-long record of hostility toward Iran and
because of suspected ties between Moscow and Iranian ethnic minorities

fighting for independence, such as the Kurds. Indeed, Moscow may well have been placed in a difficult position when in late October the Kurdish Democratic Party of Iran, led by Abdul Rahman Gassemlou, joined the opposition front headed by Bani Sadr and Mujahadeen leader Massoud Rajavi.[166] Moscow and Gassemlou had long maintained friendly ties and the formation of the opposition front once again posed a difficult problem of choice for the USSR.

Yet another irritant in the Soviet–Iranian relationship was Tehran's unhappiness that Moscow had taken only a neutral position on the Iran–Iraq war in the face of "flagrant Iraqi aggression" as the late Iranian Prime Minister Ali Rajai told Soviet Ambassador Vladimir Vinogradov on February 15,[167] a message repeated in October by the Iranian Ambassador Mohammed Mokri, during an Iranian delegation's visit to Moscow.[168] A third area of conflict was Iranian unhappiness with the Soviet intervention in Afghanistan, despite Soviet efforts to tie the CIA to the resistance movements in both Iran and Afghanistan. Finally, the Islamic fundamentalist regime was becoming increasingly suspicious about the activities of the communist (Tudeh) party and its ally, the majority faction of the Fedayeen guerrillas, as shown by Iranian Prime Minister Hussein Mousavi's declaration that members of the Tudeh and majority Fedayeen would be executed if, upon joining the revolutionary guards or other Islamic fundamentalist organizations, they failed to state their (communist) party affiliation.[169]

For its part Moscow was clearly not happy with a number of Iranian policies, including frequent anti-Soviet comments by Iranian leaders,[170] the continued war with Iraq, and Iran's continuing controversy with Saudi Arabia (Iranian pilgrims had been arrested for demonstrating in Mecca) which helped reinforce the tie between Saudi Arabia and the United States. While Iran's growing international isolation (in 1981 Iran quarrelled with France over a hijacked gunboat and French asylum for Bani Sadr, while Japan decided to end its $3 billion investment in a huge Iranian petrochemical plant) may have appeared to Moscow as the factor that would ultimately push Iran over to the Soviet camp, by the end of 1981 no such movement had taken place.

The US–Israel strategic cooperation agreement

If Moscow sought to exploit the domestic upheavals in Iran to reinforce anti-American feelings there, it was also to move to exploit the Israeli–American agreement in principle on strategic cooperation reached during Israeli Prime Minister Begin's visit to Washington in early September. Moscow had already deplored the reelection of Begin and the appointment of the "superhawk" Arik Sharon as Israel's Defense Minister, and sought also to exploit Reagan's decision in mid-August to finally allow the F-16s to go to Israel. Indeed, several Soviet commentators actually linked the release of the F-16s to the American–Libyan air clash which took place several days later.[171]

It was the strategic cooperation agreement (later to be formally signed when Sharon visited the United States in early December), however, which came in for the most criticism[172] as Moscow, which tends to have a military view of world events, may well have felt that the combination of the Israeli airforce and army with the American Sixth Fleet, would militarily dominate the Middle East, while the American use of Israeli air bases in the Negev and the stockpiling of equipment in Israel for the US Rapid Deployment Force would greatly enhance the ability of the US to deploy its ground forces in the Middle East.[173]

While Moscow sought to show that the Israeli–American agreement, coming after the Israeli bombings of Beirut and the Iraqi reactor and the Libyan–US clash over the Gulf of Sidra was a policy aimed at threatening the entire Arab world, the Soviet leaders themselves may have felt some need to make a gesture toward Israel before that country moved totally into the American camp. Thus, during Gromyko's visit to the United Nations in late September, he agreed to meet Israeli Foreign Minister Yitzhak Shamir.[174] It appears as if Moscow's willingness to meet with the Israeli Foreign Minister, the first such official meeting in six years, was a Soviet effort, as in the past, at a time of flux in Middle Eastern politics both to maintain some contact with the Israelis and to seek Israeli support for Moscow's idea of an international conference on the Arab–Israeli conflict.[175] While no such Israeli support for Moscow's position was to emerge from the conference, it appears that the meeting was seen as useful by both sides.[176] In any case, the Soviet–Israeli meeting was soon superseded in the thrust of Middle Eastern events by the assassination of Anwar Sadat, a development that once again put the region in an upheaval.

The assassination of Sadat and its aftermath

Relations between Sadat and the USSR had been worsening steadily since the 1973 war, but in 1981 the deterioration accelerated. Not only was Sadat openly proclaiming himself to be the leading anti-Soviet force in the Middle East, but he had also announced that Egypt was sending aid to the Afghan rebels and he had agreed to both the stationing of US troops in the Sinai (as part of the multinational force to separate Egypt and Israel after the April 1982 Israeli withdrawal), and to American use and development of the Egyptian base at Ras Banas for its Rapid Deployment Force.[177] In sum, Egypt under Sadat had become a centerpiece of the anti-Soviet Middle Eastern bloc which the United States was seeking to create and Soviet–Egyptian relations plummeted to a new low as a result.

Three weeks before Sadat's assassination, the Egyptian leader had expelled seven Soviet diplomats, including the Soviet Ambassador and about 1,000 Soviet technicians, on grounds that they were fomenting sedition in Egypt.[178] In addition, he dissolved the Egyptian–Soviet Friendship Society and arrested its President Abd As-Salam Az-Zayyat as part of a major crackdown on Egyptians opposed to his policies from both the Egyptian left and from the fundamentalist Muslim right.[179]

The assassination of Sadat by Muslim fundamentalists was greeted with considerable relief in Moscow, although there was a difference of opinion on the part of Soviet commentators on the future policies of the new regime. *Pravda* on October 14 cited the statement of the National Progressive party which opposed the referendum for the election of Hosni Mubarak to Egypt's presidency on the grounds that he intended to pursue Sadat's policies, "in particular to continue the Camp David policy and strengthen the alliance with the US." On the other hand *Izvestia* commentator Alexander Bovin, a senior Soviet analyst on the Middle East, said that he thought Egypt's policies might change after Israel completed its scheduled withdrawal from the Sinai in April 1982.[180] In any case, while Moscow saw the possibility of an improvement in relations with Egypt, and both before and after the assassination, was giving propaganda support to General Shazli, the exiled leader of the Egyptian "Patriotic Front" based in Libya (Shazli was urging Egypt to return to the Arab fold and improve ties with Moscow),[181] it expressed considerable irritation with the US response to Sadat's assassination. Perhaps hoping for a repeat of the uncertain American reaction to the collapse of the Shah's regime in Iran, Moscow seemed particularly upset by Reagan's strong response to Sadat's assassination which included the alerting of US forces in the Mediterranean along with elements of the Rapid Deployment Force in the United States, the movement of ships of the Sixth Fleet toward Egypt, and the dispatch of former US Presidents Carter, Ford, and Nixon to Egypt for Sadat's funeral.[182] On October 12 Moscow issued a warning to the United States against what it termed a "gross interference" in the internal affairs of Egypt, stating that "what is going on around Egypt cannot help but affect the security interests of the Soviet Union," which will "keep a close watch on the development of events."[183]

Unlike the situation in Iran in 1978–79, however, the US did not appear deterred by the Kremlin warning. Indeed, in addition to pledging support to Mubarak, it dispatched several AWACs radar planes to patrol the border between Egypt and Libya while also announcing that it would expand the planned US Middle East military exercise "Bright Star" scheduled for November 1981. The US also promised to step up arms shipments to both Egypt and the Sudan, both of whom were seen as being threatened by Libya.[184]

In the face of both the US pledge of support for Mubarak and the new Egyptian President's initial consolidation of power (he overwhelmingly won the referendum on October 13 and was sworn in on October 14), Moscow appeared to change course somewhat on October 15 as Brezhnev sent Mubarak a congratulatory telegram on his election, pledging that Moscow would reciprocate any Egyptian readiness to improve Soviet–Egyptian relations.[185] In making this move, Moscow may have realized that there would be no immediate change in Egyptian foreign policy despite Sadat's assassination, and the most that could be hoped for was a "change in the direction of the wind" as Bovin had stated,[186] after completion of the Israeli withdrawal in April, 1982. Nonetheless, the announcement on October 20 that the United States would replace cracked Soviet-made turbines for the Soviet-built Aswan Dam – the major symbol of Soviet–Egyptian cooperation – seemed to underline the fact that US influence was to remain dominant in Egypt, at least in the short term, although Mubarak's subsequent decision to invite some of the expelled Soviet technicians back to Egypt may have raised some hope in Moscow.[187]

The assassination of Sadat, as a major turning point in the Middle East, also gave Moscow the opportunity to again call for an international conference to settle the Arab–Israeli conflict. This was one of the themes of the visit by PLO leader Yasser Arafat to Moscow two weeks after the Sadat assassination, as the PLO leader gave strong support to Moscow's call for the conference.[188] For its part Moscow granted the PLO mission in Moscow full diplomatic status, thus conferring increased diplomatic legitimacy on the Palestinian organization. While the Soviet move was the culmination of an increasingly close Soviet–PLO relationship, and the USSR may have wished to consolidate the relationship further in the period of uncertainty following the death of Sadat, Moscow nonetheless may also have wished to counter the possibility of the development of a formal relationship between Washington and the PLO. During his mediation of the fighting in Lebanon in July, US special representative Philip Habib had, *de facto*, negotiated with the PLO (albeit via intermediaries) and in August both Anwar Sadat and former American National Security Adviser Zbigniew Brzezinski had advocated an American dialogue with the PLO.[189] Then, following Sadat's funeral, former Presidents Carter and Ford stated that at some point the US would have to begin to talk to members of the PLO, if not to Arafat himself.[190]

Less than a week after Arafat's visit came a trip to Moscow by North Yemeni (YAR) President Ali Abdullah Salah. Like Jordan and Kuwait, North Yemen was a key Centrist Arab state which Moscow wished to keep from going over to the American camp, something Moscow feared might happen after the PDRY invasion of North Yemen in February 1979 had led to a major American military supply effort to the YAR.[191] Nonetheless, a lack of coordination between the US, which was supplying the equipment and Saudi Arabia, which was paying for it and which was concerned that North Yemen might become too strong if it obtained the weapons too quickly, led the North Yemeni President to turn to Moscow for arms later that year. Complicating the North Yemeni political situation still further was the South Yemeni-supported National Democratic Front that posed both a political and military challenge to the regime in Sana. The end result was that the North Yemen government had to walk a delicate tight-rope between Saudi Arabia (which financed and influenced a number of North Yemeni tribes), and South Yemen (which supported the National Democratic Front and alternately invaded and advocated union with North Yemen) as well as between the United States, Saudi Arabia's main supporter and the Soviet Union, the primary backer of South Yemen.[192] President Salah's primary aim in the talks in Moscow, therefore, appeared to be the acquisition of additional weaponry to deal with his internal and external problems, and he was successful in his quest as the final communiqué issued at the close of his visit stated that the two countries expressed the desire to continue "broadening and perfecting their advantageous cooperation" in the military field.[193] In return, Salah thanked the USSR for its aid in strengthening North Yemen's "national independence and sovereignty," supported Moscow's call for an international conference on the Middle East, and condemned the establishment of foreign military bases in the Persian Gulf, while also supporting Moscow's peace plan for the Persian Gulf and Indian Ocean.[194] In sum, like the visits by the leaders of Kuwait and Jordan, the trip of North Yemeni President Salah can be considered a clear plus for Moscow, although Salah was to immediately visit Saudi Arabia following his visit to Moscow in an effort to secure his position with that country.

Although the North Yemeni leader's visit to Moscow was greeted with satisfaction by Moscow, as was the election of the anti-NATO Andreas Papandreou to the premiership of Greece in late October, and the failure of President Reagan to either convince Jordanian King Hussein to join Camp David or get the King to reject a major surface-to-air missile deal with Moscow in favor of an American system during Hussein's visit to Washington in early November,[195] a number of other Middle Eastern developments took place during the fall of 1981 that were not to Moscow's satisfaction. In the first place, after a long and bitter debate the United States Senate agreed to the sale of AWACs aircraft to Saudi Arabia in late October, a development that appeared to cement US–Saudi ties, at least in the short run. Second, in a major policy change, a number of European states agreed to provide troops for the Sinai multinational force, thereby at least tacitly supporting Camp David. Third, the United States successfully mounted a major military exercise in the Middle East (Bright Star), thus demonstrating that it was developing the capability of a quick intervention there to aid its friends.

The debate over the AWACs highlighted the ambivalent Soviet position toward Saudi Arabia. On the one hand, as the leading Centrist Arab state opposed to Camp David, and as a major financial and political backer of the PLO, Saudi Arabia pursued two key Middle Eastern policies which Moscow also strongly supported. On the other hand, however, as a leading opponent of Soviet policy in Afghanistan and as a nation with increasingly close military ties to the United States, as evidenced by the emplacement of US-controlled AWACs in Saudi Arabia soon after the start of the Iran–Iraq war, and as a nation which had sought to use its financial power to try to pry several Arab states out of the Soviet camp, Saudi Arabia was also a leading anti-Soviet force in the Arab world. Moscow's ambivalent position toward Saudi Arabia was especially apparent in 1981. In April Moscow warmly welcomed both Saudi Arabia's rebuttal of US Secretary of State Haig's call for an anti-Soviet alliance during Haig's visit to the Middle East and Saudi

Foreign Minister Saud al-Faisal's statement that Israel, not Moscow, was the main threat to the Arabs.[196] One month later, a key article in *Literaturnaia Gazeta*, written by Soviet commentator Igor Belyayev, noted, in discussing the failure of Haig's visit: "Arab politicians, even the conservative ones, have never refused Soviet assistance in the struggle against their real enemy – the Israeli expansionists. The Arabs will hardly become accomplices in an anti-Soviet crusade under the aegis of the US."[197]

On the other hand, in late August, Moscow's chief oil analyst, Reuben Andreasian, bitterly noted Saudi Arabia's unwillingness to act against US interests during an OPEC meeting to set oil prices, as he complained that despite the Israeli raid on the Iraqi nuclear reactor and the recent attack by US airforce planes on Libyan aircraft – "on the very day the OPEC meeting opened" – there was no agreement on prices.[198]

Moscow's central fear in the AWACs debate was that Congressional approval for AWACs would cement the Saudi–American relationship to the point that Saudi Arabia might be persuaded both to support the Camp David agreements and also provide facilities for the American Rapid Deployment Force "in direct proximity to the extremely rich Persian Gulf oil fields"[199] – a fear that was even more openly expressed after the Senate approved (by failing to vote down) the AWACs agreement. *Pravda* on October 30 noted: "The AWACs system will be effectively under direct US control, not to mention the innumerable advisers who will be sent to Saudi Arabia. All indications are that the US would now prepare Saudi Arabia for the role of bridgehead."[200] Moscow Radio Peace and Progress on October 30 went even further in its criticism, asserting that the AWACs deal was "aimed at transforming the Wahhabi Kingdom into a source of threat to the entire Islamic world."[201]

While the AWACs approval was a blow to the Soviet Middle East position since it strengthened Saudi–American ties, so too was the decision of several key European states to provide troops for the multinational force which the United States was organizing for the Sinai. The rapid evolution of the multinational force during the course of 1981 was of clear concern to Moscow which saw it as a cover for the American RDF.[202] The commitment of American troops for the force, a goal long pursued by Israel, which saw the US as a far more reliable barrier to a future Egyptian attack than the UN, was not approved by the US Congress or Sadat until well into 1981, and, for most of the year, Western Europe had held aloof from participation in the multinational force. The election of François Mitterand to the presidency of France, however, together with the assassination of Sadat galvanized the Europeans to take a more active role and by the end of November the participation of France, England, Holland, and Italy in the Sinai force, despite some initial objections by Israel on the terms of their participation, was set. As might be expected, Moscow strongly opposed both US and especially Western European participation in the multinational force. In the case of Western Europe, Moscow had long seen the Middle East as an area where, because of a much greater European oil dependency, a wedge could be driven between the US and its NATO allies.[203] Consequently, Moscow condemned what it saw as a Western European "knuckling under" to Washington's "diktat" on the multinational force.[204] In addition, because the multinational force was tied to the Camp David agreements, Moscow saw European participation in the Sinai force as a *de facto* legitimatization of Camp David, a development which ended American isolation as the sole Western state supporting the agreements.[205]

The Bright Star military exercise, which also involved some British and French participation, may be considered another gain for Washington – and concomitantly a loss for Moscow. The exercises took place in Egypt (with the participation of units of the Egyptian army and airforce), the Sudan, Somalia, and Oman. While Moscow denounced "Bright Star" as a rehearsal for the invasion of both Libya and the Middle East oil fields (the "Bright Star" exercise was commanded by the head of the RDF), as a device for intimidating "progressive" governments in the Middle East such as Libya, Ethiopia, and South Yemen, and as a technique for strengthening pro-US regimes in the region,[206] it had to be concerned about the rather impressive showing of the US military, including a bombing run by B-52 bombers on a direct flight from the United States. This stood in sharp contrast to the difficulties encountered by the US in its abortive hostage rescue mission in Iran in April 1980. Indeed, Moscow may well have been concerned that the successful US Rapid Deployment Force exercise might have a positive influence on such Arab countries as Kuwait which had turned to Moscow, in part, because it could not be sure that the US either had the capability or will to help it in case of a conflict with an unfriendly neighbor like Iran which had again bombed Kuwaiti territory in early October.[207] The conclusion of a major US–Pakistani military agreement, which held out the possibility of US use of the Pakistani naval base at Gwandar and air base at Peshewar, seemed to further enhance

US capabilities for military intervention in the Persian Gulf.[208] Finally, the Egyptian component of "Bright Star" in which 4,000 American and Egyptian troops participated also served to improve relations between the US and Egyptian militaries and between the Mubarak and Reagan governments, and Egyptian Defense Minister Abdel Halim Abu Ghazala stated that the exercises were a "rehearsal for a possible joint operation" to protect the oilfields of the Persian Gulf.[209]

As "Bright Star" was concluding its Egyptian phase on November 24, the Arab states, except for Egypt, were preparing for a major Arab summit conference in Fez, Morocco, one that was closely watched by Moscow. The central issue at the conference was the so-called Fahd Plan, a Saudi peace initiative first put forth in August, which held out, albeit somewhat vaguely, the possibility of Arab recognition and peace with Israel in return for a total Israeli withdrawal from all territories captured in 1967, including East Jerusalem, and the establishment of a Palestinian state. The assassination of Sadat, which seemed to make possible a *rapprochement* between Egypt and Saudi Arabia,[210] along with the US Senate approval of AWACs gave a new momentum to the Fahd plan which received little attention when it was first broached in August.

The Soviet reaction to the Fahd Plan was an interesting one. On August 12, Moscow Radio praised the plan, noting that it conformed in many ways to the Soviet Middle East plan (i.e. total Israeli withdrawal; the establishment of a Palestinian state; and the right to exist of all states in the region).[211] Five days later however, Moscow Radio Peace and Progress in Arabic attacked the plan because of its tie to American policy,[212] and *Izvestia* further criticized the plan on August 23 as an effort to undermine the PLO and decide the Palestinian peoples' fate "behind their backs." Moscow's criticism of Saudi Arabia and the Fahd Plan grew even harsher at the time when the AWACs deal was approved by the United States Senate as it was portrayed as a device to split the Arabs and spread Camp David,[213] but Moscow shifted its position again when Saudi Prince Faisal called for Soviet participation in the search for peace in the Middle East and sought to get Soviet support for the Saudi peace plan.[214] From Moscow's point of view, cooperation on the Fahd Plan, particularly when the Reagan administration was at best lukewarm about it, could be a means of driving a wedge between Saudi Arabia and Washington, despite the AWACs deal. From the Saudi perspective, Soviet support for the Fahd Plan may have been seen as necessary for rallying the Steadfastness Front Arab states to the support of the Fahd Plan at the Fez summit. Indeed, Riyadh made a further gesture to Moscow – possibly for the same purpose – at a meeting of the Gulf Cooperation Council in mid-November when it supported the Kuwaiti view in the final communiqué which "confirmed the need to keep the region as a whole away from international conflicts, especially the presence of military fleets and foreign bases."[215] If this was indeed Riyadh's purpose in giving strong support to the principles of nonalignment at the GCC meeting (Riyadh may also have been embarrassed by a November 1, 1981 article in the *Washington Post* describing US plans to make Saudi Arabia a major military and air command base for the US RDF,[216] and by Reagan's press conference statement on October 1 that the US would not let Saudi Arabia be an Iran)[217] it did not work since the Steadfastness Front states, and particularly Syria and Libya, were to strongly oppose the Fahd Plan at the Fez summit. Indeed, the Steadfastness Front had its own agenda at Fez – one endorsed by Moscow – which called for sanctions against Arab states making available military facilities to the US, and against European states providing troops for the Sinai force; the use of all Arab resources, including oil and petrodollars, to "resist the US–Israeli strategic alliance"; and the strengthening of relations with the USSR.[218] Neither the Fahd Plan nor the Steadfastness Front agenda, however, were to receive support at the Fez summit which was to collapse less than six hours after it had begun because of the Steadfastness Front's hostility to the Fahd Plan, leaving the Arab world in a state of major disarray. In an attempt to put a positive light on the events at Fez, a Moscow Radio Arabic language broadcast rather plaintively urged the Arabs to rebuild their unity on an anti-imperialist basis,[219] something that even the most optimistic observers in Moscow must have realized was a very distant goal. Indeed Dmitry Volsky, one of Moscow's most frank analysts of Middle Eastern affairs, in his commentary on the Fez Conference, summed up Soviet frustration with developments in the Arab world:

> The Arab world is living through difficult, troubled times full of con-
> tradictions. If additional proof of this were needed, it was provided by
> the sudden discontinuation of the summit conference that had just got
> under way in the Moroccan city of Fez. After a five-hour discussion,
> the decision to break it off was announced by King Hassan II of
> Morocco. In the opinion of the press, the pretext was disagreement
> over some points of the plan for a Middle East settlement submitted by
> Saudi Arabia – a pretext but hardly the real reason. For it is obvious
> that the disagreements over this question were indicative of different

and at times opposite views on the strategy to apply in the struggle of the Arab peoples for a just peace in the Middle East.

And on a broader plane, too, it would be putting it mildly to say that the Arab leaders are far from taking the same view of the development of their countries and of the region as a whole. To some the ideal is a sort of "America in the desert," where free enterprise would coexist with the lifestyle of the Bedouin tribes; others think that the prototype of the future can be found only in the remote past, in "pure Islam"; still others – who are quite numerous – envision a socialist perspective. All this, naturally, affects the internal and foreign policies of the Arab countries; they differ in social content, and this is inevitable in the present conditions.

What is by no means inevitable are the internecine conflicts by which, alas, the entire Arab and, indeed, the whole Muslim world is rent. Take the war Morocco has been waging for several years now against the Polisario Front in Western Sahara, the continuing hostilities between Iran and Iraq, the tension on the Sudanese–Libyan border. There are smouldering embers also in other places. Understandably, all this prevents the Arab peoples from jointly tackling the acute problems, common to all of them, connected with the elimination of the consequences of Israeli aggression and the organization of a joint rebuff to the new bellicose moves of Tel Aviv and its overseas patrons. To uphold the independence of the Arab countries and the rights of their peoples – that is now the main concern to which, in the opinion of patriotic-minded people in the Arab world, both personal and all other ambitions should be subordinated.

But this is, evidently, easier said than done, all the more so since the enemies of the Arabs are extremely adept at inciting internecine strife, speculating on the narrow class aspirations of the privileged strata, and scaring the Arabs with the old "Soviet threat" bogey. Three years ago this insidious policy found embodiment in the Camp David deal. Now Camp David has been demonstrably deadlocked. But attempts to break the deadlock not by displaying common sense but by trying doggedly to blunder ahead in the same direction can prove very dangerous. Yet that is precisely what the current Washington administration has been doing, especially since the death of Sadat. Now that this figure, odious literally to all Arabs, has gone, Washington is in a hurry in some way or other to go "beyond the Camp David framework." Not only the Somali regime and the small Arabian sultanate of Oman are already being tacked on to it factually if not formally, but also such a large Arab state as Sudan. Saudi Arabia, with its oil and petrodollars, is being assiduously courted. Attempts are being made to knock together a new bloc with a military spearhead on the coasts of the Persian Gulf and the Red Sea.

And the military spearhead is to be American. The decision on the sale to Saudi Arabia of an AWACs system which will be controlled by the Americans, the new steps to set up US bases in Oman and Somalia, the planned weapons deliveries to Sudan, the agreement on the stationing in Sinai of the notorious "multinational force" the backbone of which will be largely American, and finally the "Bright Start" exercise – all these are only the most recent facts.[220]

Volsky's rather pessimistic assessment of the state of the Arab world and its distance from the "anti-imperialist" Arab unity Moscow had wanted for so long, reflected the fact that by December 1981 the Arab world had split into three camps. First there was what might be called the "Egyptian" camp of Egypt, the Sudan, Oman, and Somalia, all of whom were pro-Western (to the point of providing facilities for the US Rapid Deployment Force [RDF]) and also to a greater or lesser degree committed to peace with Israel. At the other extreme, was the Front of Steadfastness and Confrontation, all of whose members (Syria, Algeria, Libya, the PDRY, and the PLO) were, at least on paper, opposed to any kind of peace with Israel, and were also following a pro-Soviet line on such issues as the Soviet invasion of Afghanistan. Located between the "Peace" camp and the Front of Steadfastness and Confrontation was the rather amorphous group of Arab states which could be called, for want of a better term, the "Centrists." These states had indicated a willingness to live in peace with Israel (albeit under very stringent terms) and were composed of states that ran the spectrum from being mildly pro-Western (such as Morocco, Saudi Arabia, and the United Arab Emirates) to neutralists as in the cases of the Yemen Arab Republic (North Yemen) and Kuwait. Iraq, before 1978 among the most hostile Arab states to Israel, had moderated its position to that country and by 1982 could be considered part of the Centrist bloc for this reason as well as because of its improved relationship with the United States.[221] The Centrists had in common with the Steadfastness Front an opposition to Camp David, but also had in common with the Egyptian camp opposition to the Soviet invasion of Afghanistan and support of Iraq in the Iran–Iraq war.

Given this situation, Moscow's goal was to try to move the Centrist Arab states back toward the Front of Steadfastness and Confrontation into an "anti-imperialist" bloc, much as had existed immediately after Camp David. On the other hand, however, the Soviet leadership had to be concerned about a *rapprochement* between the Egyptian camp and the Centrists, since this would leave the pro-Soviet Steadfastness Front in an isolated position in the Arab world with its individual components engaged in their own intra-Arab and regional confrontations (Algeria–Morocco; PDRY–YAR; Libya–Egypt; Syria–Iraq; Syria–Jordan; Syria–Israel; and PLO–Israel), a development that would also exacerbate some internal strains within the Steadfastness Front, especially the conflict between Syrian President Hafiz Assad and PLO leader Yasser Arafat.

Thus the USSR sought to capitalize on the Israeli annexation of the Golan Heights in December 1981, the rather heavy-handed US pressure against Libya, and the rapid expansion of Israeli settlements on the West Bank to discredit the United States and rally the Centrist Arab states around its Steadfastness Front clients. The Soviet leadership also sought to exploit the actions of a deranged Israeli who, in April 1982, fired into an Arab crowd in the Mosque of Omar in Jerusalem to achieve the same purpose. As *Izvestia* noted:

> The crime in the Muslim shrine should be viewed not as an individual terrorist act, committed by a fanatic individual, but as a logical consequence of a large scale anti-Palestinian campaign unleashed by the Zionist authorities of Israel supported by their transoceanic patrons.[222]

Nonetheless, Moscow was not particularly successful in its efforts. Because of their continuing aid to Iran in its war against Iraq (indeed, Syria reportedly stepped up its military aid to Iran during this period) Syria and Libya were isolated in the Arab world and Israeli actions on the Golan Heights and in the West Bank proved insufficient to restore the two Steadfastness Front states to the Arab mainstream.

In the case of Syria, Moscow itself did not appear willing to provide as much support as the Syrians wanted. Thus, when the Syrian Foreign Minister, Abdul Khaddam, in the aftermath of the Israeli annexation of the Golan, visited Moscow in January 1982 in quest of a Soviet–Syrian security treaty similar to the one between the US and Israel (which the US had suspended following the Golan annexation) and, reportedly also to seek Soviet aid in case Israel attacked Syrian forces in Lebanon,[223] the Soviet leadership resisted, perhaps fearing that Syria might drag it into an unwanted adventure. Hence, the joint communiqué issued after the visit noted that the talks had proceeded in a "spirit of understanding" – the usual Soviet code words to indicate disagreement.[224] Another issue of dispute between the two countries was Moscow's insistence on

Israel's right to exist, a point made explicitly by Gromyko in his luncheon address during the talks.[225]

While Moscow seemed to be fending off Syria's desire for a closer military relationship, it was seeking a closer tie of its own with Syria's ally, the Islamic fundamentalist regime of Ayatollah Khomeini in Iran. Consequently, the Soviet leadership welcomed the visit of Iranian Energy Minister, Hasan Ghafurifarad in February, and his statement at a news conference that Iran regarded the Soviet Union as a friendly country and that his visit had laid the basis for greater Soviet–Iranian cooperation.[226] The Ghafurifarad visit at which a protocol on accelerated economic and technical cooperation in the construction of two gas-fired power plants was signed, was, however, to be the high point of Soviet–Iranian relations in 1982. Less than a month later, senior *Pravda* Middle East correspondent Pavel Demchenko, issued the strongest Soviet criticism of the Khomeini regime since Alexander Bovin had personally criticized Khomeini himself in September 1979.[227] While noting the increase in Soviet–Iranian trade, and the fact that the USSR was assisting Iran in the construction of a number of industrial projects, including the Isfahan Metallurgical Works, Demchenko openly complained that Soviet–Iranian relations had been damaged in a number of spheres in the period since the Khomeini regime took power because of Iran's "unilateral acts."[228] These included the reduction in the size of the diplomatic staff of the Soviet Embassy in Tehran, the closing of the Soviet consulate in Resht, the refusal to grant entry visas to Soviet newspaper correspondents, and the closing of the Iranian Society for Cultural Relations with the USSR (where the Russian language was taught), along with the Russian–Iranian Bank and the branches of the Soviet Insurance Society and Transport Agency. In addition, Demchenko complained of an atmosphere of "greatly intensified anti-Soviet propaganda" and of anti-Soviet demonstrations outside the Soviet Embassy in Tehran, and he blamed these anti-Soviet activities on "conservative groupings" around Khomeini.

It is not clear whether the *Pravda* article was merely a reflection of growing Soviet frustration with Iran or whether its main purpose was to serve as a warning to Iran about its anti-Soviet activities. If the latter, it was not particularly successful, as Soviet–Iranian relations continued to deteriorate in the spring and summer despite the dispatch of a new Soviet Ambassador, V. K. Boldryev, who had extensive experience in Iran.[229]

While Moscow may have drawn some consolation from the arrest and subsequent execution of former Iránian Foreign Minister Sadegh Ghotbzadeh, since Ghotbzadeh had been the most anti-Soviet of the Iranian secular leaders, the Khomeini regime's increasing crackdown on the Tudeh party and the banning of its publication *Ittihad al-Marddom*, its continued refusal to export natural gas to the USSR unless it received a much higher price, the expansion of its economic ties with Pakistan, Turkey, and Western Europe which meant a lessened economic dependence on the USSR (indeed, an Iranian–Turkish natural gas pipeline deal, signed in September, may have caused concern in Moscow that Iran was seriously considering a permanent redirection of its natural gas sales from the USSR to Western Europe), its continued opposition to Soviet policy in Afghanistan, and, perhaps most of all, its continued prosecution of the war with Iraq and its refusal to seriously consider mediation efforts to end the war, clearly angered Moscow[230] which was frustrated by the continuation of the war which reinforced the divisions in the Arab world and, particularly after Iran went on the offensive and threatened Iraqi territory in May, 1982, helped reinforce the American military and diplomatic position in the Persian Gulf while also accelerating the *rapprochement* between Egypt and a number of Centrist Gulf states (see below, pp. 131–32).

While Moscow was witnessing a deterioration in its relations with Iran, it proved unable to make much progress in improving its ties with the post-Sadat regime in Egypt. While Egypt's new President, Hosni Mubarak made a number of gestures toward the USSR, including the proclamation of nonalignment as Egypt's foreign policy goal and the invitation to a number of Soviet technicians to return to Egypt to help operate some Soviet-built equipment,[231] Egypt still remained in the American camp although Mubarak was less overtly pro-American than Sadat had been. In addition, while there was a toning down of anti-Soviet propaganda, and more of an emphasis on the public sector of the Egyptian economy, the Mubarak regime continued Egypt's state of emergency and continued to arrest Egyptian communists,[232] while Egypt's Defense Minister Abu Ghazala, much to the consternation of Moscow, emphasized the Soviet threat to the Persian Gulf and Saudi Arabia.[233] The continued chill in the Soviet–Egyptian relationship was best symbolized by Mubarak's unwillingness to allow a Soviet ambassador to take up residence in Cairo.

One of the issues which, from Moscow's perspective, irritated Soviet–Egyptian relations was the stationing of American troops in the Sinai as part of the multinational force which patrolled the region to help

maintain peace between Egypt and Israel following the Israeli withdrawal from the Sinai on April 25. While Moscow complained that the
American troops would be part of the US Rapid Deployment Force –
and the fact that the first US contingent came from the crack 82nd
Airborne Division gave some credence to Soviet complaints[234] – the
Soviet leaders had no one but themselves to blame for this development. In 1979, in the period following the Egyptian–Israeli peace treaty,
the US had sought to create a multinational force, based on UN troops,
to patrol the Sinai in the aftermath of the Israeli withdrawal. Had
Moscow acceded to the US effort, the end result would probably have
been a military force made up essentially of Third World troops patrolling the Sinai – a force that would not have enhanced the American
military position in the region. The USSR, however, refused to agree to
such a UN force lest it legitimize the Israeli–Egyptian peace treaty and
the end result in 1982 was to be a combat-ready American military
force, one that could be relatively easily transferred to the Persian Gulf,
that was to be emplaced in the Sinai.[235]

The stationing of US troops in the Sinai was not the only strategic
problem facing Moscow in the region during the spring. The opening of
talks between India and Pakistan and a warming of relations between
China and India had to concern Moscow because it was the fear of
China and hostility toward US-backed Pakistan which had moved India
to sign a Treaty of Friendship and Cooperation with the USSR in 1971
and which had kept India favorably disposed toward Moscow ever since.
Indeed, it was no accident that Brezhnev had proclaimed his plan for the
neutralization of the Indian Ocean during a visit to New Dehli in
December 1980, since India played a key role in Soviet policy toward
the Indian Ocean.[236] Moscow's concern about the future direction of
Indian policy could only have risen during Prime Minister Indira
Ghandi's largely successful visit to Washington in August, and despite
the Indian leader's subsequent trip to Moscow in September, the Soviet
leaders may well have worried that India, where the 1983 non-aligned
conference was scheduled to be held, might adopt a more genuinely
non-aligned policy.[237]

The negative developments in India's foreign policy were only part of
Moscow's concern as Middle Eastern dynamics took a distinctly anti-
Soviet direction during the first half of 1982. In the first place, Moscow's
client Libya was discredited when the anti-Kaddafi forces of Hassan
Habre consolidated their control over most of Chad, and Moscow could
also not have been too happy when Kaddafi called for the overthrow of

the Saudi regime – an action which led Riyadh radio to state that Kaddafi was "the perfect example of a communist agent."[238] Secondly, the Morocco–Algerian confrontation over the Spanish Sahara intensified as Morocco signed a major military agreement with the US in which it provided transit facilities for the US RDF in an apparent *quid pro quo* for increased shipments of military equipment.[239] In addition, Morocco boycotted meetings of the Organization of African Unity, a pan-African organization which Moscow also hoped could unify on an "anti-imperialist" basis, because some OAU members recognized the Algerian-backed Polisario rebels. Additional problems for Moscow lay in the increasingly severe difficulties that both Syria and the PLO were encountering. In the case of Syria, there was an anti-regime uprising by the Muslim Brotherhood in the city of Hama in February (blamed by Assad on Iraq and the United States)[240] in which as many as 20,000 people are reported to have been killed. Two months later, Syria blocked the Iraqi oil pipeline which ran through Syria, an event which, while weakening Iraq, exacerbated the Syrian–Iraqi conflict and made Moscow's hopes for an "anti-imperialist" Arab unity dim further. Meanwhile the Lebanese-based PLO, already under heavy Syrian pressure, found itself fighting against Shiite forces in Southern Lebanon who were protesting PLO activities in their section of the country. This conflict was of particular worry to Moscow both because the Shiites, as the poorest element in the Lebanese population, were a prime recruiting ground for the Lebanese communist party and other leftist Lebanese elements who were allied with the PLO, and also because the Shiite militia, AMAL, was now also fighting against leftist and communist forces.[241] Perhaps the greatest problem for Moscow, however, was the gradual *rapprochement* between Egypt and the Centrist Arabs. Induced in part by the Israeli withdrawal from the last part of the Sinai on April 25, 1982, the *rapprochement* was accelerated by Iran's success in its war with Iraq as the Iranians took the offensive and threatened Iraqi territory in the late spring. The Iranian advance frightened the Gulf states who turned both to the US and to Egypt for support (fear of Iran had caused Saudi Arabia to agree to establish a joint defense planning committee with the United States in February). Iraq had long been a recipient of Egyptian military equipment and had moderated its position toward Egypt as a result,[242] and now other Gulf states moved in the same direction. In addition, the warm official greetings by Jordan and Morocco to Egypt after the final Israeli Sinai withdrawal also appeared to signal their interest in improved ties with Egypt.[243] In the case of

Jordan, there was evidently hope of Egyptian support against Jordan's enemy Syria (as well as a hope for increased Egyptian aid to Iraq), while in the case of Morocco, there seemed hope for Egyptian support against Algeria. In any case, by the time of the Israeli invasion of Lebanon, there was a clear move toward *rapprochement* between Egypt and the Centrist Arabs. Indeed, a special meeting of the Steadfastness Front took place at the end of May 1982 to try to reverse this trend (this may also have been one of the purposes of Libyan Foreign Minister Abdul Jalloud's visit to Moscow following the Steadfastness Front meeting), as the Front proclaimed its opposition to any normalization of relations with Egypt until it renounced Camp David.[244]

The Israeli invasion of Lebanon

It was thus a badly disunited Arab world, whose pro-Soviet members were isolated and whose Centrist states were gradually moving toward a reconciliation with Egypt, which faced Soviet policy makers on the eve of the Israeli invasion of Lebanon. The invasion itself on June 6, 1982, which had been predicted both by Western and Soviet commentators, clearly came as no surprise. Israel had long proclaimed its desire to rid itself of the PLO artillery which threatened its Northern towns, while the SAM missiles which Syria had emplaced in the Bekaa Valley of Lebanon in April 1981 had also been cited by Israeli spokesmen as targets for destruction.

This being the case, it is surprising that there was no contingency planning among Syria, the PLO, and Moscow for an invasion. While the lack of coordination between Syria and the PLO can perhaps be explained by the conflict between Assad and Arafat who feared the Syrian leader was trying to take over the PLO, and the lack of contingency planning between Syria and the USSR may possibly be explained by Moscow's publicly proclaimed unwillingness to extend the provisions of the Soviet–Syrian treaty to cover Syrian forces in Lebanon,[245] the lack of Soviet–PLO preparation is somewhat surprising. Perhaps Moscow felt that any Israeli invasion would, because of Western and Arab pressure, be at most a repetition of the limited 1978 Litani operation; perhaps Moscow hoped that the PLO, which had frequently proclaimed its readiness for an Israeli assault (Arafat reportedly made an inspection of PLO military positions on June 2),[246] could indeed cause so many casualties among the casualty-sensitive Israelis that the invasion would halt after only a few days; or perhaps Moscow simply did not wish to run the risks of too close a military involvement with such a fragmented organization.[247]

Indeed it must have been clear by as early as the end of the first day of the invasion when Israeli forces pushed by Tyre and drove well past the Litani River, or at least by the second day when the Israeli army had pushed past Sidon and headed toward Damour that this was not to be a repetition of the Litani operation of 1978 when Israel drove only to the Litani River and never captured Tyre. Despite spirited resistance, the PLO forces were unable to withstand the Israeli attack and rapidly fell back toward Beirut.[248] It is not surprising therefore that Arafat made appeals to Moscow for aid, via the Soviet Ambassador to Lebanon, Aleksander Soldatov, on each of the first four days of the Israeli invasion.[249] While Soldatov was quoted on Beirut radio as saying on June 6 that Moscow "will take all measures inside and outside the Security Council and will also resort to all the means and courses available to it to denounce the aggressors,"[250] the USSR was to be rather hesitant in its response to the early stages of the Israeli invasion – a hesitancy that was to be maintained throughout the war. Thus, while *Pravda* noted on June 7 that Syrian President Hafiz Assad had promised Arafat that Syria would not let anyone destroy the Palestinian revolution and that "the Syrian people and troops would fight side by side with the Palestinian warriors," Moscow made no mention of its own troops. Instead, the USSR emphasized the role of the United Nations in stopping the invasion by trying to get the UN Security Council to force an Israeli withdrawal. By going to the UN, Moscow avoided the necessity of direct action, although it was to try to obtain propaganda value from the vetoes cast by the US to protect Israel while also using the Security Council debates to split the US from its NATO allies – particularly France – who were far more critical of Israel. In addition, the official Tass statement on June 8, although denouncing the Israeli invasion and emphasizing what it termed American complicity in it, contained only general threats, merely warning that the "adventure" may cost Israel and its people dearly and that Israel's aggression could threaten world peace.[251] The USSR's unwillingness to take further action was reflected in the comments of the PLO representative in Moscow, Mohammed Shaer, who in a press conference on June 8 in which he praised the Tass statement, also noted that the USSR would not send troops.[252]

The war heated up further on June 9 as Syria, which despite Assad's pledge to Arafat, was only giving the PLO limited assistance, suddenly found itself involved in a full-scale war with Israel in the Bekaa Valley as

Israeli planes destroyed the disputed SAM missile emplacements. A major Israeli–Syrian dogfight ensued with Syria losing scores of planes, and a series of tank battles also took place. The same day, Soviet Foreign Minister Andrei Gromyko, who was in New York, met with Farouk Kaddoumi, head of the Political Department of the PLO Executive Committee, and pledged that the USSR would invariably support "the just struggle of the Palestinians."[253] At the same time, a delegation of Arab Ambassadors from Jordan, Algeria, Kuwait, and Tunisia and the Chargé d'Affaires of Lebanon, visited the Soviet Foreign Ministry where they met with Deputy Soviet Foreign Minister Viktor Shukatev.[254] Given the increased intensity of the fighting, it is quite possible that the Arab diplomats, who came from both the Steadfastness and Centrist blocs in the Arab world, were calling for more Soviet support against Israel. Indeed, a Kuwaiti broadcast on June 10 went so far as to report that "an extensive Soviet political move was expected within the next 24 hours."[255] It is possible that the Arab demand for increased Soviet activity, and the escalation of the fighting in Lebanon, induced Brezhnev to send a letter to Reagan on June 10 in which the Soviet leader reportedly expressed his concern "that a most serious situation had been created which contained the possibility of wider hostilities."[256] Reagan, however, reportedly responded to the letter by warning of the dangers if outside powers became involved in the war.[257]

As the fighting escalated and Israeli forces approached Beirut, while also pushing Syrian troops back in the Bekaa Valley, the Soviet leadership received one bit of positive diplomatic news – that Iraq had announced it was pulling its troops out of Iran and was calling for an unconditional end to the Iran–Iraq war so that all energies could be devoted to the battle against Israel. Moscow applauded the Iraqi move which was clearly a face-saving measure by Saddam Hussein to terminate Iraqi involvement in what had become a disastrous war for Iraq. While the Soviet leaders may have hoped that the Iraqi announcement would indeed bring an end to the war – which was perhaps the most divisive element in intra-Arab relations – such was not to be the case as Iran pledged to continue the fighting until Saddam Hussein was overthrown. To counteract the political impact of Iraq's call for a united effort against Israel, however, Iran announced the dispatch of Iranian volunteers to Lebanon to fight the Israelis, a development that was ultimately to have more influence on internal politics in Lebanon than on the Arab–Israeli conflict.

Following the loss of one-fifth of its airforce, the destruction of its

SAM emplacements in Lebanon, and heavy losses to its tank forces, including the highly sophisticated T-72, the Syrians called for a cease-fire on June 11 and Moscow may have been pleased that the possibility of a wider war was thereby averted. While PLO–Syrian relations were further strained by the fact that Syria agreed to the cease-fire while the PLO was still fighting, one day later, with its forces virtually surrounded in Beirut, the PLO also called for a cease-fire.

With the worst of the fighting apparently now over, Moscow had to decide its next moves. Hitherto the USSR had acted in a manner which US Secretary of State Alexander Haig had publicly called "encouragingly cautious."[258] In truth, Moscow's options did not look too promising. In the first place, from a purely military standpoint there were serious obstacles to any commitment of Soviet troops to the conflict. While in the past decade, the USSR had committed its troops and/or those of surrogates such as Cuba to Third World conflicts no less than three times (Angola in 1976; Ethiopia in 1978; and Afghanistan in 1979), in each case the opponent was not a significant military power, with a first-rate airforce, a highly trained army, and possessing the latest in military technology, some of which was supplied by the United States. In addition, given US President Ronald Reagan's statement that outside powers should not intervene in the conflict, the Soviet leadership could not be sure that the US would not actively intervene if Soviet troops entered the fighting. Third, the destruction of Syria's SAM missiles and its most modern tank, the T-72, in battles with the Israelis, along with eighty-five Syrian planes, had to give Moscow pause since these were the same weapons on which the defense of the USSR was based and because Soviet military equipment was a prime export commodity earning the USSR billions of dollars a year in hard currency.[259] Finally, it should also not be overlooked that the destruction of the SAM system in the Bekaa Valley, and, by implication, Israel's ability to similarly destroy the SAMs located in Syrian territory meant that Israel had virtually complete air supremacy in the region of the fighting – a significant deterrent to any major Soviet operation.

This having been said, there were still a number of things Moscow could have done that it did not do, especially the airlifting of elements of an airborne division to Syria, and the dispatch of "volunteers" via Syria to aid the PLO in areas of Lebanon such as Tripoli to which the Israeli army had not yet penetrated. Both moves would have been seen as major deterrents to further Israeli activity and would have been a demonstration to the Arabs as a whole that Moscow was indeed aiding them – and a reinforcement of the position of Moscow's Steadfastness Front allies. Such moves, however, entailed serious risks of involvement in the fighting, and the possible escalation into a superpower confrontation as indeed occurred during the 1973 war. In 1973 Moscow, by actively supplying the Arabs during the fighting and openly threatening armed intervention in the later stage of the war when Israel had successfully gone on the offensive, had been willing to take such risks.[260] In 1982, even when its strategic power had increased markedly *vis-à-vis* the United States, Moscow was to prove unwilling to risk an escalation of the fighting.

This lack of significant Soviet action during the Israeli invasion of Lebanon as the Israeli army soundly defeated both an important Soviet client, the PLO, and Moscow's most important Arab ally, Syria, aroused a great deal of comment in the West. One group of analysts attributed the Soviet hesitancy to the succession crisis and former Soviet General Secretary Brezhnev's deteriorating health. Another group pointed to Soviet logistical difficulties in the conflict, and Soviet unwillingness to deploy troops abroad in the face of significant opposition. Others contended that Moscow was preoccupied with the continuing crises in Poland and Afghanistan, the strategic arms negotiations, and efforts to encourage nuclear freeze forces both in the United States and Western Europe. While there may well be some validity in all of these contentions, it would appear that there is perhaps an even more important reason for the lack of vigorous Soviet action during the Lebanese crisis – the inability of the Arab states themselves to take coordinated action to aid Syria and the PLO. Indeed, in seeking to explain Soviet behavior, one can point to one major difference between 1973 and 1982. In 1973 the Arabs were united behind Cairo and Damascus in their war effort against Israel and had placed an oil embargo against the United States, and Moscow may well have seen the possibility of a decisive blow being struck against US influence in the region. In 1982, however, the Arabs were so disunited that they proved unable to even call a summit conference to take action against Israel during the war. It must have seemed to Moscow that the bulk of the Arab world, unhappy with Syria because of its backing of Iran in the Iran–Iraq war, were not going to rally behind the Syrian regime of Hafiz Assad or, for that matter, behind the PLO which many distrusted.[261] In addition, given the increasingly severe Iranian military threat against Iraq and the Arab Gulf states as a whole, Saudi Arabia and its Gulf Cooperation Council allies were not about to place an oil embargo on the United States to whom they might have to turn for protection against Iran, especially at a time when an oil glut was forcing down prices. Under these circumstances, Moscow evidently decided that if the Arabs were not going to help themselves, Moscow was not going to take any risks to help them. Nonetheless, as a superpower eager to have a hand in developments throughout the world and especially in the Middle East, a region Soviet leaders frequently reminded the world is in "close proximity to the southern borders of the USSR," Moscow had to at least give the appearance that it was taking an active role as events developed, particularly since the US was sending its Middle East trouble shooter Philip Habib back to the region to try to peacefully end the Beirut siege. Were Habib's efforts to prove successful, this would further enhance US diplomatic credibility in the region while reinforcing the view of the late Egyptian President Anwar Sadat that the United States held "99% of the cards in the Arab–Israeli dispute." Moscow, therefore, adopted a two-tier diplomatic approach. On the one hand it issued a series of warnings to Israel about the consequences of its actions in Lebanon, and sought wherever possible to link the United States to the Israeli invasion so as to discredit American diplomatic efforts to end the Lebanese crisis. On the other hand, it also began to openly appeal to the Arabs to unite so as to confront the Israelis. The official Tass statement issued on June 14 echoed both of these themes. Published after the bulk of the fighting had ended (the PLO–Israeli cease-fire came into being on June 12) Moscow, as it had done in the 1956 Suez conflict, sought to obtain diplomatic credit for taking strong action when the most serious fighting had already died down. Thus Moscow warned Israel that the Middle East was an area lying in close proximity to the southern borders of the USSR and that "developments there cannot help but affect the interests of the USSR." In addition, using terminology the Soviet leaders may later have regretted, the statement said "the USSR takes the Arab side not in words but in deeds." Moscow also blamed the US for aiding in Israel's "genocide" in Lebanon through its "strategic cooperation" with Israel. Finally the statement publicly deplored Arab disunity, and asserted "In carrying out its plans, Israel is using the fact that a number of Arab countries are virtually observing indifferently the destruction of the Palestinians in Lebanon."[262]

Interestingly enough, however, despite its strong words, there were two major omissions in the Tass statements. Thus there was no mention of the Soviet–Syrian treaty (Moscow may well have remembered past Syrian efforts to embroil the USSR in Lebanon), or of the PLO. These omissions, coupled with the termination of the fighting, indicated that the Soviet statement was essentially just rhetoric.

Nonetheless, Moscow did not totally refrain from military action during this period as the First Deputy Commander-in-Chief of Soviet air defense forces was sent to Damascus on June 13 in an obvious attempt by Moscow to see what had gone wrong with the Soviet-supplied air defense system. In addition, the Soviet Ambassador to Lebanon announced on June 15 that Soviet warships, including a nuclear submarine, were being sent to the Eastern Mediterranean and that Moscow was resupplying both the PLO and Syria.[263] Still, Moscow was clearly playing down the possibility of its becoming openly involved in the fighting as a Soviet official, speaking with the *Christian Science Monitor* on June 16, stated that he thought a wider war between Israel and the Syrians could be avoided because "We, the US, Syria, and Israel are against it."[264] Similarly, on June 18, Moscow agreed to a two month extension of the UN force in Lebanon, despite previous unhappiness with its "ineffectiveness" for allowing Israeli forces to move unimpeded through its territory.[265]

While downplaying the possibility of its military intervention, Moscow stepped up its rhetoric. Moscow Radio Peace and Progress, the most radical of Soviet broadcast media, which had appealed to the Arabs for an oil embargo on June 12, three days later denounced "feeble and apathetic Arab countries who do not even raise a finger to halt this ugly crime against Palestine."[266]

While calling for the Arabs to unite against Israel, Moscow was beginning to come in for some serious Arab criticism for its own failure to provide more substantive support for the Arab effort against Israel. Thus, at a press conference on June 22,[267] Gromyko when asked the meaning of the term "standing behind the Arabs not in words but in deeds" stated "there is no need to expand on this theme." This clearly was not what the Palestinians, now completely surrounded in Beirut, wanted to hear. Thus, in an interview on Radio Monte Carlo, the number two man in Fatah, Abu Iyad (Salah Khalaf) stated in response to a question about the significance of the June 14 Soviet warning:

> Actually, I personally cannot understand the Soviet Union's stand. I say this from the position of friendship between the Palestinian revolution and the Soviet Union. I say I cannot understand this silence and sluggishness. They can tell the United States to stop this massacre being committed against the Lebanese and Palestinian peoples, but it seems we are not included within the framework of the red line. I hope

I am wrong, but so far this is the feeling of the Lebanese and Palestinian peoples.[268]

The PLO leader was even more critical of the USSR in a *Le Monde* interview on June 23:

The Soviet attitude is even more inexplicable. We have questioned Moscow publicly and in secret. We have only received symbolic encouragement: "We are with you, we are exerting pressure ..." How can the Soviet Union even show such passiveness when the United States is such a blatant party to the battle? I do not understand it.[269]

Moscow also came in for criticism from Naef Hawatmeh, leader of the Marxist Popular Democratic Front for the Liberation of Palestine who was cited by Monte Carlo Radio as "indignant" at the Soviet position on Israel's invasion.[270] "The Soviets could have done more," he stated, "they could have resorted to other means, including military, to deter the aggressors."[271] Hawatmeh's criticism must have been particularly worrisome to the USSR because he had been considered one of the closest of all the PLO leaders to Moscow. But it was not only PLO spokesmen who were raising questions with Soviet policy – Libyan leader Muammar Kaddafi, perhaps the most outspoken of all of the Soviet clients in the Arab world, openly berated a group of Soviet bloc Amabassadors on June 26, complaining:

The friendship between Arab progressive forces and the Socialist countries is passing through danger, like the danger that surrounds the Palestinian resistance. This friendship is almost ready to go up in flames the way Beirut is going up in flames, and we have no answer to those Arabs in the street who ask about the posture of our friends *vis-à-vis* the Zionist–American aggression.[272]

As Arab criticism mounted, Moscow felt constrained to reply. In the first place, Tass gave prominent coverage to the press coverage of Syrian Information Minister Ahmad Iskander of June 20. The Syrian official praised the USSR as a "sincere friend" of Syria who had "helped us defend our lands, wives and children" and he called for a strategic alliance with the Soviet Union.[273] While the Syrians appeared to be using their battle losses against Israel and the Iskander press conference in yet another effort to obtain the strategic alliance with the Soviet Union they had long wanted,[274] Moscow utilized the press conference to demonstrate its continuing importance in Arab affairs and the major role in aiding in Arab defense efforts it had already played. Similarly, Moscow Radio, in an Arabic language broadcast on June 28, played up the visit of a second-level PLO official, Yasser Abd Raboo, who was cited as praising the USSR "for opposing in words and deeds the US–Israeli aggression in Lebanon."[275] Moscow also publicized a series of public demonstrations throughout the USSR opposing the Israeli invasion, cited a series of foreign reports praising Soviet weaponry, and announced the dispatch of doctors, medicine, and bandages to aid the relief effort in Lebanon.[276] Interestingly enough, however, it was to be Jordan, one of the Centrist Arab states which in the past had been close to the United States, that was to play the largest role in this stage of Moscow's propaganda efforts. Thus, during an "unofficial visit" to the Soviet Union in late June, King Hussein thanked the USSR for its help to the Arabs and joined Soviet Prime Minister Tikhonov and Foreign Minister Gromyko in calling for Israel's immediate withdrawal from Lebanon and in stressing the need to "unite the efforts of all Arab countries and all Arab peoples, in order to confront the aggressor from a common position."[277] Perhaps even more to Moscow's liking was an article which appeared in the semi-official Jordanian newspaper *Ar-Ra'y* on June 28 (it was broadcast by Tass the next day) which stated:

> The USSR cannot send armies to fight on behalf of a nation such as the Arab nation which is one of the richest in the world and whose population allows it to mobilize 30 million fighters. It is Soviet arms which defend the USSR and the Socialist bloc countries. It was with these arms that the barefoot Vietnamese defeated the US war machine ...

> What has happened and is still happening in Lebanon is not due to Soviet failure but to our own failure. It is due to the wooden swords which we use against one another ... the USSR has every right to accuse us of failure for humbling its weapons and friendship and enabling Israel and the United States to make our miserable situation a lesson for the friends of the Russians.[278]

As Moscow was seeking to defend itself from Arab charges of insufficient aid, diplomatic developments began to overshadow those on the battlefield which had become relatively quiet. The first major diplomatic event occurred on June 25 as Secretary of State Alexander Haig suddenly resigned. A Tass broadcast, reacting to the resignation, noted that the event "evoked in Arab conservative circles dangerous illusions and hopes for positive changes and a more balanced approach" in US Middle East policy.[279] One day later an emergency meeting of Arab foreign ministers began in Tunis to try to deal with the Israeli invasion. Despite pleas from the PLO representative Farouk Kaddoumi for an

Arab economic and financial boycott of the US, an oil embargo, and the break-off of diplomatic relations (Kaddoumi's call was given extensive press coverage by Moscow),[280] no such moves were taken by the sharply divided foreign ministers. Instead, a six state ministerial committee was appointed to both contact the permanent members of the UN Security Council in an effort to work out the modalities for an end to the Israeli invasion, and also to prepare for a special Arab summit.

With the new diplomatic momentum underway, a major Tass commentary, by Grigory Vasilyev, was released on July 1. In his commentary, Vasilyev concentrated on the two themes that were central to Moscow's concern at this time. In the first place, he deplored the fact that "US–Zionist" efforts to discredit Soviet manufactured weapons and "instill in the Arabs scepticism concerning their own strength" had met a positive response in "certain Arab circles leaning toward the United States." Secondly he reminded the Arabs that they had "huge potentialities" that could be used – if intra-Arab differences could be resolved. Vasilyev then openly called for the use of the oil weapon against the United States and also cited the "impressive military potential" possessed by the Arabs.[281]

The stage was thus set for the July 5 trip to Moscow of the three-man Arab delegation representing the newly established Arab League Ministerial Committee. The delegation consisted of Kuwaiti Foreign Minister Sheik Sabah, Moroccan Foreign Minister Mohammed Boucetta and the PLO political department chief Farouk Kaddoumi. There is little doubt that the Arabs were in Moscow seeking increased Soviet support. Indeed, Kaddoumi was quoted in the Kuwaiti newspaper *Al-Anba* on June 30 as stating that the PLO expected more political support from the Soviet Union:

> We expect a stricter tone with stronger warnings to the United States. The Soviet Union cannot turn a blind eye to events that are taking place at its southern borders and infringe on its national security. Therefore, some brothers have gone to the Soviet Union to urge it to escalate the degree of its warning to the US and Israel because of their attack. We hope the Soviet Union will intensify its political warning.[282]

It is doubtful whether the delegation got what it wanted. Thus, the *Pravda* report of the talks, while citing Soviet efforts to get Israel out of Lebanon and Arab praise for the Soviet stand, also noted that the discussions between the Arab delegation and Gromyko had taken place in a "businesslike, friendly atmosphere" – the usual Soviet code words

for very limited agreement.[283] This interpretation of the talks was confirmed by Arab diplomats in Moscow who told *Washington Post* correspondent Dusko Doder that Gromyko had ruled out Soviet military
involvement in the Lebanese fighting.[284]

Nonetheless, one day after the visit, when word of the possible dispatch of American Marines to Lebanon was made public, Moscow felt
compelled to take action. On July 8, Brezhnev, after calling on Reagan
"to do everything in the United States power to end the bloodshed,"
openly warned the US President not to send troops to Lebanon. As
Pravda noted:

> In connection with statements to the effect that the US is prepared in
> principle to send a contingent of American troops to Lebanon, L. I.
> Brezhnev warned the US President that if this actually takes place, the
> Soviet Union will construct its policy with due regard to this fact.[285]

Soviet propaganda agencies gave extensive coverage to Brezhnev's
warning,[286] with an Arabic language broadcast by Aleksandr Timoshkin
on July 9 noting that "this warning has aroused widespread comment in
the world, especially in the US with which the message is primarily
concerned."[287] It is, of course, possible that Moscow had several
purposes behind the July 8 warning. At the minimum, it would be both a
response to Farouk Kaddoumi's call of June 30 for the USSR to escalate
the degree of warning to the United States, and a response to the Arab
League delegation's visit of July 5. Moscow may also have hoped that
Reagan would respond as former US President Jimmy Carter did when
another major warning on a Middle East trouble spot was issued by the
USSR – in November 1978. At that time Brezhnev warned Carter not to
get involved in the turmoil that was then gripping Iran. Indeed, in a
Persian language broadcast to Iran on July 14, 1982, Soviet commentator Vera Lebedeva made an explicit comparison between the two
warnings.[288] Nonetheless, Reagan was not Carter, and the US simply
shrugged off the warning and continued with its diplomatic efforts to
solve the Beirut siege – efforts that included the emplacement of US
troops, as part of a multinational force, to ensure the safe departure of
the PLO.

As Moscow was continuing its warnings about the dispatch of US
troops to Beirut (it warned the Arabs that any US troops in Lebanon,
even as part of a multinational force, would serve as a bridgehead for
the US RDF, much as the US troops in the Sinai were doing), it faced a
deteriorating diplomatic situation in the Arab world. The OPEC meet-

ing of July 10 ended in failure, as it was not able to fix production quotas, and whatever hopes that Moscow might have had for the Arab members of OPEC securing an oil embargo against the United States proved unfounded. Then, on July 13, Tunisian President Habib Bourgiba, in whose country the proposed Arab summit to deal with the Israeli invasion of Lebanon was supposed to have taken place, announced its cancellation, because of insufficient Arab cooperation.[289] A Tass commentary expressed Moscow's disappointment with this development: "It is therefore not surprising that the disorder and vacillation, the inability of the Arab states to display political will and even a minimum degree of unity in the present stage arouses profound regret and anxiety amidst the Arab public."[290]

The situation took a further negative turn as far as Moscow was concerned with the announcement that the Foreign Minister of Syria, the leading Steadfastness Front state, and the Foreign Minister of Saudi Arabia, the leading Arab Centrist state, were journeying to Washington for discussions with Reagan. Not only did this development underline the continued centrality of the United States in Middle East diplomacy, Moscow may also have worried that Syria, seeing the changing balance of military and political power in the region, was making a change in its diplomatic orientation. The fact that rumors about a collapse of the Steadfastness Front had already begun to circulate in Arab circles, may have heightened Moscow's concern.[291] Nonetheless, the problem before Moscow remained as it had been in the past – how to react. To add to the pressure on the Soviet leadership, DFLP leader Naef Hawatmeh was again complaining about insufficient Soviet assistance calling it "incomprehensible," and asserting that "we believe that the Soviet Union should resort to direct pressure, including sending troops in accordance with the Soviet–Syrian pact."[292] Moscow, however, was to react the opposite way, and, in addition to not sending troops, began to de-escalate its rhetoric. In a series of answers to questions from *Pravda* on July 21, Brezhnev, perhaps seeing that the US would not back down from its plan to send troops to Beirut despite Soviet threats, suggested a compromise: the use of a UN force to help in the disengagement of forces in Beirut as a first step toward an Israeli withdrawal from Lebanon. (Moscow was to suggest a similar ploy in 1987 for a UN fleet to replace US forces in the Gulf). While again stating the USSR's categorical opposition to the dispatch of American troops to Lebanon, the tone of his comments was far milder than his July 8 warning. Thus Brezhnev noted that "more and more people in Israel itself" were beginning to realize that the invasion of Lebanon was turning into a major political and moral defeat for Israel, and that the world was realizing that the best solution to the Palestinian problem was the creation of a Palestinian state. The Soviet leader also repeated Moscow's call for Arab unity in the present "crucial situation," and again urged the convening of an international conference on the Middle East, with the participation of the PLO, to achieve a Middle East settlement.

Brezhnev's comments of July 21 proved no more efficacious however, than his warning of July 8, and, as the Israelis grew impatient with PLO stalling during the Beirut negotiations, fighting again escalated. By early August Israel had begun to penetrate West Beirut. At this point, Brezhnev did nothing but issue yet another appeal to Reagan in which the Soviet leader called on the US President to "most urgently use the possibilities at his disposal to prevent the continuing annihilation of the people in Beirut."[293] The Brezhnev appeal again underlined the centrality of the US diplomatic role, and when the Soviet leader, on August 6, would do nothing more than send a telegram[294] to Arafat praising the PLO leader's courage as the Israeli pressure increased, Arafat and his colleagues must have realized that neither the USSR nor their fellow Arabs would save them. Rejecting a call from Kaddafi to become martyrs, the PLO leaders began to negotiate in earnest for their departure from Beirut. Indeed, two days before the Brezhnev telegram to Arafat, Moscow had hinted that the PLO position in Beirut could no longer be maintained. Thus a *Pravda* editorial on August 4 cited French President François Mitterand's statement that "even if Israel succeeds in neutralizing the PLO as a military force, this will not change the people's right to have their own country." On August 20, with the PLO about to leave Beirut, *Pravda* simply noted that the evacuation plan had been approved by the PLO and the Lebanese government and that an international force with units from the United States, Italy, and France, would be in place to monitor the evacuation.

Thus the event that Moscow had long feared, and which it had committed some of its prestige to prevent – the emplacement of US troops in Lebanon – had taken place. This diplomatic defeat for Moscow was followed by what it feared would be yet another blow to its waning Middle East position. With the US now ever more clearly holding the diplomatic initiative in the Arab world following the PLO departure from Beirut, President Reagan, on September 1 – the eve of the long-delayed Arab summit – announced his plan for a Middle East peace settlement. In a clear effort to gain Centrist Arab support for his plan,

Reagan called for a stop to Israeli settlement activity on the West Bank and announced US refusal to accept any Israeli claim to sovereignty over the West Bank. To satisfy the Israelis, Reagan emphasized US concern for Israel's security, asserted that Israel's final borders should not be the pre-1967 war boundaries, called for the unity of Jerusalem and direct Arab–Israeli negotiations, and reaffirmed US opposition to a Palestinian state on the West Bank. In his most controversial statement, and one also aimed at obtaining Centrist Arab support, Reagan called for a fully autonomous Palestinian entity linked to Jordan. Moscow, while denouncing the Reagan plan – and denigrating Begin's rapid rejection of it – was concerned that the plan might prove attractive in the Arab world. Indeed *Izvestia* correspondent Vladimir Kudravtzev noted that "judging from press reports 'moderate' and 'pro-Western' Arab regimes find positive elements in the American initiative."[295]

Given this situation, Moscow seemed pleased by the outcome of the Arab summit at Fez, Morocco, which not only indicated that the Arab world had regained a semblance of unity[296] but also that it brought forth a peace plan which, except for its lack of explicit clarity as to Israel's right to exist, was quite close to the long-standing Soviet peace plan.[297] Thus the Fez plan called for (1) Israeli withdrawal from all territories occupied in 1967, including Arab Jerusalem; (2) the dismantling of settlements established by Israel in the occupied territories; (3) guarantees for worship and the exercise of religious rites for all religions; (4) affirmation of the right of the Palestinian people to self-determination, and the exercise of their inalienable national rights under the leadership of the PLO, their sole legitimate representative, with compensation to be paid for those who do not wish to return; (5) a transition period for the West Bank and Gaza under the supervision of the UN for a period not exceeding a few months; (6) the establishment of an independent Palestinian state with Jerusalem as its capital; (7) the guarantee of the peace and security of all states in the region, including the Palestinian state, by the UN Security Council; and (8) the guarantee of the implementation of these principles by the UN Security Council.[298] Moscow also was pleased that the Sudanese proposal to formally re-admit Egypt to the Arab League was rejected.[299] Nonetheless, the Fez conference did not reject the Reagan plan, thereby leaving it, along with the Fez plan, as one of the solutions which the Arabs would consider to resolve the post-Beirut diplomatic situation in the Middle East. With both the Reagan and Fez plans now being considered, Moscow evidently felt that it too had to enter the diplomatic competition, and in a speech on September 15, during the visit of PDRY leader Ali Nasser Mohammed, one of Moscow's few remaining Arab allies, Brezhnev announced the Soviet Union's own peace plan.[300] While a number of its points were repetitions of previous Soviet proposals, others seem to have been added to emphasize the similarity between the Fez and Soviet plans. The elements of the Soviet peace plan which repeated earlier Soviet proposals were Moscow's call for the withdrawal of Israeli forces from the Golan Heights, the West Bank, the Gaza Strip, and Lebanon to the lines which existed before the June 1967 war; the establishment of a Palestinian state on the West Bank and Gaza; the right of all states in the region to a secure and independent existence; and the termination of the state of war between Israel and the Arab states. While these points in many ways resembled the Fez plan, except for Moscow's more explicit call for Israel's right to exist and an end to the state of war between Israel and the Arab world, the new elements in the Brezhnev peace plan seemed to be virtually modeled on the Fez plan. Thus Moscow called for the Palestinian refugees to be given the right to return to their homes or receive compensation for their abandoned property, for the return of East Jerusalem to the Arabs and its incorporation into the Palestinian state, with freedom of access for believers to the sacred places of the three religions throughout Jerusalem, and for Security Council guarantees for the final settlement. Brezhnev also took the opportunity to repeat the long-standing Soviet call for an international conference on the Middle East, with all interested parties participating, including the PLO, which the Soviet leader again characterized as "the sole legitimate representative of the Arab people of Palestine."

In modeling the Soviet peace plan on Fez, Brezhnev evidently sought to prevent the Arabs from moving to embrace the Reagan plan. Nonetheless, with the United States clearly possessing the diplomatic initiative in the Middle East after the PLO pull-out from Beirut, and both Jordanian King Hussein and PLO leader Arafat, along with other Arab leaders, expressing interest in the Reagan plan, Moscow was on the diplomatic defensive. Given this situation, it is not surprising that Brezhnev seized upon the massacres in the Sabra and Shatilla refugee camps to point out to Arafat "if anyone had any illusions that Washington was going to support the Arabs ... these illusions have now been drowned in streams of blood in the Palestinian camps ..."[301]

Nonetheless, despite the massacres, Arafat evidently felt that there was value in pursuing the Reagan plan (the US, meanwhile, had again dispatched troops to Lebanon, and was joined by France and Britain, although the mission of the troops, sent in reaction to the massacres was unclear) and he began to meet regularly with his erstwhile enemy, King Hussein of Jordan, to work out a joint approach to the United States.[302] Such maneuvering infuriated Syria, which sought to use pro-Syrian elements within the PLO to pressure Arafat into abandoning his new policy, a development which further exacerbated relations between Assad and Arafat. In addition, evidently fearing the weakening of the Steadfastness Front and the possibility of the PLO (or at least Arafat's Fatah wing) defecting from it, Moscow continued to warn the Arabs about what it called US efforts to split the PLO and to draw Jordan and Saudi Arabia into supporting the Reagan plan, which the USSR termed a cover for Camp David. Despite the Soviet warnings, however, many Arabs were clearly interested in giving the Reagan plan a chance – and getting the US to ensure Israel's departure from Lebanon. Under these circumstances there was little overt criticism of the Reagan plan, and it was a deteriorating Middle East situation that Brezhnev, who died on November 11, 1982, was to bequeath to his successor, Yuri Andropov.

3 The interregnum: Moscow and the Middle East under Andropov and Chernenko

The interregnum between Leonid Brezhnev, who led the Soviet Union from October 1964 to November 1982, and Michail Gorbachev, who took over the leadership of the Soviet Union in March 1985, lasted twenty-eight months. In that period first Yuri Andropov and then Konstantin Chernenko served as interim leaders of the USSR, but ill-health prevented either leader from making a dramatic impact on Soviet politics or foreign policy.[1] Nonetheless, each was to influence Soviet policy toward the Middle East in a significant way. Thus Andropov, in sending SAM-5 and SS-21 missiles to Syria, escalated the Syrian–Israeli arms race while in the process giving Syria the impression of heightened Soviet support, something which Syrian leader Hafiz Assad was to exploit. For his part Konstantin Chernenko, faced by the possibility that Jordan might embrace the Reagan Plan, modified the Soviet peace plan to make it more acceptable to Jordan and also actively courted Kuwait as an escalation of the Iran–Iraq war threatened to move Kuwait to take a more pro-American stance in Middle East politics.

Yuri Andropov, having inherited a deteriorating Middle East situation from Brezhnev, immediately sought to rebuild the Soviet position in the region. Andropov faced three major problems. In the first place, due to its inactivity during the Israeli invasion of Lebanon and the siege of Beirut in 1982, Soviet credibility as an ally of the Arabs had been called into question, even by such pro-Soviet regimes as Libya. Second, due to the poor performance of Soviet-made weaponry in the hands of Syria, the quality of Soviet military equipment had become suspect. This was a major problem for Moscow both because the provision of modern weaponry was the single most important element of Soviet influence in the Middle East, and also because the sale of weapons earned Moscow badly needed hard currency. A final Middle East problem for Andropov at the start of 1983 was the fact that the United

States, which at the beginning of January had established a new "Central Command" to oversee its Rapid Deployment Force (RDF) in the Middle East, was clearly holding the diplomatic initiative in the region. By contrast, Moscow's own peace plan had received little support. In addition, as shown by the Fez II Arab summit, Moscow's main Arab allies – Libya, South Yemen, Syria, and the PLO – seemed to have little clout in Arab politics, while they had serious disagreements among themselves, with Libyan leader Muammar Kaddafi and Syrian President Hafiz Assad at odds with PLO leader Yasser Arafat who was publicly flirting with the Reagan plan.

Andropov very quickly received first-hand knowledge of the diminution of Soviet influence in the Middle East, and the rise of American influence, when an Arab delegation, headed by King Hussein, journeyed to Moscow in early December 1982 soon after Brezhnev's death to discuss the Fez plan with the new Soviet leader. Thus while *Pravda* gave page one coverage to the talks and to the significance of the Arab delegation's visit, its report that the discussions took place in a "businesslike and friendly atmosphere," and that there was "an exchange of opinions," reflected the fact that the Soviet leader was unable to get the Arab leaders to either criticize the Reagan plan or agree to Moscow's proposal for an international conference.[2]

At least one positive result from the Arab leaders' visit, for Moscow, was the fact that Soviet Foreign Minister Gromyko had a face-to-face meeting with Saudi Foreign Minister, Prince Saud al Faisal, who was the first Saudi official to visit the USSR since the 1930s.[3] Nonetheless, following the visit Saudi Information Minister Mohammed Abdu Yamani stated that Saudi Arabia was not considering diplomatic relations with the USSR because "the time was not ripe for such links."[4] In addition, the fact that Moscow subsequently invited a delegation from the Popular Front for the Liberation of Bahrain – an organization anathema to the Saudis – to an anniversary celebration in Moscow was an indication that the USSR did not foresee any rapid improvement of relations with Saudi Arabia.[5]

Meanwhile, Moscow faced yet another negative Middle Eastern development – the resumption of the momentum for a reconciliation between Egypt and the Centrist bloc, which had been temporarily interrupted by the Israeli invasion of Lebanon. Indeed, the visit of Iraqi and UAE military delegations to Cairo in December 1982,[6] and the calls by both Arafat and Iraqi Deputy Prime Minister Tariq Aziz for Egypt to reenter the Arab world without having to renounce Camp David[7] seemed to signal that the end of Egypt's isolation in the Arab world might soon be at hand.

Meanwhile, Andropov also had to face increasingly severe problems in the Soviet relationship with Iran. Despite a number of public and private calls by the USSR for Iran to end its war with Iraq, the Iranians refused and Moscow continued to be frustrated by the continuation of the war which was now characterized by Iranian attacks against Iraqi territory. In addition, as the Iranian regime stepped up its crackdown on the Tudeh, a Soviet diplomat stationed in Iran, Vladimir Kuzichkin, defected to England, possibly bringing with him reports of Tudeh operations in Tehran and elsewhere in Iran.[8] Finally, on the third anniversary of the Soviet invasion of Afghanistan, there was a major demonstration outside the Soviet embassy in Tehran in which, according to an irate Soviet report, "a gang of hoodlums with the obvious connivance of the (Iranian) authorities, tried to force their way into embassy grounds and tore down the Soviet flag."[9] The report also noted that the USSR had issued a "vigorous protest" over the incident to the Foreign Ministry of Iran.

As Soviet–Iranian relations deteriorated, there were reports that Moscow was increasing its shipments of arms to Iraq,[10] although Iraqi leader Saddam Hussein in late November publicly complained that Iraq's Treaty of Friendship and Cooperation "has not worked" during the Iran–Iraq war.[11] The Iraqi President also asserted that the USSR, like the US, was opposing the end to the war because both superpowers were allowing weapons to flow to Iran. Perhaps in an effort to gain increased Soviet support for Iraq's war effort, a top level Iraqi delegation composed of Taha Yassan and Tariq Aziz journeyed to Moscow in December for meetings with Gromyko and Boris Ponomarev which reportedly were more successful in obtaining arms than the last visit of high-ranking Iraqi officials to the Soviet capital on June 4, on the eve of the Iranian invasion of Iraq.[12] In any case, despite its increased arms shipments to Iraq, Moscow could not have been pleased with Iraq's growing *rapprochement* with Egypt, or with the repeated gestures by the hard-pressed Iraqis for an improvement of relations with the United States.[13]

Andropov was to receive additional evidence of Moscow's diminution of influence in the Middle East, and the rise of American influence, when PLO leader Yasser Arafat journeyed to Moscow in mid-January 1983. Arafat, who had long been a close Soviet ally in the Arab world, now was openly praising some aspects of the Reagan plan, and had stated that he was resigned to dealing with the United States as the dominant superpower in the Middle East.[14] As a result, his visit to Moscow revealed a number of major Soviet–PLO differences. Thus, while in the past Arafat had supported Soviet plans for an international conference to solve the Arab–Israeli conflict, now he only conceded that such a conference "might open a road to a settlement."[15] Even more discouraging for Moscow must have been the PLO leader's announced agreement to the establishment of a confederation between Jordan and "an independent Palestinian state after its creation." While Moscow was in favor of the creation of an independent Palestinian state the fact of its linkage to Jordan, a Centrist state, not only seemed to associate the PLO at least partially with the Reagan plan, but also appeared to mean its defection from the Steadfastness Front, which had been already badly weakened by the Israeli invasion. Consequently, the USSR only expressed its "understanding" of the PLO position – a diplomatic way of demonstrating its opposition.[16]

Under these circumstances, with Soviet influence in the Middle East at a low ebb, Andropov took action to rebuild the Soviet position in the region. His first action was the deployment of several batteries of SAM-5 missiles to Syria – along with the Soviet soldiers to operate and guard them.[17] This Soviet move went far beyond the Soviet resupply effort of tanks and planes to Syria which had been going on since the end of the Israeli–Syrian fighting in 1982. Indeed, by sending Syria a weapons system that had never been deployed outside the USSR itself, a system that had the capability of engaging Israel's EC-2 aircraft which had proven so effective during the Israeli–Syrian air battles in the first week of the Israeli invasion of Lebanon in June 1982, Moscow was demonstrating to the Arab world – and especially to Syria – that it was willing to stand by its allies.[18] Nonetheless, by manning the SAM-5 missiles with Soviet soldiers, Moscow was also signalling that it, and not Syria, would determine when the missiles would be fired.[19] Given the fact that both in November 1980 and April 1981 Assad had tried to involve the USSR in his military adventures, this was probably a sensible precaution.[20] Yet another cautionary element in the dispatch of the missiles was that Moscow never formally announced that its own troops were involved in guarding the missiles, thus enabling the USSR to avoid a direct confrontation with Israel (and possibly the United States) should Israel decide to attack the missile sites.

By acquiring the missiles, however, Syria's military position *vis-à-vis* Israel was strengthened and it was not to be long before Assad was to use his new Soviet weaponry to enhance his political position both in

Lebanon and in the Middle East as a whole. Indeed, less than two weeks after the arrival of the SAM-5s, Syria joined with Libya and Iran not only in pledging support for the end of the Israeli occupation of Lebanon, but also in calling for the ouster of Iraqi leader Saddam Hussein[21] – a move which underlined the continuing hostility between Iraq and Syria, which made Soviet hopes of an "anti-imperialist" Arab unity seem even more remote.

While moving to bolster the USSR's primary Arab ally, Syria, with new weaponry, Andropov also sought to strengthen the position of Libya, another key Soviet client state, after it once again found itself in a confrontation with the United States. Acting in response to reports of a planned Libyan-supported coup against the Sudan in mid-February, the United States sent four AWACs aircraft to Egypt for what was first called "training maneuvers" and also dispatched the aircraft carrier Nimitz from Lebanon to a position close to Libya, although outside the disputed Gulf of Sidra where the US had shot down two Libyan planes in 1981.[22] Following the American moves, no Libyan coup attempt took place and US Secretary of State George Shultz bluntly stated that Kaddafi had been "put back into his box where he belonged."[23]

While, as in the 1981 Gulf of Sidra incident, Moscow kept a low profile during the crisis itself, the Soviet leadership evidently felt that if the USSR was to rebuild its Middle East position, something more than merely a denunciation of US policy was called for. Thus Moscow took a significant, but not irreversible, step toward deepening relations with Libya by coming to "an agreement in principle" to conclude a Treaty of Friendship and Cooperation with Libya, one month after the Libyan–US confrontation.[24] The agreement was reached during the mid-March Moscow visit of the number two man in the Libyan leadership, Abdel Salam Jalloud, who was a frequent visitor to the USSR. To be sure, Moscow was not yet ready to fully endorse all of Kaddafi's adventures. Thus Soviet Prime Minister Tikhonov noted, in a dinner speech welcoming Jalloud, that the Soviet Union wanted to see Libya "as an economically developed state playing a weighty, positive role in international affairs and capable of repulsing all outside encroachments on its independence," and the Soviet Prime Minister went on to say that "the all around assistance given by us to your country, the fulfillment of a number of promising projects of much importance for the development of Libya's economy, are called upon to facilitate the attainment of this aim."[25] Tikhonov's emphasis was clearly on the Soviet–Libyan economic relationship (Soviet–Libyan trade had passed the 1 billion rouble mark for the first time in 1982),[26] while it would appear that the Libyans were more interested in a strong military relationship.[27] This difference in emphasis was reflected in the joint communiqué which described the talks as taking place in a spirit of "frankness and mutual understanding" and said that there was a "thorough exchange of opinions" on the international situation.[28] While Moscow condemned US "provocative and dangerous aggressive actions against Libya," it issued no threats against the United States, stating only that "actions of this kind were aimed at undermining the universally accepted principles of relations between sovereign states." In addition, while both Libya and the USSR condemned the establishment of the US Central Command, along with Israeli actions in Lebanon, the only detailed areas of cooperation mentioned in the communiqué were in the economic sphere, thus indicating that Moscow's emphasis had prevailed. In any case, while at the close of the communiqué mention was made of the agreement "in principle" to conclude a Treaty of Friendship and Cooperation, the failure of the Soviet press to report any further progress toward concluding the treaty during the remainder of 1983 may well have been an indication that Moscow had had second thoughts about even appearing to give a military guarantee to Kaddafi whose mercurial behavior was well known in Moscow, and whose adventure in Chad was soon to embroil Moscow in unwanted complications.

Nonetheless, in mid-March, when it consented to the "agreement in principle," Moscow was still in an assertive mood as it sought to rebuild its Middle East position, and it was to follow up its promise to Libya with a public warning to Israel not to attack Syria. This Soviet warning, issued on March 30, came after a series of Syrian warnings, yet was limited in nature.[29] Thus, while Moscow warned that Israel was "playing with fire" by preparing to attack Syria, it made no mention of the Soviet–Syrian treaty. Indeed, in listing those on Syria's side in the confrontation with Israel, the Soviet statement merely noted "on the side of the Syrian people are Arab patriots, the Socialist countries, and all who cherish the cause of peace, justice and honor." The statement also emphasized the need to settle the Arab–Israeli conflict, politically, not through war.

This rather curious Soviet warning can perhaps be understood if one assumes that Moscow did not seriously expect an Israeli attack on Syria. With the more cautious Moshe Arens as Israel's new Defense Minister, and with rising opposition to Israel's presence in Lebanon being felt on Israel's domestic political scene, it appeared unlikely that Israel would attack Syria, even to take out the newly installed SAM-5 missiles. Indeed, even the hawkish Israeli Chief of Staff, General Eitan, in an interview on Israeli armed forces radio, stated that Israel had no intention of starting a war.[30] If Moscow, therefore, basically assumed that Israel would not go to war, then why the warning? Given the fact that Moscow's credibility in the Arab world had dropped precipitously as a result of the warnings it had issued during the Israeli invasion of Lebanon in the June/July 1982 period – warnings that had been ignored by both Israel and the United States – Moscow possibly saw a chance to increase its credibility in the region. Thus, if Moscow, assuming Israel would not attack Syria, issued a warning to Israel not to attack Syria and Israel then did not attack Syria, Moscow could take credit for the nonattack and could then demonstrate to the Arab world that Soviet diplomacy was effective *vis-à-vis* Israel, at least as a deterrent. If this, in fact, was Moscow's thinking, however, not all the Arabs were convinced. Indeed, the Saudi paper *Ar-Riyad* expressed a lack of trust in the Soviet warning, noting that the limited value of Soviet statements had been proven during the Israeli invasion of Lebanon "which dealt a sharp and severe blow to the Kremlin when the Soviet missiles became no more than timber towers in the face of the sophisticated weapons the United States had unconditionally supplied to Israel."[31]

In any case, only three days after the Soviet warning to Israel, Soviet Foreign Minister Andrei Gromyko, who had recently been promoted to Deputy Prime Minister, held a major press conference in Moscow.[32] While the main emphasis of Gromyko's press conference was on strategic arms issues, he also took the opportunity to make two major points about the Middle East situation. In the first place, in response to a question from a correspondent of the Syrian newspaper *Al-Ba'ath*, Gromyko stated "the Soviet Union is in favor of the withdrawal of all foreign troops from the territory of Lebanon, all of them. Syria is in favor of this."[33] Secondly, Gromyko noted once again that the USSR was in favor of Israel's existing as a state. "We do not share the point of view of extremist Arab circles that Israel should be eliminated. This is an unrealistic and unjust point of view."[34] The thrust of Gromyko's remarks were clear. The Soviet leader, by urging the withdrawal of all foreign troops from Lebanon – including Syrian troops – and reemphasizing the Soviet commitment to Israel's existence, seemed to be telling Syria that despite the provision of SAM-5 missiles, Moscow was not desirous of being dragged into a war in Lebanon on Syria's behalf. If this was indeed the message Gromyko was trying to get across, the rapid pace of Middle Eastern events was to pose new challenges, as well as opportunities, for Soviet policy.

On the one hand, Moscow had to be pleased by developments within the PLO, which challenged Arafat's opening to Washington, and the subsequent slowing of the momentum in support of the Reagan plan. Indeed, Moscow's interest in preventing a PLO turn to the United States was shared by both Syria and Libya which actively moved to undermine Arafat's position.[35] The efforts of the anti-Arafat forces were to prove successful as the Palestine National Council which, after a number of postponements, finally convened in mid-February in Algiers, formally stated its refusal to consider the Reagan plan "as a sound basis for a just and lasting solution to the Palestine problem and the Arab–Israeli conflict."[36] Needless to say, Moscow viewed this development positively with *Pravda* correspondent Yuri Vladimirov praising the council's policy document as a reaffirmation of the organization's determination to continue the struggle against imperialism and Zionism.[37]

As sentiment within the PLO hardened against the Reagan plan, King Hussein of Jordan, who on January 10 had stated that he would make his decision about joining peace talks with Israel by March 1, began to back away. Indeed, on March 19, after delaying any official statement, the King indicated, during a visit to London, that unless the United States succeeded in getting all of the foreign troops out of Lebanon and got Israel to stop building settlements on the West Bank, the talks could not get started.[38] Under these circumstances, and having linked (unwisely) progress on a troop withdrawal agreement in Lebanon to the Reagan plan, the United States stepped up its efforts to keep the plan alive. Thus President Reagan both tied the promised sale to Israel of seventy-five F-16 fighter bombers to an Israeli agreement to withdraw from Lebanon, and promised King Hussein that if Jordan joined the Middle East peace talks, the US would try to bring about a halt to the building of Israeli settlements on the West Bank.[39]

Despite these US actions, by the end of March it appeared that the Reagan plan was in deep trouble. On March 30, speaking at a Palestinian rally in Damascus, Arafat himself rejected the Reagan plan.[40] The Arafat rejection cast a predictable pall on the final round of the Arafat–Hussein talks in Jordan and it was not surprising that on April 10 King Hussein, claiming that Arafat had reneged on an earlier agreement, stated that Jordan would not enter into the peace negotiations.[41] Hussein's statement was greeted with great relief by Moscow which had long feared that Jordan would be attracted to the Reagan plan which the Soviet leadership saw as an extension of Camp David. As *Pravda* correspondent Pavel Demchenko noted on April 13:

> The authors of the "Reagan Plan" have especially been counting on Jordan. The government of that country has announced, however, that it would make a final decision only after meetings with the leaders of the Palestine Liberation Organization and would act only in concert with it. And now, after those meetings have ended, Amman has published a statement saying that, as in the past, Jordan will not hold talks on behalf of the Palestinians and refuses to take separate action to establish peace in the Middle East.

> As the *New York Times* writes, Jordan's answer "killed President Reagan's plan."[42]

Although the Reagan plan was not yet dead, the American diplomatic position deteriorated still further in mid-April as, one week after King Hussein had announced his refusal to enter into peace negotiations, the US embassy in Beirut was blown up by a car bomb, with a massive loss of life. Reacting to both events, President Reagan dispatched his Secretary of State, George Shultz, to salvage the stalled Israeli–Lebanese talks and regain the momentum for the United States in Middle East diplomacy. As Shultz toured the region, and shuttled back and forth between Beirut and Jerusalem, prospects for a Lebanese–Israeli agreement began to improve. Both Moscow and Damascus, for different reasons, wanted to see the Shultz mission fail. The USSR did not want to see any more Arab states following in Egypt's footsteps and agreeing to a US plan for Middle East peace. Syria, for its part, had long sought the dominant position in Lebanon and feared that any Lebanese–Israeli agreement would strengthen the Israeli position in Lebanon at Syria's expense. In addition, Syria also did not wish to see any more Arab states moving to make peace with Israel, since this would leave Syria increasingly isolated among the Arab confrontation states facing Israel. The end result was a rise in tension and a war scare in which Moscow was to play a role, albeit perhaps a somewhat unwilling one.

Less than a week after King Hussein refused to enter the peace talks, the Syrian government raised its price for a Lebanese troop withdrawal. While as late as January Syria had been willing to have a simultaneous withdrawal of Israeli, Syrian, and PLO forces, on April 16 the Syrian government, strengthened both by its new Soviet weapons and by the

Soviet warning to Israel, stated that Syria would not even discuss the withdrawal of its troops from Lebanon until all Israeli troops had left the country.[43] While the United States sought to assuage Syrian opposition in a letter from Reagan to Assad in which the US President indicated that the United States was still pressing for Israeli withdrawal from the Golan Heights,[44] the US ploy was not successful. Indeed, Syria appeared to step up tension by allowing guerrillas to infiltrate into Israeli lines to attack Israeli troops while simultaneously accusing the Israeli government of reinforcing its troops in Lebanon's Bekaa Valley and of staging "provocative" military exercises on the Golan Heights.[45] Meanwhile although Israeli Foreign Minister Shamir called the Syrian-induced tension "artificial,"[46] Israeli Defense Minister Arens, concerned about Soviet and Syrian intentions, put Israeli troops on alert and indicated that Israel would not leave Lebanon until Syria did.[47] Syria then stepped up its pressure on April 26 when Syrian forces opened fire on an Israeli bulldozer near the cease-fire line.[48]

Meanwhile, despite the rise in Syrian–Israeli tension, US Secretary of State Shultz continued to work for an Israeli–Lebanese troop withdrawal agreement and on May 6 his efforts seemed to be successful as the Israeli government accepted, in principle, a troop withdrawal agreement that had already been agreed to by Lebanon.[49] The next US goal was to try to gain Arab support for the agreement so as to pressure Syria into also withdrawing its forces from Lebanon. As might be expected, neither Moscow nor Syria was in favor of a rapid Syrian withdrawal. Moscow, although interested in Syria ultimately withdrawing its troops from Lebanon, did not want any precipitate withdrawal in the aftermath of the Israeli–Lebanese agreement lest the United States reap the diplomatic benefit. Syria complained that Israel had obtained too much from the treaty and Damascus Radio asserted that Lebanon had "capitulated to the Israeli aggressor."[50] It appeared at this point that President Assad was posturing so as to improve his bargaining position *vis-à-vis* the Arab world (Syria, long isolated because of its support of Iran in the Iran–Iraq war was now openly confronting Israel and should, thereby, merit Arab support), and *vis-à-vis* the United States (so as to get US pressure on Israel for a withdrawal from the Golan Heights). Indeed, as the crisis was played out until the end of May, with military maneuvers and threats of war (almost all from the Syrians) it seemed clear that Assad was enjoying the opportunity to play a major role once again in Middle East events.[51]

As Syria was exploiting the Lebanese situation for its own ends,

Moscow was cautiously supporting its Arab ally. Thus, on May 9, three days after Israel had agreed in principle to the accord, the Soviet Union issued an official statement denouncing the agreement, and, in a gesture of support for Syria, demanded that "first and foremost" Israeli troops be withdrawn from Lebanon. The statement added, however, that "American and other foreign troops staying in Lebanon also must be withdrawn from it," an oblique reference to Moscow's continuing desire to see Syrian troops leave the country.[52] At the same time, perhaps to enhance the atmosphere of crisis, Soviet dependants were withdrawn from Beirut, although the Soviet ambassador to Lebanon stated that the departure of the dependants had occurred because of the beginning of summer camp in the USSR.[53] In helping to enhance the atmosphere of crisis, Moscow may also have seen that the situation could be used as a means of once again playing a role in the Middle East peace process after having been kept on the diplomatic sidelines since Sadat's trip to Jerusalem in 1977. Indeed, on May 10, Shultz openly urged Moscow to use its influence to get Syria to withdraw its troops and stated he might meet Soviet Foreign Minister Gromyko to discuss the Middle East along with other international issues.[54] Shultz, however, indicated that the United States was not yet ready for an international conference on the Middle East, still a goal of Soviet diplomacy.[55]

Nonetheless, even in giving Syria a limited degree of support, Moscow had to be concerned as to the possibility of war erupting, especially as Syria began to issue increasingly bellicose threats – threats which involved Soviet support for Syria in case of war.[56] Thus, on May 9, Syrian Foreign Minister Khaddam, in an interview, noted that in case war between Israel and Syria broke out, "We believe that the USSR will fulfil its commitments in accordance with the [Soviet–Syrian] treaty." The next day, Syrian Radio warned that any Israeli attack against Syrian forces anywhere, even in Lebanon, would mean an "unlimited war."[57] The Syrian bellicosity, however, may have overstepped the bounds of propriety insofar as Moscow was concerned. Thus, in a broadcast over Beirut Radio, Soviet Ambassador to Lebanon, Aleksander Soldatov, when asked about Khaddam's assertion that Moscow would fully support Syria if war with Israel broke out, replied that "the USSR does not reply to such hypothetical questions."[58] Soldatov added that the USSR continued to support the withdrawal of all foreign forces from Lebanon. These themes of caution were repeated during the visit of a Soviet delegation to Israel in mid-May to attend ceremonies marking the 38th anniversary of the defeat of Nazi Germany. One of the leaders of the delegation, the well-known Soviet journalist Igor Belyayev took the opportunity to state upon arrival at Ben Gurion airport that Syria's recent military moves in the Bekaa Valley were purely defensive and that Syria had no aggressive intent toward Israel.[59] Similarly, Karen Khachaturev, deputy director of the *Novosti* news agency, noted that the USSR favored a peace treaty between Israel and Lebanon – but only after all Israeli soldiers departed – and Khachaturev reiterated Moscow's support of Israel's right to live in peace and security.[60]

While Moscow was trying to play down the possibility of war, the US Secretary of Defense Caspar Weinberger, in a speech to the American Jewish Committee in New York, was publicly warning Moscow and Syria about their behavior in Lebanon: "I want to make it very clear to the Soviets and any proxies they might have in Syria that any aggression by them would be met by a retaliatory force that would make the aggression totally unworthwhile, totally lacking in any hope of gain to the aggressor."[61] While the State Department sought to somewhat tone down Weinberger's remarks several days later,[62] there was no question but that despite friction between US and Israeli troops in Lebanon, the US commitment to Israel remained strong. Indeed, following Israel's signing of the US-mediated agreement with Lebanon, US–Israeli relations improved markedly and the US government decided to release the seventy-five F-16 fighter bombers for sale to Israel.

As might be expected, Moscow seized on Weinberger's comments and the end of the F-16 embargo to highlight the US–Israeli relationship and to underline the close relationship between Israel, "an occupier of Arab lands," and the United States.[63] This was part of Moscow's efforts to try to prevent an Arab consensus from building up behind the Israeli–Lebanese accord, and Moscow hailed the statement by Saudi Defense Minister Prince Sultan Ibn Abd al Aziz that his country refused to put pressure on Syria on behalf of the United States.[64]

Meanwhile, Syria continued to escalate the political and military pressure to undermine the Israeli–Lebanese agreement. On the political front it formed an alignment with a group of Lebanese leaders opposed to the agreement including former Lebanese Premier Rashid Karami, former President Suleiman Franjieh, Druze leader Walid Jumblatt, and Lebanese communist party First Secretary George Hawi.[65]

While moving to strengthen his political position, Assad also stepped up the political and military pressure in the Bekaa. After refusing to see US Envoy Philip Habib, Assad, on May 23 predicted a new war with

Israel in which Syria would lose 20,000 men.[66] Two days later Syrian
planes fired air-to-air missiles against Israeli jets flying over the Bekaa
Valley – the first such encounter since the war in 1982.[67] Assad followed
this up by conducting military exercises in the Golan and Bekaa, and the
danger of war appeared to heighten.[68] Nonetheless, despite a limited
countermobilization, Israel kept very cool during the crisis while for its
part Moscow kept a very low profile (although it did send a new aircraft
carrier into the Mediterranean), supporting Syria politically but issuing
no threats against the United States or Israel, and again appealing for a
full withdrawal of all forces in Lebanon. In any case, by the end of May
the crisis had subsided and the dangers of a Syrian–Israeli war in
Lebanon had, at least for the time being, receded.

While Andropov had to be pleased that the crisis ended without an
escalation of the Syrian–Israeli conflict, and that US efforts to gain
Centrist Arab support for the May 17 treaty appeared stymied, Moscow
faced another serious Middle East problem, the very sharp deterioration of its position in Iran. The Soviet–Iranian relationship had been
deteriorating since 1982,[69] despite Soviet efforts to cultivate the regime
of Ayatollah Khomeini. In part this had occurred because of an increase
in the supply of Soviet military equipment to Iraq – something publicly
noted by Iraqi Foreign Minister Tariq Aziz in late February 1983[70] – but
another major irritant in the relationship was the communist party of
Iran, the Tudeh, which Khomeini and the majority of his followers held
in deep suspicion. In February 1983, the First Secretary of the Tudeh,
Nureddin Kianuri, and a number of other top party leaders were
arrested on charges of espionage. Moscow vehemently denied the
charge with a *Pravda* article on February 19 blaming the arrest on the
increased activity of "reactionary conservative forces in Iran which are
trying to deal a blow against the progressive patriotic forces and at the
same time damage Iranian–Soviet relations." The *Pravda* article went
on to list the areas in which the Soviet Union had been aiding Iran since
the fall of the Shah, but also pointedly cited the comments by the late
Soviet Party Secretary Leonid Brezhnev on the need for reciprocity in
the Soviet–Iranian relationship.[71] If the *Pravda* article and its call for
reciprocity was aimed at deterring the Khomeini regime from moving
further against the Tudeh, it was not to prove successful. On April 30
Kianuri made a public confession on Iranian TV of spying for the Soviet
Union.[72] Four days later Iran expelled eighteen Soviet diplomats and
dissolved the Tudeh party, declaring that "any activity on behalf of the
party is now illegal."[73] Adding to the anti-Soviet atmosphere in Iran

were such slogans as "Britain is bad; America is worse than Britain; and the Soviet Union is worse than both of them."[74]

The first Soviet response to the Iranian action came in the form of a *Pravda* editorial on May 6 which not only denied that the Tudeh members had been spying for the USSR, but also asserted that their confessions had been extracted by torture. In addition, the editorial noted that the USSR had lodged a "resolute protest" against the Iranian government's "arbitrary" and "groundless" expulsion of the Soviet diplomats. Nonetheless, it was still in Moscow's interest to preserve some ties with Iran, lest Iran begin to gravitate toward the West, a possibility noted by the *Pravda* editorial. For this reason, Moscow's counter actions against Iran were limited to (1) editorial denunciations of the Iranian authorities as a whole, without mentioning Khomeini by name; (2) a more sympathetic treatment of the Iraqi position in the Iran–Iraq war which Moscow continued to deplore as it had since the war erupted in 1980; and (3) expelling three Iranian diplomats from Moscow.[75] Nonetheless, Moscow's displeasure with Tehran was noted in Gromyko's speech on foreign policy to the Supreme Soviet in mid-June:

> We have relations of friendship with Iraq. We are for normal relations of friendship with Iran as well. The USSR would like to continue to see it an independent state and has always striven for good neighborly relations with it. Regrettably, actions like those recently taken by the Iranian side with regard to a group of employees of the Soviet mission in Iran by no means contribute to the development of such contacts between our countries. In short, the USSR will be guided in its actions by whether Iran wants to reciprocate its action or whether it has different intentions.[76]

While Moscow was exhibiting its concern about the deterioration of relations with Iran, it again had to come to grips with the actions of Muammar Kaddafi with whom it had agreed, in principle, to sign a Treaty of Friendship and Cooperation in mid-March. Denied the presidency of the Organization of African Unity which he had long coveted, and having suffered a second African defeat in June when the Libya-backed Polisario rebels were pressured by the other African states to withdraw from an OAU meeting so that it could begin free of the threatened Moroccan boycott,[77] Kaddafi decided to move once again to control Chad as he had from 1980 to 1981 before withdrawing under OAU pressure.[78] His tool for the conquest of Chad was Goukouni Oueddi, a Chadian leader whom Kaddafi had been supporting against Hissine Habre who had taken power in Chad in 1982 after driving out the forces of Oueddi. Initially, the battle went well for Oueddi's Libyan-supported troops who drove down into Chad from their base in the Libyan-controlled Aouzou strip of territory in northernmost Chad. By June 24 the Oueddi forces had seized the northern oasis city of Faya Largeau and then continued south capturing Oum Chalouba and then Abache by July 10. At this point, following the arrival of 250 Zairan paratroopers to aid Habre, the United States and France stepped in and provided large amounts of military equipment which enabled Habre to go on the offensive. He succeeded in recapturing Abache and Oum Chalouba and by the end of July had recaptured Faya Largeau. At this point, however, Libya escalated the conflict by employing fighter bombers which succeeded in helping Oueddi's troops to drive Habre's forces out of Faya Largeau once again. As it appeared that the Libyan-backed Oueddi forces might again drive deeper into Chad and threaten the capital of N'Djamena, first the United States and then an initially reluctant France undertook an escalation of their military presence in Chad with the US sending AWACs aircraft and F-15s to Sudan to monitor the Libyan-backed offensive and then France sending paratroopers and, subsequently, fighter planes to bolster Habre's forces. The end result was a stalemate as Habre was able to recapture Oum Chalouba and, with French military aid, to hold most of the country (by August 20, there were 1,000 French troops in Northern Chad along the Salal–Abache line).[79] Oueddi, with Libyan aid, was able to entrench himself at Faya Largeau, some 200 miles to the north of the French position.

As the crisis developed, Moscow was again faced with a dilemma. On the one hand, a victory for Libya's client, Oueddi, would enhance Libya's strategic position in Africa, a development which Moscow might well exploit. On the other hand, however, the Libyan move once again raised the possibility of a direct US–Libyan confrontation, something Moscow wished to avoid. In addition, given Libya's continuing difficulties in Africa, too close an identification between Moscow and the Libyan move into Chad would raise problems for the USSR's overall position in Africa. It would appear, therefore, that Moscow decided to take a cautious position on the developing Chad situation. Soviet caution took the form primarily of publicly denying that Libyan forces were involved in the fighting in Chad.[80] Such a denial served two purposes. First, in case a conflict between Libya and either the US or France occurred, Moscow would not be constrained to aid its North African ally, and Soviet prestige would, therefore, not become involved in the conflict. Secondly, Moscow could point to the events in Chad as another example of a "colonialist intervention" by the imperialists. Indeed, this was the central theme of a Tass statement printed in *Pravda* on July 13, when Habre had begun his offensive, in which Moscow "strongly denounced the escalation of imperialist intervention in the internal affairs of the Republic of Chad."[81]

Nonetheless, there was some evidence that Libya was not satisfied with the limited level of Soviet support, particularly in early August after there was another encounter in the Mediterranean between US F-14 aircraft and Libyan MIGs at the height of the crisis.[82] Indeed, several days later Libya announced that a military delegation had gone to Moscow for talks.[83] The fact that there was no report of the visit in the Soviet media, however, was another indication that Moscow wished to play down its involvement in the crisis. About all Moscow did was issue yet another Tass statement, this time on August 3.[84] The statement mentioned "far fetched" accusations against Libya that were being used to justify French and US activity in Chad, and went on to assert that the US, with its aircraft carrier off Libya's shores, was trying to find a pretext for an armed clash and was virtually giving Libya "ultimatums." The statement concluded with a Soviet condemnation of both US press-ure on Libya, and the US–French intervention in Chad, but no Soviet warning was issued. Essentially, therefore, it was yet another *pro forma* statement in support of Libyan sovereignty, but one which clearly did not support Libyan activity in Chad. The fact that the Chad crisis was not followed by any further movement toward the conclusion of the expected Soviet–Libyan Treaty of Friendship and Cooperation was perhaps indicative of the fact that the Soviet leadership, by August, might have grown a bit more wary of Libyan adventurism. In addition, with its position in the Middle East now strengthened by the erosion of support for the Reagan plan, and the impasse over the Israeli–Lebanese agreement of May 17, Moscow may have felt less need to support its mercurial North African ally. Indeed, some of the Soviet leaders may have felt that, at least politically, Libya was often more a liability than an asset to the USSR, given the problems Kaddafi had caused in the Organization of African Unity (which the USSR had hoped would unite on an anti-imperialist basis) in general, and North Africa in particular.

Indeed, North Africa was to prove a particular area of difficulty for the Soviet Union in 1983, in part due to Kaddafi's machinations. Morocco, despite its close economic ties with the Soviet Union, was moving ever closer to the United States, in large measure because of Kaddafi's aid to the Polisario guerrillas which by 1983 had surpassed the assistance given to the rebel group by Algeria.[85] US–Morocco military maneuvers took place for the second consecutive year in 1983 and the US was providing direct assistance to Morocco in the form of electronic surveillance equipment and other military supplies to assist it in its battles against the Polisario.[86] Perhaps even more serious for Moscow was the growing *rapprochement* between the United States and Algeria, a member of the Arab Front of Steadfastness and Confrontation which had hitherto been pro-Soviet in its policies. In late December 1982, a US Cabinet official, Secretary of Commerce Malcolm Baldridge, led a trade and investment mission consisting of representatives of thirty-five major American companies to meet with Algerian President Chadli Benjedid – the first such visit to Algeria by a US Cabinet official since 1974.[87] Then, in September 1983, Vice-President George Bush also used his visit to speak out on behalf of "genuine non-alignment."[88] At the same time Algerian–US relations were improving, so too were Algerian–French relations. Algerian President Benjedid made a highly publicized visit to France in November, where he laid a wreath at the tomb of France's unknown soldier, thereby symbolizing an end to the strained relations caused by the Algerian war for independence. What made this *rapprochement* a problem for Moscow was the fact that France was now actively backing US policy in Chad and Lebanon, as well as in Europe, and the warming of Franco-Algerian ties, when coupled with the improvement of US–Algerian relations may have led the Soviet leaders to believe that Algeria, which had helped the US in the hostage crisis with Iran in the 1980–81 period, was leaving the Soviet orbit and becoming more nonaligned. Still another problem for Moscow in Algeria's new foreign policy line lay in its *rapprochement* with Morocco. On the one hand, the USSR had long called for an end to the Saharan war and an improvement in ties between Algeria and Morocco as a major step toward "anti-imperialist" Arab unity. Yet the normalization of ties between the two countries, which took place following a face-to-face meeting between Benjedid and King Hassan of Morocco in February, did not provide for an end to the war between Morocco and the Palisario, although Morocco was later to give lip service to an OAU recommendation for a referendum in the former Spanish Sahara.[89] Instead, when coupled with an agreement between Algeria and Tunisia, the Algerian–Morocco *rapprochement* seemed to be leading toward a larger Mahgreb union – with Libya, which was in conflict with all three other Mahgreb countries, being frozen out despite belated efforts by Kaddafi who visited both Morocco and Tunisia in 1983.[90] Such a development would further isolate Kaddafi, while also weakening the Front of Steadfastness and Confrontation in which both Libya and Algeria participated.

North Africa, however, was not the only area of Libyan–Algerian conflict in 1983. Both nations also found themselves on opposite sides during the conflict which broke out in Fatah in mid-May when Syria, backed by Libya, moved to undermine Arafat's authority within the most important of the PLO's numerous factions, Fatah, by aiding a rebel movement in that organization. The revolt was led by Abu Musa, a hardliner who vehemently opposed any settlement with Israel.[91] Abu Musa was also outspoken in his opposition to a Jordanian–PLO negotiating arrangement. The anti-Arafat uprising took place in the Syrian-controlled Bekaa Valley of Lebanon, and it soon became clear that Assad was utilizing the revolt within Fatah to try to bring the PLO under Syrian control once and for all.

The revolt against Arafat underlined the PLO leader's weakened position in the aftermath of the Israeli invasion of Lebanon which had eliminated his main base of operations. While he was supported by the bulk of Palestinians living outside Syria and Syrian-controlled regions in Lebanon, and while both Iraq and Algeria gave him support in the Arab world's diplomatic arena, he had no real power to resist Syria's crackdown against him. Thus, as the summer wore on, the positions of Arafat's supporters in the Bekaa Valley were overrun, and Arafat himself was expelled from Syria. In early August, the Palestine Central Council, meeting in Tunis, called for an "immediate dialogue" to rebuild relations with Syria[92] but this effort, along with others attempted during the summer, proved to no avail and in early September, Arafat, who had once again begun to meet with Jordanian officials, admitted that all attempts at negotiations with Syria had failed.[93]

As the revolt within Fatah developed, Moscow was faced by another of its serious problems of choice. On the one hand, a victory for Fatah hardliners would make it even more difficult for Moscow to succeed in promoting its Middle East peace plan. In addition, the very split within Fatah, and the fact that Iraq and Algeria, key Arab countries, were backing Arafat against the Syrian-supported opposition, further outlined the disunity in the Arab world. This was one more obstacle in the way of the "anti-imperialist" Arab unity Moscow had sought for so long. On the other hand, however, Moscow could not have been too unhappy with the fact that Arafat was being punished for his flirtation with the Reagan plan. In any case, in a showdown between Assad and Arafat, *realpolitik* impelled Moscow to side with Syria, who in the aftermath of the Israeli invasion of Lebanon was the main Arab state opposing US diplomacy in the Middle East and who had granted to Moscow the use of Syrian naval and air force facilities as well.[94]

Given this situation, about all Moscow could do was to plead for Palestinian unity and PLO cooperation with Syria. Nonetheless, a Radio Peace and Progress Arabic language broadcast early in the revolt, indicated Soviet frustration with the split in Fatah:

> The US exploits the smallest possible chance to weaken the PLO or at least split it if its total destruction proves impossible. In this context, one cannot ignore the irresponsible statements made in some Arab political quarters which help to deepen some of the disputes within the PLO.
> ... The hasty and shortsighted calls in which the ambitions of certain political quarters in the Arab world are reflected have nothing to do with the real interests of the Palestinian resistance movement and they in fact benefit imperialism.[95]

A series of PLO officials including Salah Khalaf, Naef Hawatmeh, and Farouk Kaddoumi, journeyed to Moscow in June and July in an apparent effort to get the USSR to intervene, but to no avail. While PLO media frequently reported that the USSR was backing Arafat,[96] no public statement of support from Moscow was forthcoming. The most Moscow would do was to denounce the split within the PLO, as the *Pravda* description of Kaddoumi's talks in Moscow noted:

> The Soviet side expressed its firm opinion about the impermissibility of strife and internecine dissension among the Palestinians faced with the Israeli aggressor, for they weaken the forces of the Palestinians and decimate the ranks of the Arabs. Discord within the PLO can and should be overcome by political means, through a dialogue.[97]

The fact that the talks were described as having taken place in an atmosphere of "mutual understanding" indicates that the two sides remained far apart, and this may have been the reason that Arafat did not undertake a rumored visit to Moscow after Kaddoumi's trip.[98] About the only positive development Moscow may have seen from the conflict within the PLO was the decision by Naef Hawatmeh's Democratic Front for the Liberation of Palestine and George Habash's Popular Front for the Liberation of Palestine to establish a single military and political leadership, as this was a step, albeit a small one, toward Palestinian unity.[99]

One of the reasons why Moscow was standing on the sidelines during the clash between Assad's forces and those of Arafat may have been because the Soviet leadership was concerned that the unpredictable Assad might yet strike a deal with the United States over Lebanon. While Syria indicated that long-time mediator Philip Habib was *persona non grata* in Damascus, it did receive US Secretary of State George Shultz in July and Habib's replacement Robert McFarlane, in August for talks about a Syrian troop withdrawal from Lebanon. In addition, while Assad continued to denounce the May 17 Israeli–Lebanese agreement and to assert that Syria would not pull its forces out of Lebanon unless all Israeli forces left "without any political gains," he did agree to establish a working group with the United States to consider the restoration of Lebanon's unity and independence.[100] He also helped secure the release of the kidnapped President of the American University of Beirut, David Dodge, who had been abducted in the summer of 1982.[101]

While maintaining contact with the United States, Assad was also strengthening Syria's position in Lebanon. In addition to bringing Arafat's forces in the Bekaa under his control, he was profiting from the growing war-weariness of Israel which was planning a unilateral withdrawal of its forces from the Chouf Mountains and seemed in no mood to go to war to throw the Syrians out of Lebanon. Indeed, on June 1, Prime Minister Begin had stated that Israel was not preparing to attack Syria[102] and a week later Israel's Deputy Foreign Minister Yehuda Ben-Meir ruled out military action to remove Syrian forces from Lebanon.[103] One month later Shultz stated that US Marines would not fill any vacuum created by a unilateral withdrawal by Israel in Lebanon.[104] Under these circumstances Assad was able to fill the vacuum with Syrian-backed forces, in large part because of mistakes by the Lebanese government. By July, the Lebanese government of Amin Gemayel had alienated two of the major forces within Lebanon, the Druze and the Shiites. In part because he did not establish an equitable power-sharing system and in part because Phalangist policies in the Chouf Mountains and in Shiite areas of Beirut angered the Druze and Shiites, they entered into an alignment with Syria. Druze leader Walid Jumblatt did this explicitly by leading a newly proclaimed "National Salvation Front" (which also had as members Rashid Karami, a Sunni Muslim, and Suleiman Franjieh, a Christian opponent of Gemayel), while Shiite leader Nabih Berri gave tacit support to the organization.[105]

The strengthening of the Syrian position in Lebanon was, on balance, a plus for Moscow since by the end of August US diplomatic efforts to secure a troop withdrawal agreement from Lebanon had all but collapsed and Moscow was again raising the possibility of a joint US–Soviet effort to bring about a Middle East peace settlement.[106] Yet the situation also had its dangers from the USSR. As Israel stepped up its planning to withdraw its troops from the Chouf Mountains, the possibility that new fighting would erupt became increasingly strong, particularly since no agreement had been reached between the Druze and Gemayel about deploying the Lebanese army in the Chouf to replace the departing Israelis. Exacerbating the situation was the Syrian government statement on August 27 that it would defend its allies against the Lebanese army.[107] The danger for Moscow was that since the United States was backing the Gemayel government, a direct US–Syrian confrontation could occur and then Moscow would again be faced with the problem of how to react to a military conflict in which its principal Arab ally was involved. This time, however, the opponent would most likely not be Israel, backed by the United States, but the United States itself. In short, Moscow faced the prospect of a superpower confrontation over Lebanon, but when the crisis did occur, the USSR adopted a very cautious policy so as to avoid any direct involvement.

The crisis began at the end of August when warfare broke out between the Lebanese government and the Shiites of Western and Southern Beirut who resisted a Lebanese army push into their neighborhoods on August 30 and 31. The scale of fighting escalated sharply, however, after the Israeli redeployment of September 3 with Syrian-supported Druze forces clashing both with the Maronite (Phalange) militia and the Lebanese army. While the Phalangist forces were all but driven from the Chouf Mountains, the Lebanese army proved a tougher opponent for the Druze and a battle was fought for the strategic mountain town of Souk el-Gharb which overlooked Beirut. While Israel held off from intervening both because of pressure from its Druze minority and because of assurances from Druze leader Walid Jumblatt that he would not permit the PLO to occupy positions in Druze-controlled areas, the United States decided to play an active role in the fighting in support of the Lebanese army which it was training. US involvement in the conflict had actually begun before the Israeli withdrawal, as US helicopters had fired on sniper and mortar positions that had harassed the Marines. The US role escalated during the fighting in the Chouf as guns from US warships in Beirut harbor were fired both in support of

Lebanese army troops fighting in Souk el-Gharb[108] and against artillery positions that were firing on or near US positions.[109] After holding aloof from the fighting, France also got involved when its forces came under fire.[110] As the fighting escalated, Syria felt constrained to issue threats against the US so as to back up its clients in the Chouf Mountains,[111] particularly as the US battleship New Jersey, whose 16-inch guns appeared to have the capability of seriously damaging Syrian positions, neared Beirut.[112]

As the crisis developed, Moscow reacted very cautiously. A Tass statement published in *Pravda*, on September 1, merely noted that the Soviet Union was "deeply concerned" over the US armed intervention in Lebanon. It also called for an end to US intervention, the unconditional withdrawal of Israeli forces from Lebanon, and the withdrawal of US troops and "the foreign troops that arrived with them." Interestingly enough there were no Soviet threats against the US, although Moscow may have balanced its lack of activity with the implicit support of Syria's right to remain in Lebanon, because there was no mention of any Syrian withdrawal in the Tass statement – a clear change from earlier Soviet policy.

The rapid escalation of the crisis, however, posed both problems and opportunities for the USSR. On the one hand Moscow seized on the US involvement in the fighting to discredit American policy in the Middle East by asserting that the US was now directly fighting the Arabs. Vladimir Kudravtzev, one of *Izvestia*'s more colorful commentators, emphasized this Soviet propaganda line with the statement, "By shedding the blood of Arab patriots, the United States has *de facto* declared war on the Arabs."[113] In addition, Soviet commentators also utilized the intervention to discredit the US RDF, whose forces it claimed were fighting in Lebanon.[114] Moscow also sought to exploit the Lebanese fighting to divert attention from its shooting down of a Korean airliner in early September. Nonetheless, as American participation in the fighting grew, Moscow faced the dilemma of whether or not it should get directly involved, particularly as Syrian positions came under American fire. The Soviet press noted the escalation of the fighting, and also noted Syria's warning to the US that it would fire back if fired upon, perhaps to prepare the Soviet public for a heightened crisis.[115] Nonetheless, on September 20, the day after *Pravda* published the Syrian warning, the same Soviet newspaper published a Tass statement that carefully avoided any hint of Soviet involvement in the fighting. While it accused the US of trying to intimidate Syria, and of seeking to establish its own hegemony in the Middle East, it issued no warning to the US other than to state that Washington would not "evade responsibility" for the consequences of the escalated fighting.[116] To be sure, Moscow did not deny reports in the Kuwaiti press that the USSR had placed its forces in the southern part of the USSR on alert, and that a joint Soviet–Syrian operations room was monitoring the situation in Lebanon.[117] In addition, Moscow rejected a US request to cooperate in limiting Syrian participation in the conflict.[118] Nonetheless, Moscow refused to formally offer military support to Syria; nor did it react to statements by Syrian officials that Damascus might turn to the USSR for help.[119] It also ignored the leftist Lebanese newspaper *As-Safir*'s report that Assad had made a secret trip to Moscow in mid-September.[120] Perhaps most important of all, during the crisis Moscow failed to publicly mention the Soviet–Syrian treaty. In sum, Soviet behavior during the crisis was very cautious indeed, and it is not surprising that Moscow, which feared a superpower confrontation over Lebanon – an area of only tertiary interest to the USSR – warmly welcomed the cease-fire that ended the crisis.[121]

In looking at the September 1983 crisis, it is clear that it differed substantially from the one four months earlier. In May, Assad had been basically in control of the situation and he maneuvered accordingly. Since that crisis was essentially a *political* one over the Israeli–Lebanese treaty, Syrian mobilizations and threats of war were essentially political acts, unlikely to get out of control. In September, the crisis was essentially a military one that escalated rapidly. Under these circumstances, it is not surprising that the USSR refrained from giving Syria overt support during the crisis; nor did Syria complain publicly about a lack of Soviet aid (thus repeating the strategy it followed during the Israeli invasion of June 1982) although Damascus could not have been too happy with the lack of Soviet support. Syria expressed its anger more openly against its fellow Arabs, intimating that whatever the position of the Arab governments, the Arab masses supported Syria.[122] The lack of Soviet and Arab support, coupled with the US Congress's agreement to extend the stay of US Marines in Beirut for an additional eighteen months, and the arrival near Beirut of the US battleship New Jersey, seem to have persuaded Assad that at least a temporary compromise was in order and he agreed to a Saudi-mediated cease-fire plan that held out the possibility of a new distribution of power in Lebanon.[123] No sooner had the cease-fire been achieved, however, than Assad moved to strengthen Syria's position in Lebanon further by expelling the remaining troops loyal to Arafat from the Bekaa Valley, and forcing them to go over the mountains to Tripoli where Arafat had suddenly appeared in mid-September.

In the aftermath of the cease-fire, the Soviet Union adopted what, on the surface, appeared to be a contradictory policy toward Syria. On the one hand, perhaps to assuage Syrian unhappiness at the lack of support during its confrontation with the US in September, Moscow dispatched to Syria modern SS-21 ground-to-ground missiles with a range of seventy miles – long enough to strike deep into Israel, and with greater accuracy than the previously supplied SCUD or Frog missiles.[124] On the other hand, perhaps out of concern that if the Lebanese cease-fire should break down Syria might become involved in a major confrontation with the US, Moscow downplayed its military relationship with Syria. With Andropov ill, a major Soviet campaign to prevent the deployment of US Pershing II and cruise missiles underway in Western Europe, and Moscow still trying to overcome the negative effects of the Korean airliner incident, the time was not opportune for the USSR to become involved in a Middle Eastern war. Thus Soviet treatment of the third anniversary of the Soviet–Syrian treaty was kept in very low key as far as Soviet military aid was concerned. A *New Times* article commemorating the treaty, for example, emphasized that Soviet aid had enabled Syria to enhance its defense potential and that the Syrian leaders had themselves repeatedly stressed that they possessed the means to repulse an aggressor.[125] Similarly, a *Pravda* commentary by Yuri Glukhov on October 8 cited the Syrian Prime Minister's statement that Syria relies on its own efforts first, and only then on the assistance of its friends. Perhaps to reinforce the point that the first friends Syria should look to for help were its fellow Arabs, an Arabic language broadcast commemorating the 10th anniversary of the 1973 Arab–Israeli war asserted that the effectiveness of aid from the socialist countries is increased manyfold if the Arab states themselves united to fight the aggressor.[126]

As the crisis in Lebanon was cooling off, albeit temporarily, the war in the Persian Gulf was again heating up. Armed with new French Super-Entard fighter bombers and Exocet missiles, Iraq was threatening to destroy Iranian oil facilities, a threat which brought an Iranian counter threat to close the Gulf of Hormuz if Iraq disrupted Iranian oil shipments.[127] The crisis had a number of negative implications for Moscow. In the first place, the Iranian threats once again had the effect of forcing such Arab states as Saudi Arabia and Kuwait to look to the

US for protection against Iran.[128] Indeed, an *Izvestia* article on October 24 noted that "the aggravation of the situation in the Persian Gulf is seen as a convenient reason to expand the range of US activities in the Middle East." In addition, as the Iraqi position grew weaker, Baghdad appeared to be turning to the West for support. Thus not only did Iraq sign an oil-for-arms deal with France (in January, in a *Le Monde* interview, Iraq's Foreign Minister Tariq Aziz stated that France was Iraq's "main political, economic, military, and trading partner")[129] and improved relations further with Egypt (see below, p. 000), Iraq also began to cultivate the United States. Thus, in early January President Saddam Hussein of Iraq, in a major policy change, publicly indicated that "it was necessary to have a state of security for the Israelis" in any peace settlement.[130] Then, in May, Iraqi Foreign Minister Aziz met US Secretary of State Shultz in Paris for what the Iraqi leader later said were "useful talks."[131] Despite continuing US–Iraqi friction over the presence of Palestinian terrorist Abu Nidal in Iraq,[132] Iraqi–US relations continued to improve as an Iraqi Foreign Ministry representative visited Washington in early September[133] and the new US Middle East envoy Donald Rumsfeld visited Baghdad in December, the first visit of such a senior US official to the Iraqi capital since the June 1967 Arab–Israeli war.[134]

As Franco-Iraqi and US–Iraqi relations improved, the USSR moved to improve its relations with Iraq to counterbalance the Iraqi move to the West. Thus, while continuing both to maintain official neutrality in the Iran–Iraq war and to call for as rapid as possible an end to the conflict from which it claimed "only the imperialists" benefited, Moscow stepped up its arms shipments to Iraq and began to more openly criticize Iran for continuing the war. Thus, while praising Iraq's cease-fire proposal of June 1983, a commentary in *Pravda* by Yuri Glukhov on November 14 criticized Iran's rejection of it, blaming the rejection on "chauvinistic attitudes" in Tehran. In addition, Moscow publicized a visit by Tariq Aziz to the Soviet Union in late November, during which the USSR again called for a rapid end to the Iran–Iraq war and stated that Moscow would continue to work for a political settlement of the conflict.[135] Nonetheless, the visit was clearly marked by disagreement on a number of issues as the *Pravda* report described the talks as having taken place in a "frank and friendly atmosphere," and stated that there had been "an exchange of views" on the situation in the Middle East and on Soviet–Iraqi relations.[136] Interestingly enough, however, Moscow appeared willing to make a gesture toward Iraq which was backing Arafat in his conflict with Syria by endorsing the PLO as the "sole legitimate representative of the Palestinian people" and calling for the "end to the dissension" and for the restoration of unity within the ranks of the Palestinian people. Perhaps in response, Aziz agreed to the statement that "no one had any right to interfere in the affairs of coastal states under any pretext, including freedom of navigation."

The Tariq Aziz visit to Moscow came at the time both of a sharp escalation of the Arafat–Syria conflict and of the Lebanese crisis as a whole. On October 24 the US Marine headquarters in Beirut was blown up with over 240 Marines killed, and the US was subsequently to blame Syria for being at least indirectly responsible. While *Pravda* senior Middle East correspondent, Pavel Demchenko, attributed the explosion to the work of "Lebanese patriots," and asserted that it was the direct result of Reagan's "adventurist policy,"[137] the deputy director of the CPSU International Department, Vadim Zagladin, in a *Le Monde* interview on October 25, tried to play down the possibility of a Syrian–US confrontation, calling the Beirut attack a "tragedy" and emphasizing that Soviet aid to Syria was defensive, and that Moscow had always told the Syrians that it was in favor of a peaceful solution to the Middle East conflict. Zagladin, however, also utilized the interview to emphasize, in light of the explosion, that Soviet participation in a Middle East peace settlement would be useful.[138]

Soviet commentary on US policy in Lebanon became more shrill, however, after the US invaded Grenada, with the Soviet media warning that even such moderate Arab states as Saudi Arabia, Morocco, and even Oman might be next.[139] Meanwhile as threats of retaliation for the destruction of the Marine headquarters were repeated, and the US began flying reconnaissance missions over Syrian lines in Lebanon, the possibility of a Syrian–US clash grew stronger. At this point, as if to disassociate Moscow from the possibility of intervening, a major Arabic language broadcast minimized the Soviet military presence in Syria, repeating the now-familiar Soviet practice of citing Syrian statements that "Syria has enough means at its disposal to defend itself." In addition, the broadcast asserted that "there is no Soviet military presence in Syria at all, only experts helping Syria bolster its defense capability" and that Syria had "repeatedly replied vehemently to the lie of the alleged Soviet military presence on its soil."[140]

Nonetheless, as tension rose in Lebanon, Moscow evidently felt constrained to issue another warning to the US, if only to show its support for the "progressive" Lebanese forces which were backed by Syria. Thus on November 4 a Soviet government Tass statement, citing remarks by Reagan, Weinberger, and Shultz, stated that the US was planning a "massive strike against Lebanese national patriotic forces" and warned the US "with all seriousness" about taking such action.[141] As in the case of the March 30 warning to Israel, the Soviet warning of November 4 was very limited. Not only was there no mention of Syria, let alone the Soviet–Syrian treaty, but there was not even the usual Soviet statement that the Middle East lay close to the southern borders of the USSR. While *Pravda* commentator, Pavel Demchenko, two days later mentioned specifically that the US was preparing "an act of retribution against Syria," he omitted any Soviet warning to the US and also failed to mention the Soviet–Syrian treaty.[142]

While Moscow was seeking to limit its involvement in the period of rising tensions, Assad was exploiting the possibility of an escalated US–Syrian confrontation to crack down on the last redoubt of Arafat's supporters, the refugee camps north of Tripoli. At the same time it was announced that Syrian Foreign Minister Abdul Khaddam would shortly visit the Soviet Union.[143] It is not known whether the Khaddam visit was at the initiative of Moscow, which was unhappy at Assad's crackdown on Arafat's forces, or of Damascus. Whoever initiated it, it was clearly Damascus which was to exploit the atmosphere surrounding the visit. Thus, despite American and Israeli statements that they were not going to attack Syria, Assad mobilized his army on November 8.[144] While Moscow noted the Syrian mobilization in an Arabic language broadcast on November 9, and also stated that Syria was exerting its additional defense efforts with the help of the USSR, on the basis of their bilateral treaty, the broadcast also stated that "the substance of this treaty is very well known."[145] The purpose of this qualification to the treaty may well have been to remind the Arabs that the treaty did not cover Syrian activities in Lebanon. Indeed, the latter part of the broadcast was devoted to a call for the Arabs to strengthen their unity and act collectively in the face of the US threat. Interestingly enough, in a possible backhand slap at Syria, the broadcast also noted Soviet support "for the efforts of some Arab states aimed at healing the rift in the ranks of the Palestinian resistance movement and at consolidating the ranks of the Arabs."

While Moscow was urging the Arabs to unite on an "anti-imperialist" basis, Assad appeared to be painting his Soviet allies into a corner in which they had no choice but to support him, regardless of what he did to Arafat's forces. Thus, on the eve of Khaddam's visit to the USSR,

Syrian forces opened fire on four American reconnaissance planes.[146] At the same time the Syrian Ambassador to Britain was stating in a TV interview that a conflict caused by US "aggression" against Syria would not be confined to one area, but would be "large scale because of the help which we are supposed to get from our brothers and friends."[147]

Thus Syrian Foreign Minister Khaddam flew on to Moscow in the midst of a crisis which, like the one in May, seemed to have been orchestrated by Assad who at this critical moment, however, suddenly became seriously ill. For its part Moscow could not have been too pleased either with Syrian claims to Soviet aid in a widened conflict or to Syria's crackdown on Arafat's forces in the Tripoli area since Moscow still appeared to wish to see Arafat, and the PLO, as independent actors in the Middle East who would need Soviet support, rather than as a dependent element of the Syrian army. Gromyko's luncheon speech to Khaddam made this point very clear: "We regard as highly important and urgent the need for overcoming strife and restoring unity within the ranks of the liberation movement of the Arab people of Palestine which must remain an active and effective factor of the anti-imperialist struggle in the Middle East."[148] Gromyko also pointedly called for increased Arab unity, stating "the fact is that the enemies of the Arabs seek, in no small measure, to rely on their aggressive policy precisely on this disunity." While Gromyko also condemned US and Israeli threats against the Lebanese National Patriotic Forces and Syria, he pointedly refrained from mentioning the Soviet–Syrian treaty. Khaddam, in his return speech, totally ignored the Palestinian issue while pointedly mentioning, in a segment of his speech ignored by *Pravda* but reported by Damascus Radio, that Soviet support "helped Syria in its steadfastness" and "enabled it to confront aggression."[149] Khaddam did, however, state Syrian aims in Lebanon that seemed to coincide with those of the Soviet Union – the renunciation of the May 17 agreement; the full withdrawal of Israeli and multinational forces; and the achievement of national unity and the restoration of security in Lebanon. The joint communiqué issued at the conclusion of the talks reflected the clearly differing viewpoints of the two sides as it reported an exchange of opinions – the usual Soviet code words for disagreement – "regarding the US and Israeli threats against Syria and the danger of aggression against Syria in this connection."[150] Moscow did, however, give a general statement of support for Syria against "the intrigues of imperialism and Zionism", and "confirmed its adherence" to its commitments under the Soviet–Syrian treaty.

If Moscow felt that it had succeeded in getting Syria to moderate its pressure on Arafat as a result of the Khaddam visit to Moscow, this proved not to be the case. Indeed soon after Khaddam's return to Damascus, Syrian-backed troops stepped up their attacks on Arafat's forces and drove them out of the two Palestinian refugee camps north of Tripoli into the city itself. It is possible that Assad felt able to withstand Soviet pressure because at the same time his forces were fighting Arafat's followers near Tripoli, US National Security Adviser, Robert McFarlane, was warning Syria that the US would retaliate if Syria continued to fire on US reconnaissance planes (he specifically reminded Damascus of what the US had done on Grenada),[151] and French and Israeli planes were attacking purported terrorist bases in parts of Lebanon under Syrian control.[152] Indeed, at the height of the fighting in Tripoli, Syrian Defense Minister Mustafa Talas was threatening suicide attacks against US warships and proclaiming that the USSR would never allow Syria to be defeated.[153] At the same time, Assad, in a Syrian TV broadcast of his interview with the American columnists Evans and Novak, was stressing the possibility of a Soviet–American confrontation if a new war broke out.[154]

As the twin Lebanese crises escalated, Moscow increased its rhetorical activity. An article by Demchenko in *Pravda*, on November 17, citing McFarlane's comments on Grenada, noted that the US and Israel counted "on deriving the maximum advantage from the present situation in the region, which is complex enough as it is, with the senseless Iran–Iraq war continuing, inter-Arab discord exacerbated, and the PLO's internal differences having led to bloody clashes between rival groupings." He then appealed for cooperation among all "anti-imperialist" forces to counter the "dangerous development of events" and the US–Israeli threats. Two days later, a *Pravda* editorial discussing the fighting in Tripoli made the point even more strongly: "It is no accident that the inter-Palestinian discord is being exploited in the framework of the anti-Syrian campaign unleashed by imperialist circles. In these conditions, the senseless and perverse nature of the fratricidal clashes in Northern Lebanon are particularly vivid."[155] The editorial also repeated the section of Gromyko's luncheon address during Khaddam's visit in which the Soviet Foreign Minister had stressed that the PLO "had to continue to operate as an active and effective factor of the anti-imperialist struggle in the Near East." The editorial went on to say that Moscow was taking "active political steps to end the conflict."

As the Tripoli fighting escalated further, despite the Soviet pleas, Moscow stepped up the level of its public complaints with an appeal from the Soviet Afro-Asian Peoples Solidarity Organization. Reminiscent of similar pleas at the time of Syrian–PLO fighting during the Syrian intervention in Lebanon in 1976,[156] the AAPSO called for an end to the "senseless bloodshed" and the restoration of unity in the ranks of the Palestinians, and the consolidation of all Arab anti-imperialist forces "in the face of the mounting military and political pressure on the part of the USA, Israel and their allies."[157]

Perhaps as a gesture to Arafat, Gromyko received Farouk Kaddoumi, one of Arafat's closest allies in the PLO, on November 23. The fact that *Pravda* described the talks as having taken place in a "friendly, businesslike atmosphere," however, indicated that little agreement was reached – a probable indication that Kaddoumi was told that Moscow would not take action against Syria – although Gromyko promised to help "in any way possible" to achieve a settlement among the Palestinian factions.[158] Fortunately for Moscow, however, an uneasy cease-fire was achieved in Tripoli several days later, although to what degree Assad agreed to halt the fighting due to Saudi inducement, Soviet pressure, or the realization that Arafat continued to have widespread support in the Arab world and among Palestinians, is not yet clear. In any case, Moscow warmly praised the cease-fire in an Arabic language "Window on the Arab World" broadcast on November 26,[159] and three days later, a joint Soviet party–government statement on the "international day of solidarity with the Palestinian people" saluted Arafat as the Chairman of the PLO executive committee.[160] At the same time it called for unity within the organization and its "close collaboration" with "those countries that are in the forefront of resistance to the US and Israel," i.e. Syria, as Moscow continued to try to maintain good relations with both Arafat and Assad.

While Moscow was clearly relieved by the Tripoli cease-fire, however tentative it may have been, it had to be concerned with the rise in US–Syrian tensions. US Defense Secretary Weinberger had asserted on November 22 that the attack on the Marine headquarters had been undertaken by Iranians with the "sponsorship and knowledge and authority of the Syrian government."[161] While Syria rejected the charge,[162] it also again asserted that its planes had driven off US jets flying over Syrian-controlled areas.[163] At this point, with the cease-fire holding in Tripoli, Moscow moved again to champion Syria, as a *Novosti* article by Demchenko that was distributed to Western correspondents warned that Syria was an ally of Moscow with whom it had a Treaty of Friendship and Cooperation, and that aggression against Syria was an "extremely dangerous venture." He also noted that the potential of forces opposing US and Israeli policy in Syria and Lebanon did not compare "in any way with what the Pentagon faced on Grenada."[164] This was the strongest warning given by Moscow to the US thus far in the Lebanese crisis, and was perhaps aimed at deterring the US from any strike against Syria, although the fact that it took the form of a *Novosti* article, and not a Tass statement, indicated it was still low level. Nonetheless, such a warning again raised questions of Soviet credibility should a Syrian–American confrontation take place, either in the form of an American retaliation for the Marine headquarters explosion or an attack on Syrian positions in Lebanon in retaliation for the firing on US reconnaissance planes. Syrian government statements such as the one broadcast on Syrian Radio on November 29 that "Syria expresses its pride – before the Arab nation and the world – at the fact that it agitates a superpower" appeared to make some form of confrontation even more likely.[165]

The US attack came on December 4, following Syrian anti-aircraft fire on US reconnaissance planes the previous day. The fact that the US lost two planes, and had one of its pilots killed and another captured did not detract from the fact that the US had openly attacked Syrian forces in Lebanon and that a major confrontation was underway. Under these circumstances Moscow was again faced with the dilemma of either supporting its client's policies in Lebanon – policies that the USSR did not thoroughly agree with – or else once again losing some of its diplomatic credibility, particularly since Reagan was threatening to strike Syrian positions again if US forces continued to come under attack.[166] Once again Moscow was to take a cautious stand, although its diplomatic credibility was to suffer. Thus a Tass statement just noted that the Soviet Union "declared its solidarity with the peoples of Lebanon, Syria, and other Arab countries in defending their independence" and that "the aggressive actions of the United States against Syria constitute a serious threat to peace not only in the Middle East region."[167] While the Tass statement also sought propaganda advantage by tying the US attack to the strategic cooperation agreement concluded between Reagan and Israeli Prime Minister Yitzhak Shamir a week earlier, and claimed that by its attack the US no longer qualified as an "honest broker" in the Middle East, the failure of the Tass statement to mention the Soviet–Syrian treaty indicated that Syria could not expect more than

Soviet moral support against the US so long as the confrontation was limited to Lebanon.

While Moscow was not willing to aid Syria militarily to confront the US, it did seek to utilize the American attack against Syria to try to undermine the US position in the Middle East. Thus a *Pravda* editorial on December 10 repeated the Tass statement themes that the US no longer qualified as a mediator in the Arab–Israeli conflict and that the US attack was the outgrowth of US–Israeli strategic cooperation. The editorial went on to assert that the US was now being opposed even in conservative Arab countries, and Moscow once again appealed for Arab unity on an "anti-imperialist" basis. An Arabic language broadcast on December 12 carried this theme further, asserting that when the US signed its "strategic alliance" with Israel, it challenged "all Arabs without exception, the progressives and moderates alike."[168] Interestingly enough, however, the broadcast mentioned Soviet support for Syria only in passing and again called on the Arabs to unite and use their economic pressure against the US. It seems clear that Moscow, with Andropov gravely ill, was unwilling to use force to aid Syria and had gone back to the course of action it had pursued since the September crisis – an appeal to the Arabs to help Syria themselves. Unfortunately for the USSR, which hoped that the US attack would force the Centrist Arabs to again rally around Syria and what was left of the Steadfastness Front, this was not to happen. With Syria's ally Iran again threatening to close the Straits of Hormuz, the Centrist Arabs, and particularly the members of the Gulf Cooperation Council, had no choice but to rely on the US for help. Syria, to its apparent bitter disappointment, also realized this soon after the US attack as the Syrian media bewailed the lack of Arab support. As *Al Ba'ath* noted on December 8: "It is illogical to have Arab resources remain idle, waiting for the circle of aggression to reach them. It is also illogical to restrict the role of this or that Arab country to mere condemnation or denunciation of the aggressor."[169]

The end result was that Syria, without Soviet or Arab support against the US and with its efforts to topple Arafat as leader of the PLO only moderately successful (the PLO leader, who continued to command widespread Palestinian support, left Tripoli under the UN flag), moved to deescalate the tension. Thus it returned the body of the dead US airman to the US, agreed to talk to US mediator Donald Rumsfeld – despite the fact that the battleship New Jersey was firing on Syrian positions after US reconnaissance planes were again fired upon – and, finally, in a gesture which it said was aimed at "creating a circumstance conducive to the withdrawal of US forces in Lebanon", released the captured US airman.[170] This was a major Syrian concession, given the fact that Syrian leaders had earlier said that he would not be released until after the "war" was over and US forces had withdrawn from Lebanon.[171]

While it is clear that Assad, who had now recovered from his illness, was trying to exploit the rising tide of opposition in the United States to the Marine presence in Lebanon; nonetheless, to release the airman at a time when US naval guns were still pounding Syria positions indicated that the Syrian leader realized that his confrontation with the US held the danger of getting out of control at a time when he could not count on either Soviet or Arab support. Meanwhile, Assad's enemy, Yasser Arafat, appeared to at least temporarily take the initiative in intra-Arab politics away from the Syrian leader by his surprise meeting with Egyptian President Hosni Mubarak following his departure from Tripoli, a meeting that held out the possibility of a new alignment in Arab politics. Indeed the Arafat visit to Egypt came at a time when Egypt was again moving toward a *rapprochement* with a number of Centrist Arab states. Iraqi–Egyptian relations had been improving since 1982, and on July 23, 1983 Iraqi Foreign Minister Tariq Aziz had paid a formal visit to Cairo. The following month, a financial accord was signed between the two countries as Egyptian Foreign Trade Minister Mustafa Kamel Said visited Baghdad in the first such official visit by an Egyptian Minister since Camp David.[172] Then, following the surprise trip of Yasser Arafat to Cairo, Jordan announced the end of its five-year trade boycott against Egypt,[173] and on December 25 Jordan signed a trade protocol to upgrade its trade with Egypt to a level higher than the pre-boycott era.[174]

As the events took place, Moscow had to be concerned that the Steadfastness Front, already weakened by the Libyan–Algerian, Libyan–PLO, and Assad–Arafat rifts was crumbling further and a new Arafat-Egypt-Jordan-Iraq alignment in the Arab world might be forming. Such an alignment would mean that, in effect, Egypt was being accepted back into the Arab world without having to renounce Camp David. Given the fact that Egypt continued to maintain close ties with the US (the US continued to provide extensive military and economic aid to Egypt and joint military maneuvers again took place in 1983 after a hiatus in 1982 due, in part, to the Israeli invasion of Lebanon), such a reconciliation would be considered a victory for American diplomacy at a time when the US was having very serious problems in Lebanon.

Meanwhile, Egyptian–Soviet relations remained strained. Despite occasional rumors,[175] there was no exchange of ambassadors between the two countries and the most positive development for Moscow in Soviet–Egyptian relations in 1983 was the signing of a trade protocol which called for a large increase in trade.[176] Egypt remained suspicious of Soviet aid to Libya (the Egyptian Defense Minister indicated that half the Egyptian army was deployed on the Libyan border because of the presence of Soviet and Cuban forces there),[177] while Egypt's ties both to the United States and to Britain (with which Cairo also conducted military maneuvers in 1983) came in for sharp Soviet criticism. Indeed, an *Izvestia* article on October 18 noted that under Mubarak Egypt remained "the prisoner of Camp David." A feature article in the Soviet foreign policy weekly *New Times* at the end of December 1983 titled "Changes Without a Change" summed up Moscow's displeasure with Mubarak, noting that Egypt was "shackled" by US economic and military aid, and was increasingly being run by an American-educated elite. For this reason, the journal lamented:

> Any marked deviation from the foreign and domestic policies inherited from Sadat is bound to provoke a sharply negative reaction on the part of influential forces – a considerable section of the ruling clique and its US benefactors. This explains why anti-Soviet attacks appear in pro-government newspapers, why the Egyptian regime sticks to the Camp David agreements, and why its position on the Palestinian problem and the situation in Lebanon is much closer to the US than to the pan-Arab view. Moreover, Washington is trying to build a bridge between Cairo and the so-called "moderate" Arab regimes and draw them into its strategic game.[178]

Thus, as 1983 came to a close, Moscow had to again be concerned about the reintegration of a pro-American Egypt into the Arab world. Fortunately for Moscow, however, early in 1984 the US position collapsed in Lebanon and Moscow may well have hoped that not only the Centrist Arabs, but perhaps Egypt itself would have lost confidence in the United States because of its mishandling of the Lebanese situation.

The crumbling of the US position began with the publication of the Long Commission report which analyzed the American political and military mistakes in Lebanon in the period leading up to the destruction of the US Marine headquarters in Beirut in October 1983.[179] The report increased the clamor in the United States for a pullout of the Marines from Lebanon, a clamor that was reflected in the US Congress.[180] At the same time, the position of Amin Gemayel weakened considerably as negotiations for a disengagement plan among the various warring Lebanese factions broke down at the end of January. The diplomatic impasse was followed by heavy fighting in the Beirut area between the Lebanese army and Druze and Shiite forces, a development which led to the virtual collapse of the Lebanese army, the resignation of Prime Minister Wazzan, and the seizure of West Beirut by Moslem militias. As chaos appeared to reign in Beirut, President Reagan suddenly announced the "redeployment" of US Marines to navy ships off the coast of Lebanon.[181] The US redeployment which was soon to be followed by the other members of the multinational force, was accompanied by American naval shelling of anti-government positions in the vicinity of Beirut, although the rationale for the shelling was never clearly explained by the Reagan administration.[182] Indeed, the general course of US policy during this period seemed confused at best, and whatever the mistakes the US had made in backing the Gemayel government up until this point, the hurried exodus of the Marines from Beirut, coupled with what appeared to be the indiscriminate artillery fire into the Lebanese mountains, could only hurt the US image, not only in Lebanon, but in the Middle East as a whole. Naturally, such a weakening of the US position was welcomed by Moscow which moved to coordinate policy directly with Syria following the Muslim takeover of West Beirut. On February 8, *Pravda* announced that Geydar Aliyev, the only Politburo member of Shii Muslim extraction, would be going to Syria for a "working visit." Just before Aliyev was to depart, however, Andropov died, the second Soviet leader to die during the Lebanese crisis. The succession of Konstantin Chernenko to power was, nonetheless, quite rapid and the new Soviet leader soon moved to exploit the US defeat in Lebanon.

The first issue pertaining to the Lebanese crisis facing Chernenko was a French proposal to replace the multinational force in Beirut with a United Nations force. Moscow, which had called for such a force in 1982, vetoed the French plan, ostensibly because it would not prevent the US from shelling Syrian and pro-Syrian forces in Lebanon behind the screen of the UN troops. It would appear, however, that the primary reason for the Soviet veto of the French proposal was to prevent the US from using the insertion of the UN force as a cover for the American retreat from Lebanon, a development which might diminish the impact of the US defeat.[183]

Moscow was to achieve another success for its Lebanese policy when Amin Gemayel, now virtually bereft of US military support, could only turn to Assad for help in staying in power. Assad proved willing to do so – for a price. The price was the abrogation of the May 17 Israeli–Lebanese agreement, and Gemayel announced its abrogation on March 5. Yet even as Moscow was hailing this development (Soviet commentators were to call it a major blow to the entire Camp David process), and Aliyev was again getting ready to journey to Damascus, there were a number of problems which the new Soviet leadership had to face despite the collapse of the US position in Lebanon. In the first place a power struggle had erupted in Damascus over the succession to President Hafiz Assad who apparently had not fully recovered from his heart attack. Secondly, despite its victory in Lebanon which the Syrian media was hailing as equivalent to Nasser's nationalization of the Suez Canal,[184] Syria remained in diplomatic isolation in the Arab world, while Egypt continued to improve its ties to Centrist Arab states. As noted above, Egypt's *rapprochement* with the Centrist Arabs was expedited by the surprise visit of Arafat to Cairo after his expulsion from Lebanon in December 1983 (Arafat later went to Jordan where he resumed discussions with King Hussein), and the *rapprochement* was highlighted by the decision of the Islamic Conference to readmit Egypt to its ranks in mid-January, a development attributed by Moscow to the "pressure of conservative Moslem regimes."[185] Nonetheless the fact that Libya, Syria, and South Yemen walked out of the conference indicated the continuing isolation of Moscow's closest Arab allies, while the USSR had to be concerned about the possible formation of a new Arab front that would move to reincorporate Egypt into the Arab League and possibly revive the Reagan plan. Indeed, following the Arafat visit to Cairo, *Izvestia* noted unhappily:

> Behind the scenes some "moderate" Arab regimes are using all kinds of tricks and lies to induce the PLO leadership to adopt the Reagan plan for the resolution of the Palestinian problem... This is why, out of necessity, they are playing up to Cairo which, as a participant in Camp David, is trying to urge other Arab countries onto this path.[186]

Soviet concern with such a development could only have increased with Mubarak's visit to King Hassan of Morocco – the first official visit to an Arab country by the head of the Egyptian state since the 1979 Peace Treaty, as Moscow TV unhappily noted[187] – and by Mubarak's meeting with King Hussein in Washington in mid-February as the two Arab leaders prepared for talks with President Reagan.

Meanwhile, as Egypt's relations with Centrist Arab nations

improved, Syria, despite its victory in Lebanon, appeared to remain isolated. Thus not only was its influence insufficient to prevent the Islamic Conference from readmitting Egypt, it was again in isolation when the Arab League Foreign Ministers, in a meeting in mid-March which Syria and Libya boycotted, took a strongly anti-Iranian position, condemning Iran for its continuing "aggression against Iraq," and warning Iran that the continuation of the war would force the Arab states to reconsider their relations with it.[188] For its part, Moscow could only have been concerned with Syria's continued Arab isolation, not to mention that of Libya whose heavy-handed actions against the Sudan (the bombing of Obdurman) and Jordan (the storming of the Jordanian embassy in Tripoli) served only to alienate two regimes Moscow was seeking to win over. Compounding Moscow's difficulties in exploiting the US failure in Lebanon was the situation in the Persian Gulf. Iran had again undertaken a major offensive against Iraq and was threatening the key southern Iraqi city of Basra, while at the same time repeating its threats to close the Straits of Hormuz if Iraq, using its newly acquired Super-Entendard bombers interfered with Iranian oil exports. Moscow, at a time when its relations with Iran were at a low ebb in part because of the Khomeini regime's persecution of the Tudeh party, was clearly concerned that the United States, which had again pledged to keep the Straits open and which had increased the size of its fleet near the Gulf, would exploit the Iranian threats to reinforce its position in the Arab states of the Gulf, and thereby divert attention from its failure in Lebanon. As *Krasnaya Zvezda* noted on March 4, "Washington is trying in [the Persian Gulf] to compensate at least somehow for its political and military errors in Lebanon."[189] In a counter to the stepped-up US deployment near the Gulf, the Soviet government issued a statement on March 8 denouncing US activity in the Gulf as a "grave threat to peace and international security," and stating that the USSR would not abide by any restrictions imposed by the US in the Gulf region.[190]

Thus, when Geydar Aliyev came to Damascus, the overall Middle East picture was not as bright as Moscow would have wished, despite the failure of US policy in Lebanon. In addition, the dinner speeches during Aliyev's visit reflected continued tension in Soviet–Syrian relations. Thus, Khaddam, in hailing the defeat of American and Israeli policy in a dinner speech welcoming Aliyev, gave more credit to Syrian action than to Soviet aid, while also praising those Palestinian "patriotic forces who courageously opposed the policy of sliding, fragmentation, and departure from the decisions of the Palestine National Council, pursued by some Palestinian leaders to satisfy the Americans and Israelis."[191] In his speech in response Aliyev praised the Lebanese National Patriotic Forces for resisting US pressure before mentioning the Syrian role although he did have words of praise for the Soviet–Syrian treaty. He also called for the Arab people of Palestine, "under the leadership of the PLO, its sole legitimate representative, to be given an opportunity to establish its own state."[192]

The final communiqué issued after Aliyev's talks with Syrian leaders (Moscow made special mention of Aliyev's meeting with Rifat al-Assad who was "heartily congratulated" on his appointment as Vice-President, perhaps as a gesture to show that Moscow had confidence in Rifat)[193] referred to a "spirit of friendship and mutual understanding," the usual Soviet code words for disagreement.[194] Thus while the two sides hailed the abrogation of the May 17 Israeli–Lebanese agreement as a great success, and also expressed their aspirations to further strengthen Soviet–Syrian relations, the final communiqué noted "an exchange of opinions" regarding US and Israeli threats against Syria, thereby, as in the visit of Khaddam to Moscow in November 1983, probably indicating disagreement over the degree of Soviet support Syria might expect if it became involved in a war with the US or Israel. An even more serious Soviet–Syrian disagreement was revealed over the Palestinian issue by the communiqué's notation that "a thorough exchange of opinions took place on questions relating to the state of affairs in the Palestinian Resistance movement." Nonetheless, perhaps reflecting Moscow's displeasure with the Arafat–Mubarak meeting, and the resumption of Arafat's talks with Hussein, the communiqué also noted:

> The Soviet Union and Syria are convinced of the need to preserve the unity of the Palestinian resistance movement and to overcome as speedily as possible the disagreement within the PLO, which is the sole legitimate representative of the Arab people of Palestine, on a *progressive-patriotic and anti-imperialist basis*.

> The sides believe that the implementation of the Palestinian National aspirations is impossible without observance of the Palestine National Council's decision aimed at countering the Israeli aggression and the Camp David policy of separate deals, including the "Reagan plan" and without close cooperation by the PLO with Syria, all progressive Arab states, and patriotic forces of the Arab world.[195] (emphasis added)

Another area of Soviet–Syrian disagreement was most probably Syria's continuing support for Iran at a time when Moscow was trying to end the Iran–Iraq war. While no mention of this dispute was made in the joint communiqué, the Kuwaiti periodical, *al-Qabas*, asserted that such differences had surfaced during the discussions.[196]

On balance, however, it appeared that Aliyev's visit helped to solidify Soviet–Syrian relations following the succession in Moscow and the power struggle in Damascus. As might be expected, Soviet broadcasts to the Arab world highlighted the Aliyev visit, citing Syrian newspaper declarations of praise for Soviet–Syrian and Soviet–Arab relations.[197] Nonetheless, as far as Lebanon was concerned, Moscow did not appear ready to cede it to Syria as a satrapy. In the first place, despite the departure of the US Marines and the abrogation of the May 17 agreement, Syria was not yet in a position to fully control events in Lebanon, as the failure of the Lausanne National Reconciliation Conference, which was held under Syrian supervision, indicated. Indeed, while both Druze leader Walid Jumblatt and Shii leader Nabih Berri had cooperated with Syria against Amin Gemayel, neither was a Syrian stooge (according to most reports, Jumblatt's father had been killed by Syria) and both might act in an increasingly independent manner should a genuine power sharing system ever be worked out in Lebanon. Under these circumstances Moscow evidently felt it was useful to develop its own ties with key Lebanese groups. Thus, Walid Jumblatt, whose father had close ties to Moscow before his assassination, was invited to visit the Soviet capital in January 1984,[198] there were frequent meetings between Soviet leaders and Lebanese communist party officials, and, at the end of March, Karen Brutents, deputy chief of the CPSU Central Committee's International Department journeyed to Lebanon where he met Berri, Jumblatt, Lebanese Foreign Minister Elie Salim, and Lebanese communist party leader George Hawi, as well as Lebanese President Amin Gemayel. Moscow's goal in Lebanon at this time appeared to be to gain first-hand knowledge of the complex political situation there in order to help consolidate the victory of those Lebanese forces opposed to American influence so as to keep Lebanon out of the American-directed peace process. To be sure, at this time the United States was having more than its share of difficulties in its Middle East diplomacy. Not only had it suffered a débâcle in Lebanon, but the Reagan plan suffered a major blow in mid-March when King Hussein of Jordan announced he would not enter into talks with Israel, even if the Israelis froze the construction of settlements in occupied territories, because the US had lost its credibility and was no longer a trusted mediator.[199] Needless to say, Moscow was delighted with this development with some Soviet commentators attributing the King's action to the failure of US policy in Lebanon,[200] although Syrian commentators dismissed the King's speech as insignificant unless Hussein broke his ties with the United States.[201]

The Syrian commentators may well have been closer to the mark, given King Hussein's statement at a March 30 press conference express-ing interest in a possible Labor Party victory in the just-announced Israeli elections, a development that might once again breathe life into the Reagan plan and the US-mediated peace process.[202]

All in all, despite the collapse of US policy in Lebanon, and its other diplomatic difficulties in the Arab world,[203] by the end of March it did not appear as if either Moscow or Syria was able to convert the events in Lebanon into larger victories in the Arab world. Indeed as Damascus Radio, quoting *al Ba'ath*, noted somewhat ruefully on March 28:

> We and the masses of the [Arab] nation had expected some kind of an official Arab move toward Syria to reinforce this victory [the abro-gation of the Israeli–Lebanese agreement], so as to take the nation to another, more important victory represented by the abrogation of the Camp David accords prior to achieving the greater victory, the libera-tion of the occupied Arab territory from the Zionist invaders.
>
> But the current moves between the Egyptian, Jordanian, and Iraqi capitals involving Arafat among others are only part of the US–Israeli plan to abort the victory in Lebanon.
>
> At any rate Syria will continue to work for revolutionary Arab solidarity against the enemies of the nation. We will not allow a solidarity sponsored by the US and Israel.[204]

Essentially, therefore, Moscow had two major problems in the spring of 1984: (1) dealing with an escalating Iran–Iraq war in such a way as to prevent the United States from rebuilding its position in the Middle East and (2) preventing any further moves toward the reintegration of Egypt in the Arab world and thereby preventing the expansion of the Camp David process.

As far as the situation in the Gulf was concerned, Moscow moved quickly to exploit the sudden chilling of US–Iraqi relations (after a slow but steady improvement since 1981) which had been caused by US accusations that Iraq had employed poison gas in its war against Iran. In addition to denying reports of Soviet supply of chemical weapons to Iraq, and castigating the Iranian government for spreading the rumors,[205] Moscow sought to strengthen its ties with Iraq by signing an intergovernmental agreement on economic and technical cooperation which involved Soviet assistance in the construction of two major projects in Iraq – a heat and power station and a hydroelectric complex.[206] A month later, Iraq's Deputy Prime Minister Taha Ramadan was invited to Moscow for talks. The fact that in addition to meeting with Prime Minister Tikhonov, Ramadan also met with both the then Soviet deputy Defense Minister and Chief of Staff, Nikolai Ogarkov and the Chairman of the State Committee on Foreign Economic Relations, Yaakov Ryabov, who is responsible for foreign arms sales, appeared to mean that the Iraqi leader was interested in more arms from the USSR.[207] Subsequent reports of increased Soviet arms shipments indicate that Ramadan may well have been successful in his quest, although it is interesting to note that while the *Pravda* description of the talks stated that Ramadan had criticized US "imperialist intrigues,"[208] the Iraqi news agency description cited no such statement,[209] as Iraq clearly had no wish to unnecessarily alienate the United States, with Iran, whose February offensive had scored some costly gains, reportedly preparing yet another major offensive.[210]

Another purpose of Ramadan's visit may have been to alert the USSR to Iraq's plan to wage a war of attrition against Iran's oil exports so as to weaken Iran's ability to finance its war effort. Having proclaimed a 50-mile air and sea blockade around Iran's main oil export terminal on Kharg Island in February, Iraq now began to attack oil tankers and other vessels that entered the zone. Iran responded by using its airforce to attack Kuwaiti and Saudi tankers, and the Gulf war escalated further. Moscow's continuing concern during the war's escalation was that the US would exploit the situation to improve its ties with the Gulf states which might have to turn to the US for protection.[211] Indeed, just such a development was to take place in the case of Saudi Arabia. As a result of Saudi unhappiness over US policy in Lebanon, the increasingly close US tie with Israel, the US Congress's opposition to the sale of Stinger anti-aircraft missiles to Saudi Arabia, and the possible move of the US embassy in Israel to Jerusalem, Saudi–US ties had cooled considerably by April 1984,[212] and such incidents as the Saudi public consideration of the purchase of a $4.5 billion air defense system from France rather than the US, and the invitation of Soviet Ambassador Anatoly Dobrynin to a dinner at the Saudi embassy in Washington were cited in some quarters as evidence of Saudi Arabia's move away from the United States.[213] Nonetheless, the Iranian attack on a Saudi oil tanker in mid-May quickly reversed this trend. Two days after the tanker was hit, Saudi Ambassador Bandar Bin Sultan met with US Secretary of State George Shultz, reportedly to obtain a US commitment to come to Saudi Arabia's aid in case a crisis occurred.[214] The US was quick to respond. President Reagan sent a letter to King Fahd reportedly reaffirming US support for the kingdom as well as reaffirming US support for freedom of navigation in the Gulf, and stating that the US would back up its commitment with military power if requested to do so by friendly nations in the area.[215] Reagan, citing the demands of "national security" (which obviated the need for Congressional approval), then sent 400 Stinger missiles and 200 launchers to Saudi Arabia, along with a KC-10 tanker aircraft to augment the three KC-135 tankers already there. The US idea was to enable Saudi F-15s and the Saudi-based US AWACs to stay in the air for longer periods, thereby, in the words of the State Department spokesman Alan Romberg, "to lower the risk of a broader conflict by providing a deterrent against hostile activities."[216] Thus strengthened, and perhaps angered by comments in the US and elsewhere that they would not fight even to defend their own interests (except perhaps against Israel), the Saudi leaders sent up their F-15s against Iranian F-4s hunting for oil tankers near the Saudi coast, and shot down one Iranian plane while driving off a number of others. The fact that the Saudis had acted with US AWACs assistance, and that more American assistance was on the way in the form of extra fuel tanks for the F-15s, along with more advanced AWACs capable of detecting slow moving ships and aircraft,[217] clearly improved the US–Saudi relationship, and the Saudis were to reciprocate soon afterwards by freeing many of the Americans held in Saudi jails as part of a general amnesty.[218] The Saudi–US relationship improved still more in August when the US promptly responded to Saudi requests to clear the Red Sea of mines which, apparently laid by Libya, hampered not only maritime trade in the Red Sea and through the Suez Canal, but also the *Hajj* which Saudi Arabia, as the keeper of the Holy places of Mecca and Medina, took great pride in hosting.

While Moscow could do little about the US success in exploiting the escalation of the Iran–Iraq war to improve ties to Saudi Arabia, it was to work energetically to prevent a similar development in US–Kuwaiti relations. As the most neutralist of the Gulf Cooperation Council states, and the only one then to have diplomatic ties with and receive military equipment from the Soviet Union, Kuwait occupied a special place in Soviet strategy toward the GCC. Moscow had long feared that the GCC both because of the invasion of Afghanistan and because of Iranian victories in the Iran–Iraq war, might gravitate to the US for protection and the Soviet leadership had sought to cultivate Kuwait's neutralist leanings, and its basically anti-American press, to prevent such a development. On the eve of the escalation of the tanker war in mid-May, a Kuwaiti delegation headed by the Under-Secretary of the Foreign Ministry, Rashid ar-Rashid, visited Moscow for discussions on the Gulf war and to arrange the visit to Moscow of Kuwaiti Defense Minister Sheikh Salem as-Sabah.[219] The delegation also met with Yaakov Ryabov, possibly for a preliminary discussion on new arms sales, and also signed an agreement on cultural cooperation. Then, however, the Saudi and Kuwaiti tankers were hit and questions were raised among the elite in Kuwait about the desirability of its nonalignment policy in the face of the Iranian threat. Possibly noting that Reagan had been willing to buck Congressional opposition to quickly send Stinger missiles to Saudi Arabia, the Kuwaiti Foreign Minister Sheikh Sabah as-Sabah also asked for the missiles.[220] Unfortunately for Kuwait, however, its refusal to accept an American Ambassador the year before because of his previous service in the US consulate in East Jerusalem, and the generally anti-US tone of the Kuwaiti press, did not particularly endear the Kuwaitis to President Reagan who clearly had no desire to alienate Congress further by sending Stingers to Kuwait. Other arguments against the sale were the relatively small US stockpile of Stingers for export and US fears that the Stingers might wind up in the hands of terrorists.[221] The end result was that the US announced in the words of State Department spokesman John Hughes that while "no final decision had been made on the sale, we don't contemplate a sale at this time."[222] The US, however, did offer to improve the quality of the US-made Hawk anti-aircraft missiles that Kuwait already possessed (a US team which had made a survey of Kuwait's defense needs had recommended this) while also offering to share with Kuwait the information gathered by US AWACs based in Saudi Arabia. While, on the eve of the trip to Moscow by its Defense Minister, Kuwait made no formal response to the US offer to improve the Hawks, Sheikh Sabah did announce Kuwait was already making use of the AWACs-gathered information.[223]

It was under these circumstances that Sheikh Salem as-Sabah, the Kuwaiti Defense Minister, journeyed to Moscow in early July. The Soviet leadership, noting that the Kuwaitis had been denied the weapons system they really wanted, and had been embarrassed in the process (the Kuwaiti Foreign Minister, after being privately denied the missiles, had made a public appeal to the US Congress, going so far as to say that the missiles were only for defensive purposes and not "to declare war" against Israel)[224] moved to demonstrate that they could treat a client far better than the US had done. Thus, Sheikh Salem, besides reportedly being offered a wide variety of weapons,[225] was taken to visit Leningrad, Tbilisi, Sevastopol, Tashkent, and Samarkand, and in addition to being invited to witness live-fire exercises (including a combined land, air, and naval exercise), also was shown a number of archaeological sites and Soviet museums.[226] The Soviet leadership seemed to have gone out of its way to demonstrate warm hospitality to the Kuwaiti official, and while the end result of the visit appears not to have been the $347 million arms deal initially rumored, the Kuwaiti Defense Minister ultimately did agree not only to purchase Soviet air defense missiles[227] but also to invite a small number of Soviet advisers to Kuwait – the first time this had ever happened – to train Kuwaitis on the use of the anti-aircraft missiles.[228]

Nonetheless, despite the decision to buy the weapons from Moscow, Kuwait was clearly keeping open its ties to Washington and in the fall an agreement was made with the US both to train 150 Kuwaiti pilots in the United States and for the US to establish a pilot training school in Kuwait.[229] At the same time, the Kuwaiti government reportedly gave red-carpet treatment to the new US Ambassador to Kuwait, Anthony Quinton, and also toned down the usually anti-US Kuwaiti press.[230] Finally, during the hijacking of a Kuwaiti plane to Iran, the Kuwaiti government stood firm and refused to free the imprisoned terrorists accused of the attacks on the US and French embassies in December, 1983, as demanded by the hijackers, thereby earning warm praise from President Reagan.

While the escalation of the Iran–Iraq war was, somewhat paradoxically, to lead to an improvement in Kuwait's ties to both the USSR and the US, on balance Washington gained more – much to the displeasure of Moscow which continued to see the Arab world as a zone of zero-sum game competition with the United States. Nonetheless, Moscow must have been heartened by the fact that the Gulf Cooperation Council, thanks at least in part to Kuwait's opposition and to a lessened fear of Iran due to a prolonged postponement of the expected Iranian offensive, did not move to establish a joint defense treaty or even a joint air defense system at its meeting in late November although its constituent members did not agree to earmark troops for a GCC Rapid Deployment Force.[231] As *Literaturnaia Gazeta* commented on December 5: "this means that the GCC will remain an economic organization as its founders intended and will not become a military organization, a kind of defensive pact, over which the US seeks to gain control."[232]

While Moscow proved unable to move Saudi Arabia away from the US, and while it had only limited success in reinforcing Kuwait's neutralist leanings, it continued to be frustrated by the Iran–Iraq war, and, in particular, by the Khomeini regime in Iran. Moscow's relationship with Iran had reached a new low on the eve of 1984, as shown by an extensive article in *Pravda* which, in addition to criticizing the regime for arresting 8,500 Tudeh members, noted that the anti-Soviet circles in Iran were trying to entice the Iranian government "onto a path of blind fanaticism" and warned the Khomeini regime to stop the "filthy campaign of slander" against the USSR.[233] Similarly, a feature article in *New Times* analyzing the first five years of the new Iranian government complained that the political revolution did not develop into a social revolution and blamed Iran for the continuation of the Iran–Iraq war. It also noted the growing trade ties between Iran and the US and other NATO members and the anti-socialist hostility which "the conservative wing of the Iranian religious and political leadership has always harbored." The article also condemned Iran for its support of "Afghan counterrevolutionaries" and for arresting and imprisoning Tudeh members as terrorists.[234] Interestingly enough both the *Pravda* and *New Times* articles also appealed to Iran for an improved relationship, much as Moscow previously did at times of Soviet–Iranian conflict.

If Moscow's ties with Tehran were strained, US–Iranian relations (except in the area of trade which had risen to $1 billion in 1983) were far worse. The US had blamed Iran for the terrorist attack on the Marine headquarters in Lebanon in October 1983 and had officially classified Iran as an exporter of terrorism, thus necessitating a close scrutiny of all exports to Iran[235] and possibly making Iran a target for a US retaliatory strike. Nonetheless, as in the past, a hostile relationship with the United States did not drive Iran any closer to the USSR as, despite Soviet warnings, Iran announced the execution of ten Tudeh members in late February.[236] Moscow grew increasingly angry as Iran went on the offensive in its war with Iraq the same month, fearing, as mentioned above, that such a development would push the Gulf Arabs toward the United States. *Krasnaia Zvezda* noted in its review of the war on April 21, that the escalation of the war created "a pretext" (though a false one) for a further build-up of the US military presence in the Gulf.

The outbreak of the tanker war however, and a possible split in Iran's ruling elite over the desirability of Iran's continuing its "go it alone policy" may have caused Iran to partially change its policy toward the USSR in June. In the first major diplomatic gesture to Moscow since the expulsion of eighteen Soviet diplomats the year before, Tehran sent Seyed Mohamed Sadr, the director general of the Iranian Foreign Ministry to Moscow on June 6 where he met with Soviet Foreign Minister Andrei Gromyko.[237] In commenting on the trip, Iran's newly re-elected speaker of Parliament, Hashemi Rafsanjani, stated that the visit was "unrelated to the war" but that it helped improve relations. He also observed that Iran did not want its relationship with the USSR to become "darkened."[238] Following the visit, there did seem to be somewhat of a warming of Soviet–Iranian relations as there were reports that Moscow's allies Bulgaria, Czechoslovakia, and North Korea had stepped up their shipments of arms to Iran,[239] and on June 21 the Soviet Union's Deputy Power and Electricity Minister Aleksei Makukhim led a delegation to Iran – the highest level Soviet delegation to Iran in over a year. Moscow's purpose in sending the delegation, in addition to reciprocating the visit of the Iranian Foreign Ministry official, seemed to be to try to build upon its economic relationship with Tehran, hoping perhaps that this might be the foundation for improved political relations in the future. One of the central themes of Moscow Radio's Persian language broadcasts to Iran since the Khomeini regime took power had been the benefits that would accrue to Iran from increased trade with Moscow (one broadcast went so far as to urge Iran to allow the rebuilding of the bridges on the border rivers "which were built in the early years of World War II and are now old"[240] – as if the Iranians might have already forgotten how the bridges were used to facilitate Soviet occupation of Northern Iran at the time). Another goal of the Soviets may have been to try to save the lives of imprisoned Tudeh leaders, as a Persian language broadcast to Iran on the eve of the Soviet delegation's visit cited the appeal of the Arab communist and workers' parties to free the Tudeh members.[241]

Nonetheless, while moving to improve its ties with Moscow somewhat, Iran was making gestures to the West as well, with the visit to Tehran in late July of Hans Dietrich Genscher, the West German Foreign Minister who said after his visit – the first by a major NATO state Foreign Minister since the fall of the Shah – that the Iranian government had expressed a "clear wish" to gradually reestablish contacts with the West.[242] In addition, despite the fact that France was harboring many exiles opposed to Khomeini, Rafsanjani was quoted as saying that "not all doors with France were closed."[243]

In the following months, the central issues causing strain in Soviet–Iranian relations continued – the persecution of the Tudeh party; anti-Soviet propaganda in Iran; continued Iranian aid to the Afghan guerrillas; and, especially, the continuation of the Iran–Iraq war. The Soviet press, in describing the fifth anniversary of the outbreak of the war in September, continued to call for the war's end as soon as possible since the conflict "only benefits the imperialists."[244] Dmitry Volsky, writing in *New Times*, summarized Moscow's unhappiness with the conflict:

> The protracted war between Iran and Iraq has upset the fragile military-political balance throughout the vast area from the Atlantic to the Indian Ocean and served as a catalyst of the religious and national strife dating back to the Middle Ages which had seemed to have become a matter of the past. More, the new seat of war became something of a connecting link between the zones of older local conflicts. It gave added impetus to the adventurism of the Tel Aviv rulers, who saw their chance in the growing division in the Arab world owing to the Iranian–Iraqi war and hastened to take advantage of this to invade Lebanon. On the other hand, the Gulf war fanned Moslem extremism, which is capitalized on in the undeclared war against Afghanistan and in intrigues against India.[245]

Moscow itself was to suffer from this extremism not only in Afghanistan, but in Lebanon where Islamic fundamentalists fired a grenade at the Soviet embassy in Beirut, and in the Red Sea where the shadowy Islamic "holy war" group took credit for laying mines in August.[246] This action was directly counterproductive to Soviet strategy since not only were the United States and other Western nations called in to help clear the mines – thus shoring up ties with Saudi Arabia and Egypt – but also, because the USSR itself depended on the Red Sea for its seaborne trade, and Soviet ships and those of its Warsaw Pact allies were also at risk because of the mines. Interestingly enough, the Iranian leadership seemed to be at cross purposes over the mining, with Tehran Radio praising the mining (while saying Iran was not involved), but Khomeini himself condemning it several days later.[247]

As Moscow was encountering difficulties with Iran, and the fundamentalist Islam which had been encouraged by the Khomeini regime, it could at least draw comfort from the fact that US–Iranian relations appeared to be worsening. Thus the US–Iranian claims panel was suspended after two Iranian judges physically attacked a Swedish judge whom they accused of pro-American bias,[248] and the Iranian

Foreign Minister, Ali Akhbar Velayati, noted in an interview that he saw no hope of improving ties with the United States.[249] Interestingly enough, possibly in a gesture to Moscow when Iran was undertaking a minor offensive against Iraq, Velayati also stated "our relations with the USSR are exactly what relations between two neighboring states should be. The Tudeh party is an internal problem for us that had absolutely nothing to do with any foreign government."[250]

If the Soviet leadership could perhaps take some small comfort from the words of Velayati, it was less positively inclined to developments in Iraq. Despite increased Soviet shipments of arms, especially tanks and planes, the Iraqi regime which also had been receiving sophisticated aircraft from France (Super Entendards and Mirage F-1s) had decided to renew its strategy of seeking a balance among the superpowers.[251] Thus, in an interview in early October, Iraqi Foreign Minister Tariq Aziz noted that "a very agreeable atmosphere" now existed in US–Iraqi relations and he hinted that full diplomatic relations would be restored after the US presidential elections.[252] It was perhaps for this reason that, on his visit to Moscow two weeks later, the discussions which he had with Gromyko were described as having taken place in a "frank and friendly atmosphere."[253] At the end of November the US and Iraq announced the restoration of full diplomatic relations, a development which the Prime Minister of Iran, Hussein Mousavi, stated would increase anti-US sentiment in Iran.[254] Interestingly enough, however, less than a week later it was reported that Iran had agreed to replace the two Iranian judges who had physically abused their Swedish colleague at the US–Iran claims tribunal,[255] a development which enabled Iran to keep at least one line of negotiation open with the United States, while also resuming the process of regaining its credit-worthiness in the Western world.

All in all the Persian Gulf proved to be a major problem area for Soviet policy in 1984, one in which the Soviet leadership, now headed by the aged and infirm Chernenko, tended to be reacting to events caused by the Iran–Iraq war rather than formulating any new initiative of its own. Moscow was to take more of an initiative, however, in trying to deal with a possible revival of the Reagan plan.

As far as the Reagan plan was concerned, the centerpiece of Moscow's concern was King Hussein of Jordan whose agreement, along with that of the Israeli government, was needed if the Reagan plan had any hopes of being put into effect. So long as the Likud party ruled Israel, there was little likelihood of any progress on the Reagan plan since both Prime Minister Menahem Begin and his successor Yitzhak Shamir opposed it. In addition, there was an increasingly tense relationship between the United States and Jordan which was characterized by the stinging attack by King Hussein on US policy mentioned above and the subsequent US denial of Stinger missiles to Jordan, and the US abandonment of a plan to equip a Jordanian army detachment to act as a surrogate Rapid Deployment Force for use in the Persian Gulf.[256] Moscow greeted these developments enthusiastically, with *Izvestia* commentator Stanislav Kondrashev going so far as to state on March 28 that:

> With American prestige sinking rapidly and relentlessly [after the US débâcle in Lebanon], Hussein disassociated himself from the Reagan Administration's Middle East policy. He rejected the prospect of becoming the third Camp David victim. As a result, the entire policy of separate deals has been deprived of any future.[257]

Yet Kondrashev's optimism was premature. Before the month was out, the Likud government had fallen, and the rival Labor Party soon assumed a commanding lead in the Israeli public opinion polls. What made this a problem for Moscow was that not only had Labor Party leader Shimon Peres welcomed the Reagan plan, but that King Hussein, in commenting on the collapse of the Likud government, had stated that a Labor victory would be a healthy change[258] – an indication that the Jordanian monarch, as always, was keeping his options open. For this reason, during the spring and summer of 1984 Soviet Middle Eastern diplomacy had a special Jordanian focus. Thus Moscow assiduously wooed King Hussein with numerous Soviet delegations visiting Jordan and Jordanian delegations visiting the USSR in the hope of keeping Jordan from embracing the Reagan plan in the event, as the polls predicted, that the Labor Party scored a major victory in the July Israeli elections.[259] In addition, the Soviet leadership prepared a new variant of its Middle East plan, one that might prove more amenable to King Hussein than previous Soviet peace plans had been. While the Jordanian monarch had long shared the Soviet goal of an international conference to settle the Arab–Israeli conflict, he also had long desired a link between any Palestinian entity or state on the West Bank and Jordan, whose population was more than 60 percent Palestinian. The Soviet peace plan of July 29, which mentioned such a link, therefore, can be considered a major gesture to Hussein.

Modeled on the Brezhnev peace plan of September 15, 1982, which had combined the basic three-point Soviet peace plan (total Israeli withdrawal to 1967 boundaries; a Palestinian state on the West Bank and Gaza; and the right of all states in the region to exist) with the major components of the Arab program announced at Fez in 1982,[260] the new Soviet plan had one additional key element – the acknowledgment that the new Palestinian state could decide to form a confederation with a neighboring country.[261] Given the clash with Arafat over this issue during the PLO leader's visit to Moscow in January 1983, the Soviet leadership's inclusion of this element in its peace plan may also be seen as a gesture to Arafat who, in the summer of 1984, was engaged in a prolonged political battle to win over the Marxist elements of the PLO (the so-called "Democratic Alliance" of the PFLP, DFLP, and Palestine Communist Party),[262] while struggling to isolate the so-called "National Alliance" of Palestinian factions controlled by Syria.

In addition to the new content in the Soviet peace plan of July 29, its timing is also significant. Apparently prepared to coincide with the July 23 Israeli elections, Moscow evidently hoped to use it to help keep King Hussein from joining the Reagan plan. The fact that, contrary to expectation, the Labor victory was so narrow that it did not appear as if Peres, even if he could manage to form a narrow parliamentary majority, would be able to make the concessions that the Reagan plan would require, was a bonus for the USSR, as Moscow now sought to use the plan as a rallying point for Centrist and Steadfastness Front Arabs to draw them together and away from the US and its Egyptian-camp allies.

Not unexpectedly, Israel quickly rejected the Soviet peace initiative. Israel, in addition to refusing to participate in an international conference where the PLO would be present, also opposed the Soviet concept of an international conference on the Middle East because it feared that at such a conference the Arabs would be reduced to their lowest common denominator – opposition to Israel's right to exist – and that the superpowers would impose an unfavorable peace agreement on Israel. The United States, whose Reagan administration was deeply suspicious of Soviet motivations in the Middle East, also rejected the Soviet proposal.

Much to Moscow's satisfaction, however, its peace initiative was warmly received in the Arab world, especially by such Centrist Arab states as Jordan and Kuwait. Arafat's wing of the PLO also accepted the plan, as did Lebanon, and it also received favorable comment from North and South Yemen, Syria, and Saudi Arabia. The Arab League Secretary General Chedli Klibi called it "a positive approach for solving the crisis," and in line with the (Fez) Arab peace plan.[263] Buoyed by the basically positive Arab reaction for the plan – although the various Arab states tended to be more supportive of the Soviet plan for an international conference on the Middle East than for the specific elements of the Soviet proposal – Moscow moved ahead during the summer to garner increased backing for it. In following this policy it appears doubtful if the Soviet leadership really thought a Middle East conference was obtainable in the near future, given the opposition of both Israel and the United States. Indeed, it seems as if Moscow was capitalizing on US and Israeli opposition as it put forth a basic framework on which both the Steadfastness Front and Centrist groupings in the Arab world might agree, thereby if not reuniting the two Arab camps then at least slowing the *rapprochement* between Egypt, which was then, at best, lukewarm about the Soviet plan,[264] and the Centrist Arab states, while at the same time highlighting the United States as the opponent of the Arab consensus on the peace program. Indeed, Radio Damascus in its commentary on the Soviet plan seemed to follow this interpretation:

> It becomes clear from the viewpoint of world observers and politicians that the Soviet peace program in the Middle East will frankly expose the stands of the enemies of peace, particularly the stands of the United States ... The Soviet peace program in the Middle East gives all the Arab states an opportunity to put the US and the USSR in the Arab balance.[265]

In its efforts to gain support for its peace plan, and isolate the United States and Israel, Soviet propaganda also exaggerated the close ties between Israel and the United States, going so far as to allege that Israel was going to deploy Pershing missiles on its soil to enable it "to intimidate Arab countries."[266] Interestingly enough, however, there were numerous hints in the Israeli press of Soviet feelers to get Israel to accept an international conference on the Middle East, holding out the prospect of a resumption of diplomatic relations, but these came to naught.[267]

Moscow continued its efforts to gain support for its peace plan in the late summer and early fall, as the leaders of North and South Yemen journeyed to Moscow along with the President of Syria and the deputy Prime Minister of Iraq. The first three Arab leaders endorsed the Soviet peace plan (the visit of the President of North Yemen was also highlighted by the signing of a Soviet–Yemeni Treaty of Friendship and Cooperation),[268] as did Chadli Ben-Jedid of Algeria, during a visit to Algiers by Soviet Politburo member Boris Ponamarev in mid-October.

In the case of Syria, however, there was continuing disagreement on the Palestinian question, and the fact that Gromyko, in a meeting with Arafat in East Berlin in late September had persuaded the PLO leader to back the Soviet peace initiative strongly, may have served to induce Assad to at least give lip service to it.[269] Nonetheless, the fact that the communiqué issued after Assad's visit referred to "an atmosphere of friendship and mutual understanding," and "an in-depth exchange of opinions on questions concerning the state of affairs in the Palestine Resistance Movement," probably indicated that Moscow and Damascus remained far apart on this issue, although the two sides jointly condemned the attempt to "activate" the policy of Camp David type separate accords.[270]

Despite Moscow's tactical success in garnering at least verbal support from most of the Arab world for its peace plan, the pace of Middle Eastern events once again seemed to confound Soviet strategy. Thus, in late September, soon after President Reagan, from the rostrum of the United Nations, had again emphasized the Reagan plan as US policy in the Middle East, and a Peres-led National Unity government with Shamir as Vice-Prime Minister and Foreign Minister had taken office in Israel, King Hussein, whom Moscow had been courting, suddenly reestablished full diplomatic relations with Egypt. This move, which was the final stage of a steady improvement of Jordanian–Egyptian relations since December 1983, appeared to be a major step in the *rapprochement* between the Centrist Arab camp and Egypt. To be sure, Moscow may have hoped that given the continuing tension in US–Jordanian ties, and the steady development of Soviet–Jordanian relations, Jordan might pull Egypt away from its close tie to the United States instead of being pulled by Egypt toward the Reagan plan. Nonetheless, despite resuming full diplomatic relations on the ambassadorial level with the Soviet Union in July,[271] and making such small gestures to the USSR as allowing the reopening of a Soviet bookstore in Cairo, Egypt continued its close military and economic relationship with the United States as exemplified by Mubarak's call for the US to help in the clearing of mines from the Red Sea in August and the joint military exercise "Sea Wind" carried on by the two nations in early November. Indeed the low level treatment given to the resumption of Egyptian–Jordanian diplomatic relations in the Soviet press seemed to indicate that Moscow was trying to play down the development while continuing to cultivate Jordan. Nonetheless, an *Izvestia* editorial on October 14 by one of Moscow's most outspoken commentators, Vladimir Kudravtsev, seemed to indicate Moscow's true feelings about the Jordanian monarch's moves:

> Availing itself of the fact that certain Arab countries have taken an ambiguous stand – condemning the US for its pro-Israel policy in words, while actively undermining the emerging Arab unity in deeds – US propaganda is stressing the need for creating some sort of bloc of "moderate" Arab states. The US intends to use this bloc against the anti-imperialist and anti-Zionist unity of Arab countries and against Syria, which takes a firm anti-imperialist stand, and to deepen the contradictions that have recently emerged within the Palestinian resistance movement.

> In this connection, the US press is devoting a great deal of attention to Jordan's re-establishment of diplomatic relations with Egypt (all Arab countries severed diplomatic relations with Egypt by decision of the Baghdad conference of those countries' heads of state and government, in response to Cairo's Camp David capitulation). Amman's step was viewed in the Arab countries as a flagrant violation of Arab unity.

> Egyptian President Mubarak's trip to Jordan did even more to put the Arab states on their guard. The American press considers it a possible stone in the foundation of a US-inspired organization of "moderate" Arab countries. At the same time, this appraisal of the Egyptian President's visit is being used on the other side of the Atlantic in an effort to resurrect the "Reagan Plan." That plan made its appearance in September 1982 and set itself the goal of eliminating the Palestinian problem by assigning the task of "solving" it to Jordan, the country that until 1967 included the Palestinian West Bank of the Jordan River. Thus in its aggressive plans, the US is trying to make the most of Amman's violation of the Arab decision on Egypt, while disregarding (for the time being) Jordanian representatives' statements specifically opposing US policy in the Middle East, including its policy on the Palestinian problem ...

> It would be appropriate to recall the decision of the summit meeting of Arab countries that was held in the Moroccan city of Fez in September 1982. It demands, as an essential condition for the elimination of the Middle East crisis, the withdrawal of Israeli troops from Arab territories that Israel seized in 1967 and after, as well as the implementation of the legal rights of the Arab people of Palestine to create a sovereign state on Palestinian soil.

> Soviet proposals on ways to resolve the Middle East crisis in a just manner are in keeping with these decisions ...[272]

Interestingly enough, however, despite resuming diplomatic relations with Egypt, Hussein appeared to go out of his way to demonstrate that he was not succumbing to the blandishments of the US or Israel. Thus, in a speech at the opening of the Jordanian Parliament on October 1 he rejected Peres's call to join in peace negotiations, as "an exercise in subterfuge and deception" and repeated his approval of the Soviet Union's call for an international conference on the Middle East.[273] One month later, in an interview with the London-based Saudi newspaper *al Sharq al Awsat*, Hussein announced that he would go to Moscow for weapons.[274]

Nonetheless, despite these statements, the resumption of diplomatic relations with Egypt was not to be the only action taken by King Hussein which was to discomfit the Soviet Union, not to mention Moscow's chief ally, Syria, which bitterly attacked Hussein for reestablishing ties with Egypt. In November, King Hussein agreed to the convening of the Palestine National Council in Jordan. Arafat was eager to convene this meeting in a friendly capital (he had been turned down by Algeria and South Yemen), and managed to achieve a quorum in Amman despite the boycott of the session by the Syrian-backed Palestinian National Alliance, and the Marxist Democratic alliance which included the pro-Soviet Palestinian communist party. Moscow's displeasure with the meeting was exemplified not only by the failure of the Palestine communist party to attend, but also by the failure of the Soviet Ambassador to Jordan to attend the session and by the pro-Soviet Israeli communist party's opposition to it.[275] In addition, both PFLP leader George Habash and DFLP leader Naef Hawatmeh announced their opposition to the PNC meeting after hurried visits to Moscow,[276] and both an article in *Pravda* marking Palestinian Solidarity Day on November 29 and a Tass report on the Palestine National Council meeting the following day contained muted criticisms of the meeting, with the Tass report noting:

> as is known, a number of the Palestinian organizations did not attend the Amman session of the National Council of Palestine. They published statements pointing out that the time for the convention of the session was not suitable due to the lack of unity among the Palestinians and did not meet the interests of the Arab people of Palestine.[277]

While the PNC meeting, which was orchestrated by Arafat to demonstrate his control over the PLO while also offering a renewed tie to both the Democratic and National Alliances, did not, for precisely that reason, make any dramatic moves toward peace (indeed, Arafat emphasized the need for armed struggle),[278] the very fact that the meet-

ing took place when and where it did held out the possibility of a final
split in the PLO between Arafat's backers and those of Syria.[279] Indeed,
Assad's speech at the Syrian Ba'ath Congress in January 1985 in which
he implied that Syria would take command of the Palestine Movement,[280] and the assassination of PLO Executive Committee member
Fahd al Qawasmi, which Arafat blamed on Assad,[281] seemed to hasten
such a split, which seemed to foreshadow an alignment of Egypt,
Jordan, Arafat's wing of the PLO, and Iraq (which had just resumed
diplomatic relations with the United States) as well. Under these
circumstances, Moscow had to be concerned that Arafat might yet move
again toward the Reagan plan, much as he appeared to be doing in the
fall of 1982 prior to the Syrian-engineered plot in the PLO against him.
Such a development would breathe new life into the US initiative given
both Egypt's preference for the US to play a major role in the peace
process, and the avowed position of Israeli Prime Minister Shimon
Peres, long a supporter of the "Jordanian option," who had begun to
consolidate his position in Israel and had started to withdraw Israeli
troops from Lebanon. Given the fact that King Hussein, while publicly
unhappy with recent US policy in the Middle East, had always kept his
options open, the formation of an Egyptian-Jordanian-Arafat wing of
the PLO bloc in the Arab world appeared to provide both Hussein and
Arafat with sufficient strength to move ahead with the peace process.
Indeed, in mid-February 1985 Hussein and Arafat reached an agreement on a joint negotiating strategy for the Middle East peace process.
Moscow's reaction to the agreement, and its rapid endorsement by
Mubarak, was a very negative one. While not immediately attacking
Jordan or Egypt directly – Moscow still had hopes of ultimately weaning
both away from the United States (a Soviet–Jordanian arms agreement
had just been signed)[282] – the Soviet displeasure was clear. *Pravda*, on
February 20, noted that while the accord had received favorable comment from "official circles" in Egypt, Morocco, and Saudi Arabia, it
had been "resolutely condemned" in Syria, Democratic Yemen, and
"certain other Arab countries" as well as by leaders of "most Palestinian organizations." In an indirect critique of Hussein and Arafat, the
Pravda article went on to cite the opponents of the agreement, noting:
"The agreement will result in a further exacerbation of differences
within the Palestinian Resistance Movement, will subvert the authority
and role of the PLO as the sole legitimate representative of the
Palestinian people, and will weaken the PLO's ties to the forces fighting
for liberation and progress." The *Pravda* article concluded by noting

what it considered the very positive reactions of the US and Israel to the agreement: "Judging from reactions to the Amman agreement in the US and in Israel – two countries that, as is known, are attempting to impose unequal and separate deals on the Arabs – people there are expecting Jordan and the PLO to abandon the policy of resistance to US–Israeli plans in the Middle East."[283]

One week later, the Soviet response became sharper as Tass quoted the joint statement of a meeting of Arab communist parties in Damascus: "The Amman agreement threatens the cause of the Palestinians and the Palestinian revolution, deepens the split among the ranks of the Palestine Liberation Organization, leads to a deepening of the differences between the Arab states and opens the way to strengthening American–Israeli influence in the region."[284] Soviet propaganda continued to sharpen in tone in subsequent weeks. *Pravda* on March 8 complained that the Amman agreement failed to deal with two critical issues: the creation of an independent Palestine state and the PLO's participation in the settlement process as the sole legitimate representative of the Palestinian people. The *Pravda* article also asserted that the agreement contradicted the decision of the Arab summit at Fez, Morocco in 1982.

With the announcement of Assistant Secretary of State Richard Murphy's trip to the Middle East to help arrange for a joint Palestinian–Jordanian negotiating team acceptable to Israel, Moscow began to directly criticize Egyptian President Mubarak's efforts to expedite the peace process. Writing in the Soviet foreign policy weekly *New Times*, O. Famin noted:

> President Mubarak's initiative has been rightly interpreted by the Arab progressive forces as a call for direct separate talks between Israel and a Jordanian–Palestinian delegation under the American–Egyptian aegis, and as an attempt both to get the Camp David process going again and to draw other countries into it thereby proving that Sadat's policy was, in fact, correct. If this initiative proves successful, they note a second phase of the Camp David process would be complete. The Palestinians would be granted administrative autonomy – a substitute for their legitimate national rights.

> In short, those Arab circles who reject the Amman agreement and the Mubarak initiative and who call for an uncompromising struggle for a just solution of the Palestinian problem – the key aspect of a Middle East settlement – are proved to be correct. The facts show once again that the Arabs can win their just cause not by relying on the United

States or Western Europe, but by forming a united front of their countries against the American–Israeli "strategic cooperation," against imperialism and Zionism.[285]

This, then, was the rather negative Middle East situation which greeted the new Soviet leader, Mikhail Gorbachev, as he took power in March and it is to an analysis of the energetic new Soviet leader's response to the problematic Soviet position in the Middle East that we now turn.

4 Moscow and the Middle East under Gorbachev: "new thinking" in theory and practice

Mikhail Gorbachev, who took power in the Soviet Union in March 1985, was the most energetic Soviet leader since Khrushchev and the most willing to undertake domestic reforms since Lenin instituted the New Economic Program of the 1920s. As the new Soviet leader consolidated his hold on power in 1985 and 1986, he came to see that the economic problems facing the Soviet Union were so great that a respite was needed in the arms race with the United States so that resources could be diverted from Soviet military to civilian needs. To accomplish this task he had to convince the NATO powers, and especially the United States, that the "Soviet threat" had diminished. This would not only improve the chances for new arms control agreements, but also give encouragement to the advocates of reduced military spending in NATO nations and undermine the support for such projects as the US Strategic Defense Initiative. Gorbachev set about trying to win over the NATO states in four ways. First, there was the rhetoric about "new thinking" in Soviet foreign policy (see below p. 206). Second, Moscow made a number of concessions in Third World conflict areas such as Angola, Cambodia, and, above all, Afghanistan. Third, Gorbachev backed off from the previous Soviet hardline position opposing arms control negotiations so long as the US continued its deployment of cruise missiles and Pershing II missiles in Europe. Instead, Gorbachev actively promoted an Intermediate Range Missile agreement that was to be signed in 1987. Fourth, he instituted what became known as *glasnost* in the Soviet Union where, for the first time in the history of the USSR, the Soviet media was allowed to report the situation as it actually was, rather than either covering up problems such as train wrecks and airplane crashes, or reporting events through the prism of Marxist–Leninist ideology. Gorbachev evidently decided that for there to be real reform in the USSR – he used the word *perestroika* – people first had to realize just how bad the situation actually was. The policy of *glasnost* was also aimed at mobilizing the Soviet intelligentsia behind Gorbachev, and his decision to bring Andrei Sakharov back to Moscow from internal exile in Gorky in December 1986 may be seen as a major step in signalling the intelligentsia that he was giving more than lipservice to *glasnost*. Needless to say, the return of Sakharov, who was the Soviet Union's most famous dissident, also had major public relations value in the West, and contributed to improving the Soviet image in NATO states, as did the rehabilitation of Nobel Prize winner Boris Pasternak.

It should be emphasized, however, that the "new thinking" in Soviet foreign policy did not begin in 1985 with the advent of Gorbachev – indeed some of the hardline policies undertaken in his first year in power such as intensifying the Soviet war effort in Afghanistan and sending SAM-5 missiles to Libya led a number of Western observers to comment that his policy was "Brezhnevism without Brezhnev."[1] By the beginning of 1987, however, with Gorbachev having consolidated his position, the "new thinking" in Soviet foreign policy was officially in place. Essentially, the "new thinking" had five major principles.[2]

1 The danger of nuclear war impels the superpowers to realize that human survival should take precedence over the interests of states, classes, and ideologies.
2 There is a need to abandon such concepts as "spheres of influence," "vital interests," "positions of strength," and the "zero-sum game" approach to the Third World.
3 A new concept should lie at the heart of international relations, the "balance of interests" which would take into account the legitimate interests of the USSR, the US, and regional states.
4 Primary reliance should be placed on political means for the resolution of regional conflicts.
5 There is an organic connection between regional conflicts and confrontation between the superpowers and, hence, there is a need for joint action by the superpowers to settle the most serious regional conflicts because there will be no possible detente in US–Soviet relations if there is no settlement of the most serious regional conflicts especially in the Middle East.

In looking at the "new thinking," it is clear that there is indeed much that is new. First, the linkage between superpower relations and Third World conflicts is a marked departure from the Brezhnev period when the Soviet leadership felt it could act freely in the Third World in places like Angola and Ethiopia, without having a major effect on detente.[3] Second, there is a downgrading of Marxist–Leninist ideology in Gorbachev's approach to world affairs. Since it did not seem possible to separate ideology's internal role in the Soviet Union as the legitimizer of the rule of the CPSU, from its role in shaping the Soviet view of world affairs, Gorbachev's domestic critics within the party, already angry at his other reform efforts which threatened their power, took issue with the policy change on ideology as did the leaders of self-proclaimed Marxist–Leninist states in the Third World such as Fidel Castro of Cuba who feared a loss of Soviet support under Gorbachev.

Yet for all of the newness of the "new thinking," it is important to separate the rhetoric from the reality. Consequently one of the themes of this chapter will be to show where the "new thinking" has – and has not – been reflected in Soviet policy actions.

When Gorbachev took power, the two central problems facing Soviet policy in the Middle East were the Hussein–Arafat agreement which, as mentioned above, seemed to be closely connected to the Reagan plan and which reinforced Egypt's reintegration into the Arab world, and the escalating war in the Gulf that helped the United States reinforce its position among the Gulf Arabs despite the débâcle it had suffered in Lebanon. Fortunately for Gorbachev, however, an event occurred in early April which weakened both the American and the Egyptian Middle Eastern positions – the overthrow of the regime of Ja'afar Nimeri in the Sudan. Nimeri had long had close ties with both Egypt and the United States,[4] and the regime which replaced him quickly moved to distance itself from both countries despite its initial statements that it favored continued close relations with them.[5] Thus one week after the coup, the new Sudanese leader, General Abdelrahman Sawar-Dhahab noted that he had moved to improve relations with the USSR and its two major African allies, Ethiopia and Libya,[6] and a week later, Libya and the Sudan restored diplomatic relations. While this seemed aimed at ending Libyan support for Sudanese rebel leader Joseph Garang, the US became more concerned when the renewal of diplomatic relations was followed by a visit to Khartoum by Libyan leader Muammar Kaddafi[7] in May and then by a military logistic agreement between Libya and the Sudan in July.[8] Sudan further discomfited the United States by refusing to participate during the summer in joint military maneuvers – it had done so under Nimeri.[9] As a further demonstration of the Sudan's new neutrality in East–West affairs (despite a heavy dependence on US food aid), General Sawar-Dhahab announced his intention to send high-level delegations to both the United States and the Soviet Union.[10] Further complicating US–Sudanese relations was a Sudanese probe into CIA assistance in the airlift of Ethiopian Jews from refugee camps in the Sudan to Israel during the Nimeri regime,[11] and US charges that the Sudan had allowed "known Libyan terrorists" to enter the Sudan.[12]

While Moscow clearly was pleased at the deterioration in US–Sudanese relations, it also profited diplomatically from the more limited weakening of Sudanese–Egyptian ties. As might be expected, Mubarak was not pleased with the new warmth in Sudanese–Libyan relations, or the Sudanese demands for the extradition of Nimeri who was living in exile in Egypt.[13] Sudan's much harsher position on peace with Israel was also a problem for Mubarak, as the Sudan demonstrated that it had moved to the Centrist wing of Arab politics by criticizing Camp David, banning Coca-Cola (it was on the Arab boycott list because it was sold in Israel)[14] and by staging a major trial of officials involved in the airlift of Ethiopian Jews to Israel.

As the Sudan changed its foreign policy stance to one more accept-able to Moscow, the tone of Soviet reporting about the Sudan became increasingly favorable.[15] Indeed, a November article in *New Times* by A. Agaryshev aptly titled "From Despair to Hope" praised the developments in the Sudan, putting particular emphasis on the new regime's denunciation of the Camp David accords, with Prime Minister Dafalla quoted as saying: "We are against the Camp David agreements signed between Egypt and Israel, and against all other separate agree-ments that lead to Arab retreat and disunity." The article concluded with a call for the unity of all the anti-Nimeri forces in the Sudan to prevent another Nimeri-style dictator from coming to power.[16]

All in all, Moscow could only be pleased by the events in the Sudan. While it would have been premature for Moscow to hope the Sudan would shift back to its pre-1971 pro-Soviet stance, the Sudan had moved far enough from both the United States and Egypt for Moscow to consider the overthrow of Nimeri a clear gain in what it continued to see as a "zero-sum game" competition for influence with the United States in the Arab world.

While the new Soviet leadership could only have been pleased with developments in the Sudan, events in Lebanon posed continuing prob-lems for Moscow. To be sure, the withdrawal of Israeli forces from that country, announced in January 1985 and completed in early June (except for a 5–8 mile "security zone" north of the Israeli border), was viewed favorably by Moscow which saw it as a victory for "Lebanese patriotic forces," as well as for its major Arab ally, Syria.[17] In addition, the withdrawal of Israeli troops seemed to lessen the possibility of a serious clash between Israel and Syria – especially since Syria was careful not to move troops south as Israel was withdrawing – thereby, in turn, decreasing the possibility of Syria calling on Moscow to aid it in a war against Israel that could erupt into a superpower confrontation. Yet the Israeli withdrawal, far from bringing calm to Lebanon, seemed to exacerbate the internecine conflict there which Syria either could not, or would not, suppress. In March came an intra-Christian conflict as Samir Geagea openly opposed Amin Gemayel (Moscow blamed the rebellion on Israel);[18] but, as far as the USSR was concerned, a much more serious conflict erupted in late May as the Shiite militia, Amal, acting almost certainly with Syrian support, attacked the Palestinian refugee camps in Beirut into which Arafat's forces were reinfiltrating. The fighting got so bad that Arafat was later to refer to it as "the second massacres of Sabra and Shatilla."[19] For Moscow, the incident must have seemed to be the rerun of a bad dream as the dilemma of two of its allies fighting each other reappeared. In 1976, during the civil war in Lebanon, and again in 1983, Moscow had been confronted with fighting between Syria and the Arafat-led PLO, and both times the Soviet leadership (under Brezhnev in 1976 and under Andropov in 1983) faced a difficult problem of choice. In both cases, as Syria suffered increased Arab isolation because of its actions, Moscow essentially chose to be neutral while calling for an immediate end of the fighting which "only benefited the imperialists." In addition, both in 1976 and 1983 the Soviet Afro-Asian Solidarity Committee issued statements calling for an end to the fighting.[20] The new Soviet leader, Mikhail Gorbachev, was to react in an identical way.

In 1985, as in previous times, Syria was badly isolated in the Arab world because of its actions, even though in this case it did not attack the PLO with its own troops. Both Libya and Iran were critical of their ally's support of Amal, while even the anti-Arafat Abu Musa Palestinians supported by Syria switched sides and aided their fellow Palestinians against the Amal.[21] While Moscow was increasingly critical of Arafat because of his agreement with King Hussein, the PLO leader still had considerable support among Palestinians, and, in the Arab world, among the Centrist and Egyptian-camp states. For this reason, as well as because the Amman agreement at this stage was far from becoming the American-brokered peace settlement which Moscow feared, the

USSR again took a neutral position in the fighting while publicly calling for its immediate end, as once again the Afro-Asian Peoples Solidarity Organization issued a plea to end the fighting. An editorial in *New Times* titled "Senseless Bloodshed" summed up the Soviet position:

> The present flare-up of violence, irrespective of who sparked it off, is causing enormous damage to Lebanon's national interests. In connection with the tragic events in Beirut, the Communist and Workers' parties of the Arab East have issued a statement calling for an immediate end to the fighting. The statement points to the existence of a conspiracy aimed at preventing the settlement of the Palestine problem and stresses that the continuation of the bloodshed is diverting attention away from the crimes committed by the Israeli invaders in Southern Lebanon and from the struggle for the country's independence and unity.

> The Soviet Afro-Asian Solidarity Committee has emphasized that the latest developments primarily play into the hands of the enemies of Lebanon's sovereignty, independence, and territorial integrity, who have long sought to shift the blame for the unsettled situation in the country on the Arabs. Soviet public opinion urges the conflicting sides to put an end to the senseless fratricide without delay.[22]

Fortunately for Moscow and Syria, however, the fighting between Amal and the Palestinians was temporarily stopped by a ceasefire.[23] It was replaced in the headlines by the hijacking of an American TWA plane to Beirut by Shiites who claimed they did it to get Israel to return their comrades who, as prisoners, were taken back over the border when Israel was completing its withdrawal from Lebanon. The hijacking provided both an opportunity and a dilemma for Moscow. On the one hand the crisis held the potential of another Lebanese humiliation for the United States, one that would again weaken the America Middle East position. On the other hand, however, Moscow could not rule out the possibility of a US military action to free the hostages, one that would pit the United States against the Syrian-backed Amal militia which had taken control over both the plane and the majority of the hostages after the plane had landed in Beirut. This would mean a repetition of the Soviet dilemma of December 1983 when it faced the problem of aiding Syria in its confrontation with the US in Lebanon or doing nothing, and when it chose the latter option in 1983, it lost credibility in the Arab world.[24] As the hijacking dramas unfolded, Soviet propaganda blamed Israel as the main cause of the problem, and warned of a possible US military attack on Lebanon.[25] Gorbachev also took the opportunity to invite Syrian President Hafiz Assad to Moscow for the first official visit between the two leaders. Tass described the talks as having taken place in a "friendly atmosphere" – a Soviet term that indicates that the two sides took different positions on a number of issues.[26] What these areas of disagreement were can be seen from the Tass statements that "a thorough exchange of opinions was held on issues concerning the situation in the Middle East, Soviet–Syrian relations, and the international situation," and "during an exchange of opinions on questions pertaining to the situation in the Palestine Resistance Movement, the Soviet side especially accentuated the importance of preserving the unity of the Palestine Liberation Organization and overcoming the disagreements between Palestinians as soon as possible on a principled anti-imperialist platform." Interestingly enough, the Syrian version of the talks portrayed a much warmer meeting, stating that the talks had taken place in an atmosphere of warm cordiality and mutual trust, making no mention of an "exchange of opinions," and indicating that "regarding the situation in the Middle East and Lebanon, the Syrian and Soviet views were identical."[27] It seems clear that the Syrian propaganda move was aimed at demonstrating Soviet support for Syrian positions in the Middle East – above all on the Palestinian question. Nonetheless, Moscow was not above using the positive Syrian portrayal of its ties to Moscow as a tool to enhance its own Middle Eastern position, by showing the importance Syria placed on the role of the USSR in the Middle East and the world.[28]

As far as the hijacking situation was concerned, it is not yet known whether or not Gorbachev used his influence with Assad to arrange the hostage release although there were rumors that this in fact took place.[29] In any case, Syria's intervention was a key factor in the hostage release and Moscow could only have been pleased with the outcome. Not only had a military confrontation between Syria and the US been avoided, but Moscow's ally Syria had emerged from the crisis with increased prestige. This was a clear reversal of the situation of only two weeks earlier when Syria had been severely criticized in the Arab world and abroad for aiding Amal attacks against Palestine refugee camps.

Nonetheless, despite the sudden improvement in its ally's position, Moscow still faced the dilemma that the Amman agreement was on course despite the hijacking and that American diplomats continued to work to arrange a Palestinian–Jordanian negotiating team acceptable to Israel. Indeed, in late June, perhaps as an early sign of *glasnost*, unusually frank analyses began to appear in the Soviet press of the problems facing Moscow in the region.[30] An article appearing in *Sovietskaia Rossiia* by Genady Kusayelian seemed to mirror Soviet concerns:

> The decision by the United States and Israel to escalate their aggress-
> ive actions at the present moment is no accident: they are trying to take
> maximum advantage of the lack of unity among the Arab states and
> within the ranks of the Palestinians and the PLO – their sole legitimate
> representative. And it is no coincidence that the US press has called
> the agreement signed in Amman between King Husayn and Y. Arafat
> and the "Mubarak initiative," put forward by the Egyptian president,
> "encouraging events" in the region. We should also mention the
> acutely negative factor represented by the Iran–Iraq conflict. It has
> frightened the rulers of a number of Arab states, particularly in the
> Persian Gulf, and diverted their attention and resources from the
> Israeli front.
>
> Thus, the strengthening of unity is the key to the Arab peoples' success
> in the struggle against imperialist and Zionist aggression. Of course, it
> is virtually impossible to achieve unanimity on all problems, given the
> effect of certain factors and the differences in state ideology and social
> system, and, ultimately, in the level of activeness of progressive forces
> in the countries in question. But there ought to be another and broader
> factor here: loyalty to pan-Arab interests, rejection of narrow short-
> term solutions, defense of political and economic structures against
> imperialist and Zionist dominance, preservation of national pride and
> dignity, formulation of a joint pan-Arab stance on the most important
> global problems, and steadfast adherence to it.[31]

Given these problems, Gorbachev evidently decided that if Moscow were not to once again be on the sidelines when a major Middle East peace effort was underway, he had to make some gestures to Israel to be included in the negotiations. To be sure the USSR and the US had met in February for high-level talks to discuss the Middle East (the first such superpower meeting on the Middle East in seven years), but President Reagan gave no indication of wanting to include the USSR in the peace process.[32] Indeed, the most a US official would concede was that the talks were "merely an exchange of thoughts in the hope of reducing misunderstandings. Even to call them explorations would be an exaggeration."[33] Not unexpectedly, therefore, no agreement was achieved in the talks, and the US representative, Assistant Secretary of State Richard Murphy, noted that the USSR lacked credibility as a mediator because of its refusal to resume diplomatic relations with Israel and because its treatment of Soviet Jews had alienated the Israelis. He also stated that while the USSR was pressing for an international conference involving Security Council members and interested parties in the Middle East including the PLO, the US felt that such large meetings would be counterproductive and called instead for direct talks between Israel and its neighbors.[34]

Following a late May visit to Washington by King Hussein who, perhaps both as a sop to Moscow, and as a means of diplomatically protecting his flank, continued to call for an international conference with Moscow's participation, State Department spokesman Edward Djerejian listed a number of specific actions which Moscow could take to show that it was ready to play a "constructive role" in the Middle East peace process. These included resuming full diplomatic relations with Israel, ending Soviet anti-Semitic propaganda, improving the treatment of Soviet Jews, and ending arms aid to militias in Lebanon.[35] Interestingly enough, however, while Soviet Middle East specialist Yevgeny Primakov, at the time Director of the Soviet Institute of Oriental Studies, in an interview in Moscow predicted that the USSR would not accept "one side setting preconditions for the other to meet," and stated that it was premature to ask the USSR to recognize Israel as a condition for holding an international conference on the Middle East,[36] Gorbachev was to move in just such a direction.

While signals about the possibility of the resumption of diplomatic relations had been sent from Moscow to Israel almost from the time relations were broken off during the 1967 war,[37] the signals increased in intensity soon after Gorbachev took power. Soviet gestures to Israel were to come despite a series of Israeli actions that bound the Jewish state even more tightly to the United States, including its signing of strategic cooperation and free trade agreements with the US, and its agreement to allow the United States to build a Voice of America transmitter on Israeli territory and to enter into the American Star Wars defense scheme. Indeed, it would appear that the Soviet gestures to Israel were aimed not only at gaining entry to the Middle East peace process, but also at winning favor in the United States with which a summit was on the horizon. Given Moscow's tendency to overestimate the influence of American Jews on American policy-making *vis-à-vis* the USSR, gestures to Israel, which virtually all American Jews hold dear, could thus also be seen as part of Moscow's pre-summit maneuvering.[38]

The first major Soviet gesture came in mid-May, two months after Gorbachev took power. The gesture came in the form of *Izvestia*'s publication of Israeli President Chaim Herzog's congratulatory message to the USSR on the fortieth anniversary of the allied victory over Nazi Germany. What was significant about the *Izvestia* publication was not only that it was the first time such a message from an Israeli leader had been published since relations were broken in 1967, but also that the message itself contained a denunciation of the Nazis, as Herzog declared that the Jewish people "will never forget the huge contribution of the Red Army in the final destruction of the Nazi monsters in Europe and her assistance in the freeing of Jews who survived the concentration camps."[39] Given the fact that the Soviet propaganda media had long equated Israeli and Nazi activities, and had even accused Zionists of actively aiding the Nazis,[40] the publication of this message seemed to be a major reversal of Soviet policy on this issue.[41]

A far more important Soviet signal was to come in mid-July. With Arafat and Hussein calling for an Arab summit and with a review session commemorating the tenth anniversary of the signing of the Helsinki agreements due to open at the beginning of August – a session that was likely to see the issue of Soviet Jewry raised – Gorbachev apparently decided that a major discussion between Soviet and Israeli diplomats on the subject of both renewing diplomatic relations and increasing the flow of Soviet Jewish emigration to Israel was in order. The meeting took place in Paris at the home of Israeli-born pianist Daniel Barenboim between the Israeli Ambassador to France, Ovadia Sofer, and his Soviet counterpart, Yuli Vorontsov. Sofer's description of the meeting was leaked to Israeli radio, which promptly broadcast it. Given the importance of the Israeli radio broadcast – even though Moscow publicly denied any deal was made[42] – it is reprinted here in full:

> There has been a signal – and not just a minor one – from the Soviet Union. This time it is a real flashing light. The Israeli Ambassador to Paris recently met with the Soviet Ambassador to France. The Soviets, under a fresh, new administration, are hinting about a package deal for the emigration of Jews. They are ready for a compromise over the Golan Heights. There is a hint about the renewal of diplomatic relations, and a genuine chance for high-level meetings. Our political correspondent Shim'on Schiffer has the details of this disclosure:
>
> [Schiffer] I should say at once that reference is to a Soviet initiative – not a coincidental meeting at a cocktail party, but a lengthy meeting that lasted for more than two hours and took place on Monday of this week. It was full of political content and genuine signals. Ambassador Sofer went to the meeting, which was held in Daniel Barenboim's

residence, provided with directives he had received from Israel. The Soviet Ambassador, Yuli Vorontsov, admitted that he is the candidate to replace his country's Ambassador to Washington. He is leaving for Moscow next week and will be prepared to convey to the Kremlin leaders the details of the Israeli position.

When will relations between the two countries be renewed, Sofer asked? The Soviet Ambassador said the relations had been severed following the Israeli conquest of the territories, and so Israel would have to do something about this. I quote: There must be some sort of movement on the matter of the Golan Heights; negotiations with Syria would supply the Soviet Union with a pretext for the renewal of relations. We will not oppose a section of the Golan Heights remaining in Israeli possession, if this is achieved through negotiations with Syria. Ambassador Sofer asked if it was a coincidence that the Soviet speaker was not mentioning Judea and Samaria. No, it is no coincidence, the Soviet Ambassador said. In any event, he added, the severance of relations with Israel was a grave error and a sensitive, ill considered move that harmed the Soviet Union.

It seems that the clearest and most amazing things were said on the issue of Soviet Jewry. The problem of Jewish emigration from the Soviet Union can be solved within the framework of a package deal, in return for an end to the anti-Soviet propaganda Israel is conducting in the United States and Europe, the Soviet speaker said. We would be prepared for the Jews to leave if we are promised that they will emigrate to Israel, not the United States. The Soviet Union fears a brain drain to the West. The Soviet Ambassador admitted that mistakes had been made by the authorities in their attitude toward refuseniks. Those errors, he said, originated in the behavior of Soviet Jewry and the pressures applied to the Soviet Union. As for the continuation of the political process, the Soviet Ambassador again raised the proposal regarding the convening of an international conference with the participation of the Soviet Union. My country, he said, cannot agree to negotiations under the sole aegis of the Americans. On the Palestinian issue, the Soviet Ambassador said it was hard to see how it would be possible to find a solution to the Palestinian problem while also satisfying Israel's security demands. Vorontsov repeated his emphasis on the Soviet Union's commitment to Israel's existence, while expressing concern at the continued freeze in the peace process. Ovadia Sofer asked the Soviet Ambassador to organize an urgent meeting between Vice Prime Minister Yitzhak Shamir and his new Soviet counterpart, as early as the UN General Assembly session in New York in September.

The report on the meeting was received with satisfaction and amaze-
ment in Jerusalem, while, at the same time, it confirmed earlier evalua-
tions that Mikhail Gorbachev's rise to power in the Soviet Union
presages a change in the relations between Israel and the Soviet Union.
However, and this is yet another evaluation, the policymakers here will
– after having studied the material – have to deliberate and make far-
reaching decisions on these issues.[43]

In evaluating the Israeli Ambassador's description of the meeting, it
is of course necessary to treat it with some skepticism, given the normal
tendency of ambassadors to portray themselves and their countries in
the best light in such dispatches. Nonetheless, the fact that Dobrynin
was soon to leave Washington (although he was not replaced by Vorontsov) and that Vorontsov repeated a number of Soviet Middle East
positions, including the call for an international conference with
Moscow's participation, does lend some credence to the report. In any
case, the most interesting aspect of Vorontsov's discussion is that he
seemed to indicate that diplomatic relations could be restored if there
was at least a partial Israeli withdrawal on the Golan Heights, and that
large-scale emigration of Soviet Jews could take place if they emigrated
to Israel and not the United States, and if Israel ended the anti-Soviet
propaganda it was undertaking in the United States and Europe. Here
again, Moscow apparently saw an improvement of relations with Israel
as a key to improving relations with the West.

Yet the Soviet hint of renewed relations, while welcome in Israel, was
received in a highly negative way by Moscow's Arab allies, especially
Syria. Syria, the USSR's main bastion in the Arab world, was incensed
that the USSR would consider renewing ties with Israel while even part
of the Golan Heights seized during the 1967 war remained in Israeli
hands. As a result, the USSR in both official visits and radio broadcasts
to the Arab world repeated the old Soviet position that diplomatic
relations would not be restored until Israel gave up all the land con-
quered in 1967.[44] At the same time, however, Moscow continued to hint
to Israel that relations could be restored if Israel agreed to Moscow's
inclusion in a Middle East peace conference.[45] For his part, Israeli
Prime Minister Shimon Peres expressed a keen interest in improving ties
with the USSR,[46] much as his predecessor Yitzhak Shamir had done.

Moscow's primary concern at the time of the Sofer–Vorontsov meeting was that the Arafat–Hussein agreement might receive acceptance
from the Centrist Arab states, and this concern was heightened in late
July when an Arab summit was scheduled for Casablanca in early

August. While Syria and its Steadfastness Front allies (the PDRY, Algeria, and Libya) and its protectorate, Lebanon, boycotted the session, the fact remained that both Hussein and Arafat were actively seeking support for their agreement at the conference, while Egypt was also hoping that the summit would restore it to full membership in the Arab League.[47] Meanwhile, the United States continued to play an active role in the Arab world, as on the one hand it continued its efforts to form a Jordanian–Palestinian negotiating team acceptable to Israel, and on the other hand it sought to reinforce its ties to Egypt, Jordan, Oman, and Somalia by carrying out joint military exercises with them.

The summit, however, did not meet the needs of Hussein and Arafat or the United States. While it did not denounce the Amman accord, neither did it endorse it. The absence of both King Fahd and Saddam Hussein (lower-ranking Saudi and Iraqi figures took their places) were factors limiting the effectiveness of the meeting. The most the summit would do in its final communiqué was to "take note" of the Amman agreement by stating that the summit "viewed with understanding the explanations it has been given by King Hussein and Yasser Arafat who consider that the Jordanian–Palestinian initiative is in conformity with the resolution of the 1982 Arab Summit of Fez."[48] Moscow may have been pleased also that the summit established a committee to seek reconciliations between Iraq and Syria and between Syria and Jordan,[49] thus indicating not only that the Centrist Arabs attending the summit did not want to alienate Syria by endorsing the Amman accord, but also that the Arabs were again trying to restore a semblance of unity which Moscow hoped would be the "anti-imperialist" unity it had long sought. Finally, the fact that Egypt was not readmitted to the Arab League by the summit was also pleasing to Moscow.[50]

Nonetheless, the Soviet media continued to express concern that US efforts to obtain an accord between Israel and a Jordanian–Palestinian negotiating team might succeed.[51] It was perhaps for this reason that Moscow made yet another gesture to Israel, this time in the form of an agreement between its close Eastern European ally, Poland, and Israel, whereby the two countries agreed in principle to establish "interest sections" in foreign embassies in each other's capitals – the first stage in the process of reestablishing diplomatic relations.[52] While Moscow was not yet resuming diplomatic ties itself, this appeared to be a signal that it was prepared to do so, and Gorbachev, during his visit to Paris in early October, noted "as far as re-establishing relations [with Israel] is concerned, I think the faster the situation is normalized in the Middle East, the faster it will be possible to look at this question.''[53] The announced resumption of low-level diplomatic relations with Poland, World Jewish Congress President Edgar Bronfman's visit to Moscow carrying a message from Peres, the Peres meeting with Soviet Foreign Minister Edward Shevardnadze at the UN in October, and Gorbachev's visit to Paris reinforced the rumors circulating in Israel that Moscow was about to release 20,000 Soviet Jews and allow them to be flown directly to Israel, on French planes.[54]

The momentum toward even a partial Soviet–Israeli *rapprochement* – if that indeed was Gorbachev's goal – was slowed and then stopped, however, as the peace process fell by the wayside in the face of an escalation of Middle East terrorism. While Moscow itself was to suffer both embarrassment and physical loss as a result of the Middle East terrorism, the end result was that the peace process, centered around negotiations between Israel and a Jordanian–Palestinian delegation, was halted, a development from which Moscow was to profit diplomatically.

The root of the problem lay in the fact that Arafat, in an effort to maintain credibility with the hardliners in his organization, stressed the escalation of "armed struggle" (terrorism) soon after concluding the Amman agreement with King Hussein.[55] For his part Peres was vulnerable politically even for considering negotiations with Palestinians close to the PLO and he was frequently attacked by the opposition Likud party for being "soft on terrorism" and "soft on the PLO." As a result, when a wave of terrorist murders struck Israel during the spring and summer of 1985, Peres not only found it increasingly difficult to negotiate with any Palestinian closely linked to the PLO, he also came under increasing pressure to respond. Thus, when three Israelis were murdered in Cyprus at the end of September 1985 by terrorists who proclaimed they were fighting for the Palestinian cause, Peres authorized an attack on PLO headquarters in Tunis on October 1, 1985, perhaps signalling to Arafat that if the PLO leader wished to fight while he was negotiating, Israel could play the same game.

Moscow lost little time in exploiting the Israeli attack to try to undermine the US position in the Middle East, and once again appealed for Arab unity against Israel and the United States. The lack of Arab unity was a particular problem for Moscow at this time because Libya had become even more isolated in the Arab world at the end of September when Tunisia had broken relations with it (Iraq had broken relations with Libya in June), and turned to the United States and Algeria for support.[56] Complicating the North African situation even more for Moscow in the period before the Israeli raid was the warming of relations between the United States and Steadfastness Front member Algeria, whose President, Chadli Benjedid, had made a very successful visit to the United States in April which had resulted in the Reagan administration's decision to agree to sell arms to Algeria.[57] Indeed, the Algerian Ambassador to the United States, Mohamed Sahnoun, was quoted as saying at the time that Algeria was interested in purchasing US weapons to reduce its dependence on its main arms supplier, the USSR.[58]

Thus the raid came at a propitious time for Moscow. Even more propitious was Reagan's initial endorsement of the raid, an American position which was bitterly attacked even in Arab countries friendly to the United States. Not only did the raid chill US–Algerian relations, it harmed, albeit only temporarily, US–Tunisian relations as well, as a reported plan whereby the US would supply arms to Tunisia in exchange for use of Tunisian bombing ranges was put on hold.[59]

As the Arab reaction to the bombing intensified, Moscow did what it could to link the Israeli action to the United States. Thus in a radio broadcast in Arabic on October 2, the day after the attack, the Soviet commentator alleged not only that the US had used its radar posts in the Mediterranean to direct Israeli planes to PLO headquarters in Tunis, but also that the Israeli bombers took off from a US aircraft carrier – a classic case of Soviet disinformation. In addition, linking the Israeli action even more closely to American aid, the Arabic language broadcast asserted:

> Official terrorism has become the main weapon in the strategic American–Israeli alliance. Here too it is not easy to say who is more responsible. Is it the killer, or the one who put the weapon in the killer's hands and helped him carry out his crime? How is it possible to pull the carpet from underneath the feet of those who are planting death and blood in the Arab lands for the sake of their imperialist and hegemonistic ambitions?[60]

Even before the uproar over the Israeli attack had died down, another terrorist event from which Moscow was to profit diplomatically took place. This was the hijacking of the cruise ship Achille Lauro and the murder of a Jewish passenger, Leon Klinghoffer, by a PLO faction headed by Mohammed Abbas, a hard-line PLO leader who was linked to Arafat because of their mutual opposition to Syrian leader Hafiz

Assad.[61] The hijacking had two major diplomatic benefits for Moscow. In the first place, the action of the United States in forcing down an Egyptian plane carrying the hijackers and Abbas inflamed US relations not only with Egypt but also with Italy where the plane was forced to land, when Italian Premier Bettino Craxi allowed Abbas to leave his country. While subsequent US aid to Egypt when one of its aircraft was hijacked to Malta somewhat smoothed over the strain in US–Egyptian relations, there was no question but that serious diplomatic damage had been done, a development which Moscow evidently hoped would lead to a weakening of US–Egyptian relations. As *Izvestia* noted on October 18:

> When President Mubarak talks about the humiliation of his country by the United States' actions, he seems to be transferring his personal sense of insult to the entire people. The US, no matter how powerful it may be, is not capable of humiliating a nation. It has blatantly violated Egyptian sovereignty but has humiliated only those who were cooperating with it and trusted it.

> President Mubarak has said more than once that Egypt's actions to save the hostages were begun only after the concurrence of all interested parties had been obtained. He emphasized that the decision to turn the abductors over to the PLO leadership for trial was also taken with Reagan's concurrence.

> But, as is now obvious to everyone, the American partners were quite simply deceiving the Egyptian leadership. As a White House official admitted, all available means were set in motion for this purpose. The well-informed British newspaper, *The Observer*, writes bluntly that the operation attests to the highly effective work of US intelligence in Cairo. It in fact traced the entire route of the four Palestinians through its agents in appropriate agencies of a government friendly to the US.

> Did the US leadership foresee that the act of intercepting the airplane would put the Egyptian President in a humiliating position? Unquestionably.[62]

In addition to profiting from the strain in US–Egyptian relations, Moscow also obtained diplomatic benefit from Shimon Peres's policy change on the Middle East peace process. Apparently concluding that Arafat and the PLO had discredited themselves so badly in the United States by the Achille Lauro episode[63] as well as by Arafat's failure to go ahead with a previously arranged agreement with British Prime Minister Margaret Thatcher,[64] under which British Foreign Secretary Sir Geoffrey Howe would meet in London with a joint Palestinian–Jordanian delegation which contained PLO members if it agreed to recognize Israel, Peres sought to sidestep the PLO and make a direct deal with Jordan. Realizing that Hussein had become displeased with Arafat because of the diplomatic débâcle in London, but also that the King needed some sort of diplomatic cover for his dealings with Israel, Peres proposed at the UN, on October 21, Israeli–Jordanian talks under "international auspices."[65] Unfortunately for Peres, however, King Hussein was not to opt for the Israeli offer and moved instead to improve relations with Syria, as the King in a major speech at the opening of Jordan's parliament on November 2 noted that the Saudi-sponsored meetings between Jordanian Prime Minister Zaid Rifai and Syrian Foreign Minister Abdul Rauf Qasim over the past two months had marked a "good beginning" toward improving Syrian–Jordanian relations.[66] Indeed, relations were to rapidly improve in November and December with Hussein publicly apologizing for Muslim Brotherhood attacks on Syria which had used Jordan as a base of operations, and visiting Syria at the end of December in the first meeting between the two leaders in Damascus in six years. Nonetheless, the fact that no communiqué was issued after the meeting indicated that there were still major areas of disagreement between the two countries, with Syria unhappy because of Hussein's close relations with Egypt and Iraq and his continued, albeit somewhat weakened, ties with Arafat.[67] Nonetheless, Moscow was clearly pleased with even the limited Syrian–Jordanian *rapprochement*, as was noted by Soviet Middle East specialist Dmitry Volsky in a *New Times* article summarizing the Soviet view of Middle East trends at the close of 1985.[68]

Yet the spiral of Middle Eastern violence, while paying diplomatic dividends for the USSR, was not without its costs for Moscow. On September 30, three Soviet diplomats stationed in Beirut and the embassy doctor were kidnapped, and two days later one of them, Consular official Arkady Katkov, was killed. What made this particularly embarrassing for Moscow was that the incident occurred on the eve of the much heralded Gorbachev visit to France and the Soviet leader was clearly embarrassed by the kidnapping when he arrived in Paris.[69] The kidnappers, apparently from a shadowy group called the Islamic Liberation Organization called on the USSR to pressure Syria to stop an offensive against Tripoli, Lebanon, by its leftist Lebanese allies, which included the Lebanese communist party.[70] The Syrian-backed forces were attacking the Sunni Muslim fundamentalist group known as the

Unification Movement which had ties to Arafat's wing of the PLO and which had clashed with Alawites – the ruling Shiite Muslim sect in Syria – who lived in Tripoli. The incident could only have embarrassed the USSR as photographs were published in Beirut and Western newspapers of the Russians with guns at their heads, thus demonstrating the impotence of the USSR in the face of Middle East terrorism. The Soviets reacted bitterly to the abduction and subsequent murder, with a Tass statement blaming Israel for "inciting the strife in Lebanon," and also blaming "the immediate organizers and perpetrators of the act of atrocity against the Soviet citizens," and "those who could have stopped the criminal action and prevented violence against the Soviet people but did not do everything possible to this effect." This last group, the Tass statement warned, "should not hope that this conduct of theirs would not have a most negative effect on the Soviet Union's attitude to them."[71] Whether or not this last message was aimed at the Syrians is not clear.

Nonetheless, the Syrians ended the offensive against Tripoli and a cease-fire was put into effect in the city, although the Syrians played a role in supervising it. The surviving hostages, however, were not immediately released and Moscow ordered a partial evacuation of its embassy, with the evacuees proceeding overland to Damascus – just as did the victims of the TWA hijacking on their way to freedom in July.[72] The USSR also suspended operations at its Narodny Bank branch[73] and barricaded its embassy in the face of threats to destroy it. While the hostages were released one month after their abduction (reportedly with Syrian and Iranian help),[74] the experience was clearly a negative one for Moscow and this may have been a factor in Soviet willingness to support a UN General Assembly resolution on December 9 that condemned all acts of terrorism as "criminal,"[75] as well as a unanimous UN Security Council resolution on December 18, which, for the first time in the organization's history, condemned "unequivocally all acts of hostage-taking and abduction" and called for "the immediate release of all kidnap victims wherever and by whomever they were held."[76]

In sum, the abduction of four of their embassy staffers and the murder of one of them was clearly a bitter experience for Moscow. Nonetheless, on balance, the escalation of Middle East terrorism benefited the USSR as it led to the sidetracking of the American-brokered peace process, a cooling of ties between Arafat and Hussein, and a sharp dispute between the United States and Egypt.

As the chances for a Middle East peace settlement brokered by the

United States receded, Moscow took a much harder line with Israel as the mid-November summit between Reagan and Gorbachev in Geneva approached, despite reported calls by Egypt and Jordan for Moscow to restore diplomatic relations with Israel as a way to advance prospects for Middle East peace talks.[77] Indeed, on the eve of the summit, a Soviet government spokesman, Albert Vlasov, demanded as the price of renewed relations that Israel agree not only to allow the USSR to participate in the international peace conference, but also to allow the PLO to participate as well – clearly something that Peres was unwilling to accept.[78] Perhaps because of this condition Peres again shifted his position, and now stated that the resumption of Soviet Jewish emigration from the USSR was much more important than the restoration of diplomatic ties. "If they agreed to renew Aliya," he stated, "we shall waive our objections to their taking part in an international conference on the Middle East."[79]

Peres thus presented Moscow with an interesting choice. As far as its position in the Arab world is concerned, it is far less costly for Moscow to release Soviet Jews than it is for it to reestablish ties with Israel, and Moscow has long wanted to participate in an international conference on an Arab–Israeli settlement. On the other hand, however, it was doubtful whether the USSR would settle in 1985 for just a symbolic role in an international conference – the most Israel seemed to be ready to concede – in return for sharply increasing the number of Jews allowed to leave the Soviet Union. Nonetheless, Israel clearly did not give up on the possibility, and the attendance of Israel's President Chaim Herzog at the National Convention of Israel's communist party in early December, the first time an Israeli President had ever attended such a function, was a clear gesture to Moscow that Jerusalem was interested in continuing a dialogue with the USSR.[80]

Yet Moscow's harder line policy toward Israel may have had additional causes as well. Arab leaders, perhaps remembering the 1972 Nixon–Brezhnev summit, seemed concerned that a superpower deal might be worked out at their expense,[81] and Reagan's pre-summit demand for linkage between an arms control agreement and Soviet behavior in the Third World, may have heightened Soviet determination to prove that no such deal had taken place.[82] Indeed, in a spate of articles appearing in the Soviet media at the time of the summit, including Arabic language radio broadcasts and *Novosti* statements distributed in Beirut, the USSR dismissed as "fabrications and lies" claims that Arab interests would be compromised at Geneva.[83] An Arabic language broadcast, by a senior Soviet commentator Alexander Bovin, sought to put an end to Arab concerns about any such deal:

> Themes are put forward on the possibility of a new Yalta for the sharing of influence in the Middle and Near East during the Geneva summit meeting. These fabrications and accusations are aimed at giving rise to the idea of a possible Soviet–US collusion at the expense of the Arabs' interests. Despite the fact that the Soviet Union has firmly refuted all this, more unfounded rumors are being spread on the possibility of a Soviet–Israeli resumption of relations even if Israel does not relinquish its expansionist and aggressive line.

> Western propaganda is spreading rumors to the effect that the Soviet Union is ready to allow 500,000 Soviet Jews to emigrate to Israel upon a request from the United States. All these fabrications and accusations are aimed at making the Arabs no longer sure of Soviet support and thus compelling them to relinquish the struggle against the conspiracies of imperialism and Zionism and for the achievement of the Arabs' interests. This is the aim of Washington and Tel Aviv, who are trying to cast doubts between the Arab and the Soviet leadership and are planning schemes of separate deals with the Israeli invaders under US aegis. It should be pointed out that the weakening of the struggle of the Arab front against imperialism by way of making fabrications against the Soviet Union and thereby rupturing Soviet–Arab friendship is a well-known method of imperialism, Zionism, and Arab reactionaries.[84]

Moscow, however, was not to limit its campaign to demonstrate to the Arabs that there was no US–Soviet deal at Geneva, to mere words. Less than a month after the Geneva summit, it was revealed that the USSR had sent SAM-5 anti-aircraft missiles to Libya,[85] a clear escalation of the Soviet military commitment to that country since heretofore only Syria, of all of Moscow's Third World allies, had received such a weapon. Given the very tense relations between the United States and Libya, as well as Libya's troubled relations with virtually all of its neighbors, the decision to send SAM-5 missiles to Libya was clearly a commitment of support to the Kaddafi regime, but one that was ultimately to prove costly to Moscow.

The origin of the decision to send the SAM-5s to Libya may have been Kaddafi's visit to Moscow in early October. At the time the Libyan leader, threatened by Egypt, Algeria, and the United States, was clearly looking for increased military assistance and, most probably, a formal Treaty of Friendship and Cooperation with the Soviet Union. Indeed, in his dinner speech during the visit, Kaddafi stated "We note with satisfaction that the defense of Libya's national interests is in full accord with Soviet policy. That is why we are convinced that our multifaceted ties have by no means exhausted their potential and will continue to develop and strengthen."[86] If that indeed was Kaddafi's goal, he was not to achieve it during the visit although agreements were signed on political consultation, a consular convention, and a long-term program for the development of economic, scientific-technical and trade cooperation.[87] While Libya was a useful economic partner for Moscow (although the drop in oil prices was making it more difficult for Libya to purchase arms), Kaddafi's frequent conflicts with his Arab neighbors had often troubled the Kremlin, and it was probably not accidental that in Gorbachev's dinner speech, the Soviet leader emphasized the need for unity of action by the Arab countries.[88] Nonetheless, the joint communiqué issued after the meeting was considerably warmer in tone than previous communiqués following meetings between leaders of Libya and the Soviet Union had been, and it took the strongest stand yet demonstrating Soviet support for Libya against the United States:

> The two sides condemned the increasing military and economic pressure by the United States on the Libyan Jamahiriyah and its slanderous propaganda campaign against Libya. They opposed the increasing US military presence in the region and condemned the provocative military maneuvers, which the United States carries out in the Mediterranean, including in the Gulf of Sitre and near the eastern borders of the Mediterranean and North African regions. In this regard they stated that the use of or threat to use force in international relations is inadmissible.

> The Soviet Union expressed its support for the steps taken by the Libyan Jamahiriyah to defend its sovereignty, independence and territory.[89]

Another factor which might have prompted the USSR to send SAM-5s to Libya was the disclosure in early November that President Reagan had authorized a CIA covert operation to undermine the Libyan government.[90] While Moscow denounced the US plan, Kaddafi may well have asked the USSR to back up its rhetoric with words and the SAM-5s may have been the result. Still, Moscow was taking a major risk by escalating its aid to Kaddafi. In April Kaddafi had formed a pan-Arab command to carry out acts of violence against the United States, other Western nations, and moderate Arab regimes,[91] and a Libyan radio station calling itself "Radio of Vengeance and Sacred Hate" called on North African Arabs in Tunisia, Algeria and Morocco to kill the Jews living in their countries.[92] Under the circumstances, and particularly after Israel, which considers itself the protector of endangered Jews, had demonstrated its ability to strike at Arab targets far from its borders, Kaddafi may well have felt that an attack by the United States, Israel, or Egypt was a major possibility. By sending the missiles to Libya, however, and deepening its commitment to the Kaddafi regime, Moscow ran the risk of either a superpower confrontation or a loss of face if an attack were made against Libya without a Soviet response. Nonetheless, the USSR may have felt that the US, which in the past had rhetorically denounced both terrorism and Kaddafi but which had never taken any substantive military action (other than shooting down two Libyan planes over the Gulf of Sidra in 1981) to deal with either would confine its opposition to Kaddafi to rhetoric, such as the statement by the State Department spokesman, Charles Redman, who said, "This is a significant and dangerous escalation in the Soviet–Libyan arms relationship. We have made clear our concern about this escalation and Soviet support for an irresponsible and erratic regime."[93] If so, this was a major miscalculation, as was to be seen by the lack of any substantive Soviet response to American military attacks on Libya in 1986, which followed bloody terrorist attacks at the Rome and Vienna airports in late December 1985 which the US blamed on Libya.[94]

Yet a possible Libyan–American conflict was not the only military confrontation Moscow had to be concerned about at the close of 1985. Another missile crisis had erupted between Israel and Syria, as Assad, perhaps responding to Israel's shooting down of two Syrian planes over Syrian territory on November 19, after a confrontation over Lebanon,[95] moved SA-2 surface-to-air missile batteries close to its Lebanese border and then moved other SAM missiles into Lebanon, thereby impairing the ability of Israeli jets to fly reconnaissance missions over that country.[96] While, in its discussions of this incident, Moscow emphasized that the Syrian moves were defensive in nature,[97] the Soviet leadership nonetheless had to be concerned that the missile deployment was another factor raising the possibility of a Syrian–Israeli war. While Moscow had reportedly withdrawn its troops manning the SAM-5 missile sites in Syria as Syrians had been trained to replace them,[98] another Syrian–Israeli clash held the possibility of a rapid escalation, something Moscow appeared to wish to avoid.

While military confrontations between Israel and Syria and between the United States and Libya were still only potential problems for

Moscow in late 1985, the ongoing war between Iran and Iraq continued to plague Soviet policymakers. Not only did Moscow have no success in its efforts to end the war, but it had little to show for its attempts to improve its relations with either combatant. In addition, the war continued to split the Arab world badly and reinforce ties between the United States and the conservative sheikdoms of the Gulf.[99] Moscow did, however, obtain one benefit from the conflict. Both Oman and the United Arab Emirates established diplomatic relations with the Soviet Union as possible reinsurance against an Iranian victory that would threaten their territories, as the war escalated in 1985 with an unsuccessful Iranian offensive in the early part of the year, missile and bombing attacks against the two capitals, Iraq's attacks on the Iranian oil terminal at Kharg Island in August, and Iranian interception of neutral ships in the Gulf beginning in September.

Despite continually appealing for improved relations, Moscow took a critical stance toward Iran's Khomeini regime in 1985, not only because it continued to resist Iraqi offers to end the war but also because it was providing aid for the Afghan rebels, and was repressing the Tudeh party and other "democratic forces."[100] Indeed, although Iran and the USSR shared a common interest in keeping oil prices high and keeping the US out of the Gulf, one of the senior Soviet specialists on the Middle East, Rotislav Ulyanovsky, writing in the communist party journal *Kommunist* went so far as to call the Khomeini regime a "political despotism reminiscent of the darkest times of the Middle Ages."[101]

Moscow's relations with Iraq were not much better. While two high level Iraqi visits to the USSR took place (Foreign Minister Tariq Aziz in March and President Saddam Hussein, in his first trip since becoming President of Iraq, in December), Soviet references to an "exchange of views" during the March visit[102] and "a businesslike, frank, and friendly atmosphere" during the December visit[103] clearly indicated disagreements, despite Soviet support of Iraq's efforts to end the war. On the Iraqi side there was displeasure that the USSR had permitted Libya (or Syria) to send Soviet-supplied ground-to-ground missiles to Iran which were then used to bombard Baghdad.[104] For its part, Moscow was unhappy at the steady improvement of Iraq's ties with the United States, which was exemplified by its purchase of forty-five US helicopters which were initially developed as troop carriers for Iran.[105] While the issue of Iraq's use of poison gas remained an irritant in US–Iraqi relations,[106] commercial ties between the two countries continued to develop[107] and Moscow may well have feared that Iraq, which made repeated calls in 1985 for Egypt's reintegration into the Arab world, was moving toward the pro-American camp in the Arab world despite its continuing dependence on Soviet arms.[108]

Elsewhere in the Gulf the Soviet record was mixed. Despite continuing efforts to establish diplomatic relations with Saudi Arabia, Moscow met with no success. In addition, the Saudi decision to sharply increase oil production, which had the effect of forcing down oil prices, was a major blow to the Soviet Union which depended on oil exports for a large share of its hard currency earnings. Since the drop in oil prices came at a time when Moscow's own oil production had begun to decline, the negative impact of the Saudi action was intensified. In other areas of the Gulf, however, Moscow made gains, as both Oman in September and the United Arab Emirates in November established diplomatic relations with it. In both cases the escalation of the Iran–Iraq war appears to have been the primary motivation as both countries seem to have sought formal relations with the USSR as another possible deterrent to an Iranian attack on them. Indeed, in the words of Omani Foreign Minister Yousef bin Alawi, the escalation of the war had reached "a critical stage that was threatening the interests of states that are not party to the struggle."[109] A second possible reason for Oman's decision to establish diplomatic relations with the USSR may have been related to the sudden burst of articles in US newspapers earlier in the year that indicated that American–Omani defense ties were far greater than generally believed.[110] It is therefore possible that Oman's establishment of diplomatic ties with Moscow was a means of demonstrating to other states, especially fellow members of the Gulf Cooperation Council, that despite its close military ties with the United States, Oman had full freedom of action. As might be expected, Moscow warmly welcomed its new diplomatic ties with the two Gulf Arab states. A Soviet commentary, appearing in *New Times* after the establishment of Soviet–Omani diplomatic relations, gave Moscow's view of the significance of the event:

> The decision to establish diplomatic relations with the USSR reflects the growing desire of Persian Gulf states to pursue a more balanced foreign policy. The Soviet Union's unchanging policy of supporting the Arab people of Palestine in their just struggle and the Arab nations in their fight against Israel's aggressive expansionist policy has earned it the respect of the monarchs in the region. The constructive Soviet stance with regard to issues bearing upon the situation in the Persian Gulf has also played a definite role.

Characteristic among press comment on Oman's decision is that of the British Guardian. According to this newspaper, the news came as a telling diplomatic blow to Britain and the USA which have military agreements with the present Oman regime. In this connection it would be in place to emphasize that the agreement to establish diplomatic relations with Oman in no way attests to Soviet desires to deal "diplomatic blows" at anyone or crowd anyone out. It merely demonstrates the Soviet Union's mounting international prestige and the striving of Persian Gulf states to pursue an independent policy according with their genuine interests.[111]

In sum, Moscow's establishment of diplomatic ties with Oman and the United Arab Emirates capped a generally successful second half of 1985 for Soviet Middle East diplomacy, as the US–brokered Middle East peace process came to a standstill, and Jordan moved toward a *rapprochement* with Syria. Unfortunately for Gorbachev, however, his decision to send SAM-5 missiles to Libya in December 1985 was to cause it severe problems in 1986, as the year began with a major crisis between the United States and Libya which was blamed by the Reagan administration for a series of terrorist acts including terrorist attacks at the Rome and Vienna airports in late December 1985 that killed a total of nineteen people (sixteen in Rome and three in Vienna). Exacerbating the problem for Moscow was that Moscow's sending of the SAM-5 missiles to Libya appeared to encourage Libyan leader Muammar Kaddafi, who justified the Rome and Vienna attacks as part of the "holy struggle" of the Palestinians, and threatened to "declare war in the Middle East and in the Mediterranean zone" and "follow and harass Americans in their own streets," if there was a US or Israeli retaliation for the airport attacks.[112] The dilemma posed to Moscow by this situation was that if a confrontation took place, Moscow would have to decide whether or not to back Libya and thereby risk a confrontation with the United States. For Gorbachev, a month before the 27th Party Congress of the CPSU, this posed a very difficult choice. On the one hand, the new Soviet leader was now seeking to introduce his program of economic and political reform and was therefore beginning to pursue a foreign policy of easing world tension wherever possible. As part of this policy Moscow was seeking major arms control agreements with the United States as well as an overall improvement in the bilateral US–Soviet relationship. Needless to say, a major confrontation with the United States over Libya ran the risk of undermining Gorbachev's policy toward the US. On the other hand, however, not supporting

Libya also had risks. In 1982 when Israel invaded Lebanon, the Soviet Union, then led by Brezhnev, limited itself essentially to pro-forma protests both to Israel during the invasion and to the United States when the US deployed Marines in Beirut. Then, in 1983, when the United States and Syria came into open conflict over Lebanon, Moscow, then led by Yuri Andropov, also maintained a low profile. In both cases, Moscow lost credibility in the Arab world for not resisting the US actions. Thus, were conflict to break out between Libya and the United States, and Moscow again not to take action, the USSR ran the risk of again losing credibility among the Arabs.

As the January crisis proceeded, Gorbachev chose to keep a low profile. Following a pro-forma condemnation of US policy by the Soviet Afro-Asian People's Solidarity Organization,[113] the then Soviet Foreign Ministry spokesman, Vladimir Lomeiko, at a press conference on January 6, in responding to a question as to how the USSR would react in case a US–Libyan confrontation took place, stressed that the Soviet Union's actions were aimed at preventing conflicts, not at constructing "scenarios of its actions for their escalation."[114] Meanwhile tension had appeared to ease somewhat when Libya's Secretary for Foreign Affairs, Ali Treiki, condemned the airport attacks and denied Libyan involvement in them,[115] and President Reagan, on January 7, decided to limit the US response to the alleged Libyan involvement in the terrorist attacks to economic sanctions.[116] These measures included the freezing of all Libyan assets in the US and a ban on trade between the two countries – a move aimed at ending the participation of US oil firms in the Libyan economy.[117] Perhaps feeling that the imposition of economic sanctions meant that the US would not use military force against Libya, Moscow sharpened its tone and an *Izvestia* editorial on January 8, 1986, after citing a Libyan Foreign Ministry statement condemning terrorism, warned:

> The state of the international situation in the Mediterranean region is by no means a matter of indifference for the Soviet Union. And it is not just that the relations which exist between the USSR and Libya are of a close and lasting nature and are based on long-standing traditions and on the manifestation of profound liking and mutual respect between the Soviet and Libyan peoples. Our country's course toward this region is also determined by the fact that the USSR, as a Mediterranean power, has a vital interest in the preservation of peace in the Mediterranean basin. Our country proceeds from the conviction that in this particular region, just as anywhere on earth, all problems and all

situations that are fraught with conflict must be overcome solely by peaceful means and solely by political means.

The situation can still be controlled and still allows one to stop before the danger mark is passed. There is still time to curtail the military preparations, to renounce plans for inflicting strikes against Libya, and to rebuff Israel which is itching for adventures ... The question is simply whether Washington will manage to make a definitive decision from positions of restraint, conscious of all its responsibility for the morrow.[118]

As the USSR was counselling restraint, and asserting that Libya opposed terrorism, it could only have been embarrassed by the remarks of Salim Huweidi, Libyan Cultural Attaché to the USSR, who said at a Moscow press conference that Libya supported the attacks at the Rome and Vienna airports because they were "actions of a partisan war, committed by revolutionaries." While claiming "we are not for terrorism, we are resolutely against it," Huweidi stated "we are in support of the acts perpetrated in Rome and Vienna because we support the peoples' struggle ..."[119]

Meanwhile, as the January crisis unfolded, Moscow was making some limited military moves in the Mediterranean. It stationed a submarine tender in Tripoli harbor, and established a picket line of ships north of the Gulf of Sidra, long a bone of contention between the United States, which does not recognize Libyan sovereignty over the Gulf, and which shot down two Libyan planes there in 1981, and Libya which claims such sovereignty.[120] At the minimum, these ships had the capability of providing advanced warning to Libya in case of a US attack and Moscow may have felt also that the presence of the Soviet vessels in Tripoli harbor would deter a US attack on Libya's capital city. In any case, the January crisis ended without any US military attack on Libya, and Moscow could only have been happy at that outcome. Nonetheless, there were a number of voices in the United States, including Secretary of State George Shultz, who were advocating tougher measures toward Libya, while some American columnists were beginning to wonder if Reagan, because of his unwillingness to use force, was becoming another Jimmy Carter.[121] With Kaddafi, perhaps emboldened by the lack of US military action, on January 15, publicly pledging to train and equip Arab guerrillas for "terrorist and suicide" missions,[122] Moscow could only have been concerned that a Libyan–American military confrontation remained a real possibility.

In mid-January, however, Soviet attention was diverted from the US–

Libyan crisis to South Yemen (the Peoples Democratic Republic of Yemen) where an internecine leadership clash threatened the existence of the pro-Soviet party which ruled the country. For many years Moscow had endeavored to create a set of Marxist institutions for this backward Arabian Peninsula state which it hoped would become a model of Soviet-style socialism. The crisis, however, was to reveal the thinness of the Marxist patina Moscow had created. Essentially, it involved a struggle for power betwen PDRY President Ali Nasser Mohammed and the man he had deposed in February 1980, Abdul Fatah Ismail.[123] For reasons that are not yet fully clear, someone in the Soviet leadership permitted Ismail, then in exile in the USSR, to return to Aden in March 1985, just as Gorbachev was taking power. Following some major disagreements at the PDRY Party Congress in October 1985 where Mohammed saw his position weakened (Mohammed was in favor of improved ties with the PDRY's Arab neighbors, and more scope for private initiative, especially in agriculture),[124] the PDRY President evidently decided to eliminate Ismail once and for all by a preemptive move in which he tried to murder Ismail and his supporters at a cabinet meeting on January 13, 1986. While Ismail was killed, along with Ali Antar, Vice-Chairman of the government Praesidium, Muslih Qasim, the PDRY Defense Minister and Ali Fadi, Chairman of the Party Control Commission, the fighting between factions loyal to Ismail and Mohammed spread throughout the PDRY and Soviet advisers and dependents were hastily evacuated. Ultimately, a pro-Soviet official, the Prime Minister, Haidar Al-Attas, who was touring India at the time of the crisis, returned to become President and Soviet warnings against outside intervention and its own involvement in the fighting tipped the balance against Mohammed who was forced into exile.[125] Nonetheless, while Moscow was able to regain control of the situation, the crisis had several negative consequences for the USSR. First, with at least 4,000 members of the Yemeni communist party killed,[126] and a very pronounced degree of tribalism evident in the conflict between Ali Nasser Mohammed and Abdul Fatah Ismail, the Marxist structure of the PDRY, which Moscow was seeking to establish as a model for other Arab states, suffered a major blow. Second, the vaunted security infrastructure which Moscow had been providing to the PDRY proved faulty as both the USSR and East Germany seemed taken by surprise by the January events. (This was evident by Moscow's confused reporting at the start of the crisis).[127] Finally, the ouster of Ali Nasser Mohammed, who had sought to improve the PDRY's relations with its conservative Arab neighbors, and his replacement by more hardline elements served to slow Soviet efforts to improve relations with the conservative Arab states of the Gulf.

That the last factor was of considerable concern to Moscow was evident in its reporting of post-crisis meetings between Soviet and PDRY officials. Thus when Moscow's number two leader, Yegor Ligachev, met the PDRY delegation to the 27th CPSU Congress, headed by Ali Salim al-Bedh, the new First Secretary of the PDRY communist party, in early March, *Pravda* emphasized Moscow's reminding of the PDRY leadership of the necessity "of continuing a peace-loving foreign policy and strengthening good neighbor relations with the countries of the region."[128] Similarly, when the new PDRY Prime Minister, Yasin Numan, visited Moscow in early June *Pravda* emphasized his efforts "to develop and strengthen relations with Arab states and with neighboring countries of the region."[129] Finally, one month later, when Soviet Middle East trouble-shooter Karen Brutents, who had been promoted to deputy head of the International Department of the CPSU's Central Committee, visited Aden, *Pravda* cited the PDRY leaders as declaring their "steadfast desire to maintain and develop good relations with all countries of the region, including bordering states."[130] Moscow had good cause for its concern. As noted above, only a few months before the crisis in South Yemen had erupted, Oman and the United Arab Emirates, both of which had been targeted for PDRY-supported guerrilla attacks in the past, had established diplomatic relations with the Soviet Union, and both states were now worried about the possibility of a more radical regime in Aden resuming its pressure. Such a development, particularly when Moscow had repeatedly pledged its support for the new South Yemeni regime, would, most likely, chill relations between the USSR and the two Gulf states. To be sure, in his first interview with Western reporters, the new PDRY President al-Attas stated, "We will make our best efforts to consolidate our relations with our brothers in North Yemen, Saudi Arabia, and the six states of the Gulf Cooperation Council."[131] Nonetheless, North Yemen to which Ali Nasser Mohammed had fled, signaled its wariness about developments in the PDRY when, during a visit by Vice President George Bush in April, the North Yemeni President, Ali Abdullah Salah, told Bush his government was eager to improve relations with the United States.[132] The US position had already been strengthened as a result of a US oil company, Hunt Oil, finding oil in the impoverished country and Bush, who was warmly applauded by crowds lined up in the streets (despite a US military confrontation with Libya two weeks earlier), promised Salih a $5 million increase in economic aid and passed on an invitation from President Reagan for him to visit Washington.[133]

In sum, therefore, while Moscow had ensured that a pro-Soviet regime retained control in a country of great geopolitical importance to the USSR (the PDRY serves as the base for Soviet reconnaissance flights over the Indian Ocean, provides the main facilities for resupply and repair of the Soviet Indian Ocean fleet, and has the most extensive port accessible to the Soviet Navy between Camranh Bay and the Black Sea);[134] nonetheless, the foreign policy consequences of the events in South Yemen held potential problems for Moscow. While one could expect that reconstruction would be the main priority of the new PDRY regime in the immediate future, its neighbors were clearly suspicious of its future foreign policy and this very suspicion contained dilemmas for Moscow.

While the January 1986 Libyan–American and South Yemeni crises posed problems for the Soviet Union, Moscow was to benefit from a subsequent Middle East development, this one taking place on the eve of the 27th CPSU Party Congress. On February 19, after meeting with US Assistant Secretary of State Richard Murphy in London in mid-January, and two weeks of negotiations with PLO leader Yasser Arafat in late January and early February, King Hussein of Jordan publicly broke with Arafat and thus ended their year-long joint peace effort. In a major speech giving his view of what had happened, Hussein first noted that he had obtained a major concession from the United States by getting it to agree to have the PLO invited to attend an international peace conference on the Middle East, along with the Soviet Union and other permanent members of the Security Council, if the PLO clearly stated "on the public record that it had accepted (UN) resolutions 242 and 338, is prepared to negotiate peace with Israel and has renounced terrorism."[135] The next day, US State Department spokesman, Charles E. Redman, confirmed the accuracy of Hussein's remarks – a development that caused both surprise and consternation in Israel.[136] Arafat, however, according to Hussein wanted the US to go farther by publicly agreeing to the legitimate rights of the Palestinian people, including their right to self-determination within the context of a confederation between Jordan and Palestine. Hussein then reportedly told Arafat that "the subject of self-determination within the context of a confederation was a matter for the Jordanians and Palestinians and that no other party had anything to do with it," and intimated that such a response from the PLO indicated that the organization might be "dealing with us on a basis of lack of confidence."[137] (Hussein was probably correct, given PLO suspicions that the King would try to dominate any Palestinian–Jordanian confederation.) Hussein concluded his speech by stating that he was "unable to continue to coordinate politically with the PLO leadership until such time as their word becomes their bond, characterized by commitment, credibility, and constancy."[138]

The split between Hussein and Arafat was welcome to Moscow for several reasons. In the first place it appeared to put a final stop to the US attempt to organize talks between a joint PLO–Jordanian delegation and Israel (a possibility that had concerned Moscow following the Hussein–Arafat agreement of February 1985); although Arafat, despite considerable pressure from within Fatah,[139] was not to reciprocate the formal break with Hussein until the Palestine National Council meeting of April 1987. Second, with the Jordanian option now apparently closed to Arafat, Moscow may well have felt that the PLO leader would move to reunify his organization and move closer to the pro-Soviet Palestine Democratic Alliance of George Habash's Popular Front for the Liberation of Palestine, Naef Hawatmeh's Democratic Front for the Liberation of Palestine and the Palestine communist party, if not yet to the Syrian-controlled elements of the PLO. Indeed, with relations between the PLO and King Hussein already chilling in the latter part of 1985, Arafat evidently decided to mend his fences with the Soviet Union and sent Farouk Kaddoumi to Moscow in early January 1986, where he met with Soviet Foreign Minister Edvard Shevardnadze. *Pravda*'s description of the talks as having taken place in a "businesslike atmosphere," however, indicated considerable disagreement between the two sides, although they both called for Palestinian unity on an "anti-imperialist basis" and called for an international conference on the Middle East with the participation "of all interested sides, including the PLO."[140] Three months later Soviet Middle East specialist Vladimir Polyakov held meetings in Damascus with the Syrians and with Habash and Hawatmeh in another Soviet effort to encourage Palestinian unity.[141]

While on balance the break between Hussein and Arafat was a positive development for Moscow, Gorbachev still had to be concerned that Hussein, despite the US Congress's opposition to selling him arms until he made peace with Israel, might still make a separate deal with Israel (and, presumably, be rewarded with arms afterwards, much as Egypt had been), something that was regularly rumored in the press.[142]

Hussein's subsequent closure of PLO offices in Jordan, his arrest of Jordanian communists, and his effort to forge an alternative Palestinian leadership on the West Bank (with Israel's tacit cooperation), were all factors which appeared to incline Hussein in this direction. Indeed, three days after his public break with Arafat, Hussein noted that while he would respect a decision by Palestinians to preserve the PLO as their "sole legitimate representative," he would also welcome another "apparatus" to express their wishes.[143] Nonetheless, the murder of the pro-Jordanian Mayor of the West Bank city of Nablus, Zafir al-Masri, on March 2, 1986, illustrated Hussein's difficulties in creating an alternative Palestinian leadership on the West Bank. On balance, therefore, Gorbachev clearly gained from the split between Hussein and Arafat, and the Soviet leader could therefore enter the 27th Party Congress of the CPSU relieved that the American-orchestrated peace process appeared at a dead end.

At the 27th Party Congress itself it seemed as if Gorbachev had almost completely lost interest in the Middle East. The main emphasis of his speech was on internal reform, and his foreign policy emphases were on Soviet–American, Soviet–European, and Soviet–Asian relations in that order. He referred to the Middle East only as one of a number of "hotbeds of war,"[144] a clear contrast with Brezhnev's speeches at previous Party Congresses where the Middle East received a great deal of attention and certain Arab countries, such as Syria, were singled out for praise. Gorbachev did, however, indicate a desire to withdraw Soviet troops from Afghanistan and stated that it was in the Soviet Union's interest to have good and peaceful relations with all the states which bordered the USSR. While Gorbachev's statements may be considered gestures to China, they may also have been directed at Iran with which relations had been strained from the time of Khomeini's takeover in 1979 and which had strongly criticized Moscow's occupation of Afghanistan and had aided the Afghan guerrilla forces there.

If Gorbachev had hoped that the break between Hussein and Arafat would mean a period of reduced concern for the USSR in the Middle East, the region soon reasserted its claim for the Soviet leader's attention. On March 4, the official Libyan news agency JANA reported a call by the Libyan Parliament (the General People's Congress) for the formation of suicide squads "to wreck US–Zionist interests everywhere."[145] Two weeks later, the US announced it was planning to cross Kaddafi's self-proclaimed "line of death" at the top of the Gulf of Sidra in what was called a "freedom of navigation exercise."[146] On

March 25 a military confrontation which the USSR most probably expected[147] took place as Libyan SAM-5 missiles were fired from their base at Surt at American planes participating in the naval maneuvers in the Gulf.[148] The US responded by attacking the SAM-5 base and also hitting three Libyan patrol boats, two of which were destroyed. While the military action was a minor one (especially when compared to the US strike at Tripoli three weeks later), the USSR was nonetheless faced with the problem of how to respond, particularly since Soviet advisers had presumably been at the SAM-5 base which had been attacked.[149] The initial Soviet response to the attack was given by Vladimir Lomeiko, the same Soviet Foreign Ministry spokesman who had publicly responded to the US–Libyan confrontation in January. Lomeiko was quoted in a press conference as saying "the Soviet Union has provided moral and political support to the Libyan people and will take all measures it considers appropriate within the framework of existing treaties."[150] Given the fact that the USSR and Libya had no mutual defense treaty, or even a Treaty of Friendship and Cooperation such as Moscow had with Syria, Iraq, and South Yemen, Lomeiko's remarks made it clear that Moscow would not come to Libya's aid. Lomeiko also refused to answer a question about possible Soviet casualties in the US air strike. A *Tass* statement was also low-key, noting only that "the piratical action against Libya sharply aggravates the already explosive situation in the region and could also have serious consequences beyond its borders"; that "the Soviet people express their solidarity with the Libyan people"; and that the Soviet Union "has been and remains on the side of Libya in its just struggle for freedom and independence. It condemns the aggressive US actions in the most resolute manner and demands that they be stopped."[151] Gorbachev himself, speaking at a dinner in honor of visiting Algerian President Chadli Benjedid, also condemned the US action as "a challenge to the world public"[152] and he used the opportunity to call for the simultaneous withdrawal of the US and Soviet fleets from the Mediterranean – a proposal quickly rejected by the United States[153] – and also for a general conference on the Mediterranean with adjoining states and the US and Soviet Union participating.

While the USSR was low-key in its response to the US–Libyan military confrontation, Kaddafi was not. Speaking at a rally in Tripoli on March 28, Kaddafi warned that if the confrontation continued Libya would strike at military bases in any country aiding the US Sixth fleet, thus transforming the US–Libyan conflict into a Libyan–NATO confrontation.[154] Two weeks later, Kaddafi claimed that the USSR and Libya had an agreement to cooperate in times of conflict, and he noted that while he did not expect the USSR to aid Libya militarily if hostilities were limited to the Mediterranean, "if the war spreads widely, then naturally, the Soviet Union will not stand by with its hands tied during a war involving a superpower."[155]

As this situation developed, the Soviet leadership could not have been pleased either by Kaddafi's efforts to expand the US–Libyan conflict into a Libyan–NATO confrontation, or by his efforts to enmesh the USSR in the conflict, something Libyan Radio again tried to do on April 12 when it asserted that Libya might call on the USSR for assistance against growing pressure from the United States.[156] With another summit with the US on the horizon (Shultz and Shevardnadze were due to meet in mid-May to prepare the groundwork for the summit)[157] Gorbachev certainly had no desire to be drawn into a conflict with the US over Libya. A Soviet delegation headed by Konstantin Katushev, which left Tripoli on April 14, may have carried a message of caution from Gorbachev (in addition to investigating why the SAM-5s fired at the US planes were so ineffective).[158] Significantly, Soviet ships were pulled out of Tripoli harbor in early April in possible anticipation of another US strike.[159]

Despite these Soviet cautionary moves, presumed Libyan aid to terrorists who in early April bombed a West Berlin discotheque frequented by US soldiers precipitated another US attack on Libya which in turn posed yet another unpleasant choice for Moscow. The US air strike, which took place on April 15, was far more extensive than the one in March. Targets attacked included a PLO training base, a military barracks, and the military section of the Tripoli International airport, along with a military barracks in Benghazi and the military portion of the Benghazi airport.[160] Moscow's response to this US attack, while somewhat sharper in tone than its response to the March attack, remained primarily symbolic. Thus, in addition to denouncing the US at the United Nations, the USSR cancelled the scheduled mid-May meeting of Shultz and Shevardnadze, although Soviet press spokesman Lomeiko stated at a news conference that if the US stopped showing "contempt for international law and morality" it might be possible to set a new date for the meeting.[161] Interestingly enough, however, despite the new chill in Soviet–American relations, Moscow did not cancel the agreement resuming Moscow–Washington air flights by Aeroflot and Pan American. The first flight took place, on schedule, on

April 29.[162] Nor did Moscow cancel the technical talks for the upgrading of the US–Soviet hotline which took place a week after the April 15 attack.[163]

If Soviet action in responding to the raid was essentially symbolic, its rhetoric was more heated. Thus a Soviet government statement on April 16 branded the attack "barbaric" and "piratical" and noted that the USSR demanded an immediate end to it; "otherwise, the Soviet Union will be forced to draw more far-reaching conclusions."[164] Gorbachev followed up the government statement with a message to Kaddafi that was printed on page one of *Pravda* on April 17.[165] In it the Soviet leader, after first noting Soviet efforts to "stave off the threatening development of events surrounding Libya" which included "repeated serious warnings" to the United States, and expressing his solidarity with Kaddafi and the Libyan people, then promised to "continue to fulfill the commitments it has made with respect to the further strengthening of Libya's defense capability." Gorbachev's reply did not promise any protection for Kaddafi against the United States, and may well have disappointed the Libyan leader whose radio, in the aftermath of the US attack, had called on "the socialist community, led by the USSR" to "shoulder its international responsibilities in an actual war waged by NATO against a small, neutral people."[166] Perhaps in an effort to obtain further Soviet support, Libya's number two leader, Salaam Jalloud, told a press conference on April 18 that Libya was considering offering the Soviet Union military bases in Libya.[167] Moscow did not respond publicly to the Libyan gesture, although in claiming that five US planes had been shot down (instead of the one which the US admitted had been lost)[168] Moscow may have been trying to upgrade the reputation of its weaponry which had been called into question because of Libya's lack of effectiveness in responding to the American attacks of March 25 and April 15.

In the aftermath of the two American raids, Moscow confronted a mixed balance sheet. On the one hand the US raids were unpopular in Western Europe. Only British Prime Minister Margaret Thatcher allowed US planes to use English bases for the raid, and France refused to give the US permission to overfly its territory. Popular opinion in both Britain and West Germany opposed the attacks although Thatcher's policy did not prevent her overwhelming reelection a year later. US relations with France, Germany, and Italy were clearly strained over what Reagan perceived as a lack of allied support for his anti-terrorist policy,[169] and although the NATO alliance increasingly imposed economic and diplomatic sanctions against Libya as country after country publicly linked Libya with terrorism,[170] strains remained, and Gorbachev may have seen this as a possible weakening of the NATO alliance. In the Arab world, however, Libya called in vain for assistance. His pleas for a *jihad* and economic sanctions against the United States went unanswered (there were public demonstrations only in Tunisia and the Sudan), and the Arab League proved unable even to convene a summit meeting to deal with the American attack.[171] This development indicated just how much of a *persona non grata* Kaddafi had become to his fellow Arabs, and demonstrated that Moscow would be unable to exploit the attack to promote the kind of "anti-imperialist" Arab unity it had wanted for so long.

The two American attacks – and the lack of a substantive Soviet response to them – reportedly strained Soviet–Libyan ties[172] and also raised questions of Soviet credibility in the Arab world, although Libya was not linked to the USSR by a formal treaty. The problem for Moscow was that the US had used Libyan involvement in terrorism as a pretext for attacking it, and when another Arab country, Syria, much closer to Moscow than Libya, became heavily involved in a terrorist incident, there was the risk of either another American, or an Israeli–American retaliatory strike. Indeed, following the second attack on Libya, Reagan said that if there was "irrefutable evidence" linking Syria or Iran to terrorism, the US should attack them.[173]

Even before the terrorist incident, which involved a plan to blow up an El Al plane departing from England in mid-April, Syrian–Israeli relations had become very tense, and by May there were a number of press reports that war would break out between the two countries.[174] Contributing to the heightened tension were the Syrian decision to construct a series of artillery and tank emplacements near Israel's security zone in South Lebanon, and Israel's forcing down of a Libyan plane which contained high-ranking Syrian Ba'ath party officials (instead of the PLO officials Israel was seeking). The most serious incident however, was the attempted bombing of the El Al plane in London on April 17, by Nizar Hindawi, a man who was quickly found to have close links with the Syrian Embassy in London.

As tension rose, Moscow, which had been accused by the United States both before and after the April 15 attack on Libya, of not doing enough to stop terrorists infiltrating into Western Europe from East Berlin,[175] took action. On April 16, the day after the US attack on Libya, State Department spokesman Bernard Kalb had complained:

> On March 27, we advised Soviet officials here (in Washington) and in Berlin that we had evidence indicating Libya was planning actions against US interests and citizens in Berlin. We urged the Soviets and East Germans to restrain the Libyans. Had they done so, this entire cycle of events could have been avoided.[176]

One month after Kalb's complaint, the East German government almost certainly acting under Soviet prodding, gave assurances to the US that it would not permit any embassy operating in East Berlin to be used as a base for terrorist attacks.[177] Gorbachev himself sought to distance Moscow from terrorism – and to dissuade both Syria and Libya from employing it as state policy – during Moscow visits by Salam Jalloud of Libya and Abd al-Halim Khaddam, one of Syria's Vice-Presidents and its former Foreign Minister, at the end of May.

According to Moscow television, Gorbachev, while condemning the American attacks, warned Jalloud:

> The US moral-political defeat does not rule out further adventures, and that is why vigilance, firmness, and a high level of defense capability by states that might become the target of an imperialist attack, a sense of principle and *consistency in condemning those pretexts that the imperialists use in this regard, especially terrorism in any of its forms, are required*.[178] (emphasis mine)

Moscow's failure to agree to a Treaty of Friendship and Cooperation with Libya during the Jalloud visit – something the Libyans continued to want badly – may also be seen as a cautionary factor.

As far as the Khaddam visit was concerned, it appeared as if the Syrian leader was repeating the Libyan ploy of claiming that the USSR had an obligation to protect it, by portraying Syria as a country which stood at the forefront of the battle line against an American–Israeli alliance which, according to Khaddam, "threatens not only Syria and the Arabs, but also the security of all progressive forces in the world, including the Soviet Union."[179] For their part, the Soviets were more cautious, as Andrei Gromyko, in his dinner speech welcoming Khaddam, merely expressed "effective solidarity" with Syria and Libya and pointedly noted "in the USSR there is the conviction that if the Arabs succeed in ensuring unity in their ranks it would be an effective weapon in resisting their enemies' intrigues."[180] This was a not-so-subtle commentary on the fact that Syria, because of its role in dividing the PLO and its aid for Iran in the Iran–Iraq war, was a major cause of disunity in the Arab world. Gromyko did, however, promise continued support for

Syria, including the "strengthening of its defense capability." Nonetheless, perhaps because it was unsure of how far it could depend on Soviet support, Assad made a number of tactical moves to strengthen Syria's position following the terrorist incident in London. Thus he hinted at a reconciliation with Iraq and a turn away from Iran (a ploy, it turned out, which seemed primarily aimed at getting Iran to resume shipments of cut-rate oil). He also publicly denounced terrorism, including the attacks at the Rome and Vienna airports, and declared that Syria was willing to cooperate in combating terrorism.[181] Unfortunately for Assad, however, the Italian Interior Minister on June 24 undermined the new Syrian anti-terrorist posture by claiming that he had "concrete evidence" that Syria was one of the sources of international terrorism.[182] Two days later there was another abortive attack on an El Al Israel plane, this one in Madrid, Spain, and again Syria was implicated as one of the suspects, Nasser Hassan Ali, was shown to be a member of the pro-Syrian Abu Musa Palestinian guerrilla organization and to be travelling on a false Syrian passport.[183] While Syria publicly condemned the attack, and Assad sought to deflect US and Israeli pressure by promising to continue his efforts to free American hostages in Lebanon,[184] Syrian–Israeli tension rose. The diplomatic situation further worsened for Syria – and for the USSR – on July 14 when British authorities directly implicated Syria in the abortive bombing of the Israeli airliner in London in April.[185]

Under these circumstances, with a US–Syrian or Israeli–Syrian confrontation now a real possibility, it appears that Moscow moved to exercise some creative diplomacy in an apparent attempt to prevent a confrontation from occurring. The diplomacy was two-fold in nature. On the one hand Moscow suddenly announced its willingness to hold public consular talks with Israel. This diplomatic ploy, Moscow may well have felt, would deter an Israeli attack on Syria, lest it harm a possible improvement in Soviet–Israeli relations, which in turn held out the possibility of an increase in the number of Soviet Jews being allowed to leave the USSR, long a major Israeli goal. Secondly, it agreed to reschedule the Shultz–Shevardnadze meeting which had been postponed because of the US attack on Libya in April. Once again, such a move would presumably deter a US attack on Syria, Moscow's close ally, because the Reagan Administration had been pressing for another summit meeting with the USSR. At the same time, Moscow again began to call for an international conference on the Middle East, but one arranged by a preparatory meeting of the permanent members of the

UN Security Council – a proposal that was rapidly endorsed by both Egypt and Jordan.

There were, however, a number of other factors which may have prompted Moscow into its August 4 announcements of both diplomatic moves. First, there were serious domestic problems confronting Gorbachev: the nuclear disaster in Chernobyl at the end of April, the precipitous drop in world oil prices in mid-1986 (more than 60 percent of Soviet hard currency earnings come from oil and natural gas sales),[186] Gorbachev's efforts to restructure the Soviet economy, and the major economic difficulties facing the USSR, were all factors now moving the Soviet leader toward an arms control agreement that would prevent another expensive spiralling of the arms race and which might lead to increased trade with the United States.[187] For this reason Gorbachev sought a second summit with the United States and, given Moscow's tendency to overestimate Jewish influence in the United States, the new Soviet leader may well have felt that the gesture to Israel would help pave the way for the summit. A second factor which may have prompted the flurry of Soviet diplomatic activity was the Middle East diplomatic situation which took a sudden turn for the worse for Moscow at the end of July as Israeli Prime Minister Peres and King Hassan of Morocco held a surprise summit in Morocco – a development hailed by the United States as "a historic opportunity to further the cause of peace in the Middle East."[188] (The last surprise summit, Moscow may well have recalled, was Sadat's visit to Jerusalem in November 1977 which led to the Camp David accords less than a year later). While no agreement was reached at the summit, a joint communiqué was issued which described the talks as "exploratory" and which emphasized the Arab Fez plan as the basis for an agreement.[189] Moscow had to be concerned, particularly since the summit coincided with a visit to the Middle East by Vice President George Bush, one of several visits he made to the region in 1986. While Syria broke diplomatic relations with Morocco, no other Arab state took similar action, although Hassan did agree to resign as President of the Arab League because of the criticism he received from a number of Arab countries and the PLO.[190] Nonetheless, an additional problem for Moscow caused by the summit was Hassan's decision to cancel his 1984 treaty of union with Libya because of Libyan criticism of his meeting with Peres as an "act of treason."[191] Moscow had hoped Kaddafi's tie with Morocco would pull that country away from the United States but such a possibility seemed aborted following the dissolution of the treaty.

In sum, therefore, it would appear that Moscow, concerned both about the possibility of an unwanted war between Israel and Syria (or an American attack on Syria), and by the surprise Hassan–Peres summit, and preoccupied with domestic problems, once again decided to send a major signal to Israel by agreeing to public talks at the consular level.[192] The talks were the highest level formal bilateral negotiations between the two states since Moscow broke diplomatic relations with Israel in 1967 and the public nature of the discussions, which Moscow had agreed upon at Israeli urging,[193] served Israel's needs by striking a major blow at Arab efforts to isolate and delegitimize Israel, despite Soviet efforts to play down the significance of the meetings in its propaganda in the Arab world.[194] Nonetheless, the negotiations, which took place in Helsinki, Finland, on August 18 did not immediately produce the results either side said it wanted, although the symbolic significance of the talks was probably much more important than their content. While the Soviets wished to send a team of officials to take an inventory of Soviet property (primarily owned by the Russian Orthodox Church) in Israel, the Israeli delegation, under heavy domestic pressure from such individuals as Moshe Arens and Anatoly Sharansky (a prominent Refusenik whom Moscow had released in February), made the issue of Soviet Jewry the paramount one at the talks, and the meeting ended after ninety minutes.[195] Nonetheless, the very fact that the talks were held, and the fact that one month later Israeli Prime Minister Peres and Soviet Foreign Minister Shevardnadze held detailed (and apparently cordial) negotiations at the United Nations,[196] as well as subsequent meetings between the Soviet and Israeli ambassadors to the US, all indicated that the Soviet Union was keeping alive its contacts with Israel.

If the Helsinki meeting did not produce immediate results for Israel, a meeting between Israeli Prime Minister Peres and Egyptian President Hosni Mubarak in Alexandria, Egypt three weeks later proved considerably more successful. Despite a terrorist attack on the main synagogue in Istanbul, Turkey that killed twenty-one worshippers and may have been timed to disrupt the talks,[197] an agreement was reached to send the dispute over the Taba border area to arbitration; Mubarak agreed to return the Egyptian Ambassador to Israel (the Ambassador had been recalled following the 1982 Sabra and Shatilla massacres); and the two countries agreed to set up a committee to lay the groundwork for an international conference on the Middle East.[198] The summit ended a long chill in Israeli–Egyptian relations and the fact that follow-

ing the summit the small Arab League state of Djibouti restored diplomatic relations with Egypt[199] was a blow to Moscow which had long
sought to isolate Egypt in the Arab world because of its participation in
the American-sponsored Camp David accords.[200] While Moscow
remained interested in the convening of an international conference on
the Middle East, it took strong exception, as *Pravda* noted on September 14, to the agreement by Peres and Mubarak to create a committee
"to determine who will attend the conference and what its prerogatives
will be."[201] This was particularly irksome to Moscow because, in
August, Egyptian Foreign Minister Butros Ghali, had endorsed the
Soviet plan for a preparatory conference committee made up of the
permanent members of the UN Security Council.[202]

Nonetheless, despite its displeasure with Egypt over Camp David,
Moscow had been seeking to improve its relations with the most
populous Arab state since the assassination of Sadat in 1981, and 1986
was no exception. A group of senior Soviet government officials spent a
week in Cairo in March, meeting with Mubarak on March 24, and the
leader of the Soviet delegation, Pavel Gilashvili, deputy Chairman of
the Presidium of the USSR Supreme Soviet, was quoted as saying that
the USSR was looking for new avenues of cooperation with Egypt and
that Mubarak had "injected great optimism into bilateral cooperation
and friendship between Egypt and the Soviet Union."[203] A *Pravda*
article by Vladimir Belyakov in late April, while discussing Egypt's
serious internal problems including the police conscript uprising of late
February, noted the possibilities for future improvements in Soviet–
Egyptian relations.[204] A concrete step was taken in early December
when, after twelve days of talks with Egyptian officials, Victor Demenstev, head of the Soviet State Bank, stated that the USSR was willing to
provide Egypt with additional time to repay its military debts.[205] (An
agreement was to be reached on the debt issue in 1987). The Demenstev
visit was of particular political value to Mubarak because two weeks
later the US also offered Egypt a plan of military debt relief.[206]

On the negative side of Soviet–Egyptian relations in 1986 was Egypt's
continuing close military and economic relationship with the United
States (despite Egypt's inability to obtain the increased US economic
aid it wanted) which was highlighted by the joint military exercise "Sea
Wind" conducted in the Mediterranean near Libya, although north of
the Gulf of Sidra, at the end of August.[207] Moscow, which had praised
Egypt's unwillingness to undertake a joint attack with the US against
Libya in April,[208] showed concern that the August exercises might have

the same goal.[209] A second problem in Egyptian–Soviet relations emerged in mid-December when an Egyptian communist plot against Mubarak was revealed, and forty-four members of the illegal party were arrested.[210]

If there was a slow, but steady improvement in Soviet–Egyptian relations, the same can be said for Moscow's ties with Egypt's southern neighbor, the Sudan. As noted above, following the ouster of Nimeri in April 1985, the Sudan began to distance itself from both the United States and Egypt, and drew closer to the USSR and Libya.[211] The process continued in 1986, as the newly elected Sudanese Prime Minister, Sadiq al-Mahdi, paid an official visit to Moscow. Burdened by an overwhelming debt and by an Ethiopian-assisted rebellion in Sudan's southern provinces which was adding to the country's economic woes, al-Mahdi clearly hoped that Moscow would exert pressure on its Ethiopian ally to reduce its support to the Sudanese rebels.[212] Al-Mahdi's hope, however, did not appear to be realized as the joint communiqué described the talks as having taken place in a "spirit of friendship and mutual understanding"[213] – a sign of considerable disagreement. Nonetheless al-Mahdi put a positive face on the visit and was quoted by Tass as stating that his visit was only an "opening page" in Soviet–Sudanese relations and that contacts would be continued because "the Soviet leadership had demonstrated a constructive approach to the restoration of Soviet–Sudanese relations and had shown the readiness to develop them on the basis of equality."[214]

As Soviet–Sudanese relations improved, Sudanese ties with its main economic benefactor, the United States, continued to be severely strained. The US, unhappy at what it saw as the growing Libyan influence in the Sudan, evacuated three-quarters of its embassy staff following the shooting of an embassy communications worker in the aftermath of the US bombing of Libya in April 1986.[215] While most of the evacuated Americans had returned by the end of the year, reportedly because the Sudan had expelled the Libyans associated with terrorism about whom the US had complained,[216] US–Sudanese relations remained strained and this could only benefit Moscow, given its zero-sum game view of its Middle East competition with the United States.

While Moscow's primary attention in the Middle East at this time was concentrated in the western section of the region, the Iran–Iraq war continued to pose problems for Soviet policy because it diverted the attention of the Arab world from the Arab–Israeli conflict, isolated Moscow's major clients, Syria and Libya, who backed Iran in the war, and also contributed to the strengthening of the US position in the Gulf. Gorbachev sought to deal with this situation by seeking to improve ties with Iran, after a long period of Soviet–Iranian tension. Nonetheless, just as the Khomeini regime was later shown to have exploited US efforts to improve ties during what became known as the Iran–Contra scandal,[217] so too did it appear to manipulate similar efforts by Moscow. Thus in early February 1986, the USSR First Deputy Foreign Minister Georgii Kornienko visited Tehran – the highest ranking Soviet official to visit the Iranian capital since the ouster of the Shah. When Kornienko obtained an agreement in principle from Tehran to resume Aeroflot flights to Iran, and Iran's Foreign Minister accepted an invitation to visit Moscow, Gorbachev may well have felt he was making headway in improving the Soviet position in Iran.[218] Indeed, following Kornienko's visit, the Iranian speaker of Parliament, Hojatolislam Rafsanjani was quoted at a news conference as saying that Soviet–Iranian relations were improving and Kornienko's visit "will have a great effect on our relations with the Soviet Union and the Eastern world. One can be optimistic in fields such as technical, military, economic, and possibly political relations."[219] Less than a week after Kornienko's visit, however, Iran embarked on an offensive in its war against Iraq and scored a major success by capturing the Fao Peninsula.[220] It might well have occurred to Moscow that Tehran had exploited the Kornienko visit, and the impression of an improvement in Soviet–Iranian relations, to deter the USSR from increasing its aid to Iraq during the Iranian offensive lest Moscow lose the increased influence in Iran it had (or so it appeared) just obtained. If Moscow did not see the significance of the Iranian ploy in February, Iran was to repeat the maneuver again later in the year. Thus in June, Iran announced its agreement to the first meeting in six years of the standing commission on Iranian–Soviet joint economic cooperation,[221] and in August there were visits to Moscow by the Iranian Deputy Foreign Minister for Economic and International Affairs, and the Iranian Petroleum Minister (the latter stated Iran was planning to resume natural gas sales to Moscow, something Moscow had long sought, and also stated "we can cooperate with the Soviet Union as part of our defense strategy").[222] Then, in December, Moscow agreed to return the technicians it had pulled out of Iran in 1985,[223] during a Tehran visit by Konstantin Katushev, Chairman of the Soviet committee for foreign economic relations.

Yet once again Iran appeared to exploit the improvement of ties with Moscow by launching a major attack on Iraq, this one, at the beginning of January 1987, less than two weeks after Katushev's departure. Nonetheless its attacks on Iraq were not the only Iranian actions troubling Moscow. In September 1986 Iran had stopped two Soviet freighters in the Gulf, the *Pyotr Yemtsov* and the *Tutov*, and searched them before allowing them to continue – actions that drew a protest from the Soviet Foreign Ministry.[224] A second major irritant for Moscow, besides Iran's continued prosecution of the Iran–Iraq war and its unwillingness to accept Iraqi offers to settle it, was its aid to the Afghan guerrillas. While Moscow changed leaders in Afghanistan, in 1986, replacing Babrak Karmal with Mohammed Najibullah; announced the withdrawal of six Soviet regiments in October and its readiness to withdraw the rest of its troops if external aid to the guerrillas ceased; and on January 1, 1987 offered a cease-fire and a general amnesty,[225] Iran did not appear to be impressed, and continued its aid to the Afghan insurgents.[226] By far the most serious issue of all, however, in Soviet–Iranian relations in 1986 was the revelation in early November 1986 that the United States had been secretly selling arms to Iran and this development posed both risks and opportunities for Moscow. On the one hand the fact that the US was again shipping arms to Iran held out the possibility of a reconciliation between Iran and the United States – something that Moscow had long feared and which it had sought to prevent by trying to improve its own position in Tehran. Indeed, as the crisis unfolded, Soviet propaganda sought to undermine what it viewed as pro-American elements in Iran by claiming that the US arms deal was both a device for prolonging the war (from which Moscow asserted that the US benefited) and for interfering in the internal affairs of Iran.

On the other hand, however, the crisis put the United States very much on the defensive in the Arab world. The revelations of US arms aid to the Khomeini regime undermined the American position, not only among the Gulf Arab states (whose ties to the US were, to a substantial degree, a reflection of their need for American protection against Iran), but also in Egypt and Jordan, two friends of the United States who maintained close ties with the Gulf Arabs.[227] In addition, the Irangate affair made US efforts to isolate the Khomeini regime through operation "Staunch" – a world-wide effort to ban arms sales to Iran – look ridiculous, while the "arms-for-hostages" appearance of the US–Iranian deal undercut the US position against international terrorism. In addition, Moscow's major concern about Irangate – that it would lead to a reconciliation between Iran and the United States – quickly proved unfounded as US Secretary of State George Shultz publicly revealed in late January 1987 that there had been a secret US–Iranian meeting in December 1986 in which the US told Iran that any further improvement in relations would be based solely on Iran's "willingness to mend its ways."[228] Given Iran's active prosecution of the war with Iraq and its continued support for international terrorism, a change in Iranian policy satisfactory to the US must have seemed to Moscow to be an unlikely prospect. Indeed, Shultz, on January 29, publicly stated that Iran had "very strong ties" to the group which kidnapped three American teachers from the American University of Beirut a week before.[229] The Iranian President, Ali Khameni, two weeks later ruled out any reconciliation with the United States, unless the US ended its "hostility and hatred."[230]

Yet even as Gorbachev was seeking to exploit the US débâcle over the Iran–Contra affair, he was aware that the Soviet Middle Eastern position was not without its own problems. In the first place, the Soviet presence in Afghanistan remained a major barrier to improved Soviet ties with Muslim states, and, especially with the Arab world. This was brought home to Gorbachev not only by the continuing lopsided votes in the UN General Assembly calling for a Soviet withdrawal from Afghanistan, but also by the Islamic Conference which, meeting in Kuwait in late January 1987, called for the "total and unconditional" withdrawal of Soviet troops.[231] The Islamic nations took this action – one of the few that the divided summit could agree upon – despite the Afghan regime's proclamation of a unilateral six-month cease-fire and its establishment of a National Reconciliation Commission. *Pravda* blamed this action on the influence of the "most conservative" members of the Islamic Conference.[232] Moscow was, however, pleased by the conference's decision to endorse the Soviet plan for an international conference on the Middle East, with all permanent members of the Security Council and the PLO participating.[233]

A second problem confronting Gorbachev was closer to home, the ethnic rioting in the Soviet Republic of Kazakhstan in Soviet Central Asia (a Muslim region) on December 16–17, 1986. The rioting followed the ouster of the communist party leader, Dinmukhamed Kunaev, a Kazakh, and his replacement by an ethnic Russian, Gennady Kolbin.[234] Initially the Soviet press was quick to blame the rioting on corrupt opponents of Gorbachev's *perestroika* (restructuring) program who incited young people to take to the streets carrying nationalist banners.[235] Later in the year, however, *Pravda* was blaming the riots, in part, on the fact that "no vigorous work was done to expose the reactionary essence of Islam and its attempts to preserve outmoded traditions and notions to reinforce national aloofness."[236]

A third Middle Eastern problem facing Gorbachev at the start of 1987 was continued instability in the People's Democratic Republic of Yemen (South Yemen), which had not yet recovered from the events of January 1986. The new South Yemeni party leader, Ali Salim al Bedh, journeyed to Moscow in early February for discussions with Gorbachev.[237] The *Pravda* description of the talks as a "comradely frank discussion" where "negative as well as positive experiences in the revolutionary struggle" were discussed, indicated the tone of the talks.[238] Gorbachev lectured al-Bedh on the need to face up to past mistakes, not to move ahead too rapidly ("no revolution is secure against the desire of its vanguard to skip over unavoidable stages"), and to take into account South Yemen's "international position." This last point may well have been related to the continuing suspicions of the Aden regime on the part of its immediate neighbors North Yemen, Saudi Arabia, and Oman, all of whom Moscow was wooing. If indeed Moscow was urging a slow and cautious pace on the PDRY leadership, the lesson might not have been too well learned, despite al-Bedh's promise to "spare no effort to strengthen security and stability in both parts of Yemen" and "continue work to strengthen relations with all neighboring countries on the basis of mutual respect, non-interference in internal affairs, and constructive cooperation."[239] In mid-December 1987 the PDRY announced that thirty-five members of the previous South Yemeni regime had been sentenced to death, a development that angered North Yemen whose President, Ali Abdullah Salah, had earlier requested that the South Yemen regime cancel the trials and release the prisoners.[240] The fact that the former PDRY President, Ali Nasser Mohammed, a relative moderate who had encouraged good relations between South Yemen and its neighbors and who was now in exile in North Yemen, was among those sentenced to death, was clearly a blow to intra-Yemeni relations, and it also had the potential of damaging South Yemeni relations with its other neighbors, something that would come into conflict with Moscow's goals in the Arabian Peninsula.

Another problem facing Moscow in early 1987 was the series of defeats suffered by its client, Libya, in battles with the forces of Chad which were supported by both France and the United States. (French planes bombed a Libyan-held airfield in Northern Chad on January 7 in retaliation for Libyan bombings of Southern Chad).[241] Gorbachev, who was now actively engaged in an effort to secure a major arms control agreement with the United States, was in no mood to help the Kaddafi regime with anything other than oral support; and the USSR limited itself to urging a solution to the conflict through the Organization of African Unity (OAU), and denouncing US and French help to Chad, as an Afro-Asian Peoples Solidarity organization demanded "the immediate end to imperialist interference in Chad's internal affairs."[242]

As Libya's military situation worsened (Chadian forces first pushed Libya out of Northern Chad and, in August, invaded the disputed Aouzou Strip which lies between the two countries), the Libyan newspaper *al-Jamahir* published an editorial in early January warning that "unless the Soviet Union takes measures against the 'imperialist attack' in Africa, friends and allies of the USSR will have no arguments to defend it against its enemies."[243] However, neither this editorial, nor Kaddafi's offer to allow Soviet nuclear missiles to be based in Libya prompted the USSR to expand its support of Kaddafi's actions in Chad.[244] (The offer was made after Chadian soldiers captured a Libyan air base in Northern Chad in late March). Kaddafi then turned to Druze warlord Walid Jumblatt for support and recruited 800 Druze soldiers from Lebanon to help bolster the Libyan military position in case the tentative OAU-mediated cease-fire, finally arranged in September, collapsed.[245] Kaddafi also sought to strengthen his position by promoting a unity scheme with Algeria, but this scheme, as many of his previous efforts at Arab unity, proved unsuccessful. The one major meeting between Soviet and Libyan officials in 1987 took place in May when the Libyan Foreign Minister, Jadallah Azziz al-Tahir, visited Moscow. *Pravda*'s description of the talks as having taken place in a "business-like" atmosphere illustrated a relative lack of agreement, as did the fact that neither Kaddafi, nor Sallam Jalloud, Libya's number two leader, made the trip to Moscow.[246]

Yet another problem facing Moscow as 1987 began was the continuing low level of oil prices. Given the fact that the USSR depends on the sale of oil and natural gas for 60 percent of its hard currency earnings, the precipitous drop in petroleum prices in 1986 (at one point as low as $9 per barrel) was clearly a blow to the already overburdened Soviet economy. Consequently Moscow welcomed OPEC efforts to stabilize prices, and an *Izvestia* article in late December 1986 had noted in commenting approvingly on OPEC plans to raise oil prices to $18 a barrel: "Nor is the Soviet Union remaining aloof from efforts to stabilize and align prices on the world petroleum market. It has fought for the setting of just, stable and predictable prices and will continue to do so."[247]

One positive result for the USSR of the drop in oil prices and OPEC's subsequent efforts to restore them came in the late January visit to Moscow of Saudi Arabian oil minister Hisham Nazer. Nazer came to the USSR to discuss the recent OPEC decision and to ask Moscow's support, as an oil exporter albeit not an OPEC member, for the decision. Nikolai Ryzhkov, the Soviet Prime Minister, in his meetings with Nazer stated that "the USSR approves of OPEC's constructive efforts and takes them into account"[248] and Soviet Foreign Ministry spokesman, Gennady Gerasimov, then announced that "as a result of our talks with the Saudi oil minister, we are cutting back our exports." Nazer was later quoted as saying that the cutback would be 7 percent.[249] Given the fact that the USSR had long wanted diplomatic relations with Saudi Arabia, one of the most important countries in the Arab world, it was not surprising that Ryzhkov also took the opportunity of the Nazer visit to stress that the USSR wanted "normal relations and cooperation on an equal basis with all states," and that it favored mutually advantageous ties with Saudi Arabia, including ties in the area of trade, science, and culture.[250]

During his visit, Nazer also met with Soviet Foreign Minister Shevardnadze, and one of the subjects they discussed was the rapidly escalating Iran–Iraq war that was a subject of great concern both for the USSR and Saudi Arabia. At the beginning of 1987, Iran had launched another major offensive against Iraq, and, clearly in reaction to the offensive, Moscow began to tilt toward Iraq. Thus, on January 9, the USSR issued its most detailed condemnation of the war to date, one clearly timed as a reaction to the Iranian offensive and one that was, in its proposed solution to the war, far closer to the Iraqi than the Iranian position in that it called for a return to the pre-war borders, "non-interference in each other's internal affairs," and the right of every people "to independence and freedom" and "to choose its own way of life" – a clear rejection of the Iranian goal of deposing Saddam Hussein and setting up an Islamic republic in Iraq.[251] At the same time, the Soviet delegate to the United Nations, Alexander Belongov, blamed Iran for continuing the war, and characterized Iran as an aggressor nation that should be deprived of arms.[252] The new chill in Soviet–Iranian relations was also reflected in an article in *Pravda* which strongly criticized the mistreatment of jailed Iranian communists.[253] Meanwhile, Soviet propaganda was also exploiting a *New York Times* report that the US had provided misleading intelligence information to Iraq,[254] something Iraq's First Deputy Prime Minister, Taha Ramadan, then blamed for the loss of the Fao Peninsula to the Iranians in February 1986.[255] While the US denied Ramadan's charge, the leading Soviet Middle East commentator, Pavel Demchenko, in a *Pravda* article on January 25, cited it as evidence that the US wanted to prolong the war so as to strengthen the US position in the Gulf. Demchenko's article was also critical of Iran for launching its new offensive and it called upon Tehran to respond to the UN call for a cease-fire.

It was in this atmosphere that Iranian Foreign Minister, Ali Akhbar Velayati, journeyed to Moscow in mid-February. Velayati met first with Andrei Gromyko, the President of the USSR, who took a very tough line with the visiting Iranian (*Pravda* described the atmosphere of their talks as being "frank and businesslike"),[256] blaming Iran both for continuing the Iran–Iraq war and for aiding the Afghan insurgents from bases in Iranian territory. Gromyko warned that Iran bore "full responsibility" for allowing the Afghan guerrillas to use its territory, and urged Velayati to influence the Afghans living in Iran to accept the Afghan government's offer of national reconciliation.[257] Velayati had an apparently more successful visit with Shevardnadze in which the Iranian, utilizing a ploy Iran had employed in the past to entice the USSR into better relations, mentioned a number of economic projects in which it was interested in Soviet assistance. As in the past, Moscow apparently was willing to be enticed, with the *Pravda* report of the talks noting that the USSR stated its readiness to consider Iran's requests "in a positive manner."[258] Trade was also a major subject of Velayati's talks with Ryzhkov, with *Izvestia*'s report of the talks noting that both Ryzhkov and Velayati had agreed that the present level of Soviet–Iranian trade was below the "available opportunities."[259] Moscow's willingness to consider additional aid to Iran may also have been linked to its concern about a possible Iranian move back to the US, given the failure of the January offensive and Iraqi bombing of Iranian cities. According to a Kuwaiti report, Velayati told Soviet officials that the Iraqi bombardment of Iranian cities had caused great destruction and serious damage and that it was likely to make Iran turn openly to the US.[260]

In examining the Velayati visit there are several issues of importance to note. In the first place, while Iran's agenda was to try to convince Moscow to stop supplying arms to Iraq, Moscow had two major objectives. The USSR wanted both to end the Iran–Iraq war, and by 1987 also to reach a settlement in Afghanistan. Given Iran's position as a major opponent of the Afghan regime, and as a base of support for its enemies, Iranian help to Moscow in achieving a satisfactory settlement in Afghanistan would be very welcome. That Moscow received little support from Iran over the Afghan issue, however, became clear less than two weeks later when a Soviet Persian-language broadcast denounced Iran's leadership for holding "a special consultative meeting with leaders of Afghan counterrevolutionary bands who are ensconced in Iran," issuing "strict orders to prevent the return of Afghan emigrants to their homeland," and using the army to prevent their return.[261] Second, while Moscow was clearly angry with Iran for continuing to prosecute the war, it still had some hope of winning influence in the Khomeini regime (and positioning itself for good relations with a successor regime). For this reason, as well as because of a continuing concern that Iran might yet gravitate back to the US, a concern reinforced by the Iran–Contra affair, Moscow continued to be willing to offer economic assistance to Iran, irrespective of the serious problems that continued to impact on the Soviet–Iranian relationship.

Nonetheless, by March 1987, it was clear that Moscow was tilting to Iraq in the Iran–Iraq war, and this tilt was to continue until June 1987 when the major US reflagging of Kuwaiti tankers once again prompted Moscow to try to court Iran. During the January to June period, Moscow sought to exploit the furor in the Arab world caused by the Iran–Contra affair, by taking an increasingly public anti-Iranian stance. As mentioned above, the scandal had put the United States on the diplomatic defensive in the Middle East as many of the Arab states which had looked to it for protection against Iran became bewildered at the "arms for hostages" diplomacy carried on by the United States with Iran. This created somewhat of a vacuum in Middle East diplomacy, and Moscow sought to exploit this situation in two ways. First, by agreeing to a Kuwaiti request to charter three of its ships, Moscow sought to demonstrate that, as in the case of the Arab–Israeli conflict, while the US was arming the enemy of the Arabs, the USSR was aiding the Arabs themselves. Moscow also moved to improve ties with American ally Egypt by moving ahead with the rescheduling of Egypt's military debt. The Egyptians, perhaps reciprocating the Soviet gesture, in turn agreed not only to reestablish the Egyptian–Soviet Friendship Society but also to appoint Butros Ghali, Egypt's Minister of State for Foreign Affairs, as its chairman.[262] In addition, Anatoly Gromyko, son of the Soviet President and head of the Soviet Academy of Sciences African Institute, who was in Cairo in mid-February for a joint Egyptian–Soviet symposium on Africa (and who met with Mubarak while there), was quoted in an interview in the Egyptian newspaper *al-Jumhuriyah* as saying: "In the Soviet estimation, Egypt is a friendly country that has great weight in international affairs. We are endeavoring to deepen cooperation with it in certain fields until relations attain the level of the 1950s and 1960s."[263] Moscow, however, clearly still realized that Egypt remained an ally of the US. Indeed, an *Izvestia* article on February 19, analyzing the visit of the US aircraft carrier Nimitz to Alexandria harbor, noted somewhat ruefully that the US aircraft carrier "felt very confident in Egyptian waters." The article went on to say that the main US goal was to "irreversibly drive Egypt into the orbit of US policy in the Middle East. In its efforts to achieve this, the US is ensnaring Egypt not only by means of economic debts, but also by politically compromising it in the eyes of the Arab world, as the Nimitz has done, for instance."[264] The *Izvestia* article seemed to reflect a current of thought in Moscow which, while acknowledging the need for the USSR to improve ties with Egypt, nonetheless continued to be concerned that Egypt, without renouncing Camp David, was increasingly being accepted back into the Arab world, and that despite Irangate the danger still existed of another deal between Israel and her Arab neighbors, based on the Camp David precedent, and mediated by the United States and endorsed by Egypt. For this reason, Moscow had another major incentive to promote an internatonal conference to achieve a Middle East settlement at this time, and it began to step up its efforts to gain Israeli support for the conference.

The idea of an international conference was also increasingly welcome to Shimon Peres who, after stepping down as Prime Minister from the National Unity government in October 1986, had now become Israel's Foreign Minister and Vice Prime Minister. In addition, the United States, with an Irangate-weakened administration, came under increased pressure from Arab states such as Egypt and Jordan to agree to an international conference.[265] It was in part to deflect such pressure that Israeli Prime Minister Yitzhak Shamir traveled to the US in mid-February where he branded the idea of an international conference "a Soviet-inspired notion supported by radical Arabs."[266] (Shamir also, unsuccessfully, sought to get the US government to deny refugee status to Soviet Jews so as to deter them from coming to the United States). At the same time, however, Peres went off to Cairo where he and Egyptian President Hosni Mubarak called for an international conference in which Israel would have the right to approve the participants. Their call for an international conference was reinforced by the EEC who also called for such a conference.[267]

For his part, Shamir stepped up his criticism of the international conference further as his office, on March 11, published a formal statement repudiating the idea of such a conference. In this document he was particularly critical of Soviet efforts to achieve an international conference, claiming that rumors of Soviet efforts to improve Soviet–Israeli relations were essentially "disinformation" and noting that Moscow's goal all along had been a total Israeli withdrawal from territories captured in the 1967 war.[268]

As the internal Israeli debate on an international conference heated up, Moscow began to increase its contacts with Israel to signal its desire for improved ties. The Soviet signals took several forms. On the diplomatic front, there was a meeting in Washington between Israeli Ambassador Meir Rosenne and Soviet Ambassador Yuri Dubinin in late January in which the Soviet Ambassador reiterated the Soviet desire for an international conference and reportedly indicated Moscow was willing to be more forthcoming on Soviet Jewish emigration.[269] According to a report in the Israeli newspaper *Davar*, Dubinin also indicated that Moscow wanted to resume the diplomatic dialogue with Israel and would consider a visit to Israel by a consular delegation.[270] While these diplomatic issues were being discussed, Moscow was sending a number of non-diplomatic delegations to Israel, although given the report of their trips in the Soviet press, the visits clearly had a political function. Thus *Literaturnaia Gazeta*, on January 28, discussed the visit of a Soviet delegation that signed an agreement at the Weizman Research Center on cooperation in the spheres of genetic and cellular research.[271] In addition, *Izvestia* correspondent Konstantin Geivandov, wrote two articles describing his January 1987 visit to Israel that were far less negative about Israel than previous Soviet reporting about Israel had been. He spoke positively of his meeting with a group of Knesset members as "constructive and useful" and noted that these Knesset members had advocated the development of bilateral ties between the Israeli and Soviet publics including ties in the cultural, scientific, and sports areas. He also commented positively on his meetings with members of Israel's peace camp including Shalom Achshav (Peace Now), and Yesh Gvul (There is a Limit). While he also noted a number of negative things about Israel (especially its treatment of the Palestinians) the article was so different in tone from previous Soviet commentaries on Israel that it might be viewed both as another Soviet signal to Israel of

Moscow's interest in improved relations and also as a sign to the Soviet public and the international community that Moscow was preparing to upgrade its ties with Israel.[272]

One of the issues that Soviet delegations always encountered on their visits to Israel (and Geivandov was no exception) was the question of Soviet Jewish emigration. Given the importance of this issue to Israelis, regardless of party, any major move by Moscow toward increasing the number of Jews allowed to emigrate would be seen as a possible sign of the USSR's intention to improve relations. Clearly, however, Soviet Jewish emigration was more than just a bilateral Soviet–Israeli issue. At the Reykjavik summit between Reagan and Gorbachev in October 1986, Reagan had emphasized the issue of Soviet Jewry, thus reminding the Soviet leader that one of the ways Moscow could demonstrate its desire for an improved relationship with the United States was to permit an increase in the number of Soviet Jews allowed to leave the USSR. (Secretary of State Shultz's participation in a Passover Seder with Refuseniks during his Moscow visit in mid-April 1987 made the same point). Consequently, as Gorbachev decided to rapidly move for nuclear arms agreements with the US, he must have realized that an increase in the number of Soviet Jews allowed to emigrate would reap important political benefits in the US. At the same time, however, the increase in emigration would also, or so Gorbachev probably hoped, win important political benefits in Israel, at least from the Labor Party whose leader, Shimon Peres, when Prime Minister in 1985, as noted above, had cited increased emigration of Soviet Jews as the price for Soviet participation in an international peace conference.[273]

Thus, although a more restrictive emigration decree went into effect on January 1 that limited emigration to first degree relatives (mother, father, sister, brother, child) of people abroad, statements by a number of Soviet officials indicated that emigration would rise, and indeed, after averaging less than 100 per month in 1986, emigration shot up to 470 in March 1987 and 717 in April, with a *Novosti* official, Sergei Ivanko, predicting an exodus of 10–12,000 by the end of the year.[274] It was in this atmosphere that two major non-Israeli Jewish leaders, Morris Abram, President of both the National Conference on Soviet Jewry and the Conference of Presidents of Major Jewish Organizations, and Edgar Bronfman, President of the World Jewish Congress, journeyed to Moscow in late March and met with a number of Soviet officials including Anatoly Dobrynin, the former Soviet Ambassador to the United States, who was now the director of the International Department of the

CPSU Central Committee. According to Abram, they received "assurances" from the USSR in a number of areas pertaining to Soviet Jewry, in return for their willingness to consider changes to the Jackson–Vanik and Stevenson amendments, which limited trade with and credits to the USSR. Given the importance of this meeting, the text of the "assurances" in the Abram report is listed below:[275]

1 Soviet Jews with exit visas for Israel will travel via Romania on flights to be established.

2 All Refuseniks and their families will be allowed to emigrate to Israel within a one-year period, except for legitimate national security cases. A procedure will be established, however, to review previous visa denials on national security grounds. This procedure may involve officials on a level as high as the Supreme Soviet.

3 First degree relatives may emigrate for family reunification within an established time frame. There may be flexibility within the framework of the current narrow interpretation of "first degree relative."

4 Cases of those Refuseniks recently placed in a "never allowed to emigrate" category will be reviewed.

5 All Jewish religious books may be imported into the USSR, and a recommended list of books will be submitted.

6 Synagogues will be opened in all sites where there is a demonstrated need.

7 Soviet Jews will be allowed greater access to rabbinical training. Some may even be allowed to study in the United States.

8 The teaching of Hebrew in school or synagogue settings will be considered together with similar restrictions applied to other religious groups.

9 A kosher restaurant will be opened in Moscow, and liberal provisions will be made for ritual slaughter.

The Bronfman–Abram mission got a mixed reaction in Israel. While Peres warmly endorsed it, Shamir deprecated its value and Soviet Jewry activists such as Anatoly Sharansky, Lev Elbert, and Yuri Shtern, fearing that once the 10,000 Refuseniks were allowed to leave, the gates would close permanently, denounced it, with Elbert claiming it was a "trade of 3,500 families for 2 million people waiting to leave."[276]

In arranging the meeting with Abram and Bronfman (although subsequently denying that any "deal" had been made),[277] Moscow apparently had two goals. In the first place, with a new summit on the horizon because Gorbachev had "decoupled" SDI from other arms agreements, and with the Soviet leader now energetically pushing his plan for an intermediate range nuclear arms agreement, the sharp increase in the number of Soviet Jews allowed to leave the USSR, the promise of a still greater exodus inherent in the Bronfman–Abram visit, and the Soviet decision to free almost all the jailed prisoners of Zion (those imprisoned for wanting to go to Israel), all clearly had major public relations value in the United States. In addition, however, it also gave political ammunition to Peres who saw in the increased emigration the price which Moscow was paying to qualify for attendance at an international conference. For his part, Shamir sought to counter this development by formally separating the issue of Soviet–Israeli relations from the Soviet Jewry issue, a development that angered Soviet Jewish activists in Israel.[278]

Meanwhile, however, Peres pursued his efforts for an international conference. Meeting for the first time publicly with pro-PLO Palestinians, Peres claimed that the Palestinians expressed the desire for Palestinian representatives acceptable to Israel.[279] At the same time, China, also evidently interested in an international conference, began formal diplomatic talks with Israel at the United Nations.[280] As the momentum for the conference built up, the Soviets, following up the January talks between Dubinin and Rosenne, announced they wanted to send a consular delegation to Israel (albeit without any reciprocal visit by an Israeli delegation),[281] and Peres stated that Moscow had already requested visas for the delegation.[282]

Thus, in early April, as Peres set out for visits to Spain and to the Socialist International meeting in Rome, he was actively pushing for an international conference, and Shamir, who was just as actively opposing the conference, publicly stated that he hoped Peres's efforts to arrange an international peace conference would fail.[283] It was thus in an atmosphere of the beginning of a domestic political crisis in Israel, that Peres met with two high-ranking Soviet officials in Rome, Karen Brutents, deputy director of the International Department of the CPSU and his Middle East advisor Alexander Zotov, in what Peres was later to describe as "the first serious direct dialogue between the two nations."[284] The meeting created a major political stir in Israel with Peres, although agreeing to keep the details of the six hours of discussions secret,[285] giving the impression of major progress in the negotiations both in terms of the exodus of Soviet Jews and in the improvement of Soviet–Israeli relations, and going so far as to assert that "if there is no international peace conference within the next few months, the chance for peace could slip away."[286] He also leaked the information that the USSR had spoken against any "coercion" by the superpowers in the context of an international peace conference, or by the conference itself; that Moscow had agreed to the idea of bilateral talks as part of the international conference, and that they had spoken of Palestinian representation at the conference in more general terms than just the PLO.[287]

The Likud political counterattack was not long in coming. Even as Peres was meeting with the Soviet officials in Rome, the Likud chairperson of the Knesset subcommittee on immigration, Uzi Landau, accused Peres of creating the impression that moves toward an international conference were a condition for Jewish emigration from the USSR.[288] Shamir was even sharper in his criticism on April 10 denouncing the idea of an international conference as "national suicide."[289] The Labor Party, in a formal meeting several days later, responded by stating that it would not accept any reduction in the pursuit of the peace process and the resumption of emigration from the USSR, and asserted that Shamir's statement that the idea of an international conference was conceived by Peres during a nightmare might deal a blow to Israel's vital interests and the government's performance. The Labor Party also stated that Peres would submit a "practical proposal" for convening an international conference to the government within a few weeks.[290] For its part, the Likud Party through a spokesman, Yosi Ahimeir, issued a statement that Israel's willingness to take part in the Geneva talks (the international conference planned for 1977) became null and void with the signing of Camp David. The statement also noted that Likud was the first to start the struggle for the sake of Soviet Jewry, and that the (Labor) Alignment's claim that Likud was curbing the emigration of Soviet Jewry "is astonishing and ridiculous." Ahimeir also stated that "there is no connection whatsoever and there should be no connection between emigration and the concession of Judea and Samaria."[291] Shamir himself, seeking to rally the Soviet Jewish activists in Israel in his political battle to torpedo Peres's plan for an international conference, deprecated Peres's efforts to show there had been a real change in Soviet policy, asserting:

> there are only rumors and piecemeal reports about a few hundred Jews who have been allowed out, but this does not represent a change. If the Soviet Union wants to improve its image and attain a different attitude

from the West by changing its policy on Jewish emigration, it must open its gates and allow hundreds of thousands of Jews out without imposing any restrictions and qualifications. We must not sell the Jewish cause cheaply.[292]

While the internal Israeli debate raged in April, Moscow was not idle elsewhere in the Middle East. On the one hand it took an active role in the Palestine National Council meeting in Algiers to help the PLO regain a modicum of unity, as the Soviet ambassador to Algeria, Vasily Taratura, reportedly helped mediate disputes between Arafat and his erstwhile Palestinian enemies, George Habash of the Popular Front for the Liberation of Palestine and Naef Hawatmeh, of the Democratic Front for the Liberation of Palestine.[293] Possibly in return for Soviet help (an earlier conference in Czechoslovakia in September 1986 had begun the process of reunification),[294] or possibly because Arafat was more dependent on Moscow for support because of his poor relations with Syria (the Syrian-based Palestinian groups composed of the Abu Musa faction of Fatah, Saiqa and the PFLP-GC refused to attend the PNC meeting), and because Hawatmeh and Habash had pressured Arafat into agreeing – at least on paper – to sharply curtail ties with Egypt, as well as to publicly renounce the Hussein–Arafat agreement of February 1985, the USSR obtained a seat on the PLO Executive Committee for the pro-Soviet Palestinian communist party whose representative, Sulayman Najjab, would now play a role in PLO policy-making.[295]

On balance, the outcome of the PNC meeting in Algiers was a major success for the USSR. In the first place, the formal abrogation of the Hussein–Arafat agreement[296] seemed to remove the danger, at least for the time being, of a US-mediated deal between Israel and a Jordanian–Palestinian delegation dominated by King Hussein. Second, the partial reunification of the PLO with the effective dissolution of one of the main groups opposing Arafat, the Palestine National Salvation Front, was another step toward Palestinian unity which Moscow has seen as the *sine qua non* for the anti-imperialist Arab unity it had sought for so long. Third, the resolutions at the conference had a distinctly pro-Soviet and anti-American tone.[297] Thus not only did they call for the fostering of the joint Pan-Arab struggle against imperialism and Zionism ("particularly the strategic US–Israeli alliance"), and for "strengthening military relations of alliance with the Socialist bloc countries, foremost of which is the Soviet Union," they also supported Soviet proposals for ending the arms race. Perhaps most important, the Palestine National Council adopted the Soviet plan for an international conference on a Middle

East peace settlement with "full powers," in which the PLO would participate "on an equal footing," and also supported the Soviet plan for a preparatory committee to arrange it. Finally, Moscow had to draw satisfaction from one of the immediate results of the conference – a sharp deterioration of relations between the PLO and Egypt's President Hosni Mubarak whose reaction to what Egyptian Foreign Minister Esmat Abdel-Maguid called an act of "insolence" by the PNC, was to shut all PLO offices in Egypt except those dealing with labor and women's affairs.[298] (The PNC had "entrusted" the PLO Executive Committee to define Egyptian–Palestinian relations on the basis of the 16th PNC session of 1983, which had condemned Egypt for Camp David and stated that relations with Egypt would depend on "how far Egypt retreats from Camp David").[299] Moscow may have felt that the PNC action against Egypt (however much Arafat had tried to water it down) would pose a barrier to any future cooperation between Egypt and Arafat on a US-sponsored peace initiative, while serving to further delegitimize the Camp David peace process.

While all of these PNC developments could be seen as positive for the USSR, there was also a major problem for Moscow as a result of the PNC meeting – the increasingly severe split between Assad and Arafat. Even before the PNC meeting, relations between the two, already bad, were worsening. Syrian-supported Amal troops had besieged the Palestinian refugee camps of Shatilla and Barj el-Baranjeh from October 1986 until April 1987, as both Amal leader Nabbi Berri and Assad shared the goal of preventing the reemergence of an independent Palestinian military presence in Lebanon. The camp siege, however, as in 1985, had driven the PFLP and DFLP back toward Arafat as their forces joined together to fight Amal. Indeed, Assad may have ordered a truce and the lifting of the siege in early April in an unsuccessful effort to prevent the PFLP and DFLP leaders from reconciling with Arafat.[300] Consequently, while a *Pravda* article by Middle East commentator Pavel Demchenko took a very positive view of the PNC meeting, it also called upon the PLO to improve its ties with Syria:

> Summarizing the course of the 6 days of, at times, stormy debate and the decisions made in Algiers, one comes to the conclusion that the PLO has demonstrated that it is a real force to be reckoned with. It succeeded in resolving many organizational problems and determining its political platform. The documents adopted point out the importance of rallying the Palestinian ranks on an anti-imperialist basis, reaffirm the rejection of capitulationist deals of the Camp David type, and voice

support for the Soviet proposal to hold an international conference on the Middle East with the participation of all interested parties, including the PLO.

> Naturally, the session could not answer all the questions and untie all the knots – this applies particularly to regularizing ties with Arab governments. I would especially like to note that the effectiveness of the program outlined will depend to a large extent on what the Palestinian liberation movement's relationship is like with the other forces opposing imperialism and Zionism, *first and foremost with Syria*.[301] (emphasis mine)

Moscow had the opportunity to try to promote Syrian–Palestinian cooperation while the PNC meeting was still in progress, since on April 24 Syrian President Assad began talks in Moscow with Gorbachev. During a dinner speech, Gorbachev frankly noted that the USSR was "saddened by the disunity, friction, and conflicts in the Arab world which are vigorously exploited by imperialists and their henchmen. Naturally, we saw a good sign in the current efforts to restore the unity of the PLO."[302] For his part, Assad made no gesture toward compromise with the PLO, noting only that Syria also supported Arab solidarity to confront imperialism and Zionism and was "working for a Palestinian National will on a similar basis."[303] The joint communiqué issued after the visit merely reiterated the previous joint Soviet–Syrian position on the Palestinian question: "the need to restore unity in the ranks of the Palestinian resistance movement on a principled, anti-imperialist platform was stressed."[304]

Yet, Palestinian affairs were not the only issue of controversy to arise during the Assad visit, as the *Pravda* description of the talks noted that they had taken place "in an atmosphere of friendship and mutual understanding."[305] Gorbachev was clearly out to signal to Israel Moscow's peaceful intentions, and the Moscow visit of the Jewish state's most implacable enemy provided an excellent opportunity. Thus Gorbachev lectured Assad on the need, in the nuclear age, to solve the Arab–Israeli conflict by political means:

> Today the realities of the nuclear age face us all with the need to coexist with each other, irrespective of whether we like each other or not and regardless of differences in our political and socioeconomic systems or ideological views ... We see a just settlement of the Middle East conflict – one of the most complex and involved of the regional conflicts – along political tracks...[306]

Gorbachev also made a major point about Soviet–Israeli relations:

Much has been said lately about relations between the Soviet Union and Israel, and a lot of lies have been spread too. Let me put it straight. The absence of such relations cannot be considered as normal. But they were severed by Israel in the first place. It happened as a result of the aggression against the Arab countries. We recognize without any reservation – to the same extent as with all other states – the right of Israel to a peaceful and secure existence. At the same time, like in the past, the Soviet Union is categorically opposed to Tel Aviv's policy of strength and annexation. It should be plain – changes in relations with Israel are conceivable only in the mainstream of the process of settlement in the Middle East. This issue cannot be taken out of such a context.[307]

While Gorbachev was emphasizing the need for a political and peaceful settlement of the Arab–Israeli conflict, and indicating to Israel in the process that the resumption of diplomatic relations would not necessarily require a prior Israeli troop withdrawal, Assad was taking a much tougher line. Perhaps hoping to embarrass Gorbachev into increasing Soviet aid to Syria, to the point of the parity Assad had long wanted, the Syrian leader emphasized that increasing US aid to Israel enabled it to continue to occupy Arab territories and resist an international conference.[308] The joint Soviet–Syrian communiqué following the talks called for a total withdrawal of Israeli troops from all territories occupied since 1967, an independent Palestinian state, a return of Palestinian refugees to their homes, and echoed the Soviet call for an international conference under UN auspices, and with a preparatory committee to arrange it.[309]

Another issue discussed by the two leaders was the political influence of religious movements. In part, this may have reflected Moscow's unhappiness that a number of Lebanese communists had been murdered by Islamic fundamentalists prior to the Syrian entry into West Beirut in mid-February to put down intra-communal fighting (an action praised by Moscow).[310] It may also have related to Moscow's hope that Syria could use its influence with Iran to help bring the Iran–Iraq war to an end. One of the major barriers to Arab unity had been Syrian (and Libyan) support of Iran while the rest of the Arab world supported Iraq, and Gorbachev may have utilized the first visit by Assad to the USSR in two years to press upon the Syrian leader the need to end the war. Interestingly enough, while Gorbachev stressed this point in his speech to Assad, Assad did not mention it in his dinner speech and the joint communiqué noted only:

The cessation of the bloody conflict between Iraq and Iran, imposed upon two neighborly peoples, and which had bled the resources of these countries, would be a major contribution to the cause of the overall improvement of the situation in the Near and Middle East, and would strengthen the front of the forces struggling against imperialism and Zionism in this region.[311]

In sum, there was apparently as much controversy as cooperation during the Assad visit to Moscow, although Gorbachev's comment at the beginning of his dinner speech that the USSR had indicated its willingness to "assist Syria further in maintaining her defense capacity at the proper level" may have been aimed at reassuring the Syrian leader.[312] Nonetheless, despite a successful joint space flight in July that the Soviet media exploited to demonstrate Soviet–Syrian and Soviet–Arab cooperation, tensions clearly continued between the two countries.[313] As in the past, there were Syrian complaints about insufficient Soviet military aid, with the outspoken Syrian Defense Minister Mustafa Talas complaining in a *Washington Post* interview that during the April trip to Moscow in which he had accompanied Assad, "we had to negotiate, bargain, and fight bullet by bullet, cannon by cannon, and bomb by bomb and we still got the minimum of our needs."[314] While Western intelligence sources noted that Syria had acquired two squadrons (24) of MIG-29s from the USSR, Syria's Arab enemy Iraq got them first, and Talas admitted that a lack of financial resources was hampering Syria from reaching its goal of strategic parity with Israel. (In another *Washington Post* interview, Assad had reiterated that parity remained Syria's goal).[315] Talas also asserted that Syria paid cash for Soviet weapons and did so to maintain its independence from Moscow. (He conveniently skipped over the fact that funds from Saudi Arabia had heretofore paid for most of Syria's Soviet arms). Talas's comments may have been aimed at contrasting the Syrian–Soviet relationship with the Israeli–US one, because Israel was receiving a large part of its weaponry from the United States free of charge.

In any case, as Moscow, in late April, was seeking to profit from the decisions of the PNC and to use the Assad visit to Moscow both to encourage Syrian–PLO cooperation and to signal Israel that Moscow genuinely wanted peace[316] and was willing to directly confront its ally Syria with that fact; a full-fledged political crisis had erupted in Israel, with Peres using the issue of an international conference to try to bring down the National Unity government. Indeed, Peres went so far as to claim that Israel had "an opportunity that we have not had (for peace) since the creation of the State of Israel."[317] In using such hyperbole, however, he left open some very basic questions about the international conference such as: (1) who would represent the Palestinians (Peres claimed Jordan had agreed to abandon the PLO which had broken with it at the PNC conference in Algiers, but King Hussein, who by many accounts had met secretly with Peres in London, denied this);[318] (2) the role of the USSR at the conference (in none of its public statements had Moscow agreed to the basically ceremonial role Peres had stated for it); and (3) whether or not the conference as a whole would have to confirm the decisions of the bilateral committees (the USSR had continued to indicate it wanted the conference as a whole to approve all bilateral agreements, in short, to be an "authoratative conference"). In any case, the debate, at least in the short run, became academic as Peres found he did not have sufficient Knesset votes to bring down the government on the issue of an international conference, and by mid-May he announced he was not going to submit the plan for the international conference to the Israeli cabinet.[319] While Peres's failure was primarily due to the clever political maneuvering of Shamir, it was also due in part to the PNC meeting in Algiers where neither the resolutions of the PNC nor the rhetoric of Arafat was conducive to attracting the Israelis to participate in an international conference. Not only did the PNC resolutions advocate "armed struggle" and reject UN Resolution 242, and refer to Israel as the "Zionist enemy," but Arafat both called for a "united national state" like Canada and proclaimed that "this land, including Jerusalem, headed by Jerusalem, will remain Arab, Arab, Arab."[320] Such statements could only strengthen Israeli opposition to attending an international peace conference with members of the PLO.

Interestingly enough, however, despite the fact that Peres was unable to force new elections over the issue of an international conference, Moscow continued to demonstrate its interest in maintaining contacts with Israel. Thus immediately after Peres's political failure, the Soviet ambassador to the US, Yuri Dubinin, reportedly at Soviet request (Moscow claimed it was at Israeli request) met Peres in Washington at the apartment of Edgar Bronfman to discuss the Middle Eastern situation (and the Israeli cabinet debates about the peace process).[321] Then, in July, a Soviet consular team arrived in Israel for a three-month stay. Nonetheless, while clearly increasing the level of their diplomatic contacts with Israel, Moscow played down the significance of this development with the head of the eight member Soviet consular team, Yevgeny Antipov, deputy director of the Consular Directorate of the Soviet

Foreign Service, stating "our mission is not diplomatic, not political. It is purely a technical task (to inventory the property of the Russian Orthodox church and to handle the updating of passports)."[322] Perhaps to balance the impact of the consular delegation's visit, the USSR complained publicly about Israel's development of the Jericho II missile, which Moscow claimed could strike the USSR.[323] On balance, however, Moscow sought to slowly, if steadily, improve Soviet–Israeli ties. Thus, there were numerous conversations between Soviet and Israeli officials (the longest – ten hours – between Peres advisor, Nimrod Novik, and Vladimir Tarasov of the Soviet Foreign Ministry in mid-August),[324] and the Soviets did not even bother to deny the Soviet–Israeli contacts to the Arabs, as Yuli Vorontsov openly spoke about them in a *Rose al-Yusuf* interview,[325] as did Radio Moscow in an Arabic language broadcast in late August.[326]

In addition to the rhetoric, Moscow demonstrated its interest in improved ties with Israel by allowing a second East European ally, Hungary, to establish low-level diplomatic interest section relations with Israel in September 1987. Then after a meeting between Peres and Shevardnadze at the UN at the end of September, Peres claimed that Shevardnadze had both offered Israel a similar interest-section arrangement (which Peres rejected)[327] and that the USSR did not insist that the PLO represent the Palestinians at an international peace conference.[328] Given Peres's habit of exaggerating Soviet offers, it is not surprising that Moscow publicly denied them, as an Israeli journalist, in commenting on Peres's UN performance, noted critically.[329] Nonetheless, it was clear that Moscow was continuing to speak different things to different audiences. On the one hand, it sought to reassure the Arabs by voting to exclude Israel from the General Assembly, and hinting that Arafat would soon be coming to Moscow; at the same time, however, it moved to reassure Israel by extending the stay of its consular team there for an additional three months.[330] In sum, with both the US and Israeli elections now little more than a year away, Moscow was clearly positioning itself for a future diplomatic move by maintaining ties with all sides.

The USSR was to demonstrate a similar flexibility in its policy toward the Gulf war in the spring and summer of 1987. During the spring, Soviet–Iranian relations, which had taken a negative turn following the January 1987 Iranian offensive, continued to deteriorate. As noted above, Moscow, apparently trying to exploit Arab unhappiness with the US because of the Irangate scandal, agreed to a Kuwaiti request to charter three Kuwaiti tankers and said it would escort them with Soviet warships, if necessary, as if to demonstrate that if the US would not aid the Arabs in time of need,[331] the USSR would. Indeed, as a follow up to the charter announcement on April 14, Moscow stated that its deputy Foreign Minister, Vladimir Petrovsky, would visit Kuwait, Iraq, Oman, and the United Arab Emirates. Yet just as the US was later to encounter problems with Iran because of its reflagging operation, so too was the USSR. The day after the Soviet reflagging announcement, Iran's Foreign Ministry called the Soviet move "very dangerous",[332] and three weeks later, on May 6, a Soviet freighter, the *Ivan Karateyev*, was attacked in a daylight raid (so, presumably, the attackers knew it was a Soviet ship) by Iranian patrol boats (Tass called the attack an act of "piracy").[333] Less than two weeks after that attack, a Soviet oil tanker, the *Marshall Chuikov*, which had been chartered by Kuwait, struck a mine in the Gulf.[334] These incidents elicited an angry Soviet response, with Deputy Foreign Minister Vladimir Petrovsky, after returning from his tour of the Gulf Arab states, noting in an interview with *Moscow News* that the "USSR reserved the right to act according to international law (i.e. use self-defense) if provocative action with regard to Soviet ships were repeated."[335] But Iranian attacks on Soviet ships were not the only irritants in the Soviet–Iranian relationship in the late spring. Moscow also complained about pro-Iranian forces in Afghanistan rejecting the Afghan government's ceasefire appeal,[336] and about an article in the Iranian newspaper *Jomhur e-Eslam* which claimed that the Soviet republics of Tadjikistan, Turkmen, and Uzbekistan, as well as some districts in Georgia, were originally Iran's national territory and ought to be liberated.[337] The USSR also emphasized its opposition to Iran's efforts to export Islamic fundamentalism. Gromyko, speaking to a visiting Arab delegation in late April, asserted "no state had the right to interfere in the internal affairs of another, regardless of pretext,"[338] while a Moscow Radio Peace and Progress broadcast in Persian to Iran in early May noted sarcastically "tomorrow Afghanistan or even Turkey may be attacked on the basis of nonsensical pretexts such as a threat against traditional Islamic dress."[339]

Yet, despite the sharp Soviet criticism of Iran, Soviet–Iranian relations were to take a major turn for the better in mid-June as Moscow once again sought to improve ties with Iran, although it would appear that, just as in the past, Iran was once again exploiting the USSR for its own purposes. The cause of the Soviet policy change was the US decision not only to reflag eleven Kuwaiti tankers but also to protect them with a flotilla of the US Navy, which would convoy the ships from the Strait of Hormuz to Kuwait's territorial waters. Moscow saw in this a major American effort both to block growing Soviet influence in the Gulf and to improve its ties with the Arabs after Irangate. In a statement on May 30, Reagan took a strongly anti-Soviet as well as an anti-Iranian position, vowing "the use of the vital sea lanes of the Persian Gulf will not be dictated by the Iranians. These lanes will not be allowed to come under the control of the Soviet Union."[340] On the basis of its own experience with Iran, the USSR may have seen the US move as a source of US–Iranian tension. Given Moscow's earlier concern that Iran's need for weapons might lead it to a *rapprochement* with the United States, any US–Iranian tension over American assistance to Kuwait, a major ally of Iraq in the Iran–Iraq war, could only be welcomed. At the same time, however, as the Iran–Iraq tanker war escalated, Moscow had to be concerned that the US would use the reflagging operation not only to redeem itself in the eyes of the Gulf Arabs after Irangate, but also to obtain naval and air bases in the Gulf. Indeed, Moscow was to claim that the US used the accidental attack by Iraq on the US warship Stark in mid-May as a "Gulf of Tonkin" ploy to accomplish just such an objective.[341] In addition, were Moscow to overtly tilt to backing Iran in the Iran–Iraq war, the USSR ran the risk of alienating Gulf Arab states like Kuwait and Saudi Arabia that it had been diplomatically courting. On the other hand, however, this must have appeared to Moscow to be an opportune time to win the influence in the Khomeini regime it had long sought. Iran was now isolated as never before under the Ayatollah with not only the United States pitted against Iran's regime, but most of the Arab world and Britain and France as well. For this reason Moscow moved openly to improve relations with Iran, while at the same time seeking to end the Gulf war and get the American fleet out of the Gulf. In doing this, however, Moscow sought to avoid alienating either the Gulf Arabs, or the US which it had been urging to cooperate with the USSR in solving regional conflicts such as the Iran–Iraq war.[342] This was, however, to be a very difficult diplomatic tightrope to walk.

Moscow's first move to improve relations with Iran came during a Tehran visit by Yuli Voronstov, now First Soviet Deputy Foreign Minister, in mid-June. As if to reassure the Iranians, who have tended to see the Persian Gulf as their area of dominant influence,[343] before his trip, Voronstov on June 6 announced that the USSR would not augment its force of three warships in the Gulf.[344] During his visit to Tehran,

Voronstov reportedly emphasized four major points: (1) that the USSR does not have parallel interests to the US in the Gulf; (2) that the US was planning projects against both the USSR and Iran in the Gulf; (3) that the USSR did not want foreign (non-Gulf) military forces in the Gulf; and (4) that the USSR had a great deal of respect for the Iranian revolution.[345] The Soviet representative also discussed a number of industrial projects Moscow was interested in helping Iran develop, including the expansion of the capacity of the Isfahan metallurgical complex to 1.9 million tons and the completion and expansion of the Montagen power station.[346] In discussing these issues Moscow appears again to have been seeking to broaden the level of state-to-state economic relations which it hoped would lead to improved political relations, if not with the Khomeini regime, then with its successor.[347]

Vorontsov's reception was a relatively warm one, although Iran's Parliament speaker Hashemi Rafsanjani reportedly told him that the US used the USSR's "small action" in the Gulf as an excuse for adventurism.[348] Nonetheless, in an English language broadcast over Tehran Radio – a possible effort by Iran to signal the US that if it pushed Iran too hard it might move into the Soviet camp – Iranian Prime Minister Hussein Mousavi noted that Iran wanted "clear-cut and friendly relations with the USSR within the framework of [Iran's] principles" and he expressed the hope that "the policies of the two anti-imperialist countries would be coordinated both at the regional and international levels."[349] Nonetheless, it was clear that on the issues of the situation in Afghanistan and the Iran–Iraq war, Tehran was not changing its position. A Tehran Persian language broadcast noted that when Iranian President Ali Khameni met Voronstsov, in addition to calling for "an expansion of relations based on friendship and sincere cooperation" and "totally endorsing" Vorontsov's remarks about Soviet anxiety over US hegemony and its presence in the Gulf, Khameni repeated the "firm Iranian position on the evacuation of Soviet troops from Afghanistan." Khameni also stated "our resolve to punish the [Iraqi] aggressor has become firmer in every way"[350] – a statement unlikely to give Moscow much encouragement that Iran was considering an end to the war.

Nonetheless, following Voronstov's visit to Iran, and his subsequent visit to Iraq, Moscow, on July 3, issued a major new policy statement on the Iran–Iraq war. In it, in a clear demonstration of the similarity of Soviet and Iranian views on the issue, the USSR called for the withdrawal of all foreign ships from the Gulf. Moscow also called for Iran and Iraq to refrain from actions threatening international shipping, for a cease-fire, for the withdrawal of all forces to internationally recognized borders, and also for the UN Secretary General to play a "substantial role" in achieving a just settlement. That the Soviet effort was, in part, also an anti-American propaganda device, however, may be seen from the commentary accompanying the proposal:

> The United States wants to exploit the present alarming situation in the Persian Gulf area to achieve its long harbored plans of establishing military–political hegemony in this strategically important area of the world that Washington is trying to present as a sphere of US vital interests.

> As to several Soviet warships staying in the Persian Gulf to which they in Washington refer, they have to stay in the Gulf for they accompany Soviet merchant ships and have nothing to do with the heightening of tension in the area.[351]

Interestingly enough, however, just before Moscow issued its July 3 statement, there was a meeting in Moscow between US special envoy Vernon Walters and Deputy Soviet Foreign Minister Petrovsky to discuss the Iran–Iraq war, but it was clear from the Soviet statement of July 3 that Moscow saw the tactical advantages it might obtain from gaining influence in Iran to be more important than any joint cooperative efforts with the US to pressure Iran to end the war – a policy Moscow was to continue to follow until the war ended in 1988. Thus while Walters was to say, following his talks, that the US "can count on Moscow's vote for a UN resolution demanding a ceasefire," the US representative, in a news conference following his visit, did not note any Soviet agreement to impose sanctions against Iran if it rejected the ceasefire.[352]

As might be expected, Iran greeted the Soviet proposal for foreign forces to leave the Gulf as a "positive" one,[353] and during a visit to Moscow in mid-July, the Iranian deputy Foreign Minister, Mohammed Larijani, also discussed cooperation in economic areas, including oil and gas.[354] Soon after Larijani's departure, the UN Security Council, on July 20, 1987, unanimously adopted Resolution 598, which called for an immediate ceasefire in the Iran–Iraq war, and the release of prisoners of war. In additional articles, however, it tilted somewhat toward the Soviet July 3 statement by entrusting the UN Secretary General with a mediating mission, and urging all other states to "refrain from any act which may lead to further escalation and widening of the conflict" (Moscow was later to refer to this article to claim the US had violated it by building up its forces in the Gulf). Finally, given Iran's continuing desire to get Iraq condemned for starting the war, an article was inserted about an "impartial body" of inquiry to determine responsibility for the conflict.[355] Given the document's tilt toward the Soviet position, it is not surprising that Moscow praised it,[356] although the US simultaneously emphasized the need for sanctions against Iran if it failed to agree to a ceasefire.[357]

Following the UN resolution which also led to a pause in the tanker war, Moscow adopted a strategy of delaying any attempt to impose sanctions on Iran in an obvious effort to win Iranian goodwill.[358] Thus as the US began its convoy operation, Soviet propaganda began to assert that the US naval build-up in the gulf was as bad a cause of tension as the Iran–Iraq war itself.[359] In addition, Moscow asserted that the US build-up was a violation of the Security Council resolution. At the same time, however, perhaps concerned that the US was winning increased influence among the Arab states of the Gulf,[360] Moscow warned them that the gulf could be a second Vietnam, intimating that just as Vietnam suffered massive destruction at the hands of the US, so too might the Arabs if they got too closely involved with Washington.[361] Moscow also became concerned at this time that America's NATO allies, at first hesitant about the US naval escort program, were now sending their own ships to the Gulf.

Moscow's tilt toward Iran continued with an evenhanded reporting of the Iranian riots in Mecca in late July[362] (something that did not improve Saudi–Soviet relations as the Iranians, following the riots, called for the "uprooting" of the Saudi royal family)[363] and Vorontsov made another visit to Tehran in early August. According to the Iranian version of the visit, Khameni told Voronstov "our people will continue the war until the downfall of the aggressive Iraqi regime"[364] – a blunt rejection of Soviet efforts to achieve a ceasefire. Still, Iran needed the USSR to block follow-up UN Security Council action, including sanctions, against it. So the Iranians made further gestures to give Moscow the feeling it had won influence in Tehran. Thus during the Voronstov visit there were discussions about the export of Iranian oil through the Black Sea, a possible second railroad link, and other aspects of economic cooperation, and deputy Foreign Minister Larijani praised Iranian–Soviet relations as "progressing and developing at a very good level."[365]

Meanwhile, as Soviet–Iranian relations improved, so too did US–Arab relations, as a result of the growing American military presence in the Gulf – something ruefully noted by *Pravda* in late August.[366] During this period Moscow sought to portray Iran as more moderate than it actually was, with a Tass broadcast on August 9 citing Iran's UN representative as saying Iran did not plant mines in international waterways,[367] and asserting that Iran had not specifically rejected UN Resolution 598.[368]

By late August, with tension in the Gulf rising as Iraq resumed its air attacks on shipping heading to Iran and with Iran still rejecting a ceasefire despite the mediating efforts of the UN Secretary General, Arab criticism of Moscow began to mount. Thus, editorials in the Iraqi government newspaper *al-Thawra* called Soviet opposition to sanctions against Iran "shortsighted."[369] A delegation of the Arab League headed by a Kuwaiti official came to Moscow on September 7 to discuss the war. While Moscow sought to blame the rise in tension on the US build-up in the Gulf, and proclaimed its full support for UN Resolution 598,[370] the final communiqué described the talks as having taken place in a "businesslike atmosphere" where a "frank exchange of opinions had taken place" – a clear indication of serious disagreement.[371] Moscow's sensitivity to Arab charges that it was protecting Iran was reflected in a September 9 *Pravda* article which condemned "attempts to cast a shadow on the Soviet Union's policy and drive a wedge in its relations with the Arab states."[372]

Yet at the very same time Moscow was trying to reassure the Arabs, it was entertaining the Iranian deputy Foreign Minister Mohammed Larijani who had come to Moscow for talks on September 9 (perhaps to try to demonstrate an "evenhanded position," Soviet officials met Iraqi Foreign Minister Tariq Aziz the same day). Commentators in Tehran noted that the two countries had agreed in principle on the project for an Iranian oil pipeline through Soviet territory to the Black Sea and had also agreed to draw up plans for building a railway network in Eastern Iran and for joint shipping in the Caspian sea.[373] Clearly, Iran was offering Moscow an increased economic stake in Iran in return for its support in the UN against the US, something Moscow continued to prove willing to do. Indeed, when the US destroyed an Iranian speedboat laying mines in international waters on September 21, Moscow gave the Iranian view of the incident, claiming that the ship was carrying food.[374] Still, as tension – and Arab criticism of the USSR – rose, Moscow employed yet another diplomatic device. This was a call, by Soviet Foreign Minister Shevardnadze at the UN in late September, for a UN force to replace the US and NATO forces in the Gulf.[375] Such a ploy, if successful, might reduce Iranian–US tension, but it would also reduce US influence in the Gulf, an important plus for Moscow. In addition, it would deflect pressure for sanctions against Iran, another of Moscow's goals. Not surprisingly, therefore, the US rejected the plan. Many US observers pointed out that UN forces have historically been effective as peace-keepers, after a war has ended, not in the midst of an on-going conflict, as the history of the UN force in Lebanon (UNIFIL) has demonstrated. In addition, there were such questions as command responsibility and rules of engagement that had to be worked out, clearly a time-consuming process, that would further delay considera-tion of sanctions.

For its part, Iran was showing a measure of appreciation for the Soviet policy, which included getting the Security Council to simultaneously both look into the causes of the Iran–Iraq war to posit blame (an Iranian demand), which was article no. 6 of Resolution No. 598, and work out a ceasefire.[376] Thus on October 1, the Iranian Ambas-sador in the USSR gave a press conference in which he praised the USSR for wanting to pull Soviet troops out of Afghanistan, while criti-cizing the US for wanting the war to continue.[377] Two weeks later, the Soviet airline Aeroflot formally resumed flights to Tehran.[378] Then, in mid-October, as the US was placing an embargo on virtually all imports from Iran, the Iranian oil minister visited Moscow and signed an agree-ment in principle for the supply of Iranian oil for processing at Soviet refineries.[379]

Meanwhile, the USSR was also taking the Iranian side during the two US–Iranian military confrontations in October, with Soviet Foreign Ministry spokesman Gerasimov deeming the US attack on Iran's off-shore oil platform on October 19 "a violation of the UN charter."[380] Nonetheless, as Moscow continued to tilt to Iran, it also sought to shore up its relations with the Gulf Arabs using, as it had in the past, its special relationship with Kuwait to try to accomplish this objective. Thus on October 15, during a Moscow visit by Kuwait's oil minister Ali al-Khalifa, the two countries signed a bilateral cooperation agreement.[381] If Kuwait, despite its unhappiness with the Soviet tilt toward Iran, had arranged Khalifa's visit to Moscow in the hope of deterring Iran, the attempt did not meet with success. Indeed, the day before the agree-ment was signed, on October 14, Iran fired a missile into Kuwait, which hit a tanker located in its port. Moscow's response to the Iranian act took the form of a *Pravda* statement which condemned the attack as "unacceptable from the standpoint of international law, politics and morality."[382]

Nonetheless, as Arab displeasure with the USSR grew – the Iraqi Foreign Minister Tariq Aziz, speaking at a news conference at the UN on October 2 had rejected the Soviet effort to simultaneously effect a cease-fire and set up a commission to determine responsibility for the war,[383] and an Iraqi official was quoted as saying "there is a mini-crisis in our relations with the Soviet Union"[384] – Moscow tried once again to achieve an end to the war. Thus Yuli Voronstov at the end of October traveled to Iraq, Kuwait, and Iran but the Iranians sent a rather important signal of their unwillingness to end the war by launching a missile at Baghdad while Vorontsov was still in the Iraqi capital.[385] Following Vorontsov's return to Moscow, the Iranian Prime Minister, Hussein Mousavi, appeared to put a final end to Voronstov's effort to get Iran to accept UN Security Council Resolution 598 by publicly stating "we have no hope that the UN can do anything about the war."[386]

Mousavi's rather negative comment coincided with the opening of the Arab summit in Amman, Jordan, in early November. The Gulf war dominated the conference as its opening was punctuated by an Iranian missile strike against Baghdad, and the Arabs strongly condemned Iran in most of their resolutions.[387] The central decision of the meeting – to allow each Arab state to decide on its own about restoring diplomatic relations with Egypt – was a major defeat for Soviet efforts to keep Egypt isolated in the Arab world because of its peace treaty with Israel, as the Arabs decided that, despite Camp David, Egypt was needed as a counterweight to Iran. Indeed, in rapid succession Saudi Arabia, Kuwait, the UAE, Bahrein, Qatar, North Yemen, Morocco, and Tunisia restored ties with Egypt. In addition, relatively little attention was paid to the Arab–Israeli conflict at the summit, as the threat from Iran transcended what had heretofore been the Arab world's primary preoccupation – and the lever used by Moscow to increase its influence in the region. *Pravda*'s Middle East commentator, Pavel Demchenko, sought to put the best possible interpretation on the conference, noting that it was a step toward Arab unity and that it had endorsed the Soviet proposal to convene an international conference on the Middle East.[388] Yuri Glukhov, also writing in *Pravda*, took a somewhat more negative view, noting that "the meeting's documents do not contain a single word condemning the policy of US imperialism." He also noted that Egypt was given "an opportunity to emerge from isolation, but there was no rehabilitation of Sadat's policy of separate deals."[389] Perhaps more reflective of Moscow's true feelings about the summit was the *Izvestia* interview with PFLP leader George Habash on November 28:

> We note with profound regret that for the first time in the history of inter-Arab summit meetings, the Amman meeting's final documents for some reason did not mention support for the Palestinian people's legitimate national rights, including their right to self-determination and the creation of an independent sovereign state with its capital in East Jerusalem.

> Furthermore – the decision adopted in Amman to give each state the right to individually decide the question of restoring diplomatic relations with Egypt may lead to the involvement of other Arab countries in the Camp David cause. The meeting in no way condemned the build-up of the US military presence in the Persian Gulf. And in general, it seemed to us that the influence of progressive, patriotic forces was less perceptible in the atmosphere of the summit meeting than at previous such meetings.[390]

Given the strong anti-Iranian position taken by the Arab summit (even Syria joined the Arab call to Iran to accept a cease-fire and withdraw from Iraqi territory), Moscow evidently felt it had to respond. Thus, on November 19, Moscow Radio Peace and Progress, broadcasting to Iran in Farsi, warned:

> We see the formation of a US Middle East strategy on the establishment of bases, as well as the extension of its ambitious hegemonism. In our opinion, this is exactly the very point which should be taken into consideration by those Arab circles that are opening the doors of their countries to US military presence, as well as by those Iranian dignitaries who continue to maintain their stand of "war, war until victory," and who are – irrespective of their inclinations – working against the interests of their peoples and those of regional and international security.[391]

Then, in early December, following the signing of a protocol for the opening of joint shipping routes between Iranian and Soviet ports,[392] Gromyko held a meeting with the Iranian Ambassador to the USSR, Naser Hayrani-Nobair. Gromyko took a relatively hard line with the Iranian envoy as the Soviet President, who was to step down from office the following year, noted that "you as an ambassador and the Iranian leadership made a great number of statements about the wish to end the war. But the war goes on. Iran is practically not carrying matters toward ending the war." Gromyko went on to warn that if UN Resolution 598 were not implemented "the question of further steps toward ensuring the implementation of the decisions adopted by the Security Council might be put on the order of the day," and reminded the Iranian that at the Reagan–Gorbachev summit, which was a few days off, the Iran–Iraq war would be discussed.[393] The tension inherent in the meeting was reflected in *Pravda*'s notation that the talks took place in "a business-like and frank atmosphere."[394]

In addition to its calls to Iran to bring the war to an end, Moscow began to move on the diplomatic front to try to compensate for the events at the Arab summit which it saw as a gain for the US. Thus, Gerasimov in a press briefing on November 30 went beyond the previous Soviet position on the Iran–Iraq war by stating that the USSR would be prepared to have a UN naval force not only escort ships in the Gulf, but also act to implement sanctions.[395] To be sure Gerasimov coupled this offer with a demand that Western nations enact legislation to prohibit both overt and covert trade in arms with any nation that violated UN Resolution 598. To some Americans, mindful of the time it would take to get such legislation passed, this appeared to be yet another delaying tactic by Moscow. Other analysts again raised the problem of command and control inherent in any such UN force.[396] Nonetheless, after Moscow had agreed to a Security Council decision to consider sanctions on December 24, Iran took the Soviet policy change seriously – and in a highly negative manner. Thus on the eighth anniversary of the Soviet invasion of Afghanistan, Iran permitted a group of Afghan demonstrators to attack the Soviet consulate in Isfahan.[397] Moscow lodged a "strong protest" with Iran, claiming that the attack had been carried out by a "group of fanatical elements from the Afghan counterrevolutionaries who are based in Iran."[398] One week later, a commentator on Iranian TV took a highly caustic view of the change in Soviet strategy and warned Moscow not to continue its new policy:

> the Soviet Union feels that because of the possible threat to them posed by the continuation of the war, the reactionary Arab leaders are daily inclining more and more towards the United States and the West. The culmination of this inclination could be seen in the Amman conference and the GCC summit. The Russians feel that if they continue their previous line, they may lose the astronomic loans from the Arabs and their future economic-political presence in Arab countries. They also feel that if they do not react more strongly toward Iran, the Americans will become the only defender among the Arab reactionaries, and this will pave the grounds for the United States to take strategic steps where the future of the Middle East is concerned. At this juncture, the Soviet Union has altered its stand; it is gradually

moving away from its previous position toward a more overt stand on the war. At the same time it is trying, as much as possible, to postpone the moment of decision.

Moscow's request to the UN Secretary General to pay another visit to the region stems precisely from this. But is this a logical policy at a time when the Americans are still prepared at the slightest smile from Tehran to sell out all the Arabs for the sake of establishing a small relationship with Iran? What will the Russians gain from this stand? The United States understands very well Iran's sensitive role in the region and if, under such conditions, the Russians join in the arms embargo, they will destroy all the bridges that have been built so far. Moreover, because of their intrinsic fear of communism and the natural compatibility between their systems and capitalism, the Arabs will certainly not turn toward the Soviet Union. The only outcome of the Russians' act can be that the Americans will benefit and their position will be strengthened.

The strength that Iran has shown in the past year in the Persian Gulf proves the seriousness of the remarks by our officials that if such a plan is implemented, all Persian Gulf ports will become obsolete. If the Russians go along with the Americans in this, they will be repeating the same mistake they once made when they leased their tankers to Kuwait. The difference, though, is that it is easy to make up for some mistakes, but difficult or impossible to do so for others.[399]

In addition to its announced change of policy on the sanctions issue, and perhaps also reacting to another overwhelming defeat in the United Nations on the Afghanistan issue,[400] Moscow moved to assuage Arab unhappiness with Soviet strategy in other ways as well. Thus, it took a harder line on relations with Israel,[401] and as if to make clear that there would be no Soviet–American deal on the Middle East at the expense of the Arabs at the Reagan–Gorbachev summit, the Soviet UN ambassador, in late November, reiterated the Soviet call for the PLO to fully participate in an international conference on the Middle East.[402] In addition, Moscow, perhaps acknowledging the inevitability of Egypt's rejoining the Arab mainstream, sought to make the best of the situation. Thus, Moscow signed a cultural protocol with Egypt for the exchange of films and TV programs on October 22[403] and less than a week later Soviet consulates were reopened in Alexandria and Port Said.[404] At the end of December Moscow signed a long-term trade pact with Egypt that doubled the trade between the two countries.[405] Even more important, however, was the fact that Egypt now became a regular stop on Soviet diplomatic trips to the Middle East, with important visits by Voronstov in October 1987 and Karen Brutents in January 1988[406] as Moscow may have hoped to pull Egypt away from the US to a more neutralist position.

The main Soviet diplomatic effort, however, came with the visit of King Hussein of Jordan to Moscow in late December as the Soviet media sought to portray the visit as an important example of Soviet–Arab friendship.[407] Given the fact that *Pravda* described the talks as taking place in an atmosphere of "mutual understanding" and noted an "in-depth exchange of views,"[408] there were clearly areas of disagreement between the two sides, most probably on the Iran–Iraq war as Hussein, after making a major gesture to Moscow by rejecting US plans to solve the Arab–Israeli conflict without the help of the USSR, then urged Gorbachev to accept an embargo on weapons shipments to Iran.[409] Gorbachev hedged on this issue, noting only that the USSR was "not against discussion" of the embargo in the UN Security Council. The Soviet leader then sought to cast blame on the United States, doubting whether "those who are shouting louder than anyone else for an embargo, and who, by the way, were found to be delivering arms secretly to Iran, are ready to observe it."[410]

In February 1988, a month and a half after Hussein's visit to Moscow, Gorbachev made a major move to improve Soviet ties with both the Arab world and Iran by announcing his decision to pull out of Afghanistan. The Soviet leader sent special envoys to virtually every Arab state as well as to Iran to inform them of the withdrawal and seek their aid in assisting it, by using their influence to get Pakistan and the US to agree to Soviet conditions for the withdrawal at the Geneva talks.[411] The Khomeini regime, while welcoming the Soviet move and calling it a "positive development," nonetheless expressed reservations that it might be a ploy to keep the Najibullah regime in power and prevent the "Afghan Moslem people and revolutionaries" from controlling their own country.[412] Soviet Deputy Foreign Minister Vladimir Petrovsky flew to Iran on February 11 to explain the withdrawal to the Iranian leadership, but was told by Iranian Foreign Minister Velayati that Iran expected that the Mujahadeen would have a "fundamental and decisive" role in the future of Afghanistan which should be "independent and non-aligned."[413] Majlis speaker Rafsanjani went so far as to apparently offer Petrovsky a deal on this point, noting that "if you are determined to pull out of Afghanistan, we are prepared to assist you, so that after your departure there will be no US domination in

Afghanistan."[414] While Foreign Minister Velayati was to give an overall positive evaluation of the Petrovsky visit,[415] differences on the role of the Mujahadeen remained, and on February 23 the Afghan Muslim Council issued a strongly worded anti-Soviet statement in Tehran rejecting the idea of any compromise with "Soviet-inspired groups who are responsible for the social calamities in Afghanistan."[416] Meanwhile, Soviet–Iranian relations continued to be irritated by what Tehran saw as Soviet acquiescence in the continued US attempts to achieve an arms embargo against Iran.[417] In fact, despite extensive US and Arab pressure, the USSR continued to delay action on the sanctions, and neither the Moscow visits of Saudi Foreign Minister Prince Saud Faisal and Iraqi Foreign Minister Tariq Aziz,[418] nor repeated urgings by the US administration and Congressional leaders,[419] nor the Riyadh visit of Soviet Foreign Ministry Middle East Department head, Vladimir Polyakov, seemed to move Moscow to do anything more than give oral support to the idea of sanctions.[420]

While the Soviet Union's balancing act on the sanction issue appeared to be costing it diplomatic support both in Iran and in the Arab world, and also raising questions in Washington as to how far the "new thinking" in Moscow had really affected Soviet foreign policy, Moscow was to suffer a severe blow to its relationship to Iran at the end of February when Iraq launched a missile attack against Tehran.[421] The Iranian leadership denounced the USSR for supplying Iraq with the missiles, and Iranian protesters marched on the Soviet embassy in Tehran and the Soviet consulate in Isfahan, shouting "death to Russia."[422] While Moscow denied supplying the missiles, the Iranian leadership rejected the Soviet denials, with Rafsanjani asserting that the Iranian people would "never forget the Soviet Union's impudence" in supplying Iraq with missiles, and stating "this will definitely affect our future relations" with the USSR.[423] Rafsanjani also asserted at a news conference that the Soviet Union was "currently pursuing a policy of hypocrisy and duplicity" by putting the missiles at Iraq's disposal, and providing parts to modify the missiles and increase their range.[424] Meanwhile, Iran's Deputy Foreign Minister, Javad Larijani, also speaking at a press conference in Tehran, noted that on his recent trip to Moscow he "clearly told the Soviet President and Prime Minister that any missile or bomb given to the tottering regime of Iraq by the Soviet Union will first hit Tehran–Moscow relations before hitting Iranian soil."[425]

The Soviet Union, clearly troubled by the Iranian response to the Iraqi missile barrage, sought to assuage Iranian anger by leading an effort in the UN Security Council to achieve an end to the "war of the cities"[426] although the Soviet effort was to prove ineffective. One month later, Tehran denounced the US–Soviet agreement on Afghanistan that was signed in mid-April in Geneva, because it did not include the Mujahadeen.[427] Moscow was then to use another ploy to try to improve ties with Iran as on April 20 it sought to politically exploit the US attack on Iranian off-shore oil platforms which followed the mining of a US warship. The US attack coincided with a major Iraqi offensive in the Fao Peninsula;[428] and Radio Tehran, claiming that the US attack was aimed at giving "direct support" to Iraq, denounced the "Eastern and Western superpowers" for aiding Iraq.[429] Soviet commentators criticized the American action, which quickly escalated into a battle between the US and Iranian navies, with Tass commentators calling the attack "an act of aggression" and "a gangsterlike act."[430] A Soviet Foreign Ministry spokesman, Vadim Perfilyev, labelled it a "gross violation of international law" taken in "total disregard for world public opinion."[431]

The ploy, however, did not appear to meet with too much success, as Tass news analyst Valery Vavilov somewhat ruefully acknowledged, as he deplored Rafsanjani's claim that the US attack was part of a "coordinated campaign of the United States, the Soviet Union, and Kuwait."[432] A Radio Peace and Progress broadcast, in Persian, to Iran on April 25 made this point more clearly, denouncing Iranian claims that the USSR was "hand-in-hand" with the US in a coordinated effort to destroy the Islamic republic, and that Iran was now a target of hostile actions agreed to by the Soviet Union and the United States.[433] Moscow also deplored Iran's role in splitting Muslim unity through its refusal to end the war (diplomatic relations between Iran and Saudi Arabia had just been broken by Riyadh), with another Moscow Radio Peace and Progress broadcast in Persian going so far as to assert:

> Those who support a protraction of the Iran–Iraq conflict hide their spiteful programs under the shield of religious slogans. They regard war as a decisive means in the struggle for leadership in the Islamic world. Such a policy can yield the most dangerous results under current international conditions.[434]

By June, Soviet–Iranian relations had sharply deteriorated and this development was spelled out in detail by the Iranian newspaper *Kayhan International*, in an editorial on June 27:

> The Iranian nation and leadership have been alarmed at the rate Iraq's

arsenals have been stock-piled after Gorbachev took the helms of power. Long-range Soviet missiles have rained on innocent Iranian civilians. Soviet MIGs are responsible for a very large number of Iranian non-military casualties. And these inhumane events have unfolded parallel to Mr. Gorbachev's image-building efforts at home and abroad ... As things appear to be, the Soviets have failed to win substantial influence in Tehran. Nearly 10 years of diplomatic, political and economic relations with the Islamic republic has surely not placed the Kremlin in a better position than the White House in the eyes of 50 million Iranians.[435]

Moscow was to try to again exploit a US–Iranian clash in early July when a US cruiser, after a battle with Iranian gunboats, accidentally shot down an Iranian civilian airliner. Soviet commentators, again strongly endorsing the Iranian version of the incident, condemned the action, with one hinting that it was "premeditated aggression"[436] and others, including *Pravda*, calling it "cold-blooded murder" and an attempt to intimidate Iran.[437] Moscow also sought to use the airbus affair to mobilize diplomatic pressure on the United States to pull its naval forces out of the Gulf – a goal shared by Iran.[438]

In any case, less than three weeks after its airliner was shot down, Iran agreed to accept UN Resolution 598. Suffering major losses on the battlefield in the April–July 1988 period, including the loss of the Fao Peninsula, and in the face of both missile and poison gas attacks by Iraq, Iran changed its previous position and reluctantly accepted the UN resolution without conditions, in an action which Khomeini himself called "more lethal for me than poison."[439] As might be expected, the USSR warmly welcomed an end to the war that had caused it so many problems in the Middle East for the past eight years.[440] Yuli Voronstov flew to Tehran to immediately consult with Iranian leaders and reportedly took the opportunity to condemn the shooting down of the Iranian airliner as an "act of barbarity," as he sought to once again exploit US–Iranian hostility and open a new page in Soviet–Iranian relations.[441] According to the Soviet account of the visit, Voronstov also urged the Iranian leadership to help to "normalize the situation in Afghanistan."[442] Rafsanjani, however, in a speech on August 11 claimed that the Soviets had offered to cut their arms shipments to Iraq if Iran agreed to support "the subservient government in Afghanistan" – an action which Iran rejected "on principle."[443]

Meanwhile, Iran's agreement to UN Security Council Resolution 598 did not immediately end the war as both Iran and Iraq continued their military efforts to gain political advantage while UN Secretary General Perez de Cuellar sought to work out a cease-fire. In the midst of the fighting another Arab delegation came to Moscow on August 10 seeking Soviet support to end the war. While Moscow sought to use the visit to gain support for the ouster of the US fleet from the Gulf, the Arab delegation, composed of the Kuwaiti Foreign Minister Sheikh Sabah al-Ahmad As-Sabah and the Iraqi Minister of State for Foreign Affairs, Sadun Hammadi, clearly wanted the USSR to pressure Iran, with Sheikh Sabah stating that the role of the superpowers should be "to back the direct negotiations between the two parties and pressure, in the event those negotiations fail, the party that is not prepared to achieve peace and that exploited the 598 Resolution to realize a truce."[444]

On August 20, a month after Iran formally accepted UN Resolution 598, a cease-fire finally came into effect although the Iran–Iraq conflict appeared to simply move from the battlefield to the bargaining table as the two sides disputed such issues as the validity of the 1975 Algiers Treaty which set their boundary along the midpoint of the Shatt al-Arab shipping channel, the return of prisoners of war, and the clearing of the Shatt al-Arab of mines and sunken ships.[445] Nonetheless, despite the wrangling, the fighting had stopped, and in an official government statement welcoming the cease-fire Moscow sought to capitalize on the situation by offering, once again, to withdraw its small force of warships from the Gulf if the US and its NATO allies also removed their fleets. The USSR also suggested that the security of the sea lanes in the Gulf could be ensured by a system of guarantees by the permanent members of the UN Security Council – a proposal reminiscent of Shevardnadze's call for a UN Gulf fleet in September 1987. So as not to alienate Iran by its proposal, however, Moscow promised to "carefully take into account the considerations of the Persian Gulf states which, needless to say, have the principal and greatest stake in turning the Persian Gulf into a zone of security, good-neighborliness, and cooperation."[446]

In evaluating their position in the Middle East once the cease-fire had gone into effect, the Soviet leadership evidently saw it as a much improved one. On the one hand, the bulk of the Arab states, while angered, had not been totally alienated by Moscow's tilt to Iran, and with the Palestinian Intifada now raging, could be expected to begin to shift their attention back to the Israeli–Palestinian conflict, an arena where there was a great deal of room for cooperation with Soviet diplomacy, particularly in the effort to bring about an international conference. On the other hand, while Iran had clearly been angered by the extensive Soviet arms shipments to Iraq (Rafsanjani's speech on August 11 had noted this point clearly as had a number of statements by other Iranian officials), the Iranian government had also benefited by the Soviet delaying tactics that prevented the imposition of an arms embargo, and Moscow evidently hoped it could begin to build a more positive postwar relationship with Tehran. Indeed, a senior Soviet diplomat, Alexander Zotov, writing in *New Times* after Iran had formally accepted UN Resolution 598, sought to justify this aspect of Soviet diplomacy during the war:

> It goes to its (Soviet diplomacy's) credit that it showed restraint over the demands of a number of Western and other countries that Iran be "punished" for procrastination over the acceptance of Resolution 598 and a blockade be imposed on it under an appropriate Security Council resolution. Such a resolution would hardly have worked – it is enough to recall the Irangate affair – and, worse still, it could only have encouraged Iran's belligerent rejection of outside pressure.[447]

Nonetheless, the Soviet Union had a number of obstacles to overcome before there could be any significant improvement in Soviet–Iranian relations. Besides Iran's continuing unhappiness over Soviet arms supplies to Iraq, Moscow had to be concerned that as Iran began its postwar reconstruction it would become economically dependent on the Western states and Japan and this would cause Iran to move toward the West politically. Indeed, as the war ended, a major debate broke out in Tehran as to the proper course to take in reconstruction, with Khomeini himself, in a major speech on September 4 urging Iran not to become dependent on the US or USSR stating: "God willing, the warrior Iranian people will maintain their revolutionary and sacred rancor and anger in their hearts and use their oppressor-burning flames against the criminal Soviet Union and the world-devouring United States and their surrogates."[448]

While the debate raged in Tehran over whether or not to incur foreign debts in reconstruction,[449] Moscow Radio sought to influence the debate by noting:

> Some in Tehran fear that Western companies may exploit Iran's weakened economy and may possibly impose unsuitable conditions on Iran when concluding agreements with it... There are several ways to resist the pressure by Western companies. *As was justly and timely noted in Tehran*, one of these measures is the balanced expansion of economic relations with the West and the East, namely with the Soviet Union ...[450] (emphasis mine)

The Iranian leadership in fact was to choose to balance its economic ties between East and West, but Moscow was not to be the sole major communist economic partner. China, which had supplied Iran with Silkworm missiles during the war, was actively courted as a postwar economic partner. When the Chinese Deputy Foreign Minister for political affairs, Qi Huaiyaun, visited Iran in mid-August he was told by Hamid Mirzadeh, the Iranian Deputy Prime Minister for Executive Affairs who was also the Iranian head of the Tehran–Beijing economic commission, that the good wartime relations between China and Iran could improve further in postwar times.[451] Mirzadeh told a visiting Chinese economic delegation one week later that he hoped China would play a major role in Iran's economic relations with foreign countries.[452] Agreements between the two countries were not long in coming. On September 3 an agreement was signed on cooperation in dam construction and energy;[453] and on September 27 Mirzadeh announced on his return from a trip to Beijing for the fourth session of the Iran–Beijing economic commission that an agreement had been reached to boost Sino-Iranian trade from $500 million in 1988 to $600 million in 1989, that discussions were held on building two Iranian power stations, and that an Iranian consulate would be opened in Shanghai.[454]

Moscow, whose total trade with Iran in 1987 was only $250 million[455] – half the Sino-Iranian 1988 figure – also sought to capitalize on Iran's desire to develop economic cooperation. For its part, as in the past, Iran appeared to be exploiting Moscow's policy of seeking improved political relations by first strengthening economic ties. Thus, Deputy Foreign Minister Javad Larijani, in a meeting with the Soviet Deputy Minister of Foreign Economic Relations, Benjamin Korolev, who had come to Iran for the 14th Tehran International Trade Fair in September, and who had declared Moscow's eagerness "to upgrade mutual economic, technical and cultural ties with Iran,"[456] told the visiting Soviet official that Iran's policy *vis-à-vis* the USSR had always been based on mutual interest and understanding and "non-interference in each other's internal affairs," and that he hoped that the joint Iranian–Soviet economic commission session to be held in the near future in Moscow would be a "turning point" in mutual relations.[457] The economic commission, which met in early December, did reach a number of agreements including the resumption of Iranian natural gas shipments to the USSR and the building of two dams across the Aras River which serves as a border between Iran and the USSR. Moscow and Tehran also signed a protocol on other types of economic cooperation, including the development and upgrading of transport links between the two countries.[458] Heading the Iranian delegation to Moscow was Mohammed Iravani, Iran's Minister of Economy and Finance, and he was invited to meet with Soviet Prime Minister Nikolai Ryzhkov on December 6. The talks took place in what was described as a "businesslike and friendly atmosphere" where a "thorough exchange of views" took place – Soviet parlance for disagreement.[459] Among the areas of probable disagreement was Iran's aid to the Afghan rebels, which had led to increasingly critical treatment of Iran by the Soviet media. While not all Soviet commentators were as critical of Iran as Igor Belyayev, who in a *Literaturnaia Gazeta* article on November 2 stated that Iran, having failed in its efforts to export the Islamic revolution to Iraq, was now trying to reroute the "Islamic march" to Afghanistan, and was making use of the 2 million Afghan refugees on Iranian soil to accomplish this task,[460] many were quite critical of Iran. Thus Belyayev's *Literaturnaia Gazeta* colleague, Konstantin Kapitonov, took a similarly dim view of Iran, noting that there were many more prisons there under Khomeini than in the Shah's day and that the government of Iran had been trying to turn "most of the population into robots who, on orders from above, mindlessly apply pressure on any dissidence or the slightest expression of opposition."[461] But it was not only the increasingly free Soviet press that was unhappy with Iran's policy, whether domestic or foreign. *Pravda*, on November 2, reflecting Soviet government policy, reported a "resolute protest" by Afghanistan to Iran because of Iranian Foreign Minister Velayati's meeting with Afghan rebel leaders whom he urged to continue the war.

In addition to Iranian aid to the Afghan rebels, Moscow had two other concerns with Iran in the period following the cease-fire. One was the possibility that in the postwar period there might be a reconciliation between Iran and the US, given the fact that many of Iran's factories had been built by US firms, and Iran was now in the process of planning its reconstruction. While the shooting down of the Iranian airliner had embittered Iranian–US relations, once Iran had accepted Resolution 598, the US sent a message to Iran proposing normalization of relations.[462] Although Iran's initial reply did not satisfy the United States,[463] the strong US position condemning Iraq's use of poison gas against its Kurdish minority (both the Senate and House called for sanctions) held out the possibility of improved ties. Continuing to play the zero-sum game political competition with the United States over Iran – despite all its talk about "new thinking" – Moscow deprecated the US action, with a Radio Peace and Progress broadcast in Persian to Iran claiming it was only a tactical move by the US to motivate Iranian "extremist circles" to impede the Geneva talks (between Iran and Iraq) and "drag Iran into the orbit" of US policy.[464] Moscow also sought to play down the Iraqi action as based on "vague reports"[465] in part because of fear that the issue might cause the still tenuous peace talks to break off, a concern Moscow had shown since the peace talks had begun. While Iranian leader Rafsanjani criticized the US condemnation of the Iraqi use of poison gas, claiming the US should have shown this concern earlier when Iraq had used chemical weapons against Iran; he was also highly critical of the USSR for not openly protesting the Iraqi use of poison gas.[466] The end result of the poison gas episode was that it did not lead to an improvement in US–Iranian relations, and for this Moscow may well have been grateful; yet Soviet behavior on the poison gas issue could only have raised questions in Tehran about how much Moscow could be trusted in the postwar period.

A final problem Moscow had with Iran in the latter part of 1988 was the Iranian treatment of the Iranian communist party, the Tudeh. Once Iran accepted UN Resolution 598, the Iranian regime cracked down hard on opposition groups, and executed a number of political prisoners including members of the Tudeh party. While Moscow's initial complaints were limited to the clandestine "Radio of Iranian Toilers" in Persian,[467] it escalated its criticism in November with a Radio Peace and Progress broadcast to Iran discussing the UN Human Rights Commission report which denounced Iran for mistreatment of political prisoners.[468] On December 7 Moscow took another step as *Pravda* published a Tudeh party statement which condemned the executions and appealed to the UN to save the political prisoners still alive in Iranian jails. Coming at the same time as the Iranian economic delegation was in Moscow, the *Pravda* report was clearly meant to signal Soviet displeasure at the Iranian executions. The Soviet leadership, despite its *perestroika*, *glasnost*, and "new thinking" (which minimized the role of ideology in world affairs) evidently felt it could not stand idly by while communists who looked to Moscow were killed, without at least noting Soviet unhappiness with the development. On balance, however, as in the past, the Soviet leadership felt that state-to-state relations took precedence over the fate of any foreign communist party, and Moscow quickly resumed its efforts to improve ties with Iran. Indeed, in a Moscow Radio broadcast on December 10 – only three days after the *Pravda* article – the Soviet commentator hailed the success of the joint economic commission's meeting which "elevated Soviet–

Iranian relations to a new stage" and appealed for Iranian help in securing a settlement in Afghanistan.[469]

While Moscow worked to improve relations with Iran, it was also mindful of its ties with Iraq which emerged as a major Arab power with its military victories over Iran at the end of the war. Moscow's supply of modern weapons to Iraq, a Soviet policy which continued to be denounced by Iran, had assuaged the Iraqis during the USSR's tilt to Iran, but in the postwar situation, with military supplies less politically useful, and with Moscow's continuing efforts to woo Iran, problems in Soviet–Iraqi relations loomed on the horizon. Indeed, the meetings between Soviet and Iraqi diplomats once Iran had accepted UN Resolution 598 were described by the Soviet media as taking place in an atmosphere "of frankness and friendliness" and as being "constructive and businesslike."[470] Nonetheless, Moscow could take solace from the fact that the dispute over poison gas led to a deterioration in US–Iraqi relations,[471] as did US efforts to prevent Argentina from developing the medium-range Condor II missile that was being developed with Iraqi financial assistance.[472] Reflecting the deteriorating relations, Iraqi Foreign Minister Tariq Aziz declared on September 19 that he would not agree to New York as the site of Iran–Iraq peace talks both for security reasons and because "I cannot go to a town where there is a campaign against the Arabs."[473] In addition, a projected plan for Iraq to buy an idle USX steel plant in Texas fell through.[474] Although the anti-Iraqi economic sanctions were never enacted by Congress, US–Iraqi relations deteriorated further in mid-November as a senior US diplomat was expelled from Iraq and the US, in turn, expelled an Iraqi diplomat.[475]

While Moscow was able, at least in the short run, to profit diplomatically from the deterioration in US–Iraqi relations, it was to take actions of its own to improve its position elsewhere in the Gulf. On August 1, the Soviet Union and Qatar announced the establishment of diplomatic relations, with Qatar being the fourth GCC state (after Kuwait, the United Arab Emirates, and Oman) to establish ties with the USSR.[476] As in the case of Oman's establishment of diplomatic ties with the USSR in 1985, Qatar's move appeared, at least in part, to stem from a dispute with the United States. In March 1988 the US had protested Qatar's illegal acquisition of US Stinger missiles and asked for their return. When Qatar (involved in a territorial dispute with neighboring Bahrain) to whom the US had agreed to sell Stingers in December 1987, wanted the US to get Bahrain to relinquish its claim to the settlement of Zubara on Qatar's Western coast, in return for giving back the Stingers or at least telling the US their serial numbers (so the US could trace the illegal diversion), the US refused, reportedly because such US action would infringe on Bahrain's sovereignty.[477] The end result of the episode was that Qatar moved to establish diplomatic relations with the USSR, and Moscow, in turn, used the Qatari action to try to strengthen its position in the Gulf. In early November, Qatar's Foreign Secretary, Sheikh Hamad Ibn Sulhaym al Thani, journeyed to Moscow and met with a number of Soviet officials, including Foreign Minister Shevardnadze, and the joint communiqué issued at the end of his visit supported the Soviet proposal for a UN regional security system to ensure the safety of shipping in the Gulf.[478] Moscow also used the opportunity provided by the Qatari official's visit to appeal for the establishment of diplomatic relations with Bahrain and Saudi Arabia, the only two remaining GCC countries not to have diplomatic relations with the Soviet Union.[479]

Moscow's relations with Kuwait, long the friendliest GCC state to Moscow, also showed improvement in 1988 although, as in the past, Kuwait cleverly moved to improve its relations with both superpowers to maximize its security. In what was in some ways a repetition of the events of 1984, Kuwait appealed to the United States for weapons, ran into Congressional opposition, was courted by Moscow which signed an arms deal with it, and then went on to sign a major arms deal with the United States.[480] Unlike 1984, however, by 1988 US–Kuwaiti relations were much closer both because of the tanker reflagging and because of Kuwait's tough stand against terrorism (a Kuwaiti airliner had been hijacked in March 1988, but Kuwait refused the demands of the hijackers). Consequently, the Reagan administration actively fought Congressional opposition and ultimately secured Congressional support for an arms sale worth almost $2 billion, which included forty F-18 fighter planes and anti-ship Maverick missiles. The fact that Saudi Arabia, which had also been seeking a major arms deal with the US, turned instead to Britain as a result of Congressional opposition, was another factor influencing the Congressional decision to approve the sale, but Kuwait also compromised by agreeing not to have refueling capability for the F-18s and to forego the air-to-ground version of the Maverick missiles, thus satisfying Congressional critics who feared that otherwise the weapons could be used against Israel by Kuwait or another Arab state to which the weapons could be transferred.[481]

While Congress debated the arms sale, Kuwait signed a deal with the Soviet Union on July 9, reportedly for an estimated $300 million, with the Kuwaiti Defense Minister Sheikh Nawaf al-Ahmad stating that the agreement included 245 Soviet BMD-2 armored personnel carriers.[482] Following the arms agreement, the Kuwaiti Chief of Staff, Major General Mizyad al-Sani journeyed to Moscow where he met with the Soviet Chief of Staff Marshall Sergei Akhromeyev who was quoted by the Kuwaiti news service as saying that Moscow would "consider" any specific arms request by Kuwait and indicated that the response would be "positive."[483]

In sum, therefore, Moscow's position in the Gulf may be considered to have been strengthened in the aftermath of the cease-fire. The end of the war led to an improvement in Soviet–Iranian relations while Moscow did not lose any significant diplomatic ground in Iraq, in part because of the sharp deterioration of US–Iraqi relations. In addition, Soviet–Kuwaiti relations remained good while Moscow scored a gain to its position by establishing diplomatic relations with Qatar, although both Saudi Arabia and Bahrain continued to resist Soviet offers to establish diplomatic ties.

Moscow was to face a more difficult set of problems in dealing with the Arab–Israeli conflict in 1988. On the one hand, it wanted to cultivate good relations with Israel (or at least the appearance of good relations) so as to both positively influence the United States and also create the conditions for convening an international conference on the Middle East. On the other hand, however, it was also again cultivating the PLO, now that the Arafat–Hussein agreement had been declared null and void by the 1987 Palestine National Council meeting in Algiers. In addition, the Palestinian uprising, or Intifada, which broke out in December 1987, caught the Soviet Union – as well as Israel – by surprise, and it was to take almost six weeks for Moscow to react officially to it.

To be sure the USSR did quickly move, from a propaganda point of view, to try to exploit the Intifada. Thus a Soviet government report linked the Israeli "repression" of the protestors with a newly signed US–Israeli military cooperation agreement,[484] and Moscow also sought to exploit the US abstention on a UN Security Council resolution condemning Israeli actions on the West Bank and Gaza.[485] Yet, aside from condemnation of Israeli policy – and constantly linking the US to Israeli actions – Moscow took no substantive action in regard to the uprising until mid-January, despite Arab urgings.[486] There were, of course, the usual Palestinian solidarity meetings, a World Federation of Trade Unions (WFTU) declaration, a statement by Soviet Muslims, an Afro-

Asian Peoples Solidarity Organization condemnation, and even a message from Gorbachev to Arafat noting that the "violent measures Israelis were using against the Palestinians aroused anger and indignation in the Soviet people."[487] Interestingly enough, however, the Gorbachev message also noted "one must not ensure one's own rights and security by flouting the rights of others" – a statement which foreshadowed Gorbachev's later remarks to Arafat in Moscow that the PLO had to take into consideration Israel's security needs. In addition, perhaps concerned that its consular delegation in Israel might be terminated by Israeli officials demanding a reciprocal Israeli mission in Moscow – just at the time when it was of the highest importance for Soviet officials to have accurate information on what was going on in Israel – Moscow agreed in principle in mid-January to receive an Israeli consular delegation, although no date was set for the visit,[488] and the Foreign Ministry press spokesman, Gennady Gerasimov, in a press briefing, stated that the resumption of Soviet–Israeli relations would be possible "within the process of a Middle East settlement."[489]

The major Soviet response to the uprising came six weeks after it had begun. On January 20, Soviet Foreign Minister Shevardnadze wrote a letter to the UN Secretary General, in which he called for the Security Council to begin consultations at the Foreign Minister level, both to establish and to start up a mechanism for an international conference on the Middle East.[490] This was an effective propaganda ploy for Moscow, given the fact that both Israel and the United States rejected the Shevardnadze proposal while the Arab states generally supported it.[491] Nonetheless, the US was galvanized by the Palestinian uprising to the point that Secretary of State Shultz, after first dispatching Philip Habib and Richard Murphy to the Middle East, set out himself on what was to be the first of four trips in the winter and spring to bring about a peace agreement. Moscow's negative public reaction to the peace efforts of the American envoys generally emphasized two points. First, that the US efforts were just another attempt to make a "separate deal," like the Camp David agreement, while in the process diverting attention from the Palestinian uprising.[492] Second, with Moscow increasingly supporting Arafat following the 1987 Algiers PNC conference, the USSR asserted that US efforts to claim that the uprisings were "spontaneous" were merely an effort to undermine and discredit the PLO.[493] Indeed, on the latter point, PFLP leader Naef Hawatmeh, invited to Moscow in early February by the Afro-Asian Peoples Solidarity Organization, and interviewed in *Izvestia* noted: "The aim of all these allegations is clear –

to discredit the PLO as allegedly not enjoying authority and influence among the population of the occupied territories and instill mistrust of this organization. To our deep regret, some Arabs have fallen into this propaganda trap."[494] In addition, Soviet propaganda which all along had been linking Israel's repression of the Palestinians on the West Bank and Gaza to US support of Israel, cited the US plan to close the PLO mission to the United Nations as yet another anti-Palestinian and anti-Arab action undertaken by the US.[495]

Meanwhile, the Soviet position in the Arab world had been strengthened by Gorbachev's announcement in early February that he was pulling Soviet troops out of Afghanistan. Reportedly, in his messages to Arab heads of state about the withdrawal, Gorbachev also warned them against accepting the Shultz Middle East peace plan, while stating that the withdrawal from Afghanistan "would help the USSR devote more time to other Middle East problems like the Gulf war and the Palestinians."[496]

Meanwhile, Shultz was having a difficult time during his journeys to the Middle East. While no side, including Syria, gave an out-and-out "no" to his plan (which consisted of a foreshortened period of Palestinian autonomy and talks between Israel and its neighbors at a ceremonial international conference), there was little support for it outside of Shimon Peres and Hosni Mubarak with Shamir, Syria, and Jordan, to say nothing of the PLO which denounced the plan, opposing it. As it became clear both that the Palestinian uprising was continuing and Shultz's efforts had proved unsuccessful, and with another US–Soviet summit again on the horizon, Moscow took a less negative role in Middle East diplomacy, seeking to win Israeli and American support for an international conference. Thus in its description of the meeting between Shevardnadze and the seven-man Arab committee which came to Moscow in mid-March to discuss Middle Eastern problems, Tass, while emphasizing that Israel had to withdraw from *all* occupied territory, nonetheless also stated that the participants in the talks agreed on the need to ensure the right of *all* states and peoples of the region to a safe existence and in giving at least rhetorical support for the "new thinking" also expressed the view that in evaluating the US peace proposals, the main criterion should be the extent to which "they accord with the task of achieving a comprehensive and lasting Middle East settlement with due regard for *the balance of interests of all the parties* [emphasis mine] involved in the conflict."[497] The Tass report also noted that the sides agreed that the international conference "should be a permanently functioning forum within the framework of which talks would be held and *mutually acceptable decisions taken*" (emphasis mine). Then Gorbachev himself, meeting in early April with the General Secretary of the Italian communist party, Alessandro Natta, appeared to further soften the Soviet position on renewing diplomatic relations with Israel when he stated that "within the framework of preparing to hold the (international) conference, a way will be found also toward renewing normal relations between the USSR and Israel." And, in an obvious effort to demonstrate that the conference would not be a coercive one, Gorbachev also reportedly noted that "the most varied multilateral and bilateral talks could take place within it," and, instead of calling for PLO representation at the conference, referred only to representatives of the Palestinian people.[498]

The main Soviet signal to Israel was to come during PLO leader Yasser Arafat's visit to Moscow in early April. During talks with Shevardnadze and Gorbachev, the PLO leader was told that Israel's interests, including its security interests, had to be taken into consideration in any peace settlement along with those of the Palestinians. Specifically, Gorbachev noted:

> The Palestinian people has extensive international support and this is the earnest of the solution of the main question for the Palestinian people – the question of self-determination. Just as *recognition of the State of Israel and account for its security interests*, the solution of this question is a necessary element of the establishment of peace ... in the region on the basis of the principles of international law.

> The Soviet Union [Mikhael Gorbachev said] persistently works for a just and all-embracing settlement *with due account for the interests of all – both Arabs, including Palestinians, and Israel*. It is prepared to interact constructively with all the participants in the peace process.

> The Soviet view of the essence of the settlement [he said] is the following:

> The withdrawal of Israeli troops from territories occupied in 1967 – the West Bank of the Jordan, the Gaza Strip and the Syrian Golan Heights – is the key precondition of a settlement.

> The Palestinian people *has the right to self-determination in the same measure as it is ensured for the people of Israel*. How will the Palestinians exercise this right is exclusively their own business.

> An international conference under the aegis of the United Nations organization is the most effective mechanism of a settlement. *Recog-*

nition by all its participants of resolutions 242 and 338 of the United
Nations Security Council and the lawful rights of the Palestinian people,
including the right to self-determination, should become the legal basis
of the conference.

The conference should be attended by representatives of all sides
drawn into the conflict, including the Arab people of Palestine, and
also the permanent members of the United Nations Security Council.

The conference presupposes most diverse forms of interaction of its
participants. As to the role of the permanent members of the United
Nations Security Council, it will be to create a constructive atmosphere
for the conduct of talks at the conference. For this purpose, in particu-
lar, they can collectively or individually table proposals and
recommendations.

The invitations to all participants in the conference are to be sent by
the United Nations Secretary General.

Mikhail Gorbachev showed an understanding attitude to the idea of a
single Arab delegation at the international conference.[499] (emphasis
mine)

While Gorbachev's comments may have been aimed at convincing
Israel it had nothing to fear from an international conference, it would
appear that Arafat, despite his assertion that this was "the most successful of all his visits" and that there was "complete unity of views," did
not like all that he heard.[500] Thus not only did the Tass statement note
that there was a "businesslike atmosphere" (the usual Soviet term for
very low-level agreement), but Arafat, after leaving the USSR, asserted
that Gorbachev did not ask him to recognize Israel, an assertion that
would appear to be inconsistent with both the tone and content of
Gorbachev's public statement.[501] Two of the issues that may have irked
Arafat were Gorbachev's unwillingness to state that the PLO was the
sole legitimate representative of the Palestinian people or to use the
term "Palestinian state," as the Soviet leader limited himself to the
more ambiguous term "self-determination." These may well have been
further tactical gestures to the Israeli leadership which was united on its
opposition to the PLO and to a Palestinian state, if on little else, as well
as to the US, which also opposed the PLO and a Palestinian state.
Indeed, in an interview with the Kuwaiti newspaper *al-Siyasah*, a Soviet
Foreign Ministry official, Alexander Ivanov-Golitsyn, in response to a
question about a Palestinian state, noted "it was the first time the Soviet
leadership did not discuss a Palestinian state. This is not a rescindment

of the Soviet stand, but we believe some flexibility should exist."[502] He then went on to state in response to a question about Palestinians who were dispossessed in 1948: "We as realistic politicians can only discuss the establishment of a state in the West Bank and Gaza. Palestinians living abroad can return to this state. Israel is a *fait accompli*. Talking about the repatriation of the 1948 Palestinians is something extreme."

Gorbachev's gesture to Israel during the Arafat visit was accompanied by a further low-level improvement in state-to-state relations between the USSR and Israel. Thus the Soviet Party Youth Organization, Komsomol, invited a group of Mapam (a left-of-center party, but non-communist) youth to visit the USSR,[503] Soviet HAM operators were permitted to talk to their counterparts in Israel,[504] a famous Soviet singer, Alla Pugachova, gave concerts in Israel,[505] and the Soviet Union even began to allow Soviet Jews to visit Israel as tourists.[506] There appeared to be a brief cooling of ties in April after the assassination of Abu Jihad, which the Soviet media blamed on Israel and, lapsing back into the "old thinking' of zero-sum game competition, linked to the signing of a memorandum on security cooperation between the United States and Israel, in what appeared to be yet another example of Soviet disinformation aimed at weakening the US position in the Arab world.[507] Still, Moscow also welcomed the apparent reconciliation between Assad and Arafat that was precipitated by the assassination (it was, however to be short-lived), with Moscow Radio, in Arabic, hailing it as "a very important event."[508] It was also possibly because Moscow felt it had to demonstrate a tougher Middle Eastern stance in the aftermath of the Abu Jihad assassination (Abu Jihad was, after all, a close comrade of Arafat, who had just visited Moscow), that Soviet negotiators took a hard line on the Middle East during Shultz's visit to Moscow in late April. Whatever the reason, Richard Murphy reportedly told Israel's UN Ambassador Moshe Arad that the talks were "not productive" and that the Soviets were "rigid" in their attitudes.[509]

By the beginning of May, however, with a US–Soviet summit less than a month away, Moscow again began to send signals to Israel. Thus Shimon Peres made a surprise visit to Hungary – the first such visit by a major Israeli leader to a Soviet bloc state (other than Romania) since the 1967 war. Peres, who had been interviewed by the Hungarian government newspaper in April (a month after the formal establishment of the diplomatic interest sections agreed upon in 1987),[510] met with a number of top Hungarian officials, including the Prime Minister, Karoly Grosz.[511] Given the then very close ties between the USSR and Hungary, it is difficult to believe that the Soviet Union had not approved the visit, despite Shevardnadze's assertion at a news conference in mid-May, that "the visit by the Israeli foreign minister to Hungary has no bearing on Soviet–Israeli relations. This was an independent step, taken within the framework of bilateral relations."[512]

From Hungary, Peres went on to Madrid, to a meeting of the Socialist International where, as in 1987, he had meetings with Soviet officials. This time he was reportedly assured by Soviet Middle East specialist Alexander Zotov that the proposed international conference would not have the authority to impose a settlement.[513] Interestingly enough, to make sure Shamir got the same message (lest he perhaps assume that Peres was using the meeting for partisan political purposes given the fact that an Israeli election was on the horizon), World Jewish Congress President Edgar Bronfman, who was visiting the USSR, was given a message to carry to the Israeli Prime Minister that emphasized the same point.[514] Meanwhile, to improve the atmosphere further, there was another marked increase in the exodus of Soviet Jews with 1,086 leaving in April and 1,145 departing in May – both figures higher than any month since 1981.[515]

As the date of the summit neared, Moscow stepped up its diplomatic activity. On May 18 Peres met with the Soviet Ambassador to the US, Yuri Dubinin, in Washington, and was read a Soviet position paper on the Middle East.[516] Once again Peres was told that, in Moscow's view, an international conference could not impose a settlement, and also that any negotiations had to be based on UN Resolution 242.[517] While Dubinin again pressed the issue of Palestinian self-determination, he also promised to look into the delay in the Soviet issuing of visas for Israel's consular delegation that was due to go to Moscow. A week later, Peres's advisor Nimrod Novick was told by Vladimir Tarasov, deputy director of the Soviet Foreign Ministry's Middle East department, that Moscow would issue visas for the Israeli consular delegation after the superpower summit.[518] Peres, predictably, sought to get the maximum political benefit from the Tarasov statement, stating that the USSR had come a long way in its relations with Israel, while Shamir's supporters, also predictably, sought to minimize the move with Yossi Ben-Aharon, director general of Shamir's office, accusing Peres of "constant theatrics" in depicting the USSR as moving toward a more favorable attitude toward Israel.[519] It should be noted that Shamir and his Likud backers were not the only ones skeptical about the amount of genuine movement in the Soviet position. A number of US officials, including Secretary of State Shultz expressed skepticism, with one American close to the Middle East negotiations remarking that Peres was engaged in "wishful thinking."[520]

It was perhaps to quiet such skeptics that Gorbachev, in his press conference following the summit (where little progress was made on the Middle East, although Reagan pressed the issue of Soviet Jewry) went further than ever before in seeking to reassure Israel that Moscow would take Israeli interests into account at an international conference:

> We stand for a political settlement of all issues, *with due account for the interests of all sides concerned and, of course, for the principled provisions of the relevant UN resolutions.* We are talking about the fact *that all the Israeli-occupied lands be returned* and the Palestinian people's rights be restored. We said to President Reagan how we view the role of the United States, but we cannot decide for the Arabs in what form the Palestinians will take part in the international conference. *Let the Arabs themselves decide, while the Americans and we should display respect for their choice.*
>
> Furthermore, *we ought to recognize the right of Israel to security and the right of the Palestinian people to self-determination. In what form – let the Palestinians together with their Arab friends decide that. This opens up prospects for active exchanges, for a real process.* Anyway, it seems to me that such an opportunity is emerging.
>
> I will disclose one more thing: we said that *following the start of a conference – a normal, effective conference, rather than a front for separate talks – a forum which would be inter-related with bilateral, tripartite, and other forms of activity, we will be ready to handle the issue of settling diplomatic relations with Israel.*
>
> We are thus introducing one more new element. This shows that we firmly stand on the ground of reality, on the ground of recognition of the balance of interests. Naturally, there are principal issues – the return of the lands, the right of the Palestinian people to self-determination. I should reiterate: *We proceed from the premise that the Israeli people and the State of Israel have the right to their security because there can be no security of one at the expense of the other. A solution that would untie this very tight knot should be found.*[521]
> (emphasis mine)

When one analyzes the Soviet leader's statement, it appears to be a Soviet version of an "evenhanded" position on the Arab–Israeli conflict. Thus while he called for the return of all lands occupied by Israel and the Palestinian people's rights of self-determination, he did not stipulate a specific role for the PLO at the conference, leaving that for the Palestinians and the Arabs to decide. In addition, he stated that Soviet–Israeli diplomatic relations could be restored following the start of the conference, and that the USSR recognized Israel's right to security. To be sure, much of what Gorbachev said was vague; nonetheless, the tone toward Israel was positive, something recognized even by Shamir who noted in New York that Gorbachev was a "great man and a great leader,"[522] and that the tone of Soviet statements had changed.[523] He questioned, however, whether the substance of the Soviet position had changed, and he indicated that, having been invited to meet with Shevardnadze in New York, he would, as in the past, press for increased emigration of Soviet Jews to Israel and the restoration of diplomatic relations.

The Soviet leadership, in deciding to arrange the Shevardnadze–Shamir meeting, seems to have been motivated by one major consideration. With Shamir's Likud party gaining in the polls against Labor, there was a good chance that Shamir would form Israel's next government, and Moscow may well have wished to signal its willingness to deal with him. The Soviets sent Shamir a further signal during the talks – which both sides publicly characterized as "useful and constructive" – by announcing the time of the forthcoming Israeli consular visit to Moscow (mid-July).[524] This enabled Shamir to demonstrate to the Israeli public that he too could obtain benefits from Moscow, not just Peres. Several days later Israel agreed to renew, for an additional three months, the visas of the Soviet consular delegation in Israel, thus enabling Moscow to keep a diplomatic presence in Israel,[525] and on July 28 the Israeli diplomatic delegation arrived in Moscow.[526]

While Moscow was moving to improve its ties with Israel, it was not neglecting the Arab world. Indeed, on the eve of the Arab summit in Algiers in early June, the Soviet leadership could probably draw satisfaction from a number of developments that seemed to improve Moscow's position among the Arabs – despite the warming of Soviet–Israeli relations. First and foremost, its decision to leave Afghanistan had removed a great deal of the perception of a Soviet "threat" to the Arab world, and on May 14, three weeks before the Arab summit, the Soviet commander in Afghanistan, Lt.-General Boris Gronov, promised that 25 percent of the Soviet force would be out of Afghanistan by the end of May.[527] Second, a number of the intra-Arab and regional disputes that had plagued Soviet policy in the past seemed on their way to resolution. Thus, on April 4 Ethiopia and Somalia agreed to normalize relations,[528] and on May 16 Algeria and Morocco announced their decision to restore diplomatic relations after a break of twelve years because of the conflict over the former Spanish Sahara.[529] Next, Libya, on May 26, declared an end to its war with Chad and Kaddafi stated he would recognize the Habre government of Chad with which he had long been in conflict.[530] (Diplomatic relations were restored between the two countries at the beginning of October, 1988). In addition, Kaddafi moved to improve ties with Tunisia, another country with which he had been in conflict, and the move toward greater cooperation in the Maghreb was seen as a positive development by Moscow, not only because it reduced conflict in the region and laid the foundation for greater intra-Arab cooperation, but also because the Soviet leadership may have felt that acting together, such major North African states as Algeria and Morocco could curb Kaddafi's often erratic behavior.[531] It should be noted, however, that serious problems continued to exist in the Maghreb. In September, a major battle took place between Polisario forces and the Moroccan army, and in October large-scale rioting erupted in Algeria, which threatened the regime of Chadli Ben-Jedid, a development which greatly concerned Moscow since Algeria was one of its closest Arab friends.[532]

A third development improving the Soviet position in the Arab world was Moscow's *rapprochement* with Egypt, which reached its culmination with the visit of Egyptian Foreign Minister Esmat Abdel-Maguid to Moscow on May 19 for a three-day official visit. Maguid, the highest ranking Egyptian to make an official visit to the Soviet Union since 1977, met both with Shevardnadze and Gorbachev (according to an Egyptian source, a change was made in Maguid's itinerary by Soviet officials so Gorbachev could personally meet with Maguid to symbolize the improvement in Soviet–Egyptian relations).[533] During the visit the two states signed an agreement whereby the USSR would expand the annual production capacity of the steel mill at Helwan from 850,000 tons to 1.5 million tons and would complete the aluminum plant at Nag Hammadi.[534] In addition, Egypt and the USSR signed an agreement to establish an intergovernmental commission on trade and economic cooperation.[535]

In seeking to explain the rapid warming of Soviet–Egyptian relations, it would appear that a decision had been made in Moscow to reject the old policy of trying to isolate Egypt because of the Camp David agreements, if only because Egypt had successfully reintegrated into the Arab world by the beginning of 1988 despite Camp David. Instead, given the fact that Egypt had now become an active supporter of an international conference to solve the Arab–Israeli conflict, Moscow evidently decided to work with Egypt and capitalize on its increased influence in the Arab world to help arrange for the conference or, at the minimum, to politically isolate and bring diplomatic pressure on Israel and the United States who continued to oppose the conference. Indeed, the decision of Moscow's closest Arab ally, South Yemen, to restore diplomatic relations with Egypt in early February, may be seen as a major signal of the change in Soviet policy.[536] As a sign of the new *rapprochement*, Moscow Radio broadcast an Arabic language interview with Maguid in which he praised the improvement in Soviet-Egyptian relations, and the Egyptian Foreign Minister invited Shevardnadze to visit Egypt, a trip he was to make in early 1989.[537]

The improvement in Soviet–Egyptian relations, like the improvement in Soviet–Israeli relations, was not greeted warmly by the two Arab states most strongly opposed to both Egypt and Israel – Libya and Syria. While Libya made its opposition known in editorials and radio broadcasts which raised questions about Soviet policy,[538] it continued its close military relationship with the Soviet Union as visits by the Soviet Air-Defense Commander at the end of December 1987[539] and the Commander-in-Chief of the Soviet Navy in mid-March 1988 indicated.[540] Nonetheless, Kaddafi's decision to at least temporarily moderate his foreign policy and improve his ties with neighboring states may have been due, in part, to the fact that he received nothing but oral support from Moscow during his confrontations with the United States in 1986, and he felt he would be better protected by becoming part of a Maghrebi alignment.

Syrian opposition to the Soviet policy was a more serious problem for Moscow. While Syria was the primary Soviet ally in the Arab world, its quarrels with Iraq, Egypt, and the PLO (the *rapprochement* between Assad and Arafat after the assassination of Abu Jihad had been a short-lived one) continued to hamper Soviet efforts to achieve Arab unity, and Syria's continued confrontational approach to Israel raised the prospect of an Israeli–Syrian war at a time not desired by Moscow. Thus, throughout 1988, the USSR continued to repeat the message Gorbachev had given Assad in 1987 – that in the nuclear age, political solutions had to be found for regional conflicts.[541] For their part, the Syrians publicly noted that there had been no change in Israeli policy and that Syria had to receive more weapons to keep up with the weapons supplied to Israel by the United States or, like the new Israeli satellite, developed by Israel itself.[542] There were a number of reports of major arms deals between the Soviet Union and Syria in 1988 which – if true – would indicate that Moscow had decided to continue to arm Syria with modern weaponry so as to maintain its influence in that country even as Moscow was improving ties with Egypt and Israel and urging Damascus to refrain from going to war.[543] The Soviet Union did deny however that it was supplying poison gas equipment to Syria as had been charged by the *New York Times*,[544] and Soviet commentators played down the agreement reached with Syria in May 1988 that gave the USSR quasi-base rights for its fleet to use the Syrian port of Tartus. *Krasnaia Zvezda* called it a "material and technical supply point" which included "two tenders and two storehouses on dry land" that was to be used by the Soviet fleet for preventive maintenance and for rest and relaxation for Soviet sailors.[545] Interestingly enough, however, possibly because it was not getting all the weaponry it wanted from the Soviet Union, Syria was rumored to be trying to acquire M-9 missiles from China.[546]

In any case, on the eve of the Arab summit the Soviet position in the Arab world had been strengthened despite the intra-Arab conflicts that remained, and the lack of Syrian and Libyan support for the Soviet policy of *rapprochement* with Egypt and Israel. Gorbachev's message to the Arab summit called for Arab unity on a "constructive and realistic basis" – a change in the previous Soviet call for Arab unity on an "anti-imperialist basis" – and he called both for Palestinian self-determination and for free development and safe existence for all states and peoples in the region.[547]

As far as the summit itself was concerned, Soviet Middle East commentators hailed what they perceived as the unity in the Arab world displayed by the conference, unity highlighted by the fact that Kaddafi attended an Arab summit for the first time in fifteen years.[548] The summit also met the Soviet policy goals of calling for an international conference on the Middle East, with the PLO represented on an equal footing supporting Palestinian self-determination and national independence, calling for the complete withdrawal of all Israeli troops from the occupied territories, and criticizing US support of Israel.[549] Nonetheless the summit did not reject the Shultz plan and, while giving the PLO oral support, did not provide it with the funding it requested to support the Intifada. In addition, the degree of Arab unity was something less than the Soviet commentators had indicated as Arafat, in a *New Times* interview, somewhat caustically noted.[550] Indeed, with the rise of *glasnost*, such journals as *New Times* felt free to break with the *Pravda* and Tass lines on the summit, with Leonid Medvenko asserting: "My impression was that effective unity as regards the Palestinian uprising was patently lacking. Not just cooperation, but even mutual understanding between the Arab patriotic organizations is only just beginning to take effect ..."[551]

So matters stood until King Hussein changed the diplomatic equation in the Middle East by publicly severing Jordan's connection with the West Bank at the end of July 1988. Whatever the King's motivations,[552] his action, together with pressure from the leaders of the Intifada on the West Bank and Gaza, led the PLO in less than four months to call for an independent Palestinian state at the Palestinian National Council meeting in Algiers in mid-November 1988. In the interim period, Moscow took a cautious stand. Unwilling to alienate Jordan, with which relations had been slowly improving, and concerned about the continuing divisions within the PLO, the Soviet leadership issued no formal Soviet government statement on the King's action, and Soviet commentators were circumspect in their analysis of it. An *al-Ittahad* interview in late August with Karen Brutents, deputy director of the CPSU Central Committee's International Department, appeared to reflect Moscow's hopes as to what might happen:

> It is difficult now to discuss this action ... its results are unclear and ... the Palestinian stand on it is not specified ... however, if the Jordanian move consolidates the Palestinian stand, leads to an active and effective Palestinian participation in the international peace conference, and secures further Jordanian support for this direction, then the results of this move will be positive.[553]

During the three and a half months between the King's severing of ties with the West Bank and the November Algiers PNC, Moscow played host to a number of different Palestinian groupings from the mainstream Fatah to the Marxist DFLP as strategy was being worked out for the PNC. That Moscow was in favor of the PLO declaring publicly its support for a two-state solution for the Arab–Israeli conflict, was in little doubt, because precisely this solution had been part of the Soviet Middle East peace plan since 1976. Writing in *Izvestia* in mid-September, as Palestinian thinking moved toward a two-state solution, *Izvestia* commentator Konstantin Geivandov, made this point clear:

> The Palestinian uprising on the Israeli-occupied West Bank of the Jordan river and in the Gaza Strip, now in its 10th month, could not

better illustrate the new realities that have arisen in recent decades in this region of the Middle East. And against that backdrop, the step taken by the Jordanian leadership in announcing an end to its administrative and legal ties to the West Bank of the Jordan was a logical one – logical in so far as it is intended to help some people rid themselves of persistent illusions and remind others of their historical responsibility.

First, King Hussein's decision dashed the hopes of those who were counting on the "Jordanian scenario" to settle the Palestinian problem and identified the real people who must be dealt with in negotiations on this problem, i.e., the Palestinians. Second, it offered the Palestine Liberation Organization (PLO) the status of sole legitimate representative of the Palestinian people, a fact that was confirmed at the recent Arab summit meeting in Algiers, and it made possible a whole series of political and diplomatic initiatives aimed at securing the Palestinians' right of self-determination.

One would like to believe that the PLO will use the existing situation for the good of its people. Specifically, an extraordinary session of the Palestine National Council is planned for October, at the PLO's initiative, for the proposed purpose of discussing ways and means of restoring the Palestinian Arabs' national rights. *The possibility of declaring an independent Palestinian state and creating a government in exile is one such means that is under discussion. In the given case, what is intended?*

First of all, let us return to the 1947 United Nations Resolution No. 181 on the partition of Palestine, which became the legal foundation for the appearance of the State of Israel. But this resolution stipulated the creation of two states from the partition of Palestine: Jewish and Arab. And each was assigned territory of appropriate dimensions. The second part of this UN resolution has yet to be fulfilled, and it must be acknowledged that the leaders of certain Arab states are by no means the least to blame for this. *Therefore, it is proposed that if the PLO, in acting to gain the Palestinians' right to self-determination, now declares the creation of an independent Arab state on the grounds of Resolution 181, it will rectify an injustice permitted more than 40 years ago. Moreover, the PLO's recognition of Resolution 181 would lay the groundwork for the observance of international law in the Arab–Israel conflict.*[554] (emphasis mine)

The PNC, however, was held not in October but in mid-November (this may well have been a tactical mistake because holding it after the November 1, 1988 Israeli election instead of in October as originally planned, cost the PLO a chance to influence Israeli public opinion prior to the election).[555] In any case, the PNC decided to declare a Palestinian state, renounce terrorism, and accept UN Resolution 242 (which implicitly recognizes Israel's right to exist) on the proviso that an international peace conference was held. The vote in favor was 253:46 with the DFLP and PFLP opposing the acceptance of 242 but agreeing to go along with the consensus[556] – reportedly, in part, because of intensive lobbying by the Soviet Union.[557]

In any case the PLO action did not go far enough to meet US conditions for talks with the PLO, which included the *unambiguous* acceptance of UN Resolution 242, renunciation of terrorism (the PLO document obfuscated this somewhat), and recognition of Israel's right to exist. Interestingly enough, Moscow itself exercised some ambiguity in reacting to the PNC declaration, perhaps in an effort not to alienate either Israel or the United States, both of whom continued to oppose a Palestinian state, and also to mollify the Israelis who were angered by the USSR's vote to exclude Israel from the UN in October. The official Soviet government statement, printed below, noted only that the USSR recognized the declaration of the state – not the state itself:

> Resolutions adopted by the extraordinary session of the Palestine National Council held in Algiers have met with interest and approval in the Soviet Union. Taken together, these resolutions, which are infused with the lofty sense of realism and responsibility demonstrated by the leadership of the Palestine Liberation Organization, are a great contribution to the process of a just political settlement in the Middle East.

> As a result, a situation has developed in which all parties directly involved in the conflict proceed from a recognition of the fact that the path to peace and peaceful co-existence among Arabs and Israel lies through negotiations based on Security Council Resolutions Nos. 242 and 338, and of the equal rights of Jewish and Arab states to exist in Palestine. It is important that the highest representative body of the Palestinian people proclaimed its adherence to generally accepted principles of international intercourse.

> The Soviet Union has unfailingly supported the Palestinian people in its efforts to secure its inalienable national rights, including the right to create an independent state of its own. Our people understand the feelings of political uplift and enthusiasm that the Palestinians and their brother Arabs are expressing in connection with the decisions taken by the Algiers session of the Palestine National Council. The Soviet Union, true to the fundamental principle of freedom of choice,

recognizes the proclamation of a Palestinian state, guided by the under-
standing that the achievement of a comprehensive settlement will also
result, in practice, in the culmination of the historically important pro-
cess of that state's creation.

The way is being cleared for the immediate convening of an international conference on the Middle East. The Soviet Union appeals to
all interested states to step up efforts aimed at accelerating preparations for this conference. The United Nations and the UN Security
Council and its permanent members have a particularly great role to
play in this matter. The common task is to not miss the chance that has
presented itself, to get down to practical work with the goal of
establishing an enduring peace in the Middle East, with the result that
the Palestinian people will find a homeland, the Israeli people will find
dependable security, and the entire region and international community will extinguish one of the most dangerous hotbeds of tension.[558]
(emphasis mine)

Moscow also hailed Egypt's decision to formally recognize the
Palestinian state, claiming that it was a serious blow against Camp
David and a contribution to the strengthening of Pan-Arab unity.[559]

Meanwhile, the United States, still considering Arafat a terrorist,
denied him a visa to visit the United States to address the UN – an
action severely criticized in the Arab world, and by Moscow.[560] Gorbachev, in a major address to the United Nations in December, took the
opportunity to criticize the US for its action and expressed Moscow's
"solidarity" with the Palestine Liberation Organization which had
taken a "constructive step facilitating the search for an untangling of the
Middle East knot." In another part of his speech, however, Gorbachev
made his most extensive statement to date on the deideologization of
international relations. Given the importance of this section of his
speech – and the negative effect it was to have on Moscow's relations
with the radical self-proclaimed socialist states of the Arab world (and
not just the Arab world) who feared that with this policy change
Moscow would have less reason to support them – Gorbachev's words
are worth noting in detail:

The deideologization of interstate relations has become a requirement
of the new stage. We are not renouncing our convictions, our philo-
sophy or traditions. Neither are we calling on anyone else to give up
theirs. Yet we are not going to shut ourselves up within the range of
our values. That will lead to spiritual impoverishment, for it would
mean renouncing so powerful a source of development as sharing all

the original things created independently by each nation. In the course
of such sharing, each should prove the advantages of his own system,
his own way of life and values, but not through words or propaganda
alone but through real deeds as well.

That is indeed an honest struggle of ideology, but it must not be carried
over into mutual relations between states. Otherwise we will simply
not be able to solve a single world problem; arrange broad, mutually
advantageous and equitable cooperation between peoples; manage
rationally the achievement of the scientific and technical revolutions;
transform world economic relations, protect the environment, overcome underdevelopment or put an end to hunger, disease, illiteracy
and other mass ills. Finally, in that case, we will not manage to eliminate the nuclear threat and militarism.[561]

Meanwhile, Arafat was continuing to gather support for his
Palestinian state, and the US became increasingly isolated because of its
denial of a visa to the PLO leader. The UN overwhelmingly (154:2)
voted to move to Geneva, Switzerland, for a special session where
Arafat could freely address the organization.[562] In Geneva, however,
Arafat, in a speech and press conference statement, finally met the
American conditions for a US–PLO dialogue,[563] and the dialogue was
begun in mid-December with a meeting between the American Ambassador to Tunisia, Robert Pelletreau and one of the senior PLO leaders
Yasser Abd-Raboo.[564] Moscow's reaction to this event was ostensibly
positive but the Soviet leadership may well have been concerned that
just as the US had successfully mediated peace between Egypt and
Israel in the 1973–79 period, and in the process moved Egypt from the
Soviet to the American orbit, it would have a similar effect on the PLO
by mediating peace between the Palestinians and the Israelis. It was
possibly for this reason that the official Soviet statement on the US
decision to begin a dialogue with the PLO followed its praise of the
American action as an "important positive step" with a call for convening of the international conference – a move to try to preempt any
unilateral role by the US in the peace process.[565]

Meanwhile, just as US–PLO relations had begun to improve, so too
did Soviet–Israeli relations. This was due however less to Soviet actions
– the Israeli consular mission in Moscow was severely circumscribed in
its activities[566] – but to Israeli policies. Thus, at the beginning of December, Israel promptly returned a group of four hijackers who had flown to
Israel after seizing a busload of children as hostages and releasing them
in return for an aircraft. Moscow warmly praised Israel for its role in the

affair and Israel, for the first time since the 1967 war, got a very positive treatment in the Soviet press.[567] Gorbachev himself, during his UN visit which took place after the hijacking, was photographed by *Agence France Press* shaking hands with Israel's UN Ambassador Yochanan Bein.[568] Gorbachev reportedly told Bein, "I want to thank the Israeli people for the efficient cooperation we received with regard to the hijacked airplane ... Please tell the Israeli government and the people of Israel that there is a lot of good will and friendship in the Soviet Union toward Israel."[569] Gorbachev had to cut short his stay in the United States because of a massive earthquake in Armenia, and here again Israel proved helpful to the USSR. Israel sent medical teams and four tons of medical supplies, and set up a field hospital in the city of Kirovakan. The Israeli team, which was praised in the Soviet press, found and saved three women who had been buried alive in the rubble.[570] Nonetheless, despite Israel's assistance in these two episodes, there was little let up in Soviet criticism of Israeli actions in the Middle East as a *Pravda* article on December 30 took a dim view of the policies of Israel's newly formed coalition government. Interestingly enough however, on the same day, *Izvestia* published an article critical not only of Israeli "terror in the occupied territories" but also of a meeting of Islamic fundamentalists who were planning to wage a Jihad (holy war) against Israel, and of Damascus-based PLO factions which were trying to undermine Arafat's leadership in the PLO.

As 1989 began, Gorbachev, while still scoring major political successes in the United States and Western Europe, was increasingly beset by domestic turmoil within the USSR. With his *perestroika* program not yet taking hold, the Soviet economy got into deeper and deeper trouble and its problems were now openly admitted by the Soviet press as *glasnost* became increasingly evident.[571] In addition, ethnic turmoil on the periphery of the Soviet Union, which had become a major problem for Gorbachev in 1988, continued into 1989. In addition to violence in Central Asia, pitched battles took place between Armenians and Azerbaizhanis, Soviet Georgians demonstrated for independence, and the Baltic republics of Estonia, Latvia, and Lithuania pushed for increasing autonomy, a development that threatened the ethnic Russians living in the Baltic. Gorbachev sought to meet these problems by first carrying out a mini-purge of his opponents in the Politburo in the fall of 1988, and then orchestrating a change in the Soviet system of government whereby a new Supreme Soviet (over which he would preside as President) was to be elected in quasi-Western style democratic election conditions. Gorbachev promised the new Supreme Soviet, which he hoped would help stimulate *perestroika*, real input in the government decision-making process, although it remained to be seen whether the Soviet leader was genuinely willing to limit the communist party's monopoly on political power.

If it was not yet clear whether these government changes would so stimulate the Soviet populace that *perestroika* would be saved, it was already clear that change was underway both in the mechanisms of Soviet foreign policy and in some of the policies themselves. At the end of 1988 Foreign Minister Shevardnadze held a meeting with Soviet consular officials and ordered that a new approach should be used toward Soviet *émigrés*. Instead of treating them as traitors, he asserted that they should be treated as potential assets for the improvement of ties between the Soviet Union and the *émigrés'* new homelands. Shevardnadze also urged consular officials to encourage business contacts between the USSR and firms owned by these "compatriots."[572] Given the fact that more than 170,000 Soviet *émigrés* lived in Israel, the new Soviet policy held out the possibility for a further improvement in Soviet–Israeli relations. Indeed, less than a week after the consular conference, Shevardnadze met Israel's new Foreign Minister, Moshe Arens, in Paris where both were attending a conference on the control of chemical weapons. In talks which Arens termed "very friendly, open and sincere," Shevardnadze reportedly promised to upgrade Israel's consular delegation in Moscow and to allow Israeli diplomats to conduct political talks there.[573] The Soviet Foreign Minister also indicated that the Israeli consular delegation could move from its crowded quarters in the Dutch embassy to the old Israeli embassy building which had been occupied by Israel prior to the severing of relations in 1967. For his part, Shevardnadze, who again urged Israel to participate in the international peace conference as soon as possible since "all parties' interests" would be taken into account there,[574] also noted in a *Le Figaro* interview that he agreed with Arens that Israeli–Soviet contacts should be stepped up in order to achieve a settlement in the Middle East.[575] Other signals of an improvement in Soviet–Israeli relations at the time included an end to the jamming of Kol Israel (Radio Israel) broadcasts to the USSR,[576] the granting of visas to 175 Israelis to attend a Soviet–Israeli basketball game in Moscow,[577] and the offer by the Soviet ambassador to Egypt to help establish a dialogue betweeen Israel and the PLO.[578] In addition, in its clearest signal to the Arabs to date, Vladimir Tarasov, interviewed in Kuwait's *Al-Anba*, noted that since Israel was a party to the Middle

East conflict, there had to be dialogue with it. Tarasov then listed three objectives to be obtained from the Soviet–Israeli meetings:[579]

1 the most important is that the Israelis become familiar with the USSR stand from the original sources, as it is well known that there are some in Israel and in the West who try to cast doubts on the USSR stand;
2 another objective is to become familiar with the Israeli stand from the original source as well;
3 a third objective is to try to influence the Israeli stand as much as possible and encourage it to become constructive and realistic with respect to a Middle East settlement.

While Moscow intensified its contacts with Israel, it was not neglecting the PLO. Indeed, less than two weeks after the Paris discussion between Shevardnadze and Arens, Soviet and PLO officials, meeting in Tunis, reached an agreement "making Soviet–Palestinian consultations more regular and intensive."[580]

While Moscow was moving to improve relations with both Israel and the PLO, one aspect of its "new thinking," the "deideologization" of foreign policy, which had been heralded by Gorbachev in his UN speech in December 1988, received added emphasis.[581] Moscow's new approach was clearly unpopular among the radical Arab states as a *Pravda* article describing a Soviet–Arab forum in Cairo on February 18, 1989 noted:[582]

The revolutionary restructuring in the USSR has provoked diverse and often diametrically opposed attitudes from various political forces. Both the enemies and the supporters of socialism are following it carefully. No one is merely indifferent to it. Even rightists are forced to acknowledge the attractive force of the new political thinking, which is broadening the base for cooperation between the Soviet Union and the Arabs, although it is by no means weakening the USSR's close and intimate ties with the states where revolutionary democrats are in power. At the same time, this does not prevent rightists from repeatedly making assertions regarding the "crisis of socialism and Marxist ideology" and the "unacceptability of Marxism and socialism" in Arab society ...

Let's be frank: the new ideas in Soviet foreign policy have confused some of our traditional close friends – the representatives of revolutionary democrats, communists, and other left forces. How does class struggle correlate with the priority of common human values, the struggle for mankind's survival, and pooling of efforts in resolving global problems? *Doesn't the development of relations with the West mean that the USSR is renouncing cooperation with the Nonaligned Movement? Doesn't the course of settling regional conflicts entail withdrawing support from national liberation movements and the struggle to strengthen the peoples' security?* Soviet participants in the Cairo forum were asked these and other questions. Left, right, friend, and enemy of the Soviet Union are discussing them. (emphasis mine)

But while deideologization was viewed with displeasure in some Arab circles, it was clearly welcome in Iran. Soviet–Iranian relations had grown warmer in early 1989 as Yuli Voronstov visited Iran for talks with Afghan rebel leaders,[583] and Khomeini evidently became convinced that Moscow was indeed withdrawing from Afghanistan.[584] Immediately after Voronstov's visit, Khomeini sent a message to Gorbachev via a special envoy Ayatollah Javadi Amoli (who was accompanied by Deputy Foreign Minister Mohammed Larijani) calling for improved Soviet–Iranian relations, and congratulating Gorbachev for changing Soviet policies, especially in allowing more freedom for Islam in the USSR.[585] Khomeini went on to say, however, that since communism was intellectually bankrupt ("I hope that you will achieve true glory for eradicating the rotten layers of the last seventy years of deviousness of world communism from the face of history and from your own country"),[586] Gorbachev should study Islam and Islamic philosophers to find the true path for the Soviet Union ("a serious study of Islam may save you forever from the issue of Afghanistan and similar issues in the world").[587] Khomeini also offered the services of Iran, "as the greatest and most powerful base in the Islamic world" to "easily help fill up the ideological vacuum of your system."[588] While Gorbachev no doubt simply disregarded the religious content of Khomeini's special message, he had to be concerned about the Ayatollah's comment that "we regard the Muslims of the world as the Muslims of our own country, and we always regard ourselves as partners in their fate,"[589] since that statement raised serious questions about Iran's long-term intention toward the Muslims of the USSR.[590]

In the short run, however, the message from Khomeini set the stage for a significant improvement in Soviet–Iranian relations and Iran's Deputy Foreign Minister Javad Larijani noted that Soviet–Iranian relations "had entered a new phase."[591] From the Soviet point of view, Iran could be helpful in insuring that a post-withdrawal Afghanistan would not be hostile to the USSR (Larijani, in Cuba, was cited in *Pravda* as stating that Iran agreed that no anti-Soviet government should be set up in Afghanistan)[592] while from Iran's point of view, Moscow could be helpful in pressing Iraq to reach a peace agreement to finally end the war (the peace talks had remained stalled with Iraq unwilling to compromise on the Shatt al-Arab border, or pull its troops back from Iranian territory) and in providing economic aid. Moscow proved willing to aid Iran economically in an effort to gain influence in Iran especially in the post-Khomeini era (Khomeini was, in fact, to die on June 3, 1989) while Iran, facing major postwar construction needs, could use Soviet economic assistance to balance Western aid, so as to maintain Iran's independence of East and West. In sum, the Iranian–Soviet *rapprochement* reflected the interests of both partners, but it remained to be seen whether, as in the past, it would be a temporary phenomenon or whether this time it would become a long-range development.

While the Khomeini regime may have said that it was impressed by the "new thinking" in Moscow, some of the "old practice" in Soviet foreign policy continued to be evident. This was particularly clear in Soviet reporting of the incident in which United States F-14s shot down two Libyan MIG-23 jet fighters which US officials said were threatening patrolling US aircraft.[593] In some ways reminiscent of the 1981 incident,[594] this battle appeared more serious because the US was in the midst of a campaign to stop Libya from building a poison-gas factory, with President Reagan publicly noting that the US was "discussing" with its allies the possibility of destroying the factory through military action.[595] As in the past, the Soviet media sought not only to justify the policies of Libya, but to demonstrate that the US attack on the Libyan aircraft (and its possible attack on the Libyan gas factory) was not just an attack on Libya but an attack on the entire Arab world.[596] In addition an Arabic language broadcast used the incident to again demand that all foreign fleets and all foreign military bases be removed from the Mediterranean sea.[597] Given the propinquity to the Mediterranean of Soviet military power in the Black Sea, this call, together with Soviet efforts to rally the Arab world in support of Libya and against the US, would seem another example of Moscow's continued zero-sum game competition for influence in the Arab world, however much the new Soviet rhetoric tried to dress up the Soviet policy as reflecting "the basic interests of mankind."[598] Top Soviet diplomats, as well as the Soviet media carried on the anti-American propaganda campaign. Thus while an English language broadcast by Moscow Radio called the US military action "murder in cold blood, little different from the shooting down by the American cruiser of the (Iranian) passenger airliner last year,"[599] Soviet Foreign Minister Shevardnadze called it "air piracy,"[600] while Gennady Gerasimov, the Foreign Ministry spokesman called it "political adventurism and state terrorism."[601] Moscow was, however, clearly sensitive to the US rejoinder that the USSR had reverted to the "old thinking" in handling the incident. An article in *Pravda* on January 10 sought to justify the Soviet reaction:

> The US press has begun to voice annoyed comments: Oh, those Russians! They themselves are striving to abandon the terms and stereotypes of "cold war" times. But it only took the American downing of two Libyan aircraft for the Soviet mass media to start rivaling one another with tales of air piracy and state terrorism. It looks as though everything is reverting to its former state because of a single incident. What about the constructive approach and the new thinking that people in Moscow are so fond of mentioning?
>
> I want to tell my American colleagues plainly that their reproaches are misdirected. It is not the sharp tone of the Soviet press and television that runs counter to the new positive tendencies in USSR–US relations, but the US administration's illegal military action in the Mediterranean. It is hard to tell who needed this latest flare-up of anti-Libyan hysteria, or why it was needed, against the backdrop of reassuring changes in the process of a Near East settlement leading, in particular, to the start of a US–Palestinian dialogue.[602]

It should be pointed out, however, that, as in the past, while Moscow gave Libya a great deal of rhetorical support, it did not come to its aid militarily and Soviet spokesmen told the Arabs that Moscow was seeking to prevent the spread of the conflict.[603]

The Libyan incident soon faded from the front pages and there was no US attack on the Libyan poison-gas factory. Kaddafi may well have precipitated the aircraft battle to deflect the US from such an attack, given the fact that the aerial dogfight took place on the eve of the Paris conference on the control of chemical weapons, and the US was put on the diplomatic defensive at the conference because of the shooting down of the two Libyan fighter planes.[604] In any case, by the latter part of January, Soviet attention was fixed on pulling out its remaining troops from Afghanistan, an action that was completed on February 9. Thus ended the longest Soviet military action ever undertaken in a Third

World state. After the ouster of Soviet troops from Egypt by Sadat in 1972, the Soviet withdrawal from Afghanistan was the most significant "roll-back" of Soviet power in the Third World since World War II. The USSR suffered heavy casualties in the war, from 15,000 dead by one "official" estimate to as many as 50,000 dead by another estimate, with an estimated 1 million Afghans being killed or wounded as well and another 5 million Afghans made refugees.[605] In addition to the cost in human life, both Soviet and Afghan, the Soviet invasion had major political effects as well. Inside the Soviet Union, it helped lead to the emergence of the "new thinking" in Soviet foreign policy, as the new leadership under Gorbachev moved to undo the damage to the Soviet position in the world caused by the invasion, both in terms of relations between the Soviet Union and the United States, and in the Soviet position in the Middle East. Gorbachev may well have felt that the Soviet exit from Afghanistan would lead to an improvement both in Soviet–American relations and in Soviet relations with Middle Eastern states such as Iran which were the most threatened by the invasion. Indeed, as the last Soviet troops were leaving Afghanistan, Soviet Foreign Minister Shevardnadze was setting out on a major visit to the Middle East (he visited Syria, Jordan, Egypt, Iraq, and Iran) as he sought to consolidate Moscow's position in the region following the withdrawal. His first stop was Syria which, at least symbolically, was honored as "the Soviet Union's leading partner" in the Near East both by Shevardnadze's words and by being the first stop in his tour.[606] Yet with the Soviet media reporting the visit as taking place in an atmosphere of "friendly frankness,"[607] there clearly remained significant differences between the two sides as Shevardnadze emphasized the need for Syria to improve its ties with the PLO, Iraq, and Egypt. He also urged a meeting between the representatives of Jordan, Syria, Egypt, Lebanon, and the PLO[608] (a suggestion he repeated in Jordan, his next stop) as a means of coordinating Arab efforts.

Indeed, as Shevardnadze noted in his dinner speech to Assad: "There can be no two views: a fair settlement cannot be achieved without having secured the unity of the Arab countries."[609] Perhaps also reflecting concern about the development of the US–PLO dialogue, Shevardnadze called for the preparation of an international conference on the Middle East in no more than nine months.[610] As to the key issue of Syria's desire for military parity with Israel, while Shevardnadze did talk to Assad about "the development of ties in various fields, including the military field,"[611] he also repeated to Assad what Gorbachev had told the Syrian leader in 1987 – that the Arab–Israeli conflict had to be solved peacefully.

> We see how much peoples can give each other when they cooperate in the creation of a modern economy, the use of national resources, and the professional training of young people.
>
> We see how much people are deprived of by war and hostility. The bitter memory of the past, embodied in the ruins of Kuneitra, echoes like a sharp pain today. But however unbearable it may be, it cannot but be overcome by concern for the future, which is concern for peace and not for war.
>
> We see how different cultures, which stood in opposition in the past, have now merged into a single civilization, calling for the search for the path that should lead us to the supremacy of values common to all of mankind.
>
> The present generation will have to fulfill an historic mission and lay the foundations for a secure future for all mankind. To bring this about, one must master the difficult art of living in peace and respect for one another while preserving one's national, political, spiritual, and religious values in all their diversity and originality. Movement toward this noble goal is only possible given the rejection of strong-arm approaches in politics and the transfer from confrontation to dialogue, from rivalry to codevelopment and the search for a balance of interests. Mankind has been given no other alternative. This relates to global as well as regional affairs. The reality of today's interdependent world is such that any flare-up in one region throws a worrisome atmosphere over our whole planet.
>
> *The new thinking is powerfully knocking at the door of the Near East, too. Through suffering, its peoples have achieved the right to a peaceful and safe life. It is time to build the bridges of mutual understanding and peaceful coexistence in this region too.*[612] (emphasis mine)

While Assad could not have been too happy with the Soviet Foreign Minister's message, Shevardnadze himself proved unsuccessful in forging a Syrian–PLO reconciliation during his visit to Damascus as Soviet efforts to arrange an official invitation for Arafat to visit Syria to meet with Shevardnadze fell through.[613] Arafat did meet the Soviet Foreign Minister however in Cairo, in what must have appeared as a double blow to Syria. Not only did the Shevardnadze visit to Cairo (the first by a Soviet Foreign Minister in fifteen years) cap the Soviet–Egyptian *rapprochement*, it further legitimized Egyptian leader Hosni Mubarak's policies, including the maintenance of peace with Israel, since not only did Shevardnadze meet Arafat and Mubarak in Cairo, he also met Israeli Foreign Minister Moshe Arens there as well, thus putting Egypt, not Syria, at the center of Soviet Middle East diplomacy. Indeed, Shevardnadze was lavish in his praise of Egypt as he noted:

> In the Soviet Union, it is assumed that Egypt, as a major country of the Arab world with rich historical, cultural, and political traditions, is called upon to occupy a fitting place in the community of nations. On the Soviet side a positive assessment is made of Egypt's role in the Nonaligned Movement; its constructive and carefully weighed approach to solving urgent international problems is noted; and acknowledgement is expressed of Egypt's support for Soviet peace initiatives.[614]

The Soviet Foreign Minister also highlighted the Soviet–Egyptian *rapprochement*:

> We can with full justification place the full normalization of Soviet–Egyptian relations, which has now become a fact, on a level with the greatest political achievements of the recent period, which have so greatly promoted radical changes in the nature of world politics and in the maintenance of a dialogue common to all mankind.[615]

Shevardnadze also utilized his visit to Egypt to emphasize the new thinking in Soviet foreign policy and especially its deideologization:

> Traditional and – we'll be blunt – obsolete standards and outlooks are being reviewed. It is indicative that in this common channel the Soviet Union, aspiring to the democratization of interstate communication, is reducing, or even completely excluding from it the previously predominant ideological component. The world can be saved from nuclear, ecological, economic, and other catastrophes only by acting together and being guided by the priority of values common to mankind. We have a vital interest in the construction of international relations on innovative designs, and we are gladdened that the ideas and proposals M. S. Gorbachev set out in his speech at the United Nations General Assembly session are meeting with a well-disposed and committed response, as has been shown by our conversation with President H. Mubarak. This is also not the least important factor in strengthening our hope that Egypt, as one of the authoritative and influential members of the international community and the Nonaligned Movement, will continue to actively assist the process of improving the situation, including that in the vicinity.[616]

The visit of Shevardnadze to the Middle East, which occurred immediately after the final withdrawal of Soviet troops from Afghanistan, is a good point of departure for evaluating Soviet policy toward the Middle East since the invasion of Afghanistan.

5 Conclusions: continuity and change in Soviet policy toward the Middle East

Gorbachev and his predecessors: a comparison

In the period between the Soviet invasion of Afghanistan in December 1979, and the final withdrawal of Soviet troops from that country in February 1989, four different Soviet leaders ruled the USSR: Leonid Brezhnev, who died in November 1982; Yuri Andropov, who died in February 1984; Konstantin Chernenko, who died in March 1985; and Mikhail Gorbachev, who has been in power since 1985 and who oversaw the withdrawal from Afghanistan.

In this period of almost ten years, two main conclusions can be drawn about Soviet policy toward the Middle East. First, as in the past, Soviet policy toward the Middle East continued to be a reaction to a series of regional developments that Moscow not only had not caused, but that successive Soviet leaders were essentially unable to shape to fit Soviet goals in the region. Second, despite the rhetoric of Mikhail Gorbachev, there would appear to be more continuity than change in Soviet policy toward the Middle East.

The Soviet invasion of Afghanistan itself had a negative impact on the Soviet political position in the Middle East. At the time of the invasion, the Arab world was basically united in opposing the US–supported Camp David accords, and, except for its ties with Egypt and Israel, the US position in the Middle East was a weak one. Pro-Soviet regimes had emerged in Ethiopia and South Yemen, America's ally, the Shah of Iran, had fallen, to be replaced by the virulently anti-American Khomeini regime that was holding American diplomats hostage, and even in Arab countries that had once been close to the United States, such as Saudi Arabia and Jordan, there were deep misgivings about the nature and steadfastness of US policy in the Middle East. Given the fact that Moscow has looked upon the Arab world as a region of zero-sum game influence competition with the United States, it appeared clear that the Soviet Union was winning, and the United States was losing, the influence competition.

The Soviet invasion of Afghanistan changed the basic political equation in the Arab world. While Moscow's Steadfastness Front allies, particularly Libya, Syria, and South Yemen, supported the invasion, as did Ethiopia, the vast majority of other Arab states opposed it, and the post Camp David "anti-imperialist" Arab unity that Moscow had sought for so long was broken, with even Steadfastness Front members Algeria and the PLO voicing reservations about the Soviet invasion of a Muslim country. Iran, too, opposed the invasion, which became a barrier to Moscow's attempt to exploit the US–Iranian conflict over the hostages to improve the Soviet position in Iran. Meanwhile, the United States, through the Carter Doctrine, had pledged to protect the Persian Gulf against further Soviet incursions and the US pledge, backed up by an expanded US Rapid Deployment Force, served to partially rebuild the US position in the Middle East as a number of Arab states, confronted by the Soviet threat, began to look to the US for protection – despite Camp David.

Moscow's regional position received another jolt when Iraq invaded Iran in September 1980 and thus began an eight-year-long war that was to be, after the Soviet invasion of Afghanistan, perhaps the largest obstacle to the increase in Soviet influence in the Middle East. Initially unwilling to back either side for fear of alienating the other, Moscow adopted a position of neutrality only to see the United States position in the Middle East improve significantly because of the war. This was to be the case first because the Arab world further split, with Steadfastness Front members Syria and Libya strongly backing Iran (South Yemen did so somewhat less strongly), while the PLO shifted from a pro-Iranian to a pro-Iraqi position and Algeria tried to remain neutral. The end result was that with the rest of the Arab world, including Egypt, strongly backing Iraq, Moscow's main Arab clients, Syria and Libya, became increasingly isolated in the Arab world while the main American client, Egypt, was to begin the process of *rapprochement* with its fellow Arabs, a process that was speeded up following the assassination of Anwar Sadat in October 1981. A second problem for Moscow from the war was the sharp improvement of US–Saudi relations, symbolized by the US stationing of AWACs reconnaissance planes in Saudi Arabia to help protect the Arab Gulf states from Iranian threats to close the Gulf. A third problem for Moscow was the establishment of the Gulf Cooperation Council, one of whose members, Oman, was advocating closer military cooperation with the US in the face of the Soviet and Iranian threats. A final problem for Moscow was the diversion of Arab attention from the Arab–Israeli conflict, where Moscow's position basically coincided with the Arabs, to the Persian Gulf where the US position on the war was far closer to the Arabs than was Moscow's.

The next regional problem which faced Moscow was the Israeli invasion of Lebanon in 1982, one of whose aims was to root out the state-within-a-state which the PLO had established in Southern Lebanon. While Moscow was to oppose the Israeli invasion only with rhetoric, the PLO was expelled from Lebanon and PLO leader Yasser Arafat began to entertain the possibility of working with the US, and the newly proclaimed Reagan plan, to obtain his long-desired Palestinian state – much to the consternation of Moscow.

The Israeli invasion of Lebanon was to be followed by two American military interventions, the first to escort the PLO guerrillas out of Beirut and the second, a more ill-defined mission to help secure the new Lebanese government of Amin Gemayel, and arrange for the withdrawal of foreign troops from Lebanon. When the latter mission failed, and the US withdrew ignominiously from Lebanon in 1984, US prestige in the Middle East again plummeted. Unfortunately for Moscow, however, the sudden escalation of the Gulf war with Iran and Iraq attacking oil tankers sailing in the Gulf, diverted attention from the US failure in Lebanon and also further strengthened US ties with the Gulf Arabs who again looked to the US for protection despite Moscow's decision in 1982 to resume military sales to Iraq. For its part, as its fortunes seemed to ebb in the war, Iraq moved to improve its ties with the United States, and, despite Israel's use of American planes in its attack on the Iraqi nuclear reactor in 1981, reestablished full diplomatic relations with the US in 1984.

The next regional problem facing Moscow was the Hussein–Arafat agreement of February 1985 which came after Jordan had reestablished full diplomatic relations with Egypt in September 1984, and after PLO leader Yasser Arafat had himself moved to restore relations with Egypt after being expelled a second time from Lebanon, this time by Moscow's ally Syria, in 1983. With Egypt actively backing the Hussein–Arafat agreement, and Iraq giving it support as well, it appeared as if a new Arab axis had emerged in the Arab world, one that would further isolate Syria. As the US took an active role in trying to bring about talks between a Jordanian–Palestinian delegation and Israel, Moscow responded by beginning its own contacts with Israel. Fortunately for the USSR's new

leader, Mikhail Gorbachev, however, the terror process quickly replaced the peace process in the Middle East, and although a Soviet
diplomat was killed and several others kidnapped, the wave of Middle
East terrorism in the summer and fall of 1985 helped to derail the US-
supported peace process.

Perhaps the most important regional event in the mid 1980s to which
Moscow had difficulties in reacting was the Iran–Contra affair. Initially
Moscow feared that the US supply of arms to Iran would lead to the
long-feared US–Iranian *rapprochement*, and Moscow denounced the
arms sale and "pro-American" forces in Iran that supported it. When
no *rapprochement* took place, however, Moscow then seized the opportunity to charter three Kuwaiti tankers (on Kuwait's request), and
denounced Iran's new offensive in the war, as the USSR sought to
demonstrate that while the US, as in the case of the Arab–Israeli conflict, was helping the enemy of the Arabs by arming Iran, the Soviet
Union, by chartering the Kuwaiti tankers and arming Iraq, was backing
the Arabs. Unfortunately for Moscow, however, the US sought to atone
for Irangate by reflagging eleven Kuwait tankers (also on Kuwait's
request, as the Kuwaitis skillfully exploited the US–Soviet rivalry to
gain protection from Iran), and escorting the tankers with a large naval
flotilla which soon became involved in a series of clashes with Iran. The
end result of the process was that while US–Iranian relations deteriorated – especially after the US mistakenly shot down an Iranian passenger plane during a naval battle in the Gulf – US relations with the Gulf
Arabs, and especially Kuwait, improved.

While these regional events essentially worked against Moscow's
interests, a number of other regional events took place which Moscow
had not initiated but appeared to benefit from, at least initially. Thus for
example Syria's growing isolation in the Arab world led Assad to sign a
Treaty of Friendship and Cooperation with Moscow in October 1980
that he had long resisted. Yet this treaty turned out to be a two-edged
sword for Moscow. In November 1980, with a Soviet official in
Damascus for the exchange of treaty papers, Assad mobilized his troops
on the border with Jordan which was both hosting an Arab summit
(which Syria boycotted) and backing Iraq, Syria's enemy, in the Iran–
Iraq war. Given the fact that Moscow was seeking to weaken the US–
Jordanian relationship at the time, the actions by Moscow's new treaty
ally were counterproductive to Moscow's regional goals. Similarly, in
the spring of 1983 as Syria was seeking to sabotage the US–brokered
Israeli–Lebanese agreement, Assad threatened a war involving the

USSR, and in the fall of 1983, when Syrian–American clashes took place in Lebanon, Assad once again sought – albeit unsuccessfully – to extend the mantle of Soviet protection to Syria's activities in Lebanon. While Moscow was undoubtedly happy that Syria was the primary force successfully opposing US policy in Lebanon, Soviet leaders, nonetheless, despite the arms they had sent to Syria, saw the danger inherent in the Syrian leader's activities and in both the spring and fall of 1983 played down Moscow's treaty tie to Syria while, especially in the fall of 1983, emphasizing that Syria had enough military equipment to protect itself and urging the other Arab states to come to Syria's aid. Since 1983, while continuing to supply Syria with sophisticated arms, Moscow has not enabled it to have the parity with Israel that Assad has long wanted, and Gorbachev's blunt statement to Assad during the Soviet leader's Kremlin visit in April 1987 that no matter how serious a conflict was, in the nuclear age the conflict had to be solved politically, seemed to underscore Moscow's unwillingness to back Syria in an offensive war against Israel, as did a similar statement by Shevardnadze in Damascus in February 1989.

Moscow has encountered similar problems with Libya. While Soviet–Libyan relations have clearly improved since 1980, in part because of Libya's isolated regional position and its conflict with the United States, many of the actions of the Libyan leader have clearly discomfited Moscow. Thus, Kaddafi's open encouragement of terrorism, his pressure against neighboring Tunisia, his military incursion into Chad and, above all, his threats to expand the US–Libyan conflict into a NATO–Warsaw Pact confrontation have clearly clashed with larger Soviet global and regional objectives. Indeed, Kaddafi's decision in 1988 to integrate with his North African neighbors into a larger Maghrebi entity, may have been due, in part, to the Libyan leader's realization that he could not obtain sufficient Soviet support for his regional objectives. If the Maghrebi union serves to contain Kaddafi's adventurism, however, the union's formation may turn out to be a positive development for Moscow.

Developments within the PLO in recent years have also worked to Moscow's advantage. When Hussein denounced the Hussein–Arafat agreement in February 1986, Arafat found himself in conflict not only with Syria, but with Jordan as well. This prompted the PLO leader to seek to broaden his base of support within the PLO and he tried to win over two of the Marxist elements of the PLO, Habash's PFLP and Hawatmeh's DFLP, that were close to Moscow, so as to keep them from an alliance with Syria against him. The end result of the process was that Moscow, which had taken a very negative view of the Hussein–Arafat agreement, improved its relations with Arafat. Moscow also benefited from the outbreak of the Intifada in December 1987 as it partially refocused Arab attention on the Arab–Israeli conflict at a time when the Arabs seemed almost totally preoccupied with the Iran–Iraq war. Moscow was particularly pleased with the PLO decision in November 1988, under the pressure of the Intifada, to declare its own state and accept a two-state solution to the Palestinian–Israeli conflict because the Arafat-sponsored PNC decision coincided with Moscow's own peace plan. Moscow had to be concerned, however, that the start of the PLO–US dialogue in December 1988 could lead to US mediation of the Israel–Palestinian conflict, just as the US had been instrumental in bringing Egypt and Israel from war in 1973 to peace in 1979. For this reason, in the first few months of 1989, Moscow pushed very hard for the rapid convening of an international conference on the Middle East where it would play a co-equal role with the United States.

The final regional event that appeared, at least initially, to work to the benefit of Moscow was the cease-fire ending the Iran–Iraq war in August 1988. While tensions remained high between Iran and Iraq after the cease-fire and the threat of renewed conflict continued to exist, the end to the fighting removed a major obstacle to the improvement of Soviet–Iranian relations, since the supply of Soviet weapons to Iraq was the primary factor enabling the regime of Saddam Hussein to fight the war against Iran. Indeed, Soviet–Iranian relations improved rapidly after the ceasefire, while US–Iraqi relations which could have been expected to improve in response, became strained over Iraq's use of poison gas and its persecution of its Kurdish minority – a net gain in the US–Soviet influence competition for Moscow, albeit perhaps only a short-term one. At the same time, however, all the Gulf Arab states remained wary of a resurgent Iran and possibly a newly aggressive Iraq as well, and despite disputes over arms sales to countries like Saudi Arabia, the US position among the Arab Gulf states, fortified by the US reflagging and escorting of Kuwaiti tankers, was far stronger in 1989 than it was on the eve of the Soviet invasion of Afghanistan ten years before.

Nonetheless, with the end to the Iran–Iraq war (and the subsequent Soviet withdrawal from Afghanistan) Moscow could expect Arab attention to shift back to the Arab–Israeli conflict, from which it had been diverted both by the Soviet invasion of Afghanistan and then by the outbreak and escalation of the Iran–Iraq war. Should the United States, which is closely linked to Israel, not take an effective role in mediating a peace agreement between Israel and the Palestinians, the US position in the Middle East, which greatly benefited from the Soviet invasion of Afghanistan, and the Iran–Iraq war, and which, as mentioned above, was far stronger in 1989 than it had been in 1979, might again begin to deteriorate.

In turning to the question of continuity and change in Soviet policy toward the Middle East, when one compares the policies of Mikhail Gorbachev with those of his predecessors Brezhnev, Andropov, and Chernenko, it would appear that, at least until February 1989, when the USSR pulled its last troops out of Afghanistan, there was considerably more continuity than change. The main areas of continuity were: (1) the Soviet plan for a settlement of the Arab–Israeli conflict; (2) Soviet unwillingness to use military force to challenge either Israeli or American activities in the Middle East; (3) Soviet inability to effect reconciliations between Syrian leader Hafiz Assad and his two Arab opponents, PLO leader Yasser Arafat and Iraqi President Saddam Hussein; (4) the Soviet policy of tilting first to one side and then to the other during the Iran–Iraq war; and (5) the Soviet disinformation campaign against the US in the Middle East.

The Soviet plan for a settlement of the Arab–Israeli conflict, first made public in 1976 under Brezhnev, has remained essentially the same under Gorbachev. The Soviet Union, in 1976 as in 1989, has called for an international conference to solve the Arab–Israeli conflict and has stipulated three central points for such a settlement:

1 the total withdrawal of all Israeli forces from territories captured in the 1967 war;
2 the establishment of an independent Palestinian state on the West Bank and Gaza strip;
3 the right to a secure existence for all states in the Middle East, including Israel.

While minor modifications of this plan have been made for tactical reasons from time to time, such as in 1982 under Brezhnev with the addition of a number of the principles of the Arab summit conference peace plan at Fez, in an effort to win Arab support following the Israeli invasion of Lebanon; under Chernenko in 1984 with the affirmation of the Palestinian state's right to form a confederation with another state, a gesture aimed at Jordan which Moscow was courting at the time; and under Gorbachev in 1986 when the Soviet leader, seeking to broaden support for the Soviet peace plan, proposed a preliminary conference made up of the permanent members of the UN Security Council to plan the international peace conference; the Soviet peace plan has nonetheless remained essentially unchanged. In 1989, as in 1976, Moscow evidently felt that an independent Palestinian state sandwiched between a hostile Israel and a possibly hostile Jordan would turn to the USSR for support, especially if relations between such a state and Israel resembled those between North Korea and South Korea, instead of being genuinely normalized with trade, tourism, cultural, and diplomatic relations according to the model of the Israeli–Egyptian peace treaty. At the same time, in 1989, as in 1976, Moscow has continued to support Israel's right to exist both for fear of alienating the United States and because the existence of Israel has provided Moscow with a convenient rallying point for anti-Western agitation in the Arab world. What was somewhat different in 1989, however, was that most of the Arab world now supported the Soviet plan for an international conference, and this should be considered a success for Soviet diplomacy.

A second major area of continuity in Soviet policy toward the Middle East has been Moscow's unwillingness to challenge either American or Israeli military activity in the region in such a way that a direct military confrontation might take place. Thus, just as Brezhnev did not oppose with anything more than rhetoric the Israeli invasion of Lebanon in 1982 and the American troop deployments there, and Andropov did not come to Syria's aid when its troops in Lebanon were attacked by American forces in December 1983, so too did Gorbachev stand by while American planes twice bombed Libya in 1986 and clashed with Iran on a number of occasions during the convoy operation in the Gulf in 1987 and 1988. Interestingly enough, in each of the first three cases, Moscow sent weapons to the targeted group prior to the Israeli or US military action (artillery to the PLO in Lebanon; SAM-5s and SS-21s to Syria; and SAM-5s to Libya). Yet the increased military supplies did not serve to deter the attacks, and, in the case of the Israeli invasion of Lebanon in 1982, the Soviet aid may have been a factor in precipitating the military action. This lack of Soviet military activity stands in sharp contrast to Moscow's active role in the Egyptian–Israeli War of Attrition along the Suez Canal in 1969–70 and its threats to intervene in the 1973 Yom Kippur war. Moscow's inactivity can in part be explained by its higher priorities elsewhere in the 1979–89 period. Burdened by its entanglement in Afghanistan, Moscow's highest priority in the early and mid-1980s appeared to be first to prevent the deployment of US Pershing II and cruise missiles in Western Europe by mounting a huge peace campaign and, when this failed, to try to reverse the deployments. As soon as Gorbachev took over, this became his highest foreign policy priority and, beset by the nuclear disaster at Chernobyl and the sharp drop in oil prices – both of which were body blows to an already weakened Soviet economy – Gorbachev sought to reduce international tensions so as to achieve an arms agreement, cut military spending and divert resources to *perestroika*. Under the circumstances, military clashes with the US or the US ally, Israel, would have been counter-productive to the larger Soviet interests.

A third area of continuity in Soviet policy toward the Middle East has been Moscow's inability to terminate the quarrels between Syrian leader Hafiz Assad and PLO leader Yasser Arafat on the one hand, and between Assad and Iraqi President Saddam Hussein on the other. These quarrels, along with Syrian backing of Iran in the Iran–Iraq war, helped to prevent the "anti-imperialist" unity in the Arab world sought by Gorbachev and his predecessors. Indeed, just as Brezhnev was caught between Assad and Arafat during the Lebanese civil war of 1976, so too was Andropov in 1983 when Syrian forces pushed Arafat out of Lebanon, and so too was Gorbachev during the camps war of 1985 and 1986–7 when the Lebanese Shiite militia, Amal, which was supported by Syria, sought to prevent Arafat's followers from reestablishing their positions in Lebanon. In each of these cases Moscow proved unwilling to fully back either Syria, a treaty ally, or the PLO, a significant force in the Arab world and in world politics. Moscow's failure to secure a compromise agreement between Assad and Arafat highlights the limits of Soviet influence in the Arab world as does the inability of successive Soviet leaders to work out a lasting *rapprochement* between Assad and Saddam Hussein. The one significant *rapprochement*, precipitated by the Camp David agreements of September 1978, lasted only until July 1979, and Syria's help to Iraq's enemy Iran, in the Iran–Iraq war, further embittered the Syrian–Iraqi relationship.

A fourth area of continuity has been Soviet policy toward the Iran–Iraq war which began in September 1980 and ended with a cease-fire in August 1988. Despite all the Soviet rhetoric about "new thinking" and "balance of interests" in solving Third World problems, there was far more continuity than change in Soviet policy when one compares Gorbachev's policy with that of his predecessors Brezhnev, Andropov, and Chernenko. Thus as Brezhnev first tilted to Iran from 1980 to 1982 and then back to Iraq from 1982 to 1985, Gorbachev was to tilt to Iran in 1986, back to Iraq in the first six months of 1987, and then back to Iran again. In addition, like his predecessors, Gorbachev tried – and failed – to end the Gulf war which, as mentioned above, caused numerous problems for Soviet strategy in the Middle East such as dividing the Arab world and enhancing the US political/military position in the Gulf. The ceasefire which ended the war in August 1988 was due to Iranian war-weariness and defeats on the battlefield, not to Soviet diplomacy, although the weaponry supplied to Iraq by the USSR played a role in the Iranian decision to accept a cease-fire. To be sure, Gorbachev demonstrated more diplomatic flexibility than his predecessors in dealing with Iran, although it is an open question as to whether or not he has been any more successful. Thus in 1986, Iran made a series of gestures to the USSR which Moscow eagerly reciprocated, only to find out that Iran had exploited the Soviet drive for influence to mount major offensives against Iraq. Then Moscow sought to exploit the Irangate crisis by denouncing Iran and championing the Arabs against it, going so far as to agree to charter three Kuwaiti tankers. Once the US moved in a major way to redeem itself for Irangate by reflagging eleven Kuwaiti tankers and building up its naval armada in the Gulf, however, Moscow switched positions again, trying to exploit the rise in US–Iranian tension to enhance its own position in Tehran. Its peace initiative of July 3, 1987, which was marked by anti-American propaganda, and its efforts to delay the imposition of UN sanctions against Iran, clearly reflected the pro-Iranian tilt in its policy. Moscow's policy alienated the Arab states of the Gulf, while initially winning it very little new influence in Iran. Indeed relations between the Soviet Union and Iran appeared to fall to their lowest point since Gorbachev took power when, in March 1988, the Iranian leadership blamed Moscow for supplying Iraq with the missiles it used to bombard Tehran. Soviet–Iranian relations were to improve however, once the war came to an end and Moscow pulled its troops out of Afghanistan. In any case the overtly anti-American policy of the USSR in the Gulf from the US reflagging of Kuwaiti tankers in July 1987 to the cease-fire one year later would appear to raise serious questions about Soviet claims to demonstrate "new thinking" in the solution of such Third World crises as the Iran–Iraq war.

In examining the tactics used by Moscow in seeking to improve ties with Iran, again there is more continuity than change. Thus, just as his predecessors sought to exploit a perceived Iranian economic vulnerability to improve ties with Tehran, so too did Gorbachev. Yet it would appear that although Iran was, in fact, in need of economic assistance, the Khomeini regime very cleverly exploited the Soviet offers of economic cooperation to entice the USSR through rhetorical declarations into thinking it was on the verge of a political breakthrough in Tehran. On no less than three separate occasions (before the 1986 Fao offensive, before the 1987 offensive, and during the US naval build-up in the Gulf in the summer of 1987), Iran appears to have manipulated Moscow and achieved its own political ends without making any concessions to the USSR. Indeed on such basic issues as the continuation of the Iran–Iraq war and aid to the Afghan Mujahadeen, Iran demonstrated that Moscow had little influence over it, although once Moscow pulled its troops out of Afghanistan, Iran said it did not want an anti-Soviet regime there and Moscow may have hoped for Iranian support in establishing an Afghan government that would not be hostile to the USSR. Gorbachev may also have taken some satisfaction from the fact that, despite the shipments of US weapons to Iran during the Irangate affair, Washington and Tehran remained very far from any political *rapprochement*, and this was at least a negative achievement for Gorbachev. Once the Iran–Iraq war came to a close, and Iran embarked on a major postwar reconstruction program, the pattern of Iranian–Soviet relations seemed to be repeated as the Soviet Union again offered economic assistance, and Iran again offered encouraging rhetoric. Whether the death of Khomeini will alter this pattern and lead to the closer Soviet–Iranian relationship Moscow has long wanted, remains very much in doubt.

In looking at Soviet policy toward Iran in the period from Gorbachev's coming to power in March 1985, there is one apparently new facet of Soviet policy that is observable. This is Moscow's new emphasis on the role of the UN, and, especially, the UN Secretary General, in settling the dispute. It is interesting to note, however, that Moscow's new emphasis on the UN came at a time when the US had made a major military committment in the Gulf. Thus, by first working for the passage of UN Resolution 598 and then calling for a UN fleet in the Gulf to escort shipping, Moscow appeared to be trying to use the world organization to prevent the United States from making major political gains with the Arab Gulf states. At the same time, however, Moscow's refusal to agree to the implementation of sanctions against Iran deprived UN Resolution 598 of any real political force. Similarly, the Soviet suggestion that the proposed UN Gulf fleet be the instrument to impose sanctions was so limited by qualifications that it seemed merely a propaganda ploy to assuage Arab opinion at a time when the Gulf Arabs were increasingly critical of Moscow's pro-Iranian tilt.

Gorbachev's effort to employ the UN for tactical purposes is in many ways similar to his predecessors' attitude toward UN Middle East activities. While all the Soviet leaders have supported the UN force on the Golan Heights and UNIFIL in Lebanon, most probably as barriers against renewed Syrian–Israeli conflict, it should be remembered that Brezhnev opposed the deployment of UN forces between Israeli and Egyptian troops as part of the Egyptian–Israeli peace agreement of 1979. Then, in an action very similar to the proposal for a UN fleet in the Gulf, Brezhnev proposed a UN force to escort PLO forces out of Beirut in 1982 in an apparent effort to prevent the US from gaining the diplomatic credit for accomplishing this task. Brezhnev's successors, however, then opposed the installation of a UN force in Beirut as the US and other members of the multinational force were in the process of a rather ignominious withdrawal, in an apparent Soviet effort to reinforce their humiliation by preventing the deployment of a UN force that would help the US and its NATO allies to more gracefully exit from Lebanon. In sum, therefore, it remains to be seen whether Gorbachev, as part of the "new thinking' really wants to utilize the United Nations to help cool crisis spots in the Middle East – thereby enabling the crisis to be settled without either superpower fully committing its prestige and risking the concomitant dangers – or whether Gorbachev's use of the UN, much as his predecessors, is primarily tactical in nature and is aimed at enhancing the Soviet position while weakening that of the US.

Another area in which continuity, rather than change, would appear to be the norm in Soviet policy toward the Middle East is Moscow's continued use of disinformation – the deliberate telling of lies – to undermine the US position in the region and enhance that of the USSR in the zero-sum game influence competition that is still evident in Soviet policy, if not in Gorbachev's rhetoric. In Brezhnev's day, on the eve of the final settlement of the hostage crisis between Iran and the US in 1981, the Soviet press spread false reports of an impending US military attack on Iran – a clear effort to sabotage the completion of the agreement and prevent a possible US–Iranian *rapprochement*. In October 1985, in the first year of the Gorbachev era, Moscow Radio told the Arab states that the Israeli aircraft that bombed PLO headquarters in Tunis, had taken off from US aircraft carriers, a classic case of disinformation because the aircraft involved, F-15s and F-16s do not have the capability of taking off from aircraft carriers, something most Arabs (and, for that matter, most Europeans and Americans) could not be expected to know. Even during the high point of the "new thinking," disinformation continued, with Moscow Radio stating in April 1988 that the Israeli assassination of the PLO leader Abu Jihad was arranged with US help, and that the shooting down of the Iranian passenger plane in July 1988 by the US warship was "deliberate murder." So long as Moscow persists in practicing disinformation on this scale, it will be difficult for US policy makers to take seriously any Soviet offer of cooperation in settling Middle Eastern crises because the suspicion will remain that Moscow will seek to manipulate the settlement of the crisis to enhance its own position while weakening that of the US. In other words, so long as Moscow continues to give the appearance of actively following a zero-sum game influence competition strategy in the Middle East, it is doubtful that it will qualify as a partner for peace in the region.

While there are thus major areas of continuity in Soviet policy toward the Middle East from 1979 to 1989, there are a number of changes as well. First and foremost was the decision to pull Soviet forces out of Afghanistan. More than any other act, the Soviet invasion poisoned Soviet–American relations and created a new "cold war" atmosphere in the early 1980s, leading not only to a major build-up of US military power, but also to the establishment of a strategic relationship between the US and Israel which included Israeli participation in SDI and joint military exercises between the two countries, but also to the deepening of suspicion as to Soviet aims in the Middle East by most Arab states, Turkey, and Iran. After Gorbachev intensified the Soviet military effort in his first year in power, he evidently decided that the war was unwinnable and decided to pull out. The Soviet exodus from Afghanistan, he may have reasoned, could be expected to have a salutary influence not only on US–Soviet relations, but also on Moscow's relations with the Muslim world, and especially Iran since the invasion had led to Soviet troops, already on Iran's northern border, to be emplaced on Iran's eastern border as well. The very positive reaction of the states of the Middle East to the Soviet withdrawal set the stage for Moscow to try to improve its position in the region through Shevardnadze's trip to the Middle East in the immediate aftermath of the withdrawal as he visited Syria, Jordan, Egypt, Iraq, and Iran, and met with the Israeli Foreign Minister Moshe Arens and PLO chief Yasser Arafat. It is too early to determine, however, to what degree the Soviet pull-out from Afghanistan will improve the Soviet position in the Middle East although it is already clear that Soviet–Iranian relations have been somewhat improved by the withdrawal.

A second highly significant change in Soviet policy toward the Middle East under Gorbachev has been Moscow's *rapprochement* with Egypt. Although diplomatic relations on the ambassadorial level which had been terminated by Anwar Sadat in 1981 during the Brezhnev era, were restored by Sadat's successor Hosni Mubarak while Chernenko was in power in 1984, the real improvement in Soviet–Egyptian relations did not come until the advent of Mikhail Gorbachev. While under Brezhnev, Andropov, and Chernenko, the Soviet Union had sought to keep Egypt isolated in the Arab world because of Camp David, Gorbachev came to realize that the pressures of the Iran–Iraq war, and Mubarak's clever diplomacy, were causing Egypt to be reintegrated into the Arab world despite Camp David and Egypt's peace treaty with Israel. By 1987, therefore, Gorbachev evidently decided to accept the inevitable and to exploit the desire of Mubarak for an international conference to work with Egypt, which had influence on both the United States and Israel (particularly when Peres was Prime Minister), to bring about an international conference or, failing that, to try to pull Egypt away from the United States. The *rapprochement* was a rapid one. Moscow rescheduled Egypt's military debt, Soviet consulates were reopened in Alexandria and Port Said, the Soviet–Egyptian Friendship Society was revived with Butros Butros Ghali, Egypt's Minister of State for Foreign Affairs, as the Egyptian leader of the organization, cultural ties proliferated, trade increased sharply, a cooperative agreement was signed between the Soviet and Egyptian Chambers of Commerce and Moscow agreed to give Egypt renewed economic aid. Perhaps most important, however, Egypt was now included in Soviet diplomatic tours of the Middle East, with the October 1987 Cairo visit by Soviet First Deputy Foreign Minister Yuli Voronstov one of the early signals of the changed Soviet policy. The *rapprochement* increased in intensity in 1988 with the visit of Egyptian Foreign Minister Maguid to Moscow and reached its culmination in February 1989 when Soviet Foreign Minister Shevardnadze not only visited Cairo, but also met PLO leader Yasser Arafat and Israeli Foreign Minister Moshe Arens there, thus putting Egypt once again very much on the Middle Eastern diplomatic map and further legitimizing the policies of Mubarak – much to the consternation of Assad. To be sure, despite the *rapprochement* with the Soviet Union, Mubarak's Egypt remained closely aligned with the United States as shown by the annual "Bright Star" military exercises and the $2.3

billion in American economic aid. On balance, however, the *rapprochement* helped both Gorbachev and Mubarak. From the Soviet viewpoint, as noted above, Egypt could be an ally in helping to arrange an international conference and was an important link to such countries as Israel and Saudi Arabia; for Mubarak, the closer tie with the USSR enhances his "non-aligned" appearance, a development that has helped him domestically as well as in the Arab world.

While Egypt was the most important Arab country successfully courted by Gorbachev, three small Gulf Arab states also established diplomatic relations with the USSR during his tenure in office. The United Arab Emirates and Oman established ties with the Soviet Union in 1985 and Qatar did the same in 1988. In the first two cases Moscow was able to capitalize on the small Arab states' desire for "reinsurance" against Iran as the Iran–Iraq war escalated, while in all three cases friction with the United States also seemed to play a role in the decision to establish ties with Moscow. Interestingly enough, however, while all three states followed the Kuwaiti example of non-alignment in establishing relations with the Soviet Union, Kuwait itself, the most neutralist of the Gulf Cooperation Council states, moved closer to the United States as a result of the US decision to reflag Kuwaiti tankers and protect them against Iranian attack. It should also be noted that Saudi Arabia, despite an increased level of diplomatic contacts with the Soviet Union in 1987 and 1988, did not, despite Soviet urging, establish diplomatic relations with Moscow. This may, in part, have been due to the reestablishment of a radical regime in the PDRY in January 1986 following the failure of the relatively moderate Ali Nasser Mohammed to eliminate his opponents in a preemptive palace coup. In any case, while Moscow was able to reestablish a pro-Soviet regime in Aden following the bloodbath there, the Soviet decision to allow Ali Nasser Mohammed's opponent, Abd al Fattah Ismail to return to Aden from exile in Moscow and the failure to foresee that Ali Nasser Mohammed would react violently to Ismail's challenge, raised questions about Soviet intelligence capabilities as well as about the suitability of the Marxist model which Soviet advisers had sought to establish in the PDRY. In addition, while Moscow repeatedly urged the new PDRY leadership to cooperate with its neighbors, it remained to be seen, once the new regime had fully recovered from the aftermath of the January 1986 events, whether it would again support dissident groups in North Yemen and in the Arab Gulf as it had in the past. Should such a development occur, Moscow's newly established relations with Oman, Qatar, and the UAE may well be threatened and Soviet hopes to establish ties with Saudi Arabia might be further from realization despite Gorbachev's claims to have "deideologized" Soviet foreign policies.

A final change in Soviet policy toward the Middle East under Gorbachev that is worthy of examination is the Gorbachev approach toward Israel. One cannot, however, in examining Soviet–Israeli ties look only at relations between the two countries to try to determine Moscow's goals. Given the very close tie between Israel and the United States, Soviet gestures to Israel may be seen to have a positive impact in the United States as well, and, particularly as Gorbachev's efforts at *perestroika* took hold in 1987 and 1988, one can see this factor playing an increasingly important role in Soviet relations with Israel.

In the period prior to Gorbachev, while occasional Soviet delegations visited Israel, and the Soviet and Israeli Foreign Ministers met from time to time at the United Nations, relations between the two countries remained highly strained. Moscow had broken off diplomatic relations with Israel during the 1967 war, and while continuing to proclaim that Israel had a right to exist, stated that diplomatic relations would not be restored until Israel withdrew from all the territories it had occupied in the 1967 war. The Israeli invasion of Lebanon in 1982, in which it fought a series of battles with Syria as well as the PLO, further exacerbated relations as did Moscow's sharp cut in the number of Soviet Jews allowed to leave the USSR, from a high of 51,320 in 1979 to a low of 896 in 1984, along with Moscow's political and military support not only for Syria but also for the PLO which Israeli leaders saw as equally bent on Israel's destruction. Additional problems vexing Soviet–Israeli relations were the annual efforts of the Soviet Union to exclude Israel from the UN General Assembly, and Israel's increasingly close military cooperation with the United States including its decision to join in the SDI project and to allow Voice of America and Radio Liberty radio transmitters to be built on Israeli soil.

Gorbachev's diplomatic efforts to improve Soviet–Israeli relations began in July 1985 with a secret meeting between the Israeli and Soviet ambassadors to France, continued in 1986 with public consular-level talks in Helsinki, Finland, in August and an extended meeting between the Israeli Prime Minister Shimon Peres and Soviet Foreign Minister Shevardnadze, at the United Nations in September. The pace of contacts increased in 1987 with numerous meetings between Soviet and Israeli officials, culminating in April with a six-hour meeting between Peres and the Soviet delegation to the Socialist International Conference headed by the deputy director of the CPSU's International Department, Karen Brutents. Moscow's dispatch of a consular delegation to Israel in July 1987 and its permitting Warsaw Pact allies Poland and Hungary to reestablish diplomatic relations with Israel, albeit at the low level of diplomatic interest sections, were other signals of its interest in improving relations with Israel, as were its actions in 1988 which included permission for an Israeli consular delegation to come to the Soviet Union, public comments by Soviet leaders that Israel's interests had to be taken into account in any peace settlement, and Shevardnadze's meeting with Israeli Prime Minister Yitzhak Shamir in New York – all of this despite the Palestinian uprising which began in December 1987 and which the USSR severely criticized Israel for repressing. At the same time, beginning in 1987 Moscow sharply increased the number of Soviet Jews leaving the USSR, with 8,155 departing in 1987 and 18,965 leaving in 1988. In addition, all the "Prisoners of Zion" (those Soviet Jews jailed for wanting to go to Israel) were released, and a number were permitted to go to Israel along with prominent Refuseniks like Anatoly Sharansky and Ida Nudel.

In seeking to explain these changes under Gorbachev, there appear to be two major factors to consider – Middle East politics and Soviet–American relations. When Gorbachev took office, the Middle East peace process appeared to be well underway as a result of the Hussein–Arafat agreement of February 1985 and US efforts to broker a Palestinian–Jordanian negotiating team acceptable to Israel. Consequently, Gorbachev, a far more flexible leader than his predecessors, felt an opening to Israel was necessary for Moscow to enter the peace process from which it had been excluded since 1973. While the peace process came to a halt because of the rise in Middle East terrorism and the break between Hussein and Arafat, Moscow continued its contacts with Israel, in part because it was seeking Israeli support for an international peace conference which Gorbachev, as his predecessors, felt was the best way to resolve the Arab–Israeli conflict (and enhance the Soviet position in the Middle East in the process), and in part because Moscow, seeing an escalation of Syrian–Israeli tension due to Syria's involvement in terrorist attacks against Israeli aircraft, wished to deter a possible Israeli attack on Syria. By the fall of 1986, the threat of a Syrian–Israeli war had receded (although with the spread of modern missiles – some Chinese-supplied – to the region, and the use of chemical weapons in the Iran–Iraq war, Moscow continued to worry about the outbreak of a military conflict between Israel and Syria), but Moscow now saw the opportunity to go on the diplomatic offensive in the Middle East as the Iran–Contra scandal dealt a major (if temporary) blow to the US position in the Arab world. Consequently Gorbachev stepped up Soviet efforts to convene an international conference on the Middle East (gaining the support of Egypt and Jordan in the process) and these efforts involved expanded contacts with Israel.

Fortunately for Moscow, Soviet interests in convening an international conference were reciprocated by Peres who saw in such a meeting, particularly after he stepped down as Prime Minister in October 1986, a means of bringing down the National Unity government and moving Israel to new elections. Yet in advocating such a conference, and claiming that important changes had taken place in Soviet policy, such as its promise not only not to allow an international conference to impose a settlement on Israel but also to take Israeli interests into consideration, Peres left open a series of questions to which the Soviets, in speaking to different audiences (Israeli, Arab, US) had given very ambiguous answers. To be sure, Gorbachev had now promised to settle the issue of reestablishing diplomatic relations with Israel once the international conference had begun. This was a considerable change from the previous Soviet position which had gone so far as to refuse to consider reestablishing diplomatic relations until after Israel had withdrawn from all occupied territories. In addition, Gorbachev's public comments to Israel's most implacable enemies, Syrian President Hafiz Assad, to whom the Soviet leader urged a political (not military) settlement of the Arab–Israeli conflict, and who was told that the lack of Soviet–Israeli diplomatic relations was "abnormal," and Yasser Arafat, who was told that recognition of Israel and concern for its security would have to be part of any peace settlement, could be pointed to by Peres as significant changes in Soviet policy. The Israeli Foreign Minister could also point to the increase in Soviet Jewish emigration, the release of the "Prisoners of Zion," and the reestablishment of interest section diplomatic relations with two of Moscow's East European clients, Poland and Hungary, the latter nation to which Peres paid a formal visit in May 1988 – the first such visit by an Israeli leader to a Soviet bloc state (albeit an increasingly independent one) since the 1967 war.

Nonetheless, despite these moves, the Soviet Union continued to take an ambiguous position on two of the key questions involved in the peace process. First, would Moscow be satisfied with merely a formal role at the international conference or would it demand the right for the conference as a whole to approve any agreements reached in the bilateral or multilateral talks between Israel and her neighbors. The Soviet Union's change in terminology from calling for an "authoritative" conference to calling for an "effective" conference, does not really end its ambiguity on this question. Second, would Moscow back PLO representation at the conference – something still anathema to most Israeli leaders. Having invested a considerable amount of effort in helping to bring some of the disparate factions of the PLO back together, and given the increased prestige of the PLO because of the Palestinian Intifada (uprising) in the occupied territories and the PLO recognition of Israel in 1988, it appeared unlikely that Moscow would throw away the political capital it had gained in the organization by excluding it from an international conference. Indeed, Gorbachev's comments at the post-summit press conference in June 1988 that the Palestinians themselves and the other Arabs would decide Palestinian representation seemed to be just a tactical deflection of the question, as did his call for Palestinian "self-determination" rather than for a Palestinian state, and, later, the Soviet recognition of the Palestinian proclamation of a state in November 1988, rather than the state itself. To be sure, the ambiguity of the situation fitted Moscow's goals well; so long as there was no conference, it could continue to pursue a number of policy options simultaneously (Israel, PLO, Arab states) without having to commit to any one, while giving the impression of being actively involved in the peace process, a policy which was calculated to bring Moscow dividends not only in the Middle East but in the United States as well. This was the case because Moscow's opening to Israel, along with its policy toward Soviet Jewry in 1987 and 1988, seemed aimed at influencing public opinion in the United States.

Following the CPSU party conference in February 1986, with his position in the party reinforced, Gorbachev set about to undertake major economic and political reforms in the USSR. To succeed in his program, however, particularly at a time of declining hard currency earnings due to the drop in oil prices, Gorbachev, as noted above, clearly wanted to slow down the arms race to free resources for Moscow's lagging economy. He was also interested in getting credits from the US, as well as investments in joint enterprises, and this necessitated changes in the Jackson–Vanik and Stevenson amendments. Given the fact that Moscow has long overestimated Jewish influence in the United States, and that it understands the close tie between American Jewry and the State of Israel, Soviet gestures to Israel, which included in 1988 and 1989 a large number of cultural and athletic exchanges, coupled with the increased exodus of Soviet Jews, seemed aimed at improving the Soviet image in the United States for arms control purposes and positioning Moscow for US trade benefits. Indeed, the very fact that National Conference on Soviet Jewry President Morris Abram was invited to Moscow, and that he indicated a willingness to support changes in the Jackson–Vanik and Stevenson amendments if the Soviet Jewish exodus increased, indicated that Moscow was actively using the issue of Soviet Jewry as well as the appearance of an improved relationship with Israel to improve its standing in the US. For its part, Israel, by promptly returning to the Soviet Union the hijackers of a plane which was flown to Tel Aviv in December 1988 and actively aiding in the search for victims of the Armenian earthquake later that month, was doing its best to improve ties with the USSR. Yet it appeared Moscow was getting the better of the relationship, with the Soviet Union giving the appearance of having full relations with Israel as a result of the large amount of publicity it received for even limited cultural contacts with the Jewish state, but keeping formal diplomatic contacts with Israel at the very low level of consular ties and explaining the limited contact to the Arabs as necessary for the pursuit of peace.

In sum, therefore, Soviet policy toward Israel under Gorbachev has been an active and flexible one. Moscow has sharply increased contacts of all kinds with Israel, yet formal diplomatic relations would appear to be a long way off unless an international peace conference is convened, still a doubtful possibility. In addition, there has been a sharp increase in the exodus of Soviet Jews, but a continuation of this increase may be hostage to both the diplomatic situation in the Middle East and progress in the arms control negotiations between the US and USSR, and Soviet policy could be reversed if Gorbachev is unable to maintain himself in power.

Future prospects for Soviet policy in the Middle East

In looking to the future of Soviet policy toward the Middle East, much will depend on whether Gorbachev's *perestroika* policy is successful and whether the Soviet leader succeeds in staying in power. With Soviet domestic politics in a state of flux due to a combination of ethnic unrest and economic crisis, the Soviet leader is concentrating his foreign policy attention on relations with the NATO states, East Europe (also in a state of flux), and China, and is trying as much as possible to avoid crises in the Third World. For this reason Moscow has moved to help settle conflicts in Cambodia and Angola – areas far from the Soviet Union. Having withdrawn from Afghanistan (although still supplying the communist government there with weaponry), Gorbachev has clearly sought to limit a number of the economically and politically costly Soviet involvements in the Third World. Yet of all the Third World regions, the Middle East is closest to the USSR, and as mentioned above, there has been more continuity than change in Soviet policy toward the region when one compares the policies of Gorbachev with his predecessors. What then could lead the USSR to significantly change its policy and move from a policy of zero-sum game competition (in practice, if not in rhetoric) with the United States to one of regulated competition and possibly even cooperation with it in the Middle East. The two superpowers do have a number of common interests in the Middle East which range from preservation of freedom of navigation (the USSR uses Middle East waterways to link its Eastern and Western segments, while America's NATO allies use the region's waterways to acquire oil supplies); to maintaining free access to oil (crucial for the NATO alliance now and possibly of increasing importance to the USSR and its Warsaw Pact allies in the future); to concern about the spread of Iranian-backed militant Islamic fundamentalism (whether into allies of the US like Egypt and Saudi Arabia or into Afghanistan and the Soviet Union itself). In addition, neither side wants the outbreak of another Syrian–Israeli war which would raise the danger of a superpower confrontation. Assuming Gorbachev stays in power, what would it take to convince Moscow that genuine rather than rhetorical cooperation in solving Middle East problems would be in its best interest? One increasingly important factor is the spread of advanced military technology to the region in the form of ground-to-ground missiles and chemical weapons. In the hands of a Kaddafi or a militant Islamic fundamentalist in Iran, such weaponry might precipitate a major regional conflict from which both superpowers could suffer, whether or not their own forces became targets of the regional states' increasingly sophisticated weaponry. Similarly, as Assad, possibly with Chinese help, acquires long-range ground-to-ground missiles, technology, and chemical weapons, he could be tempted to fire the missiles at Israeli cities, air bases, and mobilization points, a development that would lead the Israelis not only to retaliate but also to preemptively attack Syria if they thought Assad was likely to launch an attack. The outbreak of a Syrian–Israeli war would run a major risk of involving the two superpowers and could possibly lead to a major confrontation, something that neither of them would appear to want. Given these problems, the Soviet leadership may decide that a major effort to join the United States and its NATO allies to limit the spread of advanced technology to the Middle East would be worthwhile. Given the fact that weapons sales earn the USSR a significant amount of hard currency as well as at least the appearance of influence, any Soviet decision to limit arms sales would be a difficult one. Nonetheless the limitations on the sale of sophisticated arms to countries like Libya, Syria, and Iran would appear to be the *sine qua non* for effective Soviet–American cooperation in crisis management in the region, and would underlie any system of limited influence competition. A second requirement would be for Moscow to end its disinformation campaign which, more than almost any other Soviet policy, appears to demonstrate Moscow's continuing interest in a zero-sum game influence competition with the US in the region. Third, Moscow should come out for a genuine normalization of relations between Israel and a future Palestinian state and stipulate that such a state would have to be essentially demilitarized. This, along with resuming full diplomatic relations with Israel, would help convince the United States and many Israelis that Moscow is genuinely interested in an equitable Arab–Israeli settlement. A fourth policy that Moscow could take to convince the US that it is interested in limiting its competition with the US in the Middle East would be to arrange, in advance, with the United States for a UN military force that would be empowered to move rapidly (with the help of both US and Soviet transport aircraft) to a regional crisis area to defuse a tense situation. With command and control systems worked out in advance, such UN forces could be useful tools in crisis management. Soviet agreement to the establishment of such forces, and to the conditions of their employment, would go a long way toward removing Western suspicion that Moscow's new interest in the UN is merely a tactical ploy to improve the Soviet position in the Middle East.

In sum, while continuity rather than change highlighted Soviet policy toward the Middle East in the period from the Soviet invasion of Afghanistan in 1979 to the Soviet exodus from that country in 1989, one cannot rule out a turn in Soviet policy from zero-sum game competition to regulated competition and even cooperation with the United States if a combination of domestic problems in the Soviet Union, and the threat of increasingly sophisticated weaponry in the hands of regional states, convinces the Soviet leadership that a change in policy toward the Middle East is called for.

Notes

Introduction

1 For general studies of Soviet policy in the Middle East, see Robert O. Freedman, *Soviet Policy Toward the Middle East Since 1970*, 3rd edn (New York: Praeger, 1982); Jon D. Glassman, *Arms for the Arabs: The Soviet Union and War in the Middle East* (Baltimore: Johns Hopkins, 1975); Galia Golan, *Yom Kippur and After: The Soviet Union and the Middle East Crisis* (London: Cambridge University Press, 1977); Yaacov Ro'i, *From Encroachment to Involvement: A Documentary Study of Soviet Policy in the Middle East* (Jerusalem: Israel Universities Press, 1974); Amnon Sella, *Soviet Political and Military Conduct in the Middle East* (New York: St. Martins, 1981); and Adeed Dawisha and Karen Dawisha (eds.), *The Soviet Union in the Middle East: Policies and Perspectives* (New York: Holmes and Meier, 1982). See also Yaacov Ro'i (ed.), *The Limits to Power* (London: Croom Helm, 1979); Steven Spiegel, Mark Heller, and Jacob Goldberg (eds.), *The Soviet–American Competition in the Middle East* (Lexington: D.C. Heath, 1988); Helena Cobban (ed.), *Military Dimensions of Soviet Middle East Policy* (College Park, Maryland: Center for International Security Studies, 1988) and Mark Kauppi and R. Craig Nation (eds.), *The Soviet Union and the Middle East in the 1980s* (Lexington: D.C. Heath, 1983), and Alvin Z. Rubinstein, *Soviet Policy Toward Turkey, Iran and Afghanistan* (New York: Praeger, 1982).

For Arab viewpoints see Mohammed Heikal, *The Sphinx and the Commissar* (New York: Harper and Row, 1978) and Mahrez Mahmoud el Hussini, *Soviet–Egyptian Relations 1945–1985* (New York: St. Martins, 1987). The most authoritative Soviet scholar writing on the Middle East, now a member of the Politburo is Yevgeny Primakov. His books include *Anatomia Blizhnevostochnogo Konflikta* (Anatomy of the Middle East Conflict) (Moscow: Mysl, 1978), and *Istoriia Odnogo Sgovora* (History of The [Camp David] Deal) (Moscow: Political Literature Press, 1985). See also his article "Soviet Policy Toward the Arab–Israeli Conflict," in William B. Quandt (ed.), *The Middle East: Ten Years After Camp David* (Washington, D.C.: Brookings, 1988), pp. 387–409. See also Rashid Khalidi, "Arab Views of the Soviet Role in the Middle East," *Middle East Journal*, vol. 39, no. 4 (Autumn 1985), pp. 716–32.

For general studies of Soviet policy toward the Third World, see Robert H. Donaldson (ed.), *The Soviet Union in the Third World: Successes and Failures* (Boulder: Westview Press, 1981); Andrzej Korbonsky and Francis Fukuyama (eds.), *The Soviet Union and the Third World: The Last Three Decades* (Ithaca: Cornell University Press, 1987); Daniel Papp, *Soviet Policies Toward the Developing World During the 1980s* (Maxwell Air Force Base, Alabama: Air University Press, 1986); *The Soviet Union in the Third World 1980–85: An Imperial Burden or Political Asset* (Washington: Congressional Research Service, 1986); Stephen T. Hosmer and Thomas W. Wolfe, *Soviet Policy and Practice Toward Third World Conflicts* (Lexington: D.C. Heath, 1983);

Carol Saivetz (ed.), *The Soviet Union in the Third World* (Boulder: Westview Press, 1989); and Carol Saivetz and Sylvia Woodby, *Soviet–Third World Relations* (Boulder: Westview Press, 1985). See also Alvin Z. Rubinstein, *Moscow's Third World Strategy* (Princeton: Princeton University Press, 1988).

2 The main representatives of this school of thought are Dennis Ross and Uri Ra'anan. See, for example, Dennis Ross, "The Soviet Union and the Persian Gulf," *Political Science Quarterly*, vol. 99 (Winter 1984–85), pp. 615–35. See also Alvin Z. Rubinstein, "Soviet Success Story: The Third World," *Orbis*, vol. 32, no. 4 (Fall 1988), pp. 551–65.

3 Political science models dealing with the exertion of influence in Soviet foreign policy in general and Soviet foreign policy toward the Middle East in particular are still relatively rare. For a general study of influence the interested reader is advised to consult J. David Singer, "International Influence: A Formal Model," in the influence theory section of *International Politics and Foreign Policy*, ed. James N. Rosenau (New York: Macmillan, 1969). Singer makes the useful distinction between influence leading to behavior modification in a target state and influence leading to behavior reinforcement. Another useful study, which examines the phenomenon of influence from a perspective of the target state is Marshall R. Singer, *Weak States in a World of Powers* (New York: Free Press, 1972), especially chapters 6–8. See also Richard W. Cottam, *Competitive Interference and Twentieth Century Diplomacy* (Pittsburgh: University of Pittsburgh Press, 1967). For an attempt to analyze Soviet influence in the Third World, see Alvin Z. Rubinstein (ed.), *Soviet and Chinese Influence in the Third World* (New York: Praeger, 1975). For an effort to measure Soviet influence in Egypt, see Alvin Z. Rubinstein, *Red Star on the Nile: The Soviet–Egyptian Influence Relationship since the June War* (Princeton: Princeton Universty Press, 1977).

4 The main representatives of this school are Galia Golan and George Breslauer. See Galia Golan, *Yom Kippur and After*, and George Breslauer, "Soviet Policy in the Middle East 1967–1972: Unalterable Antagonism or Collaborative Competition?" in Alexander L. George (ed.), *Managing U.S.–Soviet Rivalry: Problems of Crisis Prevention* (Boulder: Westview Press, 1981), pp. 65–105.

5 Cf. Robert O. Freedman, *Soviet Policy Toward the Middle East Since 1970*.

6 For an excellent analysis of Tsarist Russian foreign policy, see Barbara Jelavich, *A Century of Russian Foreign Policy 1814–1914* (Philadelphia: J.B. Lippencott, 1964). See also Rubinstein, *Soviet Policy Toward Turkey, Iran and Afghanistan*, chapter 1 and Malcolm Yapp, *The Making of the Modern Near East 1792–1923* (New York: Longman, 1987).

7 This point is discussed cogently in Pedro Ramet, *The Soviet Presence in Syria* (Boulder: Westview Press, 1990).

8 See, for example, Rajan Menon, *Soviet Power and the Third World* (New Haven: Yale University Press, 1986); Andrew T. Pierre, *The Global Politics of Arms Sales* (Princeton: Princeton University Press, 1982); Abraham S. Becker, "A Note on Soviet Arms Transfers to the Middle East," in Spiegel *et al.*, *The Soviet-American Competition in the Middle East*, pp. 49–60; Michael Brzoska and Thomas Ohlsen, *Arms Transfer to the Third World 1971–1985* (New York: Oxford, 1987), and Alexander T. Bennett, "Arms Transfers as an Instrument of Soviet Policy in the Middle East," *Middle East Journal*, vol. 39, no. 4 (Autumn 1985), pp. 745–74. For information on Soviet arms transfers to the Middle East, it is necessary to check a number of sources because the available information is sometimes in dispute. The best sources are the annual compilations in the Stockholm International Peace Research Institute (SIPRI) Yearbook; The International Institute for Strategic Studies (London) *Military Balance*; and The Jaffee Center for Strategic Studies (Tel Aviv) *Middle East Military Balance*. Other useful sources are publications by the US government including *World*

Military Expenditures and Arms Transfers, published by the US Arms Control and Disarmament Agency and the Congressional Research Service's, *Trends in Conventional Arms Transfers to the Third World by Major Suppliers*.

9 Richard F. Grimmett, *Trends in Conventional Arms Transfers to the Third World by Major Suppliers 1981–88* (Washington: Congressional Research Service, 1989), p. 54.

10 *Ibid.*, p. 46.

11 Moscow TV, July 2, 1989 (*Foreign Broadcast Information Service Daily Report: The Soviet Union* (hereafter *FBIS:USSR*), July 5, 1989, p. 16).

12 For an excellent study of Soviet aid and trade policy in the Third World, see Elizabeth K. Valkenier, *The Soviet Union and the Third World* (New York: Praeger, 1983).

13 These developments are discussed in Freedman, *Soviet Policy Toward the Middle East*.

14 See Paul Henze, *Ethiopia: Crisis of a Marxist Economy – Analysis and Text of a Soviet Report* (Santa Monica: Rand 1989), Francis Fukuyama, "Patterns of Soviet Third World Policy," *Problems of Communism*, vol. 36, no. 5 (September–October 1987), pp. 1–13 and Valkenier, *The Soviet Union*.

15 This incident is discussed below, pp. 232–33.

16 Both incidents, along with other examples of Soviet disinformation, are discussed below. See also Richard Shultz and Ray Godson, *Dezinformatsia: Active Measures in Soviet Strategy* (Washington: Pergamon-Brassey's, 1984).

17 The first two cases are discussed in Freedman, *Soviet Policy Toward the Middle East*; the case of the Tudeh party is discussed below. See also Robert O. Freedman, "The Soviet Union and the Communist Parties of the Arab World: an uncertain relationship," in Roger E. Kanet and Donna Bahry (eds.), *Soviet Economic and Political Relations with the Developing World* (New York: Praeger, 1975), pp. 100–34; John K. Cooley, "The Shifting Sands of Arab Communism," *Problems of Communism*, vol. 24, no. 2 (April 1975), pp. 22–42; and Arnold Hottinger, "Arab Communism at a Low Ebb," *Problems of Communism*, vol. 30, no. 4 (July–August 1981), pp. 17–32.

18 See Mark N. Katz, *Russia and Arabia* (Baltimore: Johns Hopkins Press, 1986), p. 91.

19 For a good introduction to Soviet thinking about Islam, see Carol R. Saivetz, *The Soviet Union and the Gulf in the 1980s* (Boulder: Westview Press, 1989), ch. 1. See also Yaacov Ro'i (ed.), *The USSR and the Muslim World* (London: Allen and Unwin, 1984).

20 Translated in *FBIS: Middle East Iran Supplement*, no. 070, March 24, 1980, p. 7.

21 See Alexandre Bennigsen and Marie Broxup, *The Islamic Threat to the Soviet State* (New York: St. Martin's, 1983) and Michael Rywkin, *Moscow's Muslim Challenge: Soviet Central Asia* (New York: M.E. Sharp, 1982).

22 For a very balanced analysis of the dynamics of Islam in a Soviet Republic, see Muriel Atkin, *The Subtlest Battle: Islam in Soviet Tajikistan* (Philadelphia: Foreign Policy Research Institute, 1989).

23 See below, pp. 86–91.

24 Key sources, in English, include *The Middle East Journal*, the *International Journal of Middle East Studies*, the *Journal of Palestine Studies*, *The Middle East Review*, *The Middle East* (London), *The Middle East Economic Digest* (London), *The Jerusalem Post* and *Middle East International* (London). Translation of the speeches of Middle Eastern leaders, and of key articles from the media of Middle East states can be found in *FBIS: Middle East and South Asia*. A particularly useful source of information is the *Middle East Contemporary Survey*, published annually by the Dayan Center of Tel Aviv University.

25 In preparing this book, I had the opportunity to interview Soviet diplomats and scholars during an IREX exchange visit to the USSR in January 1988. I have also interviewed Soviet officials attached to the Soviet embassy in the United States, and Soviet scholars on visits to the United States. On the Middle East side I had the

opportunity to interview Israeli Foreign Ministry officials, PLO leaders including Yasser Arafat, and Abu Iyad, the Kuwaiti ambassador to the Soviet Union, the Jordanian ambassador to the United States, and a number of Arab and Israeli scholars specializing in Middle Eastern politics.

26 See Robert E. Hunter, "Western Europe and the Middle East since the Lebanon War," in Robert O. Freedman (ed.), *The Middle East After the Invasion of Lebanon* (Syracuse: Syracuse University Press, 1986), pp. 93–113 and Frederick Zilian, "The U.S. Raid on Libya – and NATO," *Orbis*, vol. 30, no. 3 (Fall 1986), pp. 499–524.

27 See Dina Rome Spechler, "The USSR and Third World Conflicts: Domestic Debate and Soviet Policy in the Middle East 1967–1973," *World Politics*, vol. 38, no. 3 (April 1986), pp. 435–61. See also David E. Albright, "The USSR and the Third World in the 1980s," *Problems of Communism*, vol. 38, no. 2–3 (March–June 1989), pp. 50–70.

28 Andrei Gromyko, *Pamiatnoe* (Moscow: Politizdat, 1988).

29 Jerry F. Hough, *The Struggle for the Third World: Soviet Debates and American Options* (Washington: Brookings, 1986), p. 262. See also Yury Polsky, *Soviet Research Institutes and the Formulation of Foreign Policy* (Falls Church, Virginia: Delphic Associates, 1987).

30 Valkenier, *The Soviet Union*.

1 On the eve: Soviet policy toward the Middle East from World War II until the invasion of Afghanistan

1 For an analysis of Soviet policy toward the Middle East between 1917 and 1945, see Ivan Spector, *The Soviet Union and the Muslim World* (Seattle: University of Washington Press, 1956). This book also contains a useful survey of Tsarist foreign policy toward the Middle East from 1552 to 1914. For an analysis of Soviet policy toward the communist parties and radical movements of the Middle East in the interwar period, see Walter Laqueur, *The Soviet Union and the Middle East* (New York: Praeger, 1959), pp. 1–134. For an excellent treatment of Western involvement in the Middle East, see William R. Polk, *The United States and the Arab World*, 3rd rev. edn (Cambridge, Mass.: Harvard University Press, 1975).

For a study of Soviet policy toward the Northern Tier see Alvin Z. Rubinstein, *Soviet Policy Toward Turkey, Iran and Afghanistan* (New York: Praeger, 1982). For a study concentrating on Soviet policy toward the Arab world in the 1970–80 period, see Robert O. Freedman, *Soviet Policy Toward the Middle East Since 1970*, 3rd edn (New York: Praeger, 1982).

2 For a detailed examination of Soviet pressure against Iran and Turkey, see Howard M. Sachar, *Europe Leaves the Middle East 1936–1954* (New York: Alfred A. Knopf, 1972), ch. 9.

3 According to Khrushchev's memoirs, Stalin considered the Near East part of Britain's sphere of influence and felt that Russia did not have the power to challenge Britain there directly. See Strobe Talbott (ed.), *Khrushchev Remembers* (Boston: Little, Brown, 1970), p. 431. Soviet support for the ouster of British and French troops from Lebanon and Syria in 1946 seems to have been motivated by the same considerations as its early support for Israel. A collection of Soviet documents pertaining to its relations with the Arab world from 1917 to 1960 is found in *SSSR i arabskie strany* (The USSR and the Arab states) (Moscow: Government Printing Office of Political Literature, 1960). The documents pertaining to Soviet support of Lebanon and Syria are found on pages 87–96 of that volume.

4 For a detailed analysis of the USSR's relations with Israel, see Avigdor Dagan, *Moscow and Jerusalem* (New York: Abelard-Schuman, 1970). For an analysis of Soviet behavior during the Israeli struggle for independence, see Robert O. Freedman, "The Partition of Palestine: Conflicting Nationalism and Power Politics," in

Thomas Hachey (ed.), *Partition: Peril to World Peace* (New York: Rand McNally, 1972).

5 In the 1955–56 period, while there were already some strains in Sino-Soviet relations, Russia was still the unquestioned leader of the socialist bloc. In addition, the *rapprochement* between Yugoslavia and the USSR that took place at the time seemed to many observers to bring Yugoslavia back into the Soviet sphere of influence. (Yugoslavia had been ousted from the socialist bloc by Stalin in 1948 and had subsequently turned to the West for aid). Thus, Khrushchev apparently considered that any state that became Communist would automatically come under Soviet leadership. This situation was to change radically with the onset of the Sino-Soviet conflict several years later. For an excellent survey of Soviet policy toward the Middle East under Khrushchev, see Oles M. Smolansky, *The Soviet Union and the Arab East under Khrushchev* (Lewisburg, Pa.: Bucknell University Press, 1974).

6 Two useful analyses of the background to the arms deal are Uri Ra'anan, *The USSR Arms the Third World* (Cambridge, Mass.: MIT Press, 1969), and Amos Perlmutter, "Big Power Games, Small Power Wars," *Transaction*, vol. 7, nos. 9–10 (July–August, 1979), pp. 79–83.

7 For an analysis of the Middle East arms race as a cause of the Arab–Israeli wars, see Nadav Safran, *From War to War* (New York: Pegasus, 1969). For a description of Soviet efforts to avoid participation in the 1956 conflict, see J. M. Mackintosh, *Strategy and Tactics of Soviet Foreign Policy* (London: Oxford University Press, 1963), pp. 185–87. The Soviet threats against Britain, France, and Israel were not issued until after the crisis had abated, and seemed primarily directed toward a propaganda advantage with respect to the United States, which had also opposed the attack on Egypt. In 1967 Nasser's claim that American and British planes were involved in the attack on Egypt seemed to be a ploy to get the Russians to intervene on his behalf. For a discussion of Soviet behavior in the 1973 war, see Freedman, *Soviet Policy Toward the Middle East Since 1970*. For an analysis of Soviet arms shipments to Egypt prior to each conflict, see Jon Glassman, *Arms for the Arabs: The Soviet Union and War in the Middle East* (Baltimore: Johns Hopkins Press, 1975).

8 *Al-Jarida* (Beirut), August 16, 1955, cited in Laqueur, *The Soviet Union and the Middle East*, pp. 219–20.

9 Press Release 50/59 (March 20, 1959), UAR Information Department, Cairo. Document found in Walter Laqueur, *The Struggle for the Middle East* (New York: Macmillan, 1969), p. 235.

10 Data are available only on the economic aid, which consisted of an $87.5 million loan for a dam and power plant on the Euphrates River, and other projects. Kurt Mueller, *The Foreign Aid Programs of the Soviet Bloc and Communist China* (New York: Walker, 1967), p. 225.

11 For a detailed discussion of the events leading up to the union, see Patrick Seale, *The Struggle for Syria* (London: Oxford University Press, 1965); and Malcolm Kerr, *The Arab Cold War* (New York: Oxford University Press, 1970).

12 *New Times*, the Soviet foreign affairs weekly, stated on February 21, 1958: "The Soviet people rejoice in the progress achieved by the friendly Arab nations. The USSR has never interfered in the internal affairs of any country, Arab or otherwise," *New Times*, no. 7 (1958), p. 6.

13 On March 6, 1959, the Soviet Union gave Iraq a $137.5 million loan for thirty-five industrial and agricultural facilities, and on August 18, 1960, a $45 million loan for construction and equipment for the Baghdad–Basra railroad. Data from Mueller, *Foreign Aid Programs*, p. 223.

14 Nasser was incensed at Soviet support for Kassem, whom he considered a dangerous rival. The Egyptian leader was even more angry at the Russians for opposing the

efforts of the Nasserites in Iraq who wished to have their country join the UAR. The Russians apparently felt that their influence would grow faster in an independent Iraq. In a reception for a visiting Iraqi delegation in March 1959, Khrushchev pointedly remarked in a general attack on Nasser: "Untimely unification ultimately undermines the unity of the people, rather than strengthens it ... What ensues is not greater unity but a division of forces. Who profits from this ... only the imperialists." *Pravda*, March 17, 1959, translated in *Current Digest of the Soviet Press*, vol. 11, no. 11 (April 15, 1959), p. 8.

15 Cited in Aryeh Yodfat, *Arab Politics in the Soviet Mirror* (Jerusalem: Israel Universities Press, 1973), p. 211.

16 For an Egyptian perspective on these events, see Mohammed Heikal, *The Cairo Documents* (New York: Doubleday, 1973), pp. 152–53.

17 For an examination of Kassem's activities, see Majid Khadduri, *Republican Iraq* (New York: Oxford University Press, 1969); and Uriel Dann, *Iraq under Kassem* (New York: Praeger, 1969), ch. 11 in M. S. Agwani, *Communism in the Arab East* (Bombay: Asia Publishing House, 1969), is also worthy of examination, as it deals in detail with Kassem's manipulation of the Iraqi communist party.

18 The Russians got a late start in developing relations with the FLN because Khrushchev did not wish to antagonize French President Charles de Gaulle, whom he hoped to wean away from NATO. The loans that the USSR promised Algeria ($100 million in 1963 and $128 million in 1964 – Mueller, *Foreign Aid Programs*, p. 226) seem also to have been aimed at gaining the USSR admission to the second Bandung Conference of Afro-Asian states, which was scheduled to be held in Algeria in 1965. For an overall discussion of Soviet–Algerian relations see David and Marina Ottaway, *Algeria: The Politics of a Socialist Revolution* (Berkeley: University of California Press, 1970).

19 In the first installment of his memoirs, Nikita Khrushchev referred to those members of the Soviet leadership who opposed his policy toward Egypt as "those skunks, those narrow-minded skunks who raised such a stink and tried to poison the waters of our relationship with Egypt." See Talbott, *Khrushchev Remembers*, p. 450.

20 For analyses of the Soviet ideological convolutions, see Richard Lowenthal, "Russia, the One-Party System and the Third World," *Survey*, no. 58 (January 1966), pp. 43–58; Yodfat, *Arab Politics*, ch. 1; and Phillip Mosley, "The Kremlin and the Third World," *Foreign Affairs*, vol. 46, no. 1 (October 1967), pp. 64–77. See also Jaan Pennar, *The USSR and the Arabs: The Ideological Dimension* (New York: Crane Russak, 1973).

21 "Socio-Economic Changes in the Arab Countries and 'Arab Socialism' Concepts," *World Marxist Review*, vol. 7, no. 9 (1964), p. 60.

22 *Ibid.*, p. 63.

23 *Ibid.*, p. 62.

24 Heikal, *Cairo Documents*, pp. 155–57.

25 This sizable loan, like similar loans to Algeria, may have been related to Soviet efforts to gain entry into the second Bandung Conference of Afro-Asian states. The Chinese communists strongly opposed the admission of the USSR to the conference and offered loans of their own in an effort to prevent it. A very useful chart comparing Chinese and Soviet loans to Afro-Asian countries in the 1963–65 period is found in Marshall Goldman, *Soviet Foreign Aid* (New York: Praeger, 1967), p. 190. The loan may also have been related to Nasser's decision to free a large number of imprisoned Egyptian communists (an action taken before Khrushchev's visit) and may have served as an incentive for the Egyptian leader to allow some of them to serve in his regime.

26 The Russians justified their assistance to the feudal regime of the Imam of Yemen on

the basis of his "anti-imperialist" policy toward British-controlled Aden. Following the death of the Imam in 1962, a civil war broke out in which the Egyptians intervened with large numbers of troops. The USSR supported the Egyptian intervention, although it maintained a number of military advisers there as well.

27 The loan was for a number of projects, the most important of which was a dam. Data from Mueller, *Foreign Aid Programs*, p. 224.

28 For a more detailed description of the Shah's problems, see Laqueur, *The Struggle for the Middle East*, pp. 30–35.

29 *Ibid.*, p. 17.

30 Nodari Alexandrovich Simoniya, "On the Character of the National Liberation Revolution," *Narodi Azii i Afriki*, no. 6 (1966), translated in *Mizan*, vol. 9, no. 2 (March–April 1967), p. 48.

31 *Ibid.*, p. 45. A Soviet evaluation of the role of the national bourgeois in the "noncapitalist way" that appeared soon after Nasser's death is found in R. Ulianovsky, "Nekotorie voprosy nikapitalisticheskogo razvitiia" (Some problems of noncapitalist development), *Kommunist*, no. 4 (1971), pp. 103–12.

32 For a detailed description of the new Soviet leadership and its policies, see Sydney Ploss, "Politics in the Kremlin," *Problems of Communism*, vol. 19, no. 3 (May–June 1970), pp. 1–14.

33 For an excellent analysis of the factors, both domestic and foreign, that led to Khrushchev's fall, see Carl Linden, *Khrushchev and the Soviet Leadership 1957–1964* (Baltimore: Johns Hopkins Press, 1966).

34 For a description of the US position in the Middle East at this time, see Polk, *United States and the Arab World*, ch. 19. Another useful source for examining the post-1967 situation is John Badeau, *An American Approach to the Arab World* (New York: Harper and Row, 1968).

35 An examination of Soviet policy toward sub-Saharan Africa during the early years of the Brezhnev–Kosygin leadership is found in Robert Levgold, "The Soviet Union's Changing View of Sub-Saharan Africa," in W. Raymond Duncan (ed.), *Soviet Policy in Developing Countries* (Waltham, Mass.: Ginn-Blaisdell, 1970), pp. 62–82.

36 For an analysis of Soviet military strategy during the 1965–69 period, see Thomas W. Wolfe, *Soviet Power and Europe* (Baltimore: Johns Hopkins Press, 1970). For an examination of Soviet policy in the Mediterranean, see Kurt Gasteyger, "Moscow and the Mediterranean," *Foreign Affairs*, vol. 46, no. 4 (July 1968), pp. 676–87.

37 Badeau, *American Approach to the Arab World*, p. 158.

38 See William B. Quandt, *Decade of Decisions: American Policy Toward the Arab–Israeli Conflict 1967–1976* (Berkeley: University of California Press, 1977), p. 38.

39 The competition was becoming very expensive, as indicated by a large number of Soviet loans to Afro-Asian countries in the 1963–65 period. These loans appear to have been motivated, at least in part, by the Soviet effort to gain admission to the second Bandung Conference of Afro-Asian states, which was scheduled to be held in Algeria in 1965.

There is some indication that Nasser was able to secure a Soviet promise to accelerate the construction of the Aswan Dam in return for supporting Soviet admission to the conference. On this point, see Sevinc Carlson, "China, the Soviet Union and the Middle East," *New Middle East*, no. 27 (December 1970), p. 34. In addition the Soviet decision to give $250 million in loans to Algeria during the 1963–64 period may have been motivated by the same considerations.

40 Interestingly enough, the only Chinese ambassador not to be called home during the cultural revolution was Huang Hua, China's ambassador to Egypt. For a useful survey of Communist China's policies toward the Middle East until 1964, see Malcolm Kerr, "The Middle East and China," in A. M. Halpern (ed.), *Policies*

toward China: Views from Six Continents (New York: McGraw-Hill, 1965), pp. 437–56. For a more recent analysis, see Carlson, "China," pp. 32–40.

41 A detailed analysis of Soviet policy toward Sukarno's regime is found in Ra'anan, *The USSR Arms the Third World*, p. 2. For a case study of the Soviet experience with Nkrumah, see W. Scott Thompson, "Parameters on Soviet Policy in Africa: Personal Diplomacy and Economic Interests in Ghana," in Duncan, *Soviet Policy*, pp. 83–106.

42 It appears that this decision was a ploy to get Soviet support for the narrowly based regime. Whatever the reason, the Russians pledged in April 1966 to help build the large Euphrates Dam and extend the Syrian railroad network (Laqueur, *The Struggle for the Middle East*, pp. 89–90). For an excellent study of the rise of the Ba'ath to power in Syria, see Itamar Rabinowich, *Syria under the Ba'ath 1963–1966* (Jerusalem: Israel Universities Press, 1972).

43 Cited in Shimon Shamir, "The Marxists in Egypt: The 'Licensed Infiltration' Doctrine in Practice," in Michael Confino and Simon Shamir (eds.), *The USSR and the Middle East* (Jerusalem: Israel Universities Press, 1973), p. 295.

44 For a description of these events, see Ottaway and Ottaway, *Algeria*, ch. 9.

45 For a description of the effect of this incident on Soviet–Algerian relations, see Ottaway and Ottaway, *Algeria*, p. 234; and the report by John Cooley in the *Christian Science Monitor*, April 2, 1966.

46 It was the Syrian communist party's turn to embarrass the Russians in 1968. During the Budapest Consultative Conference of Communist Parties, the Syrian delegate, Khalid Bakdash, attacked Romania's position on the Arab–Israeli conflict, calling the Romanians "tools of the Zionists," and even went so far as to claim that the Romanians were "putting themselves outside the communist movement." It is doubtful that the Russians, who had convened the conference in an effort to garner support for the expulsion of the Chinese communists from the international communist movement, wished to provoke the Romanians to such an extent, and Bakdash was compelled to retract his remarks. The Romanians walked out anyway. A detailed description of the conference is found in *World Communism 1967–1969: Soviet Efforts to Reestablish Control* (Washington, DC: US Government Printing Office, 1970), pp. 63–91. For a study of the effect of the Arab–Israeli conflict on Soviet relations with Eastern Europe, see Andrew Gyorgy, "Eastern European Viewpoints on the Middle East Conflict," paper delivered to the National Meeting of the American Association for the Advancement of Slavic Studies, Denver, Colorado, March 25, 1971.

47 Shamir, "The Marxists in Egypt," pp. 298–310.

48 For a different view of these events, see George Lenczowski, *Soviet Advances in the Middle East* (Washington, DC: American Enterprise Institute, 1971), pp. 113–14.

49 For an excellent study of relations between the Arab states at this time, see Kerr, "The Middle East and China," chs. 5 and 6.

50 Laqueur, *The Struggle for the Middle East*, p. 36. For the importance of this type of agreement for a developing country, see Robert O. Freedman, *Economic Warfare in the Communist Bloc* (New York: Praeger, 1970), pp. 5–6.

51 Mueller, *Foreign Aid Programs*, p. 224.

52 For a description of Western speculation on this point, see Laqueur, *The Struggle for the Middle East*, p. 40. There is also evidence that both Morocco and Jordan used the same ploy to acquire more military equipment from the United States.

53 Aaron S. Klieman, *Soviet Russia and the Middle East* (Baltimore: Johns Hopkins Press, 1970), p. 51.

54 Khomeini's Iran was to use the same ploy. See below, pp. 247–48.

55 See the report by Hedrick Smith in the *New York Times*, May 18, 1966.

56 For a useful description of the triangular relations between the USSR, the Kurds, and the Iraqi government at this time, see R. S. Rauch, "Moscow, the Kurds and the

Iraqi Communist Party," *Radio Free Europe Research Report* (September 1, 1966).

57 *Pravda*, November 22, 1966, had the following comment about the treaty: "The defense treaty signed by the UAR and Syria is called upon to play an especially important role in rebuffing the intrigues in imperialism and Arab reaction."

58 Perhaps the best study of the events leading up to the war is found in Walter Laqueur, *The Road to Jerusalem* (New York: Macmillan, 1968). See also Charles Yost, "The Arab–Israeli War: How It Began," *Foreign Affairs*, vol. 46, no. 2 (January 1968), pp. 304–20. For a collection of Arab viewpoints on the June war, which tends to minimize the role of the USSR in the outbreak of the conflict, see Ibrahim Abu-Lughod (ed.), *The Arab–Israeli Confrontation of June 1967: An Arab Perspective* (Evanston, Ill.: Northwestern University Press, 1970). For a description of the military preparations and tactics of the opposing armies, see David Kimhe and Dan Bawly, *The Six-Day War: Prologue and Aftermath* (New York: Stein and Day, 1971), and Chaim Herzog, *The Arab–Israeli Wars* (New York: Random House, 1982), pp. 145–91.

59 See the report by Paul Wohl in the *Christian Science Monitor*, August 1, 1967, for a description of Chinese activity in the Middle East at this time.

60 Heikal, *The Cairo Documents*, p. 313.

61 L. Sedin, "The Arab Peoples' Just Cause," *International Affairs*, vol. 13, no. 8 (August 1967), p. 28, cited in Lincoln Landis, *Politics and Oil: Moscow in the Middle East* (New York: Dunellen, 1973), p. 64.

62 For an analysis of Soviet policy toward the Arab oil "weapon" during the 1967 war and its aftermath, see Landis, *Politics and Oil*; Abraham S. Becker, "Oil and the Persian Gulf," in Confino and Shamir, *The USSR and the Middle East*, pp. 191–94.

63 Igor Belyayev and Yevgeny Primakov, "The Situation in the Arab World," *New Times* (September 27, 1967), p. 10, cited in Landis, *Politics and Oil*, p. 64.

64 For an analysis of the highly complicated situation in Aden (South Yemen) at the time of the British withdrawal, see Humphrey Trevelyan, *The Middle East in Revolution* (Boston: Gambit, 1970), p. 3. Trevelyan was in charge of the British withdrawal from Aden. See also Mark N. Katz, *Russia and Arabia* (Baltimore: Johns Hopkins Press 1986), ch. 2.

65 For an account of the diplomatic attempts to fashion a peace settlement after the 1967 war, see Yair Evron, *The Middle East* (New York: Praeger, 1973), ch. 3.

66 For a description of Nasser's visit to Moscow, and of Brezhnev's decision to send troops to Egypt, see Mohammed Heikal, *The Road to Ramadan* (New York: Quadrangle, 1975), pp. 83–88.

67 According to Heikal, Nasser wanted the cease-fire so that he could finish building the missile wall that would not only protect Egyptian armed forces on the West Bank but also give protection over a strip 15–20 kilometers wide on the East Bank and thus cover an Egyptian crossing – as indeed happened in the 1973 Arab–Israeli war. See Heikal, *The Road to Ramadan*, p. 93. For a detailed study of the war of attrition, see Lawrence L. Whetten, *The Canal War* (Cambridge, Mass.: MIT Press, 1974). For examinations of the Soviet role during the war of attrition and the violation of the cease-fire, see Robert O. Freedman, "Detente and Soviet–American Relations in the Middle East during the Nixon Years," in Della W. Sheldon (ed.), *Dimension of Detente* (New York: Praeger, 1977); and Alvin Z. Rubinstein, *Red Star on the Nile* (Princeton: Princeton University Press, 1977). The Soviets have now openly admitted participating in the Egyptian–Israeli fighting in the 1969–70 period (*Ekho Planety*, cited in *Jerusalem Post*, July 7, 1989).

68 Georgi Mirsky, "Israeli Aggression and Arab Unity," *New Times*, no. 28 (1967), p. 6.

69 Shamir, "The Marxists in Egypt," p. 302.

70 Cited in Jaan Pennar, "The Arabs, Marxism and Moscow: A Historical Survey,"

Middle East Journal, vol. 22, no. 3 (September 1968), p. 446.

71 For sympathetic treatments of Nasser's attempts to keep some freedom of maneuver during the post-1967 period, see Anthony Nutting, *Nasser* (New York: Dutton, 1972), ch. 21; and Robert Stephens, *Nasser: A Political Biography* (New York: Simon and Schuster, 1971), ch. 19.

72 For an excellent study of these events, see Avigdor Levy, "The Syrian Communists and the Ba'ath Power Struggle 1966–1970," in Confino and Shamir, *The USSR and the Middle East*, pp. 395–417.

73 *Jerusalem Post*, April 11, 1969, cited in Lawrence J. Whetten, "Changing Soviet Attitudes Toward Arab Radical Movements," *New Middle East*, no. 28 (March 1970), p. 25.

74 *Trud*, July 18, 1970.

75 For studies of the Soviet need for Middle Eastern oil and natural gas, see Landis, *Politics and Oil*; Becker, "Oil and the Persian Gulf"; and Robert W. Campbell, "Some Issues in Soviet Energy Policy for the Seventies," *Middle East Information Series*, no. 26–27 (Spring–Summer 1974), pp. 92–100. See also Arthur J. Klinghoffer, *The Soviet Union and International Oil Politics* (New York: Columbia University Press, 1977), Marshall Goldman, *The Enigma of Soviet Petroleum* (Boston: Allen and Unwin, 1980), and Ed A. Hewett, *Energy, Economics and Foreign Policy in the Soviet Union* (Washington: Brookings, 1984).

76 On this point, see Uriel Dann, "The Communist Movement in Iraq Since 1963," in Confino and Shamir, *The USSR and the Middle East*, pp. 377–91.

77 For a general examination of Soviet–Iraqi relations during this period, see Y. A. Yodfat, "Unpredictable Iraq Poses a Russian Problem," *New Middle East*, no. 13 (October 1969), pp. 17–20. A detailed listing of the oil agreements between Iraq and the USSR is found in "The Broad Soviet Interest in Iraqi Oil," *Radio Liberty Report* (April 17, 1972), p. 2.

78 *Pravda*, September 21, 1969. The agreement between the Kurds and the Iraqi government in 1966 never materialized.

79 Translated in *Current Digest of the Soviet Press*, vol. 22, no. 31, p. 10.

80 For an analysis of these aid agreements, see Y. A. Yodfat, "Russia's Other Middle East Pasture – Iraq," *New Middle East*, no. 38 (November 1971), pp. 26–29.

81 For studies of the highly complex situation in the Sudan, see Haim Shaked, Esther Souery, and Gabriel Warburg, "The Communist Party in the Sudan 1946–1971," in Confino and Shamir, *The USSR and the Middle East*, pp. 335–74; and Anthony Sylvester, "Mohammed vs. Lenin in the Revolutionary Sudan," *New Middle East*, no. 34 (July 1971), pp. 26–28.

82 *Sudan News*, January 13, 1970, cited in *Record of the Arab World*, 1970, p. 419.

83 Tass, January 2, 1970, cited in *Record of the Arab World*, 1970, p. 418.

84 According to Aryeh Yodfat, "The USSR and the Arab Communist Parties," *New Middle East*, no. 32 (May 1971), p. 33, the USSR advised the Sudanese communist party to dissolve as early as May 1969. Shaked *et al.* argue that the party was urged to dissolve in 1970, after Nimeri had shown the first signs of turning against it.

85 Cited in Shaked *et al.*, "The Communist Party in the Sudan," p. 354.

86 For an excellent study of the activities and problems of the Palestinian guerrilla organizations, see William B. Quandt, Fuad Jabbar, and Ann Lesch, *The Politics of Palestinian Nationalism* (Berkeley: University of California Press, 1973), especially pts. 2 and 3.

87 For an analysis of the relations between China and the Palestinian guerrillas, see "Peking and the Palestinian Guerrilla Movement," *Radio Free Europe Research Report* (September 1, 1970). Another useful source is R. Medzini, "China and the Palestinians," *New Middle East*, no. 32 (May 1971), pp. 34–40. See also Yitzhak

Shichor, *The Middle East in China's Foreign Policy 1949–1977* (London: Cambridge, 1979).

88 Cited in Paul Wohl, "New Soviet Revolutionary Stance in the Middle East," *Radio Liberty Dispatch* (May 25, 1970), p. 2. For a study of Soviet policy toward the PLO, see Galia Golan, *The Soviet Union and the PLO: An Uneasy Alliance* (New York: Praeger, 1980).

89 For analyses of the Soviet dilemmas in dealing with the Palestinian guerrillas, see Y. A. Yodfat, "Moscow Reconsiders Fatah," *New Middle East*, no. 13 (October 1969), pp. 15–18; and John Cooley, "Moscow Faces a Palestinian Dilemma," *Mid East*, 11, no. 3 (June 1970), pp. 32–35.

90 Naim Ashhab, "To Overcome the Crisis of the Palestinian Resistance Movement," *World Marxist Review*, vol. 15, no. 5 (May 1972), p. 75.

91 For a description of these events, see Kerr, "The Middle East and China," ch. 7, especially pp. 144–48.

92 For an analysis of American policy during the Jordanian civil war, see Evron, *The Middle East*; and Robert J. Pranger, *American Policy for Peace in the Middle East, 1969–1971* (Washington, DC: American Enterprise Institute 1971), pp. 39–48.

93 For an analysis of Soviet policy during this crisis, see Freedman, "Detente and Soviet–American Relations in the Middle East during the Nixon Years."

94 For a description of the atmosphere during the cease-fire talks, see Heikal, *The Cairo Documents*, p. 4.

95 Klieman, *Soviet Russia and the Middle East*, p. 78.

96 An official description of the Rogers Plan, which basically calls for the withdrawal of Israeli forces from all but "insubstantial" portions of the territory captured in 1967 in return for a binding peace settlement, is found in United States Department of State, *United States Foreign Policy 1969–1970: A Report of the Secretary of State* (Washington, DC: US Government Printing Office, 1971). For an analysis of American attempts to implement the Rogers Plan, see Pranger, *American Policy for Peace*; and Quandt, Jabbar, and Lesch, *The Politics of Palestinian Nationalism*, ch. 3.

97 For an analysis of Nasser's role as a "broker" of Soviet interests in the Arab world, see Malcolm Kerr, *Regional Arab Politics and the Conflict with Israel* (Santa Monica, Calif.: Rand Publication RM-5966-FF, 1969).

98 Freedman, "Detente and Soviet–American Relations," pp. 92–101.

99 For an analysis of the Soviet exodus from Egypt, see Galia Golan, *Yom Kippur and After: The Soviet Union and the Middle East Crisis* (New York: Cambridge, 1977), pp. 23–26.

100 *Ibid.*, ch. 3.

101 Cf. Freedman, "Detente and Soviet–American Relations," pp. 101–9.

102 For a thorough analysis of Soviet policy during the Yom Kippur War, see Galia Golan, *Yom Kippur and After*. For the view of the Soviet Ambassador to Egypt during the war, see Igor Tirofeyev (citing former Ambassador Vladimir Vinogradov) "War on the Day of Atonement 15 Years On: Facts, Opinions, Lessons," *New Times*, no. 45 (1988), pp. 18–22.

103 For accounts of Kissinger's efforts, see William B. Quandt, *Decade of Decisions: American Policy Toward the Arab–Israeli Conflict 1967–1976* (Los Angeles: University of California Press, 1977), ch. 7; Matti Golan, *The Secret Conversations of Henry Kissinger* (New York: Bantam Books, 1976); and Edward R. F. Sheehan, *The Arabs, Israelis and Kissinger* (New York: Reader's Digest Press, 1976). See also the first two volumes of Kissinger's memoirs.

104 Cf. Matti Golan, *Secret Conversations*, pp. 137–42.

105 For an account of Soviet aid to Syria during this period, see Freedman, *Soviet Policy Toward the Middle East Since 1970*, pp. 163–67.

106 *Ibid.*, pp. 198–203. For a discussion of many such Soviet signals to Israel, see Yaacov Ro'i,"The Soviet Attitude to the Existence of Israel," *The Limits to Power* ed. Yaacov Ro'i, (London: Croom Helm, 1979), pp. 232–53.

107 For an analysis of Soviet policy toward the PLO, see Galia Golan, *The Soviet Union and the Palestine Liberation Organization* (New York: Praeger, 1980).

108 For an analysis of the evolution of Soviet peace efforts up until this point, see Robert O. Freedman, "The Soviet Conception of a Middle East Peace Settlement," in Ro'i (ed.), *The Limits to Power*, pp. 282–327.

109 For a discussion of Soviet policy during the civil war in Lebanon, see Freedman, *Soviet Policy Toward the Middle East Since 1970*, ch. 7.

110 *Ibid.*, pp. 271–73.

111 For a discussion of the events leading up to the October 1, 1977 joint statement, and for an evaluation of it, see *ibid.*, pp. 307–11.

112 The Soviet foreign policy weekly, *New Times*, asserted in an editorial in 1977: "It is no secret that by 'real peace' the Tel Aviv expansionists mean the notorious 'open borders' between Israel and its Arab neighbors, the 'free movement of peoples and goods' and even 'cooperation in respect of security' – all of which would make Tel Aviv the center of a huge neo-colonialist 'empire' in the Middle East." (*New Times*, no. 36 [1977], p. 1).

113 In 1975, Moscow exported 274.1 million worth of goods to Iraq, while importing 325.4 million roubles from it (*Vneshniaia Torgovlia SSR* 1976).

114 *Foreign Trade* (Moscow), no. 10 (1975), pp. 8–14.

115 Majid Khadduri, *Socialist Iraq* (Washington, DC: Middle East Institute, 1978), p. 160.

116 Freedman, *Soviet Policy Toward the Middle East Since 1970*, p. 235.

117 *Ibid.*, pp. 247–50.

118 *Ibid.*, p. 323.

119 See Fulvio Grimaldi, "The PLO–Iraq Conflict," *Middle East*, no. 47 (September 1978), pp. 38–39.

120 *Middle East*, no. 45 (July 1978), p. 63. Total US–Iraqi trade in 1978 was $592,400,000.

121 See comments by Iraqi Trade Secretary Mahdi al-Ubaidi, *Middle East*, no. 41 (March 1978), p. 101.

122 On this point see David Albright, "The War in the Horn of Africa and the Arab–Israeli Conflict," in Robert O. Freedman (ed.), *World Politics and the Arab–Israeli Conflict* (New York: Pergamon, 1979), pp. 147–91.

123 Cf. Baqir Ibrahim, "The Masses, The Party and the National Front," *World Marxist Review*, vol. 19, no. 8 (August 1976), pp. 49–56 and Aziz Mohammed, "Tasks of the Revolutionary Forces of Iraq," *World Marxist Review*, vol. 19, no. 9 (September 1976), pp. 10–18.

124 Tewfiq Mishlawi, "Crackdown on Communists in Iraq," *Middle East*, no. 45 (July 1978), pp. 29–30.

125 For a list of Iraqi actions against enemies of the regime, see the article by J. P. Smith, *Washington Post*, August 6, 1978.

126 Cited in *ibid.*

127 Cited in Mishlawi, "Crackdown on Communists in Iraq," p. 30.

128 Cf. *Pravda*, September 10, 1979.

129 *Pravda*, September 23, 1978.

130 Leonid Medvenko, "Middle East: Fictions and Realities," *New Times*, no. 40 (1978), p. 6.

131 A. Stepanov, "Hour of Trial for the Palestinians," *New Times*, no. 41 (1978), p. 7.

132 *Pravda*, October 7, 1978.

133 Radio Moscow (Domestic Service), October 28, 1978 (International Diary Program).

134 For a report on the results of the Baghdad Conference, see Baghdad INA, November 5, 1978, in *FBIS: Middle East and North Africa*, November 6, 1978, pp. A-13–A-15.

135 Radio Moscow (in Arabic to the Arab world), November 6, 1978.

136 Cf. Reuters report in the *Jerusalem Post*, November 24, 1978; AP report in the *New York Times*, November 24, 1978; and the article by Ned Temko, *Christian Science Monitor*, November 30, 1978. See also the broadcast by Radio Kuwait (KUNA) on December 13, 1978 of an *Ar-Ra'y Al-'am* article challenging the USSR to give more military assistance to Iraq and Syria.

137 AP report from Moscow, *Jerusalem Post*, January 5, 1979.

138 If so, the incident is reminiscent of Moscow's unwillingness to provide Egypt with the weaponry Sadat wanted in 1971 and 1972. There were also reports that following Camp David, the USSR felt it had greater leverage over Iraq and Syria and it could exercise that leverage to obtain improved treatment of the ICP from Iraq and the long-sought friendship and cooperation treaty from Syria. (See the Western sources mentioned in note 136 above). It should also be noted that at this time Moscow was close to signing the SALT II agreement with the United States.

139 *Pravda*, December 14, 1978.

140 Tass, in English, December 12, 1978. (*FBIS*, vol. 3, December 13, 1978, p. F-3).

141 *Pravda*, January 13, 1979.

142 On this point, see Freedman, "The Soviet Union and the Communist Parties of the Arab World."

143 Cited in report by Ned Temko, *Christian Science Monitor*, April 11, 1979.

144 For an analysis of the Soviet role in the PDRY invasion of North Yemen, see Freedman, *Soviet Policy Toward the Middle East Since 1970*, pp. 352–54.

145 This incident is discussed in Tewfiq Mishlawi, "Iraq's Foreign Policy Headaches," *The Middle East*, no. 57 (July 1979), p. 10.

146 The growing tension between Iraq and Iran in 1979 is discussed in Freedman, *Soviet Policy Toward the Middle East Since 1970*, pp. 360–62.

147 Cf. report in *Washington Post*, June 15, 1979.

148 Cited in AP report from Tehran, *Baltimore Evening Sun*, June 6, 1979.

149 Cited in report by William Branigin, *Washington Post*, June 16, 1979.

150 Cf. report by Ned Temko, *Christian Science Monitor*, June 18, 1979.

151 Cited in AP report from Tehran, *Baltimore Evening Sun*, June 6, 1979.

152 For an analysis of the resumption of the Iraq–Syria dispute, see Graham Benton, "After the Coup Attempt," *The Middle East*, no. 59 (September 1979), pp. 13–14.

153 Gary Sick, in his book *All Fall Down: America's Tragic Encounter with Iran* (New York: Penguin Books, 1986) has written that Khomeini "was at least generally aware of the plans for an attack on the embassy and consciously exploited it for his own domestic political purposes" (p. 231). See also Paul H. Kreisberg (ed.), *American Hostages in Iran: The Conduct of a Crisis* (New Haven: Yale University Press, 1985).

154 *Pravda*, November 5, 1979.

155 Commentary by Vera Lebedeva, *FBIS:USSR*, November 7, 1979, p. H-4.

156 Translated in *CDSP*, 1979, vol. 31, no. 49, pp. 4, 26.

157 For an analysis of the Soviet evaluation of Carter, see Robert O. Freedman, "The Soviet Image of the Carter Administration's Policy Toward the USSR from the Inauguration to the Invasion of Afghanistan," *Korea and World Affairs*, vol. 4, no. 2 (Summer 1980), pp. 229–67. For Carter's view of the Soviet Union, see Jimmy Carter, *Keeping Faith: Memoirs of a President* (New York: Bantam Books, 1982).

158 Cf. *New Times*, no. 47 (1979), p. 7.

159 *Pravda*, November 11, 1979.

160 For an analysis of the Iranian action, see Robert Rand, RL Report No. 337/79,

November 7, 1979. For the Soviet view of the treaty, see B. Ponamarev *et al.*, *History of Soviet Foreign Policy 1917–1945* (Moscow: Progress Publishers, 1969), pp. 42–48.

161 *World Marxist Review Information Bulletin*, nos. 1–2, 1980, pp. 86–87.
162 *Pravda*, November 23, 1979.
163 Cf. *New Times*, no. 2 (1980), p. 13.

2 Soviet policy from the invasion of Afghanistan until the death of Brezhnev

1 For an excellent background history of Afghanistan, see Louis Dupree, *Afghanistan* (Princeton: Princeton University Press, 1978). For analyses of the communist coup and the ultimate Soviet decision to invade Afghanistan, see Henry S. Bradsher, *Afghanistan and the Soviet Union* (Durham: Duke University Press, 1985); Thomas T. Hammond, *Red Flag Over Afghanistan: The Communist Coup, the Soviet Invasion, and the Consequences* (Boulder: Westview Press, 1984); Anthony Hyman, *Afghanistan Under Soviet Domination 1964–1983* (New York: St. Martin's Press, 1984); and Alvin Z. Rubinstein, *Soviet Policy Toward Turkey, Iran and Afghanistan* (New York: Praeger, 1982). For a solid journalistic view of the war, see Edward Giradet, *Afghanistan: The Soviet War* (New York: St. Martin's Press, 1985). For Soviet views, see Yuri Gankovsky (ed.), *A History of Afghanistan* (Moscow: Progress Publishers, 1985) (originally published in 1982, the book is highly critical of the role of Hafizullah Amin, who "used inadmissable methods in carrying out major reforms," p. 315), and O. G. Cherneta, *Afghanistan: Borba i Sozidanie* (Afghanistan. Struggle and Creation) (Moscow: Voenizdat, 1984). For initial Western analyses of the invasion, see John C. Griffiths, *Afghanistan: Key to a Continent* (Boulder, Colorado: Westview Press, 1981); Selig Harrison, "Dateline Afghanistan: Exit Through Finland?" *Foreign Policy*, no. 41 (Winter 1980–81) pp. 163–82; Zalmay Khalilzad, "Soviet Occupied Afghanistan," *Problems of Communism*, vol. 29, no. 6 (November–December 1980), pp. 23–40; and Shirin Tahir-Kheli, "The Soviet Union in Afghanistan: Benefits and Costs," in Robert H. Donaldson (ed.), *The Soviet Union in the Third World: Successes and Failures* (Boulder: Westview Press, 1981), pp. 217–31.
2 Brezhnev made this assertion during a dinner speech honoring the visit of Taraki for the signing of the Soviet–Afghan Treaty of Friendship and Cooperation (*Pravda*, December 6, 1978).
3 Cf. AP report in *New York Times*, May 4, 1979 citing United States intelligence sources.
4 Cf. reports by Richard Burt, *New York Times*, April 13, 1979, and Jonathan C. Randal, *Washington Post*, May 10, 1979. It should be noted that the US protested ineffectually as the Soviet military involvement in Afghanistan deepened.
5 *Pravda*, March 29, 1979.
6 Cf. report by Don Oberdorfer, *Washington Post*, April 3, 1979.
7 Cited by Dmitry Volsky, "The Target: Afghanistan's Revolution," *New Times*, no. 24 (1979), p. 13.
8 Cf. Harrison, "Dateline Afghanistan," pp. 170–71.
9 For a description of the growing Soviet involvement in Afghanistan, see Griffiths, *Afghanistan*, and Bradsher, *Afghanistan and the Soviet Union*.
10 For the Soviet reaction to Carter's moves, see *Pravda*, January 7, 1980.
11 Cf. *Baltimore Sun*, January 16, 1980 for a list of the states supporting Moscow or abstaining in the UN vote.
12 Cited in report by Douglas Watson in the *Baltimore Sun*, January 21, 1980.
13 Cited in report by Michael Weisskopf, *Washington Post*, January 2, 1980. Afghanis

and Iranians stormed the Soviet Embassy in Tehran but were driven off by Iranian police. One year later, however, the Iranian authorities were much slower to come to the defense of the Embassy (see below, p. 96).

14 For the text of the Steadfastness Front declaration, see Radio Damascus Domestic Service, January 16, 1980 (translated in *Foreign Broadcast Information Service* [hereafter *FBIS*]: *Middle East*, January 17, 1980, pp. A2–6).

15 *Pravda*, January 30, 1980 (translated in *Current Digest of the Soviet Press* [hereafter *CDSP*], 1980, vol. 32, no. 4, pp. 19–20).

16 Cited in report by Drew Middleton, *New York Times*, March 14, 1980.

17 Cited in report in *Washington Post*, February 10, 1980.

18 On this point see Mark Katz, *Russia and Arabia* (Baltimore: Johns Hopkins Press, 1986), p. 93. In January 1986, however, Moscow was to temporarily lose control of the situation in South Yemen (see below, ch. 4).

19 For a description of the actions taken at the Steadfastness Front Conference, see the report by Edward Cody in the April 16, 1980 issue of the *Washington Post*.

20 Editorial comments, *New Times*, no. 17 (1980), p. 15.

21 See the report by Richard Burt in the December 19, 1979 issue of the *New York Times* and the report by Edward Cody in the June 5, 1980 issue of the *Washington Post*. For a good analysis of this development, see Nimrod Novik, *Between Two Yemens* (Tel Aviv University Center for Strategic Studies, Paper no. 11 [December 1980]).

22 India also called for the United States to leave Diego Garcia and return it to Mauritius. For an analysis of Soviet–Indian relations, see Robert H. Donaldson, "The Soviet Union in South Asia: A Friend to Rely On?" *Journal of International Affairs*, vol. 34, no. 2, pp. 235–58.

23 Cf. report by William Branigin, *Washington Post*, January 17, 1980.

24 Cited in *New York Times*, January 17, 1980.

25 Cited in report by Dusko Doder, *Washington Post*, January 18, 1980.

26 Cited in *Baltimore Evening Sun* Wire Service Report, January 28, 1980.

27 The text of the Islamic Conference declaration is found in the *New York Times*, January 30, 1980.

28 Cited in Reuters Report, *New York Times*, February 5, 1978.

29 *Ibid*.

30 Cf. *Pravda*, February 12, 1980; *Izvestia*, March 26, 1980.

31 Leonid Medvenko, "Islam: Two Trends," *New Times*, no. 13 (1980), pp. 23–25.

32 "Political Shifts in the Middle East: Roots, Factors, Trends," *World Marxist Review* (February 1980), pp. 58–64. The failure of the Soviet-sponsored Islamic conference in Tashkent in September 1980 probably reinforced this view. *Izvestia*, on October 2, 1980, complained that the meeting had been boycotted by certain Muslim countries "because of excessive dependence on US imperialism or a certain political myopia." It also asserted that the Tashkent meeting "facilitated the further consolidation of the Muslim anti-imperialist forces."

33 Translated in *FBIS: Middle East Iran Supplement*, no. 070, March 24, 1980, p. 7.

34 *Ibid*.

35 AP report in *Baltimore Sun*, March 18, 1980.

36 Cited in report by Kevin Kose, *Washington Post*, April 18, 1980.

37 *Pravda*, April 26, 1980.

38 *Pravda*, May 1, 1980. This was to be a persistent theme in Soviet propaganda throughout the 1980s.

39 Translated in *CDSP*, 1980, vol. 32, no. 17, p. 9.

40 Dmitry Volsky, "Turban or Helmet," *New Times*, no. 20 (1980), p. 18.

41 Cited in report by Marvine Howe, *New York Times*, May 22, 1980.

42 Cited in report by Marvine Howe, *New York Times*, May 19, 1980.

43 Cited in report by Marvine Howe, *New York Times*, May 20, 1980.

44 The text of the resolution is found in the *New York Times*, May 23, 1980.

45 Cf. editorial comments, *New Times*, no. 22 (1980), p. 15.

46 *Pravda*, August 22, 1980 (translated in *CDSP*, 1980, vol. 32, no. 34, p. 13).

47 Cf. Khalilzad, "Soviet Occupied Afghanistan," pp. 35–39.

48 *Literaturnaia Gazeta*, July 9, 1980 (translated in *CDSP*, vol. 32, no. 28, pp. 1–3, 19). There was one important difference between the Middle East positions of Moscow and Riyadh. The USSR already formally recognized Israel's existence; Saudi Arabia was not yet willing to do so although it made some hints to that effect in the summer of 1980. For recent scholarly Soviet views of Saudi policy, see L. V. Valkova, *Saudovskaia Aravia v Mezhdunarodnykh Otnosheniiakh (Saudi Arabia in International Relations)* (Moscow: Nauka, 1979), R. M. Tursunov, *Saudovskaia Araviia v Mezharabskikh Otnosheniiakh v Period 1964–1975 (Saudi Arabia in Intra-Arab Relations in the 1964–75 Period)* (Tashkent: Fail, 1987), and L. B. Valkova, *Saudovskaia Araviia: Neft', Islam, Politika (Saudi Arabia: Oil, Islam, Politics)* (Moscow: Nauka, 1987).

49 On Soviet–Saudi ties, see Karen Dawisha, "Moscow's Moves in the Direction of the Gulf – So Near and Yet So Far," *Journal of International Affairs*, vol. 34, no. 2, p. 224.

50 The election of Andreas Papandreou as Greece's Premier the following year, however, once again raised questions as to Greece's participation in NATO.

51 Translated in *CDSP*, 1980, vol. 32, no. 28, p. 13.

52 For a discussion of Iranian politics during this period, see Eric Rouleau, "Khomeini's Iran," *Foreign Affairs*, vol. 59, no. 1 (Fall 1980), pp. 12–17, and Nikki Keddie and Eric Hooglund (eds.), *The Iranian Revolution and the Islamic Republic* (Syracuse: Syracuse University Press, 1985), pp. 17–54.

53 Cited in reports by Jay Ross in the *Washington Post*, July 1, 1980 and July 3, 1980.

54 Cited in Reuters report in *New York Times*, July 5, 1980.

55 *New Times*, no. 28 (1980), p. 3.

56 Cited in *Baltimore Sun*, July 22, 1980. The embassy was, however, to be temporarily seized at the end of December (see below, p. 96).

57 L. Skuratov, "Iran: Where the Threads of the Plot Lead," *New Times*, no. 30 (1980), p. 8.

58 *Ibid.*

59 Cf. *Pravda*, June 19, 1980.

60 Cited in *Washington Post*, August 15, 1980 and AP report in *Baltimore Sun*, August 14, 1980.

61 Pavel Mezentsev, "USA–Iran: Threats and Blackmail," *New Times*, no. 38 (1980), pp. 10–11.

62 Dmitry Volsky, "Iran: Sidetracking Attention," *New Times*, no. 35 (1980), p. 21.

63 Cited in *Middle East Intelligence Service*, April 1–15, 1980. The 1975 treaty signed in Algiers, ended a border war between the two countries.

64 *Ibid.*

65 Tass report April 19, 1980 and *Izvestia*, April 12, 1980, which cited foreign news services that Iraq had allowed Iranian *émigrés* to form armed groups on Iraqi soil to overthrow Khomeini.

66 Cf. Dmitry Volsky, "Middle East: Turban or Helmet," *New Times*, no. 20 (1980), p. 19.

67 Translated in *FBIS: South Asia*, May 8, 1980, pp. 1–5.

68 Cited in report in *Washington Post*, August 9, 1980.

69 Cited in report in *Baltimore Sun*, August 23, 1980.

70 Cf. Zakhar Kuznetsov, "In Unison with Imperialism," *New Times*, no. 52 (1979), pp. 21–22.

71 Iraq, perhaps seeing war on the horizon with Iran, appears to have backed away from its severe criticism of Moscow by April when the Afghan Foreign Minister Shah Mohammed Dost visited Baghdad. See Robert Rand, *Radio Liberty Report*, no. 346/80 (September 22, 1980).

72 The text of the Pan-Arab Charter may be found in *The Middle East*, April 1980, p. 20.

73 See Alexandre Benningsen, "Soviet Muslims and the World of Islam," *Problems of Communism*, vol. 29, no. 2 (March–April 1980), pp. 38–51. It should also be noted that the Afghans, except for the Shiite Hazara minority, are Sunni Muslims, and Afghans are not popular in Iran.

74 Cf. Tass report, September 16, 1980.

75 Libya had criticized Saudi Arabia's decision to allow the stationing of US AWACS aircraft on Saudi soil where they could be used against Iran.

76 Alexandre Usvatov, "Put Out the Fire," *New Times*, no. 40 (1980), p. 12.

77 Cf. *Izvestia*, October 3, 1980.

78 For analyses of the Gulf Cooperation Council, see Judith Perea, "Caution: Building in Progress," *The Middle East*, April 1981, pp. 8–12; John A. Sandwick (ed.), *The Gulf Cooperation Council* (Boulder: Westview Press, 1987); and Shireen Hunter (ed.), *Gulf Cooperation Council: Problems and Prospects* (Washington: Center for Strategic and International Studies, 1984).

79 Translated in *FBIS:USSR*, October 14, 1980, p. H-3.

80 Cf. Tass report, in English, October 3, 1980 (*FBIS:USSR*, October 6, 1980, p. H-4).

81 Cf. report by David K. Willis, *Christian Science Monitor*, October 14, 1980 and *Middle East Intelligence Survey*, October 1–15, 1980. See also Tass report in English, October 10, 1980 and Radio Moscow, in Persian, October 10, 1980 (*FBIS:USSR*, October 14, 1980, p. H-1).

82 For initial Western analyses of the impact of the Iran–Iraq war, see Claudia Wright, "Implications of the Iran–Iraq War," *Foreign Affairs*, vol. 59, no. 2 (Winter, 1980–81), pp. 275–303 and Adeed I. Dawisha, "Iraq: The West's Opportunity," *Foreign Policy*, no. 41 (Winter 1980–81), pp. 134–53. For Soviet analyses, see L. Medvenko, "The Persian Gulf: A Revival of Gunboat Diplomacy," *International Affairs* (Moscow), no. 12 (1980), pp. 23–29; A. K. Kislov, "Vashington i Irako–Iranskii Konflikt" ("Washington and the Iran–Iraq Conflict"), *SSha*, no. 1 [1981], pp. 51–56; and N. Poliakov, "Put' K. Bezopasnosti v Indiiskom Okeane i Peridskom Zalive" (The Way to Security in the Indian Ocean and Persian Gulf), *Mirovaia Ekonomika i Mezhdunarodnie Otnosheniia*, no. 1 [1981], pp. 62–73. For later studies of the conflict that was to last until August 1988, see Shahram Chubin and Charles Tripp, *Iran and Iraq at War* (Boulder: Westview Press, 1988); Anthony Cordesman, *The Gulf and the West* (Boulder: Westview Press, 1988); Shirin Tahir-Kheli and Shaheen Ayubi (eds.), *The Iran–Iraq War* (New York: Praeger, 1983); M. S. El Ezhary (ed.), *The Iran–Iraq War* (New York: St. Martin's Press, 1984). For an analysis of Soviet policy toward the Gulf war from its outbreak until 1987, see Carol R. Saivetz, *The Soviet Union and the Gulf in the 1980s* (Boulder: Westview Press, 1989). For a Soviet view that relates the war to energy crises, see Aleksei Vasilev, *Persidskii Zaliv v Epitsentre Buri* (*The Persian Gulf in the Center of the Storm*) (Moscow: Political Literature, 1983).

83 Cf. Reed, "Dateline Syria: Fin de régime," pp. 177–85.

84 For an analysis of the changing alliances of King Hussein, see Adam M. Garfinkle, "Negotiating by Proxy: Jordanian Foreign Policy and U.S. Options in the Middle East," *Orbis*, vol. 24, no. 24 (Winter 1981), pp. 847–80. For the earlier Syrian–Jordanian alignment, see Robert O. Freedman, *Soviet Policy Toward the Middle East Since 1970* (New York: Praeger, 1982), pp. 208–9.

85 For the text of the treaty, see *Pravda*, October 9, 1980. For a discussion of Soviet–Syrian relations from 1970–78, see Freedman, *Soviet Policy Toward the Middle East Since 1970*, Galia Golan, "Syria and the Soviet Union Since the Yom Kippur war," *Orbis*, vol. 21, no. 4 (Winter 1978), pp. 777–801 and Efraim Karsh, *The Soviet Union and Syria: The Assad Years* (London: Chatham House, 1988).

86 *Pravda*, October 11, 1980.

87 *Pravda*, October 9, 1980.

88 *Pravda*, December 6, 1978.

89 There were numerous rumors of such secret clauses. Cf. report by Anan Safadi, *Jerusalem Post*, October 10, 1980.

90 See below, p. 105–8.

91 *Pravda*, December 3, 1980.

92 Cited in report of an interview with King Hussein by Pranay B. Gupte, *New York Times*, December 2, 1980. Hussein also stated that he had put aside plans to explore arms purchases from Moscow.

93 Cf. Moscow Radio Arabic Broadcast, December 5, 1980.

94 For an analysis of the events surrounding the proclamation of the Soviet peace plan of April 1976, see Freedman, *Soviet Policy Toward the Middle East Since 1970*, p. 264.

95 Press Trust of India News Agency, December 11, 1980, cited in report by Carol Honsa, *Christian Science Monitor*, December 12, 1980. Moscow reportedly increased shipments of oil by 1,000,000 metric tons.

96 For the text of the final communiqué, see *Pravda*, December 12, 1980.

97 The text of the declaration is found in *FBIS:USSR*, December 11, 1980, p. D-7.

98 For a Soviet analysis of the significance of Brezhnev's plan, see the commentary by Igor Pavlovich, Moscow Radio Domestic Service (International Round Table), December 21, 1980 (*FBIS:USSR*, December 22, 1980, pp. CC-2).

99 For the text of the note, which was broadcast by Tass in English on December 28, 1980, see *FBIS:USSR*, December 29, 1980, p. H-1.

100 For the reports of the comments of Behzad Nabavi, Iranian government spokesman, on Radio Tehran Domestic Service, December 20, 1980, see *FBIS: South Asia*, December 30, 1980, pp. I-5–I-6.

101 Cf. Tass report, January 12, 1981 in *FBIS:USSR*, January 13, 1981, p. H-1.

102 Cf. *Pravda*, January 17, 1981 and Moscow Radio Persian Language broadcast January 17, 1981 (*FBIS:USSR*, January 19, 1981, pp. A-2–A-3). Former Secretary of State Henry Kissinger's trip to the Middle East in early January was linked by Moscow to the invasion plan.

103 Cf. Reuters report, *New York Times*, January 18, 1981.

104 For the text of Brezhnev's speech to the 26th Party Congress, see *Pravda*, February 23, 1981 (translated in *CDSP*, 1981, vol. 33, no. 8, pp. 7–13).

105 For an analysis of the development of Inter-Arab politics to early 1981, see Bruce Maddy-Weitzman, "The Fragmentation of Arab Politics: Inter-Arab Affairs Since the Afghanistan Invasion," *Orbis*, vol. 25, no. 2 (Summer 1981), pp. 389–407.

106 For an analysis of Libyan policy, see Ronald Bruce St. John, "Libya's Foreign and Domestic Policies," *Current History*, December 1981, pp. 426–29, 434–35.

107 See *Pravda*, April 28, 1981, for Kaddafi's banquet speech in which he portrayed himself as the representative of the Steadfastness front. See *Al-Watan* (Kuwait), April 29, 1981, for his frank interview about areas of agreement and disagreement with Moscow (*FBIS: Middle East and Africa*, May 4, 1981, pp. Q-4–Q-5).

108 Cf. *Pravda*, April 28, 1981 and *Pravda*, April 30, 1981. A Libyan Arabic broadcast made a major point of this (cf. Radio Tripoli Voice of the Arab Homeland, April 29, 1981) (*FBIS: Middle East and Africa*, April 30, 1981, p. Q-1).

109 During his banquet speech, Kaddafi had stated that the Steadfastness Front con-

sidered it necessary "to obtain information" about the Soviet proposal for an international conference on the Palestinian problem.

110 For an analysis of Algerian policy under Chadli Benjedid, see Robert Mortimer, "Algeria's New Sultan," *Current History*, December 1981, pp. 418–21; 433–34. For a Soviet view of Algerian development at this time that stresses the government role in economic development, see I. K. Smirnov, *Alzhir* (Moscow: Nauka, 1981).

111 Statement by Morris Draper, Deputy Assistant Secretary of State for Near Eastern and South Asian Affairs, as cited in the report by Bernard Gwertzman, *New York Times*, March 26, 1981.

112 For an analysis of the natural gas situation and other problems of US–Algerian relations, see the report by Jonathan C. Randal, *Washington Post*, March 25, 1981.

113 *Pravda*, June 11, 1981.

114 Soon after Benjedid's visit to Moscow, Morocco was to agree to a cease-fire and a referendum to determine the future of the former Spanish Sahara (cf. report by Jay Ross, *Washington Post*, June 27, 1981), but the modalities of the proposed referendum led a number of observers to believe that this was just a Moroccan ploy. For analyses of the Saharan problem, see William H. Lewis, "Western Sahara: Compromise or Conflict?" *Current History*, December 1981, pp. 410–13, 431; John Damis, *Conflict in Northwest Africa* (Stanford: Hoover Institution Press, 1983); and Tony Hodges, *Western Sahara: The Roots of a Desert War* (Westport: Laurence Hill, 1983).

115 For a description of Moscow's Mediterranean plan, see A. Usvatov, "USSR–Algeria: Common Approach," *New Times*, no. 25 (1981), p. 7. Moscow, through the UN, was making a similar effort for the Indian Ocean, but without success.

116 At the Islamic summit in Taif, Saudi Arabia in late January, for example, the emphasis was on Islamic opposition to Israel and the "Soviet threat" was played down, as was the Soviet invasion of Afghanistan (cf. Claudia Wright, "Islamic Summit," *The Middle East*, March 1981, pp. 6–10). The absence of Iran which had played a militantly anti-Soviet role in the previous Islamic conference in May 1980, however, may have been a factor in the downplaying of the Soviet threat along with Saudi Arabian efforts to achieve an Islamic consensus, which meant it had to have the support of Moscow's Steadfastness Front allies.

117 UPI report in *Jerusalem Post*, April 9, 1981. As a gesture to the US, however, Saudi Arabia broke diplomatic relations with Afghanistan on the eve of the Haig visit (cf. Reuters report, *New York Times*, April 8, 1981).

118 For an analysis of the 1975 visit, see Freedman, *Soviet Policy Toward the Middle East Since 1970*, pp. 220–21.

119 For an interview with Sheik Sabah, see *The Middle East*, March 1981, p. 18. For an analysis of the domestic situation in Kuwait at the time of Sheik Sabah's visit to the USSR, see Helena Cobban, "Kuwait's Elections," *The Middle East*, April 1981, pp. 14–15. Kuwait's foreign policy problems and strategy are discussed in Claudia Wright, "India and Pakistan Join in Gulf Game," *The Middle East*, June 1981, pp. 31–32. According to Wright, Sheik Sabah also went to Moscow to get a non-aggression treaty negotiated between the PDRY and Oman so as to lessen Omani depndence on the US. On this point, see also *Al-Hadaf* (Kuwait), May 7, 1981 (translated in *FBIS: Middle East and Africa*, May 13, 1981, p. C-5). For a view of Kuwait's position by a Kuwaiti scholar, see Hassan Ali Al-Ebraheem, *Kuwait and the Gulf* (Washington: Center for Contemporary Arab Studies, Georgetown University, 1984). Both in 1984 and especially 1987 with the escalation of the tanker war, Kuwait was to play an important role in the US–Soviet influence competition in the Gulf. See below, chs. 3 and 4.

120 *Pravda*, April 26, 1981.

121 *Ibid.*
122 For an analysis of the changing alliances of King Hussein, see Adam M. Garfinkle, "Negotiating by Proxy," pp. 847–80.
123 See below, pp. 105–8.
124 The joint communiqué was printed in *Pravda*, May 30, 1981.
125 *Pravda*, May 27, 1981.
126 Alexander Usvatov "King Hussein's Visit," *New Times*, no. 23 (1981), p. 10. One additional issue on which Jordan and the USSR obviously did not agree, however, was the Iran–Iraq war, where Jordan continued to strongly back Iraq while Moscow continued to profess a neutral position.
127 Cf. report of Jonathan Randal, *Washington Post*, April 13, 1981.
128 Translated in *CDSP*, 1981, vol. 33, no. 15, p. 18.
129 See above, p. 93.
130 By the end of the first week in May, Arab army chiefs, meeting in Tunis, had pledged to aid Syria as had Kuwait and Saudi Arabia (cf. report by Pranay Gupte, *New York Times*, May 8, 1981 and AP report, *Baltimore Sun*, May 3, 1981). *Tass* on May 8 and *Pravda* and Moscow Radio (Arabic language broadcast) on May 9 carried stories about the missiles, referring to them as a defensive measure. The stories coincided with the end of a visit to Damascus by Soviet First Deputy Foreign Minister Georgii Kornienko. For a somewhat different view of Soviet behavior, see Karsh, *The Soviet Union and Syria*, pp. 58–61.
131 The Reagan administration had decided to reinforce US–Saudi relations by selling Saudi Arabia 5 AWACs aircraft, advanced air-to-air missiles, and other sophisticated military equipment.
132 Cf. report by Don Oberdorfer, *Washington Post*, April 30, 1981.
133 Soviet radar on Lebanese mountain peaks would aid Moscow's air deployments in the Eastern Mediterranean.
134 To at least one Soviet commentator, the situation was somewhat reminiscent of June 1967. See Dmitry Volsky, "May 1981 is not June 1967," *New Times*, no. 21, (1981), pp. 5–6.
135 See Freedman, *Soviet Policy Toward the Middle East Since 1970*, pp. 151–59.
136 Cf. Moscow Radio in Arabic, May 13, 1981 (*FBIS:USSR*, May 14, 1981, p. H-1).
137 Cited in Robert Rand, "The USSR and the Crisis over Syrian Missiles in Lebanon: An Analysis and Chronological Survey," *Radio Liberty Report*, no. 227/81 (June 3, 1981), p. 6. Rand's study is an excellent analysis of the missile crisis from April 28, 1981 to May 29, 1981. (Note: *Tass* of May 5 denied that Soldatov had said the USSR regarded the Al Bekaa Valley [where Zahle is located] as a sector of substantial importance to the security of Syria).
138 Cited in report in *New York Times*, May 13, 1981.
139 *Pravda*, May 17, 1981.
140 *Pravda*, May 23, 1981.
141 *Pravda*, May 27, 1981.
142 Cited in *Jerusalem Post*, May 24, 1981. The "total" support was, however, to evaporate when Israel attacked Syrian forces in Lebanon in June 1982.
143 Cited in *Pravda*, May 26, 1981.
144 Moscow, however, had not forgotten the missile crisis and in early July carried out a joint military exercise with Syria including, for the first time, naval landings. For a report on the exercise which could be seen as a Soviet show of support for Syria after Begin's reelection, see the UPI report in the *New York Times*, July 10, 1981.
145 Cf. *Pravda*, June 10, 11 and 16, 1981.
146 Translated in *CDSP*, 1981, vol. 33, no. 24, p. 17.
147 Cf. report by Nathaniel Harrison, *Christian Science Monitor*, April 1, 1981.

148 Cf. Andrei Stepanov, "Taking Up a Point" (Soviet Neutrality in the Iran–Iraq War), *New Times*, no. 17 (1981), p. 31.

149 Cf. report by Michael J. Berlin, *Washington Post*, June 19, 1981.

150 Cited in report by Edward Cody, *Washington Post*, June 29, 1981.

151 Aziz Mohammed's speech was also printed in *Pravda*, March 3, 1981.

152 Cited in report by Bernard Gwertzman, *New York Times*, March 20, 1981.

153 Cf. report by Don Oberdorfer, *Washington Post*, April 11, 1981.

154 *Ibid.* Permission for the sale of the planes had been previously refused.

155 In early November, the *Daily Telegraph* (London) reported the shipment of 650 tanks from Poland (*Baltimore Sun*, November 12, 1981).

156 Cf. Tass statement in *Pravda*, July 22, 1981.

157 For an analysis of the background to this incident, see the report by Bernard Gwertzman, *New York Times*, August 21, 1981. For an examination of Kaddafi's attempt to improve his diplomatic position, see Claudia Wright, "Libya Comes in From the Cold," *The Middle East*, August 1981, pp. 18–25.

158 If this was one of his goals, he was unsuccessful as Saudi Arabia, despite the aircraft incident, stood firm on its price demands, something which Moscow also complained about (see below, p. 121).

159 Tass International Service, in Russian, August 20, 1981 (translated in *FBIS:USSR*, August 20, 1981, p. H-2).

160 Translated in *FBIS:USSR*, August 28, 1981, p. H-6.

161 *Pravda*, August 23, 1981. Criticism of the US action came from such Centrist Arab states as Jordan, Kuwait, Bahrain and the United Arab Emirates and from the Secretary of the Gulf Cooperation Council, and the Organization of African Unity (cf. *FBIS: Middle East and Africa*, August 20 and 21, 1981).

162 Cf. Moscow Radio in Turkish to Turkey, August 20, 1981 (*FBIS:USSR*, August 21, 1981, p. H-2).

163 Oman denounced the treaty in very strong terms (cf. Muscat Domestic Service, August 26, 1981 and Salalah Domestic Service, August 27, 1981, *FBIS: Middle East and Africa*, August 27, 1981, pp. C-1–C-2) and strongly criticized the decision by the Secretary of the Gulf Cooperation Council to denounce the US attack on the Libyan aircraft without consulting the membership (cf. *FBIS: Middle East and Africa*, August 31, 1981, p. C-2). For an interview with the GCC's Secretary General, Abdullah Bishara, who was trying to push the organization toward non-alignment, see *The Middle East*, September 1981, pp. 35–36. At its August ministerial meeting, however, several days after the Tripartite Treaty, the GCC decided "to strengthen political and security coordination between the member states" (see Nadia Hijab, "Gulf Council Shifts Into Second Gear," *The Middle East*, October 1981, pp. 25–26).

164 For Soviet attitudes toward the Iranian leadership, see Robert O. Freedman, "Soviet Policy Toward the Middle East Since the Invasion of Afghanistan," *Journal of International Affairs*, vol. 34, no. 2, pp. 290–91 and 295–97.

165 Translated in *FBIS:USSR*, September 3, 1981, p. H-1.

166 Cited in AP report, *New York Times*, November 7, 1981. Syrian communist leader Khalid Bakdash, however, was critical of Gassemlou (cf. *World Marxist Review*, November 1981, p. 33). Gassemlou was to be murdered, apparently by an Iranian "hit team," in July 1989 (cf. story by Jonathan Randal, *Washington Post*, August 2, 1989).

167 Cited in report in *Washington Post*, February 16, 1981.

168 Tehran Domestic Service, October 20, 1981 (*FBIS:USSR*, October 22, 1981, p. H-7).

169 Cited in Reuters report, *New York Times*, November 23, 1981.

170 Cf. A. Ulansky, "Presidential Election in a Tense Atmosphere," *New Times*, no. 40 (1981), p. 10. A statement by the Tudeh party was even more critical (cf. "For a

Return to Peace in a Society Based on Legality and Social Justice," Information Bulletin, *World Marxist Review*, November 1981, p. 21).

171 Cf. Radio Moscow, in English, August 29, 1981 (*FBIS:USSR*, August 31, 1981, p. H-4).

172 Cf. *Pravda*, September 8, 12, 14, 25, 1981.

173 The actual agreement, signed in December was far more modest but Moscow sought to extract the maximum in propaganda value from it both when Begin came to the United States in September to negotiate the general principles of the agreement and when Sharon came in December to sign the detailed agreement.

174 The meeting was at Shamir's initiative. Israel had long sought to improve ties to Moscow, but it was not until Gorbachev came to power in 1985 that any real diplomatic movement took place (see ch. 4).

175 Cf. Tass International Service in Russian, September 25, 1981 (*FBIS:USSR*, September 25, 1981, p. CC-3) and Radio Moscow in English to North America October 5, 1981 (*FBIS:USSR*, October 6, 1981, p. H-4).

176 Cf. report by William Clayborn, *Washington Post*, September 26, 1981.

177 For articles summarizing Moscow's displeasure with Sadat at the time of the Egyptian President's visit to Washington in early August, see *Izvestia*, August 9, 1981 and August 28, 1981.

178 *Pravda*, September 18, 1981.

179 Moscow Radio announced, however, on October 1, 1981 that the Soviet branch of the Friendship Society would continue to operate (*FBIS:USSR*, October 1, 1981, p. H-1).

180 Bovin's comments came on Moscow television on October 25 (*FBIS:USSR*, October 26, 1981, p. H-1).

181 Cf. Moscow Radio Peace and Progress in Arabic, September 7, 1981 (*FBIS:USSR*, September 10, 1981, p. H-1); Tass, in English, October 8, 1981 (*FBIS:USSR*, October 9, 1981, p. H-1), and Moscow Radio in Arabic, October 26, 1981 (*FBIS:USSR*, October 27, 1981, p. H-6).

182 For an analysis of Soviet and US policy during the fall of the Shah, see Freedman, *Soviet Policy Toward the Middle East Since 1970*, pp. 349–50, and Rubinstein, *Soviet Policy Toward Turkey, Iran and Afghanistan*, pp. 92–94.

183 *Pravda*, October 12, 1981.

184 Cf. report by Don Oberdorfer, *Washington Post*, October 15, 1981.

185 *Pravda*, October 16, 1981.

186 Cf. note 180. In a speech on November 8, however, Mubarak hinted at non-alignment, stating "Egypt will not rotate in the orbit of any state" (Radio Cairo, November 8, 1981, cited in Robert Rand, "Mubarak on the USSR," *Radio Liberty Report*, no. 462/81 [November 17, 1981]).

187 Cited in report by Don Oberdorfer, *Washington Post*, October 21, 1981. For a good analysis of Moscow's initial approaches to Mubarak and his attitude toward the USSR, see Rand, *ibid*.

188 Moscow Radio Domestic Service, October 20, 1981 (*FBIS:USSR*, October 21, 1981, p. H-1). Arafat was quoted as saying at a press conference "We fully endorse the Soviet proposals advanced at the 26th CPSU Congress and we view them as the basis for a just settlement of the Palestinian problem." *Pravda*, on October 21, 1981, reported the Joint Soviet–PLO support for the international conference and the granting of official diplomatic status to the PLO mission in Moscow.

189 Cited in report by Bernard Gwertzman, *New York Times*, August 13, 1981.

190 The text of the former Presidents' comments is in the *New York Times*, October 12, 1981.

191 For an analysis of this event, see Freedman, *Soviet Policy Toward the Middle East Since 1970*, pp. 352–54 and Katz, *Russia and Arabia*, pp. 35–39.

192 For a detailed study of North Yemen's problems, see Katz, *ibid.*, ch. 1.
193 *Pravda*, October 29, 1981.
194 Salah may have also wished to have Moscow's support in controlling the South Yemeni drive for the unification of the Yemens, following the strengthening of the PDRY by its alliance with Ethiopia and Libya.
195 Cf. reports by Bernard Gwertzman, *New York Times*, November 3, 1981; Don Oberdorfer, *Washington Post*, November 6, 1981; and Reuters, *Washington Post*, November 9, 1981.
196 *Pravda*, August 26, 1981.
197 *Literaturnaia Gazeta*, May 27, 1981 (translated in *CDSP*, vol. 33, no. 21, p. 11).
198 Ruben Andreasian, "Disagreement in OPEC," *New Times*, no. 35 (1981), p. 13. See also Ruben Andreasian, *Opek v Mire Nefti* (OPEC in the world of Oil) (Moscow: Nauka, 1978).
199 *Pravda*, August 26, 1981.
200 Translated in *FBIS:USSR*, November 3, 1981, p. A-3.
201 *FBIS:USSR*, November 2, 1981, p. H-2.
202 *Pravda*, March 29, 1981.
203 This, of course, had happened during the 1973 Arab–Israeli war. Cf. *Izvestia*, January 8, 1981.
204 Tass, November 1, 1981 (*FBIS:USSR*, November 2, 1981, p. H-3).
205 Cf. *Izvestia*, October 31, 1981. For a study of West European policies toward the Middle East, see Robert Hunter, "Western Europe and the Middle East Since the Lebanon War," in Robert O. Freedman (ed.), *The Middle East After the Israeli Invasion of Lebanon* (Syracuse: Syracuse University Press, 1986), pp. 94–103.
206 Cf. Moscow Radio in Arabic, November 8, 1981 (*FBIS:USSR*, November 9, 1981, pp. H-1 – H-2).
207 It may have also had a favorable impact on North Yemen.
208 As might be expected, Moscow was highly critical of Pakistan's increasingly close military tie to the United States (cf. *Pravda*, September 27, 1981).
209 Cited in AP report, *Baltimore Sun*, November 24, 1981.
210 Unlike Sadat, who by 1981 was on very poor personal terms with the Saudi ruling family, Mubarak had kept up good personal relationships.
211 Radio Moscow in Arabic, August 12, 1981 (*FBIS:USSR*, August 13, 1981, p. H-1).
212 Cf. *FBIS:USSR*, August 20, 1981, p. A-3.
213 *Izvestia*, November 5, 1981.
214 Cf. Moscow Radio in Arabic, November 5 and 6, 1981 (*FBIS:USSR*, November 6, 1981, p. H-1 and p. H-4).
215 The text of the communiqué is found in *FBIS: Middle East and Africa*, November 12, 1981, p. C-4. Moscow, however, at least as reflected in a Moscow Radio Peace and Progress Arabic broadcast on November 12, 1981 was critical of the GCC meetings (*FBIS:USSR*, November 13, 1981, p. H-4). One of the key issues not settled in the GCC meeting was Oman's proposal regarding Gulf security. If adopted, the proposal would have moved the GCC closer to the United States.
216 Cf. article by Scott Armstrong, *Washington Post*, November 1, 1981.
217 Cf. *New York Times*, October 2, 1981.
218 Cf. *Pravda*, September 20, 1981 and Moscow Radio Peace and Progress in Arabic, October 20, 1981 (*FBIS:USSR*, October 21, 1981, p. H-7).
219 Moscow Radio, in Arabic, November 27, 1981 (*FBIS:USSR*, December 1, 1981, pp. H-5–H-6).
220 Dmitry Volsky, "There is Light at the End of the Tunnel," *New Times*, no. 49 (1981) pp. 12–13.
221 For assessments of the policies of individual Arab states, see *The Middle East*

Contemporary Survey's Annual Yearbook.

222 *Izvestia*, April 15, 1982.

223 Cf. report by David Ottaway, *Washington Post*, January 15, 1982.

224 For the text of the communiqué, see *Pravda*, January 17, 1982.

225 Cf. *Pravda*, January 16, 1982.

226 Cf. report by Dusko Doder, *Washington Post*, February 16, 1982, and *Izvestia*, February 11, 1982 which discusses the rise in Soviet–Iranian trade and Iranian oil sales to the USSR.

227 Bovin, a senior correspondent for *Izvestia*, delivered his criticism in *Izvestia*'s weekend supplement, *Nedeliya*, September 3–9, 1979.

228 *Pravda*, March 9, 1982.

229 For Boldryev's background, see Moscow Radio, Persian Language Broadcast to Iran, June 2, 1981 in *FBIS:USSR*, June 3, 1982, pp. H-7–H-8.

230 For an analysis of Soviet–Iranian relations at this time, see Karen Dawisha, "The USSR in the Middle East: Superpower in Eclipse," *Foreign Affairs*, vol. 61, no. 2 (Winter 1982–83), pp. 447–48.

231 Cf. A.P. report, *Baltimore Evening Sun*, January 26, 1982.

232 Cf. *Pravda*, February 16, 1982.

233 Cf. *Izvestia*, May 8, 1982.

234 Cf. report in *Washington Post*, March 18, 1982.

235 Cf. Freedman, *Soviet Policy Toward the Middle East Since 1970*, pp. 368, 420.

236 *Ibid.*, pp. 397–98.

237 Cf. *Pravda*, July 31, 1982.

238 Cited in *New York Times* report, March 7, 1982.

239 For Moscow's highly negative reaction to this development, see the Moscow Radio Arab language broadcast on May 28, 1982, *FBIS:USSR*, June 1, 1982, p. H-3.

240 Cf. *New York Times* report, March 8, 1982.

241 For a description of the increasingly severe problems facing the PLO in Lebanon on the eve of the war, see David Butler, "In the Same Trench," *The Middle East*, June 1982, p. 6. See also his report, "Shiites in Beirut Clashes," *The Middle East*, February 1982, p. 14. For an excellent study of the Lebanese Shia, see Augustus Richard Norton, *Amal and the Shia* (Austin: University of Texas Press, 1987).

242 Cf. remarks by Taha Ramadan, First Deputy Prime Minister of Iraq, Baghdad Radio, June 1, 1982, *FBIS:MEA*, June 2, 1981, p. E-2.

243 The Moroccan Foreign Minister, Mohammed Boucetta, paid a visit to Cairo on June 7, 1982 thus further ending Egypt's ostracism, as did Egyptian President Mubarak's attendance at the funeral of King Khalid of Saudi Arabia later that month.

244 Cf. *Pravda*, May 26, 1982.

245 Cf. Robert O. Freedman, "Soviet Policy Toward Syria Since Camp David," *Middle East Review*, vol. 14, nos. 1–2 (Fall 1981–Winter 1982), pp. 28–30).

246 Cf. Voice of Palestine, June 2, 1982, cited in *FBIS:MEA*, June 3, 1982, p. E-1.

247 For a detailed analysis of the difficulties inherent in the Soviet–PLO relationship, see Galia Golan, *The Soviet Union and the Palestine Liberation Organization* (New York: Praeger, 1980). See also Raphael Israeli (ed.), *PLO in Lebanon: Selected Documents* (New York: St. Martin's Press, 1983), ch. 5.

248 For Israeli military analyses of the war, see *Israel Defense Forces Journal*, vol. 1, no. 2 (December 1982), pp. 11–28; and Chaim Herzog, *The Arab–Israeli Wars* (New York: Random House, 1982), pp. 339–59. For a view from the Palestinian side, see the special issue of the *Journal of Palestine Studies*, no. 44/45 (Summer/Fall 1982) devoted to the war, especially the chronology, pp. 135–92, and Rashid Khalidi, *Under Siege: PLO Decisionmaking During the 1982 War* (New York: Columbia University Press, 1986).

249 Cf. Voice of Palestine, June 7, 1982; June 8, 1982 (*FBIS:MEA*, June 8, 1982, p. A-2); June 9 (*FBIS:MEA*, p. ii) and June 10 (*FBIS:MEA*, p. A-3). For other studies of the war see Ze'ev Schiff and Edud Ya'ari, *Israel's Lebanon War* (New York: Simon and Schuster, 1984); Itamar Rabinovich, *The War for Lebanon: 1970–1983* (Ithaca: Cornell University Press, 1984); Dan Bawly and Eliahu Salpeter, *Fire in Beirut: Israel's War in Lebanon With the PLO* (New York: Stein and Day, 1984); Jonathan Randal, *Going All The Way: Christian Warlords, Israeli Adventurers and the War in Lebanon* (New York: Random House, 1984), and Halim Barakat (ed.), *Toward a Viable Lebanon* (London: Croom Helm, 1988). One result of the war was the capture of documents on PLO activities in Lebanon. See *PLO in Lebanon: Selected Documents*.
250 Voice of Lebanon, June 6, 1982 (*FBIS:MEA*, June 7, 1982, p. G-9).
251 *Pravda*, June 8, 1982.
252 Tass, June 8, 1982 (*FBIS:USSR*, June 9, 1982, p. H-2) and AP report in *New York Times*, June 9, 1982.
253 Tass, June 9, 1982 (*FBIS:USSR*, June 9, 1982, p. H-2).
254 Tass, June 9, 1982 (*FBIS:USSR*, June 10, 1982, p. H-2).
255 *KUNA*, Kuwait, June 10, 1982 (*FBIS:MEA*, June 11, 1982, p. A-1).
256 Cf. report by David Shipler, *New York Times*, June 20, 1982, citing Israeli Prime Minister Menahem Begin, who also said he had received two messages from Moscow asking Israel not to hit the Soviet Embassy in Beirut.
257 Cf. report by Hedrick Smith, *New York Times*, June 11, 1982. There is some evidence, however, that in transmitting the Soviet message to Israel it was embellished to try to stop the Israeli invasion (interview, former member of the US National Security Council, May 1986). Karsh, *The Soviet Union and Syria*, p. 69, seems to think it led Israel to accept the ceasefire. On the limited Soviet role during the first days of the invasion, see Khalidi, *Under Siege*, and Galia Golan, "The Soviet Union and the Israeli War in Lebanon," Research Paper no. 46, Soviet and East European Research Center, The Hebrew University of Jerusalem.
258 Haig interview on ABC program "This Week With David Brinkley," June 13, 1982, reprinted in *Journal of Palestine Studies*, nos. 44/45 (Summer–Fall 1982), p. 330.
259 For an analysis of the economic benefits to Moscow of arms sales, see Andrew J. Pierre, *The Global Politics of Arms Sales* (Princeton: Princeton University Press, 1982), pp. 78–80. On Soviet military logistics in aiding the PLO, see Amnon Sella, "The Soviet Attitude Towards the War in Lebanon – mid 1982," Research Paper no. 47, Soviet and East European Research Center, The Hebrew University of Jerusalem.
260 For the best analysis of Soviet strategy during the war, see Galia Golan, *Yom Kippur and After: The Soviet Union and the Middle East Crisis* (London: Cambridge University Press, 1977).
261 *Pravda*, June 15, 1982. Khalidi, *Under Siege*, also emphasizes PLO disappointment with the lack of Arab help saying that Palestinians were more angry at their fellow Arabs than at the Israelis (p. 14).
262 *Pravda*, June 14, 1982.
263 Cf. Moscow Domestic Service, June 13, 1982 (*FBIS:USSR*, June 16, 1982, p. H-1 and *FBIS:MEA*, June 15, 1982, p. i).
264 Cf. report by Ned Temko, *Christian Science Monitor*, June 18, 1982.
265 Cf. Tass, June 17, 1982 (*FBIS:USSR*, June 18, 1982, p. H-2).
266 Moscow Radio Peace and Progress, in Arabic, June 15, 1982 (*FBIS:USSR*, June 16, 1982, p. H-2).
267 *Pravda*, June 23, 1982.
268 Radio Monte Carlo, in Arabic, June 18, 1982 (*FBIS:MEA*, June 21, 1982, pp. A-3, 4).

269 *Le Monde*, June 23, 1982, cited in *FBIS:MEA*, June 23, 1982, p. A-2.

270 Cited in *FBIS:MEA*, June 28, 1982, pp. ii.

271 Cited in *FBIS:MEA*, June 29, 1982, p. A-3.

272 Tripoli, *JANA*, June 26, 1982 (*FBIS:MEA*, June 26, 1982, pp. Q-2, 3).

273 Tass, June 22, 1982 (*FBIS:USSR*, June 22, 1982, p. H-3).

274 Freedman, "Soviet Policy Toward Syria Since Camp David."

275 *FBIS:USSR*, June 29, 1982, pp. H-1, 2.

276 Cf. Moscow Radio, June 30, 1982 (*FBIS:USSR*, July 1, 1982, p. H-3); Tass, June 30, 1982 (*FBIS:USSR*, July 1, 1982, p. H-1), and Moscow Radio, June 28, 1982; June 30, 1982; July 1, 1982 (*FBIS:USSR*, July 2, 1982, pp. H-5, 6, 7).

277 *Pravda*, June 27, 1982.

278 Cf. *FBIS:MEA*, June 30, 1982, p. F-3, and *FBIS:USSR*, June 30, 1982, p. H-1.

279 Tass, June 27, 1982 (*FBIS:USSR*, June 28, 1982, p. H-3).

280 Cf. Tass, June 27, 1982 (*FBIS:USSR*, June 28, 1982, p. H-6).

281 *FBIS:USSR*, July 2, 1982, p. H-3, 4.

282 *FBIS:MEA*, July 1, 1982, p. A-3.

283 *Pravda*, July 6, 1982.

284 Cf. report by Dusko Doder, *Washington Post*, July 6, 1982.

285 *Pravda*, July 9, 1982 (translated in *CDSP*, vol. 34, no. 27, p. 3).

286 Cf. Moscow Radio in Arabic to the Arab world, July 8, 1982 (Rafael Arutounov commentary) and Moscow Radio Domestic Service, July 9, 1982 (Yuri Kornilov commentary).

287 Moscow Radio in Arabic, July 9, 1982 (*FBIS:USSR*, July 12, 1982, p. H-6).

288 *FBIS:USSR*, July 15, 1982, pp. H-1, 2.

289 Tunis Domestic Service, July 13, 1982 (*FBIS:MEA*, July 14, 1982, p. Q-6).

290 Tass, July 15, 1982 (*FBIS:USSR*, July 16, 1982, p. H-6, 7).

291 Cf. *Al-Anba* (Kuwait), July 1, 1982 (*FBIS:MEA*, July 2, 1982, p. A-8).

292 Cited in AFP (Paris), July 15, 1982 (*FBIS:MEA*, July 16, 1982, p. A-3).

293 *Pravda*, August 3, 1982.

294 *Pravda*, August 6, 1982. On PLO decision making to leave Beirut, see Khalidi, *Under Siege*.

295 *Izvestia*, September 10, 1982.

296 Cf. Dmitry Volsky, "Fez and the Bekaa Valley," *New Times* (Moscow), no. 38 (1982), pp. 7–8.

297 For an analysis of the status of the Soviet Middle East peace plan prior to the Israeli invasion of Lebanon, see Robert O. Freedman, "Moscow, Washington and the Gulf," *American–Arab Affairs*, no. 1 (Summer 1982), pp. 132–34.

298 Cf. *Middle East Journal*, vol. 37, no. 1 (Winter 1983), p. 71.

299 Cf. *Pravda*, September 11, 1982. The summit did agree, however, that any Arab countries that wished to renew ties with Egypt on a bilateral basis could do so. Jordan was to renew relations in September 1984.

300 *Pravda*, September 16, 1982.

301 *Pravda*, September 21, 1982. For the Israeli investigation of the massacres, see *The Beirut Massacre: The Complete Kahan Commission Report* (Princeton: Karz-Cohl, 1983).

302 During an interview with a senior PLO official in Tunis in February 1989, I was told that the failure of the Soviet Union to aid the PLO in 1982 led Arafat to move away from the Marxist groupings of the PLO and toward Jordan and the United States.

3 The interregnum: Moscow and the Middle East under Andropov and Chernenko

1 For studies of Andropov, see Zhores A. Medvedev, *Andropov* (New York: Penguin

Books, 1984); Vladimir Solovyov and Elena Klepikova, *Yuri Andropov* (New York: Mcmillan, 1983), and Ilya Zemtsov, *Andropov: Policy Dilemmas and the Struggle for Power* (Jerusalem: IRICS Publishers, 1983). See also *Y. V. Andropov: Speeches and Writings* (New York: Pergamon Press, 1983) and *K. U. Chernenko: Speeches and Writings* (New York: Pergamon Press, 1984).

2 *Pravda*, December 4, 1982.

3 For a background analysis of the visit, see Robert Rand, Radio Liberty Report No. RL 498/82, December 10, 1982.

4 Cf. report in *Washington Post*, December 12, 1982.

5 Cf. report in *Christian Science Monitor*, December 21, 1982.

6 UPI report, *Washington Post*, December 5, 1982.

7 Cf. report by David Ottaway, *Washington Post*, December 30, 1982 and comments by Yasser Arafat as recorded in the *Washington Post*, January 18, 1983.

8 Cf. report by Steven Rattnor, *New York Times*, October 24, 1982. For a discussion of Soviet policy toward Iran during this period, see Shahram Chubin and Charles Tripp, *Iran and Iraq at War* (Boulder: Westview Press, 1988), ch. 11, and Carol R. Saivetz, *The Soviet Union and the Gulf in the 1980s* (Boulder: Westview Press, 1989), ch. 2.

9 *New Times* (Moscow), no. 1 (1983), p. 4.

10 Cf. Robert Rand, Radio Liberty Report No. RL 31/83, January 13, 1983. Both the *IISS Military Balance* and the *SIPRI Yearbook* show increased deliveries to Iraq in 1983 and 1984, as does the Jaffee Center Middle East Military Balance.

11 See the reports by Drew Middleton, *New York Times*, November 17, 1982 and Robert J. McCartney, *Washington Post*, November 17, 1982.

12 Rand, *Radio Liberty Report*, no. 31/83.

13 Cf. Chubin and Tripp, *Iran and Iraq at War*, ch. 10.

14 Cited in report by Loren Jenkins, *Washington Post*, November 13, 1982. According to a high-ranking PLO adviser to Arafat in Tunis, during the 1982 Israeli siege of Beirut PFLP leader George Habash told Arafat that the USSR would send troops to the Bekaa Valley in Lebanon to help Syria and the PLO. When this proved to be false, both Habash and the USSR were discredited and Arafat began to diplomatically move toward the United States (interview, Tunis, February 1989).

15 *Pravda*, January 13, 1983.

16 *Ibid.*

17 Cf. report by Edward Walsh, *Washington Post*, January 5, 1982 and Thomas L. Friedman, *New York Times*, March 21, 1983.

18 It is also possible that the Soviet move, in part, was a response to the emplacement of US troops in Beirut, as well as a means of hampering US air operations in the Eastern Mediterranean near Lebanon.

19 For an analysis of the military implications of the Soviet–Syrian arms supply relationship, see Cynthia A. Roberts "Soviet Arms-Transfer Policy and the Decision to Upgrade Syrian Air Defenses," *Survival*, July–August 1983, pp. 154–64.

20 See above pp. 94 and 105–8 for a discussion of these events.

21 Cited in Reuters report, *New York Times*, January 24, 1983.

22 For an analysis of the alleged coup attempt in the Sudan, see the report by Lou Cannon and George Wilson, *Washington Post*, February 19, 1983. Nimeri was, in fact, to be overthrown in 1985. See below pp. 207–8.

23 Cited in report by Bernard Gwertzman, *New York Times*, February 21, 1983. For a Soviet view of the crisis, see "Sabre Rattling," *New Times*, no. 9 (1983), p. 11.

24 *Pravda*, March 20, 1983.

25 Tass report, cited in *Foreign Broadcast Information Service Daily Report: The Soviet Union* (hereafter *FBIS:USSR*), March 18, 1983, p. H-1.

26 Tass report, March 17, 1983 (*FBIS:USSR*, March 18, 1983, pp. H-3, H-4).

27 Following the 1981 Gulf of Sidra incident, Kaddafi, speaking on Tripoli radio on the anniversary of the Libyan revolution, had stated "We desperately need to be in military alliance with any ally who will stand by us against the United States." (Tripoli Domestic Service, September 1, 1981, cited in Ellen Laipson, "Libya and the Soviet Union: Alliance at Arms Length," unpublished paper, p. 6).

28 *Pravda*, March 20, 1983.

29 *Pravda*, March 31, 1983.

30 Cited in *Christian Science Monitor*, March 30, 1983. The author was in Israel during the middle of March 1983 where he noted the rapid disenchantment with the Lebanese invasion, a disenchantment that was highlighted by the release of the Kahan Commission's report on Israel's role in the Sabra and Shatilla massacres.

31 Riyadh *SPA*, April 2, 1983 (*FBIS:MEA*, April 4, 1983, p. C-6).

32 The text of Gromyko's press conference may be found in *FBIS:USSR*, April 4, 1983, pp. AA-1–AA-17.

33 *Ibid.*, p. AA-15.

34 *Ibid.*, p. AA-16.

35 The rise in opposition to Arafat within the PLO is discussed in Asher Susser, "The Palestine Liberation Organization," in *Middle East Contemporary Survey 1983* (hereafter *MECS*; ed. Colin Legum *et al.*, London: Homes and Meier, 1985), pp. 275–330 and Rashid Khalidi, "Palestinian Politics After the Exodus from Beirut," in Robert O. Freedman (ed.), *The Middle East After the Israeli Invasion of Lebanon* (Syracuse: Syracuse University Press, 1986), ch. 8.

36 Cited in report by Thomas L. Friedman, *New York Times*, February 23, 1983. The fact that PLO moderate Issam Sartawi, who publicly advocated a compromise between Israel and the PLO, was forbidden to speak at the meeting was a further indication of the erosion of Arafat's position. Sartawi was subsequently assassinated in April while attending the Socialist International Congress in Portugal. For general discussions of the PNC Council session, see Judith Perera, "Hammering Out a Compromise," *The Middle East*, no. 101 (March 1983), pp. 8–9 and Cheryl A. Rubenberg, "The PNC and the Reagan Initiative," *American–Arab Affairs*, vol. 4 (Spring 1983), pp. 53–69.

   For an analysis of trends within the PLO, see Aaron David Miller, "Palestinians in the 1980s," *Current History*, January 1984, pp. 17–20, 34–36, and "The PLO Since Camp David," in Robert O. Freedman (ed.), *The Middle East Since Camp David* (Boulder, Colorado: Westview Press, 1984).

37 *Pravda*, February 25, 1980.

38 Cited in report by Peter Osnos, *Washington Post*, March 20, 1983.

39 Cf. report by Bernard Gwertzman, *New York Times*, April 9, 1983.

40 Cited in Reuters report, *Washington Post*, March 31, 1983.

41 Cf. report by Herbert H. Denton, *Washington Post*, April 11, 1983. For a provocative interpretation of Hussein's decision, see the articles by Karen Elliott House in the *Wall Street Journal*, April 14, 1983 and April 15, 1983. For an analysis of Jordan's position *vis-à-vis* the Palestinians, see Adam M. Garfinkle, "Jordanian Foreign Policy," *Current History*, January 1984, pp. 21–24, 38–39. See also Khalidi, "Palestinian Politics," and Aaron David Miller, *The Arab States and the Palestine Question* (New York: Praeger, 1986), ch. 3.

42 *Pravda*, April 13, 1983 (translated in *CDSP*, vol. 35, no. 15, p. 9).

43 Cited in Reuters report, *New York Times*, April 17, 1983.

44 Cf. report by David Landau, *Jerusalem Post*, April 20, 1983.

45 Cf. report by Herbert Denton, *Washington Post*, April 22, 1983.

46 Cited in *Jerusalem Post*, April 24, 1983.

47 Cited in *Jerusalem Post*, April 26, 1983.

48 Cf. *Jerusalem Post*, April 27, 1983.

49 For an analysis of the dynamics of the process leading to the Israeli–Lebanese agreement, see Itamar Rabinovich, "Israel and Lebanon in 1983," *MECS 1982–1983*, pp. 135–49.

50 Cf. report by Herbert Denton, *Washington Post*, May 7, 1983.

51 For an analysis of the Syrian role in Lebanon at this time, see Yosef Olmert, "Syria," *MECS 1982–83*, pp. 795–829.

52 Tass report, May 9, 1983 (*FBIS:USSR*, May 10, 1983, p. H-1).

53 Cf. reports by Thomas L. Friedman, *New York Times*, May 10, 1983 and Nora Boustany, *Washington Post*, May 10, 1983.

54 Cf. report by Bernard Gwertzman, *New York Times*, May 11, 1983.

55 Cf. report by John Goshko, *Washington Post*, May 11, 1983.

56 Damascus, *SANA*, May 9, 1983 (*FBIS:MEA*, May 9, 1983, p. H-2).

57 Reuters report, *New York Times*, May 11, 1983.

58 Beirut Domestic Service in Arabic, May 10, 1983 (*FBIS:MEA*, May 16, 1983, p. H-8).

59 Cited in *Jerusalem Post*, May 15, 1983.

60 *Ibid.*

61 Cited in report by Sam Roberts, *New York Times*, May 14, 1983.

62 Cf. report by John Goshko, *Washington Post*, May 17, 1983.

63 Cf. Radio Moscow, Window on the Arab World, May 19, 1983 (*FBIS:USSR*, May 23, 1983, p. H-4).

64 Radio Moscow, Window on the Arab World, May 12, 1983 (*FBIS:USSR*, May 16, 1983, p. H-6).

65 Cf. report by Robin Wright, *Christian Science Monitor*, May 17, 1983.

66 Cf. report in *Jerusalem Post*, May 24, 1983.

67 Cf. report by William E. Farrell, *New York Times*, May 26, 1983.

68 Cf. report by Hirsh Goodman, *Jerusalem Post*, May 27, 1983.

69 For a Soviet view of the causes of the deterioration in Soviet–Iranian relations, see *Pravda*, March 23, 1983. See also Dmitry Volsky, "The Revolution at the Crossroads," *New Times*, no. 2 (1983), pp. 13–14.

70 Cited in Reuters report, *New York Times*, February 25, 1983.

71 Brezhnev had made these comments at the 26th CPSU Party Congress in February 1981. See above, p. 99.

72 *Washington Post*, May 5, 1983.

73 AFP report, *Washington Post*, May 5, 1983. The Soviet diplomats who were expelled included two minister counsellors, four first secretaries and three military attachés.

74 For a description of the anti-Soviet atmosphere in Iran at this time, see the report by Shireen T. Hunter, *Christian Science Monitor*, July 27, 1983.

75 Cited in report in *Christian Science Monitor*, May 26, 1983. See also Chubin and Tripp, *Iran and Iraq at War*, pp. 221–23.

76 *Pravda*, June 17, 1983.

77 See the report by Leon Dash, *Washington Post*, June 9, 1983.

78 For a study of the Libyan leader's policy toward Chad, see Rene Lemarchand, "The Case of Chad," in Lemarchand (ed.), *The Green and the Black: Qadhafi's Policies in Africa* (Bloomington: Indiana University Press, 1988), ch. 6.

79 Cf. report in *Baltimore Sun*, August 22, 1983. See also David S. Yost, "French Policy in Chad and the Libyan Challenge," *Orbis*, vol. 26, no. 4 (Winter 1983), pp. 965–97.

80 Cf. *Izvestia*, July 6, 1983.

81 *Pravda*, July 13, 1983.

82 For a description of the confrontation, see the report by Ian Black, *Washington Post*, August 3, 1983.

83 For a description of Soviet–Libyan relations at this time, see Robert Rand, *Radio Liberty Report*, no. 307/83 (August 11, 1983).

84 *Pravda*, August 4, 1983.

85 For a Soviet view of Soviet–Moroccan ties in early 1983, see V. Shlepin, "USSR–Morocco: Links Many and Varied," *New Times*, no. 11 (1983), pp. 10–11. For a solid study of the Sahara conflict, see John Damis, *Conflict in Northwest Africa* (Stanford: Hoover Institution Press, 1983).

86 For a description of the US–Moroccan military relationship, see the reports by James Clarity, *New York Times*, February 1, 1983, and Jonathan Randal, *Washington Post*, February 24, 1983.

87 Cf. report by Claudia Wright, *Christian Science Monitor*, March 1, 1983.

88 Cited in Reuters report, *New York Times*, September 15, 1983.

89 Cf. report by Mary Fitzgerald, *Washington Post*, June 12, 1983. *Izvestia*, on July 17, 1983 complained that King Hassan had rejected the possibility of direct negotiations with the Polisario and had stepped up its attacks in the former Spanish Sahara.

90 Cf. report by James Rupert, *Washington Post*, August 22, 1983. A Maghreb union of sorts – with Kaddafi – was to be achieved in 1988. See below p. 299. See also Mary Jane Deeb, "Inter-Maghribi Relations: A Study of the Modalities of Unions and Mergers," *Middle East Journal*, vol. 43, no. 1 (Winter 1989), pp. 20–33.

91 Cf. report by Herbert Denton, *Washington Post*, July 5, 1983. See also sources in note 23, above.

92 Cf. *FBIS:MEA*, August 5, 1983, p. A-1.

93 Cf. *Al-Watan Al-Arabi*, cited by INA (*FBIS:MEA*, September 2, 1983, p. A-1). For a sympathetic account of Arafat's difficulties at this time, see Alan Hart, *Arafat* (Bloomington: Indiana University Press, 1989), ch. 19.

94 For a description of Soviet military facilities in Syria, see *Near East Report*, vol. 27, no. 23 (June 10, 1983), p. 2. Moscow was later to admit it used the Syrian port of Tartus as a base. See below, p. 301.

95 Radio Peace and Progress, May 26, 1983 (*FBIS:USSR*, June 1, 1983, p. H-3). See also A. Stepanov, "To Safeguard Palestinian Unity," *New Times*, no. 28 (1983), pp. 14–15.

96 WAFA, June 4, 1983, cited in *Jerusalem Post*, June 5, 1983.

97 *Pravda*, July 14, 1983.

98 Cf. report by Loren Jenkins in the *Washington Post*, August 3, 1983, and reports in the *Baltimore Sun*, July 10, 1983; *New York Times*, July 15, 1983; and *Washington Post* (AFP report), July 17, 1983.

99 Stepanov, "To Safeguard Palestinian Unity," p. 14. The third Marxist group within the PLO, the PFLP-GC, remained under Syrian control however.

100 Cited in report by Don Oberdorfer, *Washington Post*, July 7, 1983. For a European view of the Shultz visit, see *The Economist*, July 9, 1983, p. 31.

101 AP report in *Washington Post*, July 24, 1983.

102 Cited in report by David Shipler, *New York Times*, June 2, 1983.

103 Reuters report, *Baltimore Sun*, June 8, 1983.

104 Cited in report by Don Oberdorfer, *Washington Post*, July 8, 1983.

105 Cf. report by Nora Boustany, *Washington Post*, July 24, 1983. For a study of Lebanese events during this period, see Halim Barakat (ed.), *Toward a Viable Lebanon* (London: Croom Helm, 1988).

106 *Novosti* article by Pavel Demchenko, cited in AP report in the *Jerusalem Post*, August 3, 1983. *Novosti* reports are often used as a direct means of trying to influence Western nations. See below, p. 177–78.

107 *Tishrin* editorial, cited in Reuters report, *Washington Post*, August 28, 1983.

108 Cf. report by E. J. Dionne, Jr., *New York Times*, September 20, 1983.

109 Cf. report by David Ottaway, *Washington Post*, September 18, 1983.

110 Cf. report by Thomas L. Friedman, *New York Times*, September 23, 1983.

111 Cf. report by Trudy Rubin, *Christian Science Monitor*, September 19, 1983.

112 When fired, however, the guns proved ineffective.

113 *Izvestia*, September 4, 1983 (*FBIS:USSR*, September 7, 1983, p. H-4).

114 Editorial, *New Times*, no. 38 (1983), p. 1.

115 *Pravda*, September 19, 1983.

116 *Pravda*, September 20, 1983.

117 Cf. *Al-Qabas* (Kuwait), September 20, 1983 (*FBIS:USSR*, September 22, 1983, p. H-1).

118 Cited in report by Bernard Gwertzman, *New York Times*, September 23, 1983.

119 Cf. *Tishrin*, September 12, 1983, cited on Radio Monte Carlo (*FBIS:MEA*, September 13, 1983, p. H-1).

120 Radio Monte Carlo, September 23, 1983 (*FBIS:MEA*, September 23, 1983, p. H-1).

121 Andropov himself praised the cease-fire (*Pravda*, September 30, 1983), in a page 1 report of his meeting with PDRY leader Ali Nasser Mohammed. A Tass statement published in *Pravda* on September 29 noted that the cease-fire had been "favorably received" in the Soviet Union, and again opposed both the Israeli and American troop presence in Lebanon, and the May 17 Israeli–Lebanese agreement. Andropov's meeting with Ali Nasser Mohammed was to be the Soviet leader's last public appearance, as he soon became gravely ill.

122 Cf. Damascus Domestic Service, September 15, 1983 (*FBIS:MEA*, September 15, 1983, p. H-1), September 18, 1983 (*FBIS:MEA*, September 19, 1983, p. H-3), and September 14, 1983 (*FBIS:MEA*, September 20, 1983, pp. H-1, H-2).

123 For the text of the cease-fire agreement, see the AP report, *New York Times*, September 27, 1983.

124 Cf. report by Michael Getler, *Washington Post*, October 7, 1983. A report in the Arabic language *Al-Majallah* asserted that Moscow had told Damascus that the missiles could only be used in self-defense (*FBIS:MEA*, October 31, 1983, p. ii). For a study of the impact of the missiles on the Syrian–Israeli military balance, see Mark A. Heller (ed.), *The Middle East Military Balance* (hereafter *MEMB*) 1985 (Tel Aviv: Jaffee Center for Strategic Studies, 1986), pp. 279–83.

125 A. Stepanov, "Consistent Support," *New Times*, no. 42 (1983), p. 13.

126 Moscow Radio in Arabic, commentary by Alexander Timoshkin, October 6, 1983 (*FBIS:USSR*, October 7, 1983, pp. H-2, H-3).

127 Cf. report in *New York Times*, October 10, 1983.

128 Reuters report, *Washington Post*, October 12, 1983. Iranian threats to close the Gulf had been issued, off and on, since July 1983 but were stepped up when Iraq announced it had acquired the Super Entendard aircraft.

129 Cf. interview by Eric Roueau, *Le Monde*, January 8, 1983 (translated in *Manchester Guardian Weekly*, January 23, 1983). Such a statement could only have angered Moscow.

130 This was done by making public an August 25, 1982 conversation between Saddam Hussein and US Congressman Steven Solarz (cf. *Washington Post*, January 3, 1983). See also Steven B. Kashkett, "Iraq and the Pursuit of Non-Alignment," *Orbis*, vol. 26, no. 2 (Summer 1982), pp. 477–93.

131 Cited in *New York Times*, May 19, 1983.

132 Cf. report by Drew Middleton, *New York Times*, July 21, 1983.

133 Cf. report by Ian Black, *Washington Post*, September 9, 1983.

134 Cf. Reuters report, *Washington Post*, December 21, 1983.

135 *Pravda*, November 22, 1983.

136 *Ibid.*

137 *Pravda*, October 25, 1983.

138 Cited in *FBIS:USSR*, October 28, 1983, p. H-2.

139 Cf. Moscow Radio in Arabic, commentary by Aleksey Zlatorunsky, November 2, 1983 (*FBIS:USSR*, November 3, 1983, pp. H-1, H-2).

140 Moscow Radio in Arabic, Rafael Artonov commentary, November 3, 1983 (*FBIS:USSR*, November 4, 1983, p. H-3).

141 *Pravda*, November 5, 1983.

142 *Pravda*, November 6, 1983.

143 Tass, November 4, 1983 (*FBIS:USSR*, November 8, 1983, p. H-2).

144 Cf. report by Bernard Gwertzman, *New York Times*, November 11, 1983.

145 *FBIS:USSR*, November 10, 1983, p. H-2.

146 Cf. report by Thomas L. Friedman, *New York Times*, November 11, 1983.

147 *FBIS:MEA*, November 9, 1983, p. i.

148 *FBIS:USSR*, November 15, 1983, p. H-2.

149 *FBIS:MEA*, November 14, 1983, p. H-2.

150 *Pravda*, November 13, 1983.

151 Cited in AP report, *New York Times*, November 14, 1983.

152 For Moscow's reaction, see *Pravda*, November 18 and 19, 1983.

153 Radio Free Lebanon, November 19, 1983 (*FBIS:MEA*, November 21, 1983, p. H-1).

154 Damascus TV, November 15, 1983 (*FBIS:MEA*, November 16, 1983, p. H-1).

155 *Pravda*, November 19, 1983 (*CDSP*, vol. 35, no. 46, p. 8).

156 Cf. Robert O. Freedman, *Soviet Policy Toward the Middle East Since 1970* (New York: Praeger, 1982), pp. 255 and 261.

157 Tass, November 20, 1983 (*FBIS:USSR*, November 21, 1983, p. H-2).

158 *Pravda*, November 24, 1983.

159 *FBIS:USSR*, November 29, 1983, p. H-8. There was some indication that Arafat was publicly angry with the lack of Soviet aid, but he moved quickly to deny the report published to that effect in the Egyptian newspaper *al-Akhbar* (cf. Kuwait *KUNA*, November 29, 1983 (*FBIS:USSR*, November 29, 1983, p. H-1).

160 *Pravda*, November 29, 1983.

161 Cited in report by Richard Halloran, *New York Times*, November 23, 1983.

162 UPI report, *Washington Post*, November 24, 1983.

163 Cited in report by David Ottaway, *Washington Post*, November 27, 1983.

164 Cited in AP report, New York Times, November 27, 1983.

165 Damascus Domestic Service, November 29, 1983 (*FBIS:MEA*, November 30, 1983, p. H-2).

166 Cited in *New York Times*, December 5, 1983.

167 *FBIS:USSR*, December 6, 1983, p. H-1.

168 *FBIS:USSR*, December 14, 1983, p. H-1.

169 The article was read on Damascus Radio, December 8, 1983 (*FBIS:MEA*, December 8, 1983, p. H-4).

170 Damascus Domestic Service, January 3, 1984 (*FBIS:MEA*, January 3, 1984, p. H-2).

171 This point had been repeatedly emphasized by Defense Minister Mustafa Talas, while Syrian Foreign Minister Khaddam only a few days earlier had linked the airman's release to the suspension of US reconnaissance flights over Syrian positions (Radio Monte Carlo, January 1, 1984) (*FBIS:MEA*, January 3, 1984, pp. H-1, H-2).

172 Cited in *Washington Post*, August 17, 1983.

173 Cited in UPI report, *New York Times*, December 23, 1983.

174 Cited in UPI report, *Washington Post*, December 26, 1983.

175 See, for example, the reports in the *New York Times*, March 6, 1983 and May 5, 1983 and in the *Christian Science Monitor*, March 8, 1983.

176 *Pravda*, December 3, 1983.

177 Cited in Reuters report, *New York Times*, November 17, 1983.

178 A. Stepanov, "Changes Without a Change," *New Times*, no. 51 (1983), pp. 22–24.

179 Excerpts of the Long report were published in the *New York Times*, December 29, 1983. The report, issued on December 20, 1983 was officially titled "Report of the DOD (Department of Defense) Commission on Beirut International Airport Terrorist Act, October 23, 1983" and emphasized errors in the US chain of command.

180 House Speaker Tip O'Neil was especially vocal. See the report by Philip Taubman, *New York Times*, December 30, 1983.

181 For an analysis of US behavior at this time, see Thomas L. Friedman, "America's Failure in Lebanon," *New York Times Magazine*, April 8, 1984. See also Eric Hammel, *The Root: The Marines in Beirut, August 1982 – February 1984* (New York: Harcourt Brace Jovanovich, 1985).

182 Cf. reports by E. J. Dionne, *New York Times*, February 12, 1984; David Hoffman, *Washington Post*, February 12, 1984; and David Hoffman, *Washington Post*, February 15, 1984. For an excellent study of the problems facing the multinational force, see Anthony McDermott and Kjell Skjebsback (eds), *The Multinational Force in Lebanon* (Oslo: Norwegian Institute of International Affairs, 1988).

183 For a Soviet explanation of the veto, see Moscow World Service in English, March 2, 1984 (*FBIS:USSR*, March 5, 1984, p. H-2).

184 Cf. Damascus Domestic Service, February 29, 1984 (*FBIS:MEA*, March 1, 1984, p. H-3).

185 Tass, January 20, 1984 (*FBIS:USSR*, January 23, 1984, p. H-5).

186 Article by Konstantin Geivandov, *Izvestia*, January 5, 1984 (*FBIS:USSR*, January 6, 1984, p. H-7).

187 Moscow TV service, February 8, 1984 (*FBIS:USSR*, February 9, 1984, p. H-6).

188 Baghdad INA in Arabic, March 14, 1984 (*FBIS:MEA*, March 15, 1984, p. A-2).

189 Translated in *FBIS:USSR*, March 7, 1984, p. H-4.

190 *Krasnaya Zvezda, March 8, 1984 (FBIS:USSR*, March 8, 1984, p. H-1).

191 For a translation of the speeches, see *FBIS:USSR*, March 13, 1984, pp. H-3, H-4.

192 *Ibid.*

193 *Pravda*, March 15, 1984. Rifat, then involved in a power struggle, was a possible successor to his brother. See Yosef Olmert, "Domestic Crisis and Foreign Policy in Syria: The Assad Regime," *Middle East Review*, vol. 20, no. 3 (Spring 1988), pp. 17–25; Moshe Maoz and Avner Yaniv (eds), *Syria Under Assad* (London: Croom Helm, 1986) and Alasdair Drysdale, "The Succession Question in Syria," *Middle East Journal*, vol. 39, no. 2 (Spring 1985), pp. 246–57.

194 *Pravda*, March 14, 1984 (translated in *FBIS:USSR*, March 14, 1984, pp. H-1 to H-2).

195 *Pravda*, March 14, 1984 (translated in *FBIS:USSR*, March 14, 1984, pp. H-1, H-2).

196 *Al-Qabas* (Kuwait), March 19, 1984 (*FBIS:MEA*, March 21, 1984, p. H-2). The article also asserted that the USSR had promised to "revolutionize" the Syrian air force to allow it to go on the offensive, as well as to improve the electronic defense system of Syria to compensate it for a reported Israeli link to the US satellite system.

197 Cf. Moscow Radio in Arabic to the Arab world, March 14, 1984 (*FBIS:USSR*, March 15, 1984, p. H-2).

198 For the Soviet view of the Jumblatt visit, see *Pravda*, January 15, 1984.

199 Hussein's statement came in an interview in the *New York Times*, March 15, 1984 in which he also called for a Soviet role in the peace talks.

200 Cf. *Izvestia*, March 28, 1984.

201 *Al Ba'ath*, Damascus, March 18, 1984 (*FBIS:MEA*, March 22, 1984, p. H-1).

202 Cf. *FBIS:MEA*, April 2, 1984, p. ii.

203 In March 1984, a major effort had been mounted in the US Congress to move the US embassy in Israel from Tel Aviv to Jerusalem – a development that aroused Arab anger.

204 Translated in *FBIS:MEA*, March 28, 1984, p. H-2.

205 *Krasnaia Zvezda*, March 22, 1984.

206 *Pravda*, March 20, 1984. According to a report by David Ottaway in the July 21, 1984 issue of the *Washington Post*, the agreement involved $2 billion in Soviet credits.

207 *Pravda*, April 26, 1984; see also report by Dusko Doder, *Washington Post*, April 28, 1984.

208 *Pravda*, April 26, 1984.

209 Cited in *FBIS:MEA*, April 26, 1984, p. i.

210 Both *The Military Balance* and *SIPRI* note a sharp increase in Soviet arms shipments to Iraq in the 1984–87 period, as does *MEMB*.

211 Cf. *Izvestia*, May 23, 1984.

212 For a Saudi evaluation of Saudi–US relations at this time, see the Reuters interview with Prince Bandar Bin Sultan, Saudi Ambassador to the United States, *Washington Post*, April 11, 1984.

213 For a description of the Saudi–French arms deal, see the article by Paul Lanier, *New York Times*, January 17, 1984. For a study of the US–Saudi arms purchase relationship, see Anthony Cordesman, *The Gulf and the West* (Boulder: Westview Press, 1988), ch. 9.

214 See report by Bernard Gwertzman, *New York Times*, May 18, 1984.

215 Cf. report by Don Oberdorfer, *Washington Post*, May 22, 1984.

216 Cited in report by David Ignatius, *Wall Street Journal*, May 30, 1984.

217 *Ibid.*

218 See report by Judith Miller, *New York Times*, August 4, 1984.

219 *Kuna*, May 14, 1984 (*FBIS:USSR*, May 16, 1984, p. H-1). For a Soviet view of Kuwait at this time, see V. Yuryev, "Kuwait Facing the Future," *International Affairs* (Moscow), March 1984, pp. 141–47.

220 See report by Jonathan Randal, *Washington Post*, June 5, 1984.

221 See report by John Goshko and Rick Altison, *Washington Post*, June 20, 1984. A high-ranking official in the Kuwaiti Embassy in Moscow told me that it was a "blunder" not to accept the US Ambassador, because Algeria subsequently accepted him. (Interview, Kuwaiti Embassy, Moscow, January 1988).

222 Cited in report by Bernard Gwertzman, *New York Times*, June 20, 1984.

223 Cited in report by David Ottaway, *Washington Post*, June 19, 1984.

224 Cited in report by Bernard Gwertzman, *New York Times*, June 20, 1984.

225 See *Kuna*, July 9, 1984 (*FBIS:USSR*, July 10, 1984, p. H-2).

226 See *Kraznaia Zvezda*, July 15, 1984 (*FBIS:USSR*, July 17, 1984, p. H-3) and *Kuna*, July 15, 1984 (*FBIS:USSR*, July 16, 1984, p. H-3).

227 The agreement was signed in mid-August (*Kuna*, August 15, 1984 [*FBIS:USSR*, August 16, 1984, p. H-1]). According to the 1985 *SIPRI* yearbook, Kuwait obtained 100 SA-7s and 48 SA-8s (p. 405).

228 See *Kuna*, July 18, 1984 (*FBIS:USSR*, July 19, 1984, p. H-1). According to data cited by Cordesman, *The Gulf and the West* (p. 77), there were five Soviet advisors in Kuwait between 1985 and 1987).

229 See report by David Ottaway, *Washington Post*, December 1, 1984.

230 *Ibid.*

231 See reports by David Ottaway, *Washington Post*, November 30, 1984 and Judith Miller, *New York Times*, November 30, 1984.

232 Translated in *FBIS:USSR*, December 5, 1984, p. H-1.

233 *Pravda*, December 31, 1983.

234 V. Komarov, "Highways and Byways," *New Times*, no. 2 (1984), pp. 18–21.

235 Cf. report by Gerald Sieb, *Wall Street Journal*, January 23, 1984.

236 Iranian news agency report, cited in *Washington Post*, February 24, 1984.

237 *Pravda*, June 7, 1984.

238 Cited in *FBIS:MEA*, June 12, 1984, p. i.

239 See report by Jack Anderson, *Washington Post*, August 4, 1984.

240 Radio Moscow, in Persian, to Iran, April 12, 1984 (*FBIS:USSR*, April 18, 1984, p. H-4).

241 Radio Moscow, in Persian, to Iran, June 19, 1984 (Igor Sheftunov commentary) (*FBIS:USSR*, June 22, 1984, p. H-7).

242 Cited in AP report, *New York Times*, July 22, 1984.

243 Cited in report by Robert Ruby, *Baltimore Sun*, August 3, 1984.

244 Cf. *Izvestia*, September 24, 1984.

245 Dmitry Volsky, "Horizontal Escalation," *New Times*, no. 45 (1984), p. 11.

246 Despite the claim, however, it appears on the basis of the limited evidence available that Libya was responsible.

247 See the report in the *New York Times*, August 10, 1984.

248 See the report by William Pruzik, *Washington Post*, October 3, 1984.

249 Cited in report by Elaine Scolino, *New York Times*, October 4, 1984.

250 *Ibid.* Iran was to repeat this ploy on a larger scale in 1986.

251 See report by Drew Middleton, *New York Times*, October 18, 1984. According to the 1986 *SIPRI* yearbook (p. 383), Moscow signed an estimated $25 billion deal with Iraq in May 1984 for 50 MIG-23s and 15 MIG-25s.

252 Cited in report by Don Oberdorfer, *Washington Post*, October 7, 1984. As part of the growing US–Iraqi relationship, the US Information Office was reopened in Baghdad for the first time since the Iraqi revolution of 1958 (*Washington Post*, October 24, 1984) and the US increased its agricultural exports to Iraq.

253 Tass, October 19, 1984 (*FBIS:USSR*, October 22, 1984, p. H-1).

254 Cited in report by Don Oberdorfer, *Washington Post*, November 29, 1984.

255 Cited in report in *Washington Post*, December 5, 1984.

256 See the report by Robert Greenberger and David Rogers, *Wall Street Journal*, March 22, 1984. The projected force was reported to total 8,000 men and to be equipped at a cost of $220 million (*Baltimore Sun*, May 24, 1984).

257 *Izvestia*, March 28, 1984 (translated in *CDSP*, vol. 36, no. 13, p. 18).

258 Cited in *FBIS:MEA*, April 2, 1984, p. ii.

259 Thus for example the head of Jordan's armed forces visited Moscow, as did delegations from the Jordanian–Soviet Friendship Society, and the Jordanian National Assembly.

260 See above, p. 145.

261 For the text of the 1984 peace plan, see *Pravda*, July 30, 1984 (translated in *CDSP*, vol. 36, no. 30, pp. 9–10). See also Larry C. Nappen, "The Arab Autumn of 1984: A Case Study of Soviet Middle East Policy," *Middle East Journal*, vol. 39, no. 4 (Autumn 1985), pp. 733–44.

262 He had signed an agreement with them in Aden in July (for the text of the agreement, see *FBIS:MEA*, July 13, 1984, p. A-1) which included a provision calling for strengthening ties with the USSR.

263 Cited in Baghdad *INA*, August 1, 1984 (*FBIS:MEA*, August 2, 1984, p. A-2).

264 Cairo Radio on July 30 called it "a constructive addition to efforts being executed by the UN to solve the crisis, but seven years too late" (*FBIS:MEA*, July 31, 1984, p. D-1).

265 Damascus Radio, July 30, 1984 (*FBIS:MEA*, July 31, 1984, p. H-1).

266 Radio Moscow, in Arabic, September 30, 1984 (*FBIS:USSR*, October, 1984, p. H-3).

267 Cf. interview with Prime Minister Shamir in *Maariv*, July 15, 1984 and article in *Hadashot*, June 22, 1984.

268 The text of the treaty is found in Saivetz, *The Soviet Union and the Gulf*, pp. 119–120. Article 4 included "The Struggle Against Zionism."

269 *Pravda* on October 8, 1984 noted that Gromyko had met with Arafat in East Berlin at the latter's request and that the PLO leader strongly praised the Soviet stand on a Middle East peace settlement.

270 *Pravda*, October 19, 1984. There was, however, an apparent agreement on arms shipments to Syria.

271 Egyptian Prime Minister Kamal Hassan Ali, stated in an interview at the time that this would not affect US–Egyptian ties (see the AP report in the *New York Times*, July 24, 1984). This was, however, to be the beginning of the Soviet–Egyptian *rapprochement*.

272 *Izvestia*, October 14, 1984 (translated in *CDSP*, vol. 36, no. 41, p. 19).

273 Cited in report by Judith Miller, *New York Times*, October 2, 1984.

274 Cited in UPI report, *Washington Post*, October 31, 1984.

275 *Jerusalem Post*, November 20, 1984.

276 It is possible that Habash and Hawatmeh used the opportunity of the trip to Moscow to play for time so as to avoid a final decision on the PNC until the last possible moment. From the Soviet perspective, consultation with the members of the Democratic Alliance was important at a major turning point in PLO fortunes. See Asher Susser, "The Palestine Liberation Organization" in *MECS 1984–1985*, pp. 181–233, and Khalidi, "Palestinian Politics."

277 Tass, November 30, 1984 (*FBIS:USSR*, December 4, 1984, p. H-1).

278 The speeches and resolutions of the PNC are found in the *FBIS:MEA* issues of November 23–30, 1984.

279 Another blow to Assad was the transfer of the PNC headquarters from Damascus to Amman, where the new PNC speaker resided. The warm reception at the Congress for the large Egyptian delegation must have also angered the Syrian President. Indeed, the Syrian-backed Palestine Liberation Front was particularly vituperative in describing the evolving ties between Arafat and the leaders of Jordan and Egypt as "an alliance with the Black September butcher's regime in Amman and the Camp David regime in Egypt" (*FBIS:MEA*, January 3, 1985, p. A-3).

280 For the text of Assad's address of January 5, 1985, see *FBIS:MEA*, January 7, 1985, pp. H-1 to H-5. By stating "we are sure that those capitulationists and conspirators will never represent the Palestinian Arab people" (p. H-4) Assad implied that he would back his own Palestinian leadership and, in effect, seek to take over the PLO.

281 Cf. *FBIS:MEA*, December 31, 1984, p. i.

282 Cited in report by Jonathan Randal, *Washington Post*, January 7, 1985. Jordan's difficulties in obtaining weapons from the United States, difficulties which escalated in 1985 due to the American Congress's opposition to arms sales to Jordan, were factors in Hussein's keeping open his options with the USSR. The 1986 *SIPRI* yearbook (p. 403) cites Jordan's purchase of SA-7, SA-8, and SA-9 anti-aircraft missiles.

283 *Pravda*, February 20, 1985 (translated in *CDSP*, vol. 37, no. 8, p. 19). Interestingly enough, according to a senior PLO advisor to Arafat, the agreement was drawn up "to coincide as much as possible with the Reagan plan." (Interview, Tunis, February 1989).

284 Tass report, in English, February 27, 1985 (*FBIS:USSR*, February 28, 1985, p. H-1).

285 O. Fomin, "Trying to Revive the Camp David Deal," *New Times*, no. 18 (1985), pp. 14–15.

4 Moscow and the Middle East under Gorbachev: "new thinking" in theory and practice

1 Cf. *Soviet Foreign Policy* (ed. Robin F. Laird) (New York: Academy of Political Science 1987). For a study of Gorbachev's early tactics in Afghanistan, see Zalmay Khalilzad, "Moscow's Afghan War," *Problems of Communism*, vol. 35, no. 1 (January–February 1986), pp. 1–20. For a study of Soviet politics under Gorbachev, see Dusko Doder, *Shadows and Whispers: Power Politics Inside the Kremlin from Brezhnev to Gorbachev* (New York: Penguin Books, 1988).

2 The most important source of information on the "new thinking" is Gorbachev's own book, *Perestroika: New Thinking for Our Country and the World* (New York: Harper and Row, 1987), especially chs. 3 and 5. See also G. A. Trofimenko, "Novye Real'nosti i Novoe Myshlenie" (New Realities and New Thinking), *Ssha*, no. 2 (1987), pp. 3–15; Yevgeni Aleksandrov, "New Political Thinking: Genesis, Factors, Prospects," *International Affairs*, no. 12 (1987), pp. 87–95; Rodimir Bogdanov, "From the Balance of Forces to a Balance of Interests," *International Affairs*, no. 4 (1988), pp. 81–87; Aleksander Kislov, "Novoe Politicheskoe Myshlenie i Regional'nye Konflikty" (New Political Thinking and Regional Conflicts), *MEIMO*, no. 8 (1988), pp. 39–47; Alexei Izyumov and Andrei Kortinov, "The Soviet Union in the Changing World," *International Affairs*, no. 8 (1988), pp. 46–56; E. Primakov, V. Martynov, G. Duligenskii, "Nekotorye Problemy Novogo Myshleniia" (Some Problems of the New Thinking), *MEIMO*, no. 6 (1989), pp. 5–18; and Walter Laqueur, "Glasnost Abroad: New Thinking in Foreign Policy," *Washington Quarterly*, vol. 11 no. 4 (Autumn 1988), pp. 75–93.

3 Cf. Robert O. Freedman, *Soviet Policy Toward the Middle East Since 1970*, 3rd edn (New York: Praeger, 1982).

4 For a Soviet evaluation of the "evils" of the Nimeri regime, and its initial hopes for the new Sawar–Dahab government, see V. Bochkaryov, "Exit Nimeri: What Happens Now?" *New Times*, no. 17 (1985), pp. 10–11. For a balanced study of Nimeri and the post-Nimeri period in the Sudan, see Peter Bechtold, "The Sudan Since Nimeri," in Robert O. Freedman (ed.), *The Middle East from the Iran–Contra Affair to the Intifada* (Syracuse: Syracuse University Press, forthcoming). See also Haim Shaked and Yehudit Ronen, "The Democratic Republic of Sudan," *Middle East Contemporary Survey* 1985 (hereafter *MECS*) (ed. Itamar Rabinovich and Haim Shaked) (Boulder: Westview, 1987), pp. 614–42.

5 Cited in report by Judith Miller, *New York Times*, April 8, 1985.

6 Cited in report by Christopher Dickey, *Washington Post*, April 16, 1985.

7 Kaddafi was the first foreign head of state to visit the new government.

8 See reports by Christopher Dickey, *Washington Post*, July 9, 1985 and Clifford D. May, *New York Times*, July 10, 1985.

9 Cf. report by Bill Keller, *New York Times*, August 1, 1985.

10 Cited in report by Neil Chase, *Washington Post*, August 16, 1985.

11 Cited in report by Christopher Dickey, *Washington Post*, July 20, 1985.

12 Cf. report by David Ottaway, *Washington Post*, November 21, 1985.

13 Cf. report by Christopher Dickey, *Washington Post*, July 11, 1985. By October, however, there appeared to be a limited improvement in Sudanese–Egyptian relations. (Cf. report by Jeffrey Bartholet, *Washington Post*, October 30, 1985).

14 Cited in Associated Press Report, *Jerusalem Post*, December 12, 1985.

15 Cf. Moscow International Service in Arabic, May 31, 1985 (*FBIS:USSR* June 3, 1985, p. H-2) and *Izvestia*, July 10, 1985.

16 A. Agaryshev, "From Despair to Hope," *New Times*, no. 47 (1985), pp. 14–15.

17 Cf. *Pravda*, January 16, 1985 and Dmitry Volsky, "Behind the Prospective Israeli Pull-out from Southern Lebanon," *New Times*, no. 5 (1985), pp. 14–15.

18 *Pravda*, March 17, 1985 and Dmitry Volsky, "Calculated Brutality," *New Times*, no. 13 (1985), p. 10. On the events in Lebanon in 1985, see Yosef Olmert, "Lebanon," *MECS 1986*, pp. 528–54.

19 Arafat was quoted on Rabat (Morocco) Domestic Service in Arabic, August 7, 1985 (*Foreign Broadcast Information Service: Middle East and South Asia* [hereafter *FBIS:ME*], August 8, 1985, p. A-4).

20 For an account of the 1976 events, see Freedman, *Soviet Policy Toward the Middle East Since 1970*, ch. 7.

21 Cf. reports by John Kifner, *New York Times*, May 25, 1986 and June 12, 1986.

22 *New Times*, no. 23 (1985), p. 15.

23 There was a report in *Al-Ray Al-Am* on June 4, 1985 that Moscow had sent a "strongly worded" message to Amal leader Nabih Berri (*FBIS:ME*, June 7, 1985, p. A-1). As might be expected, Moscow warmly praised the cease-fire (*Pravda*, June 20, 1985).

24 See above.

25 Cf. *Pravda*, June 22, 1985 and *Izvestia*, June 24 and 28, 1985.

26 Tass (in English), June 19, 1985 (*FBIS:USSR*, June 20, 1985, p. H-1).

27 Damascus Domestic Service in Arabic, June 19, 1985 (*FBIS:USSR*, June 20, 1985, p. H-1, H-2).

28 *Pravda*, June 22, 1985.

29 *Al-Qabas* (Kuwait), cited in *FBIS:ME* June 24, 1985, p. i. It appears Iran also played a helpful role in the hostage incident.

30 See, for example, an article in *Pravda* on June 6 by Soviet Middle East specialist Pavel Demchenko.

31 *Sovietskaia Rossia*, June 20, 1985 (translated in *FBIS:USSR*, June 27, 1985, p. H-2).

32 Cf. Reagan press conference, *Washington Post*, February 22, 1985.

33 Cited in an article by Henry Trewitt, *Baltimore Sun*, February 20, 1985. The talks took place between Assistant Secretary of State Richard Murphy and the head of the Soviet Foreign Ministry's Near East Division, Vladimir Polyakov.

34 Cited in report by Bernard Gwertzman, *New York Times*, February 22, 1985.

35 Cited in report by David Ottaway, *Washington Post*, May 31, 1985.

36 Cited in report by Jim Hoagland, *Washington Post*, June 8, 1985.

37 For an excellent survey of Soviet–Israeli relations, see Arthur J. Klinghoffer, *Israel and the Soviet Union: Alienation or Reconciliation* (Boulder: Westview Press, 1985).

38 This is particularly true on the issue of Soviet Jewry. On this point, see Robert O. Freedman, "Soviet Jewry and Soviet–American Relations: A Historical Analysis," in Robert O. Freedman (ed.), *Soviet Jewry in the Decisive Decade 1971–1980* (Durham, North Carolina: Duke University Press, 1984), pp. 38–67. See also Robert O. Freedman, "The Issue of Soviet Jewry in Israeli Foreign Policy," in Robert O. Freedman (ed.), *Soviet Jewry in the 1980s* (Durham: Duke University Press, 1989), pp. 61–96.

39 Cited in report by Dusko Doder, *Washington Post*, May 14, 1985.

40 Cf. *Pravda*, April 14, 1985.

41 It turned out to be a signal to Israel, but the Soviet media's equating of Zionism and Nazism continued for another year. See William Korey, "The Soviet Anti-Zionist Committee," in Freedman, *Soviet Jewry in the 1980s*, pp. 26–50.

42 Tass, English, July 20, 1985 (*FBIS:USSR*, July 22, 1985, p. H-2).

43 Jerusalem Domestic Service, in Hebrew, July 19, 1985 (*FBIS:USSR*, July 19, 1985, pp. H-1, H-2).

44 Cf. comments by Soviet Chargé d'Affairs in Kuwait, Vladimir Zentchner, as reported in KUNA on July 23, 1985 (*FBIS:USSR*, July 26, 1985, p. H-1) and comments by Leonid Zamyatin, head of the International Information Department of the Communist Party Central Committee, as reported in KUNA, July 27, 1985 (*FBIS:USSR*,

July 29, 1985, p. H-1).

45 Cf. *Novosti* report, cited in *New York Times*, August 7, 1985. See also Moscow Radio Peace and Progress, in Hebrew, July 22, 1985 (*FBIS:USSR*, July 23, 1985, p. H-3).

46 Cf. report of Peres's comments in the article by Michael Eilan, *Jerusalem Post*, July 22, 1985.

47 For analyses of the diplomatic background of the summit, see the articles by Christopher Dickey, *Washington Post*, August 6, 1985; Mary Curtis, *Christian Science Monitor*, August 7, 1985; and Judith Miller, *New York Times*, August 7, 1985 and Bruce Maddy-Weizman, "Inter-Arab Relations," *MECS 1985*, pp. 111–16. For a description of the issues concerning Moscow, see O. Fomin, "The Casablanca Summit," *New Times*, no. 34 (1985), pp. 10–11; *Pravda*, August 7, 1985; and *Tass* report in English, August 8, 1985 (*FBIS:USSR*, August 9, 1985, p. H-1).

48 Cited in article by Jean Gueyras, *Le Monde*, August 11, 1985 (*Manchester Guardian Weekly*, August 25, 1985).

49 Manama Wakh, in Arabic, August 8, 1985 (*FBIS:USSR*, August 8, 1985, p. A-8).

50 Fomin, "The Casablanca Summit."

51 Cf. Moscow Radio, in Arabic, "Window on the Arab World" (Alexander Timoshkin), August 10, 1985 (*FBIS:USSR*, August 12, 1985, p. H-1).

52 For a background analysis of this development, see the report by Thomas Friedman, *New York Times*, October 18, 1985. (A preliminary version of the agreement was broadcast over Israel radio on October 5, 1985). Of course, Poland, which also wished to influence US Jewish opinion, had its own reasons for making this move, but it could not have done so in 1985 without Moscow's approval. There was a dispute at the time in the Israeli Foreign Ministry between those opposing an interest-section relationship for fear it would set a precedent for only low-level relations with the Soviet Union, and those wanting an immediate break-through in ties with Moscow's allies. The latter won the dispute. (Interview, Israeli Foreign Ministry, July 1988).

53 Cited in *Jerusalem Post*, October 6, 1985.

54 Cf. reports by Michael Eilan and Joshua Brilliant, *Jerusalem Post*, October 31, 1986 and Judith Miller, *New York Times*, October 26, 1985. The rumor was renewed after a December 1985 Bronfman visit to the Soviet capital (see the reports in the *Washington Post*, December 23 and 24, 1985). Bronfman, it should be noted, was closer to Prime Minister Peres than to Foreign Minister Shamir who often took a dim view of the World Jewish Congress President's quasi-diplomatic activities. The rumors about direct flights turned out to be false, and mass emigration from the USSR was not to begin until 1987.

55 For a background analysis of the rise in terrorism, see the report by Thomas L. Friedman, *New York Times*, October 2, 1985. A major seaborne attack on Israel in late April, authorized by Arafat's deputy Khalil Wazir (Abu Jihad) was prevented when the Israeli Navy sank the PLO ship carrying the guerrillas. (See reports by G. Jefferson Price, *Baltimore Sun*, April 23, 1985 and Reuters, *Jerusalem Post*, May 10, 1985).

56 Cf. reports by Christopher Dickey, *Washington Post*, September 27, 1985 and Bernard Gwertzman, *New York Times*, August 27, 1985.

57 Cf. report by David Ottaway, *Washington Post*, April 20, 1985.

58 Cited in report by David Ottaway, *Washington Post*, April 16, 1985. Algeria was, of course, also interested in driving a diplomatic wedge between Morocco and the United States which shared Algeria's displeasure with the 1984 Libyan–Moroccan treaty.

59 Cited in report by George C. Wilson, *Washington Post*, October 22, 1985.

60 Moscow International Service in Arabic, October 2, 1985 (*FBIS:USSR*, October 4, 1985, p. H-3). The disinformation was at least partially successful as Arafat was

quoted as claiming that the US helped the Israelis refuel. (Cf. report by Jonathan C. Randal, *Washington Post*, October 3, 1985). Arafat also claimed the US was out to kill him.

61 Cf. report by David Hirst, *Manchester Guardian Weekly*, November 3, 1985.

62 Translated in *Current Digest of the Soviet Press*, hereafter *CDSP*, 1985, vol. 37, no. 42, p. 17.

63 To make matters worse for the PLO, Farouk Kaddoumi claimed, at the UN, that there was no evidence of Klinghoffer's murder and later asserted that "it might (have been Klinghoffer's) wife who pushed him overboard to get his insurance" (cited in Joshua Teitelbaum, "Armed Operations," *MECS 1985*, p. 93).

64 Cf. Associated Press report, *Washington Post*, September 21, 1985; *FBIS:ME*, October 15, 1985, p. i and October 16, 1985, p. i; and report by Jo Thomas, *New York Times*, October 15, 1985.

65 It was rumored at the time that Hussein was seriously considering dropping Arafat (cf. report by Jolin Kifner, *New York Times*, October 27, 1985), as indeed he was to do in February 1986.

66 Cited in report by Samira Kawar, *Washington Post*, November 3, 1985. The Syrian and Jordanian Foreign Ministers had first met in mid-September under the auspices of the reconciliation committee set up by the Casablanca summit.

67 Cf. report by Samira Kawar, *Washington Post*, January 1, 1986.

68 Dmitry Volsky, "Spring of Terrorism in the Mechanism of Tension," *New Times*, no. 50 (1985), p. 11.

69 Cf. report by Nora Boustany, *Washington Post*, October 3, 1985. Gorbachev was asked during a Paris news conference whether Moscow was just as helpless as Western states in dealing with Beirut kidnappings. (*Pravda*, October 5, 1985. Translated in *CDSP*, vol. 37, no. 41, p. 10).

70 Cf. reports by John Kifner, *New York Times*, October 1, 1985 and by Ihsan Hijazi, *New York Times*, October 2, 1985.

71 Tass in English, October 2, 1985 (*FBIS:USSR*, October 3, 1985, p. H-1).

72 Cf. reports by Ihsan Hijazi, *New York Times*, October 5, 1985 and Nora Boustany, *Washington Post*, October 5, 1985.

73 Cited in Reuters report, *Jerusalem Post*, October 22, 1985.

74 Cf. report by Ihsan Hijazi, *New York Times*, October 31, 1985. There were also unconfirmed reports of Soviet threats to mutilate relatives of the kidnappers. In questioning this report during a visit to Moscow in January 1988, I was told by a Soviet specialist on Lebanon that "all measures" had been used to free the kidnapped Soviet officials. For a Soviet view on Lebanese developments at this time, see Sergei Stoklitsky, "The Causes of the Conflict in Lebanon," *International Affairs* (Moscow), no. 6 (1987), pp. 53–61.

75 Cf. report by Elaine Sciolino, *New York Times*, December 10, 1985.

76 Cited in report by Michael Berlin, *Washington Post*, December 19, 1985.

77 Cf. report by Bernard Gwertzman, *New York Times*, October 31, 1985.

78 Cited in report by Walter Ruby, *Jerusalem Post*, November 17, 1985. Vlasov was the deputy Soviet spokesman at the summit. Evgeny Primakov made the same point at another press conference in Geneva. (KUNA, November 16, 1985 [*FBIS:USSR*, November 18, 1985, p. H-7]).

79 Cited in report by Asher Wallfish, *Jerusalem Post*, November 19, 1985.

80 Cf. report in *Jerusalem Post*, December 4, 1985. The head of the Soviet delegation to the Israeli Communist Party Conference, Mikhail Menashev, however, said Herzog's attendance at the convention would not influence Russia's policy on the exit of Soviet Jews or hasten the renewal of diplomatic ties. (Cited in *Jerusalem Post*, December 8, 1985).

81 Cf. report by Ihsan Hijazi, *New York Times*, November 20, 1985. See also the report by David Ottaway, *Washington Post*, November 8, 1985.

82 For the text of Reagan's speech on this subject, see *New York Times*, October 25, 1985.

83 Arafat was particularly suspicious. See report by Ihsan Hijazi, *New York Times*, November 20, 1985.

84 Moscow Radio International Service in Arabic, November 17, 1985 (*FBIS:USSR*, November 19, 1985, Reportage on the Reagan–Gorbachev Summit, p. 3).

85 Cf. report by Bob Woodward and Lou Cannon, *Washington Post*, December 21, 1985.

86 *Pravda*, October 13, 1985 (translated in *FBIS:USSR*, October 15, 1985, p. H-7).

87 *Pravda*, October 16, 1985.

88 *Pravda*, October 13, 1985 (*FBIS:USSR*, October 15, 1985, p. H-6).

89 *Pravda*, October 16, 1985 (*FBIS:USSR*, October 16, 1985, p. H-3).

90 See the report by Bob Woodward, *Washington Post*, November 3, 1985.

91 Cf. report in *New York Times*, April 3, 1985.

92 Cited in Reuters report, *Washington Post*, April 13, 1985. While Kaddafi denied hosting the radio station, he praised its message, and the available evidence indicates it was located in Libya.

93 Cited in report by Bob Woodward and Lou Cannon, *Washington Post*, December 21, 1985.

94 See below, pp. 237–40.

95 Cf. report by Thomas L. Friedman, *New York Times*, November 20, 1985.

96 Cf. reports by William Claiborne, *Washington Post*, December 16, 1985 and December 27, 1985, and *New York Times* report, December 27, 1985.

97 Cf. Moscow Radio, in French, to Maghreb states, December 28, 1985 (*FBIS:USSR*, December 30, 1985, pp. H-2, H-3).

98 See reports by Christopher Dickey, *Washington Post*, April 29, 1985 and Hirsh Goodman, *Jerusalem Post*, May 8, 1985.

99 For a Soviet view of the problems it faced because of the war, see Dmitry Volsky, "The Hidden Springs of a Senseless War," *New Times*, no. 40 (1985), pp. 26–28.

100 Cf. *Pravda*, March 6, 1985, Moscow Radio in Persian, March 27, 1985 (*FBIS:USSR*, March 28, 1985, p. H-2), and *Izvestia*, August 26, 1985.

101 Rotislav Ulianovsky, "The Fate of the Iranian Revolution," *Kommunist*, no. 8 (1985) (translated in *CDSP*, vol. 37, no. 36, p. 19). Ulianovsky was one of the most anti-Khomeini of Soviet academicians and party officials. The *Kommunist* article was to be the low point in Soviet–Iranian relations in 1985, and they were to improve as Gorbachev consolidated his power. For an analysis of Soviet–Iranian relations at this time, see Shahram Chubin and Charles Tripp, *Iran and Iraq at War* (Boulder: Westview Press, 1988), pp. 224–26.

102 *Pravda*, March 30, 1985.

103 *Pravda*, December 17, 1985.

104 Cf. Deutsche Presse-Agentur report, *Washington Post*, March 30, 1985 and report by Celestine Bohlen, *Washington Post*, December 17, 1985.

105 Cf. report by David Ottaway, *Washington Post*, Deptember 13, 1985.

106 Cf. report by Bernard Gwertzman, *New York Times*, March 26, 1985.

107 See the report by Barbara Rosewicz in the *Wall Street Journal*, March 5, 1985, and the AP report in the *Jerusalem Post*, October 6, 1985.

108 For an analysis of Soviet–Iraqi relations at this time, see Carol R. Saivetz, *The Soviet Union and the Gulf in the 1980s* (Boulder: Westview Press, 1989), pp. 58–60.

109 Cited in report by Christopher Dickey, *Washington Post*, November 4, 1985.

110 Cf. reports in the *New York Times*, March 25 and 26, 1985 and the report by Gerald

F. Seib, *Wall Street Journal*, April 11, 1985. There was also US–Omani friction over their joint facilities agreement of 1980. See Dore Gold, "Oman," *MECS 1985*, pp. 44–45.

111 D. Zgersky, "Establish Relations," *New Times*, no. 41 (1985), p. 9.

112 For analyses of Kaddafi's speech, see the report by James M. Dorsey, *Washington Post*, January 2, 1986 and the Knight Ridder News Service report, *Baltimore Sun*, January 2, 1986.

113 Cf. *Izvestia*, January 5, 1986.

114 Tass, in English, January 6, 1986 (*FBIS:USSR*), January 7, 1986, p. H-3.

115 Cf. report by Christopher Dickey, *Washington Post*, January 4, 1986.

116 Reagan announced the sanctions at a news conference. See *New York Times*, January 8, 1986.

117 See report by Don Oberdorfer and David Ottaway, *Washington Post*, January 8, 1986.

118 Translated in *FBIS:USSR*, January 8, 1986, p. H-6.

119 Cited in report by Celestine Bohlen, *Washington Post*, January 15, 1986.

120 See reports by Bill Keller, *New York Times*, January 14, 1986 and George C. Wilson, *Washington Post*, January 15, 1986.

121 See, for example, "Ronald Reagan Speaks Loudly, Carries a Small Stick" (Joseph C. Harsh, *Christian Science Monitor*, January 29, 1986); "Reagan's Carter Policy on Handling Terrorism" (Joshua Muravchik, *New York Times*, January 15, 1986); and "Big Mouth, Little Action Diplomacy" (Hodding Carter III, *Wall Street Journal*, January 16, 1986).

122 Cited in report by Christopher Dickey, *Washington Post*, January 16, 1986.

123 For an analysis of Soviet efforts to create a Marxist society in the PDRY, see Norman Cigar, "State and Society in South Yemen," *Problems of Communism*, vol. 34, no. 3 (May–June 1985), pp. 41–58. For solid analyses of the 1986 crisis see Mark N. Katz, "Civil Conflict in South Yemen," *Middle East Review*, vol. 19, no. 1 (Fall 1986), pp. 7–13, and David Pollock, "Moscow and Aden: Coping with a Coup," *Problems of Communism*, vol. 35, no. 3 (May–June 1986), pp. 50–70. See also Joseph Kostiner, "The People's Democratic Republic of Yemen," *MECS 1986*, pp. 527–42. For a view of Soviet–PDRY relations on the eve of the crisis, see Norman Cigar, "South Yemen and the USSR: Prospects for the Relationship," *Middle East Journal*, vol. 39, no. 4 (Autumn 1985), pp. 775–95.

124 Moscow was later to criticize Mohammed for favoring private enterprise. See Vitaly Naumkin, "South Yemen After the January Tragedy," *New Times* (Moscow), no. 48 (1986), pp. 28–29.

125 *Pravda*, on January 31, 1986, denied reports of Soviet intervention.

126 The new South Yemeni government reported in early December, 1986 that 4,230 members of the party had been killed and that there had been $115 million in property damage (AP report, *New York Times*, December 7, 1986).

127 As late as January 24, 1986, Pavel Demchenko, writing in *Pravda*, reflected considerable confusion in describing the events in the PDRY.

128 *Pravda*, March 4, 1986.

129 *Pravda*, June 5, 1986.

130 *Pravda*, July 23, 1986.

131 Cited in report by John Kifner, *New York Times*, February 1, 1986.

132 Cited in report by David Ottaway, *Washington Post*, April 12, 1986.

133 *Ibid*. For an analysis of the YAR's foreign policy in 1986, see Joseph Kostiner, *The Yemeni Arab Republic*, *MECS 1986*, pp. 668–71.

134 For a description of the Soviet military presence in South Yemen, see the report by Karen deYoung, *Washington Post*, January 22, 1986 and Anthony H. Cordesman,

The Gulf and the West (Boulder: Westview Press, 1988), p. 100.

135 For the text of Hussein's speech, see *FBIS:ME*, February 20, 1986, pp. F-1 to F-16.

136 Cited in report by David Ottaway and John Goshko, *Washington Post*, February 21, 1986.

137 *FBIS:ME*, February 20, 1986, p. F-14.

138 *Ibid.*, p. F-16.

139 Cf. report by Ihsan Hijazi, *New York Times*, March 8, 1986.

140 *Pravda*, January 8, 1986.

141 Cited in *Jerusalem Post*, April 3, 1986.

142 Cf. report by Karen deYoung, *Washington Post*, January 25, 1986. For an analysis of the King's policies, see Adam Garfinkle, "Jordan," in *The Middle East From the Iran–Contra Affair to the Intifada.*

143 Cited in report by Judith Miller, *New York Times*, February 23, 1986.

144 Gorbachev's speech was printed in *Pravda*, February 25, 1986.

145 Cited in AP report, *Washington Post*, March 5, 1986.

146 Cf. report by George C. Wilson, *Washington Post*, March 21, 1986.

147 An article in *Krasnaia Zvezda* on March 22, 1986, virtually predicted a US attack (*FBIS:USSR*, March 24, 1986, p. A-1).

148 A description of the battle is found in the *Washington Post*, March 26, 1986.

149 As to whether the Soviets were warned in advance, White House Press Secretary Larry Speakes said only that the USSR had been briefed, "at the onset of the freedom of navigation exercise." (*New York Times*, March 25, 1986). According to a report in the *New York Times* on April 14, 1986, Soviet advisers had deliberately avoided the fighting by staying in underground bunkers.

150 Cited in report by Celestine Bohlen, *Washington Post*, March 26, 1986.

151 *Pravda*, March 26, 1986 (*CDSP*, vol. 38, no. 12, p. 28).

152 Tass report, March 26, 1986 (*FBIS:USSR*, March 27, 1986, p. H-5).

153 Cf. report by Gary Lee, *Washington Post*, March 27, 1986.

154 Cited in report by John Kifner, *New York Times*, March 29, 1986.

155 Cited in report by Kevin Costello, *Washington Post*, April 10, 1986.

156 Cited in report by Edwin Schumacher, *New York Times*, April 13, 1986.

157 Cf. report by Richard Darbyshire, *Christian Science Monitor*, April 9, 1986.

158 Cited in report by Celestine Bohlen, *Washington Post*, April 17, 1986.

159 Cf. report by Don Oberdorfer, *Washington Post*, April 15, 1987.

160 A description of the attack is found in the *New York Times*, April 18, 1986. One of Kaddafi's homes was also apparently hit in the attack.

161 Cited in *New York Times*, April 17, 1986.

162 Cited in AP report, *New York Times*, April 19, 1986. Aeroflot service to the US had been terminated by Ronad Reagan because of the imposition of martial law in Poland in 1981.

163 Cf. report by Don Oberdorfer, *Washington Post*, April 27, 1986.

164 *Pravda*, April 16, 1986.

165 *Pravda*, April 17, 1986 (*CDSP*, vol. 38, no. 15, p. 4).

166 Cited in article by Antera Pietila, *Baltimore Sun*, April 17, 1986.

167 Cf. article by Christopher Dickey, *Washington Post*, April 19, 1986.

168 Cited in report by Gary Lee, *Washington Post*, April 23, 1986. One should not rule out the possibility that had Kaddafi been killed in the US attack, a Libyan leader, both actually willing to grant Moscow bases, and more circumspect in his foreign policy behavior, might have succeeded him – a net benefit to the USSR.

169 For an analysis of the allied reaction, see the report by James M. Markham, *New York Times*, April 25, 1987. See also Robert Hunter, "Western Europe," *The Middle East From the Iran–Contra Affair to the Intifada.*

170 Cf. AP report, *New York Times*, May 13, 1986.

171 Cf. report by Christopher Dickey, *Washington Post*, May 3, 1986.

172 Cf. report by Ihsan Hijazi, *New York Times*, May 6, 1986.

173 Cited in report by Gerald M. Boyd, *New York Times*, April 24, 1986.

174 Cf. reports by Joanne Omany, *Washington Post*, May 15, 1986; Mary Curtius, *Christian Science Monitor*, May 19, 1986; and Thomas L. Friedman, *New York Times*, May 19, 1986. For a Soviet view, see *Pravda*, May 15, 1986.

175 Cf. report in *New York Times*, April 12, 1986.

176 Cited in report by John Goshko, *Washington Post*, April 17, 1986.

177 Reuters report, *Washington Post*, May 17, 1986.

178 Moscow TV, in Russian, May 27, 1986 (*FBIS:USSR*, May 28, 1986, p. H-1).

179 Moscow International Service in Arabic, May 28, 1986 (*FBIS:USSR*, May 29, 1986, p. H-7). Syria had used this ploy in 1983 as well, during its prolonged confrontation with the US in Lebanon.

180 Moscow International Service in Russian, May 28, 1986 (*FBIS:USSR*, May 29, 1986, p. H-6).

181 Cited in *Jerusalem Post*, May 29, 1986.

182 Cited in *New York Times*, June 25, 1986.

183 Reuters report, *Washington Post*, June 28, 1986.

184 AP report, *New York Times*, July 1, 1986.

185 Cf. report by Karen deYoung, *Washington Post*, July 15, 1986.

186 By April 1986, the price of oil had fallen to $12.40 a barrel, less than half of what it had been in January. (Cf. report by Lee Daniels, *New York Times*, April 9, 1986). See also the Zygmunt Magorski article, *New York Times*, March 31, 1986. See also Allan Kroncher, "Oil Prices and the Soviet Economy," *Radio Liberty Research Report*, no. 298/86 (August 7, 1986).

187 On March 23, 1986 the American Committee on East–West Accord had called for a relaxation of the trade restrictions imposed on the USSR (cited in report by Clyde H. Farnsworth, *New York Times*, March 24, 1986).

188 Cited in report by John Goshko, *Washington Post*, July 23, 1986.

189 The text of the communiqué is found in the *New York Times*, July 25, 1986. For the negative Soviet reaction to the summit, see *Izvestia*, July 26, 1986, which condemned Israeli efforts to drive a wedge between the Arab countries.

190 For an analysis of the King's actions, see the report by David B. Ottaway, *Washington Post*, August 5, 1986.

191 Reuters report, *Washington Post*, August 30, 1986.

192 For a description of the events leading up to the talks, see the article in the *Jerusalem Post*, August 5, 1986.

193 Moscow, in raising the idea of the talks in the early spring, had insisted that they be private (interview with Israeli consular official, New York City, August 29, 1986). It would appear that the Soviet concern with the possibility of an Israeli–Syrian war induced Gorbachev to agree to public talks.

194 Cf. *Izvestia*, August 13, 1986 and *New York Times*, August 18, 1986.

195 For the Soviet view of the talks, see the *Tass* report, in English, August 19, 1986 (*FBIS:USSR*, August 20, 1986, p. CC-1). For the Israeli view, see Helsinki Domestic Service, in Finnish, August 18, 1986 (*FBIS:ME*, August 19, 1986, p. I-1) and Tel Aviv, IDF Radio in Hebrew, August 18, 1986 (*FBIS:ME*, August 19, 1986, p. I-1, I-2). One effect of Sharansky's coming to Israel had been to raise the political stature of the Soviet Jewry movement which now had such important politicians as Moshe Arens on its side. Hitherto, the main Knesset activists were fringe politicians, such as Tehiya's Geula Cohen. Interviews with Israeli Foreign Ministry officials in July 1988 confirmed the influence of domestic pressure in raising the issue of Soviet Jewry to the

top of the Israeli agenda at the talks.

196 See the report by Bernard Gwertzman, *New York Times*, September 23, 1986. In his UN speech, Shevardnadze noted that Israel owed its existence "to among others, the Soviet Union," and also reiterated Moscow's call for a preparatory committee "set up within the framework of the Security Council" to do the necessary work for convening an international conference on the Middle East. Moscow's report of the meeting is found in *Pravda*, September 23, 1986.

197 Cf. report by Joel Greenberg, *Christian Science Monitor*, September 9, 1986.

198 Cf. report by Glen Frankel, *Washington Post*, September 13, 1986. The joint communiqué was published in the *New York Times*, September 13, 1986.

199 Reuters report, *Jerusalem Post*, October 1, 1986.

200 For a Soviet view of the meeting, see the article by Yuri Glukhov in *Pravda*, September 14, 1986.

201 *Ibid.*

202 Cited in *Jerusalem Post*, August 12, 1986.

203 AP report, March 24, 1986 cited in Wayne Brown, *Radio Liberty Report*, no. 144/86 (March 26, 1986).

204 *Pravda*, April 28, 1986. For an analysis of domestic developments in Egypt in 1986, see Ami Ayalon, *The Arab Republic of Egypt*, MECS 1986, pp. 261–75.

205 Reuters report, *Jerusalem Post*, December 9, 1986.

206 Cf. report by David Ottaway, *Washington Post*, December 24, 1986. The US proposal would allow Egypt to postpone paying as much as $3 billion in interest until the year 2009.

207 For a description of the joint exercise, see the report by George C. Wilson, *Washington Post*, August 24, 1986.

208 The alleged attack plan is discussed in a report by Bob Woodward, *Washington Post*, April 2, 1986. For the Soviet praise of Egypt's rejection of it, see *Pravda*, April 1, 1986.

209 *Izvestia*, August 27, 1986. Moscow was especially sensitive at this time because the US was in the midst of a major (if somewhat confused) disinformation campaign against Libya. (See the article by Charlotte Saikowski, *Christian Science Monitor*, October 3, 1986).

210 AP report, *New York Times*, December 17, 1986.

211 See above, p. 207.

212 For a background report on Soviet–Sudanese relations at this time, see Daniel Abele, *Radio Liberty Research Report*, no. 395/86 (October 20), 1986.

213 *Pravda*, August 18, 1986 (*FBIS:USSR*, August 19, 1986, p. H-4).

214 Tass, August 16, 1986 (*FBIS:USSR*, August 19, 1986, p. H-2).

215 Cf. report by Jonathan Randal, *Washington Post*, July 6, 1986.

216 Cf. report by Patrick Tyler, *Washington Post*, December 2, 1986.

217 See *The Tower Commission Report* (New York: *New York Times*, 1987), especially pp. 36–39.

218 Cf. report in *Washington Post*, February 5, 1986.

219 Cited in Reuters report, *New York Times*, February 10, 1986.

220 AP report, *New York Times*, February 11, 1986. For a Soviet view deploring the Iranian attack and urging a speedy end to the war, see *Pravda*, February 14, 1986.

221 For a survey of Soviet–Iranian interactions in 1986, see Bodhan Nahaylo, *Radio Liberty Report*, no. 47/87 (February 3, 1987).

222 Cited in Reuters report, *Jerusalem Post*, August 19, 1986. See also the report by Youssef Ibrahim, *Wall Street Journal*, August 26, 1986. Clearly, Iran also had its own interest in resuming natural gas sales, not least of which was the desire for hard currency to prosecute the war.

223 Cf. AP report, *Washington Post*, December 13, 1986.

224 AP report, *Washington Post*, September 5, 1986.

225 For an overview of Gorbachev's efforts to end the Afghan war in 1986, see Bodhan Nahaylo, *Radio Liberty Research Report*, no. 16/87 (January 11, 1987).

226 Cf. *Izvestia*, December 2, 1986 for a strong Soviet critique of "flagrant interference" by Iran in Afghanistan's internal affairs. The article claimed more than sixty attacks into Afghanistan by Iranian air and ground forces.

227 For a description of the development of the Iran–Contra (Irangate) scandal, see *Report of the Congressional Committees Investigating the Iran–Contra Affair* (Washington: US Government Printing Office, 1987).

228 Cited in report by David Shipler, *New York Times*, January 22, 1987.

229 Cited in report by Elaine Sciolino, *New York Times*, January 30, 1987.

230 Cited in AP report, *Washington Post*, February 12, 1987. See also Reuters report, *New York Times*, February 12, 1987.

231 Cited in report by Jonathan Randal, *Washington Post*, January 30, 1987.

232 *Pravda*, January 30, 1987.

233 *Ibid.*

234 For a Western view of the riots and their aftermath, see the reports by Celestine Bohlen, *Washington Post*, February 19, 1987 and February 22, 1987. Bohlen cites figures of 2 dead and 200 injured in the rioting.

235 Cf. *Izvestia*, January 10, 1987 and *Literaturnaia Gazeta*, January 14, 1987. The latter is translated in *CDSP*, vol. 39, no. 2 (1987), pp. 8–9.

236 *Pravda*, July 16, 1987 (*CDSP*, vol. 39, no. 28, p. 15). My interviews with Soviet scholars in Moscow in January 1988 also reflected this viewpoint, although the scholars were divided on the question as to how serious a threat Islamic fundamentalism was to the USSR. One particularly well-informed Soviet scholar stated that the problems in Kazakhstan and Uzbekistan stemmed from a combination of opposition to *perestroika*, tribalism, and Islamic fundamentalism. Given the fact that Khomeini's brand of Islamic fundamentalism which was Shia in nature had not expanded into the largely Sunni Arab world, it is not surprising that it also did not spread in any signifcant way to the largely Sunni Muslim population of the USSR. On this point see Emmanuel Sivan, "Sunni Radicalism in the Middle East and the Iranian Revolution," *International Journal of Middle East Studies*, vol. 21, no. 1 (February 1989), pp. 1–30.

237 In an article in *New Times* (Moscow), Dmitry Zgersky noted that Al-Bedh had stated that the PDRY's government was still busy coping with the consequences of the "fractricidal conflict" (*New Times*, no. 8 [1987], p. 9). See also Donald Ramotar, Salem Said, and Andrei Olitsky, "Democratic Yemen: After a Tragic Trial," *World Marxist Review*, vol. 31, no. 1 (January 1988), pp. 132–39. For a more upbeat Soviet view, see Lidya Valkova, "PDRY: The Revolution Gets Stronger in Struggle," *Asia and Africa Today*, no. 4 (July–August 1988), pp. 52–56.

238 *Pravda*, February 11, 1987.

239 *Pravda*, February 12, 1987, *FBIS:USSR*, February 13, 1987, p. H-5.

240 Cf. report by Patrick Tyler, *Washington Post*, December 14, 1987.

241 Cf. report by Richard Bernstein, *New York Times*, January 8, 1987.

242 *Izvestia*, January 8, 1987.

243 Cited in *FBIS:ME*, January 12, 1987, p. i.

244 Cited in report by James Baron, *New York Times*, March 23, 1987.

245 Cf. report by Nora Boustany, *Washington Post*, September 21, 1987. For a Soviet view of the fighting in Chad, see Dmitry Zgersky, "Chad: The Background to the Conflict," *New Times*, no. 34 (1987), pp. 13–14.

246 *Pravda*, May 6, 1987.

247 *Izvestia*, December 28, 1986 (*CDSP*, vol. 38, no. 52, p. 14).

248 *Pravda*, January 22, 1987.

249 Cited in report by Gary Lee, *Washington Post*, January 23, 1987. See also report by Bill Keller, *New York Times*, January 23, 1987.

250 *Pravda*, January 22, 1987.

251 For the text of the Soviet statement, see *Izvestia*, January 9, 1987 (*FBIS:USSR*, January 9, 1987, p. H-1). *Izvestia*, on January 16, condemned Iran for "stubbornly rejecting" appeals for a cease-fire and insisting on "war until victory" and replacing the Iraqi regime.

252 Cited in report by Elaine Sciolino, *New York Times*, January 12, 1987.

253 *Pravda*, January 29, 1987.

254 Cf. report by Stephen Engelberg, *New York Times*, January 12, 1987.

255 Cited in report by Patrick Tyler, *Washington Post*, January 22, 1987.

256 Pravda, February 14, 1987.

257 *Ibid.*

258 *Pravda*, February 15, 1987.

259 *Izvestia*, February 15, 1987.

260 Kuwait *Al-Ray Al-Am*, February 15, 1987 (*FBIS:USSR*, February 24, 1987, p. H-5).

261 Radio Moscow in Persian to Iran (Igor Sheftunov, commentator), February 21, 1987 (*FBIS:USSR*, February 24, 1987, p. H-4).

262 *Izvestia*, February 16, 1987. Ghali had visited Moscow in June 1986 (see Ami Ayalon, *The Arab Republic of Egypt*, *MECS 1986*, p. 277).

263 *Al Jumhuriyah* (Cairo), February 17, 1987 (*FBIS:USSR*, February 20, 1987, p. H-2).

264 Translated in *FBIS:USSR*, February 24, 1987, p. H-7.

265 Cf. report by David Ottaway, *Washington Post*, March 29, 1987.

266 Cited in report by Wolf Blitzer, *Jerusalem Post*, February 20, 1987. As might be expected, Moscow took a dim view of the Shamir visit. See Tass English language report, February 20, 1987 (*FBIS:USSR*, February 27, 1987, p. A-2).

267 Cited in report by Benny Morris, Yossi Lempkowicz, and David Horowitz, *Jerusalem Post*, February 24, 1987.

268 For the text of this document, see *FBIS:ME*, March 23, 1987, pp. I-2, 3.

269 Cf. Jerusalem Domestic Service, in Hebrew, January 30, 1987 (*FBIS:USSR*, February 2, 1987, pp. H-1, 2).

270 *Davar*, February 3, 1987 (*FBIS:USSR*, February 3, 1987, p. H-1).

271 Cf. *FBIS:USSR*, February 3, 1987, p. H-1.

272 Translated in *FBIS:USSR*, February 18, 1987, pp. H-8 to H-11.

273 See above, p. 223.

274 Cited in Reuters report, *New York Times*, March 20, 1987; 871 Jews, the highest monthly total in six years, left in May 1987. In fact, 8,155 Jews were to emigrate from the Soviet Union in 1987 (cf. Freedman, *Soviet Jewry in the 1980s*, p. 215).

275 Cited in National Conference on Soviet Jewry Report, New York City, April 1, 1987. By mid-1989, the promises on Jewish cultural and religious rights had essentially been realized, although no direct flights had taken place and some Refuseniks were still not permitted to leave. For an analysis of Jewish developments in the USSR in 1988, see David Prital, *Yehudai Brit Hamoatzot* (*The Jews of the Soviet Union*), vol. 12, 1989 (Jerusalem: Publications on Soviet Jewry, Hebrew University of Jerusalem, 1989).

276 Cited in report by Walter Ruby and Andy Court, *Jerusalem Post*, April 2, 1987.

277 Cf. Jerusalem Radio Domestic Service interview with Soviet Foreign Ministry spokesman Genady Gerasimov, April 2, 1987 (*FBIS:ME*, April 2, 1987, p. I-1). See also the article by Henry Kamm, *New York Times*, April 3, 1987.

278 Cf. Jerusalem Radio Domestic Service interview with Yitzhak Shamir, March 26, 1987 (*FBIS:ME*, March 27, 1987, p. I-1). Shamir also downplayed the importance of

the Bronfman–Abram visit (cf. report by Thomas Friedman, *New York Times*, April 1, 1987). The activists were also unhappy about the failure of the Israeli government to establish a quality absorption program (interview with Yuri Shtern, Jerusalem, January 1989).

279 Cf. report by Joe Greenberg, *Jerusalem Post*, March 27, 1987.

280 Reuters report, *New York Times*, March 29, 1987. China's permanent UN representative Li Luye, met with the Director General of the Israeli Foreign Ministry, Abraham Tamir. See also the report by David Landau and Walter Ruby, *Jerusalem Post*, March 29, 1987.

281 Cf. Jerusalem Radio Domestic Service interview with Soviet Foreign Ministry spokesman Genady Gerasimov, April 2, 1987 (*FBIS:ME*, April 2, 1987, p. I-1).

282 Jerusalem Radio Domestic Service interview with Peres, April 2, 1987 (*FBIS:ME*, April 3, 1987, p. I-1). In the interview Peres noted other changes in Soviet policy including the release of nearly all the prisoners of Zion, the rise in exit permits from 100 to nearly 500 a month, and Soviet statements in diplomatic meetings that they wanted improved relations with Israel.

283 Jerusalem Radio Domestic Service, April 5, 1987 (*FBIS:ME*, April 6, 1987, p. I-1) and *Jerusalem Post*, April 5, 1987.

284 Cited in report by John Tagliabue, *New York Times*, April 10, 1987.

285 Jerusalem Radio Domestic Service, April 8, 1987 (*FBIS:ME*, April 9, 1987, p. I-1).

286 Jerusalem Radio Domestic Service, April 9, 1987 (*FBIS:ME*, April 10, 1987, p. I-3).

287 This information, reported by "sources close to Peres" was discussed in the *Jerusalem Post*, April 10, 1987 in the report coauthored by Wolf Blitzer, David Horowitz, Jonathan Karp, and Robert Rosenberg.

288 Jerusalem Radio Domestic Service, April 7, 1987 (*FBIS:ME*, April 8, 1987, p. I-3).

289 Cited in report by Lea Levavi and Asher Wallfish, *Jerusalem Post*, April 10, 1987.

290 Jerusalem Radio Domestic Service, April 12, 1987 (*FBIS:ME*, April 13, 1987, p. I-3).

291 *Ibid.*

292 Israeli Defense Forces Radio interview with Yitzhak Shamir, April 13, 1987 (*FBIS:ME*, April 13, 1987, pp. I-4/I-5).

293 Cited in report by Paul Kelaney, *New York Times*, April 27, 1987. The Algiers PNC meeting reportedly led to a sharp improvement of Soviet–Arafat ties (interview, PLO headquarters, Tunis, February 1989).

294 Cited in report by Peter Talmon, *Jerusalem Post*, January 21, 1987.

295 See *Journal of Palestine Studies*, no. 64 (Summer 1987), p. 191, for the formal inclusion of the PCP.

296 For the text of the abrogation, see *Jordan Times*, April 21, 1987 (translated in *FBIS: Near East-South Asia* [hereafter *FBIS:NESA*], April 21, 1987, p. A-1 to A-4).

297 For the text of the PNC resolutions, see Saana Voice of Palestine, April 26, 1987 (*FBIS:NESA*, April 27, 1987, pp. A-8 to A-11).

298 Cited in report by Paul Delaney, *New York Times*, April 28, 1987.

299 For an analysis of the 16th PNC, see Rashid Khalidi, "Palestinian Politics After the Exodus from Beirut," in Robert O. Freedman (ed.), *The Middle East Since the Israeli Invasion of Lebanon* (Syracuse: Syracuse University Press, 1986, pp. 240–41).

300 Cf. report by Jim Muir, *Christian Science Monitor*, April 9, 1988. It should also be mentioned that even Syria's Middle Eastern allies, Libya and Iran, criticized Syrian policies which had caused near starvation in the Palestinian camps.

301 *Pravda*, April 28, 1987 (*FBIS:USSR*, May 6, 1987, pp. H-2 to H-3).

302 *Pravda*, April 25, 1987 (*FBIS:USSR*, April 28, 1987, p. H-8).

303 *Pravda*, April 25, 1987 (*FBIS:USSR*, April 28, 1987, p. H-10).

304 *Pravda*, April 27, 1987 (*FBIS:USSR*, April 28, 1987, p. H-14).

305 *Pravda*, April 27, 1987 (*FBIS:USSR*, April 28, 1987, p. H-12).

306 *Pravda*, April 25, 1987 (*FBIS:USSR*, April 28, 1987, p. H-1).
307 *Pravda*, April 25, 1987 (*FBIS:USSR*, April 28, 1987, p. H-7).
308 *Pravda*, April 25, 1987 (*FBIS:USSR*, April 28, 1987, p. H-10).
309 *Pravda*, April 27, 1987 (*FBIS:USSR*, April 28, 1987, p. H-14).
310 Cf. *Pravda*, March 7, 1987. According to an article by Ihsan Hijazi, *New York Times*, March 4, 1987, Shiite Muslim clerics had issued a religious edict calling for the killing of all communists.
311 *Pravda*, April 27, 1987 (*FBIS:USSR*, April 28, 1987, p. H-14).
312 *Pravda*, April 25, 1987 (*FBIS:USSR*, April 28, 1987, p. H-5).
313 Cf. Vladimir Zhitomirsky, "A Splendid View of Syria," *New Times*, no. 31 (1987), p. 5 and *Pravda*, July 25, 1987.
314 Cited in report by Jim Hoagland and Patrick Tyler, *Washington Post*, September 25, 1987.
315 *Washington Post*, September 20, 1987. According to the *1988 SIPRI Yearbook* (p. 234 and 244) in 1987 Syria received 24 MIG-29s as did Iraq, but Iraq also got SU-25 ground attack bombers. *The Middle East Military Balance* 1987–1988 (p. 401) states that Syria received 20 MIG-29s while Iraq received an estimated 25 (p. 302).
316 During this period the USSR was also stepping up its cultural exchanges with Israel. Thus in March, Moscow had sent its Gypsy Theatre Troup to play in Israel, and in April Moscow invited a group of blind Israeli athletes to visit the USSR.
317 Cited in report by Thomas Friedman, *New York Times*, May 8, 1987.
318 Jordan's denial came in a statement by Jordanian Prime Minister Zaid Al-Rifai. The text of the denial was printed in the *Jerusalem Post*, May 5, 1987. According to a report by David Shipler, *New York Times*, May 12, 1987, Jordan had reportedly agreed to a limited role for the USSR in the conference which would be convened by the Secretary General of the UN based on UN Resolutions 242 and 338. King Hussein, over the years, had repeatedly met with Israeli leaders, but could never bring himself to completing a peace agreement with Israel. The meeting in London was just one more example of this. See Garfinkle, "Jordan."
319 Cf. report by Glen Frankel, *Washington Post*, May 15, 1987.
320 Cf. Kuwait (*KUNA*), April 25, 1987 (*FBIS:NESA*, April 27, 1987, p. A-13) and Algiers Voice of Palestine, April 26, 1987 (*FBIS:NESA*, April 27, 1987, p. A-5).
321 Cited in AP report, *Washington Post*, May 19, 1987.
322 Cited in report by Neil Lewis, *New York Times*, July 17, 1987. See also the report by Mary Curtius, *Christian Science Monitor*, July 16, 1987 and the report in the *Jerusalem Post*, July 14, 1987.
323 *Izvestia*, August 11, 1987 and numerous Moscow Radio Peace and Progress Hebrew language broadcasts to Israel in July and August 1987. The issue of the Jericho II was also discussed in private meetings between Soviet and Israeli officials as Moscow became increasingly concerned about the escalating regional arms race. (Interview, Israeli Foreign Ministry, July 1988).
324 Jerusalem TV, August 17, 1987 (*FBIS:NESA*, August 18, 1987, pp. AA-1).
325 *Rose al-Yusuf* (Cairo), August 17, 1987 (*FBIS:USSR*, August 20, 1987, p. E-3).
326 Radio Moscow in Arabic, August 21, 1987 (*FBIS:USSR*, August 24, 1987, p. E-2). The Soviets asserted such contacts were needed to expedite the peace process.
327 Cited in report in the *New York Times*, October 2, 1987. Reportedly, Peres demanded full diplomatic relations, given the Soviet Union's importance in world politics. During interviews in Moscow in January, 1988 with Soviet scholars knowledgeable about this issue, I ascertained that the offer had indeed come up in conversation, but it remains unclear whether the USSR made the offer, or whether Peres himself brought it up as a trial balloon. Israeli Foreign Ministry officials in Jerusalem, interviewed in July 1988, regretted agreeing to only interest-section level relations with

Poland as this set a precedent for Soviet–Israeli relations.

328 Cf. report in *Washington Post*, by John Goshko, October 1, 1987. See also AP report, *Washington Post*, October 3, 1988.

329 Cf. report by Moshe Zaq, *Ma'ariv*, September 28, 1987 (*FBIS:NESA*, October 1, 1987, p. 22).

330 Cf. report in *New York Times*, October 13, 1987. By now, however, Israel was demanding a reciprocal consular status in Moscow (interview, Israeli Foreign Ministry, July 1988). During this period Moscow also released two long-term Refuseniks, Ida Nudel and Vladimir Slepak, both of whom went to Israel.

331 For analyses of the Soviet decision, see the articles by Bill Keller, *New York Times*, April 15, 1987 and Gary Lee, *Washington Post*, April 15, 1987.

332 A high-ranking official in the Kuwaiti Embassy in Moscow told me that Kuwait had approached the USSR in late November 1986 about the chartering, but that it had taken the USSR several months to respond (interview, Kuwaiti Embassy, Moscow, January 1988).

333 For descriptions of the attack and the Soviet response to it, see *New York Times*, May 9, 1987, *Le Monde*, May 10, 11, 1987 (translated in *Manchester Guardian Weekly*, May 17, 1987); and AP report, *Jerusalem Post*, May 18, 1987. For a detailed Soviet description of the attack by a retired Rear Admiral, see Timur Gaidar, "The Tanker War," *New Times*, no. 13 (1988), p. 15.

334 Tass, May 25, 1987 (*FBIS:USSR*, May 26, 1987, p. H-1).

335 Tass, June 3, 1987 (*FBIS:USSR*, June 4, 1987, p. E-1).

336 Cf. *Izvestia*, June 1, 1987.

337 Moscow World Service in English, May 20, 1987 (*FBIS:USSR*, May 20, 1987, p. H-2). See also Moscow Radio in Persian to Iran, May 27, 1987 (*FBIS:USSR*, June 9, 1987, p. E-7).

338 *Pravda*, April 30, 1987.

339 Moscow Radio Peace and Progress in Persian to Iran, May 8, 1987 (*FBIS:USSR*, May 11, 1987, p. H-3).

340 Reagan's statement explaining the reflagging was printed in the *New York Times*, May 30, 1987. For background analyses on the US reflagging decision, see the reports by Don Oberdorfer, *Washington Post*, May 29, 1987 and Jonathan Randal, *Washington Post*, June 5, 1987. The US Congress had become quite critical of the reflagging effort after the Iraqi attack on the USS Stark in May 1987.

341 Cf. *Izvestia*, May 29, 1987.

342 By mid-1987 the "new thinking" now being widely proclaimed in Moscow led Soviet officials to begin to urge the US to join in efforts to control regional conflicts rather than engage in a zero-sum game competition for influence.

343 On this point see R. K. Ramazani, "The Iran–Iraq War and the Persian Gulf Crisis," *Current History*, February 1988, pp. 63–64.

344 Cited in report by Flora Lewis, *New York Times*, June 7, 1987. For a description of the activities of the Soviet Gulf flotilla, see Timur Gaidar, "On Shore and At Sea: Notes on the Tanker War," *New Times*, no. 12 (1988), pp. 16–19.

345 *FBIS:NESA*, June 15, 1987, pp. AA-1 and Tehran Domestic Service, in Persian, June 13, 1987 (*FBIS:NESA*, June 15, 1987, p. S-1).

346 Tehran Domestic Service in Persian, June 14, 1987 (*FBIS:NESA*, June 15, 1987, p. S-1).

347 Cf. Robert O. Freedman, "Soviet Policy Toward the Persian Gulf from the Outbreak of the Iran–Iraq War to the Death of Konstantin Chernenko," in William J. Olson (ed.), *U.S. Strategic Interests in the Gulf Region* (Boulder: Westview Press, 1987), pp. 43–80.

348 Tehran Domestic Service in Persian, June 14, 1987 (*FBIS:USSR*, June 15, 1987, p. S-2).

349 Tehran *IRNA*, in English, June 14, 1987 (*FBIS:NESA*, June 15, 1987, p. S-2).

350 Tehran Domestic Service in Persian, June 15, 1987 (*FBIS:NESA*, June 15, 1987, p. S-3).

351 *Pravda*, July 4, 1987 (translation in *FBIS:USSR*, July 6, 1987, pp. E-1, E-2).

352 Cited in report by Gary Lee, *Washington Post*, July 3, 1987.

353 Tehran *IRNA*, in English, July 18, 1987 (*FBIS:USSR*, July 20, 1987, p. E-3).

354 *Ibid.*, p. E-4.

355 For the text of the Resolution, see *New York Times*, July 21, 1987.

356 *Pravda*, July 22, 1987.

357 Cf. speech of US Secretary of State Shultz at United Nations, *New York Times*, July 21, 1987.

358 Philip Taubman, in a report in the *New York Times* on July 23, 1987, cites an unnamed Soviet official who stated that Moscow's interest in maintaining good relations with Iran might preclude an arms ban to force Iran to comply with the cease-fire.

359 Tass, in English, July 22, 1987 (*FBIS:USSR*, July 23, 1987, p. E-1), and Gorbachev's letter to Reagan, cited in report by Gary Lee, *Washington Post*, July 22, 1987.

360 Cf. article by Alexander Bovin, *Izvestia*, July 31, 1987.

361 Radio Moscow, in Arabic, August 1, 1987 (*FBIS:USSR*, August 3, 1987, p. A-4).

362 *Pravda*, August 4, 1987.

363 Cited in report by John Kifner, *New York Times*, August 3, 1987. For a balanced view of the riots in Mecca, see Martin Kramer, "Tragedy in Mecca," *Orbis*, vol. 32 no. 2 (Spring 1988), pp. 231–47.

364 Tehran Domestic Service in Persian, August 3, 1987 (*FBIS:NESA*, August 4, 1987, p. S-11).

365 Tehran Domestic Service in Persian, August 4, 1987 (*FBIS:NESA*, August 4, 1987, p. S-12). See also the report by Jackson Diehl, *Washington Post*, August 5, 1987 and Phillip Taubman, *New York Times*, August 5, 1987.

366 *Pravda*, August 24, 1987.

367 Tass International Service, in English, August 9, 1987 (*FBIS:USSR*, August 10, 1987, p. A-4).

368 Tass, in English, August 24, 1987 (*FBIS:USSR*, August 25, 1987, p. E-3). For a somewhat different view of the Iranian–Soviet relationship during this period which detects a greater willingness on the part of Iran to end the war, see Gary Sick, "Slouching Toward Settlement: The Internationalization of the Iran–Iraq War: 1987," in Nikki Keddi (ed.), *Neither East nor West* (New Haven: Yale University Press, 1990).

369 Cited in *New York Times*, August 22, 1987.

370 Tass, in English, September 8, 1987 (*FBIS:USSR*, September 9, 1987, p. 24).

371 *Pravda*, September 10, 1987. See also Paris AFP, September 10, 1987 (*FBIS:USSR*, September 11, 1987, p. 15). For a somewhat different view of Soviet policy toward the Iran–Iraq war, see Galia Golan, "Gorbachev's Middle East Strategy," *Foreign Affairs*, vol. 66, no. 1 (Fall 1987), p. 57. Golan's view is that Moscow took a "fully supportive role" in UN efforts to bring about an end to the war.

372 *Pravda*, September 9, 1986.

373 Tehran Domestic Service in Persian, September 8, 1987 (*FBIS:USSR*, September 9, 1987, pp. 22–23).

374 Moscow Radio, in English, September 23, 1987 (*FBIS:USSR*, September 24, 1987, p. 35).

375 Moscow Radio, in English, September 24, 1987 (*FBIS:USSR*, September 25, 1987, p. 27).

376 Cf. report by Michael J. Berlin, *Washington Post*, October 16, 1987.

377 Tass International Service in Russian, October 1, 1987 (*FBIS:USSR*, October 2, 1987, p. 15).
378 *Izvestia*, October 18, 1987.
379 Tass, in English, October 20, 1987 (*FBIS:USSR*, October 21, 1987, p. 5).
380 *Pravda*, October 21, 1987.
381 The agreement called for the creation of a permanent Soviet–Kuwaiti commission on economic, scientific, and technological cooperation in the areas of oil, pipe-line transport, irrigation, trade, health protection, and other fields. (Tass, October 15, 1987 [*FBIS:USSR*, October 16, 1987, p. 35]).
382 *Pravda*, October 17, 1987.
383 Cf. report by Elaine Sciolino, *New York Times*, October 3, 1987.
384 *Ibid.*
385 *Washington Post*, October 31, 1987.
386 Cited in AP report, *New York Times*, November 6, 1987.
387 For the text of the Amman Summit Resolutions, see Baghdad INA in Arabic, November 12, 1987 (*FBIS:NESA*, November 13, 1987, pp. 23–25).
388 *Pravda*, November 15, 1987.
389 *Pravda*, November 14, 1987 (translated in *FBIS:USSR*, November 19, 1987, p. 20).
390 *Izvestia*, November 28, 1987 (*FBIS:USSR*, December 3, 1987, p. 39).
391 Translated in *FBIS:USSR*, November 25, 1987, p. 29.
392 Cf. Moscow Radio in Persian, November 28, 1987 (Igor Sheftunov commentary) (*FBIS:USSR*, December 1, 1987, p. 47).
393 *Pravda*, December 5, 1987 (*FBIS:USSR*, December 7, 1987, p. 44).
394 *Ibid.*
395 Tass, November 30, 1987 (*FBIS:USSR*, December 1, 1987, p. 7).
396 For a discussion of the US reaction to the Soviet offer, see the reports by David Ottaway, *Washington Post*, December 16, 1987 and David Shipler, *New York Times*, December 29, 1987.
397 Cf. report by Celestine Bohlen, *Washington Post*, December 28, 1987.
398 *Pravda*, December 28, 1987.
399 Tehran Television, in Persian, January 8, 1988 (*FBIS:NESA*, January 12, 1988, p. 83).
400 On November 10, 1987, the UN General Assembly voted 123 to 19 (with 11 abstentions) for the withdrawal of foreign forces from Afghanistan. In 1986, 122 states voted in favor of the troop withdrawal (cf. report by Paul Lewis, *New York Times*, November 11, 1987). The roll-call vote was also in the November 11, 1987 issue of the *New York Times*.
401 Moscow, for example, rejected a US plan to have a meeting of Israel, and a Palestinian–Jordanian delegation at the Reagan–Gorbachev summit. Cf. Moscow TV program, "The World Today," October 29, 1987, reiterating Shevardnadze's statement following the October 1987 visit of Shultz to Moscow that "rumors and talk to the effect that the USSR is not supporting the Arabs are fictitious and groundless from start to finish." (*FBIS:USSR*, November 2, 1987, p. 31). See also the report by Thomas L. Friedman, *New York Times*, November 7, 1987. See also IDF Radio, in Hebrew, November 19, 1987 (*FBIS:NESA*, November 19, 1987, p. 30).
402 Tass, November 24, 1987 (*FBIS:USSR*, November 25, 1987, p. 16).
403 Tass, October 22, 1987 (*FBIS:USSR*, October 23, 1987, p. 23).
404 Tass, October 28, 1987 (*FBIS:USSR*, October 29, 1987, p. 36).
405 Reuters report, *New York Times*, December 28, 1987.
406 Tass, in English, January 4, 1988 (*FBIS:USSR*, January 5, 1988, p. 24).
407 *Pravda*, December 21, 1987.
408 *Pravda*, December 23, 1987.

409 *Ibid.*

410 *Ibid.* (translated in *FBIS:USSR*, December 23, 1987, p. 31). For a Soviet view of the rapidly escalating crisis in the Gulf, see N. C. Beglova, "Krizisnaia Situatsiia v Persidskom Zalive" (Crisis Situation in the Persian Gulf), *Ssha*, no. 12 (1987), pp. 52–58.

411 Tass, International Service, February 19, 1988 (*FBIS:USSR*, February 22, 1988, p. 39.

412 Tehran, in English, February 10, 1988 (*FBIS:NESA*, February 11, 1988, p. 56).

413 Tehran Domestic Service, in Persian, February 14, 1988 (*FBIS:NESA*, February 16, 1988, p. 61).

414 Tehran TV in Persian, February 12, 1988 (*FBIS:NESA*, February 18, 1988, p. 61).

415 Tehran Domestic Service in Persian, February 18, 1988 (*FBIS:NESA*, February 19, 1988, p. 44).

416 Tehran IRNA, February 23, 1988 (*FBIS:NESA*, February 23, 1988, p. 65).

417 Tehran Domestic Service in Persian, February 22, 1988 (*FBIS:NESA*, February 23, 1988, p. 65).

418 See the report by Don Oberdorfer, *Washington Post*, February 10, 1988 and the report by Patrick Tyler, *Washington Post*, February 8, 1988.

419 See the report by Warren Richey, *Christian Science Monitor*, January 14, 1988.

420 See the report in the *Washington Post*, February 22, 1988.

421 See AP report, *New York Times*, March 1, 1988.

422 For Iranian descriptions of the demonstrations, see IRNA, March 4, 1988 (*FBIS:NESA*, March 4, 1988, p. 55) and IRNA, March 6, 1988 (*FBIS:NESA*, March 7, 1988, p. 57). See also reports by Bill Keller, *New York Times*, March 7, 1988 and David Remnick, *Washington Post*, March 7, 1988.

423 Cited in *FBIS:NESA*, March 21, 1988, p. 1.

424 Tehran TV, March 24, 1988 (*FBIS:NESA*, March 25, 1988, p. 57).

425 Tehran IRNA, in English, March 6, 1988 (*FBIS:NESA*, March 7, 1988, p. 59).

426 Tehran IRNA, March 9, 1988 (*FBIS:NESA*, March 9, 1988, p. 60).

427 Tehran IRNA, in English, April 14, 1988 (*FBIS:NESA*, April 15, 1988, p. 55).

428 On the Fao offensive, see the reports by Patrick Tyler, *Washington Post*, April 18, 1988 and May 3, 1988. Up until this point, except for its air and missile attacks on ships and Iranian cities, Iraq had been very much on the defensive in the Gulf war, and the offensive surprised Iran as well as Western observers.

429 Tehran Domestic Service in Persian, March 19, 1988 (*FBIS:NESA*, April 20, 1988, p. 54).

430 Tass, April 20, 1988 (*FBIS:USSR*, April 20, 1988, p. 12).

431 Tass, English, April 20, 1988 (*FBIS:USSR*, April 21, 1988, p. 3). For more balanced descriptions of the battle, see reports by John Eishman, Jr., *New York Times*, April 19, 1988 and George C. Wilson and Molly Moore, *Washington Post*, April 19, 1988.

432 Tass, English, April 19, 1988 (*FBIS:USSR*, April 20, 1988, p. 13).

433 Moscow Radio Peace and Progress, April 25, 1988 (*FBIS:USSR*, April 26, 1988, p. 22).

434 Moscow Radio Peace and Progress, May 12, 1988 (*FBIS:USSR*, May 13, 1988, p. 17).

435 *Kayhan International*, June 27, 1988 (*FBIS:NESA*, July 13, 1988, p. 54).

436 Cf. Moscow Radio, in English, July 7, 1988 (*FBIS:USSR*, July 8, 1988, p. 29).

437 *Pravda*, July 15, 1988; *Krasnaia Zvezda*, July 10, 1988 (*FBIS:USSR*, July 14, 1988, p. 5).

438 Cf. report by Fox Butterfield, *New York Times*, July 16, 1988.

439 Cf. Khomeini's statement, Tehran Domestic Service, July 20, 1988 (*FBIS:NESA*, July 21, 1988, pp. 41–53). Khomeini, in his speech, was bitterly critical of both the US and the USSR. See also James Bill, "Why Tehran Finally Wants a Gulf Peace,"

Washington Post Outlook Section, August 28, 1988.

440 Moscow Radio, in Persian, July 18, 1988 (*FBIS:USSR*, July 20, 1988, pp. 22–23).

441 Tehran IRNA, July 21, 1988 (*FBIS:NESA*, July 22, 1988, p. 48).

442 *Pravda*, July 23, 1988.

443 Tehran, IRNA in English, August 11, 1988 (*FBIS:NESA*, August 11, 1988, p. 64).

444 Kuwait KUNA, August 10, 1988 (*FBIS:USSR*, August 11, 1988, p. 18).

445 For a Soviet view of the historical origins of the Shatt al-Arab dispute, see Yakov Borovoi and Dmitry Zgersky, "Shatt Al-Arab: The Price of Those 192 Kilometers," *New Times*, no. 37 (1988), p. 6.

446 *Pravda*, August 22, 1988, p. 1 (translated in *CDSP*, vol. 40, no. 34 (1988), p. 16).

447 Alexander Zotov, "A Burden for Perez de Cuellar," *New Times*, no. 31 (1988), p. 7.

448 Cited in report by Elaine Sciolino, *New York Times*, October 5, 1988.

449 On the debate, see Kayhan, August 18, 1988 (*FBIS:NESA*, September 19, 1988, p. 52) and the Friday Prayer Sermon by Iran's President Ali Khameni, Tehran Domestic Service in Persian, September 16, 1988 (*FBIS:NESA*, September 19, 1988, pp. 48–49).

450 Moscow Radio, in Persian, October 12, 1988 (*FBIS:USSR*, October 19, 1988, pp. 29–30).

451 Tehran IRNA, in English, August 18, 1988 (*FBIS:NESA*, August 18, 1988, p. 50).

452 Tehran IRNA, in English, August 25, 1988 (*FBIS:NESA*, August 25, 1988, p. 42).

453 Tehran IRNA, September 3, 1988 (*FBIS:NESA*, September 9, 1988, p. 40).

454 IRNA, September 27, 1988 (*FBIS:NESA*, September 27, 1988, p. 43).

455 Tehran IRNA, September 17, 1988. Trade was up, however, from the $100 million level of 1986 (*FBIS:NESA*, September 19, 1988, p. 51).

456 IRNA, September 18, 1988 (*FBIS:NESA*, September 20, 1988, p. 46).

457 IRNA, in English, September 19, 1988 (*FBIS:NESA*, September 20, 1988, p. 46).

458 Tass, December 8, 1988 (*FBIS:USSR*, December 9, 1988, p. 26).

459 Tass, December 6, 1988 (*FBIS:USSR*, December 7, 1988, p. 34).

460 Translated in *FBIS:USSR*, November 8, 1988, p. 41.

461 *Literaturnaia Gazeta*, November 30, 1988 (*FBIS:USSR*, December 1, 1988, pp. 21–22). See also Yuri Zhuravlyov, "Back to the Past or Back to the Present," *New Times*, no. 26 (1988), pp. 8–9.

462 Cited in report by David Ottaway, *Washington Post*, July 25, 1988.

463 Cf. report by Mark Mathews, *Baltimore Sun*, August 1, 1988.

464 Moscow Radio Peace and Progress, in Persian, September 12, 1988 (*FBIS:USSR*, September 15, 1988, p. 20).

465 Cf. *Pravda*, September 11, 1988.

466 Friday Prayer Sermon by Rafsanjani, Tehran Domestic Service, September 23, 1988 (*FBIS:NESA*, September 26, 1988, p. 55).

467 Radio of the Iranian Toilers, July 31, 1988 (*FBIS:NESA*, August 2, 1988, p. 55) and September 12, 1988 and September 16, 1988 (*FBIS:NESA*, September 21, 1988, pp. 40–43).

468 Radio Peace and Progress in Persian, November 5, 1988 (*FBIS:USSR*, November 30, 1988, p. 17). See also the report by Paul Lewin, *New York Times*, November 3, 1988).

469 Moscow Radio, in Persian, December 10, 1988 (*FBIS:USSR*, December 13, 1988, p. 12).

470 Cf. Tass report, July 30, 1988 (*FBIS:NESA*, August 1, 1988, p. 1) and Baghdad INA, September 14, 1988 (*FBIS:USSR*, September 15, 1988, p. 17).

471 See the report by E. A. Wayne, *Christian Science Monitor*, September 12, 1988, for an analysis of the effect of the poison gas issue on US–Iraqi relations.

472 Cf. report by Don Oberdorfer, *Washington Post*, September 14, 1988. Moscow, however, may yet move to cooperate with the US to stem the flow of missiles to the

Middle East, if the "missile race" continues to speed up.

473 Cited in report by Patrick Tyler, *Washington Post*, September 20, 1988.
474 *New York Times*, September 23, 1988.
475 Cf. reports by David Ottaway, *Washington Post*, November 17, 1988, and Elaine Sciolino, *New York Times*, November 18, 1988. Allegedly, the US official had been visiting Kurdish areas of Iraq without the requisite Iraqi government permission.
476 *Pravda*, August 1, 1988.
477 On the US–Qatar dispute, see the reports by John H. Cushman, Jr., *New York Times*, April 1, 1988, and Patrick Tyler, *Washington Post*, October 6, 1988.
478 *Pravda*, November 6, 1988.
479 Moscow Radio, in Arabic, November 4, 1988 (*FBIS:USSR*, November 7, 1988, p. 31). For a Soviet view of Saudi policy at this time, see A. Kislov and A. Frolov, "Ssha – Saudovskaia Araviia – Protivorechivoe Partnerstvo" (USA–Saudi Arabia – A Contradictory Partnership), *Ssha* no. 2 (1989), pp. 30–39.
480 See above, pp. 189–91.
481 For reports about the progress of the US–Kuwaiti arms deal, see David Ottaway, *Washington Post*, July 10, 1988; E. A. Wayne, *Christian Science Monitor*, August 5, 1988; and the AP report in the *Jerusalem Post*, August 28, 1988.
482 Cited in *Arab Times(FBIS:NESA*, July 18, 1988, p. 3).
483 Kuwait KUNA, August 31, 1988 (*FBIS:USSR*, September 1, 1988, p. 18).
484 *Pravda*, December 20, 1987.
485 *Pravda*, December 24, 1987.
486 Tass, December 28, 1987 (*FBIS:USSR*, December 29, 1987, p. 42) reported a meeting between Voronstov and a group of Arab diplomats on December 26, 1987 to discuss "the dangerous situation in the Israeli-occupied Palestinian territories."
487 Moscow Domestic Service, January 16, 1988 (*FBIS:USSR*, January 19, 1988, p. 37).
488 Tass, January 26, 1988 (*FBIS:USSR*, January 27, 1988, p. 9); Jerusalem Domestic Service, January 20, 1988 (*FBIS:USSR*, January 20, 1988, p. 19). Perhaps as a signal to Moscow, the Israeli Foreign Ministry in December had only granted a one-month extension to the visas of the Soviet consular delegation in December, 1987 (interviews Israeli Foreign Ministry, July 1988, and US embassy, Moscow, January 1988).
489 Tass, January 19, 1988 (*FBIS:USSR*, January 20, 1988, p. 5).
490 *Izvestia*, January 22, 1988 (*FBIS:USSR*, January 22, 1988, p. 23).
491 Cf. article by Pavel Demchenko in *Pravda*, February 2, 1988.
492 Cf. *Pravda*, February 26, 1988.
493 Cf. *Pravda*, February 9, 1988.
494 *Izvestia*, February 6, 1988 (*FBIS:USSR*, February 12, 1988, p. 36).
495 Tass, February 11, 1988 (*FBIS:USSR*, February 18, 1988, p. 24).
496 KUNA (Kuwait), February 23, 1988 (*FBIS:USSR*, February 24, 1988, p. 29).
497 Tass, March 18, 1988 (*FBIS:USSR*, March 21, 1988, p. 30). A Tass report on April 4, 1988 (*FBIS:USSR*, April 5, 1988, p. 22) noted that the USSR had no "fundamental objections" to the intermediate steps preferred by the US, but "such steps can yield a positive result only in the context of a comprehensive settlement."
498 Cf. Moscow Domestic Service, April 3, 1988 (*FBIS:USSR*, April 4, 1988, p. 13). See also Reuters report, *Jerusalem Post*, March 31, 1988.
499 Tass, April 9, 1988 (*FBIS:USSR*, April 11, 1988, p. 26).
500 Moscow Domestic Service, April 9, 1988 (*FBIS:USSR*, April 11, 1988, p. 27).
501 Cf. AP report, *Jerusalem Post*, April 13, 1988.
502 *Al-Siyasah* (Kuwait), April 26, 1988 (*FBIS:USSR*, May 2, 1988, p. 35).
503 Cited in report by Michael Yudelman, *Jerusalem Post*, March 8, 1988. Three days later, the *Jerusalem Post* reported a meeting between an Israeli and a Soviet diplomat at the UN, in which the Soviet diplomat reportedly stated that the PLO terrorist

attack on an Israeli bus in early March was a "tremendous mistake," and openly wondered if the PLO had any coherent policy.

504 Cited in report by Jonathan Karp, *Jerusalem Post*, April 15, 1988.

505 For a wry comment on the Pugachova tour, see the article by former Refusenik Josef Begun, *Jerusalem Post*, April 14, 1988. Begun called for more Israeli artists to tour the USSR.

506 Gorbachev's purpose in allowing such tourism may have been to lessen the pressure from Soviet Jews to permanently leave the country. An estimated 10,000 Soviet Jews were to visit Israel in 1988.

507 Cf. Tass, April 22, 1988 (*FBIS:USSR*, April 25, 1988, p. 38). For the text of the memorandum of agreement, see the *Jerusalem Post*, April 22, 1988.

508 Moscow International Service, in Arabic, April 25, 1988 (*FBIS:USSR*, April 26, 1988, p. 23).

509 Cited in report by Menachem Shalev and Wolf Blitzer, *Jerusalem Post*, April 29, 1988.

510 For a description of the interview, see AP report, *Jerusalem Post*, April 15, 1988.

511 For a description of the Peres visit, which Hungary played down, see the report by Menachem Shalev and Lisa Billig in the *Jerusalem Post*, May 10, 1988 and the article by Henry Kamm, *New York Times*, May 10, 1988.

512 Tass, May 12, 1988 (*FBIS:USSR*, May 13, 1988, p. 7).

513 Cited in *Jerusalem Post*, May 11, 1988.

514 Cf. report by Bernard Josephs, *Jerusalem Post*, May 16, 1988.

515 Cf. report by David Remnick, *Washington Post*, June 9, 1988. See also the report by Philip Taubman, *New York Times*, May 18, 1988. For an analysis of developments dealing with Soviet Jewry, see Robert O. Freedman (ed.), *Soviet Jewry in the 1980s*. The total number of Soviet Jews to emigrate from the USSR in 1988 was 18,965 (*ibid.*).

516 For the reported text of this document, see the *Jerusalem Post*, June 10, 1988. A Soviet official present at the talks, called it a "working paper" (interview, Soviet Embassy, Washington, DC, May 1988).

517 Cited in report by Wolf Blitzer, *Jerusalem Post*, May 19, 1988. An official at the Soviet Embassy in Washington told me that he thought the international conference would still have to be "effective" (interview, Soviet Embassy, Washington, DC, May 1988).

518 Cited in Jerusalem Post Diplomatic Staff Report, *Jerusalem Post*, May 25, 1988.

519 Cf. report by Glenn Frankel, *Washington Post*, May 25, 1988.

520 Cited in report by Wolf Blitzer, *Jerusalem Post*, May 20, 1988.

521 *Pravda*, June 3, 1988 (*FBIS:USSR*, June 3, 1988, p. 9).

522 Cited in report by Elaine Sciolino, *New York Times*, June 7, 1988.

523 Cited in report by Wolf Blitzer, *Jerusalem Post*, June 9, 1988.

524 For reports on the Shamir–Shevardnadze talks, see the reports by Don Oberdorfer, *Washington Post*, June 10, 1988; Elaine Sciolino, *New York Times*, June 10, 1988; and Menachem Shalev, *Jerusalem Post*, June 12, 1988. According to Israeli Foreign Ministry sources, however, Shevardnadze was "disappointed" by his talks with Shamir.

525 Cited in report by Menachem Shalev and Asher Wallfish, *Jerusalem Post*, June 13, 1988.

526 *Izvestia*, August 1, 1988, carried a description of the role of the Israeli delegation by V. P. Perfilyev, deputy press spokesman. See also AP report *New York Times*, July 29, 1988, and report by Gary Lee, *Washington Post*, July 29, 1988. It should also be noted that the Chief Rabbi of the city of Rehovot in Israel, Rabbi Simha Kook, was given a visa to visit the Soviet Union in late June, 1988 despite the fact that he put on

his visa application that the purpose of his visit was to "teach Jewish law and visit synagogues" (*Jerusalem Post*, June 24, 1988).

527 Cited in report by Steven R. Weiseman, *Washington Post*, May 15, 1988. Gronov's comments, of course, may also have been intended to influence the atmosphere of the US–Soviet summit at the end of May, 1988.

528 Tass, April 26, 1988 (*FBIS:USSR*, April 27, 1988, p. 27). Ethiopia was in deep economic trouble and Mengistu was embroiled in seemingly unwinnable internal conflicts. See Paul Henze, *Ethiopia: Crisis of a Marxist Economy: Analysis and Text of a Soviet Report* (Santa Monica: Rand, 1989).

529 Reuters report, *New York Times*, May 17, 1988. For a survey of Moscow's problems in the Maghreb at this time, see Yahia Zoubir, "Soviet Policy in the Maghreb," *Arab Studies Quarterly*, vol. 9, no. 4 (1987), pp. 399–421.

530 See report by Steven Greenhouse, *New York Times*, May 27, 1988. Moscow's positive response to this event – which averted the possibility of a Soviet–American or Soviet–French clash over Chad, may be seen in the Tass report, May 30, 1988 (*FBIS:USSR*, May 31, 1988, p. 34).

531 Cf. Moscow International Service in Arabic, July 15, 1988 (*FBIS:USSR*, July 20, 1988, p. 26). For an analysis of these North African developments, see Mary Jane Deeb, "Inter-Maghribi Relations Since 1969: A Study of the Modalities of Unions and Mergers," *Middle East Journal*, vol. 43, no. 1 (Winter 1989), pp. 20–33.

532 The concern was reflected in an article in *Pravda*, October 7, 1988. For a pre-riot Soviet view of Algeria, see V. Evgenev, "ANDR – Chetvert' Veka Nezavisimogo Razvitiia" (Algeria – A Quarter Century of Independent Development), *MEIMO*, no. 7 (1987), pp. 48–59.

533 Cairo, *al-Musawwar*, May 27, 1988 (*FBIS:USSR*, June 3, 1988, p. 42). For Gorbachev's speech welcoming Maguid, see *Pravda*, May 21, 1988.

534 AFP, May 19, 1988 (*FBIS:USSR*, May 20, 1988, p. 21).

535 *Pravda*, May 22, 1988.

536 *Washington Post*, February 10, 1988.

537 Radio Moscow, in Arabic, May 21, 1988 (*FBIS:USSR*, May 24, 1988, p. 39).

538 Cf. Tripoli JANA, in Arabic, September 16, 1988 (*FBIS:NESA*, September 20, 1988, p. 9).

539 *Krasnaia Zvezda*, December 23, 1987 (*FBIS:USSR*, December 24, 1987, p. 21).

540 Tass, March 14, 1988 (*FBIS:USSR*, March 15, 1988, p. 22).

541 Cf. Gorbachev's message to Assad on the 25th anniversary of the March 8, 1963 Ba'athist Revolution in Syria, Tass, March 7, 1988 (*FBIS:USSR*, March 7, 1988, p. 30), and Deputy Foreign Minister Yuli Voronstov's talk with Assad in Damascus in July (*Pravda*, July 21, 1988).

542 The clearest exposition of the Syrian position is found in a Tass interview with the outspoken Syrian Defense Minister, Mustafa Talas (*FBIS:USSR*, October 6, 1988, pp. 18–19).

543 *Davar* (Tel Aviv) on July 11, 1988 reported that Moscow was sending Sukhoi-24 ground attack bombers to Syria (*FBIS:NESA*, July 11, 1988, p. 25); on July 6, 1988, the *Jerusalem Post*, citing Israeli Defense Ministry sources said Moscow was sending more SS-21 ground-to-ground missiles to Syria. The SU-24 deal was also reported by *Al-Ittihad* (Abu Dhabi) on August 29, 1988 along with a sale of MIG-29 aircraft (*FBIS:USSR*, August 29, 1988, p. 18). Israeli Defense Minister Yitzhak Rabin in an interview on Israeli television on August 30, 1988, discussed a sale "at the beginning of 1988" of tanks and SS-21 missiles and possibly other aircraft (*FBIS:NESA*, August 31, 1988, p. 23). Moscow, however, did not sell Syria the longer range and more accurate SS-23 in 1988. For an assessment of Syrian military power in 1988, see Aharon Levran, "Changes in the Syrian Armed Forces and Their Impact on the

Military Balance With Israel," *MEMB* 1987–88, pp. 197–211.

544 See *Argumenty i Fakty*, September 3–9, 1988 (*FBIS:USSR*, September 2, 1988, p. 6). The story originated in the visit to Damascus of the Soviet Chief of Chemical Warfare. It is possible, given Iraq's use of poison gas and its enmity toward Syria, that the Syrian government wanted countermeasures against Iraq. It is also possible, however, that Syria was actively engaged in the development of chemical weapons itself as a countermeasure against Israel's nuclear capability. See Aharon Levran, "The Growing Threat to Israel's Rear," *MEMB* 1987–88, pp. 227–29.

545 *Krasnaia Zvezda*, September 15, 1988 (*FBIS:USSR* September 16, 1988, p. 18). For another view of the Tartus "facility," see the report by Robert Pear, *New York Times*, August 28, 1988.

546 Cf. report by Ya'acov Lamdan, *Jerusalem Post*, December 12, 1988 which cited the Lebanese weekly *al-Muharrar*, and report by David Ottaway, *Washington Post*, June 23, 1988. Reportedly, Syria's debt to the USSR for military purchases totalled $16.5 billion by the end of 1988, and Assad was having a hard time paying it, given the weakness of the Syrian economy.

547 Cited in *FBIS:NESA*, June 7, 1978, p. 1.

548 Radio Moscow, June 10, 1988 (*FBIS:USSR*, June 13, 1988, p. 39), Tass, June 9, 1988 (*FBIS:USSR*, June 10, 1988, p. 35) and *Pravda*, June 12, 1988.

549 For the summit communiqué, read by Arab League Secretary General Chedli Klibi on Algerian TV, see *FBIS:NESA*, June 10, 1988, pp. 11–14. For reports describing the atmosphere of the summit, see Youssef Ibrahim, *New York Times*, June 10, 1988 and George D. Moffet, *Christian Science Monitor*, June 10, 1988.

550 Arafat was interviewed by Leonid Medvenko, "A Time to Throw Stones and a Time to Collect Them," *New Times*, no. 36 (1988), p. 18.

551 *Ibid.*, p. 17.

552 See Garfinkle, "Jordan," for a view that Hussein still hopes for major influence on the West Bank.

553 *Al-Ittihad*, August 23, 1988 (*FBIS:USSR*, August 25, 1988, p. 11).

554 *Izvestia*, September 18, 1988 (translated in *CDSP*, vol. 40, no. 38, 1988, p. 17).

555 A terrorist attack on the eve of the election in which several Israelis were killed when their bus was firebombed hardened Israeli attitudes against the PLO. Soviet press spokesman Gennady Gerasimov condemned the attack although he also condemned "state terrorism." However, in a clear rebuke of the perpetrators of the attack, he stated "With respect to this specific act, one also has to ask: who gains from this, particularly on the eve of the parliamentary elections in Israel?" (*Pravda*, November 1, 1988, translated in *CDSP*, vol. 40, no. 44 [1988], p. 19).

556 The text of the political program of the PNC was printed in the *New York Times*, November 17, 1988. See also the report by Youssef Ibrahim, *New York Times*, November 15, 1988.

557 Cf. report by George D. Moffett, *Christian Science Monitor*, November 15, 1988.

558 *Pravda*, November 19, 1988 (translated in *CDSP*, vol. 40, no. 46 [1988], pp. 19–20). Gerasimov gave a legalistic argument for the Soviet Union's limited recognition, stating "Our practice knows no precedents when a state would be recognized while its territory was under foreign occupation and which had no government at the moment of recognition." Tass, English, November 24, 1988 (*FBIS:USSR*, November 25, 1988, p. 5).

559 Radio Moscow, November 21, 1988 (*FBIS:USSR*, November 22, 1988, p. 24).

560 Cf. *Izvestia*, November 29, 1988.

561 *Pravda*, December 8, 1988 (*FBIS:USSR*, December 12, 1988, p. 12).

562 *Washington Post*, December 3, 1988.

563 Arafat's press conference statement was published in the *New York Times*, Decem-

ber 15, 1989. See also the article by Robert Pear, *New York Times*, December 15, 1988 and the article by David Ottaway and John Goshko, *Washington Post*, December 15, 1988.

564 Cf. report by Patrick Tyler, *Washington Post*, December 17, 1988. Yasser Abd Raboo was No. 2 in the PFLP, but was personally close to Arafat.

565 *Pravda*, December 18, 1988.

566 Interview with Aryeh Levin, head of the Israeli consular mission in Moscow, Jerusalem, Israel, January 4, 1989.

567 For a Soviet account of the hijacking, see Vitaly Bordunov, "A Drama Brought to an Early Finale," *New Times*, no. 50 (1988), pp. 46–47. Aryeh Levin himself was interviewed by *New Times* and his photograph appeared in the story (*New Times*, no. 50 [1988], pp. 46–47).

568 Cf. report by Walter Ruby, *Jerusalem Post*, December 9, 1988.

569 Cited in *ibid*.

570 Cf. report by David Remnick, *Washington Post*, December 22, 1988. See also Michael Davis, "Armenia: IDF to the Rescue," *Israeli Defense Forces Journal*, no. 16 (Winter 1989), pp. 28–33.

571 Cf. report by Bill Keller, *New York Times*, November 3, 1988, citing the Soviet admission of sharply rising inflation, and the report by David Remnick, *Washington Post*, January 22, 1989 citing *Izvestia*'s admission of Soviet economic failures.

572 Moscow Domestic Service in Russian, January 4, 1989 (*FBIS:USSR*, January 5, 1989, p. 3).

573 Cf. article by Michel Zlatowski and Menahem Shalev, *Jerusalem Post*, January 9, 1989.

574 Tass International Service in Russian, January 8, 1989 (*FBIS:USSR*, January 9, 1989, p. 11).

575 Translated in *FBIS:USSR*, January 12, 1989, p. 8.

576 Tass, January 5, 1989 (*FBIS:USSR*, January 5, 1989, p. 3).

577 Tass, January 11, 1989 (*FBIS:USSR*, January 12, 1989, p. 7).

578 *Ha'aretz* (Tel Aviv) December 29, 1988 (*FBIS:USSR*, December 28, 1988, p. 8).

579 *Al-Anba* (Kuwait), January 7, 1989 (*FBIS:USSR*, January 10, 1989, p. 34).

580 Moscow Domestic Service, January 18, 1989 (*FBIS:USSR*, January 19, 1989, p. 30). According to interviews which I conducted in PLO headquarters in Tunis in February 1989, contacts had indeed been stepped up.

581 Cf. key article by Soviet Third World specialist Nodari Simoniya, *Pravda*, January 18, 1989.

582 *Pravda*, February 18, 1989 (*FBIS:USSR*, February 23, 1989, pp. 44–45).

583 Moscow Domestic Service, January 2, 1989 (*FBIS:USSR*, January 3, 1989, p. 31); Tehran TV in Persian, January 3, 1989 (*FBIS:NESA*, January 4, 1989, p. 52).

584 Tass International Service on January 4, 1989 cited Iranian Deputy Foreign Minister Mohammed Larijani as stating "the decision about the withdrawal of Soviet troops from Afghanistan was an extremely logical step of the Soviet leadership."

585 For the text of the Khomeini message, see Tehran TV, January 8, 1989 (*FBIS:NESA*, January 9, 1989, pp. 57–59).

586 *Ibid*., p. 58.

587 *Ibid*., p. 59.

588 *Ibid*., p. 59.

589 *Ibid*., p. 59.

590 *Pravda*, on January 5, 1989, carried a report on Gorbachev's comments to the visiting Iranian delegation in which he stated "the fact that we are different and hold different political and ideological principles and traditions is far from an impediment to the development of mutually advantageous Soviet–Iranian relations."

591 Tehran *IRNA*, in English, January 6, 1989 (*FBIS:NESA*, January 9, 1989, p. 59).
592 *Pravda*, January 19, 1989.
593 For the US explanation of the incident, see *New York Times*, January 5, 1989.
594 See above, p. 111–13.
595 Cited in report by Lou Cannon and David Ottaway, *Washington Post*, December 22, 1988.
596 Cf. Tass report, January 4, 1989 (*FBIS:USSR*, January 4, 1989, p. 12).
597 Moscow International Service in Arabic, January 4, 1989 (*FBIS:USSR*, January 5, 1989, p. 16) and Moscow International Service in Arabic, January 5, 1989 (*FBIS:USSR*, January 6, 1989, p. 7).
598 Moscow International Service in Arabic, January 5, 1989, *ibid.*
599 Moscow World Service in English, January 5, 1989 (*FBIS:USSR*, January 6, 1989, p. 11).
600 Tass International Service, January 6, 1989 (*FBIS:USSR*, January 9, 1989, p. 8).
601 Tass International Service, January 5, 1989 (*FBIS:USSR*, January 5, 1989, p. 2).
602 Translated in *FBIS:USSR*, January 11, 1989, p. 7.
603 Cf. comments of Soviet First Deputy Foreign Minister Alexander Bessmertnykh to a group of Arab Ambassadors, cited in Tass International Service, January 7, 1989 (*FBIS:USSR*, January 9, 1989, p. 39).
604 See the reports by Jennifer Parmelee, *Washington Post*, January 13, 1989 and Diana Henry, *Baltimore Sun*, January 15, 1989.
605 The official estimate was made by Soviet Army General Valentin Varrenikov (cited in report by Bill Keller, *New York Times*, March 19, 1989). For the larger estimate, see Valerii Konovalov, "Legacy of the Afghan War: Some Statistics," *Radio Liberty Report on the USSR*, vol. 1 no. 14 (April 7, 1989), pp. 1–3. See also *Afghanistan: Soviet Occupation and Withdrawal* (Washington: US Department of State Bureau of Public Affairs, Special Report no. 179, December 1988). *Izvestia* on August 21, 1989 cited the Afghan Ambassador to the Soviet Union as saying 1 million Afghans were killed or wounded during the war.
606 Cf. Shevardnadze's dinner speech in Damascus, *Tass*, February 19, 1989 (*FBIS:USSR*, February 21, 1989, p. 20).
607 *Pravda*, February 20, 1989 citing Shevardnadze's talks with Syrian Vice-President Khaddam, the former Syrian Foreign Minister.
608 Shevardnadze's dinner speech, *FBIS:USSR*, February 21, 1989, p. 21.
609 *Ibid.*
610 Cf. Shevardnadze news conference, Tass International Service, February 19, 1989 (*FBIS:USSR*, February 21, 1989, p. 23).
611 *Ibid.*
612 Shevardnadze dinner speech, *FBIS:USSR*, February 21, 1989, p. 20.
613 The author was in Tunis interviewing PLO officials when the Soviet effort was made and related to him.
614 *Pravda*, February 21, 1989 (*FBIS:USSR*, February 21, 1989, p. 28).
615 Tass, February 20, 1989 (*FBIS:USSR*, February 21, 1989, p. 29).
616 *Ibid.*, p. 30.

Bibliography

Books

Albright, David E., *Soviet Policy Toward Africa Revisited* (Washington: Center for Strategic and International Studies, 1987)

Andreasian, Ruben, *Opek v Mire Nefti* (OPEC in the World of Oil) (Moscow: Nauka, 1978)

Atkin, Muriel, *The Subtlest Battle: Islam in Soviet Tajikistan* (Philadelphia: Foreign Policy Research Institute, 1989)

Azhary, M. S., ed., *The Iran–Iraq War* (New York: St. Martin's Press, 1984)

Badeau, John, *An American Approach to the Arab World* (New York: Harper and Row, 1968)

Barakat, Halim, ed., *Toward a Viable Lebanon* (London: Croom Helm, 1988)

Bawly, Dan and Eliahu Salpeter, *Fire in Beirut: Israel's War in Lebanon with the PLO* (New York: Stein and Day, 1984)

The Beirut Massacre: The Complete Kahan Commission Report (Princeton: Karz-Cohl, 1983)

Bennigsen, Alexander and Marie Broxup, *The Islamic Threat to the Soviet State* (New York: St. Martin's, 1983)

Bradsher, Henry S., *Afghanistan and the Soviet Union* (Durham: Duke University Press, 1985)

Brzezinski, Zbigniew, *Power and Principle: Memoirs of the National Security Adviser 1977–1981* (New York: Farrar Straus Giroux, 1983)

Carter, Jimmy, *Keeping Faith: Memoirs of a President* (New York: Bantam Books, 1982)

Cherneta, O. G., *Afghanistan: Borba i Sozidanie* (Afghanistan: Struggle and Creation) (Moscow: Voenizdat, 1984)

Cobban, Helena, ed., *Military Dimensions of Soviet Middle East Policy* (College Park, Maryland: Center for International Security Studies, 1988)

Cordesman, Anthony, *The Gulf and the West* (Boulder: Westview Press, 1988)

Cottam, Richard W., *Competitive Interference and Twentieth Century Diplomacy* (Pittsburgh: University of Pittsburgh Press, 1967)

Dagan, Avigdor, *Moscow and Jerusalem* (New York: Abelard-Schuman, 1970)

Damis, John, *Conflict in Northwest Africa* (Stanford: Hoover Institution Press, 1983)

Dann, Uriel, *Iraq under Kassem* (New York: Praeger, 1969)

Dawisha, Adeed and Karen Dawisha, eds., *The Soviet Union in the Middle East: Policies and Perspectives* (New York: Holmes and Meier, 1982)

Donaldson, Robert H., ed., *The Soviet Union in the Third World: Successes and Failures* (Boulder: Westview Press, 1981)

Dupree, Louis, *Afghanistan* (Princeton: Princeton University Press, 1978)

Al-Ebraheem, Hassan Ali, *Kuwait and the Gulf* (Washington: Center for Contemporary Arab Studies, Georgetown University, 1984)

Freedman, Robert O., *Economic Warfare in the Communist Bloc* (New York: Praeger, 1970)

  Soviet Policy Toward the Middle East Since 1970, 3rd edn (New York: Praeger, 1982)

  ed., *The Middle East Since Camp David* (Boulder: Westview Press, 1984)

  ed., *The Middle East After the Israeli Invasion of Lebanon* (Syracuse: Syracuse University Press, 1986)

  ed., *Soviet Jewry in the 1980s: The Politics of Anti-Semitism and Emigration and the Dynamics of Resettlement* (Durham: Duke University Press, 1989)

Gankovsky, Yury, ed., *A History of Afghanistan* (Moscow: Progress Publishers, 1985)

Garthoff, Raymond L., *Detente and Confrontation: American–Soviet Relations from Nixon to Reagan* (Washington: Brookings Institution, 1985)

Giradet, Edward, *Afghanistan: The Soviet War* (New York: St. Martin's Press, 1985)

Glassman, Jon D., *Arms for the Arabs: The Soviet Union and War in the Middle East* (Baltimore: Johns Hopkins Press, 1975)

Golan, Galia, *Yom Kippur and After: The Soviet Union and the Middle East Crisis* (New York: Cambridge, 1977)

  The Soviet Union and the PLO: An Uneasy Alliance (New York: Praeger, 1980)

Goldman, Marshall, *Soviet Foreign Aid* (New York: Praeger, 1967)

Gorbachev, Mikhail, *Perestroika: New Thinking for Our Country and the World* (New York: Harper and Row, 1987)

Gosudarstvo Izrail (The State of Israel) (Moscow: Nauka, 1986)

Griffiths, John C., *Afghanistan: Key to a Continent* (Boulder: Westview Press, 1981)

Grimmett, Richard F., *Trends in Conventional Arms Transfers to the Third World by Major Suppliers 1981–88* (Washington: Congressional Research Service, 1989)

Gromyko, Andrei, *Pamiatnoe* (Memoirs) (Moscow: Politizdat, 1988)

Haig, Alexander, *Caveat: Realism, Reagan, and Foreign Policy* (New York: Macmillan, 1984)

Hammel, Eric, *The Root: The Marines in Beirut, August 1982–February 1984* (New York: Harcourt Brace Jovanovich, 1985)

Hammond, Thomas T., *Red Flag Over Afghanistan: The Communist Coup, the Soviet Invasion, and the Consequences* (Boulder, Westview Press, 1984)

Heikal, Mohammed, *The Cairo Documents* (New York: Doubleday, 1973)

  The Road to Ramadan (New York: Quadrangle, 1975)

  The Sphinx and the Commissar (New York: Harper and Row, 1978)

Henze, Paul B., *Ethiopia: Crisis of a Marxist Economy – Analysis and Text of a Soviet Report* (Santa Monica: Rand, 1989)

Herzog, Chaim, *The Arab–Israeli Wars* (New York: Random House, 1982)

Hodges, Tony, *Western Sahara: The Roots of a Desert War* (Westport: Laurence Hill, 1983)

Hosmer, Stephen T. and Thomas W. Wolfe, *Soviet Policy and Practice Toward Third World Conflicts* (Lexington: D.C. Heath, 1983)

Hough, Jerry F., *The Struggle for the Third World: Soviet Debates and American Options* (Washington: Brookings, 1986)

Hunter, Shireen, ed., *Gulf Cooperation Council: Problems and Prospects* (Washington: Center for Strategic and International Studies, 1984)

el Hussini, Mohrez Mahmoud, *Soviet–Egyptian Relations 1945–1985* (New York: St. Martin's Press, 1987)

Hyman, Anthony, *Afghanistan Under Soviet Domination 1964–1983* (New York: St. Martin's Press, 1984)

Israeli, Raphael, ed., *PLO in Lebanon: Selected Documents* (New York: St. Martin's Press, 1983)

Jelavich, Barbara, *A Century of Russian Foreign Policy 1814–1914* (Philadelphia: J.B. Lippencott, 1964)

Karsh, Efraim, *The Soviet Union and Syria: The Asad Years* (London: Chatham House, 1988)

Katz, Mark N., *Russia and Arabia* (Baltimore: Johns Hopkins Press, 1986)

Kauppi, Mark and R. Craig Nation, eds., *The Soviet Union and the Middle East in the 1980s* (Lexington: D. C. Heath, 1983)

Keddie, Nikki and Eric Hooglund, eds., *The Iranian Revolution and the Islamic Republic* (Syracuse: Syracuse University Press, 1985)

Kerr, Malcolm, *The Arab Cold War* (New York: Oxford University Press, 1970)

Khadduri, Majid, *Republican Iraq* (New York: Oxford University Press, 1969)

Khalidi, Rashid, *Under Siege: PLO Decisionmaking During the 1982 War* (New York: Columbia University Press, 1986)

Klieman, Aaron S., *Soviet Russia and the Middle East* (Baltimore, Johns Hopkins Press, 1970))

Klinghoffer, Arthur J., *Israel and the Soviet Union: Alienation or Reconciliation* (Boulder: Westview Press, 1985)

Korbonsky, Andrzej and Francis Fukuyama, eds., *The Soviet Union and the Third World: The Last Three Decades* (Ithaca: Cornell University Press, 1987)

Kreisberg, H., ed., *American Hostages in Iran: The Conduct of a Crisis* (New Haven: Yale University Press, 1985)

Laqueur, Walter, *The Soviet Union and the Middle East* (New York: Praeger, 1959)
The Road to Jerusalem (New York: Macmillan, 1968)

Lenczowski, George, *Soviet Advances in the Middle East* (Washington, DC: American Enterprise Institute, 1971)

Linden, Carl, *Khrushchev and the Soviet Leadership 1957–1964* (Baltimore: Johns Hopkins Press, 1966)

Mackintosh, J. M., *Strategy and Tactics of Soviet Foreign Policy* (London: Oxford University Press, 1963)

McDermott, Anthony and Kjell Skjebsback, eds., *The Multinational Force in Lebanon* (Oslo: Norwegian Institute of International Affairs, 1988)

Maoz, Moshe and Avner Yaniv, eds., *Syria Under Assad* (London: Croom Helm, 1986)

Medvedev, Zhores, *Andropov* (New York: Penguin Books, 1984)

Menon, Rajan, *Soviet Power and the Third World* (New Haven: Yale University Press, 1986)

Miller, Aaron David, *The Arab States and the Palestine Question* (New York: Praeger, 1986)

Norton, Augustus Richard, *Amal and the Shia* (Austin: University of Texas Press, 1987)

Ottaway, David and Marina, *Algeria: The Politics of a Socialist Revolution* (Berkeley: University of California Press, 1970)

Papp, Daniel, *Soviet Policies Toward the Developing World During the 1980s* (Maxwell Air Force Base, Alabama: Air University Press, 1986)

Pennar, Jaan, *The USSR and the Arabs: The Ideological Dimension* (New York: Crane Russak, 1973)

Pierre, Andrew T., *The Global Politics of Arms Sales* (Princeton: Princeton University Press, 1982)

Polk, William R., *The United States and the Arab World*, 3rd rev. edn (Cambridge: Harvard University Press, 1975)

Polsky, Yury, *Soviet Research Institutes and the Formulation of Foreign Policy* (Falls Church, Virginia: Delphic Associates, 1987)

Porter, Bruce D., *The USSR in Third World Conflicts: Soviet Arms and Diplomacy in Local Wars 1945–1980* (New York: Cambridge University Press, 1984)

Primakov, Yevgeny, *Anatomia Blizhnevostochnogo Konflikta* (Anatomy of the Middle East Conflict) (Moscow: Mysl, 1978)

Istoriia Odnogo Sgovora (History of the [Camp David] Deal) (Moscow: Political Literature Press, 1985)

Prital, David, *Yehudai Brit Hamoatzot* (*The Jews of the Soviet Union*), vol. 12 (Jerusalem: Publications on Soviet Jewry, Hebrew University of Jerusalem, 1989)

Quandt, William B., *Decade of Decisions: American Policy Toward the Arab–Israeli Conflict 1967–1976* (Berkeley: University of California Press, 1977)

Camp David: Peacemaking and Politics (Washington: Brookings, 1986)

ed., *The Middle East: Ten Years After Camp David* (Washington: Brookings, 1988)

Rabinovich, Itamar, *Syria under the Ba'ath 1963–1966* (Jerusalem: Israel Universities Press, 1972)

The War for Lebanon: 1970–1983 (Ithaca: Cornell University Press, 1984)

Ramet, Pedro, *The Soviet Presence in Syria* (Boulder: Westview Press, 1990)

Randal, Jonathan, *Going All the Way: Christian Warlords, Israeli Adventurers and the War in Lebanon* (New York: Random House, 1984)

Report of the Congressional Committees Investigating the Iran–Contra Affair (Washington: US Government Printing Office, 1987)

Report of the DOD (Department of Defense) Commission on Beirut International Airport Terrorist Act, October 23, 1983 (Washington, 1984)

Ro'i, Yaacov, *From Encroachment to Involvement: A Documentary Study of Soviet Policy in the Middle East* (Jerusalem: Israel Universities Press, 1974)

ed., *The Limits to Power* (London: Croom Helm, 1979)

ed., *The USSR and the Muslim World* (London: Allen and Unwin, 1984)

Rubinstein, Alvin Z., *Red Star on the Nile: The Soviet–Egyptian Influence Relationship Since the June War* (Princeton: Princeton University Press, 1977)

Soviet Policy Toward Turkey, Iran and Afghanistan (New York: Praeger, 1982)

Moscow's Third World Strategy (Princeton: Princeton University Press, 1988)

ed., *Soviet and Chinese Influence in the Third World* (New York: Praeger, 1975)

Rywkin, Michael, *Moscow's Muslim Challenge: Soviet Central Asia* (New York: M.E. Sharp, 1982)

Sachar, Howard, *Europe Leaves the Middle East 1936–1954* (New York: Alfred A. Knopf, 1972)

Saivetz, Carol R., *The Soviet Union and the Gulf in the 1980s* (Boulder: Westview Press, 1989)

ed., *The Soviet Union in the Third World* (Boulder: Westview Press, 1989)

Saivetz, Carol R. and Sylvia Woodby, *Soviet–Third World Relations* (Boulder: Westview Press, 1985)

Sandwick, John A., ed., *The Gulf Cooperation Council* (Boulder: Westview Press, 1987)

Schiff, Ze'ev and Ehud Ya'ari, *Israel's Lebanon War* (New York: Simon and Schuster, 1984)

Seale, Patrick, *The Struggle for Syria* (London: Oxford University Press, 1965)

Sella, Amnon, *Soviet Political and Military Conduct in the Middle East* (New York: St. Martin's, 1981)

The Soviet Attitude Towards the War in Lebanon – Mid 1982, Research Paper No. 47, Soviet and East European Research Center, The Hebrew University of Jerusalem

Shultz, Richard and Roy Godson, *Dezinformatsia: Active Measures in Soviet Strategy* (Washington: Pergamon-Brassey's, 1984)

Sick, Gary, *All Fall Down: America's Tragic Encounter with Iran* (New York: Penguin Books, 1986)

Singer, Marshall R., *Weak States in a World of Powers* (New York: Free Press, 1972)

Smirnov, I. K., *Alzhir* (Algeria) (Moscow: Nauka, 1981)

Smolansky, Oles M., *The Soviet Union and the Arab East Under Khrushchev* (Lewisburg: Bucknell University Press, 1974)

The Soviet Union in the Third World 1980–85: An Imperial Burden or Political Asset (Washington: Congressional Research Service, 1986)

Spector, Ivan, *The Soviet Union and the Muslim World* (Seattle: University of Washington Press, 1956)

Spiegel, Steven, Mark Heller and Jacob Goldberg, eds., *The Soviet–American Competition in the Middle East* (Lexington: D.C. Heath, 1988)

SSSR i Arabskie Strany (*The USSR and the Arab States*) (Moscow: Government Printing Office of Political Literature, 1960)

SSSR v Borbe Protiv Kolonializma i Neokolonializma (*The USSR in the Struggle Against Colonialism and Neocolonialism*) *1960 – March 1986* (Moscow: Politizdat 1986, 2 vols.)

Tahir-Knell, Shirin and Shaheen Ayubi, eds., *The Iran–Iraq War* (New York: Praeger, 1983)

Talbott, Strobe, ed., *Khrushchev Remembers* (Boston: Little, Brown, 1970)

The Tower Commission Report (New York: *New York Times*, 1987)

Trevelyan, Humphrey, *The Middle East in Revolution* (Boston: Gambit, 1970)

Tursunov, R. M., *Saudovskaia Araviia v Mezharabskikh Otnosheniiakh v Period 1964–1975* (*Saudi Arabia in Intra-Arab Relations in the 1964–75 Period*) (Tashkent: Fai'l, 1987)

Valkenier, Elizabeth K., *The Soviet Union and the Third World* (New York: Praeger, 1983)

Valkova, L. V., *Saudovskaia Araviia v Mezhdunarodnykh Otnosheniiakh* (*Saudi Arabia in International Relations*) (Moscow: Nauka, 1979)
Saudovskaia Araviia: Neft', Islam, Politika (*Saudi Arabia: Oil, Islam, Politics*) (Moscow, Nauka, 1987)

Vance, Cyrus, *Hard Choices: Critical Years in America's Foreign Policy* (New York: Simon and Schuster, 1983)

Vasilev, Aleksei, *Persidskii Zaliv v Epitsentre Buri* (*The Persian Gulf in the Center of the Storm*) (Moscow: Political Literature, 1983)

Yapp, Malcolm, *The Making of the Modern Near East 1792–1923* (New York: Longman, 1987)

Yodfat, Aryeh, *Arab Politics in the Soviet Mirror* (Jerusalem: Israel Universities Press, 1973)

Zemtsov, Ilya, *Andropov: Policy Dilemmas and the Struggle for Power* (Jerusalem: IRICS Publishers, 1983)

Articles and chapters in books

Abakov, P., "Novoe Myshlenie i Problema Iizucheniia Razvivaiushikhcia Stran" (New Thinking and the Problem of Studying Developing States), *MEIMO*, no. 11, 1987, pp. 48–62

Agaryshev, A., "From despair to hope," *New Times*, no. 47, 1985, pp. 14–15

Alaolmalki, Nazar, "The new Iranian left," *Middle East Journal*, vol. 41, no. 2 (Spring 1987), pp. 218–33

Albright, David, "The war in the Horn of Africa and the Arab–Israeli conflict," in *World Politics and the Arab–Israeli Conflict*, ed. Robert O. Freedman (New York: Pergamon, 1979), pp. 147–191
"The USSR and the Third World in the 1980s," *Problems of Communism*, vol. 38, nos. 2–3 (March–June 1989), pp. 50–70

Aleksandrov, Yevgeni, "New political thinking: genesis, factors, prospects," *International Affairs*, no. 12, 1987, pp. 87–95

Algosaibi, Ghazi, "Bahrain, the GCC and the U.S.," *American–Arab Affairs*, no. 23 (Winter 1987–88), pp. 57–59

Andelman, David A., "Andropov's Middle East," *Washington Quarterly*, vol. 6, no. 2 (Spring 1983), pp. 110–14

Anderson, Lisa, "Qadhafi and the Kremlin," *Problems of Communism*, vol. 34, no. 5 (September–October 1985), pp. 29–44

Arafat, Yasir, "The U.S., the PLO and the three formulas," *Journal of Palestine Studies*, vol. 15, no. 4 (Summer 1986), pp. 17–33

al-Assad, Hafiz, "Terrorism and the anti-Syrian campaign," *Journal of Palestine Studies*, vol. 15, no. 4 (Summer 1986), pp. 3–16

Atherton, Alfred, "The Soviet role in the Middle East: An American View," *Middle East Journal*, vol. 39, no. 4 (Autumn 1985), pp. 688–715

Batatu, Hanna, "Iraq's underground Shia movements: characteristics, causes and prospects," *Middle East Journal*, vol. 35, no. 4 (August 1981), pp. 578–94

Bechtold, Peter, "The Sudan since Nimeri," *The Middle East From the Iran–Contra Affair to the Intifada*, ed. Robert O. Freedman (Syracuse: Syracuse University Press, forthcoming)

Beglova, N. C., "Krizisnaia Situatsiia v Persidskom Zalive" (Crisis situation in the Persian Gulf), *Ssha*, no. 12, 1987, pp. 52–58

Bennett, Alexander, "Arms transfers as an instrument of Soviet policy in the Middle East," *Middle East Journal*, vol. 39, no. 4 (Autumn 1985), pp. 745–74

Bennigsen, Alexander, "Soviet Moslems and the World of Islam," *Problems of Communism*, vol. 29, no. 2 (March–April 1980), pp. 38–51

"Mullahs, Mujahadin and Soviet Moslems," *Problems of Communism*, vol. 33, no. 6 (November–December 1984), pp. 28–44

Benson, Sumner, "Soviet gas, Arab oil and Western security," *Washington Quarterly*, vol. 7, no. 1 (Winter 1984), pp. 129–37

Bochkaryov, V., "Exit Nimeri: what happens now?," *New Times*, no. 17, 1985, pp. 10–11

Bogdanov, Rodimir, "From the balance of forces to a balance of interests," *International Affairs*, no. 4, 1988, pp. 81–87

Borovoi, Yakov and Dmitry Zgersky, "Shatt Al-Arab: The Price of Those 192 Kilometers," *New Times*, no. 37, 1988, pp. 6–7

Breslauer, George, "Soviet Policy in the Middle East 1967–1972: Unalterable Antagonism or Collaborative Competition?," *Managing U.S.–Soviet Rivalry: Problems of Crisis Prevention*, ed. Alexander L. George (Boulder: Westview Press, 1981), pp. 65–105

Burg, Steven L., "Muslim Caches and Soviet Political Development: Reflections from a Comparative Perspective," *World Politics*, vol. 37, no. 1 (October 1984), pp. 24–47

Burrowes, Robert D., "The Yemen Arab Republic and the Ali Abdallah Salih Regime 1978–1984," *Middle East Journal*, vol. 39, no. 3 (Summer 1985), pp. 287–316

Campbell, John C., "Soviet Strategy in the Middle East," *American–Arab Affairs*, no. 8 (Spring 1984), pp. 74–82

Chaplin, Boris, "Forty-eight Hours of Risk," *International Affairs*, no. 4, 1989, pp. 22–30; 44

Cherkasov, P, "Frantziia i Konflikty na Afrikonskom Kontinente" (France and Conflicts on the African Continent), *MEIMO*, no. 8, 1987, pp. 41–53

Christie, John, "History and Development of the Gulf Cooperation Council: A Brief Overview," *American–Arab Affairs*, no. 18 (Fall 1986), pp. 1–13

Cigar, Norman, "South Yemen and the USSR: Prospects for the Relationship," *Middle East Journal*, vol. 39, no. 4 (Autumn 1985), pp. 775–95

"State and Society in South Yemen," *Problems of Communism*, vol. 34, no. 3 (May–June 1985), pp. 41–58

Cobban, Helena, "Kuwait's Elections," *The Middle East*, April 1981, pp. 14–15

Cordesman, Anthony H, "Arms Sales to Iran: The Strategic Implications for the United States and the West," *American–Arab Affairs*, no. 20 (Spring 1987), pp. 13–29

Cutler, Robert M., "The Formation of Soviet Foriegn Policy: Organizational and Cognitive Perspectives," *World Politics*, vol. 34, no. 3 (April 1982), pp. 418–36

Damis, John, "The Western Sahara Conflict: Myths and Realities," *Middle East Journal*, vol. 37, no. 2 (Spring 1983), pp. 169–79

David, Steven R., "Soviet Involvement in Third World Coups," *International Security*, vol. 11, no. 1 (Summer 1986), pp. 3–36

Davis, Michael, "Armenia: IDF to the Rescue," *Israeli Defense Forces Journal*, no. 16 (Winter 1989), pp. 28–33

Dawisha, Adeed I., "Iraq: The West's Opportunity," *Foreign Policy*, no. 41 (Winter 1980–81), pp. 13–53

"The USSR in the Middle East: Superpower in Eclipse," *Foreign Affairs*, vol. 61, no. 2 (Winter 1982/83), pp. 438–52

"Comprehensive Peace in the Middle East and the Comprehension of Arab Politics," *Middle East Journal*, vol. 37, no. 1 (Winter 1983), pp. 43–53

"The motives of Syria's Involvement in Lebanon," *Middle East Journal*, vol. 38, no. 2 (Spring 1984), pp. 228–36

Deeb, Mary Jane, "Inter-Maghribi Relations 1969: A Study of the Modalities of Unions and Mergers," *Middle East Journal*, vol. 43, no. 1 (Winter 1989), pp. 20–33

Demchenko, Pavel, "Middle East: In the Grip of the Crisis," *Asia and Africa Today*, no. 4 (July–August 1985), pp. 7–10, 45

Derkovsky, Oleg M., "The Soviet Union and the Middle East: The Soviet Perspective," *Middle East Insight*, vol. 5, no. 4 (December 1987), pp. 5–13

Dmitriev, E, "Mir na Blizhnem Vostoke – Utopiia ili Real'nost" (Peace in the Middle East – Utopia or Reality?), *MEIMO*, no. 5, 1987, pp. 43–56

"Palestinskoe Dvizhenie Soprotivleniia – na Novykh Rybezhakh" (The Palestinian Resistance Movement: New Frontiers), *MEIMO*, no. 8, 1987, pp. 54–67

"Mirnaia Konferentsiia po Blizhnemu Vostaku" (The Middle East Peace Conference), *MEIMO*, no. 3, 1988, pp. 52–61

Donaldson, Robert H., "The Soviet Union in South Asia: A Friend to Rely On?," *Journal of International Affairs*, vol. 34, no. 2, pp. 235–58

Drambyants, Gagik, "Middle East: Tension and Struggle," *International Affairs*, no. 7, 1987, pp. 65–72

Drysdale, Alasdair, "The Succession Question in Syria," *Middle East Journal*, vol. 39, no. 2 (Spring 1985), pp. 246–57

Dudarev, K., "Algeria Adjusts Its Course," *International Affairs*, no. 5, 1986, pp. 132–39

Dunn, Michael Collins, "Soviet Interests in the Arabian Peninsula: The Aden Pact and Other Paper Tigers," *American–Arab Affairs*, no. 8 (Spring 1984), pp. 92–98

Duran, Khalid, "The Second Battle of Algiers," *Orbis*, vol. 33, no. 3 (Summer 1989), pp. 403–21

Entelis, John V., "Algeria in World Politics, Foreign Policy Orientation and the New International Economic Order," *American–Arab Affairs*, no. 6 (Fall 1983), pp. 70–78

Evgenev, V., "ANDR – Chetvert' Veka Nezavisimogo Razvitiia" (Algeria – A quarter Century of Independent Development), *MEIMO*, no. 7 pp. 48–59

Fadlallah, Mohammad Husayn, "The Palestinians, The Shi'a and South Lebanon," *Journal of Palestine Studies*, vol. 16, no. 2 (Winter 1987), pp. 3–11

Fomin, O., "Trying to Revive the Camp David Deal," *New Times*, no. 18, 1985, pp. 14–15

"The Casablanca Summit," *New Times*, no. 34, 1985, pp. 10–11

Freedman, Robert O., "The Partition of Palestine: Conflicting Nationalism and Power Politics," in Thomas Hochey (ed.), *Partition: Peril to World Peace* (New York: Rand McNally, 1972)

"The Soviet Union and the Communist Parties of the Arab World: An Uncertain Relationship," in Roger E. Kanet and Donna Bahry (eds.), *Soviet Economic and Political Relations with the Developing World* (New York: Praeger, 1975), pp. 100–34

"The Soviet Image of the Carter Administration's Policy toward the USSR from the Inauguration to the Invasion of Afghanistan," *Korea and World Affairs*, vol. 4, no. 2 (Summer 1980), pp. 229–67

"Soviet Policy Toward Syria Since Camp David," *Middle East Review*, vol. 14, nos. 1–2 (Fall/Winter 1981–82), pp. 31–42

"Moscow, Washington and the Gulf," *American–Arab Affairs*, no. 1 (Summer 1982), pp. 127–39

"Moscow, Damascus and the Lebanese Crisis of 1982–84," *Middle East Review*, vol. 17, no. 1 (Fall 1984), pp. 22–40

"Soviet Jewry and Soviet–American Relations: A Historical Analysis," in *Soviet Jewry in the Decisive Decade 1971–1980* (ed. Robert O. Freedman) (Durham: Duke University Press, 1984), pp. 38–67

"Soviet Policy Toward the Persian Gulf from the Outbreak of the Iran–Iraq War to the Death of Konstantin Chernenko," *U.S. Strategic Interests in the Gulf Region* (ed. William J. Olson) (Boulder: Westview Press, 1987, pp. 43–80

"The Issue of Soviet Jewry in Israeli Foreign Policy," *Soviet Jewry in the 1980s* (ed. Robert O. Freedman) (Durham: Duke University Press, 1989), pp. 61–96

Fukuyama, Frances, "Patterns of Soviet Third World Policy," *Problems of Communism*, vol. 36, no. 5 (September–October 1987), pp. 1–13

Gaidar, Timur, "The Tanker War," *New Times*, no. 13, 1988, pp. 15–17

Garfinkle, Adam, "Negotiating by Proxy: Jordanian Foreign Policy and U.S. Options in the Middle East," *Orbis*, vol. 24, no. 24 (Winter 1981), pp. 847–80

"The Forces Behind Syrian Politics," *Middle East Review*, vol. 17, no. 1 (Fall 1984), pp. 5–15

Gause, F. Gregory, III, "Yemeni Unity: Past and Future," *Middle East Journal*, vol. 42, no. 1 (Winter 1988), pp. 33–47

Gevorgian, V. M., "Persidskii Zaliv: Strakhi i Nadezhdy" (The Persian Gulf: Fears and Hopes), *Ssha*, no. 10, 1988, pp. 66–69

Golan, Galia, "Syria and the Soviet Union Since the Yom Kippur War," *Orbis*, vol. 21, no. 4 (Winter 1978), pp. 777–801

"The Soviet Union and the PLO Since the War in Lebanon," *Middle East Journal*, vol. 40, no. 2 (Spring 1986), pp. 285–305

"Gorbachev's Middle East Strategy," *Foreign Affairs*, vol. 66, no. 1 (Fall 1987), pp. 41–57

Harrison, Selig, "Dateline Afghanistan: Exit Through Finland?," *Foreign Policy*, no. 41 (Winter 1980–81), pp. 163–82

Hassner, Pierre, "Gorbachev and the West," *Washington Quarterly*, vol. 11, no. 4 (Autumn 1988), pp. 95–103

Hottinger, Arnold, "Arab Communism at Low Ebb," *Problems of*

Communism, vol. 30, no. 4 (July–August 1981), pp. 17–32

Hunter, Robert E., "Western Europe and the Middle East Since the Lebanon War," *The Middle East After the Invasion of Lebanon* (ed. Robert O. Freedman) (Syracuse: Syracuse University Press, 1986), pp. 93–113

Hussein, King, "The Jordanian–Palestinian Peace Initiative: Mutual Recognition and Territory for Peace," *Journal of Palestine Studies*, vol. 14, no. 4 (Summer 1985), pp. 11–22

Ibrahim, Baqir, "The Masses, The Party and the National Front," *World Marxist Review*, vol. 19, no. 8 (August 1976), pp. 49–56

Izyumov, Alexei and Andrei Kortinov, "The Soviet Union in the Changing World," *International Affairs*, no. 8, 1988, pp. 46–56

Kapranov, I. and A. Dogayev, "The USSR and Developing Countries: Tangible Results of Economic and Technological Cooperation," *International Affairs*, no. 3, 1986, pp. 28–36

Kashkett, Steven B., "Iraq and the Pursuit of Non-alignment," *Orbis*, vol. 26, no. 2 (Summer 1982), pp. 477–93

Katz, Mark N., "North Yemen Between East and West," *American–Arab Affairs*, no. 8 (Spring 1984), pp. 99–107
"Civil Conflict in South Yemen," *Middle East Review*, vol. 19, no. 1 (Fall 1986), pp. 7–13
"Soviet Military Policy Toward the Third World," *Washington Quarterly*, vol. 9, no. 4 (Fall 1986), pp. 159–63
"The Soviet Challenge in the Gulf," *Middle East Insight*, vol. 5, no. 4 (December 1987), pp. 24–31

Kazakov, V., "Regional Conflicts and International Security," *International Affairs*, no. 2, 1986, pp. 45–50

Khalidi, Rashid, "Arab Views of the Soviet Role in the Middle East," *Middle East Journal*, vol. 39, no. 4 (Autumn 1985), pp. 716–32
"Palestinian Politics After the Exodus from Beirut," in *The Middle East Since the Israeli Invasion of Lebanon* (ed. Robert O. Freedman) (Syracuse: Syracuse University Press, 1986), pp. 233–53

Khalilzad, Zalmay, "Soviet Occupied Afghanistan," *Problems of Communism*, vol. 29, no. 6 (November–December 1980), pp. 23–40
"Moscow's Afghan War," *Problems of Communism*, vol. 35, no. 1 (January–February 1986), pp. 1–20

Kim, Georgi, "Soviet Oriental Studies in Time of Perestroika," *Asia and Africa Today*, no. 1 (January–February 1989), pp. 2–6

Kislov, A., "Vashington i Irako–Iranskii Konflikt" (Washington and the Iran–Iraq Conflict), *Ssha*, no. 1, 1981, pp. 51–56

Kislov, A., "Novoe Politicheskoe Myshlenie i Regional'nye Konflikty" (New Political Thinking and Regional Conflicts), *MEIMO*, no. 8, 1988, pp. 39–47

Kislov, A. and A. Frolov, "Blizhnii Vostok i Pentagon" (The Near East and the Pentagon), *Ssha*, no. 4, 1987, pp. 13–24

Kislov, A. and A. Frolov, "Ssha–Saudovskaia Araviia – Protivorechivoe Partnerstvo" (USA–Saudi Arabia – A Contradictory Partnership), *Ssha*, no. 2, 1989, pp. 30–39

Kiva, A., "Sotsialisticheskaia Orientatsia: Teoreticheskii Potentsial Kontseptsii i Prakticheski Realii" (Socialist Orientation: The Theoretical Potential of the Concept and Practical Realities), *MEIMO*, no. 11, 1988, pp. 62–73

Konstantinov, V., "A Middle East Settlement and Its Aftermath,"
   International Affairs, no. 1, 1986, pp. 105–9
Korey, William, "Jackson–Vanik and Soviet Jewry," *Washington Quarterly*,
   vol. 7, no. 1 (Winter 1984), pp. 116–28
   "The Soviet Anti-Zionist Committee," in *Soviet Jewry in the 1980s* (ed.
   Robert O. Freedman) (Durham: Duke University Press, 1989),
   pp. 26–50
Kosin, V. P., "Oon i Problema Ogranicheniaa Voenno Morskikh
   Vooruzhenii" (The U.N. and the Problem of Limiting Naval Armaments),
   Ssha, no. 10, 1987, pp. 56–62
Koslosovskii, A., "Regional'nye Konklikty i Globalnaia Bezopasnost"
   (Regional Conflicts and Global Security), *MEIMO*, no. 6, 1988,
   pp. 32–41
Kostiner, Joseph, "The Yemeni Arab Republic," *Middle East Contemporary
   Survey 1986* (ed. Itamar Rabinovich) (Boulder: Westview Press, 1987), pp.
   668–71
Kremeniuk, V. A., "'Ssha v Regional'nykh Konfliktakh" (The USA in
   Regional Conflicts), *Ssha*, no. 6, 1986, pp. 23–34
Kununnikov, Nikolai, "The USSR–Syria: A Firm Foundation and Good
   Prospects," *Asia and Africa Today*, no. 6 (November–December 1985),
   pp. 42–45
Laqueur, Walter, "Glasnost Abroad: New Thinking in Foreign Policy,"
   Washington Quarterly, vol. 11, no. 4 (Autumn 1988), pp. 75–93
Lavda, Robert, "Algeria: Along the Road of Revolutionary Struggle," *Asia
   and Africa Today*, no. 56 (March–April 1985), pp. 39–41
Legvold, Robert, "The Soviet Union's Changing View of Sub-Saharan
   Africa," in *Soviet Policy in Developing Countries* (ed. W. Raymond
   Duncan) (Waltham, Mass.: Ginn-Blaisdell, 1970), pp. 62–82
Levran, Aharon, "Changes in the Syrian Armed Forces and Their Impact on
   the Military Balance with Israel," *Middle East Military Balance*
   (Jerusalem), 1987–88, pp. 197–211
Lewis, William H., "Western Sahara: Compromise or Conflict?" *Current
   History*, December 1981, pp. 410–13, 431
Lukin, V. and A. Bovin, "Perestroika Mezhdunarodnykh Otnoshenii – Puti i
   Pokhody" (The Restructuring of International Relations – Paths and
   Approaches), *MEIMO*, no. 1, 1989, pp. 58–70
MacFarlane, S. Neil, "The Soviet Concept of Regional Security," *World
   Politics*, vol. 37, no. 3 (April 1985), pp. 295–316
Maddy-Weitzman, Bruce, "The Fragmentation of Arab Politics: Inter-Arab
   Affairs Since the Afghanistan Invasion," *Orbis*, vol. 25, no. 2 (Summer
   1981), pp. 389–407
   "Islam and Arabism: The Iran–Iraq War," *Washington Quarterly*, vol. 5,
   no. 4 (Autumn 1982), pp. 181–88
Medvenko, L., "The Persian Gulf: A Revival of Gunboat Diplomacy,"
   International Affairs (Moscow), no. 12, 1980, pp. 23–29
Meyer, Stephen M., "The Sources and Prospects of Gorbachev's New
   Political Thinking on Security," *International Security*, vol. 13, no. 2 (Fall
   1988), pp. 124–63
Mezentsev, Pavel, "USA–Iran: Threats and Blackmail," *New Times*, no. 38,
   1980, pp. 10–11
Miller, Aaron David, "Palestinians in the 1980s," *Current History*, January
   1984, pp. 17–20; 34–36

"The PLO Since Camp David," in *The Middle East Since Camp David*
(ed. Robert O. Freedman) (Boulder: Westview Press, 1984)

Mirsky, Georgi, "Newly Independent States: Ways of Development," *Asia
and Africa Tody*, no. 71 (September–October 1987), pp. 53–56

"K Voprosu o Vibore Puti i Orientatsii Razvivaiushchikhcia Stran"
(About the Question of a Choice of Path and Orientation for Developing
Countries), *MEIMO*, no. 5, 1987, pp. 70–81

Mishanin, Aleksandr, "Entrapped in a Senseless War: What Prevents the
Settlement of the Iran–Iraq Conflict?" *International Affairs* (Moscow), no.
4, 1987, pp. 86–90, 110

Mishlawi, Tewfiq, "Crackdown on Communists in Iraq," *Middle East*, no.
45 (July 1978), pp. 29–30

Mohammed, Aziz, "Tasks of the Revolutionary Forces in Iraq," *World
Marxist Review*, vol. 19, no. 9 (September 1976), pp. 10–18

Mortimer, Robert, "Algeria's New Sultan," *Current History*, December
1981, pp. 418–21; 433–34

Muksiemenko, V., "Sotsialisticheskaia Orientatsiia: Perestroika
Predstavlenii" (Socialist Orientation: The Restructuring of a Concept),
MEIMO, no. 2, 1989, pp. 93–103

Musaelyan, G., "Washington–Tel Aviv Military Alliance," *International
Affairs*, no. 7, 1986, pp. 130–34

Mylroie, Laurie, "The Superpowers and the Iran–Iraq War," *American–
Arab Affairs*, no. 21 (Summer 1987), pp. 15–26

Nappen, Larry C., "The Arab Autumn of 1984: A Case Study of Soviet
Middle East Policy," *Middle East Journal*, vol. 39, no. 4 (Autumn 1985),
pp. 733–44

Naumkin, Vitaly, "South Yemen After the January Tragedy," *New Times*
(Moscow), no. 48, 1986, pp. 28–29

Neuman, Stephanie G., "Arms and Superpower Influence: Lessons from
Recent Wars," *Orbis*, vol. 30, no. 4 (Winter 1987), pp. 711–29

Nikifarov, A. V., "Mirnoe Sosyshchestvovanie i Novoe Myshlenie"
(Peaceful Coexistence and the New Thinking), *Ssha*, no. 12, 1987,
pp. 3–10

Nikolaev, Yuri, "The Persian Gulf in Washington's Plans," *International
Affairs*, no. 9, 1987, pp. 64–67

Noorzay, M. Siddieg, "Soviet Economic Interests in Afghanistan," *Problems
of Communism*, vol. 36, no. 3 (May–June 1987), pp. 43–54

Olcott, Martha Brill, "Soviet Islam and World Revolution," *World Politics*,
vol. 34, no. 4 (July 1982), pp. 487–504

"Moscow's Troublesome Muslim Minority," *Washington Quarterly*, vol. 9,
no. 2 (Spring 1986), pp. 73–83

Olmert, Yosef, "Syria," *Middle East Contemporary Survey 1982–83* (ed.
Colin Legum) (London: Holmes and Meier 1985), pp. 795–829

"Domestic Crisis and Foreign Policy in Syria: The Assad Regime," *Middle
East Review*, vol. 20, no. 3 (Spring 1988), pp. 17–25

Page, Stephen, "Moscow and the Arabian Peninsula," *American–Arab
Affairs*, no. 8 (Spring 1984), pp. 83–93

"The USSR and the GCC States: A Search for Openings," *American–Arab
Affairs*, no. 20 (Spring 1987), pp. 38–56

Pajak, Roger F., "Arms and Oil, the Soviet–Libyan Arms Supply
Relationship," *Middle East Review*, vol. 13, no. 2 (Winter 1980–81), pp.
51–56

"Perestroika, the 19th Party Conference and Foreign Policy," *International Affairs*, no. 7, 1988, pp. 3–18

Petrovsky, Vladimir, "Oon i Obnovlenie Mira" (The UN and the Renewal of the World), *MEIMO*, no. 4, 1988, pp. 3–9

Poliakov, N., "Put' K. Bezopasnosti v Indiiskom Okeane i Peridskom Zalive" (The Way to Security in the Indian Ocean and Persian Gulf), *MEIMO*, no. 1, 1981, pp. 62–73

"Political Shifts in the Middle East: Roots, Factors, Trends," *World Marxist Review*, February 1980, pp. 58–64

Pollock, David, "Moscow and Aden: Coping with a Coup," *Problems of Communism*, vol. 35, no. 3 (May–June 1986), pp. 50–70

Price, David Lynn, "Moscow and the Persian Gulf," *Problems of Communism*, vol. 28, no. 2 (March–April 1979), pp. 1–13

Primakov, Yevgeni, "USSR Policy on Regional Conflicts," *International Affairs*, no. 6, 1988, pp. 3–9

"Soviet Policy Toward the Arab–Israeli Conflict," in *The Middle East: Ten Years After Camp David* (ed. William B. Quandt) (Washington, DC: Brookings, 1988), pp. 387–409

Primakov, Yevgeni, V. Martnynov and G Duligenskii, "Nekotorye Problemy Novogo Myshleniia" ("Some Problems of the New Thinking") *MEIMO* no. 6, 1989, pp. 5–18

Pronin, S., "Ideologiia vo Bzaimocviazannom Mire" ("Ideology in an Interconnected World"), *MEIMO* no. 10, 1988, pp. 5–15

Ra'anan, Uri, "Soviet Decision-Making and International Relations," *Problems of Communism*, vol. 29, no. 6 (November–December 1980), pp. 41–47

Rabinovich, Itamar, "Israel and Lebanon in 1983," *Middle East Contemporary Survey 1982–1983* (ed. Colin Legum) (London: Holmes and Meier, 1985), pp. 135–49

Rafael, Gideon, "Divergence and Convergence of American–Soviet Interests in the Middle East: An Israeli Viewpoint," *Political Science Quarterly*, vol. 100, no. 4 (Winter 1985–86), pp. 561–74

Ramazani, R. K., "The Iran–Iraq War and the Persian Gulf Crisis," *Current History*, February 1988, pp. 63–64

Ramet, Pedro, "The Soviet–Syrian Relationship," *Problems of Communism*, vol. 35, no. 5 (September–October 1986), pp. 35–47

Ramotar, Donald, Salem Said, and Andrei Olitsky, "Democratic Yemen: After a Tragic Trial," *World Marxist Review*, vol. 31, no. 1 (January 1988), pp. 132–39

"Revolution and Reform in the National Development of Eastern Countries: A Roundtable discussion," *Asia and Africa Today*, no. 1 (January–February) 1986, pp. 54–61

Roberts, Cynthia A., "Soviet Arms-Transfer Policy and the Decision to Upgrade Syrian Air Defenses," *Survival*, July–August 1983, pp. 154–64

Roeder, Philip G., "The Ties that Bind: Aid, Trade and Political Compliance in Soviet–Third World Relations," *International Studies Quarterly*, vol. 29, no. 2 (June 1985), pp. 191–216

Ross, Dennis, "The Soviet Union and the Persian Gulf," *Political Science Quarterly*, vol. 99 (Winter 1984–85), pp. 615–35

Rostovtsev, Igor, "Moslems in the USSR," *Asia and Africa Today*, no. 6 (November–December 1985), pp. 33–35

Rubenberg, Cheryl A., "The PNC and the Reagan Initiative," *American–Arab Affairs*, vol. 4 (Spring 1983), pp. 53–69

Rubinstein, Alvin Z., "The Soviet Union's Imperial Policy in the Middle East," *Middle East Review*, vol. 25, nos. 1–2 (Fall 1982 – Winter 1983), pp. 19–24

"The Soviet Union and the Peace Process Since Camp David," *Washington Quarterly*, vol. 8, no. 1 (Winter 1985), pp. 41–55

"Soviet Success Story: The Third World," *Orbis*, vol. 32, no. 4 (Fall 1988), pp. 552–66

Schneider, Eberhard, "Soviet Foreign Policy Think Tanks," *Washington Quarterly*, vol. 11, no. 2 (Spring 1988), pp. 145–55

"Scientific and Practical Conference at the USSR Ministry of Foreign Affairs," *International Affairs*, no. 11, 1988, pp. 13–62

Seeley, Talcott W., "U.S.–Syrian Relations: The Thread of Mu'awiyah," *American–Arab Affairs*, no. 4 (Spring 1984), pp. 40–45

"The Syrian Perspective on the Peace Process," *American–Arab Affairs*, no. 17 (Summer 1986), pp. 55–61

Semyonov, Vsevolod, "Under the Guise of Defending Islam," *International Affairs*, no. 2, 1987, pp. 81–88

Sergiyev, A., "The Non-Aligned Movement and Today's World," *International Affairs*, no. 9, 1986, pp. 60–66, 133

Shaked, Haim and Yehudit Ronen, "The Democratic Republic of Sudan," *Middle East Contemporary Survey*, 1985 (ed. Itamar Rabinovich and Haim Shaked) (Boulder: Westview, 1987), pp. 614–42

Shevardnadze, Eduard, "The 19th All-Union CPSU Conference: Foreign Policy and Diplomacy," *International Affairs*, no. 10, 1988, pp. 133–46

"The Important Line of Soviet Diplomacy," *International Affairs*, no. 3, 1989, pp. 3–16

Shlepin, V., "USSR–Morocco: Links Many and Varied," *New Times*, no. 11, 1983, pp. 10–11

Shoumikhin, Andrey U., "Soviet Perception of U.S. Middle East Policy," *Middle East Journal*, vol. 43, no. 1 (Winter 1989), pp. 16–19

Sicherman, Harvey, "Europe's Role in the Middle East: Illusions and Realities," *Orbis*, vol. 28, no. 4 (Winter 1985), pp. 803–28

Sick, Gary, "Slouching Toward Settlement: The Internationalization of the Iran–Iraq War, 1987," *Neither East Nor West* (ed. Nikki Keddi) (New Haven: Yale University Press, 1990)

Simoniya, Nodari, "Developing Countries: Traditional Factors and Social Progress," *Asia and Africa Today*, no. 2 (March–April 1986), pp. 59–61

Singleton, Seth, "Defense of the Gains of Socialism: Soviet Third World Policy in the mid-1980s," *Washington Quarterly*, vol. 7, no. 1 (Winter 1984), pp. 102–15

Sivan, Emmanuel, "Sunni Radicalism in the Middle East and the Iranian Revolution," *International Journal of Middle East Studies*, vol. 21, no. 1 (February 1989), pp. 1–30

Smolansky, Oles, "The Kremlin and the Iraqi Ba'ath, 1968–1982: An Influence Relationship," *Middle East Review*, vol. 25, nos. 3–4 (Spring–Summer 1983), pp. 62–67

Snyder, Jack, "Science and Sovietology: Bridging the Methods Gap in Soviet Foreign Policy Studies," *World Politics*, vol. 40, no. 2 (January 1988), pp. 169–93

Spechler, Dina Rome, "The USSR and Third World Conflicts: Domestic Debate and Soviet Policy in the Middle East 1967–1973," *World Politics*, vol. 38, no. 3 (April 1986), pp. 435–61

Spiegel, Steven L., "U.S. Relations with Israel: The Military Benefits," *Orbis*, vol. 30, no. 3 (Fall 1986), pp. 475–97

St. John, Ronald Bruce, "Libya's Foreign and Domestic Policies," *Current History*, December 1981, pp. 426–29, 434–35

Stein, Janice Gross, "The Wrong Strategy in the Right Place: The United States in the Gulf," *International Security*, vol. 13, no. 3 (Winter 1988–89), pp. 142–67

Stepanov, Andrei, "Taking Up a Point" (Soviet Neutrality in the Iran–Iraq War), *New Times*, no. 17, 1981, p. 31

Stoklitsky, Sergei, "The Causes of the Conflict in Lebanon," *International Affairs*, no. 6, 1987, pp. 53–61

Sturua, G. M., "Ukreplenie Bezopasnosti v Sredizemnomor'e: Voenno-morskoi Aspekt" ("The Strengthening of Security in the Mediterranean – the Naval Aspect"), *Ssha*, no. 12, 1986, pp. 34–43
"Borba za Ogranichenie Voenno-Morskoi Deiatel'nosti v Indiskom Okeane" ("The Struggle for Limiting Naval Activity in the Indian Ocean"), *Ssha*, no. 9, 1987, pp. 25–33

Susser, Asher, "The Palestine Liberation Organization," in *Middle East Contemporary Survey 1982–1983* (ed. Colin Legum, *et al.*) (London: Holmes and Meier, 1985), pp. 275–330

Tahir-Kheli, Shirin, "The Soviet Union in Afghanistan: Benefits and Costs," in *The Soviet Union in the Third World: Successes and Failures* (ed. Robert H. Donaldson) (Boulder: Westview Press, 1981), pp. 217–31

Taraben, Y., "Newly Free Countries and International Relations," *International Affairs*, no. 4, 1986, pp. 29–36, 46

Tarasov, N. N., "Vashington i Strany Afrikanskogo Roga" ("Washington and the States of the Horn of Africa"), *Ssha*, no. 3, 1988, pp. 33–40

Trofimenko, G. A., "Novye Real'nosti i Novoe Myshlenie" ("New Realities and New Thinking"), *Ssha*, no. 2, 1987, pp. 3–15

Turkatenko, N. D., "Iranskaia Afera i ee Pocledstviia" ("The Iranian Swindle and Its Implications"), *Ssha*, no. 1, 1987, pp. 60–67

Twinam, Joseph Wright, "Reflections on Gulf Cooperation with Focus on Qatar and Oman," *American–Arab Affairs*, no. 18 (Fall 1986), pp. 14–35

Ulianovsky, R., "Nekotorie voprosy nikapitalisticheskogo razvitiia" ("Some problems of noncapitalist development"), *Kommunist*, no. 4 (1971), pp. 103–12

Valkova, Lidya, "PDRY: The Revolution Gets Stronger in Struggle," *Asia and Africa Today*, no. 4 (July–August 1988), pp. 51–56

Van Hollen, Christopher, "North Yemen: A Dangerous Pentagonal Game," *Washington Quarterly*, vol. 5, no. 3 (Summer 1982), pp. 137–42

Vavilov, V. M., "Uregulirovanie v Afganistane i Vashington" ("A Settlement in Afghanistan and Washington"), *Ssha*, no. 6, 1988, pp. 54–58

Vinogradov, Yuri, "The Indian Ocean: The Problems of Demilitarization," *International Affairs*, no. 7, 1987, pp. 58–64

Volsky, Dmitry, "Middle East: Turban or Helmet," *New Times*, no. 20, 1980, p. 19
"Iran: Sidetracking Attention," *New Times*, 35, 1980, p. 21
"May 1981 is not June 1967," *New Times*, no. 21, 1981, pp. 5–6

"There is Light at the End of the Tunnel," *New Times*, no. 49, 1981, pp. 12–13

"The Revolution at the Crossroads," *New Times*, no. 2, 1983, pp. 13–14

"Behind the Prospective Israeli Pull-out from Southern Lebanon," *New Times*, no. 5, 1985, pp. 14–15

"The Hidden Springs of a Senseless War," *New Times*, no. 40, 1985, pp. 26–28

"Spring of Terrorism in the Mechanism of Tension," *New Times*, no. 50, 1985, p. 11

Wimbush, E. Enders, "The Muslim Ferment in Soviet Central Asia," *Global Affairs*, vol. 2, no. 3, pp. 106–18

Wright, Claudia, "Implications of the Iran–Iraq War," *Foreign Affairs*, vol. 59, no. 2 (Winter, 1980–81), pp. 275–303

"Libya Comes In From the Cold," *The Middle East*, August 1981, pp. 18–25

Yanov, Alexander, "New Thinking and American Brezhnevism I," *International Affairs*, no. 2, 1989, pp. 27–33

"New Thinking and American Brezhnevism II," *International Affairs*, no. 3, 1989, pp. 34–41, 53

Yefimov, Vladimir, "U.S.–Egyptian Relations in the 1970s and 1980s," *International Affairs*, no. 9, 1987, pp. 47–53

"Egypt's Foreign Policy in the 1980s," *International Affairs*, no. 2, 1988, pp. 68–74

Yost, David S., "French Policy in Chad and the Libyan Challenge," *Orbis*, vol. 26, no. 4 (Winter 1983), pp. 965–97

Zartman, I. W. and A. G. Kluge, "The Sources and Goals of Qaddafi's Foreign Policy," *American–Arab Affairs*, no. 6 (Fall 1983), pp. 59–69

Zevelev, Igor and Alexei Kara-Marza, "Social Ties: Dialectic of Development," *Asia and Africa Today*, no. 3 (May–June 1988), pp. 56–60 Gosudarstva i Puti O'bshechestbennogo Progressa v Stranakh Azii i Afriki" ("The State and the Path to Social Progress in Asian and African States"), *MEIMO*, no. 4, 1989, pp. 101–7

Zhuravlyov, Yuri, "Back to the Past or Back to the Present," *New Times*, no. 26, 1988, pp. 8–9

Zilian, Frederick, "The U.S. Raid on Libya – and NATO," *Orbis*, vol. 30, no. 3 (Fall 1986), pp. 499–524

Zotov, Alexander, "A Burden for Perez de Cuellar," *New Times*, no. 31, 1988, p. 7

Zoubir, Yahia, "Soviet Policy in the Maghreb," *Arab Studies Quarterly*, vol. 9, no. 4, pp. 399–421

Periodicals

American–Arab Affairs
Asia and Africa Today (Moscow)
Baltimore Sun
Christian Science Monitor
Current Digest of the Soviet Press
Current History
Foreign Affairs
Foreign Broadcast Information Service Daily Reports (USSR and Near East/South Asia)
Foreign Policy

Foreign Trade (Moscow)
International Affairs (Moscow)
International Security
Izvestia
Jerusalem Journal of International Relations
Journal of Palestine Studies
Kommunist (Moscow)
Middle East (London)
Middle East Journal
Middle East Review
Mirovaia ekonomika i mezhdunarodnye otnosheniia (*MEIMO*) (Moscow)
New Times (Moscow)
New York Times
Orbis
Pravda
Problems of Communism
Radio Liberty Reports
Soviet Jewish Affairs
Ssha (Moscow)
Washington Post
Washington Quarterly
World Marxist Review

Index